D0588727

NOV 13 '95

ART CENTER COLLEGE OF DESIGN

3 3220 00144 1000

PLOTS®

Unlimited

ART CENTER COLLEGE OF DESIGN LIBRARY
1700 LIDA STREET
PASADENA, CALIFORNIA 91103

808.3
S271
1995

PLOTS®

Unlimited

For the Writer of
Novels, Short Stories, Plays,
Screenplays and Television Episodes

A Creative Source for Generating
a Virtually Limitless Number and Variety
of Story Plots and Outlines

Tom Sawyer
and
Arthur David Weingarten

ART CENTER COLLEGE OF DESIGN LIBRARY
1700 LIDA STREET
PASADENA, CALIFORNIA 91103

ASHLEYWILDE™

Ashleywilde, Inc.
23715 W. Malibu Road, Suite 132
Malibu, California 90265
U.S.A.

Plots Unlimited, Copyright © 1994 by Ashleywilde, Inc. All rights reserved. Printed in the United States of America. Except as permitted under the Copyright Act of 1976, no part of this publication may be reproduced or distributed in any form or by any means, or stored in a database or retrieval system, without the prior written permission of the publisher.

Every effort has been made to supply complete and accurate information. However, Ashleywilde assumes no responsibility for the use of Plots Unlimited, nor for any infringement of the intellectual property rights of third parties which might result from such use.

Library of Congress Cataloging–in–Publication data
Sawyer, Tom, 1936-
Plots Unlimited: for the writer of novels, short stories, plays, screenplays
and television episodes: a creative source for generating a virtually
limitless number and variety of story plots and outlines
Written by Tom Sawyer and Arthur David Weingarten
p.   cm.

ISBN 0-9627476-0-2
1. Plots (Drama, novel, etc.) 2. Fiction—Technique
I. Weingarten, Arthur David, 1935-
II. Title.
PN3378, S29 1994
808.3—dc20   90-83939 CIP

First Edition: January 1995

Design and production
Leena Hannonen, Macnetic Design

TABLE OF CONTENTS

ART CENTER COLLEGE OF DESIGN LIBRARY
1700 LIDA STREET
PASADENA, CALIFORNIA 91103

Plots Unlimited

THE CONCEPT

Plots Unlimited helps you, the writer, to create, combine and interweave a virtually endless number and variety of story outlines or plots for any form of fiction: short stories, novels, plays, screenplays, or television episodes. It can be used in any genre: Romance, Mystery, Intrigue, Comedy, Juvenile, Speculative Fiction, etc., etc.

Plots Unlimited won't write your movie or play or novel for you - that will require the application of your unique writing abilities. What Plots Unlimited will do is stimulate and augment your creative talents in that essential, and for many, one of the most difficult aspects of fiction writing: plotting and structure.

The Plots Unlimited Method of plot suggestion is based upon three essential components: conflicts, characters and construction. These are discussed in sections to follow. By combining these components and selecting plot turns from the myriad choices Plots Unlimited offers, you will generate outlines for a series of well-structured, unified story segments which you can later combine, edit and use as the basis for your creative efforts.

While you can use these outlines verbatim, it is far more likely that the suggestions and choices presented by Plots Unlimited will spark your creativity and send your imagination off in entirely new and unexpected directions. You'll also discover that Plots Unlimited is an invaluable reference work, a compendium of plot turns and twists - and a virtually sure-cure for writer's block.

As you explore the possibilities within this book, you'll find that whatever your fiction writing aspirations may be, Plots Unlimited will prove a powerful and creative resource, a tool that will quickly become as indispensable as your dictionary or thesaurus.

ART CENTER COLLEGE OF DESIGN LIBRARY
1700 LIDA STREET
PASADENA, CALIFORNIA 91103

The Plots Unlimited Method of plot suggestion is divided into **Conflict Situations** (or Story Segments), **Character Combinations, Story Types** and **Sub-types**, and **MasterPlots** (or **Themes**).

MasterPlots

Every story has a **MasterPlot** or **Theme**, an underlying design which defines its type. The **Theme** may be specific or vague, but it's always present. Around this **Theme**, the writer can weave any number of distinctly different stories.

The writer, however, needn't start with a **Theme** or **MasterPlot.** Using this book, you can also generate your story from the inside out, starting with a **Conflict Situation** (or Story Segment), or with a group of **Characters** and their relationships. With Plots Unlimited one can start developing a story plot with the ending, the beginning — or anywhere between. In creating Mystery stories, for instance, many professional writers begin with the end, or solution to the mystery — and work forward. Inevitably, though, as the writer combines **Conflict Situations** and the plot outline builds, a **Theme** or **MasterPlot** will emerge.

The Plots Unlimited Chart of MasterPlots begins on page 15. Each Plots Unlimited **MasterPlot** classifies in general terms and in one concise sentence, a story **Theme**. Each **Theme** or **MasterPlot** consists of three **Clauses**: An **A Clause** describing the protagonist in general terms: a middle, or **B Clause** which initiates and continues the action: and a final **C Clause** continuing and concluding the action. Any **A Clause** can be combined with any **B Clause** and with any **C Clause**. Using the fifteen **A Clauses**, the sixty-two **B Clauses**, and the fifteen **C Clauses** which you will find listed in the Plots Unlimited **MasterPlot Chart**, it is possible to generate 13,950 different **MasterPlots**.

Immediately following the **MasterPlot Chart**, on page 21, is the List of

Story Types and Story Sub-Types

(**Romance, Mystery, Pretense, Mistaken Judgment, Obligation**, etc.) to be found under each of the sixty-two numbered **B Clauses**. Appended to each of these is a number indicating the first of the consecutively numbered **Conflict Situations** for that particular **Story Type** or **Sub-type**: i.e., Mistaken Judgment 768.

Plots Unlimited Characters

are listed on page 23. **Characters** in Plots Unlimited are represented by all-purpose names which the user can alter to suit his or her story. For example, **Jack** is the male protagonist. **Gary** is **Jack's** antagonist. **Carol** is the female protagonist. **Annie** is her friend. **Frank** is **Carol's** father, and so on.

The next main section of Plots Unlimited, beginning on page 25 is

Plots Unlimited Conflict Situations

The Plots Unlimited **Conflict Situations** (or Story Segments) are numbered from 1 to 1,462. These are further subdivided by letter and/or asterisk, thus providing approximately 5,600 different **Conflict Situations.** Each of these is cross-linked to several other **Conflict Situations** with which it can be combined. Thus, when the writer selects a **Conflict Situation,** he or she is offered choices of several subsequent, linked **Conflict Situations** which carry the story forward (or if one chooses, back-ward) in various directions, an increment at a time. Each of these is in turn linked to other **Conflict Situations** so that the writer can quickly build, in tree-like fashion, a well-constructed story in which **Conflict,** that most important element of fiction, is consistently maintained.

The Conflict Situations provided in Plots Unlimited **are the product of a basic premise: Objective + Obstacle = Conflict.**

For people the world over, although there are infinite variations in purpose, there is really only one basic, general objective: Happiness (or, if you will, Satisfaction). Whether we're talking about a Wall Street Tycoon pursuing his next stock market killing, or a pair of lovers trying to find the opportunity to run off together, the objective remains the same: Happiness — momentary or otherwise. The individual's circumstances, attributes and personal problems determine *how* one will try to achieve thic objective.

Plots Unlimited employs this general objective in three general areas of human endeavor:

> 1. To Find Happiness in Romance
> 2. To Find Happiness in Marriage
> 3. To Find Happiness in Activity (career, adventure, competition, etc.)

This single general objective, to find happiness, runs through all of the **Conflict Situations,** and while, obviously, the ultimate objective is to live — and the ultimate obstacle is death, in between you'll find an almost limitless number of secondary objectives, opposed by an almost limitless number of obstacles.

Therefore, the **Conflict Situations** in Plots Unlimited are classified in three major categories or **Story-types:**

> **Romance**
> **Married Life**
> **Activity**

Under **Conflicts in Romance** are the following five **Story Sub-types:**

> **Romance's Beginnings**
> **Romantic Misadventures**
> **Marriage Proposal**
> **Rejection**
> **Marriage**

These **Sub-type Conflicts in Romance** are further categorized according to applicable **B-Clauses** (from the MasterPlot Chart).

Conflicts in Married Life has no **Story Sub-types**. **Conflicts in Married Life** are categorized only by **B-Clauses**.

Conflicts in Activity are divided into the following fifteen **Story Sub-types:**

> **Misfortune**
> **Mistaken Judgment**
> **Helpfulness**
> **Deliverance**
> **Idealism**
> **Obligation**
> **Necessity**
> **Chance**
> **Personal Limitations**
> **Pretense**
> **Deception**
> **Crime/Immorality**
> **Vengeance**
> **Mystery**
> **Revelation**

These **Sub-type Conflicts in Activity** are then further categorized according to applicable **B-Clauses**.

Each of these 1,462 numbered Plots Unlimited **Conflict Situations** is linked to from two to as many as fourteen other **Conflicts** or Story Segments which will carry your story forward a step at a time (we call these Lead-outs), and a similar number which carry the story backward (Lead-ins). An exception are those Lead-outs that end in Death for your protagonist, or otherwise conclude a story. Clearly, the number of possible plot permutations the imaginative writer can generate from Plots Unlimited is an embarrassment of riches.

Immediately following the **Conflict Situations**, on page 183, is the final section of Plots Unlimited which begins with the

Index to the Table of Character Combinations

which lists groups of **Characters** in various combinations. (i.e.: Jack, Carol & Sam = male protagonist, female protagonist and male law officer)

Next, beginning on page 187 is the the Table of

Conflicts Classified by Character Combinations

This offers the writer yet another access to plot-generation, beginning with a **Character Combination** rather than with **Conflict Situation**, **Story Type** or **Sub-type**, or **MasterPlot**. Suppose the cast of characters you wish to work with consists of a male protagonist, Jack, a male antagonist, Gary, a female protagonist, Carol, and her father, Frank. By referring to the corresponding **Character Combination** Group, the writer will find several **Conflict Situations** under four **Story Type** and/or **Story Sub-type** headings: **Romantic Misadventures, Rejection, Marriage**, and **Married Life**.

If a particular group of characters proves too limiting, the writer can drop one of the minor characters and refer to the Group representing those remaining.

This technique can be extremely useful in constructing sub-plots and parallel action for such forms as novels, screenplays and teleplays. After generating a storyline for one group of characters, it can be interwoven with those of another group or with the main story-line, adding texture and bringing subsidiary characters to life.

Conflict Manipulations

As noted, **Characters** in the Plots Unlimited **Conflict Situations** are represented by all-purpose names. These names may be readily changed or transposed as an aid in manipulating the **Conflict Situation** suggestions. Thus, "261 ch Gary to Jack," suggests that the antagonist in Conflict Situation Number 261 is to be changed to the protagonist; similarly, "578b tr Carol & Laura" suggests a transposition in which the female antagonist takes the place of the female protagonist, and vice-versa.

The **Characters** are changed, or transposed, in the auxiliary **Conflict Situations** to conform with the **Characters** of the **Conflict Situation** whose ramifications are being studied.

In many instances the **Conflict Situations** are "broken" — that is, divided into two or more parts. The end of the first part is marked with a star (*), of the second part, a double star (**), of the third part, a triple star (***). Thus, "- *" indicates that the **Conflict Situation** is to be used up to the first star; "*-**" indicates that the first part of the **Conflict Situation** is not to be used, but only that part between the first star and the double star; "-**" indicates that all of the **Conflict Situation** is to be used up to the double star.

ART CENTER COLLEGE OF DESIGN LIBRARY
1700 LIDA STREET
PASADENA, CALIFORNIA 91103

Using Plots Unlimited

In the following examples, we will walk you through some of the ways Plots Unlimited allows the writer to begin building a **Story Outline** or **Plot.** In each example, you will see how the framework of a well known piece of literature or a famous motion picture can be generated by using Plots Unlimited — and it will become apparent that by combining your own creativity and imagination, you can create your own stories with a new-found freedom.

Starting a story with with a Character Combination

For our first example, we're going to demonstrate how the plot for one of the most popular movies of all time, Casablanca, could have been created through the use of the Plots Unlimited **Character Combinations.**

Casablanca, when reduced to its essentials, is about a man in love with another man's wife.

Our basic **Character Combination**, then, consists of the female protagonist, (Ilsa), her husband (Victor Laszlo), and Victor's rival, (Rick).

Scanning the Table of Conflicts Classified by **Character Combinations** under Jack, Carol and Gary (male antagonist), we find the following under Story Type-Married Life:

> (4) Carol, wife of Jack, runs into an old lover, Gary, and has no choice
> but to borrow money from him   583c

You may recall that in Casablanca, Ilsa, wife of Nazi resistance leader Victor Laszlo, encounters her former lover, Rick, from whom she must obtain the Letters of Transit that will allow them to leave Casablanca. Thus, if we were to substitute "Letters of Transit" for "money," in the above **Conflict Situation**, we'd have one of the cornerstones of the story.

First, let's substitute our character names for the all-purpose names provided by Plots Unlimited. Thus Carol should become Ilsa, Jack should become Victor, and Rick should take the place of Gary. Then, consulting Number 583c in the list of **Conflict Situations**, we find that 583c leads out to 476b:

476

(b) (398b) (449) (483b)
Victor's wife, Ilsa, finds herself in the power of a former lover, Rick
* Rick threatens to tell Ilsa's husband, Victor, a deadly secret unless
Ilsa agrees to a certain proposition Rick offers her ** (441) (447)
(455b) (492b) (446b ch Pete to Rick) (483b) (507a)

Let's eliminate the last part of this "broken" **Situation** and use only 476-*. Following one of the lead-outs suggested by Number 476 (and making the suggested character change) we discover:

446

(b) (411b ch Rick to Pete) (433b ch Rick to Pete) (449 ch Rick to Pete) Victor's wife, Ilsa, visits her lover, Rick * Victor visits his friend, Rick ** Rick hides Ilsa from Victor *** Victor finds his wife, Ilsa, hidden in Rick's apartment **** (400 ch Rick to Pete) (418 ch Rick to Pete) (446a)

Except for the fact that in the movie Rick was hardly Victor's friend, and Victor never actually realized, when he came to Rick's Cafe, that Ilsa was upstairs in Rick's apartment, our continuity is basically true to that portion of the plot of Casablanca. Therefore, let's use only 446b-***. We now have a story which runs as follows:

583c

Ilsa, wife of Victor, happens to meet an old lover, Rick, and is compelled to ask him to give her the Letters of Transit

476b-*

Victor's wife, Ilsa, finds herself in the power of former lover, Rick

446b-***

Victor's wife, Ilsa, visits her lover, Rick. Victor visits Rick. Rick hides Ilsa from Victor

In the foregoing exercise, you've seen how Plots Unlimited has helped you build a piece of your story, which you will later combine with other pieces you've created.

At this point in the reconstruction of Casablanca, as would be true if you were building your own plot, it might be wise to examine our characters and begin to flesh them out by determining what kind of people they are and how they arrived at their present situation. One useful approach is to build their backstories, their lives before the story we're telling began. We've established that Rick and Ilsa are former lovers. What drove them apart?

Again referring to the Table of Conflicts Classified by **Character Combinations,** under Jack, Carol and Gary, and scanning the conflicts under Rejection, we find the following possibility:

(1) Jack and Carol were engaged. Jack, whom Carol thinks died in an accident, returns, finds Carol about to marry Gary, and attempts to prevent the marriage   328

In the movie, when Rick and Ilsa fell in love in Paris he was unaware that she was married, and she was under the impression that her husband, Victor, a hero of the anti-Nazi Resistance, had been killed. Rick and Ilsa planned to elope to Marseille. Then, just as the Nazis moved in, Ilsa learned that Victor was alive after all.

If we substitute our character names, ignore Victor's attempt to stop the marriage, and make a note to ourselves that Victor and Ilsa are already married, this Conflict Situation closely parallels the movie.

Referring to the table of **Conflict Situations**, none of the leadouts from 328 seem to fit our story, so let's try working backwards and examine leadins. Number 777 shows some promise:

777

(624) (783) (787) (1199-*) (1342a) (1389a)
Victor, though not a criminal, is convinced he is one * Victor conceals his identity, avoids people, and leads a furtive life **
(681b) (705) (1199)

To the Nazis, you may recall, Victor Laszlo was a hunted criminal; to the Forces of Freedom, he was a hero. Let's add 777*-** to our story.

Now we'll employ an often fruitful technique in making effective use of Plots Unlimited, that of scanning the **Conflict Situations** in the general area in which we're working: Number 316, for instance, yields an interesting direction:

316

(146) (308a) (40b)
When Ilsa fails to keep a date with Victor, he takes it as a rejection
(341) (360a)

You'll recall that in Casablanca Rick waited for Ilsa in the rain at the train station, where he received her farewell note.

By substituting Rick for Victor, and selecting 316 as our leadout from 328, our backstory now reads as follows:

777*-**

Victor conceals his identity, avoids people, and leads a furtive life

328

Victor, whom Ilsa thinks died in an accident, returns and finds Ilsa about to marry Rick

316

When Ilsa fails to keep a date with Rick, he takes it as a rejection

The presence of a fugitive in our story suggests that at least one of our characters might be a law-officer. In Casablanca, he was Captain Louis Renault. Again, in the Table of Conflicts Classified by **Character Combinations**, under Burt and Sam (criminal and law officer), the following offers possibilities:

Law officer Sam asks Jack to help him arrest Burt 1015

Let's substitute Louis for Sam, Rick for Jack, and Victor for Burt. You'll notice that Rick is the protagonist of this plot thread, and Victor is the criminal. Referring to the Table of **Conflict Situations**, Number 1015 directs us to Number 1222a:

1222

(a) (266) (657) (1175b ch Jack to Gary)
Jack thinks Gary is guilty of a crime * Jack, trying to force Gary to confess to a crime, places himself and Gary in a situation where both seemingly face imminent death ** (1461a ch Jack to Gary) (1456 ch Burt to Gary)

By changing Jack to Rick and Gary to Victor, and ignoring the first part (Rick was only pretending to set up Victor), we've come up with a sequence which closely approxiamtes the outline for the climax of Casablanca:

1015

Law officer Captain Renault asks Rick to help him arrest Victor

1222a*-**

Rick, trying to force Victor to confess to a crime, places himself and Victor in a situation where both seemingly face imminent death

In the movie, Rick turns the tables and forces Captain Renault to inform the airport that there will be two people with Letters of Transit boarding the Lisbon plane. But Renault, you may remember, only pretends to phone the airport, and dials Nazi Major Strasser instead. Strasser quickly dispatches Nazi Troopers and heads for the airport himself, where, in a last-second attempt to prevent the Lisbon plane from taking off with Victor and Ilsa aboard, Louis, Rick and Victor are threatened with death.

Thus, through the use of Plots Unlimited — and some imagination — we have generated the major story elements of the motion picture classic, Casablanca.

Starting a story with a MasterPlot

For this example of Plots Unlimited's flexibility, let's do a bare-bones reconstruction of Arthur Miller's great stage play Death of a Salesman by starting with a search of the **MasterPlot Chart**.

Death of a Salesman tells the story of Willy Loman, whose reverence of certain ideals (albeit false ones), and inability to deal with reality lead to his tragic downfall.

Under Number 7 in the **A Clauses** we find the heading "**An Idealistic Person,**" a category which best describes our protagonist, Willy Loman. Moving to the **B Clauses** brings us to Number 21, "**Landing in Trouble Through Mistaken Judgement,**" a reference to Willy's fatal character flaws. Under the **C Clauses** we locate Number 6, "**Makes the Supreme Sacrifice,**" which mirrors the play's climax when Willy commits suicide.

Thus, our **MasterPlot** reads as follows:
>   **A** (7) An idealistic person,
>   **B** (21) landing in trouble through mistaken judgement,
>   **C** (6) makes the supreme sacrifice.

When generating a story from a **MasterPlot**, it is important to note that the number preceding the **B Clause** is the key to carrying your story forward. This number refers the writer to the next Plots Unlimited Table: **Conflict Situations,** Story-Types and Story Sub-Types Listed by **B Clause** Numbers. In our example we're looking for Number 21.

Scanning the Table of **Conflict Situations,** Story-Types and Story Sub-Types Listed by **B Clause** Numbers, Number 21 locates the heading "**Personal Limitations,**" which describes Willy Loman's inability to understand his situation. In turn, **Personal Limitations** directs us to a series of pertinent **Conflict Situations** beginning at Number 1057.

Scanning the table of **Conflict Situations** beginning at 1057, we find that Number 1060 offers the most promising direction:

> **1060**
>
> (768) (1134-*) (1418-*)
> Jack, with average abilities, unrealistically views himself as being superior * Jack tries ambitious ventures but loses confidence before finishing them ** (769) (1134*-**) (1187)

For our purposes, only the portion up to the first star is applicable. It specifically illustrates how Willy Loman's mistaken judgement has landed him in trouble. Our capsule outline for Death of a Salesman now reads as follows:

A

An idealistic person,

1060-*

Willy, with average abilities, unrealistically views himself as being superior,

C

makes the supreme sacrifice.

Thus, by tracking and building your story through the numbered **Conflict Situations**, the **B Clause** in your initial **MasterPlot** is replaced and expanded upon, while the **A** and **C Clauses** remain constant.

Summarizing the play, Willy Loman's world is rapidly crashing in on him: no longer able to earn his living as a traveling salesman, and aware that his two sons, for whom he had such high hopes are failures, Willy retreats into fantasy in his search for the point at which his life took a wrong turn. Scanning the numbered **Conflict Situations** in the area of Number 1418 (a lead-in to our first Conflict, Number 1060) locates

1423

(1389b) (1422a)
Late at night, Jack enters his house and sees another man, Walt,
sitting before the fireplace * Jack, thinking Walt is a friend, steps
closer and suddenly Walt vanishes ** (1332) (1424a) (1455a,b)

In the play, Willy materializes the image of his dead brother Ben, who had in earlier years urged Willy to follow him into the jungle and seek his fortune. Willy had told Ben that he was a salesman, the best there was and most important of all, he was "well liked;" if he wasn't yet making a large income then he was certain to do so one day soon. Ben went into the jungle a pauper and came out rich. Willy never achieved material success. By placing this **Conflict Situation** *after* Number 1060 our original **MasterPlot** has now expanded to the following form:

A

An idealistic person,

1060-*

Willy, with average abilities, unrealistically views
himself as being superior

1423

Late at night, Willy enters his house and sees another man, Ben, sitting before the fireplace. Willy, thinking Ben is a friend, steps closer and suddenly Ben vanishes.

C

Willy makes the supreme sacrifice.

And so on.

Thus one can see that starting with a **MasterPlot** is yet another extremely viable Plots Unlimited method for generating a story outline.

Starting a story with a Conflict Situation

Starting your story with one of Plots Unlimited's **Conflict Situations** is clearly the most random of our three examples. For this illustration, we've chosen **Conflict Situation** Number 1439c:

1439

(c) (1423) (1427b)
When it serves Jack's purposes, his alter-ego, Walt, materializes, unseen by others, in a menacing, demonic form (53) (552a, b) (606) (681a) (1424a)

Using Number 1439c as a starting point, we'll reconstruct the essential plot elements of Robert Louis Stevenson's timeless work, "Dr. Jekyll and Mr. Hyde".

"Dr. Jekyll and Mr. Hyde" is an examination of the duality of Man's nature: good and evil residing together in an uneasy partnership; the amoral Mr. Edward Hyde the alter-ego of the outwardly respectable Dr. Henry Jekyll. Dr. Jekyll (Jack), calls upon his alter-ego Mr. Hyde (Walt), whenever his need to lead a double life arises.

In Stevenson's story, Dr. Jekyll compounds a chemical that transforms him into Edward Hyde whenever the evil side of his nature seeks release. But one morning he awakens to find himself involuntarily transformed into Hyde. Aware that his evil side has gained control, Dr. Jekyll works feverishly to rid himself of Hyde — but without success. Scanning the lead-out numbers from **Conflict Situation** Number 1439c, we discover

681

(a) (49) (211)
Optimistic Dr. Jekyll suffers a critical reversal that destroys his spirit (106) (900) (918b) (963)

It's clear that the above **Conflict Situation** fits Stevenson's storyline without need for much alteration. Again, an investigation of the lead-out numbers allows us to select

963

(322b) (715a) (763) (862) (914) (922a)
Dr. Jekyll trades low ideals for high ideals * Dr. Jekyll, trading low ideals for high ideals, vainly struggles to achieve his high ideals. But, though unable to reach his goal, he becomes a better person ** (188b) (563c)

Firstly, for the purpose of our recreation, let's use only the portion up to the first star. Next, we'll transpose "high ideals" for "low ideals." Thus, Dr. Jekyll "trades high ideals for low ideals." In the story, Jekyll resigns himself to Hyde's amorality.

In **Conflict Situation** Number 963, the action described actually takes place earlier in the story of **DR. JEKYLL AND MR. HYDE.** This is an example of what the writer may often encounter when using Plots Unlimited: a **Conflict Situation** reached through a lead-in or lead-out number can, for the purposes of storytelling, frequently be more effective if it's placed in a different sequence. The writer should never feel constrained by the order in which the story elements come together; by repositioning any **Conflict Situation** the writer can alter the dramatic values of the story being generated.

To recap our re-creation of DR. JEKYLL AND MR. HYDE, the story essentials are

963-*

Dr. Jekyll trades high ideals for low ideals

1439 c

When it serves Dr. Jekyll's purposes, his alter-ego, Mr. Hyde, materializes, unseen by others, in a menacing, demonic form

681 a

Optimistic Dr. Jekyll suffers a critical reversal that destroys his spirit

While, as in our other examples, this is merely a beginning, it is obvious that generating a story plot from a selected **Conflict Situation** is yet another very effective illustration of Plots Unlimited's usefulness and versatility.

While Plots Unlimited won't write such memorable lines of dialogue as "Here's looking at you, kid," or "I remember every detail. The Germans wore gray; you wore blue," by adding your creativity and imagination, Plots Unlimited can become an essential aid for any writer of fiction.

We wish you great success.

MasterPlots with Interchangeable Clauses

NOTE

A **Plots Unlimited MasterPlot** consists of three clauses: An **"A" Clause**, a **"B" Clause** and a **"C" Clause**.

- The **A Clause** is the Protagonist Clause.
- The **B Clause** originates and continues the action.
- The **C Clause** continues and resolves the action.

Any A Clause may be used in conjunction with *any* **B Clause** and with *any* **C Clause**.

Suggestions for evolving a plot to the pattern of a selected **MasterPlot** will be found in the Plots Unlimited **Conflict Situations.** The **Conflict Situations** are listed under **Story Type** and **Story Sub-type,** and further sub-grouped under the full text of the representative **B Clause.**

On the page immediately following the list of **MasterPlots** is the Index of **Conflict Situations** grouped under **B Clauses, Story Types** and/or **Story Sub-types.** The numerals following each of these listings refer to the first **Conflict Situation** under your **B Clause** sub-group within that particular **Story Type** or **Story Sub-type.** The flexibility of Plots Unlimited allows the writer to choose from any of the **Conflict Situations** within that sub-group and still remain true to the selected **MasterPlot.**

The C, or Terminal, Clauses are also numbered in parentheses; and **Conflict Situations** suggesting these resolutions will be found opposite the **C Clause** numbers in the **Table of Character Combinations.**

MasterPlots with Interchangeable Clauses

"A" Clauses	"B" Clauses	"C" Clauses
1. **A Person in Love,**	(1) Undertaking a difficult venture when promised a reward for high achievement,	(1) Suffers a heavy penalty as the result of an ill-fated venture.
	(2) Falling in love despite conflicting obligations,	
	(3) Trying to prove love's power by a test of courage,	
	(4) Compelled by excessive desire to exercise mistaken judgment in a romance,	
2. **A Married Person,**	(5) Trying to make the best of a hopeless love affair,	(2) Emerges happily from a serious involvement.
	(6) Challenging the concept that lovers from different cultures cannot be compatible,	
	(7) Entering a love affair filled with unforeseen complications,	
	(8) Confronting a romantic situation in which a fortune can be won or lost by a particular course of action,	
3. **A Criminal Person,**	(9) Being put to a test in which love is lost if riches are gained,	(3) Outwits a scheming person and defeats an insidious plot.
	(10) Suffering loss of a relationship due to mistaken judgment,	
	(11) Facing a situation in which only courage and devotion can save a loved one,	

"A" Clauses	"B" Clauses	"C" Clauses
	(12) Suffering problems because of disloyalty in love,	
4. **An Erring Person,**	(13) Trying by deception to escape trouble,	(4) Assumes a role that leads directly to a catastrophe.
	(14) Getting into trouble because of a clever schemer,	
	(15) Finding the power to overcome problems,	
	(16) Being rescued from trouble by someone who confesses a guilty secret,	
5. **A Caring Person,**	(17) Dealing with enduring problems while ethically pursuing goals,	(5) Emerges from a difficult ordeal with hard-earned wisdom.
	(18) Rebelling against a power that controls and suppresses personal abilities,	
	(19) Running into trouble and being stranded in a primitive environment,	
	(20) Getting into a situation from which difficult problems are likely to result,	
6. **A Protecting Person,**	(21) Landing in trouble through mistaken judgment,	(6) Makes the supreme sacrifice.
	(22) Misguided by mistaken judgment,	
	(23) Becoming enmeshed in mistaken judgment and/ or suspicion,	
	(24) Becoming a victim of mistaken judgment while engaged in a venture,	

MASTERPLOTS

"A" Clauses	"B" Clauses	"C" Clauses
7. An Idealistic Person,	(25) Trying to save someone accused of a crime or offense,	(7) Reverses certain opinions when their flaws are revealed.
	(26) Secretly trying to save another from danger,	
	(27) Refusing to betray another's secret and facing persecution as a result,	
	(28) Facing a situation in which the troubles of someone highly regarded call for courage and wise planning,	
8. A Person Influenced by an Obligation,	(29) Helping another to keep a deadly secret,	(8) Gains a spiritual victory.
	(30) Selflessly aiding a needy person,	
	(31) Leading a lonely, unhappy life and looking for companionship,	
	(32) Trying to hide identity because of high ideals,	
9. A Person Subjected to Adversity,	(33) Secretly challenging a questionable convention for honorable reasons,	(9) Achieves success and happiness in a difficult under-taking.
	(34) Starting a rebellion to improve untenable conditions,	
	(35) Encountering a problem that challenges one's ideals,	
	(36) Having an experience that greatly changes character,	
10. A Resentful Person,	(37) Fighting to achieve a cherished ideal,	(10) Encounters a situation whereby a wrong is righted.

"A" Clauses	"B" Clauses	"C" Clauses
	(38) Making a serious mistake and secretly trying to live down its consequences,	
	(39) Giving up deeply held ambitions to fulfill an obligation,	
	(40) Starting a venture in which one obligation conflicts with another,	
11. A Person Deceived by Pretense,	(41) Finding an obligation at odds with ambition, inclination or necessity,	(11) Recognizes the foolishness of attempting to be other than one's true self.
	(42) Landing in trouble while trying to fulfill an obligation,	
	(43) Trying to overcome personal limitations while carrying out a venture,	
	(44) Using radical methods to overcome personal limitations,	
12. An Intellectual Person,	(45) Trying to forward a project and being obstructed by family sentiment,	(12) Salvages integrity from a difficult entanglement.
	(46) Attempting to retaliate for a serious wrong, either real or imagined,	
	(47) Finding (apparently) a much-desired object, and obtaining it (apparently),	
	(48) Posing as a criminal in an honest venture,	
13. A Person Influenced by the Occult and the Unexplained,	(49) Assuming a false identity when launching a venture,	(13) Finally confronts a puzzle with no solution.
	(50) Compelled by a special motive to behave underhandedly,	

MASTERPLOTS

"A" Clauses	"B" Clauses	"C" Clauses
	(51) Inventing a clever deception to attain an ambitious goal,	
	(52) Encountering a would-be offender and attempting to prevent an offense,	
14. **An Average Person,**	(53) Trying to defeat a devious opponent,	(14) Achieves a permanent character change.
	(54) Involved in a puzzling complication that concerns an object with mysterious powers,	
	(55) Involved in an exotic complication and trying to make the best of a bizarre experience,	
	(56) Testing the value of a mysterious communication and being drawn into bizarre complications,	
15. **Any Person,**	(57) Trying to solve a puzzling problem,	(15) Arrives at any fate, positive or negative.
	(58) Taking part in an action and mysteriously vanishing,	
	(59) Taking part in a venture and becoming entangled with the bizarre and the supernatural,	
	(60) Becoming involved due to curiosity, in a mysterious venture,	
	(61) Learning an important secret that requires decisive action,	
	(62) Becoming involved in any kind of complication,	

(1)   Romance 110
(2)   Romance 16, 119, 271
(3)   Romance 175
(4)   Romance 148
(5)   Romance 168, 313
(6)   Romance 331
(7)   Romance 333
(8)   Romance 117
(9)   Romance 116
(10) Romance 105;
        Married Life 369
(11) Romance 179; Married Life 545;
        Revelation 1462
(12) Romance 337; Married Life 547
(13) Romance 96, 244; Married Life 457;
        Misfortune 650;
        Deception 1247; Mystery 1373
(14) Married Life 471; Deception 1260;
        Misfortune 660
(15) Romance 12, 106, 265, 360;
        Married Life 496; Helpfulness 815;
        Deliverance 874; Chance 1051
(16) Helpfulness 831
(17) Idealism 934
(18) Misfortune 674
(19) Misfortune 685
(20) Romance 24, 153, 196, 280, 365;
        Married Life 571; Idealism 956;
        Necessity 1026; Chance 1036;
        Personal Limitations 1122;
        Crime/Immorality 1295;
        Misfortune 695; Mistaken Judgment 793;
        Deliverance 887; Obligation 997;
        Deception 1285; Mystery 1438;
        Revelation 1461a
(21) Romance 40, 182, 205, 342;
        Married Life 369, 386, 391, 399, 418;
        Misfortune 595; Mistaken Judgment 747;
        Helpfulness 804; Deliverance 851;
        Idealism 897; Obligation 979;
        Necessity 1023; Chance 1034;
        Personal Limitations 1057;
        Crime/Immorality 1290;
        Vengeance 1310; Mystery 1330
(22) Romance 255; Married Life 484;
        Mistaken Judgment 768
(23) Romance 21, 177, 328;
        Married Life 538;
        Mistaken Judgment 786
(24) Mistaken Judgment 794
(25) Romance 122; Helpfulness 820;
        Deliverance 894

(26) Married Life 558; Helpfulness 825;
        Misfortune 671
(27) Helpfulness 824
(28) Romance 125; Helpfulness 836
(29) Romance 147; Married Life 537;
        Misfortune 667;
        Personal Limitations 1070; Pretense 1160
(30) Helpfulness 845
(31) Idealism 910
(32) Idealism 917
(33) Idealism 958
(34) Idealism 949
(35) Romance 292; Idealism 922
(36) Romance 152; Misfortune 680; Idealism
        963
(37) Married Life 563; Idealism 965;
        Personal Limitations 1107
(38) Obligation 987
(39) Romance 123, 282;
        Married Life 508; Obligation 989
(40) Romance 287; Married Life 517;
        Obligation 1011
(41) Romance 19, 127, 294;
        Married Life 521; Obligation 1000
(42) Obligation 1018
(43) Helpfulness 835;
        Personal Limitations 1071
(44) Romance 191;
        Personal Limitations 1101
(45) Personal Limitations 1138
(46) Married Life 567; Vengeance 1312
(47) Pretense 1165
(48) Pretense 1167
(49) Pretense 1173
(50) Romance 1, 66, 185, 230, 347;
        Married Life 419; Helpfulness 813;
        Deliverance 863; Idealism 932;
        Pretense 1141; Deception 1209;
        Mystery 1365
(51) Deception 1277
(52) Deception 1275
(53) Helpfulness 834; Deception 1280
(54) Mystery 1379
(55) Mystery 1385
(56) Mystery 1394
(57) Romance 174; Married Life 560;
        Helpfulness 833; Mystery 1399;
        Revelation 1460
(58) Mystery 1414
(59) Mystery 1418
(60) Mystery 1429
(61) Mistaken Judgment 802; Revelation 1447
(62) All Conflict Situations

THE PLOTS UNLIMITED CHARACTERS

Characters in the **Plots Unlimited Conflict Situations** are represented by generic names which the user can easily alter to suit his or her story. The relationships of these characters to the protagonist(s) is usually explained in the text of the **Conflict Situations**, with the exception of **Jack** and **Carol** — these being the default names we've assigned the male, and the female, protagonists. Protagonist Jack or Carol might be a criminal, a law officer, an employer, etc., but if that is the case, the description is included in the text of the **Conflict Situation**. It's important to note that one need not be constrained by the genders suggested by **Plots Unlimited**; changing one or more of the characters from male to female, or vice-versa, can often help with a story-problem.

Jack	protagonist		**Carol**	protagonist
Pete (or Larry)	friend		**Annie**	friend
Gary (or Stan)	antagonist		**Laura**	antagonist
Dave (or Rick)	stranger		**Kate**	stranger
Burt (or Fred)	criminal		**Sally**	criminal
Sam (or Russ)	law officer		**Faye**	law officer
Matt	subordinate/employee		**Donna**	subordinate/employee
Eric	utility character		**Irene**	utility character
Carl	superior/employer		**Cleo**	superior/employer
Andy	Jack's father		**Frank**	Carol's father
Linda	Jack's mother		**Rita**	Carol's mother
Tom	Jack's brother		**Tony**	Carol's brother
Susan (or Molly)	Jack's sister		**Judy**	Carol's sister
Greg	Jack's son		**Doug**	Carol's son
Nina	Jack's daughter		**Vicki**	Carol's daughter
Milt	Jack's uncle		**Paul**	Carol's uncle
Karen	Jack's aunt		**Nancy**	Carol's aunt
Ray	Jack's cousin		**Julie**	Carol's cousin
Jim	Jack's nephew		**Nick**	Carol's nephew
Joan	Jack's niece		**Pat**	Carol's niece
Bill	Jack's grandfather		**Gene**	Carol's grandfather
Mary	Jack's grandmother		**Rose**	Carol's grandmother
Dan	Jack's stepfather		**Jeff**	Carol's stepfather
Ruth	Jack's stepmother		**Betty**	Carol's stepmother
Terry	Jack's grandchild		**Chris**	Carol's grandchild
Lee (or Kenny)	a child		**Amy**	mysterious/unusual character
Walt (or Leo)	mysterious/unusual character		**Enid**	mysterious aunt
X	inanimate/mysterious object			

(50) Compelled by a Special Motive to Behave Underhandedly

1

(a) (112) (117) (148) (656)
Jack, poor, loves wealthy Carol * Jack, in love with wealthy Carol, pretends to be rich ** (187) (228) (233) (347a-*)

(b) (171) (734) (1106-* ch Carol to Jack) (1146)
Uneducated Jack falls in love with college professor Carol * Uneducated Jack, in love with academic Carol, pretends to be part of her world ** (139) (153) (209) (1200)

(c) (918a) (926) (928a)
Jack, in love with Carol, finds that Carol thinks he's too rigid for a happy marriage * Carol thinks her lover, Jack, too rigid for a happy marriage; so Jack, hoping to change Carol's mind, adopts a less daunting facade ** (1167) (1170) (1216) (1227a, b, c)

(d) (148) (149) (160)
Jack, older, loves youthful Carol * Jack, older, in love with young Carol, tries to enhance the relationship by pretending to be young ** (40a, b) (75b) (78) (97) (156) (330a)

(e) (59) (1146) (1175a)
Criminal Jack pretends to be an honest man in order to enhance his romance with Carol (280a, b, tr Jack & Gary) (318; 236; 267) (252a, b)

(f) (230) (1060) (1101)
Politically conservative Jack loves passionately liberal Carol * Politically conservative Jack pretends to be interested in social causes ** (179a, b, c) (181a, b, c)

(g) (234a-*) (1061) (1150)
Stodgy Jack falls for Carol, a romantic * Stodgy Jack, in love with romantic Carol, tries to adopt an heroic facade ** (234a*-**) (1150; 851; 885a) (1227b, c)

(h) (43-*) (101b) (898-*)
Jack quarrels with his girlfriend, Carol, and is afraid he's losing her love * Jack, afraid he's losing Carol's love, pretends to attempt suicide ** (249) (262a, b, c) (1461b)

2

(a) (949a) (954) (968)
Bank clerk Jack crashes a high society party * Bank clerk Jack, taking a fling in high society, meets wealthy patrician Carol (1146 ch Jack to Carol) (1187 ch Jack to Carol), and they fall in love ** (1461a ch Jack to Carol) (1461a, c)

(b) (1146) (1175a) (1197)
Fugitive Jack, using an alias, falls in love with Carol * Jack, involved in a devious secret venture, falls in love with Carol (1146 ch Jack to Carol) (1169 ch Jack to Carol) who is also involved in a suspect venture ** (91) (224) (233) (876a)

(c) (232) (420) (818b)
Wealthy, socially-conscious Jack, in an effort to understand inner-city problems, pretends to be one of its citizens * Jack, posing as a citizen of the inner-city, meets Carol, and they fall in love ** (114) (220) (358)

(d) (818a) (1197) (1198)
Jack is mistaken by Carol for another man, Eric, with whom she's communicated but never seen * Jack, falling in love with Carol, pretends he's Eric ** (82a) (97) (822)

(e) (1170) (1329)
Rich Carol devotes much time to charity work; and, in conducting her voluntary enterprises, she pretends to be a retail salesclerk * Carol, while posing as a salesclerk, meets Jack, and they fall in love ** (115) (336b) (1461a ch Jack to Carol; 358 **-***)

(f) (916) (974) (1461a)
Working girl Carol unexpectedly wins a small lottery jackpot; with it she briefly pretends to be wealthy * Carol, poor but pretending to be wealthy, meets rich, influential Jack (1163c) and they fall in love ** (117) (152a)

(g) (850a) (1159 ch Dave to Jack)
Carol, a maid, uses the wardrobe of her rich employer and poses as an important person * Carol, poor but pretending to be rich and important, meets apparently rich, influential Jack (1148a) and they fall in love ** (885a) (1060)

2

(h) (876a) (1244a)
Carol, a criminal, assumes an alias and uses stolen funds to evade the law * Carol, a criminal in disguise, meets Jack (1169) (1175a) (1181) and they fall in love ** (97) (1208)

3

(a) (2h) (926) (949b)
Jack is a judge and Carol is a fugitive posing as a wealthy, fashionable woman * Jack, a judge, falls in love with Carol, a lawbreaker ** (359) (727)

(b) (106-*) (925-*)
Jack, a detective, falls in love with Carol, the criminal he has apprehended and is bringing back to the locale where the crime was committed (106*-**) (53) (359) (986)

4

(a) (298a ch Amy to Carol; 58a ch Walt to Jack; 1184) (1172)
Jack, trying to expose treachery, runs into the unexpected * Jack, trying to expose treachery, falls in love with Carol, suspected of the treachery ** (62) (64) (1167;826)

(b) (739; 1401) (1170)
Jack recovers property belonging to Carol, a woman he doesn't know * Jack unselfishly returns property to a woman, Carol, whom he's never met — and falls in love with her ** (21) (792a)

5

(168) (603b, c, d)
Jack, bringing news of the death of his friend, Pete, to Carol, the girl to whom Pete was engaged (70 ch Jack to Pete), is mistaken by Carol and her parents for Pete, who have never seen Jack or Pete (26a, b) * Jack, posing as dead Pete, falls in love with Carol and withholds mention of Pete's death ** (1385) (1461a; 73)

6

(a) (14b-*) (101b)
Jack unknowingly loses something of value in a public place * Carol, who has been attempting to meet Jack, retrieves the item he lost and returns it to him. Jack and Carol fall in love ** (54a, b) (1357)

(b) (2h) (3a-*)
Attorney Jack loses his briefcase * Carol finds a mislaid briefcase belonging to Jack, an attorney, and returns it to him. Jack and Carol fall in love ** (801) (822)

7

(a) (898) (1073)
Jack is crude and unattractive to women, although he wishes to be a ladies' man * An associate, Matt, offers Jack a mysterious object, X, that Matt insists will make Jack attractive to women. Jack accepts X and tries it out ** (8a) (1330) (1347)

(b) (1403) (1418a)
Jack loves Carol but worries that their affair has gone sour * Jack, in an effort to help his romance with Carol, obtains a mail-order love potion ** (249) (1433b; 1363)

8

(a) (7a, b) (1061)
Bland, painfully dull Jack, rejected by women, shies away from them * Shy, retiring Jack, acquiring a love charm, X, gains confidence and becomes attractive to women ** (161) (378) (454)

(b) (7a, b) (1330)
Jack's romance with Carol is going nowhere, so Jack buys an aphrodisiac and mixes it secretly in a cup of tea — which Carol's maiden aunt, Nancy, mistakenly drinks (1332) (1334a) (1375)

CONFLICT SITUATIONS

9

(a) (13a) (36)
Jack and Carol, both single, vow to keep their relationship platonic * Jack and Carol, involved in a project, vow to keep their relationship platonic; but, despite their intentions, they fall in love ** (207) (260a, b)

(b) (244 ch Carol to Laura) (325)
Jack and Carol, young and single, become business partners * Jack and Carol, entering into a business partnership, try with every legal device to preclude romance — but in vain ** (178) (212a) (213)

(c) (83) (84a)
Carol inherits her father's TV station. Each manager she hires comes on to her, and she fires him * Carol hires Jack as manager of her TV station on the condition that he keep his distance; but Carol falls for him, and is pleased to learn that Jack's sole purpose in taking the job was to win her love ** (181a) (828)

0

(a) (665) (1309a ch Jack to Eric; 1309b)
Detective Jack arrests criminal Carol * Carol, a criminal arrested by Jack, a detective, tries to seduce Jack in hope of escaping ** (3b) (230 tr Jack & Carol)

(b) (873) (876a)
Carol, impoverished and in trouble, is befriended by wealthy Jack * Carol, impoverished, tries to win the love of wealthy Jack ** (186) (230) (431)

(c) (239) (745)
Carol makes love to Jack in an effort to escape from trouble (182a) (406)

1

(a) (1279a ch Carol to Rita; 57 ch Carol to Rita) (124-* ch Carol to Rita)
Carol's mother, Rita, a middle-aged widow, introduces her young lover, Jack, to Carol * Carol's mother, Rita, plans for her young lover, Jack, to transfer his affections to Carol. Rita's plan succeeds ** (83 ch Carol to Rita) (324 ch Carol to Rita & Laura to Carol)

(b) (124-*) (168-*)
Middle-aged Carol and youthful Jack love each other * Carol, older, in love with young Jack, wants Jack to shift his affections to her rival, Laura, who is nearer Jack's age ** (11a ch Carol to Laura and "mother" to "friend") (93a)

(c) (3a, b) (4a)
Carol, who has a questionable past, discovers that she has won the love of straight-arrow Jack * Because of her questionable past, Carol tries to persuade her lover, Jack, to transfer his affections to her rival, Laura ** (263) (324)

(15) Finding The Power to Overcome Problems

12

(a) (2b) (1173) (750; 784-*)
Jack and Carol each secretly believe themselves to be criminals * Jack and Carol, believing themselves to be fugitives, meet while on the run, and fall in love ** (11c) (624) (784*-**) (1050)

(b) (688) (918a) (921) (750; 784-*)
Jack, unmarried, and Carol, married, are stranded in an isolated area * Jack, unmarried, and Carol, married, fall in love. Then Carol makes a startling discovery ** (307) (1461c)

13

(a) (32) (340)
Carol is discouraged with her love-life * Carol, discouraged with her love-life, receives a "sign" that predicts she'll be married within a year ** (56) (1342a ch Jack to Carol)

(b) (15a, b) (34) (229)
Carol is regarded as inferior (intellectually, physically, socially) * Carol, inferior, falls in love with a superior person, Jack; and Jack's apparent love for Carol gives her the strength to endure her problems ** (53) (270)

CONFLICT SITUATIONS

14

(a) (641) (645) (818a) (873)
Carol, nearly overcome by troubles, meets Jack, and they fall in love * Carol wins the love of Jack, and finds the strength to endure her misfortune ** (827) (850a) (892 ch Laura to Jack)

(b) (60 ch Jack to Gary) (647)
Carol finds herself in a strange city, broke, victimized * Carol, helpless and in dire straits, meets a stranger, Jack, and they fall in love ** (24a, d) (82a) (144)

(c) (504a ch Jack to Eric) (577 ch Carol to Irene)
Carol, an attractive young widow, meets Jack, a handsome young widower * Carol, a widow, and Jack, a widower, meet in a cemetery while paying their respects to their deceased spouses — and they fall in love ** (40a) (67)

15

(a) (23a) (31)
Carol, a "plain Jane" working girl, falls in love with handsome, successful Jack (68) (243)

(b) (29) (32)
Carol, a "plain Jane" servant, secretly adores Jack * Jack hasn't a clue that plain Carol is in love with him ** (87) (270)

(2) Falling in Love Despite Conflicting Obligations

16

(a) (453) (10a)
Jack, a detective, arrests Carol, a criminal, and is returning her to the crime locale * Detective Jack falls for criminal Carol, whom he's arrested ** (49) (986) (126)

(b) (250) (1186)
Jack's vows preclude romantic involvement with women * Jack, although his vows forbid romance, falls in love with Carol ** (224) (221a, b) (248)

17

(a) (690) (688)
Unmarried Jack and married Carol meet in an isolated environment, and fall in love (53) (438 ch Jack to Eric)

(b) (561 ch Jack to Eric & Gary to Jack) (503b ch Jack to Eric & Gary to Jack)
Carol is unhappily married to brutal Eric. Out of sympathy for Carol, unmarried Jack falls in love with her (568a ch Jack to Eric) (568b ch Jack to Eric & Gary to Jack)

18

(462 ch Carol to Laura) (3a) (4a)
Jack falls for Carol, but he's already married to Laura, whom he's never loved but feels obligated to care for (417) (557a ch Carol to Laura, 557b ch Carol to Laura) (368e tr Carol & Laura)

(41) Finding Obligations at Odds with With Ambition, Inclination or Necessity

19

(a) (117) (24a,b, c)
Jack falls in love with Carol, and gives up the wealth he would have inherited if he'd married mysterious Amy (223) (43)

(b) (118) (1041 ch Jack to Bill)
Jack, under threat of disinheritance, is ordered to perform an act damaging to a near-relative of Carol, the woman he loves. Jack refuses (130) (313)

20

(a) (1058) (1138)
Jack tries to buy an object, X, that he badly wants from Carol. Carol refuses to sell * Jack and Carol, while negotiating a commercial transaction, fall in love ** (41a, b, c)

(b) (1148a) (1153)
While running a con-game, Jack meets Carol, who astutely sees through his scheme; Carol is also involved in a scam, and Jack becomes suspicious * Jack and Carol, mutually involved in a devious venture, are attracted to one another and fall in love ** (163) (50)

CONFLICT SITUATIONS

(c) (125b) (745)
Carol retains young attorney, Jack, to settle the estate of her late father, Frank * Jack and Carol, while meeting as attorney and client, fall in love ** (107) (69)

(23) Becoming Enmeshed in Mistaken Judgment and/or Suspicion
21

(4a) (1167) (1168) (1169) (1170)
Jack meets Carol and suspects she is dishonorable; Carol, in turn, thinks Jack is guilty of the same * Jack and Carol, despite mutual suspicions, fall in love ** (69) (97)

22

(a) (850a, b) (250) (885a tr Jack & Carol)
Jack devoutly dislikes women, but Carol's actions change his opinion * Woman-hater Jack falls in love with Carol ** (153) (826)

(b) (259-1) (262a)
Jack has an experience with Carol that turns him into a woman-hater (22a) (1002 ch Carol to Laura)

23

(a) (3a) (15a, b)
Marine Corporal Carol falls in love with Captain Jack, and tries to win him in marriage (212a) (254)

(b) (331) (346-*)
Carol, a member of a racial minority, falls in love with Jack, a member of the racial majority (229) (226)

(c) (255) (282b)
Jack, a member of a racial minority, falls in love with Carol, a member of the racial majority (225) (227)

(d) (293) (330a)
Wealthy, sophisticated Jack falls in love with lower-class Carol (228) (358)

(20) Getting Into a Situation From Which Difficult Problems are Likely to Result
24

(a) (806 ch Kate to Carol) (812a ch Dave to Jack)
Jack falls for Carol, a woman he doesn't know, and wants to marry her (1d, e) (103)

(b) (818b) (788)
Jack, attracted by Carol's beauty, falls in love with her (71b) (128)

(c) (1364 a *-** ch Carol to Jack) (1410)
Jack sees a photo of Carol, a woman he doesn't know * Studying a photo of stranger Carol, Jack falls in love with her ** (27) (31)

(d) (22b ch Carol to Laura; 839 tr Jack & Pete) (22b ch Carol to Laura; 1461b)
Jack, hearing of the beauty and charms of Carol, a woman he's never met, falls in love and is determined to marry her (29) (54a,b)

(e) (74a, b) (924b)
Romantic Jack catches only a fleeting glimpse of Carol, and falls in love with her (27) (2c)

25

(101b) (24b)
Jack, falling for Carol (32) (38), whom he doesn't know, tries to get an introduction (139) (36)

26

(a) (169 tr Jack & Pete) (6a, b; ch Carol to Laura)
Jack and Carol have never seen each other but their fathers, Andy and Frank, arrange for them to marry (117 ch Amy to Carol) (118)

(b) (72) (1183)
Jack and Carol have never seen each other but they correspond, and through their letters become engaged (1461c) (31)

CONFLICT SITUATIONS

27

(946) (1203) (1208) (1258 ch Sam to Jack)
Carol, from a questionable background, wins upstanding Jack's love, resulting in tense complications (11c) (359)

28

(a) (452 ch Jack to Eric) (1248)
Carol, critically ill, becomes convinced she's in love with Jack, her doctor (162a) (1462)

(b) (688) (148 tr Jack & Carol)
Carol, sharing troubles with Jack, thinks she's in love with him (307) (147)

29

(38) (916) (925-*) (926)
Carol doesn't know Jack, but falls in love with him at first sight (31) (223) (226)

30

(32) (1185)
Secretary Carol loves Jack, a junior partner of the company that employs her (274) (754) (213)

31

(2f, h) (8a)
Carol, rescued from an accident by Jack, a stranger, falls in love with him (45a, b) (59) (207) (220) (255) (616) (801)

32

(31) (10a) (641) (765)
Carol, desiring a relationship, has never had a lover (185) (195) (850a, b)

33

(668) (670)
Carol, daughter of Rita, has sound reasons for opposing Rita's intention to remarry (59 ch Carol to Rita) (65 ch Carol to Rita)

34

(327b) (15a, b)
Shy, insecure Carol worships Jack from afar (87) (91) (186) (270)

35

(32) (10b*-**)
Wallflower Carol is persuaded by her girl-friend, Annie, to go on a blind-date with Jack (68) (96) (891 tr Jack & Gary)

36

(13a) (32)
Carol, pretty but dull, is unable to attract men * Carol, discouraged by her lack of admirers, resorts to pretense ** (83) (58a, b)

37

(1279a) (1d tr Jack & Carol)
Middle-aged Carol and youthful Jack love each other (59) (124)

38

(13a) (35) (36)
Carol considers love and marriage the ultimate adventure, and eagerly pursues them (64) (88) (143) (146)

39

(38) (15a, b)
Unmarried Carol dreams of motherhood (68) (90a; 60) (84a)

(21) Landing In Trouble Through Mistaken Judgment

40

(a) (41a, b) (129)
Jack gives his sweetheart, Carol, a novel. The book, unknown to Jack, includes passages that Carol interprets as uncomplimentary toward herself — and she assumes that Jack is sending her a not-so-subtle message (80a) (208) (210)

(b) (6a, b) (1461d)
Jack is crushed when Carol fails to respond to his message (316) (218b) (306)

41

(a) (1c) (9b)
Jack, in love with Carol, ignores Carol's astute business advice, and they break up (300) (315)

(b) (1079) (1132) (808b tr Jack & Carol)
Jack promises Carol, the woman he loves, to give up a type of behavior that Carol finds unacceptable * Yielding to temptation, Jack reneges on a promise he made to his girlfriend, Carol, and they split up (85a) (97) (163)

(c) (118) (1315 ch Gary to Frank)
Despite his girlfriend Carol's protests, Jack persists in opposing a member of Carol's family. As a result, Jack and Carol split up (43) (259-2, 3)

42

(a) (292) (3a)
Jack, who loves Carol, learns that Carol loves her girlfriend, Annie (1413a ch Burt to Annie) (315)

(b) (1330) (1368)
Carol, in love with Jack, learns that Jack is a narcissist and loves only himself (57) (1347) (1374) (1375)

43

(70) (73) (75b)
Jack, in love with Carol, quarrels with her father, Frank * Frank, Carol's father, is mysteriously killed and innocent Jack is arrested for murder ** (91) (828 tr Jack & Carol & ch Sally to Burt)

44

(a) (598 ch Jack to Dave) (1029 ch Jack to Dave)
Jack, a publisher in love with Carol, receives a fiction manuscript from Dave that describes in derogatory terms a character similar to Carol * Publisher Jack rejects a novel because of spite ** (208) (292) (317) (260a ch Gary to Dave)

(b) (44a) (131)
Jack is so wrapped up in his romance with Carol that it affects his business disastrously (311) (260a ch Gary to Dave)

45

(a) (28a, b) (29) (30) (31)
Jack learns that unhappily married Carol, with no encouragement from Jack, is in love with him (55) (61) (274)

(b) (806 ch Kate to Carol) (818a)
Jack is courteous to unassuming Carol, whom he considers merely an acquaintance. He's astonished to learn that she loves him (270; 251) (254)

46

(205) (22b)
Jack meets Carol, a former love, and is disappointed to learn that his success abroad (967) doesn't impress her; she believes success on one's home ground is what counts (207) (211) (21)

CONFLICT SITUATIONS

47

(a) (1399) (1436)
Jack asks Carol to let herself be hypnotized
so that he can learn a secret buried in her
subconscious (1394) * Jack hypnotizes Carol,
who dies while in a subconscious state **
(53) (633) (1262)

(b) (1220a) (1159)
Jack persuades his girlfriend, Carol, to assume an alias and help him in a dishonest
scheme — with unhappy results for both (50
tr Jack & Carol) (1192; 1200)

48

(606) (619) (631 ch Pete to Eric) (654)
Jack understood that he would have to live
with his guilt when, to cancel a debt, he arranged for his daughter, Nina, to marry Eric,
a man she didn't love (284ch Carol to Nina
& Gary to Eric) (313 ch Frank to Jack, Carol
to Nina, Jack to Gary & Gary to Eric)

49

(70; 73; 690 add Carol) (688-*)
Lovers Jack and Carol narrowly escape tragedy * Lovers Jack and Carol escape death in
an accident, but each believes the other has
died ** (105) (794 ch Pete to Carol)

50

(126) (1201)
Jack, in love with Carol, impersonates another man at her request * Jack impersonates
another man who, it turns out, has a wife
who insists Jack is her husband ** (95) (163)
(225)

51

(a) (1290a) (1316)
When Jack, who loves Carol, admits to Carol
that he committed murder, Carol suffers a
breakdown (1433a) (53)

(b) (68 ch Carol to Laura) (1304)
Jack's confession to his lover, Carol, of a
crime (or indiscretion), proves disastrous
(1269 ch Jack to Carol & Pete to Jack) (249)

52

(a) (1209a) (1298) (694)
Fugitive Jack hears someone approaching his
hideout and mistakenly shoots and kills
Carol, his girlfriend (746 ch Carol to Jack)
(787) (802b ch Jack to Sam)

(b) (808a) (475)
Jack, trying to help Carol, undertakes a
venture that ends in disaster (52a) (761b;
385a) (578a)

53

(11c) (14a) (17a, b)
Jack loves Carol. Carol dies and Jack, grief-
stricken, becomes mentally unbalanced *
Jack, unable to accept the reality of Carol's
death, spends years searching for her **
(1345) (1365) (1375)

54

(a) (8a) (117)
Jack loves Carol and dates her regularly. One
night when he calls on her, he discovers her
house has vanished and in its place stands a
musty old tomb — the tomb of Carol, who,
according to the inscription, died 100 years
before Jack was born (1433b) (1446c)

(b) (7a) (1441a)
Jack, investigating a psychic phenomenon,
falls for Carol * Carol, apparently in her early
20s, is gorgeous; but she's actually very old,
and remained young-looking due to a
psychic phenomenon. Jack's love breaks the
spell; and, before his eyes, Carol ages
grotesquely ** (1433b) (1461b)

55

(250) (288)
Jack loves Carol despite his vows of celibacy.
Jack comes to regret his vows (106) (205) (207)

56

(38) (766)
Carol is convinced that men are crazy about
her * Carol is unaware that she is deluding
herself ** (65) (184) (194a)

CONFLICT SITUATIONS

57

(226) (243) (264)
Carol, discouraged by a failed romance, plans suicide and writes a note explaining her motives * Carol, planning to take her own life, changes her mind — but inadvertently loses the suicide note ** (742) (758)

58

(a) (32) (36)
Carol concocts an imaginary lover, Walt; and, to her surprise, a man with Walt's name and resembling him, enters her life (1184) (4a)

(b) (32) (36)
Carol pretends that she's engaged to an imaginary lover, Walt, buys a ring, and has the engagement announced in a newspaper (298a ch Jack to Walt; 4a ch Jack to Walt) (1187 ch Jack to Walt)

(c) (62) (83)
Carol, single, pretends she's married and calls herself "Mrs.—" (1242a) (947) (946)

59

(31) (1146) (1175a)
Carol, a rich romantic, falls in love with Jack, a con-artist posing as a man of means (103; 93a) (90a) (228)

60

(90a, b) (676) (916) (55) (148) (217 tr Jack & Gary) (237) (247)
Carol runs off with Jack, who later deserts her (665) (737a) (738)

61

(82a, b) (87)
Carol, impersonating a man, is suddenly discovered by Jack, whom she loves (220) (224) (264) (359)

62

(36) (145)
Carol is victimized by false gossip about her love-life (83) (102) (14a, b, c)

63

(2f, g, h) (10b)
Carol sends her lover, Jack, a gift she mistakenly thinks will promote their mutual happiness (40a, b ch Jack to Carol) (153 ch Jack to Carol) (333 ch Jack to Carol)

64

(15a) (23a, b) (34) (38) (916) (232) (272) (302) (421)
Jack persuades Carol to marry him in secrecy (400) (415) (426)

65

(1105) (1121)
Narcissistic Carol believes herself irresistible to men * Jack bluntly accuses Carol of narcissism ** (1067) (679) (88)

(50) Compelled by a Special Motive to Behave Underhandedly

66

(a) (259-1) (259-2) (259-3) (226) (262a, b) (1105)
Jack, rejected by Carol, takes revenge by destroying something she values highly (173) (1326 ch Jack to Eric)

(b) (335) (334a)
Jack, rejected by Carol, revenges himself by becoming a reckless womanizer (96 ch Carol to Laura) (98 ch Carol to Laura)

(c) (284) (263 tr Jack & Gary)
Jack, rejected by Carol, revenges himself by romancing wealthy women for their money (387 ch Carol to Laura) (422b ch Carol to Laura)

67

(220) (330a)
Rich, elderly Jack is in love with young Carol * Jack plans a test to find out if Carol really loves him ** (93a ch Carol to Jack) (82a tr Carol & Jack)

CONFLICT SITUATIONS

68

(98) (658) (1306) (96)
Prominent Jack, once in love with Carol, secretly wronged her, then abandoned her to a life of pain and loneliness (951) (1461a)

69

(27) (1146) (1173) (1175a) (10c) (14b) (147) (61)
Jack, in love with Carol and thinking she's guilty of a crime (1172) (1206) (1292) (1293a, b, c), tells the police that he committed the crime (828) (833) (787 ch Jack to Carol)

70

(100) (129) (132) (240)
Jack's family hates Carol's family. Jack, in love with Carol, conceals his identity when calling on Carol (5) (73) (352a, b)

71

(a) (250) (1095) (101a)
Confirmed bachelor Jack frantically tries to avoid marriage * Jack, trying to avoid marriage, claims that [1] X, a department store mannequin, is his wife; [2] he's homosexual; [3] he's impotent ** (2c) (24a, b, c, d)

(b) (143) (145)
Carol, in order to avoid the complications of romance, resorts to pretense (83) (84a) (58a, b, c)

72

(70) (299)
Jack, in love with Carol, pretends to be his deceased friend, Pete (26a, b ch Jack to Pete) who was engaged to Carol. Carol, finally learning of Pete's death, decides to keep it secret from her family (73) (353) (362)

73

(70) (275) (276) (311) (312-1-2-3-4) (303-1 through 12)
Jack and Carol are in love but Carol's parents, Frank and Rita, dislike Jack, so Jack and Carol decide to run off and get married (154a, b) (314)

74

(a) (101b) (1389b)
Young, romantic Jack, sees a supposedly-deserted, rundown house on a city street * Jack, curious, covertly watches the house; one day, he sees a young woman's hand (953 ch Jack to Carol) (403) emerge from behind a tattered curtain and place something on the window sill ** (24e) (1335)

(b) (259-3) (968) (1104) (1134) (513)
Jack, hearing a woman crying for help in a house he is passing, rushes through the door — into a complicated romance (664) (407 ch Jack to Eric; 274)

75

(a) (266) (280a) (290)
Jack and Gary both love Carol. Gary deviously tries to eliminate Jack (79) (1228) (1253) (1267a) (1265a tr Jack & Gary)

(b) (75a) (76)
Deviously positioned by Gary, his rival in love, Jack is innocently drawn into a compromising situation with Sally, Gary's cohort (347a ch Carol to Sally) (315)

76

(75a) (157)
Jack and Gary are rivals for the love of Carol. Gary plans to win at Jack's expense (138) (245) (79)

77

(160) (158)
Both Jack and Gary love Carol (85a). Her father, Frank, secretly attempts to determine which suitor is more deserving (111 add Gary) (112 add Gary)

CONFLICT SITUATIONS

78

(137a) (157) (171)
Jack and Gary, in love with Carol, are persuaded by impulsive Carol to expose themselves to danger to prove their love (342)
(212b)

79

(111) (112) (115)
Pretending to be Jack's friend, his rival, Gary,
sets a deadly trap for Jack (75b) (612) (1226
ch Burt to Gary) (1228) (1229 ch Carol to
Irene) (1233)

80

(a) (157) (171) (918a) (926)
Jack wants to insure the happiness of Carol
(85a), who, he thinks, loves his rival, Gary
(177 ch Jack to Gary) (1175a ch Jack to Gary);
Jack vanishes so that he, rather than Gary,
will appear guilty of a certain crime (906 ch
Pete to Gary) (97) (122)

(b) (137a) (139 ch Pete to Gary)
Elderly Jack and Gary both love Carol, but
Jack learns that Carol prefers Gary. To
insure the happiness of Carol and Gary,
Jack kills himself and leaves them his estate
(248 ch Jack to Gary) (268 ch Jack to Gary)

81

(97) (252a, b) (260a) (283) (290) (293) (301a)
Jack abducts his sweetheart, Carol, while she
is enroute to marry his rival, Gary (206) (284)
(311) (367b)

82

(a) (103) (105)
Carol disguises herself and meets Jack, the
man she loves, without betraying her identity * Carol tries to find out if Jack really
loves her ** (142) (246a) (249) (250) (357)

(b) (103) (141) (162a)
Carol resorts to pretense in order to find out
if Jack, the man she loves, really loves her
(93a) (82a)

83

(102) (143) (145) (207) (870a)
Carol pretends she's engaged to be married
in order to avoid unwanted attentions (21)
(207 tr Jack & Carol)

84

(a) (947) (976) (1242a)
Unmarried scientist Carol, unable to find the
man of her dreams, creates an android, X, as
a substitute for a husband (354b) (2c)

(b) (101a) (1095)
Jack, annoyed by sexually aggressive women,
pretends he has an invalid wife, Amy
(71a-1) (1f)

85

(a) (114) (178) (188a)
Carol, in love with Jack, uses harsh measures
in an attempt to goad him into proving his
abilities (125a) (225)

(b) (162a) (249)
Carol uses deception to find out if Jack loves
her * Carol deliberately steers herself and
Jack into a compromising situation and then
blames Jack for it ** (876b) (212b)

86

(32) (36) (38) (68) (124) (871) (1105)
Carol, single and driven by an unusual motive, pretends that she is engaged to marry
an imaginary person, Walt, and has the announcement published in a newspaper (58a)
(1242a)

87

(34) (91) (162a) (163)
Carol poses as a boy so she can be near Jack,
whom she secretly adores (144) (146) (147)

ART CENTER COLLEGE OF DESIGN LIBRARY
1700 LIDA STREET
PASADENA, CALIFORNIA 91103

88

(291) (330a) (659) (745) (916) (993)
Carol, in order to carry out a necessary venture, offers to sell herself in marriage to the highest bidder (182a) (269) (351a)

89

(223) (225) (228) (246a, b)
Carol, convinced a keepsake of a lost love, X (1384), has magical powers, tries to regain love by wearing the keepsake (1368 ch Jack to Carol) (746)

90

(a) (240) (290) (59) (66b ch Carol to Laura) (1175a)
Naive Carol, on the promise of a show-business career, runs off with Jack (60) (142) (226) (415)

(b) (218a) (324) (678 ch Judy to Laura)
Carol, determined to hurt Laura, runs off with Jack, Laura's fiance (221a ch Carol to Laura) (224) (247)

91

(27) (29) (98) (1167) (1170) (1180)
Carol, in love with Jack, tries to save Jack from disaster (505) (608) (610) by an ingenious plan (92) (94a) (114) (125a)

92

(27) (126) (163) (1181) (1185) (1195) (1197)
Carol loves Jack, who has been arrested for a crime by Sam (753) (1084) (1101) * In order to help her lover, Jack, escape the law, Carol seduces the arresting officer, Sam ** (230 ch Jack to Sam) (866)

93

(a) (59) (103) (164)
Wealthy Carol pretends to lose all her money so she can discover which of her suitors loves her for herself (210-3) (214) (361a, b) (366)

(b) (186) (199) (200)
Carol, trying to find out if Jack really loves her (141), resorts to a deception (82a) (93a) (87)

94

(a) (3a, b) (14a, b, c) (925-*) (949a)
Carol and Jack are in love. Laura underhandedly steals Jack away from Carol (138) (215a) (216) * Carol, forced to become devious, wins Jack back from Laura ** (359) (361a, b)

(b) (337a) (340)
Carol's friend, attractive, married Annie, tries to save Carol's fiance, Jack, from a conniving woman, Laura, and restore him to Carol. Annie hopes to accomplish this by winning Jack away from Laura (337b) (322b)

95

(27) (91) (291) (113) (311)
Carol will lose her lover, Jack, if she lets Jack proceed with a venture (225) (125a) (1201) (1267a) (1278a) that she instigated. To avoid losing Jack, Carol defeats the venture by making a confession (50)

(13) Trying by Deception to Escape Trouble

96

(703) (925-*) (937) (121) (239) (947)
Jack betrays Carol by not marrying her as promised (60) (68) (98) (188b ch Jack to Eric)

97

(260a) (280a) (284)
Jack, in love with Carol, secretly uses any means to save Carol from an impending disaster (236) (267) (351a)

98

(1185) (1247)
Wealthy playboy Jack turns his back on Carol, whom he secretly betrayed (1325) (1326 ch Jack to Eric) (1328) (1349) (1262)

99

(259-1-2-3 ch Carol to Irene) (321a ch Carol to Irene) (13a) (38) (325)
Jack and Carol, both single, become business partners. They contract never to fall in love (808a) (822)

00

(275) (276) (299) (1298)
Jack, in love with Carol, is determined to be with her, knowing that he'll land in trouble unless he employs deception (1209a) (70)

101

(a) (250) (918a, b) (926)
Jack is swamped by matching-making mothers; their meddling is ruining his business. He devises a plan to thwart them (84b) (1163b)

(b) (718b) (949a)
Jack is a sentimental, unattached man who longs for a relationship * Jack is a poet, unattached, who is constantly on the alert for romance ** (14b) (24a, b, c, d, e) (25)

02

(32) (325)
Carol is falsely accused of being a homewrecker. She decides on a strategy to rid herself of suspicion (86) (952 ch Jack to Carol) (1204)

103

(164) (143)
Carol isn't sure which of her lovers love her for herself, rather than for her money; she devises a plan to find the answer (82a) (93a)

104

(188a) (189) (290) (291)
If Carol wins a certain competition, she also wins Gary, a wealthy admirer. Carol doesn't love Gary, but she does love money and social prominence. If she loses the contest, she wins Jack, a poor admirer whom she does love (356) (239) (933) (355)

(10) Suffering Loss of a Relationship Due to Mistaken Judgment

105

(49) (585a ch "Jack's wife" to "Jack's lover")
Jack is convinced that his lover, Carol, is dead; Carol, far away, learns of Jack's mistaken belief (82a) (162a) (357)

(15) Finding the Power to Overcome Problems

106

(259-1-2-3 ch Carol to Irene) (898) (681a)
Mean-spirited Jack is unable to find pleasure in life * Mean-spirited Jack falls for Carol (4a) (9a, b) and, inspired by love, undergoes a personality-change ** (41a, b, c) (131; 115) (359)

107

(131) (85a) (156)
Jack falls apart when he thinks his girlfriend, Carol, is unfaithful * Jack, learning that Carol is still true to him, reverts to his former self ** (360a) (369) (370)

108

(750) (43) (1167)
Jack, Carol's lover, is condemned to die for a crime he didn't commit * Unjustly imprisoned Jack is pardoned and released when Carol pleads with high authority, Carl ** (895) (350)

CONFLICT SITUATIONS

109

(249) (259-3) (283) (284) (291) (313)
Adventurer Jack loses his girlfriend, Carol,
and his freedom on a false charge (43) (747)
(731) (623) (608), escapes captivity, survives
a series of disasters (650) (686) (688) (690),
and finally reaches a location where something of great value is hidden (1394) (1369)
(1403) (1436) (1406; 1408) (1383). He finds
the treasure (360a) (963; 907)

**(1) Undertaking a Difficult Venture When Promised
a Reward for High Achievement**

10

(1a, g) (4b) (22a)
Jack is in love with Carol, who will be permitted to marry him if Jack: [1] succeeds in
a difficult venture (209) (225) (111) (112) (113)
(114) (115); [2] makes a great deal of money
(1374) (1377b); or [3] solves a baffling mystery (1352) (1377b) (1384) (1392) (1399)

111

(22a) (20a) (1e)
Jack, in love with Carol, is required by
Carol's father, Frank, to amass a specific
amount of money before he'll be seriously
considered as a son-in-law (628) (1101) (1269)
(1297)

12

(1f, g) (4b)
Jack loves Carol; and Carol's father, Frank,
promises to allow him to marry Carol if Jack
completes a dangerous venture (209) (313)

113

(111) (114)
Jack, in love with Carol, struggles to acquire
enough money to enable him to marry her
(117) (1001a) (1028)

114

(125a) (291) (595) (748)
Carol informs Jack, the man she loves, that
he will lose her unless he overcomes his lack
of ambition (132) (604) (606) (662) (757)

115

(1061) (1062) (1063) (1064) (1090)
Carol loves Jack; but, before she will commit
to marry him, she insists that he must perform heroic deeds (1093; 1098) (1073)

**(9) Being Put to a Test in Which Love is Lost if
Riches are Gained**

116

(117) (118)
Jack marries Carol against a rich relative's
wishes, and is disinherited (363a) (366)

**(8) Confronting a Romantic Situation in
Which a Fortune Can Be Won or Lost by a
Particular Course of Action**

117

(26a, b ch Carol to Amy) (1432 ch Jack to
Andy & Jim to Jack)
Drifter Jack is left a fortune by his father,
Andy, on condition that he can be located
and marries Amy, a woman he's never seen
(116) (132) (230 ch Carol to Amy)

118

(302) (1432 ch Jack to Bill & Jim to Jack)
Jack will be disinherited by his wealthy
grandfather, Bill, if he refuses to carry out
an act that will seriously harm Frank (276 ch
Andy to Bill), father of Carol, the woman
Jack loves (116) (116; 1041 ch Jack to Bill)

(2) Falling in Love Despite Conflicting Obligations

119

(128) (476a) (476b ch Jack to Eric & Gary to
Jack) (477 ch Jack to Eric & Pete to Jack)
Jack runs off with Carol, the wife of his best
friend, Pete (400 ch Jack to Eric & Gary to
Jack) (418 ch Jack to Eric & Gary to Jack)

120

(17a) (140) (409 ch Jack to Eric & Gary to
Jack)
Unmarried Jack falls in love with married
Carol. Carol's husband, Eric, won't divorce
Carol; nor will she divorce him (457) (129)
(133) (148; 210)

121

(27) (32) (34)
Unmarried, idealistic Carol, is determined to become a mother (945) (946)

(25) Trying to Save a Person Accused of a Crime or Other Offense

122

(260a) (280a) (1177 ch Jack to Gary) (1181 ch Jack to Gary)
Both Jack and Gary love Carol (84a) (235) (286). Jack tries to protect Gary from arrest (80a, b) (147)

(39) Giving Up Cherished Ambitions to Fulfill an Obligation

123

(70) (1315 ch Gary to Frank)
To protect his father, Andy, Jack is forced to take action against Frank, father of Carol, the girl Jack loves (41c) (248) (282a)

124

(37) (1279a) (148)
Carol, older than Jack, feels she would be doing Jack a disservice by marrying him, although she loves him deeply * Carol feels remorse after rejecting Jack ** (11a ch Carol to Laura & Rita to Carol) (11b, c) (326-1) (251) (268) (325)

(28) Facing a Situation in Which the Problems of Someone Highly Regarded Calls for Courage and Wise Planning

125

(a) (114) (158)
Carol, in love with unambitious Jack, influences him to take advantage of a certain opportunity (180) (284; 351a)

(b) (260b) (265b)
Absent-minded Jack proposes to Carol, who loves him. Carol says she will give Jack her answer if he shows up at a specific date and time. If he remembers to come, she'll marry him (367b) (284)

(c) (88) (745)
Carol is in love with Jack, who is settling the estate of Carol's deceased father, Frank * Carol's dead father, Frank, was deeply in debt and, unknown to Carol, wealthy Jack pays the debts ** (367b) (808a)

126

(27) (291) (244) (695b)
Jack's girlfriend, Carol, persuades him to commit a crime (628) (628 ch Carol to Laura) (637) (296) (701)

(41) Finding an Obligation at Odds with Ambition, Inclination or Necessity

127

(a) (291) (311)
Jack believes Carol won't marry him till he gets rich (638) (621) (850b)

(b) (1061) (1062) (1079) (1092)
Jack believes Carol won't marry him till he overcomes his personal limitations (252a) (853) (855) (857)

128

(24a, b, c, e) (25) (3a) (494 ch Jack to Eric & Gary to Jack)
Jack, who loves Carol, learns that Carol is married to Eric (134a, b) (558 ch Jack to Eric & Gary to Jack)

129

(128) (159) (170) (185) (196)
Jack and Carol are in love, but certain conditions prevent their marriage (371 ch Carol to Laura) (307) (402 ch Jack to Gary & Gary to Jack)

130

(220) (148) (330a)
Jack is enroute to marry Carol, when he runs into trouble (154a) (314) (634) (664) (711a, b)

131

(1a, b, c, d, f, g) (14a, b, c)
Jack is so consumed by his romance with Carol that his business suffers (41a) (85a) (115) (311)

132

(123) (118) (3b)
If Jack fulfills a certain obligation, he will be unfaithful to Carol and will lose her (116) (291; 700) (95) (986) (1007)

133

(17a, b) (120)
Jack loves Carol, but is helpless to stop her from embarking on a dangerous venture (516 ch Jack to Eric) (893) (956) (1137a)

134

(a) (290) (299) (300)
Jack and Carol, the woman he loves, inadvertently find themselves in a compromising situation (351b) (870a)

(b) (70) (73)
Jack and Carol, whom Jack loves, are trapped in a burning house (147) (360a, b) (876b)

135

(139 ch Pete to Andy) (75a ch Gary to Andy) (1d) (148 ch Jack to Andy)
Both Jack and his father, Andy, are in love with Carol and want to marry her (156 ch Jack to Andy) (282a) (983 ch Eric to Frank; 269 ch Gary to Andy) (351a ch Gary to Andy)

136

(997a) (1022)
Jack and Gary are in love with Carol * Jack, obliged to obey the orders of Gary, his rival for Carol's affections, is told to promote Gary's cause, or to disappear ** (209) (351a) (352b) (884a ch Burt to Gary)

137

(a) (27 add Gary) (139 ch Pete to Gary)
Twin brothers Jack and Gary both love Carol (80b) (821 ch Greg to Gary)

(b) (678) (668 ch Rita to Judy)
Twin sisters Carol and Judy both love Jack (215a ch Laura to Judy) (216 ch Laura to Judy) (238 ch Laura to Judy)

138

(94b) (238)
Jack, engaged to marry Carol, receives an invitation from Laura, his former sweetheart (170) (172) (349)

139

(885a ch Jack to Pete) (997a) (885a ch Carol to Pete; 997a)
Jack learns that Pete loves Carol, the girl Jack wants to marry (157 ch Gary to Pete) (174 ch Gary to Pete) (122 ch Gary to Pete) (75a, b, ch Gary to Pete) (175 ch Gary to Pete) (350 ch Gary to Pete)

140

(259-1 ch Carol to Irene) (259-2 ch Carol to Irene) (898) (32) (325)
Platonic friends Jack and Carol unexpectedly fall in love (22a) (97) (366) (367a, b) (837)

141

(145) (992) (55) (111) (113)
Carol loves Jack and has worn his engagement ring for years (129) (142) (162a) (234a) (249) (363a)

142

(162a) (82a, b) (87) (93a, b)
Carol, in love with Jack, learns that Jack no longer loves her. Yet he is willing to stand by his promise to marry her (324) (256) (287) (261) (325) (326-2)

143

(38) (908) (916)
Carol's time is totally consumed by her multiple romances (96) (102) (931)

144

(646) (654 ch Jack to Carol)
Carol, held captive by enemies of Jack, is being forced to obey them by violent threats against Jack, the man she loves (616) (719a, b) (666) (1010) (1135a)

145

(921) (976) (1100)
Attractive Carol is totally absorbed by her work; everything else, even love, is secondary to achieving her goals (1f) (31) (84a)

146

(142) (158) (170) (266)
Carol loves Jack; but Jack's rival, Gary, kidnaps Carol (81 tr Jack & Gary) and plans to make her marry him (352b) (851) (884a ch Jack to Carol & Burt to Gary)

(29) Helping Another to Keep a Deadly Secret

147

(644) (648) (801)
Carol shares with her lover, Jack, a secret that, if revealed, would prove disastrous to Carol (224 tr Carol & Jack) (596) (1408) (1409) (660b)

(4) Compelled by Excessive Desire To Exercise Mistaken Judgment in a Romance

148

(38 ch Carol to Jack) (949a) (954)
Jack, caught up in a romantic atmosphere (197) (210-1), becomes convinced he's in love with Carol (152a, b; 211) (69; 214) (3a; 176a, b, c)

149

(1073) (912a)
Elderly, wealthy widower Jack, swept up in the romance of Spring, imagines himself in love with Carol, one of his employees (616) (658) (33 ch Rita to Frank)

150

(120 ch Eric to Pete) (476a ch Jack to Pete & Gary to Jack) (900)
Unmarried Jack runs off with Carol, the wife of his best friend, Pete; Carol then leaves Jack to run off with Gary (405 ch Jack to Pete) (477 tr Jack & Pete; 403 ch Jack to Pete; 468 ch Jack to Pete; 784) (951) (925) (918b) (705)

151

(149) (210-2) (232) (27) (38) (220) (239)
Jack, believing that he loves Carol, changes his mind when he discovers a revealing truth about her (314) (865) (880a)

(36) Having an Experience that Greatly Changes Character

152

(a) (982a ch Jack to Eric & Jim to Jack) (916 ch Carol to Jack)
Jack is a wild, difficult youth; he falls in love with Carol (812b; 230 tr Jack & Carol) (224) and becomes a different person (234a) (289) (367a)

(b) (1220b) (1244b)
Jack's secretary, Carol, is an accomplice planted in Jack's house by criminal Burt * Criminal Carol, accomplice of criminal Burt, falls in love with her employer, Jack ** (144) (616)

CONFLICT SITUATIONS

(20) Getting into a Situation From Which Difficult Problems are Likely to Result

153

(218b) (976) (1042b)
Jack, in love with Carol, has a jeweler send Carol a valuable gift * Jack sends Carol a gift. By mistake, or by malicious intent, packages are switched; the gift Carol receives, supposedly from Jack, almost destroys their relationship ** (170) (172; 1136) (349)

154

(a) (73) (311)
Jack, planning to meet Carol at a rural church where they are to be secretly married, becomes lost in a storm and doesn't reach the church until Carol and all the others have left (261) (316) (154b)

(b) (160) (75a)
Jack's rival for Carol, Gary, learning of Jack and Carol's abrupt decision to marry, sends an ally, Burt, who lures Carol away by saying Jack sent for her (146) (885a, b)

155

(916 ch Carol to Walt) (954) (923 ch Jack to Walt) (954 ch Jack to Walt)
Walt, a handsome young man, arrives at an elegant estate where, to his surprise, he's greeted as a bridegroom, is hurried before the minister and hurriedly married to Carol, a beautiful young woman (38) (166) (421 ch Jack to Walt). After the ceremony she realizes he isn't the man she thought he was, but Walt has vanished (389 ch Jack to Walt) (432b ch Jack to Walt) (451 ch Jack to Walt)

156

(1a, b, d, f, g)
Pretentious Jack, in love with Carol, learns that Carol has been ridiculing him; indignant, he leaves Carol (320) (344) (922b) (1171)

157

(704) (1021b ch Pete to Gary) (913 ch Pete to Gary)
Jack and Gary, once buddies, become enemies because of their rivalry over Carol (122) (174) (352b) (906 ch Pete to Gary)

158

(159) (171)
Jack's rival for Carol, Gary, has more on the ball than Jack and seems to be on the winning track (85a) (177) (265a) (364a)

159

(25) (940-*) (24a, b, c, d, e) (37)
Jack loves Carol and is unaware that she prefers his rival, Gary (127a, b) (139 ch Pete to Gary) (267) (319 ch Pete to Gary; 294a ch Pete to Gary)

160

(171) (75a)
Jack has a rival/friend, Gary, whose self-confidence is the key to his extraordinary resourcefulness (158; 114; 1134; 81) (80a) (366; 1242b)

161

(7a) (1377a tr Jack & Pete)
Jack, believing that a certain "charm," X, has made him successful with women, learns that X has no magical powers; his newfound success was due solely to his increased self-confidence (182b) (350)

162

(a) (736) (740) (913 ch Pete to Carol) (928a)
Carol loves Jack, but isn't sure it's mutual (47a, b) (67) (82a, b)

(b) (39) (96) (98)
Unmarried Carol is pregnant, deceived by her lover * Carol contemplates suicide ** (188b) (945) (946)

CONFLICT SITUATIONS

63

(114) (125a) (126) (608) (623) (777)
Carol learns that her boyfriend, Jack, is in serious trouble (91) (92)

164

(564a ch Jack to Eric) (2e)
Rich widow Carol has so many admirers she can't make a choice (82a, b; 142) (102) (103)

165

(203) (201) (164)
Carol loses a locket, and asks her suitors to look for it. Inside the locket is a photo of Jack, Carol's favorite suitor (301b) (360b)

66

(64) (73) (154a)
Carol, thinking she's marrying Jack, mistakenly marries Walt, his long-missing twin brother. When she attempts to rectify her mistake, Walt is nowhere to be found (155) (402 ch Jack to Walt) (451 ch Jack to Walt)

167

(a) (280b) (634)
Jack is married to Amy, a woman he doesn't know. Carol is married to Walt, a man she's never seen (365b ch Carol to Amy) (365c) (365d); * Jack and Carol meet, fall in love, whereupon Jack discovers Amy is Carol, and Carol discovers Walt is Jack, the people to whom they're married but have never seen (166 ch Carol to Amy) **

(b) (647) (648) (665 ch Gary to Jack) (659) (18) (162b)
Carol, unsuccessful at her career, becomes Jack's mistress (279) (359) (743a)

(5) Trying to Make the Best of a Hopeless Love Affair

168

(603b, c, d)
While traveling together, Jack and his friend, Pete, have an accident and Pete is killed. Before he dies, Pete asks Jack to tell his lover, Carol, of his death (130 ch Jack to Pete) (112 ch Jack to Pete) (175 ch Gary to Pete). Jack does as he is asked (14a) (139) (5)

169

(26a, b)
Jack joins up with his friend, Pete, who is enroute to meet Carol, a girl he has never seen * Jack and Pete have an accident and Pete is killed ** (603b,c, d) (168)

170

(177) (178) (182a, b) (212a)
Lovers Jack and Carol argue violently and Carol returns a gift, X, given her by Jack (57) (208) (349)

171

(941) (944) (964a) (921) (946)
Unsophisticated Jack has a rival, Gary, for the love of Carol. Gary is a cultured man of the world (75b) (239 ch Jack to Gary) (899 ch Jack to Gary) (925-*)

172

(212a) (213) (222a)
Carol, alienated from Jack, a man she loves deeply, sends a message to another person and unconsciously addresses it to Jack (194b) (1136)

173

(215a) (216) (221a)
Carol wore a certain ornament when her two-timing lover, Jack, proposed. She is convinced that the same will happen to any other woman who wears the ornament (238) (849; 1245)

CONFLICT SITUATIONS

(57) Trying to Solve a Puzzling Problem

`174`

(160) (157)
Jack and Gary, rivals for Carol, confront her and demand that she choose between them (183) (816a; 1265b)

**(3) Trying to Prove Love's Power
by a Test of Courage**

`175`

(75a) (76) (93b add Gary)
Carol tests the love of two admirers, Jack and Gary (78) (79)

`76`

(a) (175) (93b)
Carol, to test her lover's devotion, sends him into great danger (212b) (342)

(b) (175) (59)
Carol, wanting to test her lover's devotion, impulsively places herself in danger to see if he will follow her (851) (85b)

(c) (164) (162a)
Carol promises to marry Jack if he succeeds in a difficult venture (212a, b)

(23) Becoming Enmeshed in Mistaken Judgment and/or Suspicion

`77`

(77) (112)
Jack mistakenly believes that Frank, the father of Carol, whom he loves, is his enemy (300) (311) (322a) (360a)

`178`

(29) (31) (24a, b, e)
Wealthy Carol invites her lover, Jack, to her home so that he can meet her parents. Jack, arriving before Carol, is mistaken for Matt, a candidate for the position of family chauffeur (70; 352a) (702 ch Jack to Frank; 1164 ch Jack to Frank & Eric to Jack)

(11) Facing a Situation in Which Only Courage and Devotion Can Save a Loved One

`179`

(a) (131) (1042b) (158) (170)
Jack, by ESP, learns of a terrible danger threatening Carol, the woman he loves (144) (146) (1137a)

(b) (217) (223)
Jack, in a distant country far from Carol, hears her cry of help over the telephone (483a, b ch "wife" to "lover") (1154a)

(c) (1389b) (1f)
Jack has a telepathic vision warning him that danger threatens his lover, Carol (694) (873) (1172)

`180`

(70 ch Jack to Gary) (206)
Struggling sculptor Jack and Carol are in love. Carol's wealthy father, Frank, wants his daughter to marry his protege, Gary. Frank suggests a contest between Jack and Gary, the winner to marry Carol (726b)(652b) (350) (142; 94a; 933 ch Carol to Jack)

`181`

(a) (41b) (114) (234a-*) (176b) (162a) (164)
Driving his Jeep across rugged terrain, Jack sees Carol on a runaway horse. Jack overtakes Carol, and rescues her * Jack is attracted to Carol and asks for a date ** (188a) (241) (360a)

(b) (135 ch Jack to Greg & Andy to Jack) (148 ch Jack to Greg)
Jack's son, Greg, is determined to marry Carol, whom Jack thinks isn't the proper choice * Jack, trying to deter his son, Greg, from marrying Carol, seduces her ** (241 ch Jack to Greg & Andy to Jack) (159 ch Jack to Greg & Gary to Jack) (156)

(c) (885b) (1426b)
Archaeologists Jack and Dave are prisoners in an ancient lost city. Carol, supposedly a goddess, helps them escape * Jack is in love with Carol; and Carol, rescuing Jack and Dave from their captors, escapes with them ** (157 ch Gary to Dave) (1395)

CONFLICT SITUATION

(21) Landing in Trouble Through Mistaken Judgment

182

(a) (56) (143) (235) (1105)
Carol thinks Jack has proposed to her, and she accepts (192a) (195). Later, she learns it was Gary who proposed (76) (160) (260a) (266) (318)

(b) (148) (137b ch Judy to Carol & Laura to Judy)
Jack loves Carol. Thinking that he has proposed to Carol, he later learns that it was Laura * Thinking he's proposed to Carol, Jack finds that he's mistakenly proposed to Laura, who accepts ** (137b ch Judy to Laura) (261) (284) (340)

183

(142) (162a) (659) (665) (669 ch Burt to Gary)
Impulsively, irresponsibly, Carol promises to marry Gary (1d) (239 ch Jack to Gary). Later, coming to her senses, she regrets the promise (404) (406 ch Jack to Gary & Gary to Jack)

184

(56) (62)
Carol wrongly interprets Jack's ambiguous remark (196) (288) as a marriage proposal (65) (307)

(50) Compelled by a Special Motive to Behave Underhandedly

185

(312-1-2-3-4) (299)
Jack loves Carol and is determined to propose marriage. But Carol is so closely supervised that despairing Jack can't find an opportunity * Jack contrives to create an opportunity to propose to Carol ** (81) (82a tr Jack & Carol) (352a)

186

(816B) (743A)
In order to help Carol, who is ill and destitute, Jack pretends to be in love with her and proposes marriage (142) (230) (373) (393)

187

(145) (956-*) (1105) (1119)
Frustrated Jack is unable to propose marriage because Carol is constantly on the run and never alone. He plans a deception to get her alone (163; 91) (352a)

188

(a) (85a) (114) (189)
Carol, compelled by an unusual motive, promises to marry Jack if she can defeat him in a certain test of skill [tennis, downhill racing, solving a mystery] (1343) (1364b) (1384) * Carol knows she can beat Jack in a contest of skill if she wants to ** (355) (1243) (234b)

(b) (162b) (968) (98 ch Jack to Eric) (926)
Pregnant, unmarried Carol, having decided on an abortion, is stopped by a stranger, Jack * Jack, a stranger, offers to marry Carol ** (411a, b) (963) (365d ch Amy to Carol)

189

(188a) (164)
Carol, asked by Jack to marry him, wants to know more about him before she decides * Carol challenges Jack to a contest of skill, her acceptance or rejection to be determined by the outcome ** (234b) (355) (615)

190

(641) (645) (659)
Neither Jack nor Carol love each other. But Carol, for certain reasons, asks Jack to marry her (230) (365a)

(44) Using Radical Methods to Overcome Personal Limitations

191

(185) (187) (145)
Witless Jack, desperate for an opportunity to propose to Carol, saves her from drowning and pops the question as they cling to an overturned boat (124) (227)

192

(a) (106) (99; 9a; 201)
Jack, lacking the nerve to propose to Carol
directly, proposes via fax (172) (182a tr Jack
& Gary) (182b)

(b) (139) (160 ch Gary to Pete)
Jack sends his friend, Pete, to propose marriage to Carol on his behalf * Pete proposes
to Carol on behalf of Jack; Carol assumes
Pete is speaking for himself and accepts **
(266 ch Gary to Pete) (300 ch Gary to Pete)
(318 ch Gary to Pete)

193

(203) (609)
Bumbling Jack loves Carol, but is too back-
ward and shy to propose marriage. Jack is
shocked when a child, Lee, who is aware of
his shyness, proposes to Carol for him * Jack
is thrilled when Carol accepts ** (754; 163)
(801) (842a) (893)

194

(a) (38) (56) (196)
Carol, thinking Jack loves her but lacks the
courage to admit it, proposes to him after
he's rescued her from almost certain death
(191 tr Jack & Carol) (264) (307) (325)

(b) (260b) (325; 261)
Carol sends a message to Gary accepting his
marriage proposal * Carol, accepting Gary's
marriage proposal, mistakenly sends the
message to Jack, the lover she broke up with
** (343) (381)

195

(9a, b) (160) (162a) (235)
Carol, in a storm at night, is proposed to.
Unable to see her lover, and barely able to
hear him, she still accepts — and faces an
unpleasant surprise (182a) (182b tr Carol &
Laura)

**(20) Getting into a Situation From Which Difficult
Problems are Likely to Result**

196

(1061) (1132)
Jack's shyness prevents him from proposing
marriage to Carol (127a; 628) (97) (179a, c)
(194a)

197

(686) (687) (689) (691) (714) (937) (959)
Adventurer Jack's life is threatened by savages. Queen Carol, the 300 pound tribal
leader, agrees to spare Jack if he'll marry her
(904) (973)

198

(941) (905)
Proud but poor Jack feels that he can't ask
wealthy Carol to marry him (93a, b) (1155)

199

(680a) (680b) (715b)
Disabled Jack is too proud ask the woman
he loves, Carol, to marry him (93b) (264)
(257b; 345 tr Carol & Laura)

200

(675) (1131)
Procrastinator Jack loves Carol and is eager
to marry her. But, true to form, he puts off
asking her (215b) (221b) (1075a ch Carol to
Laura)

201

(1a, b, d, f, g)
Jack, fearing rejection, can't bring himself to
propose to Carol (324) (323; 325)

202

(24a, b)
Jack loves Carol, but has reasons for not proposing to her (211) (214) (227) (245) (257a)
(272) (287) (288)

203

(1061) (1132)
Both Jack and Carol are too shy to admit
their love for one another (179a, b, c) (193)
(352b)

204

(265b) (1389b)
Jack is absent-minded * Jack forgets that he
asked Carol to marry him ** (1075a ch Carol
to Irene) (1101)

**(21) Landing in Trouble Through
Mistaken Judgment**

205

(214) (219) (221a)
Jack, winning Carol's love (23a, b) (34) (250)
in his youth and throwing it away, tries to
win it again when he's older (207) (148)
(361b) (377a-*; 378 ch Carol to Laura)

206

(260a) (280a)
Jack loves Carol, and learns that his rival,
Gary, has a dark secret. Carol apparently
favors Gary (97) (266) (236; 267)

207

(34) (55) (71b ch Carol to Jack) (1095)
Jack regrets telling Carol that he was married when he wasn't * Jack didn't think he
loved Carol, but later realizes he does ** (46)
(205) (220)

208

(1c, d) (10a)
Jack, in love with Carol, learns that she's a
dedicated flirt who is only toying with him
(176a, b, c) (320) (244; 421 tr Carol & Laura)

209

(110) (112) (180)
Jack carries out a difficult venture so that
Carol's father, Frank, will allow Jack to marry
her * Jack, learning secretly that Carol loves
a rival, Gary, refuses to hold Carol to Frank's
promise of marriage ** (267) (281b) (313) (345
tr Carol & Laura)

210

(101b) (1389b) (968)
Jack, under unusual conditions, falls in love
with Carol; returning to normal conditions,
Jack sees Carol as she really is and his love
vanishes. [1] Jack's love blossoms on a romantic cruise ship; back in port, he sees his
mistake (148) (150). [2] Jack's spring fever
tricks him romantically; but a change of sea-
son brings him back to reality (149) (151). [3]
Jack believes Carol wealthy; on learning she
is poor, his love cools (1e) (59; 93a). [4] Jack's
romantic success is due to a love "charm";
on finding that the charm is phony, romance
disappears (7a; 8a; 161)

211

(1075a, b) (898;1075a ch Carol to Laura) (205)
(315;1075a ch Carol to Laura)
For a long time Jack thought Carol was his
ideal woman. But when he returns home after
a long absence, he finds that Carol has undergone a radical character-change (921; 946;
97) (27; 359)

212

(a)   (126) (176c)
Jack is committed by Carol, the woman he
loves, to take part in a venture that will end
disastrously for him * Carol commits Jack to
a venture which, unknown to Carol, will end
disastrously for Jack ** (50) (212b)

(b)   (212a) (342)
Jack, having successfully concluded a venture instigated by unpredictable Carol, ends
the relationship (225) (746) (892 ch Laura to
Jack) (946)

213

(274) (597) (612) (623)
Jack and Carol love each other; but Matt, an
employee of Jack, tells Carol about an offense Jack has committed. Carol believes the
story * Matt is an agent of Gary, Jack's rival
in love ** (249) (262a) (315)

214

(24a, b, c) (22a)
Jack, in love with Carol, is convinced by a spiritual advisor, Walt, to avoid romance at all costs (82a, b) (352a, b) (363a)

215

(a) (239) (256) (494 ch Carol to Laura, Jack to Eric & Gary to Jack)
Jack, as a result of seductive Laura coming on to him, breaks off his engagement to Carol, whom he loves (94a, b) (220 ch Carol to Laura) (361a)

(b) (218b) (215a)
Jack loves Carol and Laura * While Jack waffles over whether to propose marriage to Carol or Laura, Carol and Laura become engaged to others ** (233) (224)

216

(218a) (170)
Jack is about to marry Laura, who has tricked him into believing his real love, Carol, is unfaithful (220 ch Carol to Laura; 865; 880a) (238)

217

(158) (160) (75a)
Jack's rival for Carol, Gary, tells her lies about Jack (213) (220; 223) (266)

218

(a) (1083) (1088) (34) (292 ch Carol to Laura)
Conceited Jack loves Carol * By flattering Jack's vanity, Laura manipulates him into a wedding engagement ** (256) (287 ch Carol to Laura)

(b) (153) (1461d)
Jack sends a gift to Carol, whom he loves; Laura intercepts the gift and replaces it with a photo of Jack, lovingly inscribed to Laura (82a; 61; 364b)

219

(718b) (24a, b)
Weak-willed Jack, under pressure from his unmarried sisters, Susan and Molly, gives up Carol, whom he loves (226) (236) (364b) (261)

220

(3a) (218b tr Carol & Laura) (305) (647) (948)
Jack's friends, Pete and Annie, try to stop him from marrying Carol, whom they believe is unprincipled (1095; 953) (870a; 851; 364b) (865)

221

(a) (24a, b) (22a)
Jack loves Carol, but gives her up when his friend, Pete, convinces him the relationship is unwise (139) (601; 163; 91) (117) (716) (671)

(b) (660b ch Burt to Gary) (664)
Jack's rival in love, Gary, kidnaps Jack and holds him prisoner to prevent him from marrying Carol (233) (280b) (875b)

222

(a) (1f) (6b) (8a)
Jack loves Carol, but becomes alienated from her due to mistaken judgment (41a, b) (49) (62) (85a, b) (153) (215a) (225) (228)

(b) (14a, b, c) (15a)
Jack, in love with Carol, is devastated to find Carol in Dave's arms * Jack, finding his girl, Carol, in Dave's arms, storms out, unaware that Dave is Carol's brother, Tony ** (708-* ch Jack to Dave) (172) (681a; 705; 879)

223

(641) (676)
Carol's father, religious fanatic Frank, throws Carol out of the house because she falls in love with Jack (6a) (14a), who is not of their faith (741; 738; 743a; 673; 817) (993-*; 125c)

224

(263) (284)
Carol, the woman Jack loves, turns out to be unfaithful; Jack is afraid Carol will reveal a secret that will cause him trouble (126; 1159; 1192) (1165 ch Jack to Eric & Burt to Jack) (923) (338) (665 ch Carol to Jack) (797-*; 818a)

225

(114) (125a)
Carol stirs her lover, Jack, out of his apathy by firing up his ambition to get ahead — with results disastrous to their relationship (237) (281c)

226

(38) (242)
Carol thinks Jack is "Mr. Right" (688; 307) (296) (324) until she learns that he has clay feet like all other men

227

(1e) (8a) (9a)
Carol cannot marry Jack because her scientist father, Frank, working with Carol in an experiment, inadvertently infects her with a deadly bacteria (43) (47a) (57; 742; 758 ch Jack to Eric; 627 ch Jack to Eric)

228

(38) (148) (171)
At Jack's request, Carol wears a particular piece of jewelry to indicate that she loves him * Carol wears a piece of jewelry to show her love for Jack; but, unnoticed by Carol, the jewelry is lost and when Jack sees her, he stalks off ** (105) (172)

229

(23b) (331) (332)
Carol, of a minority race, tries to win the love of Jack, of a majority race. She learns it's hopeless to challenge conventions (241) (247) (248)

(50) Compelled by a Special Motive to Behave Underhandedly

230

(656; 860) (155) (186)
Compelled by a special motive, Jack pretends to fall for Carol * Jack pretends to be in love with Carol, and eventually finds he has really fallen in love ** (182b) (217) (223)

231

(71a-*) (131) (1078) (1356-*)
Jack hopes that psychotherapy will cure his obsession with women (182b) (1330) (1351) (1363)

232

(24b, c, d, e)
Jack is upper class; the woman he loves, Carol, is from the working class and resents the wealthy * Upper-class Jack, in love with working girl Carol, pretends to be of her class ** (245) (254) (262a, b, c) (336a, b)

233

(27) (30) (31)
Jack loves Carol. They are to be married, but Jack mysteriously leaves town without saying where he's going, and doesn't return until after the date set for the wedding (1368) (1387) (1389a) (1040)

234

(a) (114) (164)
Jack loves Carol and wants to marry her, but Carol regards him as a wimp and keeps him dangling * Jack, to prove his courage to Carol, stages a fake rescue ** (81) (1227b, c)

(b) (260a, b) (266)
Adventurer Jack loves Carol * Adventurer Jack, in love with Carol and disliked by her parents, Frank and Rita, runs off with Carol ** (364b) (249)

235

(595) (680a) (1065)
Jack and Gary are rivals for Carol's hand (158) (160). Carol secretly prefers Jack, but because Jack is shy and less ambitious than Gary, Carol pretends to prefer Gary, hoping to spur Jack into proving himself (77) (78) (111)

236

(1059-*) (1093-*)
Jack and Gary both love Carol (59 ch Jack to Gary). Carol is about to marry Gary, whom Jack knows is a criminal * Jack persuades his rival, Gary to send Carol a certain gift, X. Then, after X is sent, Jack proves Gary stole it ** (206) (260a) (267)

237

(750) (915-*)
Jack learns that he isn't a fugitive as he thought. He returns home, deserting Carol, the woman he had said he loved (12a) while believing he was a criminal (205) (404)

238

(4b) (6a, b)
Seductive Laura tries to compromise Jack (218a, b) so his fiance, Carol will leave him. Generous Annie (844b) attempts to rescue Jack from Laura's clutches and return him to Carol (45a ch Carol to Annie) (128 ch Carol to Annie) (364b)

239

(291 ch Jack to Eric) (659) (261 ch Gary to Jack)
Carol, poor, doesn't love wealthy Jack, but would marry him to gain financial security (253) (403) (405)

240

(31; 70) (275) (276)
Carol admits that she loves Jack, whose family is feuding with Carol's. As a result, Carol's father, Frank, stops her from seeing Jack * Carol and Jack meet in secret ** (73) (154a) (362)

241

(220) (648) (946)
Carol loves Jack but she's disliked by Jack's father, Andy. Carol uses a third party to convince Andy of her grace and character (616 ch Jack to Andy) (666 ch Jack to Andy; 1010 ch Jack to Andy)

242

(13a) (947) (976)
Carol dislikes the men in her own social and business world * Disapproving of men she meets in her own world, Carol envisions her ideal man and sets off to find him (9a, b) (29) (31) (226)

243

(15a) (34)
Carol, in love with Jack, rejects him when she learns that he jilted her best friend, Annie, to pursue her (251) (277) (325)

(13) Trying by Deception to Escape Trouble

244

(687) (688) (937) (942)
Jack resists the advances of Carol (945-*), an unscrupulous woman who loves him (627) (682) (901)

245

(697b) (389 ch Jack to Andy)
Jack is accused by Gary of having a secret past (157) (75a) (1051) (1054)

246

(a) (244) (31) (229) (331) (332)
Jack loves Carol, a member of a minority, but gives her up because of misguided principles (348) (1328)

(b) (248) (259-3) (315) (322b)
Jack, embittered by a hopeless love affair, throws himself into social causes * Jack, by his selfless acts, loses his bitterness ** (368e) (360a)

CONFLICT SITUATIONS

247

(15a) (13a)
Jack betrays Carol, mistakenly believing there is no one who will avenge the wrong he's committed (1326 ch Jack to Eric; 1237a ch Jack to Eric & Gary to Jack) (1253 ch Gary to Eric) (1262) (1266 ch Jack to Eric & Gary to Jack)

248

(255) (271) (272) (288) (732)
Jack, facing an unavoidable obligation, gives up Carol, whom he loves deeply (718a; 705) (246b-*) (363a) (964a) (842a)

249

(1163b) (1167) (1186) (1187)
Carol, in love with Jack, rejects him when she becomes aware of his evil character (367b) (635) (859) (1163c)

250

(10b) (28b)
Carol loves Jack. But Jack avoids women, believing they're disciples of Satan (45a, b) (55) (71a) (101a) (363a)

251

(32) (36-*) (264) (285) (325)
Carol, unsuccessful in love, attempts to find happiness in imagined romance (58a, b, c) (271)

252

(a) (1g) (16b)
Carol turns down Jack's marriage proposal because she feels that Jack is too much of a perfectionist (1c) (1227b, c) (1237a-*)

(b) (204) (1d)
Carol refuses Jack's marriage offer because she feels Jack is irresponsible and likely to forget his vows (179a, c) (260b) (265b)

253

(291 ch Jack to Eric) (659) (261 ch Gary to Jack)
Carol is loved by wealthy Jack. Carol doesn't love Jack, but for certain reasons, she marries him (376) (403) (557b) (593)

254

(15a) (34)
Carol, despite loving Jack, realizes she's not his intellectual equal, and that their marriage would handicap him (358) (367b) (680a; 361a, b)

(22) Misguided by Mistaken Judgment

255

(718a) (959)
Only Jack knows he is of mixed race. He loves and is loved by Carol, a white woman (681a) (705) (951)

256

(215a) (218a)
Jack, in love with "plain Jane" Carol, leaves her for Laura, a beautiful woman who massages his ego and turns him on (94a, b) (238) (361b)

257

(a) (6a) (9a, b)
Jack falls in love with Carol, which for Jack violates a moral standard (255) (732) (281a)

(b) (680a, b) (681a)
Jack loves Carol, but when Jack's fortunes decline, Carol switches her affections to his rival, Gary (266) (263) (267)

258

(124 tr Jack & Carol) (149) (332) (335) (990) (1074)
Though there are reasons why Jack shouldn't marry, he still plans to do so (374) (500b) (579b)

259

Jack loves Carol. When she refuses to marry him, Jack [1] becomes aloof and cynical (224) (230) (243) (245); [2] becomes reckless, unreliable, or irrational (263) (636) (638); [3] enters into a loveless affair (109) (917) (246b)

260

(a) (59 ch Jack to Gary) (280a)
Jack loves Carol but she rejects him in favor of Gary. Jack knows Gary is a liar/criminal, but Carol is unaware (236) (265a) (266)

(b) (204) (252b)
Jack loves Carol, but he's alienated himself from her because he is overly absent-minded. Jack writes Carol a letter assuring her that he has reformed — and forgets to mail it (81) (265b)

261

(262a, b, c)
Believing she's lost the man she loves, Carol decides to marry Gary, a man she doesn't love (81) (236) (284) (290) (351a) (315; 318)

262

(a) (262b, c)
Carol receives a message from an unknown source * Carol, swayed by an anonymous communication, severs her engagement to marry Jack ** (261) (340) (870a ch Carol to Jack)

(b) (98 ch Carol to Laura) (68 ch Carol to Laura)
Carol, in love with Jack, receives an anonymous letter that claims the writer is Jack's mistress and begs Carol not to take Jack from her (364b) (1154b)

(c) (415 ch Carol to Laura) (481 ch Carol to Laura)
Carol, in love with Jack, receives an anonymous letter that says the writer is secretly married to Jack, and asks Carol to influence Jack to return to her (249) (312-1) (326-4)

263

(958) (1146 ch Jack to Gary) (1181 ch Jack to Gary)
Carol rejects her straight-arrow lover, Jack, in favor of unscrupulous Gary * Jack undergoes a radical character-change ** (819 ch Burt to Gary) (818a tr Jack & Dave)

264

(194a) (199)
Carol, desperately in love, proposes to Jack and is rejected (57) (251)

(15) Finding the Power to Overcome Problems

265

(a) (300) (1342a) (1389b)
Under hypnosis, Jack envisions his romantic rival, Gary, being discredited while he, Jack, gets the girl (1361b; 326-3) (290; 266)

(b) (260b) (1389b)
Jack is very forgetful * Jack, terminally absent-minded, forgets that Carol has rejected him and continues to pursue her ** (182a tr Jack & Gary) (182b) (189-*; 125b)

266

(206) (217)
Jack loves Carol and wants to stop her from marrying Gary, whom Jack has learned is unscrupulous (351a) (1222a; 1222b) (1232 tr Jack & Gary)

267

(59 ch Jack to Gary) (260a) (97)
Carol has promised to marry Gary. But when Jack exposes Gary's infidelities, Carol agrees to marry Jack (280b) (367b)

268

(243) (248 tr Jack & Carol) (992) (993)
Carol refuses to marry Jack, the man she loves, because of an obligation * Carol sacrifices happiness when, true to an obligation, she refuses to marry Jack, the man she loves ** (893) (976)

269

(177) (301b; 1260b ch Jack to Gary & Eric to Frank)
Carol's bankrupt father, Frank, refuses to let Carol marry wealthy Gary, a man she doesn't love, despite the fact that it would solve Frank's financial problems (993; 88) (993; 1207)

270

(30) (32) (34)
Carol secretly loves unmarried Jack (327b); when Jack vanishes and later reappears with a bride, Laura, Carol's love for Jack remains unchanged (496b tr Carol & Laura; 367b) (555b tr Carol & Laura) (368e tr Carol & Laura)

(2) Falling in Love Despite Conflicting Obligations

271

(694; 31) (255) (282b)
Jack and Carol are in love. But Jack, a member of a minority, realizes that if he marries Carol, of a majority race, it would bring great burdens to their lives (286-*) (240*-**) (87; 61; 264; 705)

272

(250) (259-1) (22b ch Carol to Laura)
Despite his vows of celibacy, Jack falls in love with Carol (55) (134a, b)

273

(139) (24b)
Jack falls in love with Carol, who is involved with his friend, Pete (122 ch Gary to Pete) (157 ch Gary to Pete) (211) (294a, b)

274

(1a, c, d, g) (22a)
Jack enters into a love affair at the same time that he is involved in a divorce proceeding (45a) as the "other man" (129; 170) (226)

275

(24a, b, c, d, e) (25) (29)
Jack and Carol fall in love despite their feuding families (53) (70) (73) (240)

276

(4b) (5) (8a)
Jack and Carol fall in love, but their fathers, Andy and Frank, are bitter foes (118 ch Bill to Andy) (117)

277

(15a) (34)
Carol falls for Jack, who jilts her friend, Annie, in order to pursue Carol (98 ch Carol to Annie) (324 ch Carol to Annie & Laura to Carol) * Annie's distress over losing Jack causes Carol to feel torn ** (243) (307)

278

(18) (281a)
Carol falls in love with Jack, who causes her great pain by keeping his marriage secret from her (279) (368e tr Carol & Laura)

279

(420 ch Carol to Laura) (464 ch Carol to Laura)
Unmarried Carol falls in love with married Jack * Unmarried Carol, falling in love with Jack, husband of Laura, is overcome with guilt. Carol leaves Jack and seeks solitude ** (921) (945) (946) (956)

(20) Getting into a Situation From Which Difficult Problems are Likely to Result

280

(a) (245) (265a)
Jack learns that Gary, his rival for Carol's love, is unscrupulous (97) (206; 157; 80a, b)

(b) (280a) (158)
Jack learns that Gary, his rival for Carol's love, has a guilty secret. To keep others from learning the truth, Gary murders Jack (951 ch Jack to Gary; 1461a ch Jack to Gary) (1344 ch Jack to Gary & Pete to Jack)

281

(a) (509 ch Carol to Laura) (486a tr Carol & Laura)
Jack wants to marry Carol, but is already secretly married to Laura (365b ch Carol to Laura) (354b) (279) (415 ch Carol to Laura) (426 ch Carol to Laura)

(b) (313) (211) (209) (271) (288)
Jack, overwhelmed by romantic problems, commits suicide

(c) (225) (176c)
Struggling Jack, in love with Carol, suddenly strikes it rich (1354b) (1394) * Jack turns his back on Carol and goes after wealthy Laura ** (287) (324)

(39) Giving up Cherished Ambitions to Fulfill an Obligation

282

(a) (276) (282b)
Spineless Jack loves Carol but gives in to the objections of his strong-willed father, Andy, and decides not to marry her (205) (241) (330b)

(b) (257a) (171)
Black Muslim Jack loves Carol, a white woman. He's ordered by his father, Andy, and by his religious leader to give up Carol (266) (271) (248)

283

(295a) (310) (334a, b) (335)
Carol loves Jack, but rejects him because of her father, Frank's feud with Jack's father, Andy (234b) (293)

284

(283) (290) (291)
Carol loves Jack but is forced by her parents, Frank and Rita, to marry Gary (81) (234b) (206)

285

(992) (995)
Carol can't marry Jack, the man she loves, because she promised to care for her widowed father, Frank (641) (676)

286

(250) (275)
Carol's parents, Frank and Rita, insist she have nothing to do with Jack * Carol lets herself be governed by parental duty when Frank and Rita order her not to see Jack, the man she loves ** (284) (261) (325)

(40) Starting a Venture in Which One Obligation Conflicts With Another

287

(302) (334a)
Jack discovers that his chosen career will suffer if he marries Carol, the woman he loves (258) (256) (248)

288

(720) (732) (1061)
Jack is afraid he's inherited an ancestor's evil traits * Jack, because he fears he's inherited an ancestor's evil traits, does not dare ask Carol, whom he loves, to marry him ** (258) (264) (705)

289

(850b) (288)
Jack is engaged to marry Carol, but feels he should give her up because of his weakness for drugs and alcohol (367a) (1126; 779)

290

(280a) (245)
Carol loves Jack, but her family disapproves of him and favors Gary, Jack's rival (104) (261) (284)

CONFLICT SITUATIONS

291

(334a) (322a)
Wealthy Carol and struggling Jack care deeply for each other, but Carol refuses to sacrifice luxury for love (134a, b) (239 ch Jack to Gary) (253 ch Jack to Gary) (341)

(35) Encountering a Problem that Challenges One's Ideals

292

(220) (330a)
Jack considers Carol the perfect woman * Jack believes Carol is perfect, seemingly unaware of her questionable character ** (302) (313) (314) (328) (211)

293

(24a, b, c, d, e) (25)
Jack is upper class and Carol, the woman he loves, comes from the working class and resents the wealthy (232) (283) (336b)

(41) Finding an Obligation at Odds with Ambition, Inclination or Necessity

294

(a) (287 ch Jack to Pete) (282a ch Jack to Pete) (274 ch Jack to Pete) (256 ch Jack to Pete)
Jack learns that his friend, Pete, is unfaithful in his relationship with Carol * Jack strongly criticizes his friend, Pete, for his infidelity to Carol ** (294b) (294b; 232)

(b) (294a) (96 ch Jack to Pete)
Angered by Pete's infidelities to his girlfriend, Carol, Jack decides to teach Pete a lesson, a course of action which places their friendship at risk (230) (232)

295

(a) (295b) (313) (350-*)
Jack loves Carol. He sues Carol's father, Frank, for damages sustained in a certain incident (41a, c) (345 tr Carol & Laura) (363b)

(b) (299) (283)
Jack loves Carol. Carol's father, Frank, disapproves of Jack and throws him out of Carol's home. Jack sues Frank for damages (41b, c) (343)

296

(220) (263-*) (266)
Jack informs Carol, whom he loves, that he has killed Gary * Jack confesses to Carol that he has killed Gary, and asks her to call the police ** (750) (787)

297

(403 ch Jack to Eric) (448 ch Jack to Eric)
Jack is the judge at a murder trial in which the defendant is Carol (10c) (14a) (27), the woman Jack secretly loves (108 tr Jack & Carol) (727)

298

(a) (24e) (22b)
Eligible young Jack is stunned by a newspaper announcement of his engagement to Amy, a woman he doesn't know (4a ch Carol to Amy)

(b) (1432 ch Jack to Milt & Jim to Jack) (606)
Jack will inherit a fortune from a deceased relative, provided he marries Amy, a woman he doesn't know (117) (19a)

(c) (669 ch Carol to Amy) (470 ch Carol to Amy) (1154a ch Carol to Amy)
Amy, a woman Jack doesn't know, asks him for help * Jack, asked for help by a stranger, Amy, refuses her, but regrets doing so when Amy mysteriously disappears. Jack feels obligated to locate Amy ** (1410) (885a ch Carol to Amy)

299

(43-*) (276)
Jack loves Carol. But Carol's father, Frank, warns Jack to stay away from Carol (70) (73) (352a, b)

300

(299) (284) (301a)
Jack loves Carol, but suddenly learns that Carol is engaged to Gary (280a; 97) (146) (81)

301

(a) (137a) (157)
Jack's rival, Gary, is preferred by Carol's father, Frank (64) (73) (75a, b) (79)

(b) (165) (162a tr Jack & Carol)
Jack's rival, Gary, finds an object that Carol has lost. The object, X, symbolizes Carol's love for Jack. Gary keeps X and says nothing about it (220) (257b) (280a, b)

302

(96) (117) (118)
If Jack marries Carol, the woman he loves, he'll be disinherited (241) (244) (305) (336b)

303

Jack's love for Carol runs into obstacles because Jack is [1] poor (291) (127a) (125a) (313); [2] too old (1d); [3] too young (37) (124); [4] of a lower class family (171) (245); [5] of an upper class family (3a, b) (232); [6] a playboy (98) (924b); [7] mentally or physically flawed (255) (288); [8] of questionable character (59) (108) (152a); [9] married/divorced (334b) (377a ch Carol to Irene) (388); [10] an ex-convict (338) (695b); [11] under suspicion (80a) (237) (274); [12] wealthy (239) (330a)

304

(285) (288) (289) (292)
Jack is determined to marry Carol, but unavoidable duty stands in his way (211) (220) (248)

305

(697b ch Jack to Carol) (818c ch Jack to Eric & Lee to Carol)
Carol knows nothing of her birth or parents * Carol's rejected lover, Jack, spreads malicious rumors about Carol's past ** (323) (364a) (255; 364c)

306

(308a) (299)
Carol, who loves Jack, is detained by her father, Frank, when she tries to keep a date with Jack (316) (64) (73)

307

(31) (36-*) (38)
Carol, forced by circumstances to be with Jack (898-*) (925-*) in an isolated place (688), loses her romantic view of men (322b) (325) 308 (a) (306) (299)

308

Carol is locked in her room by her father, Frank, to prevent her from meeting her boyfriend, Jack (316) (308b)

(b) (1461d tr Jack & Carol) (290)
Carol sends a letter to her boyfriend, Jack. The letter is intercepted by Carol's father, Frank, who disapproves of Jack (295a) (256) (43)

(c) (63)
Carol sends a gift to Jack, whom she loves *
Carol sends a gift to Jack, but her aunt, Nancy, who dislikes Jack, secretly alters the gift in such a way that Jack will be offended by it; or she exchanges it for an item that will offend him ** (81) (93b)

309

(453 ch Jack to Eric; 468 ch Jack to Eric) (470 ch Jack to Eric)
Carol and Jack are in love. Jack is unaware that Carol is already married (397 ch Jack to Eric & Gary to Jack) (400 ch Jack to Eric & Gary to Jack) (402 ch Jack to Eric & Gary to Jack)

310

(908) (1105)
Carol breaks her engagement to Jack because she doesn't feel up to the responsibilities of married life (315) (345 tr Carol & Laura)

CONFLICT SITUATIONS

311

(958) (1062)
Carol's parents, Frank and Rita, dislike Carol's boyfriend, Jack, because he lacks ambition (311) (114) (125a)

312

Carol's parents, Frank and Rita, are obstacles to her romance with Jack because [1] either Frank or Rita knows a supposedly damaging secret about Jack (98 ch Carol to Irene) (918a); [2] Rita and Frank are possessive of Carol and don't want her to marry anyone (286) (299); [3] Carol is the sole support of Rita and Frank (992) (1032); [4] Carol's career would be ruined by marriage (335) (1119)

(5) Trying to Make the Best of a Hopeless Love Affair

313

(110) (111) (112)
Jack is promised Carol in marriage by her father, Frank. But Frank reneges and forces Carol to marry wealthy Gary (234b) (315) (351a)

314

(233) (220) (330a, b-*)
Jack loves Carol and is about to marry her, but he's detained and fails to arrive in time for the wedding (130) (154a) (664) (711a) (719a) (1040) * Jack, prevented from marrying Carol as planned, makes a discovery about Carol (27) and decides not to marry her ** (337b tr Carol & Laura) (421 tr Carol & Laura)

315

(286) (310)
Carol rejects Jack. In an effort to forget Carol, Jack moves to an isolated region (24a, b, c, d, e tr Carol & Laura) (345 tr Carol & Laura) (246b)

316

(146) (308a) (40b)
When Carol fails to keep a date with Jack, he takes it as a rejection (341) (360a)

317

(316) (319) (286) (341)
Jack loves Carol, but Carol proves unfaithful (404) (177) (208; 421 tr Carol & Laura)

318

(284) (291)
Jack, who loves Carol, reads in the newspaper of her engagement to Gary (280a; 97) (236)

319

(221a) (599)
Jack, who loves Carol, secretly learns that she's about to marry his friend, Pete (168) (157 ch Gary to Pete)

320

(56) (62) (85a, b)
Jack loves Carol, but suspects she's a confirmed tease who is toying with him (421 tr Carol & Laura) (352b) (364b)

321

(a) (898) (899-*)
Jack tries to be philosophical when Carol, the woman he loves, rejects him (917) (922a-*) (922b) (246b-*)

(b) (220) (330a)
Jack falls in love with Carol and plans to marry her. Jack's parents, Andy and Linda, disapprove of Carol, and send Jack to a distant location (321a; 364b) (325 ch Carol to Jack)

322

(a) (85a) (736)
Jack loves Carol, but finds her cold, distant and inhibited (176b) (234b) (253)

CONFLICT SITUATIONS

(b) (781) (924b)
Carol tells Jack that she's rejecting him because he is selfish, cruel and obsessed with money * Carol sends Jack away with the suggestion that he reassess his life ** (246b) (963) (964a) (971)

323

(23a, b) (331) (332)
Carol, an alien, is deserted by Jack, whom she loves (229) (347a)

324

(238) (256)
Carol loses Jack's affections when Laura enters his life (94a) (325)

325

(286) (307) (324)
Carol, disappointed in love, resigns herself to her loss (14a, b) (31) (976)

326

(20a) (24a) (22a)
Carol loves Jack deeply but won't marry him because she [1] is much younger/older than Jack (37) (124); [2] learns that Jack doesn't love her (142) (162a); [3] considers Jack an impractical dreamer (958) (136b); [4] is committed to an obligation (268) (993) (995)

327

(a) (322a tr Jack & Carol) (317 tr Jack & Carol)
Carol loves Jack, but apparently Jack doesn't love her (45b) (55) (57) (68) (71a) (82a)

(b) (15a) (23a, b)
Carol loves Jack. Jack is kind to Carol but doesn't love her and is unaware that she loves him (270) (264)

(23) Becoming Enmeshed in Mistaken Judgment and/or Suspicion

328

(770a) (777) (797-*)
Jack and Carol were engaged. Jack, whom Carol thinks died in an accident, returns, finds Carol about to marry Gary (284) (339), and attempts to prevent the marriage (64) (336a; 351a)

329

(273) (330a) (292)
Jack falls for Carol despite the fact that his friend, Pete, has warned him against her (139) (314) (318 ch Gary to Pete)

330

(a) (149) (3a) (10b) (27)
Wealthy Jack loves Carol. Jack's friends, Pete and Annie, believe Carol is unscrupulous and money-hungry (239) (253)

(b) (276) (117)
Jack's father, Andy, disapproves of Jack's girlfriend, Carol * Carol, by an ingenious action (241), proves herself to Jack's father, Andy, and wins him over ** (330a; 135) (347b)

(6) Challenging the Concept that Lovers From Different Cultures Cannot Be Compatible

331

(31) (34)
Carol, from another culture/planet, challenges convention by falling in love with Jack (687) (689) (324) (336c tr Carol & Laura) (347a)

332

(23a) (23b)
Carol, an alien, tries to marry Jack, whom she loves (323) (324) (327b)

(7) Entering a Love Affair Filled With Unforeseen Complications

333

(59) (236 tr Jack & Gary) (1175a)
Jack gives a valuable gift to Carol, the woman he wants to marry. The gift, X, turns out to have been stolen (267 tr Jack & Gary) (1200)

334

(a) (8a) (4b)
Jack has a dangerous profession (astronaut, race car driver, high-steel worker) which Carol regards as an obstacle to their marriage (287) (1006b) (1356)

(b) (379 ch Carol to Irene) (377a ch Carol to Irene)
Jack loves Carol, but he's divorced and Carol's parents, Frank and Rita, are opposed on religious grounds to Carol marrying a divorced man (73) (80a, b) (134a, b)

335

(1099) (1119) (312-4)
Jack, in love with Carol, realizes that Carol's career ambitions are an obstacle to their marriage (237) (1203)

336

(a) (284) (313) (328)
Social-climber Carol loves Jack but is about to marry celebrity Gary. Jack angrily accuses Carol of blatant shallowness, and a violent argument ensues (267) (351a)

(b) (232) (2c)
Carol's lover, Jack, claims to be to be a working-stiff * Carol, who thought Jack poor, discovers that he's rich. Angered by his deception, Carol rejects him ** (340) (983 ch Eric to Frank)

(c) (331 ch Carol to Laura) (332 ch Carol to Laura)
Carol loves Jack. Laura, an alien, tries to lure Jack away from Carol (238) (688; 31; 24b ch Carol to Laura)

(12) Suffering Problems Because of Disloyalty in Love

337

(a) (256) (324)
Jack, who loves Carol, runs into trouble when he leaves her for Laura, a woman who inflates his ego (126 ch Carol to Laura; 623) (126 ch Carol to Laura; 701)

(b) (94a) (324)
Jack, living with Laura, deserts her and marries Carol * Laura sues Jack for palimony ** (393) (406)

338

(1175a) (1180) (1181)
Donna, a maid in the home of Carol, Jack's girlfriend, warns Jack that Carol has informed the police of Jack's criminal activities (1192) (1194), and that he's a former convict (1195) (1201) (568a change "wife"to "lover")

339

(233) (719a) (750) (917)
Carol, believing the man she loves, Jack, is dead, obeys the wishes of her parents, Frank and Rita, and agrees to marry Gary (334a) (336a)

340

(41a) (218a) (218b)
Jack and Carol love each other, but Laura, through her machinations, wins him away from Carol (94a) (256)

341

(261) (239)
Carol's mother, Rita, is determined that Carol marry wealth. Thus, Carol renounces the man she loves to marry the rich man she doesn't love, and finds herself miserable (373) (376) (393)

(21) Landing in Trouble Through Mistaken Judgment

342

(175) (176a, b, c)
On the eve of their marriage, Jack is placed in great jeopardy by unpredictable Carol * Carol, capriciously placing her lover, Jack, in great jeopardy, bitterly regrets her impulsiveness ** (212b) (1445)

343

(41a, b) (85a) (334a, b)
Jack is alienated from Carol, the woman he loves, because of a trivial disagreement * Jack realizes Carol was right, admits his error and they reconcile ** (408) (412) (424)

344

(145) (153) (170)
Jack breaks up with his girlfriend, Carol, who bitterly refuses to return valuables Jack had given her * Jack lands in trouble (601) (604) and Carol, from whom he's separated, rescues him by returning valuables he'd given her. They reconcile and marry ** (539a) (548a)

345

(322b ch Carol to Laura) (326 ch Carol to Laura)
Jack, rejected by Laura, travels to a distant place where he meets Carol and falls for her (9a, b) (22a) * Laura, regretting her rejection of Jack, searches for him and learns he is about to marry Carol ** (372) (458a)

346

(23a, b) (34)
Carol, an alien, rescues Jack and falls in love with him, but Jack is engaged to marry a woman of his own people, Laura * Jack leaves alien Carol, who loves him, promising to return. Instead, he marries one of his own people, Laura ** (261) (264) (323) (325)

(50) Compelled by a Special Motive to Behave Underhandedly

347

(a) (287) (288) (289) (293) (305) (323)
Jack cruelly abandons Carol (23c) (331) (332), a woman he claimed to love deeply * Jack's enemy, Gary, forces Jack to marry Carol ** (348) (377a) (379)

(b) (98) (117)
Jack is coerced by Frank, father of Carol, to marry Carol * Frank believes he is justified in forcing Jack to marry Carol ** (373) (385a)

348

(347a-*) (346-*)
Cruise-ship comic Jack is on the run from fat, ugly Carol, who desperately loves him and stows away on his ship (87). Mafia godfather Gary is a passenger on the ship and has taken a violent dislike to Jack's sense of humor * Carol makes her plight known to Mafia don Gary, who makes Jack an offer he can't refuse: marry Carol or else ** (347a*-**) (372) (385a)

349

(283) (335)
Carol and Jack, break up because of a lovers' spat * Jack and Carol's mutual friend, Pete, wanting to reunite them, arranges with each to meet him at a certain location ** Lovers Jack and Carol, at odds with each other, are reunited by Pete's surreptitious plan *** (501) (504b)

350

(1223a ch Jack to Frank & Dave to Jack) (1223b ch Jack to Frank, Dave to Jack & Eric to Gary)
Jack and Gary, rivals for Carol's affections, are put to a severe test by Carol's father, Frank * Jack and Gary are lured into an ordeal to prove themselves to Carol; Gary fails, and Jack succeeds but almost loses his life ** Frank approves of Jack, who then marries Carol *** (572) (574a)

351

(a) (266) (313)
Jack kidnaps his sweetheart, Carol (284) (300), as she's enroute to marry Gary (379) (381)

(b) (311) (335)
Jack and Carol are innocently plunged into a compromising situation (134a, b) (876b) * Jack and Carol, in order to extricate themselves from a difficult situation, are hastily married by justice of the peace, Eric ** (391) (411a, b)

352

(a) (299) (311)
Jack, posing as a salesman, calls at the home of Carol, the girl he loves, and her father Frank, who has forbidden him to see Carol * Jack, posing as a salesman, rescues Carol from an accident (181a-*) (851-*) ** Jack is exposed as Carol's lover, a man Frank has disapproved of *** Frank approves of Jack, and Jack and Carol marry **** (375) (44b)

(b) (300) (313)
Jack rescues Carol, the woman he loves, from Gary, a corrupt rival (154b). Jack marries Carol (449) (461)

353

(169) (139)
Carol's parents, Frank and Rita, mistake Jack for Pete, the man to whom Carol is engaged * Jack runs off with Carol and marries her ** (424) (430)

354

(a) (32) (36)
Compelled by an unusual motive, Carol invents a fictitious man, Walt * Walt, a fictitious man invented by Carol, "comes to life," falls for Carol (4a ch Jack to Walt) (298a, b, c ch Jack to Walt), and they marry ** (452) (462)

(b) (10c) (36)
Carol must be married by a specific age in order to receive a large inheritance * Carol has no suitors, so a marriage of convenience is arranged with Jack, on the understanding that it's to remain secret, and that Jack and Carol will part after the ceremony ** (230) (379)

355

(189) (188a)
Carol, capable of besting her lover, Jack, in a contest, deliberately loses (375) (419)

356

(104) (330a ch Jack to Gary)
Carol loses a contest she could easily have won, sacrificing great financial gain so she can marry Jack, the man she loves (410) (455a) (469)

357

(49) (105)
Carol, long lost and presumed killed in a jungle plane crash, returns incognito to spy on her former lover, Jack, a notorious womanizer (82a) (87). Much to Carol's surprise, she discovers that Jack has changed his ways (497 ch "wife" to "lover"). She reveals her true identity and they are reunited (442) (51a) (51b)

358

(232) (2c)
Working girl Carol learns that her lover, Jack, is wealthy and only pretending to be blue collar * Carol pretends to be rich, and merely posing as a salesgirl ** To win Carol, Jack must confess his true status *** Carol, having given tit-for-tat, tells Jack the truth about herself **** (391) (399)

359

(3a, b) (27)
Delinquent Carol wins the love of respectable Jack. By pretending to be respectable, Carol surprises even herself and eventually becomes respectable * Reformed delinquent Jack is rewarded with a happy marriage ** (381; 396)

(15) Finding the Power to Overcome Problems

360

(a) (177) (276) (316)
Jack, in love with Carol but adamantly rejected by her tyrannical father, Frank, conspires to have Frank killed. Suddenly Carol calls Jack with the news that her father, Frank, has relented and now blesses their marriage. Jack must race to halt Frank's murder (562) (571)

b) (20a, b) (24a, b)
Painfully shy Jack loves scatterbrained Carol, but he's unsure of her affections * Jack finds an object, X, which Carol has lost, an object (love letter, poem, etc.) that proves she loves him (165) ** Jack proposes to Carol and she accepts *** (380) (405)

361

(a) (215a) (256)
Jack betrays Carol, whom he loves, and has a passionate affair with Laura * Laura leaves Jack when his fortunes decline (606) (630) (655) (710) ** Carol, still loyal, returns to Jack. They reconcile and marry *** (585a) (589)

(b) (282a) (287)
Teenager Jack is unfaithful to his girlfriend, Carol, and they break up * Jack, middle-aged, searches for Carol, his childhood sweetheart ** (205) Jack finds Carol and they realize they're still in love *** (428) (431)

362

(70) (73)
Eloping lovers Jack and Carol are pursued by their feuding families * Jack and Carol, pursued by their feuding families, suddenly find themselves in terrible jeopardy. Jack heroically rescues Carol ** Jack's rescue of Carol results in peace between their families, and marriage for Jack and Carol *** (419) (460)

363

(a) (55) (287) (302) (329) (330a)
Jack rebels against restrictions and finds happiness by marrying Carol (473) (484a)

(b) (295a, b) (118)
Frustrated Jack stops plotting against Frank, father of Carol, the girl he loves, when Frank drops his objections to Jack and allows him to marry Carol (517) (532a)

364

(a) (245 ch Jack to Carol & Gary to Laura)
Carol takes drastic measures when she discovers a skeleton in her family closet * Jack, Carol's lover, obtains evidence that erases a shadow from Carol's past (1051) (1052a-*), and they marry ** (431) (437)

(b) (316) (320)
Carol, in love with Jack but alienated from him, discovers after several misadventures that Jack still loves her (82a) (89) * Jack and Carol, alienated, reconcile and marry ** (540) (561)

(c) (255) (282a)
Jack, an alien, loves Carol, supposedly an earth girl. About to give Carol up, Jack finds that Carol is also an alien (255 tr Jack & Carol) (1051) * Jack marries Carol ** (551) (575)

(d) (850a, b) (1075a, b)
Jack, with Carol's help, overcomes a terrible weakness * Jack's gratitude to Carol turns into love; when Jack is sure he has reformed, he proposes and Carol accepts ** (826) (828)

CONFLICT SITUATIONS

(20) Getting into a Situation From Which Difficult Problems are Likely to Result

365

(a) (9a-*) (190)
Jack and Carol, long-time friends, marry not for love but for companionship (230) (373)

(b) (101b) (599)
Jack and Carol, strangers at a party, are married in a supposedly fake ceremony which later turns out to be legal (167a) (432a)

(c) (24a, b ch Carol to Amy)
In a prearranged marriage, Jack is wedded to Amy, a woman he doesn't know, by Eric (432a, b, ch Carol to Amy) (437 ch Carol to Amy)

(d) (188b ch Carol to Amy) (365a, b, c)
Jack marries Amy, a total stranger * Jack and Amy marry, then go their separate ways immediately after the wedding ceremony ** (167a tr Carol & Amy) (432b ch Carol to Amy)

366

(302) (117)
Jack passes up an inheritance because of a restriction that he must not marry, and marries Carol (117; 116; 167a) (370)

367

(a) (289) (1075a) (1079)
Carol offers to marry Jack and to help him rebuild his wasted life (469) (524a)

(b) (24a, b, e)
Carol doubts Jack's love until, finally convincing herself of his sincerity (97) (116), she accepts Jack and they marry (369) (428)

368

(a) (285) (641)
Carol rejects Jack, the man she loves, because she feels obligated to care for her father, Frank. Frank then gets married, and Carol finds herself alone in the world (205; 361b **-***) (325)

(b) (659) (1260a, b ch Eric to Frank)
Carol marries wealthy Jack, whom she doesn't love, so that she will have money to help a desperately ill parent (403) (558)

(c) (171) (162a)
Carol agrees to marry Jack, who gets the license; then, before Jack and Carol can marry, Carol suddenly marries his rival, Gary (312-1) (313)

(d) (818d ch Jack to Eric & Lee to Carol) (1051) (1054)
Carol, an orphan, is told by Jack the secret of her lineage. Once Carol proves her parentage, she can claim a rich estate * Though Jack loves Carol, he's poor and feels he isn't worthy of wealthy Carol; but Carol convinces him of her love, and they marry ** (449) (458a)

(e) (270 ch Carol to Laura) (278 ch Carol to Laura) (528)
Jack is unhappily married to Carol and in love with Laura, but he doesn't believe in divorce * Jack's uncaring wife, Carol, is killed in an accident, leaving Jack free to marry his long-time love, Laura ** (241 ch Carol to Laura) (254 ch Carol to Laura) (307 ch Carol to Laura)

CONFLICT SITUATIONS

(21) Landing in Trouble Through Mistaken Judgment

369

(107) (367a)
Jack and Carol, married and devoted to each other, are impulsive and intolerant * Jack and Carol, married, continually quarrel (372) (373), and, as a result, separate ** (457) (460) (501)

370

(366) (367b)
Jack is devoted to his wife, Carol, but is unable to demonstrate his true feelings, often expressing them in ways that suggest their exact opposite * Carol grieves in the mistaken belief that she's lost Jack's love ** (581) (586) (575; 918b)

371

(59) (368b)
Jack is suspected of murdering his wife, Carol (385a) (416) (417) (1070 ch Carol to Irene)

372

(345) (348)
Jack and Carol are devoted to each other but because of their conflicting standards (898) (899-*) (908) (976), their marriage begins to disintegrate (369) (394)

373

(341) (365a)
Jack is so much older than Carol that after they marry, the discrepancy in their ages becomes a problem and they separate (808b) (418) (429a)

374

(9a, b) (190) (239)
During their courtship, Jack finds Carol career-oriented and highly motivated * After their marriage, Jack is disappointed to discover that Carol has lost her ambition ** (413) (441)

375

(114) (491a) (1060 ch Jack to Carol)
Jack is more capable than his wife, Carol, but she thoughtlessly treats him as her inferior (419) (427)

376

(253) (341)
Jack dominates his wife, Carol * Jack is a controlling individual who makes Carol miserable ** (403) (410)

377

(a) (347a) (421)
Jack divorces his wife, Carol * Jack owes most of his financial success to his wife Carol's loyalty and shrewd advice ** (496a) (499a)

(b) (656) (781)
Jack marries Carol, believing she is rich. After the marriage, Jack finds he was mistaken * Bankrupt Jack divorces Carol and contrives to marry wealthy Laura ** Laura, for whom Jack got a divorce, marries another man *** Carol, recently divorced by Jack, inherits a large estate **** (388) (638)

378

(59) (234a)
Jack, marrying a widow, Carol, discovers that he has married a domestic tyrant (417) (473) (480)

379

(351b) (354b)
Jack is forced by an agreement to divorce his wife, Carol (388-*) (460) (483a, b; 352b)

380

(553) (561) (562-*)
Jack is jealous of his wife, Carol * Jack foolishly starts gambling and loses money that isn't his ** Jack gambles with Gary, the man Jack thinks had an affair with his wife *** (434a) (445a) (568d) (396)

CONFLICT SITUATIONS

381

(359) (367a)
Jack finds a note (561) (562) (582 tr Carol & Jack), worded somewhat ambiguously, that causes him to mistrust the conduct of his wife, Carol * Jack angrily plots revenge ** (396) (420) (464)

382

(1002; 988) (1285b) (422a)
(4) Jack secretly cheated Carol out of money. In order to hide his crime, Jack marries Carol * After marrying Carol, Jack falls in love with Laura ** (440) (465) (572)

383

(8a) (148) (234a)
Jack's beautiful wife, Carol, has a minor physical flaw * Carol's insignificant physical imperfection is magnified out of all proportion in the mind of her husband, Jack; his love begins to fade ** (386) (391) (416) (475)

384

(574b) (1009a ch Carol to Linda; 1009b ch Carol to Linda & Doug to Jack)
Jack and his wife, Carol, live with Jack's mother, Linda * Carol battles with Linda, and with Jack over Linda ** (1067) (1067 ch Carol to Linda) (1068) (518)

385

(a) (341) (365a) (368b)
Jack and his wife, Carol, argue violently and often * Carol is mysteriously murdered (387) and Jack, innocent, is the suspect ** (520) (526)

(b) (812a ch Dave to Annie) (836 ch Jack to Carol & Pete to Annie)
Jack is asked by Annie, a friend of his dead wife, Carol, for some love letters that Annie gave to Carol for safe-keeping * Jack suspects his wife, Carol, of receiving love letters — but learns they belong to Annie and were being held by Carol for safe-keeping ** (552b; 1441b) (576a, b)

386

(539a) (542)
Jack leaves his loving wife, Carol, and runs off with Laura, a woman who flatters him * Laura is rich but shallow and Jack, following her advice, fails miserably in all his ventures ** (391) (393)

387

(484a; 490a) (370)
Jack gives his wife, Carol, a gift as a statement of his love * (1333a) Jack finds Carol dead, killed by the gift he gave her ** (385a) (474) (497) (576a; 498)

388

(464) (486a) (509) (573b)
Jack divorces Carol, then tries to remarry her * At the time Jack divorced her, Carol's health and beauty were fading ** Carol, health restored, realizes she's well rid of Jack *** (305) (319) (322b)

389

(23c, d) (27) (365b)
Jack, thinking his first wife is dead (49) (400) (486a), remarries and has children by his second wife * Jack learns that his first wife was still alive when he remarried, but that she has since died ** Jack's second marriage is unwittingly invalidated *** Jack decides to make a new will and have another wedding ceremony with his second wife, but he's killed in an accident enroute to his attorney **** The children of Jack's second marriage are illegitimate, so Jack's property goes to the relatives of Jack's dead first wife ***** (245 ch Jack to Greg) (305 ch Carol to Nina)

CONFLICT SITUATIONS

390

(709-*) (808a-* ch Carol to Pete) (1044b)
While in a dubious situation, Jack accidently loses an object, X, that belongs to his friend, Pete (711b) * X, an object belonging to Pete, is lost by Jack in questionable surroundings. X is recovered and sent by a troublemaker, Sally, to Pete's wife, with a note explaining where it was found (478 ch Jack to Pete) ** Pete, wrongly suspected of crime/immorality, is in deep trouble until Jack clears him of suspicion *** (506b ch Jack to Pete)

391

(369) (539a) (542)
Due to mistaken judgment, Jack becomes alienated from his wife, Carol " Jack has a foolish adventure with Laura (386) (540), that opens his eyes to his own immaturity ** Jack, reformed by his experience, returns to his wife, Carol *** (449) (499a)

392

(116; 53) (498) (515)
Jack thinks he sees the ghost of his dead wife, Carol * Jack attempts to catch Carol's apparition, falls from a cliff and is killed **

393

(421) (422a)
Carol's husband, Jack, is haunted by idealized fantasies about a former love, Laura * Jack's marriage to Carol is harmed by his fantasies ** Jack seeks out Laura and realizes the folly of attempting to recapture the past (244 ch Carol to Laura) (211 ch Carol to Laura). Free of his obsession with Laura, Jack returns to Carol *** (409) (454)

394

(372) (395) (408) (462)
Jack, married to Carol, finds an excuse to be absent (443-*) for a few days each month * Carol follows Jack and discovers he is merely trying to escape from her demanding nature (417) (443*-***) (478) ** Carol, realizing that her behavior has hurt Jack, promises to change, and Jack returns home ***

395

(378) (475)
Jack's idea of a happy marriage is peace and comfort * Jack's wife, Carol, is a nag, and they argue constantly ** (385a) (394) (427) (440*-**) (471) (473)

396

(380-**) (449) (553) (561) (562)
Suspicious Jack learns that his wife, Carol, has indeed been faithful * Jack learns that Gary, the man Jack thought had run off with Carol, was in a distant city at the time of the alleged affair ** (563a) (506b tr Jack & Carol)

397

(398a, b) (418)
Carol, wife of Jack, flirts with unmarried Gary * Married Carol is spending a romantic weekend with unmarried Gary when he suddenly dies ** (738) (1069 ch "daughter Nina" to "lover Gary")
(1151)

398

(a) (369) (370)
Carol feels she is neglected by her husband, Jack * Gary, by flattering and sympathizing with Carol, makes her think she loves him ** (380) (400) (418) (507a, b)

(b) (369) (370)
Carol feels she is neglected by her husband, Jack * Carol, hoping to rekindle her husband, Jack's, passion by making him jealous, flirts with Gary ** (397) (445a) (478 tr Jack & Carol)

399

(508) (524a)
Carol is the sensible, loving wife of Jack * Jack is egocentric, self-deluding ** Jack, successful because of Carol's wise advice, deludes himself that Carol envies his considerable abilities *** Jack and Carol become alienated **** (438) (457) (460) (482)

CONFLICT SITUATIONS

400

(444) (454)
Carol leaves her husband, Jack, for another man, Gary * Carol leaves her husband, Jack, for Gary, only to discover that Gary is involved with another married woman, Laura ** (418*-**) (496a) (499a)

401

(538-*) (581)
Carol worries when her husband, Jack, fails to return home * Carol, believing her husband, Jack, is in jeopardy, places herself in danger in hope of locating and rescuing him ** (538*-***) (545) (546a)

402

(49 ch "lovers" to "man and wife") (437; 548a) (572)
Carol believes her husband, Jack, is dead and marries Gary (339) * Jack, believed to be dead, returns mysteriously ** Jack tries to force Carol to give up her new husband, Gary *** (573b) (1390)

403

(368b) (376) (407) (454) (493)
Carol's husband, Jack, is a brutal tyrant * Goaded beyond her limit, Carol poisons Jack ** Carol poisons her husband, Jack, and flees before the poison takes effect *** (453; 468) (16a) (946)

404

(261) (290) (291)
Carol, after a loveless marriage with Gary, gets a divorce and searches for Jack, the man she loved and broke up with (261 ch Carol to Jack & Gary to Laura) (327a; 325) (345 tr Carol & Laura)

405

(486a tr Carol & Laura; 474 ch Carol to Laura) (578b tr Carol & Laura)
Carol is widower Jack's second wife * Jack, feeling disloyal to his first wife, Laura, makes Carol miserable with his guilt ** (496a) (504b)

406

(261 ch Gary to Jack) (284 tr Jack & Gary)
Carol, recently married to Jack, tells Jack she doesn't love him * Carol admits to her husband, Jack, that she married him out of resentment toward Gary, the man she loved, for having married Laura ** (462) (489) (499b)

407

(376) (403)
Jack beats his wife, Carol, for an act she didn't commit (445a-*) (483b) (553) (381-*) (403) (438) (470) (516) (557a, b) (558)

408

(378) (500b)
Carol's obsessive neatness makes her husband Jack's life miserable (417) (429a) (464) (486a) (473) (533)

409

(414) (422a) (436)
Carol tells her husband, Jack, that she loves Gary (423a) (457) (460)

410

(469; 532a; 1293a) (469; 532a; 583b ch Gary to Burt)
Carol commits a crime (or indiscretion) in order to help her husband, Jack * Carol finds herself in the clutches of Burt ** (411b ch Gary to Burt) (669)

411

(a) (445a-**) (434a-*) (414)
Carol, happily married to Jack, commits an indiscretion (469; 532a; 1293b) (445a**-***) (442) (446a, b) (449)

(b) (469) (492b)
Jack's wife, Carol, confidentially borrows money from a former lover, Gary * Gary tries to use his power over Carol for his own selfish goals ** (476b) (483b)

CONFLICT SITUATIONS

412

(376) (378) (405) (413)
Jack's wife, Carol, finds his odd quirks annoying: The way he slurps his coffee, his endless "unfunny" jokes, his dirty sneakers, his snoring, etc. These trivialities so aggravate Carol, that they cause bitter quarrels (404 tr Jack * Gary) (411a) (418) (557a)

413

(190) (261 ch Gary to Jack) (253)
Carol marries a much older man, Jack * Carol doesn't love Jack but thought when she married him that he would help her achieve her lifelong ambition ** Carol desperately wants a movie career *** Carol's husband, Jack, proves to be tyrannical and abusive **** (373) (404 tr Jack & Gary) (409)

414

(376) (916 ch Carol to Annie; 765 ch Carol to Annie)
Jack's wife, Carol, admires Annie's independence and wants to be like her * Jack doesn't admire Annie or her ways ** (407) (441) (442) (452)

415

(472-*) (365c, d, ch Amy to Carol)
Carol discovers that her supposed legal marriage to Jack was a sham * Jack leaves Carol penniless and alone ** (479) (481) (647) (870a) (14b ch Jack to Gary)

416

(227) (441-*) (475-*) (558) (761b)
Jack's wife, Carol, dies as the result of a venture that was started supposedly for her benefit (576a) (578a, b) (587) (588)

417

(378) (408) (420)
Carol, while raging at her husband, Jack, has a stroke and dies (371) (526) (560)

418

(530) (543) (582) (592)
After quarreling with her husband, Jack, Carol leaves him * Carol has an experience with Gary which convinces her that leaving her husband, Jack, was a mistake ** (483b) (507b) (583b)

(50) Compelled by a Special Motive to Behave Underhandedly

419

(372) (375)
To be happy, Jack needs to have his abilities acknowledged by his wife, Carol (432a) (463) * Jack abandons Carol, leaving her to run their joint business alone, hoping his absence will make Carol appreciate his talents ** (501) (519a-*) (1395) (1445)

420

(395) (406) (408) (494)
Jack is unhappily married to Carol * Jack's unhappy married life causes him to engage in reckless, destructive adventures ** (429a) (848a ch Carol to Laura) (876a ch Carol to Laura) (876b ch Carol to Laura) (1209b) (246b-*)

421

(131 ch Carol to Laura; 208 ch Carol to Laura) (176a ch Carol to Laura)
Jack marries Carol to free himself of the harmful influence of Laura * Laura is a promiscuous tease whom Jack loves ** (386) (393) (528)

422

(a) (1002; 1285b) (988)
Jack secretly cheats Carol out of a fortune (701 ch Pete to Carol) * Jack marries Carol so that he can surreptitiously replace the property he stole from her before their marriage ** (429a) (465) (486a)

422

(b) (59) (263 tr Jack & Gary) (284 tr Jack & Gary)
Jack married Carol for her money * Jack, having acquired Carol's money, tires of her ** Jack tells Carol he is a criminal, about to be arrested by the police *** Jack persuades Carol to join him in a suicide pact **** Carol, in a suicide pact with Jack, kills herself; Jack reneges ***** (371) (392) (425; 1290b ch Jack to Greg & Andy to Jack)

423

(a) (418-*) (426-*) (430) (400)
Husband Jack and wife Carol each secretly leaves home on the same day * Jack believes he has deserted Carol, and Carol thinks she has deserted Jack ** (394) (487) (500a)

(b) (429b) (484a-*)
Husband Jack and wife Carol are rich and popular * Jack and Carol are so occupied with social engagements, they have no time for each other ** Jack and Carol look for a place where they can be alone together *** Jack and Carol find the solitude they desire [1] in a lonely lighthouse; [2] on a desert island; [3] by pretending to leave on an extended trip abroad, closing their mansion and living secretly in a small apartment **** (49) (688-8) (897 add Carol)

424

(461) (484a-*) (523)
Artist Jack works secretly as a manual laborer so that he can help his wife, Carol, who is also an artist * Jack tells Carol his paintings are finally selling ** (546a) (532b) (582) (574a)

425

(349) (363a)
Jack has a son, Lee, by his wife, Carol, who dies * Jack, while traveling abroad (917), marries Laura, a woman of another race (347a ch Carol to Laura) (901 ch Carol to Laura), deserts her and returns to his own country ** Jack keeps a family secret from his son, Greg (or Lee) *** (881) (934)

426

(378) (464) (539a)
Jack, wanting to get out of his marriage to Carol, resorts to deception * Jack cons his friend, Pete, into running off with Carol ** (377b) (489) (466a ch Gary to Pete) (550 ch Gary to Pete)

427

(378) (430) (432a) (438) (463) (513)
Jack, married to Carol, is compelled by an unusual motive to surreptitiously lease a bachelor apartment in another town * Jack secretly retires to his bachelor digs where he lives, hermit-like ** (423a) (385a; 520) (502)

428

(354a) (356)
Jack and his wife, Carol, are unsuccessful artists * Jack and Carol run into severe problems. Each tries a secret method of recouping their joint finances ** (124) (455b) (532b)

429

(a) (420) (422a) (430-*) (471) (473)
Jack, married to Carol, is compelled by an unusual motive to vanish and assume a new identity (1225) (1233) (1275)

(b) (423b-*) (471) (473)
Jack and Carol, devotedly married, are propelled by an unusual motive to disappear, leave the life they know, and seek a fresh start (423b *-****) (484a)

430

(455b) (461) (491b)
Carol's husband, Jack, is heavily in debt * Jack vanishes mysteriously ** (572) (719a, b) (770a; 540)

431

(748; 700) (924a) (997b)
Jack, rich and unhappy with his wealth, is determined to get rid of it by marrying notorious spendthrift Carol (484a; 929) (488a)

432

(a) (375) (378) (382) (383)
Jack, married to Carol, devises a plan to change his unhappy marriage (377b) (393) (394) (419)

(b) (354b) (365b) (155 ch Walt to Jack)
Jack's wife, Carol, is a woman of mystery * Jack doesn't know Carol, and hasn't seen her since the day they were married ** (167a tr Walt & Jack) (486a)

433

(a) (1316) (1317 ch Eric to Gary)
Jack's enemy, Gary, who gravely victimized Jack, is dead * Jack sets out to revenge himself on Carol, Gary's widow, for a dreadful wrong committed by Gary ** (1310) (1311) (1323a ch Laura to Carol)

(b) (434a) (450) (494)
Gary loves Jack's wife, Carol * Gary deviously tries to win Carol, Jack's wife ** (444) (434a, b)

434

(a) (553) (561) (562)
Jack's wife, Carol, appears to be having an affair with Gary * Jack is manipulated by Gary into speculating with money that isn't his, and losing it ** (434b) (445a) (572)

(b) (433b) (171)
Jack is manipulated into trouble by Gary * Jack, influenced by Gary, is driven to divorce his wife, Carol ** (378 ch Jack to Gary) (385a ch Jack to Gary) (403 ch Jack to Gary)

435

(a) (402 tr Jack & Gary) (451)
Jack marries Carol, unaware that she's still married to Gary * Jack's friend, Pete, arranges for both of bigamist Carol's husbands, Gary and Jack, to meet, thus exposing the truth ** (743b; 921) (738)

(b) (466b) (510)
Jack is unaware that his wife, Carol, is cheating on him. Pete discovers Carol's infidelity and tells Jack, who is gravely ill but stubbornly refusing the treatment that might cure him * Jack, desperately ill, incensed by his wife's infidelities, decides that living will be his ultimate revenge and undergoes the treatment that cures him ** (487) (489)

436

(458b) (1061)
Jack, on the run from a relentless process-server, pretends that his showgirl wife, Carol, is his sister * Jack, having pretended that his wife, Carol, is his sister, finds himself in jeopardy when Carol's new admirer turns out to be a notorious mob figure ** (584b) (554) (557a)

437

(681b) (683) (734) (1368)
Jack, married to Carol, loses his memory * Jack assumes a false identity and marries Laura ** (402) (548a) (571)

438

(503a) (521; 1177) (521; 1178) (521; 1185) (525) (568b)
Jack searches for the cruelest way to hurt his wife, Carol * Jack mysteriously disappears, pretending he's dead ** (402) (559) (884a ch Jack to Carol & Burt to Jack)

439

(376) (403-*)
Carol's friend, Gary, tries to protect her from her brutal husband, Jack * Carol's friend, Gary, concocts a plan whereby it will appear that Carol's brutal husband, Jack, has killed Gary, will be imprisoned and thus never harm Carol again. Gary either succeeds — or is killed — by Jack — or someone else **

440

(488b) (1211; 422a)
Jack is compelled by an unusual motive to marry Carol, whom he doesn't love * Jack manages to find a way to leave his unloved wife, Carol (1204 ch Carol to Jack & Irene to Eric) (952), and, using an alias, marries the woman he loves, Laura ** (917) (963)

441

(33 ch Carol to Vicki & Rita to Carol; 258 ch Jack to Carol) (421) (422a; b-*)
Jack's wife, Carol, is a drug addict * Carol conceals her drug addiction from her husband, Jack ** (435b) (440) (442) (446a)

442

(376; 642-*) (376; 646) (403-*; 739)
Jack forbids his wife, Carol, to do a certain thing * Carol, forbidden by her husband, Jack, to do a certain thing, does it anyway when Jack is absent ** (642 *-**) (599; 534)

443

(386-*) (408)
Jack tells his wife, Carol, he's leaving town to meet a friend, Pete * Jack's friend, Pete, phones Jack, who is supposedly visiting him, and Carol finds the message on their answering machine ** Pete, friend of Jack, is abroad and Carol conceals his message from Jack. The next time Jack leaves home "to meet Pete," Carol shadows him *** (394) (486a; 552a tr Jack & Carol; 404 tr Jack & Gary)

444

(433b) (492b)
Carol runs off with Gary, who has underhandedly made Carol doubt her husband, Jack's loyalty (213-*) (476b) (540) (507a) (568a) (568b) (573b)

445

(a) (553) (561)
Jack mistakenly assumes his wife, Carol, is having an affair with Gary * Jack's wife, Carol, despises Gary, but visits him late at night at his apartment (483b) (583b) ** Carol forces Gary, at gun point, to return money he stole from Jack *** (380*-***) (396) (499a)

(b) (284) (573a)
Jack's wife, Carol, desperately tries to escape disaster * Carol drinks a potion that puts her into a deathlike state, but only after Jack's assurances that he'll revive her ** (105) (576b)

446

(a) (494) (495) (580)
Jack's wife, Carol, is guilty of an indiscretion * To avoid the consequences of her own indiscretion, Carol blames innocent Pete ** (446b ch "lover" to "friend") (507a)

(b) (411b ch Gary to Pete) (433b ch Gary to Pete) (449 ch Gary to Pete)
Jack's wife, Carol, visits her lover, Pete * Jack visits his friend, Pete ** Pete hides Carol from Jack *** Jack finds his wife, Carol, hidden in Pete's apartment **** (400 ch Gary to Pete) (418 ch Gary to Pete) (446a)

447

(90a ch Jack to Burt) (59 ch Jack to Burt)
Carol, in her teens, married a criminal, Burt * Criminal Burt is killed and Carol, his widow, tries a fresh start in a distant location ** Carol marries wealthy, prominent Jack (20a, c) (24a, b) and keeps her sordid past hidden *** (669 ch Burt to "a pal of Burt's") (669 ch Burt to "a pal of Burt's"; 738) (870b ch Burt to "a pal of Burt's") (870a)

448

(450; 550) (450; 1204; 502 tr Carol & Jack)
Carol kills her husband, Jack, to stop him from revealing a dark secret (557a) (1258) (1294)

449

(398b) (411b-*; 445a*-**) (433b; 583b)
Carol is happily married to Jack * Jack's wife, Carol, with an innocent motive, secretly meets with an old lover, Gary ** (411a-*; 410) (434a)

450

(492b-**) (494)
Carol secretly plans to free herself of Jack, her unsuccessful husband, so she can marry wealthy Gary (451) (557a) (1204)

451

(450) (418-*) (470)
Carol, married to Jack, pretends to be single * Married Carol assumes a new identity and marries Gary ** (448) (471 ch Jack to Gary) (550)

452

(376) (383; 403-*) (521)
Carol devises a plan to free herself from fear of her husband, Jack (470) (475) (516)

453

(403) (448)
Carol thinks she has killed her husband, Jack * Carol tries to save herself from the consequences of a crime by running away ** (468) (502)

454

(1a, b, d, e, f, g) (421) (422a) (440-*)
Jack married Carol under false pretenses * Carol plots revenge against her husband, Jack ** (400) (408) (451) (467) (477)

455

(a) (428) (455b) (490a-*)
Carol secretly sells a treasured possession so she can buy a gift for her husband, Jack (430) (532b) (1293c)

(b) (428) (522)
Carol and her husband, Jack, are experiencing hard times * Carol, in order to pay the bills, finds menial work but tells Jack she has a responsible position ** (424) (69) (579a)

456

(422b-*) (430-*) (525)
Carol closely resembles Irene * Carol marries Jack. Carol has property in her own name that, by a pre-nuptial agreement, will go to Jack if he outlives her ** Irene dies, and Jack makes it appear that Carol died *** Carol, manipulated by Jack, is committed to an insane asylum as Irene, and Jack inherits Carol's money **** (732) (1447 tr Jack & Eric) (1461a)

(13) Trying by Deception to Escape Trouble

457

(463) (485)
Jack and Carol are married. Finding they are incompatible, they secretly agree to a separation without divorce because of [1] their child, Lee. [2] religious beliefs. [3] inability to reach a satisfactory settlement of their estate. [4] determination on the part of husband or wife to stop the other from re-marrying. [5] fear of scandal and gossip (475) (484a) (499a) (501)

458

(a) (260b; 367b) (326-1; 363a)
Jack and Carol, just married, board a plane to start their honeymoon * Bride Carol, enroute to her honeymoon, encounters problems after the groom, Jack, gets off the plane to send a fax during a stopover, and is left behind ** (445a-*; 396-*) (583c) (589)

CONFLICT SITUATIONS

458

(b) (423b-2) (687 add Carol) (691 add Carol)
Jack and Carol, married, are stranded among
a primitive people * Jack, realizing his wife,
Carol's, beauty is a threat to himself, devises
a self-serving plan to avoid the danger **
(436) (688-*; 307) (688-*: 197 ch Carol to
Laura) (688-*; 973)

459

(376) (434a-*) (495) (503a) (559)
Carol's husband, Jack, is a tyrant * Jack plots
to kill Gary, whom Carol loves ** (439) (503b;
403)

460

(463) (553)
Jack is separated from his wife, Carol, whom
he loves deeply * Jack moves away and
struggles to overcome his problems ** (396)
(501) (539b)

461

(239) (341) (585b)
Jack deeply loves his wife, Carol * Jack faces
a business failure (491b) (606) (631) (747) —
which he knows will destroy his happy marriage ** (484b; 770b, c) (505)

462

(461) (491b)
Jack is unhappily married to Carol * Jack
singlemindedly pursues his ambitions **
(905) (907) (913) (928a) (492b)

463

(408) (420) (491b)
Jack deeply loves his wife, Carol, but rebels
against the injustice she forces him to endure (419) (427) (429a) (460)

464

(437) (509) (525)
Carol's husband, Jack, is compelled by an
unusual motive to lead a double life (486b)
(548a, b) (1200)

465

(422a; 486a) (1295)
Jack deviously tries to escape problems, re-
store property and free himself from his wife,
Carol (572) (952) (1172 ch Carol to Jack &
Sally to Burt; 1204 ch Carol to Jack & Irene
to Eric)

466

(a) (482) (493)
Carol and her husband, Jack, have one child,
Lee * Carol loves her child, Lee, but not her
husband, Jack ** Carol loves Gary and runs
off with him, leaving her child, Lee, with
her husband, Jack *** (507b; 499a) (500a)

(b) (503b ch Gary to Matt) (495 ch Gary to
Matt)
Young Carol, wife of elderly Jack, has an
affair with Jack's servant, Matt * Jack is sick
and about to die; Carol, his wife, could save
him, but she refuses ** (435b) (524b)

467

(1339) (1341)
Unbeknownst to Jack, his wife, Carol, has
seen him exchange a pair of muddy shoes
for the clean shoes of Eric * Jack attempts to
shift the blame for a crime onto innocent Eric
** (521) (540) (569-*)

468

(403) (486b) (488b)
Carol tries to poison her husband, Jack *
Carol, attempting to poison her husband,
Jack, mistakes a bottle of harmless white
powder for the poison and gives Jack some
of its contents ** (453; 502) (539b tr Jack &
Carol)

469

(428) (430-*)
Carol tries to help her husband, Jack, with a
secret venture, but lack of money stops her
(411b) (449) (455a, b) (532a, b)

470

(407) (412)
Carol tries to run away from her bullying husband, Jack (400) (418) (451) (743b)

(14) Getting into Trouble Because of a Clever Schemer

471

(450 tr Jack & Gary) (451 tr Jack & Gary)
After marrying Carol, Jack discovers that she's still married to her previous husband (473) (480) (489)

472

(476a) (488b) (503a) (521)
Jack, married to Carol, has not divorced his previous wife, Laura * Jack learns that Carol has married Gary ** (540) (568a, b, c, d)

473

(378) (420) (548a tr Carol & Laura) (572 ch Jack to Gary)
Jack becomes Carol's second husband. Carol's first husband, Gary, vanished mysteriously and is supposedly dead * After Jack and Carol are married, Carol's first husband, Gary, secretly contacts Jack ** (533; 594b) (400a)

474

(376) (378) (420)
Jack's wife, Carol, dies * Unscrupulous so-called spiritualists Burt and Sally pretend to materialize deceased Carol's spirit in order to persuade Jack to give them money ** (392) (830) (880a)

475

(383) (454)
Yuppie Jack marries wild disco queen Carol, and with each full moon, finds himself the victim of bizarre, inexplicable experiences * Carol, revealed as a vampire, draws innocent husband Jack into her demoniac world ** (1334a) (1342a) (1374) (1375)

476

(a) (398a, b) (405)
Jack's wife, Carol, is deviously persuaded by Gary, the "other man," to run off with him (397) (400)

(b) (398b) (449) (483b)
Jack's wife, Carol, finds herself in the power of a former lover, Gary * Gary threatens to tell Carol's husband, Jack, a deadly secret unless Carol agrees to a certain proposition ** (441) (447) (455b) (492b) (446b ch Pete to Gary) (483b) (507a)

477

(398b ch Gary to Pete) (446b) (580) (589)
Jack's wife, Carol, persuades his friend, Pete, to run off with her (418 ch Gary to Pete) (423a)

478

(540) (589)
Carol falsely accuses her husband, Jack, of a wrongdoing (506a,b) (507a)

479

(382) (386) (426)
Jack, secretly married to Carol, betrays her * Carol is accidently killed due to a series of events initiated by her husband, Jack ** (545) (557b)

480

(426-*) (575)
Desperately ill Carol sends her husband, Jack, for a doctor * Jack, sent for a doctor by Carol, who is seriously ill, fails to return (634) (655) (711c) (438), nor does he send a doctor **

481

(64; 415) (386)
Carol is deserted by Jack, her husband by a secret marriage * Carol is unable to prove she secretly married Jack ** (188b ch Jack to Eric) (738)

CONFLICT SITUATIONS

482

(528) (566a)
Jack's loving, supportive wife, Carol, is devastated when Jack suddenly blames her for his problems (539a) (542) * Innocent Carol's world disintegrates when she is wrongfully accused of adultery by her husband, Jack ** (546a) (581) (587) (588)

483

(a)   (410 ch Burt to Gary) (433b) (436)
Jack's wife, Carol, lands in trouble * Gary drunkenly attempts to rape Jack's wife, Carol ** (476b) (483b; 519a, b) (433a ch Carol to Irene)

(b)   (398b) (433b) (583b)
Jack's wife, Carol, is tricked by Gary, a rejected lover, into becoming a prisoner in his apartment (411b) (519b)

(22) Misguided By Mistaken Judgment
484

(a)   (429b) (436) (563c)
Jack and Carol, married, struggle to achieve a long-desired goal * Jack and Carol discover that their goal is empty (420) (457)

(b)   (375) (491b) (524a)
Jack, who adores his wife, Carol, finds himself drowning in debt because of her extravagant spending * Jack breaks the law in an effort to save himself from financial ruin ** (753) (754) (770b)

485

(395) (464)
Carol's husband, Jack, is rich, cultured and socially impeccable * Jack indulges a taste for low-life friends and questionable adventures ** (429a) (499a) (500a) (501)

486

(a)   (378) (382) (383)
Carol's husband, Jack, falls in love with Laura (386) (368e) (555b)

(b)   (395) (420) (464) (525)
Jack has two wives, Carol and Laura, two homes several miles apart, two identities in two separate communities, two circles of friends, and practices two professions (548b) (1148a) (1248)

487

(373) (412)
Jack splits up with his wife, Carol * Jack, separated from his wife, Carol, wants to reconcile, but they quarrel over who caused the breakup and the separation continues ** (391) (400) (429a)

488

(a)   (93a) (431)
Jack marries Carol because he thinks she is poor * After their marriage, Jack discovers Carol is wealthy ** (429b) (563c) (929)

(b)   (367a) (368b)
Jack marries Carol, a woman he doesn't love * Jack has committed a crime (1290a) (1301) (1304); Carol knows of Jack's wrongdoing, and Jack marries her to keep her quiet ** (528) (1291a)

489

(486a) (472)
Jack files for divorce from his wife, Carol * Jack decides to divorce Carol, hoping to find happiness in a new relationship ** (496a) (556) (886; 563a)

490

(a)   (484a-*) (966-*)
Jack and his wife, Carol, remain financially strapped because they place all their disposable income in their retirement plan * Jack and Carol remain financially strapped, investing for their retirement — but the "safe" investments they've made vanish in a stock swindle ** (484a *-**) (576a) (770a)

(b) (484b) (461)
Jack and Carol, married, are to inherit money from a rich relative, Pete, when they have a child * Jack and Carol, childless, notify a wealthy relative, Pete, that they have had a son, Lee ** Pete informs Jack and Carol that he's coming to see their child, Lee. Jack and Carol find it necessary to employ further deception *** (1057b) (1430b)

491

(a) (372) (461)
Jack's wife, Carol, loves him deeply * Carol dominates Jack in business matters ** (419) (420) (463)

(b) (510) (585b)
Jack's wife, Carol, insists on living above their means * Carol, through extravagant spending, almost ruins Jack ** (461) (505)

492

(a) (370) (372)
Jack loves his wife, Carol, deeply * Tightfisted Jack gives Carol very little money ** (492b) (593)

(b) (370) (372)
Carol's husband, Jack, is without funds * Carol loves fine clothes and jewelry that her husband, Jack, can't afford ** An old admirer, Gary, persuades Carol to accept a valuable piece of jewelry *** Carol tells her husband, Jack, that the valuable piece of jewelry given her by Gary is a fake she bought herself **** (476b) (483b)

493

(485) (486b)
Carol's husband, Jack, is affectionate and gentle in public but when he and Carol are alone, he is coarse, petty and abusive (477) (495)

494

(508) (547)
Jack's wife, Carol, is an unfaithful bimbo * Carol, married to Jack, comes on to unmarried Gary ** (503b) (568c)

495

(492a, b) (494)
Jack's wife, Carol, falls in love with youthful, reckless Gary (503b) (505-*) (507a, b)

(15) Finding the Power to Overcome Problems

496

(a) (489) (509) (539a) (553)
Jack falls ill * Jack's wife, Carol, whom he is divorcing, nurses him back to health ** (396) (379) (500a)

(b) (420) (478) (486a)
Jack's wife, Carol, leaves him and gets a divorce * Jack becomes ill. Laura, who was in love with Jack before he married Carol, nurses him back to health ** (22b; 22a ch Carol to Laura) (515 ch Carol to Laura)

(c) (473) (594b) (395) (435a)
Jack, hen-pecked husband of Carol, discovers that Carol is still married to Gary * Jack happily leaves Carol to Gary, her legal husband ** (548a ch Jack to Gary) (573b tr Jack & Gary)

497

(546a) (575)
Jack's wife, Carol, has recently died * Jack finds inspiration and the will to go on in memories of his dead wife, Carol ** (498) (1433b; 504a) (578a, b)

498

(576a) (567-*) (579a; 578a)
Jack tries to find his deceased wife, Carol * Jack believes that his dead wife, Carol, has returned to earth to comfort him ** (392) (474) (526) (560)

499

(a) (463) (460) (563a)
Jack and Carol, married, are alienated * Jack and Carol, separated, become changed through love for their child, Lee, and are reconciled ** (494; 505-*) (507b)

499

(b) (406) (510) (547)
Jack deeply loves his wife, Carol, but she doesn't love him * Jack wins his wife, Carol's love by patience, kindness and devotion ** (588) (591)

500

(a) (549) (553) (561)
Jack is divorcing Carol * Jack is reunited with Carol when she nurses him through a serious illness ** (396) (575) (956 ch Eric to Jack; 578a)

(b) (606) (656)
Jack's business is almost bankrupt. He marries Carol, a shrewd, thrifty woman * Carol reorganizes and manages Jack's affairs so that he becomes prosperous ** (419) (491a)

501

(369) (373) (457)
Jack and Carol are separated, their marriage in disarray * Jack receives a letter from Carol (1395) asking him to come home ** Jack learns that his child, Lee, has been born since he and his wife, Carol, separated; they reconcile *** (532a) (565)

502

(572; 402-*) (430)
Carol thinks that her husband, Jack, is dead * Carol, watching TV, learns that her husband, Jack, whom she thought was dead, is alive ** (548a) (550)

503

(a) (582) (590)
Carol's husband, Jack, is a tyrant * Carol, wife of tyrant, Jack, loves Gary and he loves her ** (503b) (544)

(b) (503a) (554)
Carol learns that her husband, Jack, wants to kill her lover, Gary * Carol desperately tries to save her lover, Gary, from her husband, Jack's vengeance ** (507b) (557a) (568c, d)

504

(a) (405) (485) (492a) (499b tr Jack & Carol) (579a; 565) (1133)
Carol tries to steer her husband, Jack, into a certain venture * Carol, with the help of a violent storm/flood/earthquake, etc., succeeds in guiding her husband, Jack, into a venture she has long advocated ** (534) (546a) (884b)

(b) (493 ch Carol to Laura) (528) (578b tr Carol & Laura)
Carol is Jack's second wife * Jack's grieving for his dead wife, Laura, causes his second wife, Carol, great unhappiness ** Jack's second wife, Carol, discovers that his first wife, Laura, was unfaithful *** (389) (391 ch Laura to Irene)

505

(544) (563b) (585b) (580) (484b) (908)
Jack's wife, Carol, almost dies during childbirth and undergoes a complete personality change * Carol devotes herself to her children, Lee and Kenny, and emerges from her depression ** Carol loyally helps her husband, Jack, recover his financial losses *** (474) (455b)

506

(a) (540 (541) (571) (582) (561 tr Jack & Carol, ch Gary to Laura)
Carol thinks her husband, Jack, has been unfaithful (563a) * Carol discovers through a friend, Annie, that the infidelity she accused her husband, Jack, of committing, never occurred ** (496a, b) (506b) (536) (546a)

(b) (485) (506a) (770a)
Carol, through unjust suspicion, breaks up with her husband, Jack * Carol is reconciled with her husband, Jack, when her suspicion is proved unjust ** (1451a ch Jack to Carol) (1462)

507

(a) (398a, b) (411b) (433b) (444)
Carol runs off with Gary, a man who destroyed her faith in her husband, Jack * Gary, running off with Jack's wife, Carol, encounters Jack's friend, Pete, who saves Carol from a foolish act ** (536) (568d)
(b) (466a) (543)
Jack's wife, Carol, runs off with Gary * Carol deserted her child, Lee, and her husband, Jack, but her love for the child causes her to return ** (568c, d)

(39) Giving Up Deeply Held Ambitions to Fulfill an Obligation

508

(512) (513) (521) (528) (539a) (579b)
Jack's marriage to Carol stands in the way of his happiness (510) (529b)

509

(382) (420) (500b)
Jack's marriage to Carol hinders his romance with Laura (377a) (385a) (386) (393) (426) (556)

510

(372) (375) (378)
Jack is unhappily married to Carol * Jack, despite an unhappy marriage to Carol, and having to sacrifice his goals, continues to be a good father ** (385a) (393) (435a) (511)

511

(513) (484b-*)
Jack, married to Carol, finds that supporting his wife and family prevents him from pursuing his ambitions (484b *-**) (991)

512

(513) (991) (1073)
Jack is prevented by family and business obligations from starting a new venture (900) (917) (952)

513

(511) (768)
Jack, married to dull Carol, is forced to lead a drab, monotonous, middle-class life * Jack, married to dull Carol, leads a "Walter Mitty" existence, fantasizing himself the star of daring exploits ** (771a) (773 ch Carol to Irene) (774) (1077) (1330) (1335)

514

(581) (565)
Carol's marriage to Jack, her second husband, is jeopardized by the presence of Lee, a child by her first husband (516) (503b ch "lover, Gary" to "child, Lee") (507b) (594b)

515

(585b) (1106) (1119)
Jack's wife, Carol, sacrifices her goals in order to give Jack the son, Lee, he wants * Carol dies in childbirth ** (425) (576a) (578b)

516

(514) (521) (1341; 467 ch Eric to Lee) (896 ch Doug to Lee)
Jack tries to kill his son, Lee, whom he's framed for an offense that Jack, himself, has committed. Jack's wife, Carol, allows her husband to cause her death, sacrificing her life to save their son, Lee.

(40) Starting a Venture in Which One Obligation Conflicts With Another

517

(525) (925-*) (957a)
Honest, idealistic Carol discovers that her corrupt husband, Jack, is planning a project that will severely harm the environment * Jack, rich and powerful, is determined to use his wealth and influence to carry out a corrupt project. His wife, Carol, tries in vain to dissuade him ** (403) (553) (557a-*)

CONFLICT SITUATIONS

518

(384) (543) (574b)
Jack's mother, Linda, lives with Jack and his wife, Carol * Jack and Carol quarrel over Linda, and Jack is forced to choose between Linda and Carol ** (554) (568c) (578b)

519

(a) (483a, b) (519b-*)
Jack learns that his wife, Carol, is in grave danger * If Jack leaves his post to save his wife, Carol, who is in mortal danger, he will sacrifice lives and property he is duty-bound to protect ** (519b *-**) (576b)

(b) (519a) (591)
Jack receives a desperate phone call from his wife, begging for help. Carol is in terrible danger * Jack rescues Carol **

520

(371) (449 tr Jack & Gary) (537)
Innocent Jack is arrested for murder * Jack has an alibi that can prove his innocence of a murder charge, but only by involving Laura, another man's wife ** Jack's obligation to save himself is opposed by a need to protect Laura, another man's wife *** (535-* ch Carol to Laura, Jack to Eric & Gary to Jack) (1204 ch Carol to Laura) (1151 ch Carol to Laura)

(41) Finding an Obligation at Odds With Ambition, Inclination or Necessity

521

(382) (441 tr Jack & Carol) (464) (467)
Carol's husband, Jack, pretends to be innocent of a crime (or indiscretion) but she knows he's guilty (454) (594c)

522

(574a) (601) (620) (631)
Jack and his wife, Carol, are unemployed * Jack and his wife, Carol, are faced with starvation ** (523) (532a) (532b) (579a) (583b) (628)

523

(585b) (680a) (681a)
Because of extreme poverty, Jack can't buy his wife a Christmas gift (or birthday or anniversary) (398a) (400) (411b) (455a) (628)

524

(a) (500b) (1079) (1132)
Carol's husband, Jack, gambles recklessly in the stock market * Jack, Carol's husband, is an attorney administering trust funds, and Carol is afraid he'll be tempted to gamble with them ** (380) (443) (474) (566b)

(b) (408) (466b)
Jack, elderly husband of youthful Carol, will die unless he undergoes major surgery * Jack refuses to undergo major surgery. His wife, Carol, supports his wishes ** (403) (474 tr Jack & Carol)

525

(420) (421) (461) (509)
Carol's husband, Jack, tries to carry out a shady venture despite family obligations (426) (438) (465) (486b) (548b) (556)

526

(474-*) (497)
Jack struggles to fulfill an obligation to his deceased wife, Carol (474 *-**) (498) (578b) (588)

527

(347a) (579b)
Jack tries to be loyal to his wife, Carol * Jack's wife, Carol, is an alien (ethnic or planetary) ** (585a) (588) (593)

528

(365a) (382)
Jack doesn't love his wife, Carol * Jack, married to Carol, whom he doesn't love, is haunted by memories of a former girlfriend, Laura, whom he still loves (393) (420) (555b) (246b) (368e)

529

(a) (530) (531) (540) (541)
Jack is deeply in love with his wife, Carol, who is suing him for divorce (568a) (573a) (594c) (496b)

(b) (378) (395) (408)
To overcome his wife, Carol's constant nagging, Jack assumes the unnatural role of minor tyrant * Carol is subdued by Jack's pretense of power and she becomes docile and loving ** Jack, by seeming to be cruel, secures happiness for himself and Carol *** (545) (546a)

530

(1132 ch Jack to Carol) (1334a ch Jack to Carol)
Jack's wife, Carol, is reluctant to live in a house which has a mysterious past (918b ch Jack to Carol) (1358 ch Jack to Carol) (1366 ch Jack to Carol) (1375 ch Jack to Carol) (529a)

531

(574b) (1009b ch Carol to Linda & Doug to Jack)
Jack and his wife, Carol, are forced to live with Jack's mother, Linda * Carol finds the arrangement unbearable ** (529a) (543) (557b)

532

(a) (469) (583a)
Carol needs money in order to save her husband, Jack * Carol's husband, Jack, is desperately ill and will die unless he can move to a healthier climate ** (410) (583b) (1293a, b, c)

(b) (469) (522) Carol owns a family heirloom greatly admired by her husband, Jack * To finance a certain venture involving her husband, Jack, Carol sells an heirloom which he greatly admires ** (455a) (739)

533

(378) (395)
Wimpy Jack's overbearing wife, Carol, goes out for the evening, ordering Jack to remain at home (420) (426) (435a) (471) (473)

534

(376) (378 tr Carol & Jack) (413)
Jack forbids his wife, Carol, to participate in a certain activity * Carol engages in a venture forbidden by her husband, Jack (442) (449*-**) (452) ** Carol, involved in an activity forbidden by her husband, Jack, learns that he is also involved in the activity (599). Carol uses this knowledge to forge an understanding with Jack which respects the rights and privileges of each ***

535

(667) (449; 537 ch Jack to Gary, Carol to Laura & Laura to Carol; 1070 ch Jack to Gary)
Jack's wife, Carol, saves Gary, a suspected criminal, from the law by confessing her infidelity * Jack, admiring his wife, Carol's courage in confessing her infidelity, tries to forgive her ** (695a ch Jack to Gary) (557b ch Pete to Gary)

536

(370) (372) (398a, b) (433b)
Jack's wife, Carol, is about to run off with Gary * Jack's wife, Carol, is running off with large, physically menacing Gary when they're surreptitiously spotted in an airport terminal by slightly built Pete. While Carol is in the ladies room, Pete approaches Gary and points out a large traveler, Walt, (actually a total stranger) as his hit-man buddy; unless Gary walks out of Carol's life immediately, Pete will turn Walt loose on him. It works, though Carol remains unaware of Pete's role ** (391 tr Jack & Carol & ch Laura to Gary) (396)

(29) Helping Another to Keep a Deadly Secret

537

(378) (385a) (395)
Jack's wife, Carol, is murdered at a certain time of night * Jack is suspected of murdering his wife, Carol; but, at the moment the murder was committed, Jack was with Laura (411a ch Carol to Laura) (411b-* ch Carol to Laura, Jack to Eric & Gary to Jack), a married woman with an unblemished reputation ** (520) (667 ch Carol to Laura) (535 ch Carol to Laura, Jack to Eric & Gary to Jack) (1070 ch Carol to Laura)

(23) Becoming Enmeshed in Mistaken Judgment and/or Suspicion

538

(438) (561)
Carol's husband, Jack, returning to his country home, is caught in a storm that keeps him out all night * Jack, absent from his home all night, finds on arriving home in the morning that his wife, Carol, is missing ** Jack mistakenly assumes that his wife, Carol, has run off with Gary *** (401) (545) (546a)

539

(a) (399) (954) (966-*)
Carol's husband, Jack, has delusions of grandeur and thinks he is a great man * Jack believes that the jealousy of his wife, Carol, prevents him from becoming famous ** (386) (391)

(b) (429a) (430) (460) (540)
Jack learns from a newspaper story that his wife, Carol, has divorced him * Carol divorces Jack on the grounds of desertion ** (388-* tr Jack & Carol) (496b)

540

(719a, b) (770a) (743b ch Carol to Jack)
Carol's husband, Jack, mysteriously vanishes * Carol's husband, Jack, and Laura, both vanish mysteriously at the same time ** Gossip says that Carol's husband, Jack, has run off with Laura *** (506a, b) (571) (573b)

541

(1383) (1389b) (1397) (1400) (1401)
Whenever Jack shows X, a certain mysterious object, to anyone, he gets into trouble * Jack shows X, a mysterious object, to his wife, Carol, and is astounded when she abruptly leaves him (1357) (1425)

542

(405) (420)
Jack mistakenly believes that the generosity his wife, Carol, lavishes on others is motivated by selfishness (377a) (386) (391) (555a, b)

543

(531) (574b) (994 ch Carol to Linda & Doug to Jack)
Jack's wife, Carol, is jealous of the attention Jack gives his mother, Linda * Carol mistakenly believes that her mother-in-law, Linda, is trying to come between her and Jack (507a ch "friend, Pete" to "mother, Linda") (518)

544

(462) (547)
Carol believes that her husband, Jack, takes too much credit for her accomplishments (457) (646; 594d) (644; 594d) (572; 573b) (540; 506a, b)

(11) Facing a Situation in Which Only Courage and Devotion Can Save a Loved One

545

(528) (539a; 553)
Carol's husband, Jack, doesn't return home. A blizzard rages. Carol is afraid Jack has run into trouble in the storm * Carol dies in a storm while searching for her husband, Jack ** (576a) (577) (578a)

546

(a) (706a, b, c)
Jack's wife, Carol, during his absence, sees Jack's life work threatened with destruction * Carol is killed while heroically saving the life work of her husband, Jack, from destruction ** (497) (576a)

(b) (828) (885a)
Unattractive Carol marries a blind man, Jack, who thinks she's incredibly beautiful * Carol locates a noted eye-surgeon who succeeds in restoring the sight of her blind husband, Jack ** (489) (581) (933)

(12) Suffering Problems Because of Disloyalty in Love

547

(369) (406) (529a)
Jack dearly loves his wife, Carol, but the fact that she doesn't love him causes Jack great unhappiness (499b) (563a) (573b)

548

(a) (681b) (734; 402-*)
Carol's husband, Jack, loses his memory and marries Laura * Carol's husband, Jack, recovers his memory, forgets Laura and returns to Carol ** (548b) (550)

(b) (548a) (486b)
Bigamist Jack's two wives, Carol and Laura, meet accidently and compare notes (472) (705)

549

(492a) (494 ch Gary to Pete)
Jack, married to Carol, believes in marital fidelity * Jack's wife, Carol, has an affair with his friend, Pete, who is more successful in business than Jack ** (496a, b) (507b ch Gary to Pete)

550

(540) (548a) (681b) (770a)
Carol's husband, Jack, returns after a long mysterious absence to find that Carol has married Gary (568b, c, d) (571) (573b)

551

(515) (397 ch Gary to Pete) (549) (588) (764) (79 ch Jack to Pete & Gary to Jack)
Jack learns that his wife, Carol, has borne Pete's son, Lee (585a) (392) (474)

552

(a) (510) (547) (561)
Jack learns that his wife, Carol, is unfaithful (551) (568a,b,c,d)

(b) (510) (554)
Jack finds a bundle of love letters locked in wife, Carol's, desk — letters written after Jack married Carol, but not by him * Jack, finding that his wife, Carol, is unfaithful, murders her ** (385b) (568a)

553

(410) (411a) (547)
Jack believes that his wife, Carol, loves Gary (396) (418) (496a)

554

(405) (412)
Jack discovers that his wife, Carol, is having an affair with Gary (380) (400) (434b) (438) (503b)

555

(a) (464) (481) (486a)
Jack deserts his devoted wife, Carol, to run off with younger, prettier Laura * Leaving his wife, Carol, to run away with Laura, Jack becomes remorseful and unhappy ** (377b; 408 ch Carol to Laura) (556) (552a ch Carol to Laura)

(b) (486a) (1073)
Jack, unhappily married to Carol, falls for Laura, a girl much younger than himself * Jack, married to Carol but in love with Laura, takes a long journey to try and forget Laura ** (528) (1379)

556

(485) (486a) (494 ch Carol to Laura, Jack to Eric & Gary to Jack)
Carol's husband, Jack, pretends to be single while romancing Laura * Carol's husband, Jack, is killed in an accident while enroute to an assignation with Laura **

557

(a) (398a) (413) (433b)
Carol's husband, Jack, has a weak heart. Carol allows him to be lured into over-exertion by Gary * Jack dies because of a conspiracy between Carol and Gary, and Carol is remorseful ** (665) (669) (738) (743b) (946) (956)

(b) (470; 477) (441; 477) (503a ch Gary to Pete)
Jack's wife, Carol, runs off with Jack's friend, Pete * Jack's wife, Carol, and Pete, with whom she is running off, are killed in a car accident **

(26) Secretly Trying to Save Another from Danger

558

(368b; 403-*) (376)
Carol, wife of brutal, bullying Jack, has a loyal friend, Gary, who wants to help Carol escape from Jack * Carol's husband, Jack, is a huge, powerful, belligerent man — and Gary, though he wants to help Carol, is a coward ** (1061 ch Jack to Gary; 1075a, b, ch Jack to Gary) (857 ch Jack to Gary; 557a) (568d) (403*-**)

559

(376) (403-*)
Carol's husband, Jack, is a bully who enjoys persecuting his attractive wife * Carol, wife of brutal Jack, is loved by Gary. Although she loves Gary, Carol is too principled to run off with him ** (403*-**) (438) (568d)

(57) Trying to Solve a Puzzling Problem

560

(371) (474) (498) (576a) (577) (578a)
Jack finds that his apparent sighting of the ghost of his dead wife, Carol, contains a modicum of reality * Jack hears the voice of his dead wife, Carol, and has no doubt that it's her voice ** (392) (587)

561

(428) (433b) (562)
Carol's husband, Jack, receives anonymous calls and letters concerning Carol and Gary (434a) (445a) (538) (553)

562

(381) (434a-*) (445a-*)
Each day, Carol's husband, Jack, receives a mysterious letter or phone call regarding Carol (1383) (1397) * Jack finds an anonymous message about Carol, his wife, on his computer screen (1381) (1389a) ** Jack receives poison pen letters (564b-*) about his wife, Carol *** (377a) (396) (397) (398b)

(37) Fighting to Achieve a Cherished Ideal

563

(a) (460) (547)
Jack, separated from Carol, the wife he dearly loves, works toward a reconciliation (487) (499a, b) (500a) (501)

(b) (378) (395)
Jack marries Carol, a beauty notorious for her vicious temper and scathing sarcasm * Jack deeply loves his wife, Carol, but not her bitchiness; he plans to change her personality ** (443; 394) (529b)

(c) (423b) (429b) (954 add Carol) (974 add Jack)
Jack and Carol, married, despise the superficial, money-grabbing spirit of contemporary city life * Jack and Carol, married, leave the city and explore rural areas for the ideal life ** Jack and Carol discover they're pursuing an impossible dream *** (900 add Carol) (963 add Carol)

564

(a) (557a) (569-*) (572)
Young, attractive Carol has just lost her husband, Jack * Young, attractive widow, Carol, resolves to remain single ** (14b ch Jack to Eric; 405 ch Jack to Eric) (564a tr Jack & Carol; 14c) (20a ch Jack to Eric) (31 ch Jack to Eric)

(b) (373) (376) (450) (452)
Desperate Carol, refused a divorce by her husband, Jack, writes anonymous poison pen letters about herself, and sends them to Jack * Carol, wishing to divorce her husband and make him the heavy, writes anonymous poison pen letters about her husband, Jack, and sends them to herself ** (385a) (418)

565

(975) (957a) (976) (1133; 1120)
Carol devoutly wishes for her husband, Jack, to become religious (504a) (1427b) (1445 ch Carol to Jack)

566

(a) (472-*) (473)
Carol attempts to help her husband, Jack, overcome his depression and/or discontent (410) (445a) (469) (481) (482)

(b) (524a) (579a)
Carol, afraid that her husband, Jack, will do something dishonest, attempts to discourage him from doing so * Carol pretends to be a thief, but has purchased the items that her husband, Jack, is horrified to find in her possession ** (504a) (1050)

(46) Attempting to Retaliate for a Serious Wrong, Either Real or Imagined

567

(483a, b) (492b) (583b)
Jack's wife, Carol, is raped and/or murdered by Gary * Jack's wife, Carol, is raped and/or slain during a war (or in a foreign country — or while on holiday) by Gary ** Jack tries to find Gary and avenge his wife, Carol *** (1318) (1319a, b) (1322) (1323a)

568

(a) (397) (398a) (444) (451) (494) (551) (554)
Jack discovers that his wife, Carol, has been unfaithful * Jack, realizing that his wife, Carol, is unfaithful, kills her and himself **

(b) (466a) (503a; 554)
Jack attempts to get even with his wife, Carol, for falling in love with Gary (438; 550) (503b)

(c) (446b ch Pete to Gary) (476a) (483b) (495)
Jack discovers that his wife, Carol, has been unfaithful * Jack murders Gary, his wife, Carol's lover ** (594e ch Burt to Jack & Jack to Gary) (610)

(d) (503a, b) (550) (554) (558)
Carol's husband, Jack, tries to kill Carol's lover, Gary * Attacked by Carol's husband, Jack, Gary kills Jack in self-defense ** (705 ch Jack to Gary) (712 ch Jack to Gary) (738) (895 ch Jack to Gary)

569

(730 ch Gary to Burt) (483a, b ch Gary to Burt)
Carol's husband, Jack, dies at the hands of Burt * Carol's husband, Jack, is killed by Burt but due to legal delays and technicalities, Burt gets off with a light sentence ** Carol, wanting an eye for an eye, seeks revenge on Burt for murdering her husband, Jack *** (594e) (1244b ch Jack to Burt) (1325 ch Jack to Burt)

570

(992; 641 ch Frank to Jack; 378 ch Carol to Betty) (948 ch Frank to Jack & Rita to Betty)
Carol is Jack's daughter and the step-daughter of Jack's wife, Betty * Carol plans to get even with her step-mother, Betty, because she believes Betty stole her father, Jack's, affections ** (909 ch Tony to Betty) (933)

(20) Getting Into a Situation From Which Difficult Problems are Likely to Result

571

(548a) (660a) (719a) (750) (770a)
Jack, mysteriously absent, returns home to his wife, Carol, dazed and unable to offer an explanation (540) (550) (572; 402)

572

(664) (681b) (1389a)
Carol's husband, Jack, vanishes mysteriously * Carol's husband, Jack, mysteriously disappears and is assumed dead; Carol mourns ** (402) (502)

573

(a) (70) (290)
Jack and Carol, for certain reasons, keep their marriage a secret * Carol's father, Frank, unaware that Jack and Carol are secretly married, insists Carol marry Jack's rival, Gary ** (445b) (477) (481) (483b)

(b) (572) (734; 1368; 548a)
Missing and assumed dead, Jack returns secretly and finds his wife, Carol, has married Gary * Jack, learning that his wife, Carol, deeply loves Gary, whom she married because she thought Jack was dead, quietly goes away and stays out of Carol's life ** (913) (918b)

574

(a) (601) (606)
Workman Jack tries to support his wife, Carol, and family by honest hard work; but he can't find a job, his wife is ill and his family in need (549) (579a)

(b) (522) (574a)
Carol's husband, Jack, is flat broke * Jack and his wife, Carol, are forced to live with Jack's mother, Linda, on her small income ** (518) (531) (543)

575

(421) (429b) (464)
Jack becomes aware that his wife, Carol, is dying (576a, b) (578a, b)

576

(a) (567) (591)
Jack is shattered by the death of his wife, Carol * Jack's sorrow over the death of his wife, Carol, climaxes in hallucination ** (53) (498) (1334a) (1345)

(b) (49) (445b) (460)
Jack, mistakenly thinking his beloved wife, Carol, is dead, kills himself * Carol, finding her husband dead, commits suicide **

577

(55) (376) (377a) (386) (492a)
Jack suffers deep sorrow and remorse — sorrow over the death of his beloved wife, Carol, and remorse for his infidelities * Mourning the death of his wife, Carol, Jack goes into seclusion ** (474) (497) (971)

578

(a) (420) (464) (485)
Jack is so saddened by the death of his wife, Carol, that his personality changes (918a) (922a) (923)

(b) (382) (421) (486a)
On her deathbed Jack's wife, Carol, makes Jack promise that he will marry Laura, her best friend * Laura was in love with Jack before he married Carol ** (526) (378 ch Carol to Laura) (405 tr Carol & Laura)

579

(a) (574a) (566a)
Carol, married to Jack, is convinced that their troubles stem from her husband's lack of religion (504a) (565) (884b) (1353)

(b) (347a) (508) (527)
Jack's wife, Carol, is of another culture, and is mentally Jack's inferior * Jack's wife, Carol, hinders him socially and in business ** (371) (386) (398b) (407) (491b)

580

(421) (462)
Carol is married to Jack, a friend of Pete's * Jack's friend, Pete, learns that Jack's wife, Carol, is promiscuous ** (505) (508) (443) (457)

501

(370) (482) (514)
Carol feels she has lost her husband, Jack's love and consideration (410) (445a) (515)

582

(427) (461) (464)
Carol opens a letter addressed to her husband, Jack, and discovers that he has lied to her (394) (443) (499a)

583

(a) (376) (413)
If Carol is discovered doing something she has planned, she will be at odds with her husband, Jack (442) (534)

(b) (532a) (561) (585b)
Jack's wife, Carol, desperately needs money for a certain purpose * Gary, Carol's rejected lover, promises to help Carol, wife of Jack, if she'll come to his home ** (476b) (483a, b)

(c) (458a) (470)
Jack's wife, Carol, desperately needs money for a certain purpose * Carol, wife of Jack, runs into an old lover, Gary, and has no choice but to borrow money from him ** (418) (476a, b)

584

(a) (395) (403-*)
Carol, just married to Jack, finds in a hidden place her obituary notice (written by Jack?), with only the date of her death omitted (403 *-***) (590) (1346; 1462)

(b) (421) (436) (1061)
Carol stops loving her husband, Jack, when she realizes he's a coward (409) (1082a) (1104)

585

(a) (553) (561)
Jack's wife, Carol, suddenly leaves on important business while Jack is away * Carol, leaving suddenly while Jack is away, writes a note to Jack explaining her departure. The maid inadvertently throws the note away. Carol's disappearance is considered a mystery ** (396) (538) (572 tr Jack & Carol) (755)

(b) (488b) (522) (523)
Jack's wife, Carol, is a clotheshorse * Jack's wife, Carol's happiness depends upon expensive clothes and luxurious surroundings ** (484b) (492b)

586

(1377b ch Carol to Laura) (1383) (1384 ch Carol to Jack) (1389b) (1440 ch Jack to Eric)
Carol thinks that her husband, Jack, cares less about her than a certain small statue, X, to which he attributes special powers (1352) (1408) (1425) (1444)

587

(537) (539a) (577)
An apparition of Jack's dead wife, Carol, appears to a relative of Jack's and confides secrets of her relationship with Jack (422b) (984)

588

(376) (420) (515)
Carol, dying, tells her husband, Jack, a closely guarded secret that deeply disturbs him (441) (451) (467) (492b) (503a ch Gary to Pete) (551)

589

(540) (555b)
Carol is certain that her husband, Jack, has run off with Laura (496b) (506a) (539b)

590

(426-*) (584a)
Jack's fourth wife, Carol, learns soon after their marriage that Jack's previous wives died suddenly and mysteriously (387) (403) (422b) (552b)

591

(483a, b) (1137a; 179a)
Carol, alone, helpless and in terrible danger, communicates with her husband, Jack, begging for help (519a, b) (851)

592

(398a-*) (405) (486a) (485)
Carol rebels against certain unpleasant conditions involving her husband, Jack (398a*-**) (398b*-**) (403)

593

(441) (454) (492a) (503a)
Carol steals money from her husband, Jack, for her own use (450) (484b) (491b)

594

(a) (542) (566a) (581)
Normally undemonstrative Carol arouses the suspicions of her husband, Jack, by her sudden display of affection and attention (403) (582) (593)

(b) (378) (471) (473) (550 tr Jack & Gary) (533)
Bitchy Carol, believing she's a widow, marries Jack * Gary, to whom Carol is still married, approaches her new husband, Jack, and tries to extort money from him for keeping quiet ** (417) (496c)

(c) (485) (493) (555a, b)
Carol divorces her husband, Jack, and wins custody of their child, Lee * Jack steals their child, Lee, from his ex-wife, Carol ** (499a) (500a)

(d) (410) (532a; 1293a) (1293b)
Jack's wife, Carol, innocently commits a crime * Jack, in order to save his wife, Carol, insists he's guilty of the crime she committed ** (499a,b) (500a) (695a,b)

(e) (568d ch Gary to Burt) (569)
Jack's widow, Carol, takes the law into her own hands and shoots her husband's murderer, Burt (738) (743b) (801 ch Jack to Eric)

(f) (528) (486a)
Jack's wife, Carol, wears the mask and costume of Laura, Jack's lover, and meets him as Laura at a masquerade ball (534) (1309b ch Gary to Laura)

(g) (475 ch Jack to Pete & Carol to Annie) (510 ch Jack to Pete & Carol to Annie)
Carol uses her telepathic powers to reshape the future of an unhappily married couple, Pete and Annie * Carol reconciles Pete and his alienated wife, Annie, only to realize she's in love with Pete ** (57) (279)

(21) Landing in Trouble Through Mistaken Judgment

595

(935) (1065-*)
Jack exercises poor judgment in advancing a certain undertaking * Jack loses his initiative and his business and becomes a salaried worker ** (85a) (114) (235) (1065*-**) (1088) (1243)

596

(612) (646 ch Carol to Jack & Walt to Burt) (1114)
Jack learns a closely guarded secret * Jack, learning a closely guarded secret, is hounded by a persecutor, Burt, who makes Jack's life miserable ** (705) (854 ch Carl to Burt) (884a)

597

(898) (925-*) (1159 ch Carol to Eric & Dave to Jack)
Jack's chauffeur, Matt, is ordered by Jack to drive very fast. He apparently injures a pedestrian, Eric * Jack, when his car apparently injures a pedestrian, tries to avoid consequences by telling his chauffeur, Matt, to drive on ** (669 ch Carol to Jack & Burt to Matt) (750) (775) (783) (1064)

598

(1074) (1090) (1092)
Author Jack pretends he's the criminal hero of a story he's writing so he can experience situations and "color" * Novelist Jack impersonates the criminal hero of a story he is writing and gets himself in trouble ** (2b) (786) (803a) (815a) (817) (822)

599

(442; 534-**) (793a) (838) (1168)
Jack, to help his friend, Pete, violates his own principles and suffers unpleasant results * Jack and Pete are at a costume party. Pete, suddenly called away on urgent business, promises to return shortly; Jack agrees to wear Pete's mask and costume and take Pete's place. Pete fails to return, leaving Jack in a dilemma ** (534**-***) (365b) (603a) (594f)

600

(647) (1198)
Jack, in a foreign seaport, tries to return at night to his ship. He loses his way and ends up in a tough, sleazy neighborhood (848a; 664) (12a) (31) (1218) (1226) (1230 ch Jack to Eric)

601

(111) (704) (981)
Jack, trying to help his friend, Pete, lends him all his money * Jack's friend, Pete, fails to repay money loaned him by Jack, leaving Jack broke ** (257b ch Gary to Pete) (574b) (621 ch Burt to Pete) (656) (1337)

602

(176c) (225) (1338)
Boxer Jack loses a fight and the money he bet on himself (361a) (500a) (850b) (874) (918a)

603

(a) (1273; 174 ch Gary to Pete) (426) (446b) (601) (607)
Jack loses out because his friend, Pete, fails to effectively carry out his part in a certain venture (568c, d ch Gary to Pete) (280b ch Gary to Pete) (601)

(b) (169) (779)
Jack and his friend, Pete, are attacked by thieves in a lonely place * Jack's friend, Pete, is wounded and dies ** (168) (701) (754)

(c) (770b) (793a, b)
Jack and his friend, Pete, on horseback, try to cross a flooded river. Pete is hit by floating driftwood. Jack rescues him and gets him to the river bank * Pete is so badly injured, he dies ** (794) (868)

(d) (906) (913) (1174) (1013 ch Sam to Pete)
Jack and his friend, Pete, wander around in a desert. Pete is injured and they run out of water * Jack's friend, Pete, dies ** (997a; 1007) (1160) (1168)

CONFLICT SITUATIONS

604

(299 ch Frank to Eric) (409 ch Gary to Eric)
Jack is employed by Eric, a man Jack admires * Jack, employed by Eric, arrives at work one morning and finds the office occupied by Federal Agents, Sam and Faye ** Jack's employer, Eric, is accused of a criminal act *** (750) (1279b ch Jack to Eric)

605

(652a) (1248)
Jack, stricken with fever in the wilds, is looked after by an old woman, Carol * Jack, falling ill in the wilds, is looked after by an old woman, Carol, who, just Jack's luck, Jack had once taught a fake healing technique ** (1220a) (1228-*) (1325)

606

(114) (461) (574a) (602) (958)
Jack invests all his money in a certain venture * Jack, investing all his money in a certain venture, sees the venture fail and finds himself heavily in debt ** (500b) (574b) (700)

607

(937) (1115)
Jack and his friend, Pete, are alone exploring a jungle * Jack's friend, Pete, berserk from eating the fruit of a strange plant, attacks Jack and tries to kill him ** (972) (1007)

608

Jack, in an airport in a strange city, is arrested as a criminal suspect * Jack, arrested at an airport, has innocently claimed a piece of luggage, X, staked out by the police (804) (1044a, b) (1046). The bag, X, contains contraband ** (91) (109) (163) (635) (695a)

609

(196) (201) (982b)
Jack is temporarily in charge of two unruly children, Lee and Kenny, and is faced with more problems than he can handle (193) (728-**)

610

(654) (750 (754)
Fugitive Jack is hunted by Sam, a law officer * Jack is trapped in town X. He can escape only by passing through towns Y or Z, and detectives Sam and Faye are watching for him in both places ** (651) (707) (717) (1176)

611

(a) (249) (623) (695a)
Jack's youthful escapades, thoughtless and without malice, have given him a bad reputation in his home town (864) (1275)

(b) (949a) (954)
Jack persuades his father, Andy, to advance him his inheritance * Jack leaves home, squanders his money and, dead broke, he regrets his mistake ** (815b) (818b)

612

(658) (704)
Jack accepts Burt on a forged letter of introduction from a friend, Pete, and introduces Burt into his own social circle * Jack, as Burt's sponsor, discovers that Burt is a con artist who uses Jack's sponsorship so he can cheat Jack's friends ** (635) (725) (859)

613

(926) (927) (928a)
Jack, who enjoys helping the needy, befriends a drifter, Burt * Jack befriends a drifter, Burt; and Burt, taking advantage of Jack, robs him ** (894) (998 ch Dave to Burt)

614

(709) (763) (778) (1166a)
Jack loses a priceless diamond, X * Inept Jack loses a priceless diamond, X, while at the zoo and employs desperate measures to recover it ** Jack loses a priceless diamond, X, thinks he knows where it is, but he is wrong *** (771a) (1200) (1222b)

615

(1g) (78) (857) (1061) (1150) (1219 ch Jack to Eric)
Jack is a cowardly braggart. He is manipulated into a dangerous test and must either eat his words or prove himself * Jack, a coward who has been manipulated into a dangerous test of courage, is terrified as he confronts the test ** (1104) (1227b, c)

616

(679) (743b) (946) (1244b)
Jack gives Carol the combination of his safe, X * Jack, by giving Carol the combination to his safe, X, endangers her ** (144) (666) (801)

617

(2a) (59) (412) (768) (1187)
Jack, out of ignorance of social graces, commits a gaffe before a servant, Matt, while a weekend guest at a country estate * Jack, embarrassed by his mistake, tries to save face but only makes matters worse ** (709; 786) (814)

618

(1063) (1071) (1094) (1126)
Jack is bored by certain duties he must perform * Jack, bored by certain duties he must perform, finds a way out — with disastrous results ** (1163a, b) (1184) (1164 ch Jack to Pete)

619

(601) (602) (606) (212a) (461) (1343)
Jack loses his life savings * Jack contemplates suicide, but fate intervenes ** (621) (865) (879) (1373) (1388)

620

(113) (131) (726a)
Jack loses his job * Jack lands in trouble because he deviates from a strict set of rules to pursue his own interests ** (628 ch Carol to Carl) (753) (779) (836) (832) (902) (903)

621

(127a) (522) (619) (246b ch Jack to Walt)
Jack is cheated out of a large sum by Burt * Jack, cheated out of a large sum by Burt, is on the verge of suicide when mysterious Walt returns his money ** Mysterious Walt forces Burt to hand over the money he swindled from Jack; Walt returns the money to Jack *** (1455b) (1424a)

622

(611a, b ch Jack to Greg) (928b)
Jack mistakenly thinks his son, Greg, died in a plane crash (698) (628 ch Jack to Greg & Carol to Jack) (297 ch Carol to Greg) (674) (734 ch Jack to Greg) (1053) (1056)

623

(109) (163) (513) (611a) (798) (815a)
Innocent Jack is thought to be a smuggler * Jack is thought to be a smuggler because he is caught holding contraband goods ** (859) (1168) (1228) (1264 tr Jack & Pete) (1265b tr Jack & Gary)

624

(597) (699a) (712) (750) (777) (787) (857) (1149)
Jack thinks he is a criminal until he discovers that his alleged criminal act was never committed (635) (1448) (1451a) (1456)

625

(1202a) (1220a) (1227b, c)
Jack inadvertently arouses a consuming desire in Carol to leave town, which is the opposite of what Jack wants; his impending business deal, which is of vital importance to Jack, requires Carol's presence (641) (1155)

626

(950; 966) (925-*)
While performing an experiment, scientist Jack inadvertently causes serious injury to his daughter, Nina (627 ch Carol to Nina) (227 ch Carol to Nina, Jack to Eric & Frank to Jack)

627

(416) (626 ch Nina to Carol)
Jack unintentionally causes Carol's death *
Jack, attempting to save Carol with an antidote for a poison, accidentally kills her **
(578a, b) (633; 634)

628

(111) (522) (523) (615) (838) (1086) (1101)
Jack hijacks a passenger jet * Jack, hijacking
a plane, is recognized by Carol, one of the
passengers ** (651) (699a, b)

629

(711a) (726a) (1162 ch Burt to Jack) (1163a ch
Dave to Pete)
Jack has his double, Pete, replace him in an
important venture * Jack finds himself and
his reputation ruined when his double, Pete,
fouls up an important enterprise while posing as Jack ** (635 ch Burt to Pete) (1337)

630

(1226) (1214; 1227a-**)
Jack tries to beat a conman, Burt, at his own
game * Jack, trying to beat the scam of a con
man, Burt, is betrayed by an accomplice, Pete,
whom Jack asks to help him ** Due to Pete,
Jack's accomplice in a venture, Jack sustains
a loss *** (1268) (1269 tr Jack & Pete)

631

(461) (602)
Jack is ruined when he asks his supposed
friend, Pete, for money and is turned down
(505) (619)

632

(687) (692)
In desperate danger, Jack asks a stranger,
Dave for help * Jack appeals for help to selfish, powerful Dave, who refuses to endanger a major project in order to save Jack's
life ** Dave leaves Jack to die *** (898 ch Jack
to Dave) (899-* ch Jack to Dave) (957c tr Jack
& Dave)

633

(1338) (1342a) (1344) (1347) (1356) (1357)
(1360)
The line between reality and illusion blurs
for Jack as he investigates a psychic phenomenon * The mix of illusion and reality
while investigating a psychic phenomenon
drives Jack to the breaking point ** (1391)
(1428)

634

(130) (480) (732) (776) (1350)
Jack, imagining that he sees a fast-moving
car almost upon him, leaps out of its way
and into the path of a real car which kills
him (762)

635

(249) (608) (612) (624) (629 ch Pete to Burt)
(859)
Jack is mistakenly accused of being a criminal * Jack, mistakenly accused of being a
criminal, is finally cleared by the confession
of the real criminal, Burt ** (854) (884a)

636

(763) (1166a) (1196) (1267a) (1335)
Jack is a burglar who becomes reckless in
one of his robberies * Jack, a burglar, breaks
into a research laboratory ** Jack contracts a
contagious disease *** (681b) (705)

637

(778) (1023) (1024) (1027) (1029) (1268)
Jack robs an ancient temple of its priceless
treasures * Jack, committing a robbery, is
caught and turned over to the law for punishment ** (866) (1209c tr Jack & Pete)

638

(259-2) (377b) (681a) (732) (753)
Jack, ruined financially, indulges in drugs
and dies of an overdose

639

(758-*) (768) (898) (925-*)
Jack is kidnapped by Burt and held for ransom * Jack, kidnapped and held for ransom by Burt, is an officious, disagreeable man whose family and friends are glad to be rid of him and won't pay the ransom ** Jack, kidnapped and held for ransom by Burt, makes Burt's life so miserable that he pays to have Jack taken off his hands *** (781) (880a) (918a, b)

640

(126) (488a, b) (904) (1278a)
Carol tricks Jack in a certain venture * Jack, tricked by Carol in a venture, dies as a result of his involvement ** (557a)

641

(285) (992)
Carol tries to make a home for her widowed father, Frank, but he cruelly mistreats her (14a) (223) (368a) (676) (993)

642

(491b) (585b) (766)
Carol, to please her vanity, borrows a valuable ornament from her rich friend, Annie * Carol loses a valuable ornament she borrowed from her friend, Annie ** Carol and her husband, Jack, are financially ruined when forced to replace a valuable ornament that Carol borrowed from Annie, and lost *** (767) (792a) (870a)

643

(60) (470) (1416)
Late at night in a big city hotel, Carol enters what she thinks is her room. The following morning Carol awakens, horrified to find that she's sharing a strange man's bed in a city she's never before visited (645) (870a)

644

(147) (544)
Carol innocently befriends a stranger, Dave. Later, it develops that Dave is a political radical wanted by government officials led by Sam * If Sam knew that Carol had befriended Dave, she'd be labeled an accomplice and treated accordingly ** (179a, c) (594d) (824)

645

(737b-*) (737c; 737b *-**)
Carol finds herself imprisoned in a strange bedroom * Carol, caught innocently in a compromising situation, discovers something that places her in serious jeopardy ** (648) (669 ch Burt to Jack) (1135b)

646

(147) (544)
In an effort to be helpful, Carol befriends a stranger, Walt * Carol discovers that Walt, the stranger she befriended, is a criminal on the run from the law ** (660b) (669) (743b) (211)

647

(279) (470)
Respectable, straightlaced Carol, looking for employment, takes the advice of a supposed friend, Burt, and finds herself dancing in a topless bar (14a) (738)

648

(645) (647) (1050)
Carol is accused of being a criminal (or of an indiscretion) because she is apprehended in a high-crime area, or because she possesses evidence that indicates a crime (or indiscretion) has taken place * Carol is unjustly accused of a crime ** (21) (69) (186) (817) (822) (828)

CONFLICT SITUATIONS

649

(628 ch Jack to Tony) (770b, c, ch Jack to Tony) (977a, b)
Carol, trying to prevent her brother, Tony, from dishonoring their family, unintentionally causes his death (746) (909)

(13) Trying By Deception to Escape Trouble
650

(687) (689) (690) (691)
Jack, captive of a primitive, savage tribe, saves his life by convincing them he's a god (714) (244) (878a)

651

(1193) (1282) (1298)
Fugitive Jack is surrounded by law officers Sam, Faye and Russ * Jack, a fugitive trapped by law officers, hides in an enclosure (house, cave, factory, etc.) ** (699b) (74a)

652

(a) (651-*) (153) (321b) (385a) (639-**)
Jack is trapped in a deadly complication, and faces imminent disaster if he isn't inventive enough to save himself (651*-**) (639**-***) (650) (658)

(b) (180) (212a; 726b) (793a)
Jack, is about to lose a physical contest to his rival, Gary * Jack, in an attempt to overcome his rival, Gary, meets with an accident and is killed **

653

(651-*) (652b-* (655-*) (661) (1267a) (1419b) (662 ch Pete to Burt)
Jack is held captive by Burt in a seemingly inescapable trap * in the face of impossible odds, Jack is determined to devise a plan of escape ** (651*-**) (652b*-**) (655*-**)

654

(40a) (182b) (208) (385a) (610) (615) (655-*) (732) (787)
In trouble, Jack tries desperately to avoid disaster (655*-**) (656) (657) (826) (853) (1016a) (1176)

655

(600) (758-*)
Jack, held at gun point by a thief, Burt, tries to delay handing over his valuables * Jack is shot and seriously wounded by a thief, Burt ** (619) (681a) (724) (753)

656

(751) (961) (1000) (1079)
Jack's family estate is heavily mortgaged and he is about to lose the property * Jack, by any means, tries to save his family estate ** (500b) (860) (874) (1029)

657

(23c) (245) (718a)
Jack has great ability, but for whatever reason, he is perceived to be incapable (physical disability, ethnicity, etc.) * Jack is involved in an activity and is accused of treachery ** Jack, innocent of treachery, attempts to prove his innocence *** (771b) (1222a, b)

658

(612) (1038) (1130) (1177) (1247) (1306) (1233-*) (1275-*)
Jack, above reproach, fears that unusual conditions will discredit his reputation * Jack tries to protect his reputation which is being threatened by unusual conditions ** (652b) (1233*-**) (1275*-**)

659

(10a, b, c)
Carol's mother, Rita, is an ailing widow * Rita's life hangs on a change of climate, but she and her daughter, Carol, are broke ** Carol is desperately determined to do anything necessary to raise the money to help her mother, Rita *** (88) (253) (368b) (1293b, c)

(14) Getting into Trouble Because of a Clever Schemer

660

(a) (1248) (1130 ch Walt to Dave)
Jack, a professional man, is kidnapped from his office at night by mysterious strangers, Dave, Kate and Rick. They blindfold him and take him to a secret place * Jack, grabbed by Dave, Kate and Rick, is forced to perform a service that requires his expertise ** (571) (635 ch Burt to Dave) (653 ch Burt to Dave)

(b) (646; 147) (252a, b)
Jack, captured by enemies of Carol, is threatened with death by Burt in an attempt to make him disclose a secret of Carol's * Jack, threatened with death by Burt in an attempt to force him to reveal a secret of Carol's, dares Burt to kill him ** (875b) (884a)

661

(898) (957a)
Rich, powerful Jack is alone in an isolated location * Jack is robbed by Walt, who puts on Jack's clothes and drives off in Jack's car ** (715a) (1146 ch Jack to Walt)

662

(1394 ch Jack to Pete) (1436)
Jack helps Pete hide treasure in a secret place * Jack, helping Pete hide treasure in a secret place, is left to die by Pete who takes off alone with the treasure ** (653 ch Burt to Pete) (701 tr Jack & Pete) (704)

663

(654) (883-*)
Jack's deadly enemy, Gary, has Jack at his mercy, and there is nothing for Jack to do but make the best of a bad situation (628 ch Carol to Gary) (883*-**)

664

(130) (314-*) (572) (600) (752) (786) (863a)
Jack is unexpectedly locked in a room * Jack, suddenly finding himself a prisoner, attempts to remain calm and composed ** (799) (824) (856)

665

(557a) (946)
Carol leads an exemplary life, trying to live down a troubled past * Reformed Carol has her troubled past revealed by Gary ** (669 ch Burt to Gary) (945)

666

(27) (152b) (616) (679) (1244b)
Carol knows the combination of Jack's safe, as well as the fact that it contains valuables * Thieves, led by Burt, threaten deadly harm to Carol unless she opens the safe ** (144) (885a)

(29) Helping Another to Keep a Deadly Secret

667

(50) (446a-*) (449 ch Jack to Eric & Gary to Jack) (520 ch Laura to Carol)
Unless Carol hides a past indiscretion, she will seriously compromise herself * Unless Carol reveals a personal misdeed, she will cause Jack to pay for a crime he didn't commit ** (535 ch Jack to Eric & Gary to Jack) (1461a ch Jack to Carol)

668

(285 ch Frank to Rita) (976) (978)
Carol's mother, Rita, is a narcotics addict * Carol makes a heavy personal sacrifice in order to help Rita keep a secret ** (33) (368b) (785) (892 ch Laura to Rita)

669

(410) (447 ch Burt to Eric) (557a ch Gary to Burt) (597 ch Jack to Carol) (667-*)
Carol commits a secret offense * Carol's secret offense is discovered by Burt ** Carol's secret crime or infidelity is discovered by Burt, who attempts to blackmail Carol *** (784) (870b)

670

(641 ch Frank to Rita) (740)
Carol's mother, Rita, has periods of irrational behavior * Carol helps her mother, Rita, conceal Rita's problem ** (33) (659) (720 ch Jack to Carol)

(26) Secretly Trying to Save Another From Danger
671

(663 ch Jack to Pete) (672; 764-*)
Jack's friend, Pete, is helpless against a powerful enemy, Gary * Jack devises a plan to protect helpless Pete from a powerful enemy, Gary ** Jack's friend, Pete, kills himself before Jack can help him overcome his troubles *** (672; 764) (807) (841)

672

(671-**) (853)
Jack's friend, Pete, owns a flock of sheep. Gary is a rich, powerful cattle baron. Gary's men kill almost all Pete's sheep, and Gary schemes to take Pete's land from him. Pete, deep in debt, doesn't know where to turn * Jack forms a plan to help Pete ** (671) (805 ch Dave to Pete) (807) (809 ch Burt to Pete) (839)

673

(743a) (1298)
Jack finds a U.S. Mail truck wrecked and its cargo scattered. The driver, Dave, has gone for help. Jack comes across a letter, and discovers that Carol is in trouble * Fugitive Jack tries to rescue Carol from her troubles ** (817) (869) (1209a)

(18) Rebelling Against a Power that Controls and Suppresses Personal Abilities
674

(622) (755) (1450 ch Doug to Greg)
Jack loses his son, Greg, in whom all his ambitions were centered * Jack's sorrow is so overwhelming, it affects every area of his life ** (1053) (1056)

675

(200) (1108)
Jack's constant procrastination inhibits his business and restricts his abilities * Jack learns a lesson that shows how destructive a bad habit can become ** (215b) (1134) (1163a)

676

(285) (641)
Intellectual Carol has an artistic temperament * Carol rebels against her father, Frank, and his overly strict discipline ** (14a; 223) (741) (743a) (871)

677

(145) (455b) (679)
Carol is trying to make an important venture succeed * Carol fights anxiety ** (28a) (183) (239)

678

(668 ch Rita to Judy) (670 ch Rita to Judy)
Carol is forced to live with her sister, Judy * Carol defies her bitchy, selfish sister, Judy, who makes Carol's life miserable ** (14a) (137b) (737a) (743b)

679

(1121) (1244b)
Carol is overshadowed and dominated by her less-competent employer, Jack * Carol rebels when Jack takes credit for her achievements ** (616) (677)

(36) Having an Experience that Greatly Changes Character
680

(a) (654) (734)
Jack is a war veteran * Before the war, Jack led a successful life; since returning he is physically and mentally incapable of leading a normal life ** (199) (608) (1188)

(b) (680a) (715b) (257b)
Jack starts a venture while he is prosperous; then, suffering financial loss and illness, his spirit is broken (199) (345) (690)

CONFLICT SITUATIONS

681

(a) (49) (211)
Optimistic Jack suffers a critical reversal that destroys his spirit (106) (900) (918b) (963)

(b) (313) (572)
Jack suffers a critical illness * Jack recovers from a critical illness but is left with total amnesia ** (548a) (879) (1368)

682

(687) (689) (690) (937)
Brilliant, capable Jack, fights for survival in a savage wilderness * Jack, fighting for survival in a wilderness, deteriorates in character until he sinks to the level of his primitive surroundings ** (244) (728-**) (728**-***) (901)

683

(385a; 918a) (732) (857) (897)
Jack is a radar operator at a lonely post * Jack is an astronaut, the only survivor in a spaceship hurtling across the galaxies ** Jack is a terrorist hostage in solitary confinement *** Because of loneliness, Jack gradually loses his mind **** (560) (1344) (1345)

604

(930) (921 ch Carol to Frank) (1209a ch Jack to Frank)
Carol's father, Frank, is a disreputable character who disappeared mysteriously long ago * Carol's father, Frank, long missing, returns home unrecognized and discovers that his daughter, Carol, thinks he is dead and has elevated him to sainthood ** Frank changes his mind about identifying himself and leaves Carol content with her illusions *** (922a) (681b)

(19) Running into Trouble, and Being Stranded in a Primitive, Savage Environment

685

(130) (176a, c) (212a) (438) (711c)
Traveling alone, Jack is caught in a snowstorm * Jack, caught in a snowstorm in the mountains, becomes stranded, and can't reach safety ** (713) (762)

686

(109) (718b)
Gentleman Jack is stranded in a primitive, uninhabited wilderness, and forced to fight Nature to survive (197) (918b) (904)

687

(650) (689)
Jack finds himself in a primitive, hostile culture * Jack, the only outsider in a primitive culture, finds himself a victim of local superstitions ** (682) (901) (915)

688

(49) (690 add Carol)
Jack and Carol are stranded in a desolate, primitive environment where they must fight for their survival * Jack and Carol, strangers to each other, must join forces when their lives are threatened ** (226) (244) (307) (458b)

689

(694) (926) (937)
Jack travels through a savage wilderness * Jack, traveling through a savage wilderness, is captured by natives who threaten to kill him ** (197) (331) (650)

690

(109) (957a)
Jack takes an ocean cruise in the hope of recovering his health * Jack, taking an ocean cruise, is shipwrecked and stranded on an uncharted island ** (682) (686)

CONFLICT SITUATIONS

691

(1379) (1388) (1394)
Explorer Jack is lost in a trackless wilderness (650) (689) (1426b)

692

(690-*) (719b)
Jack, without food or water, is adrift in a small boat at sea (632) (690 *-**) (878b)

693

(1082a, b) (1408)
Wandering alone in the mountains, Jack is caught in a trapper's snare, unable to free himself * Jack, caught in a trap, faces death ** (713) (728 **-***) (728-** ch Jack to Pete & Lee to Jack) (1419a)

694

(470) (676) (740) (916) (1033) (1207)
Carol drives a Land-Rover alone in the wilderness * Carol, driving alone in the wilds, crashes her vehicle and sustains injuries, leaving her helpless ** (31) (179a, c) (885a-*)

(20) Getting Into a Situation From Which Difficult Problems are Likely to Result

695

(a) (385a) (787) (822) (829)
Jack's neighbors think he is guilty of a crime for which he was tried and acquitted * Jack, tried for a crime and acquitted, attempts to free himself of suspicion ** (635) (833) (1064)

(b) (608) (623)
Jack is imprisoned for a crime he didn't commit * Jack, completing a prison term for a crime he didn't commit, discovers that being an ex-con makes life on the outside extremely difficult ** (299) (1183)

696

(715c) (695b)
Jack, a man without a country, is deprived of news of his homeland (823) (826) (859)

697

(a) (990) (1006b)
Jack's parents, Andy and Linda, insist that he study medicine, while Jack longs to enter another profession (756) (791) (950-*)

(b) (818c ch Jack to Eric & Lee to Jack) (818d ch Jack to Eric & Lee to Jack)
Jack was an abandoned child who knows nothing of his parentage * Jack knows nothing of his parentage, and finds it a handicap ** (245) (944) (1051)

698

(622) (898)
Jack finds it impossible to get past his grief over the death of his only child, Lee (674) (705) (732) (746 ch Carol to Jack) (1068 ch Carol to Jack)

699

(a) (608) (610) (623) (1298) (1300)
Fugitive Jack discovers that a relative, Eric, has died and left him a valuable estate * Jack is a fugitive who doesn't dare show up to claim his inheritance, knowing he will be arrested ** (624) (635)

(b) (651) (652a) (653)
Trapped by pursuers, Jack hides in an old house * Trapped by pursuers Sam and Faye, Jack escapes when the house in which he's hiding catches fire ** (1142b) (1209a)

700

(748) (958)
Jack has taken a vow of poverty * Jack, against his wishes, inherits a fortune from a relative, Eric ** (431) (924a)

701

(1249) (1296) (1304)
Jack tries to get rich by cheating Pete * Jack, trying to get rich by cheating Pete, is tortured by his conscience ** (832) (987) (1461a)

702

(863b, c)
Jack invites a number of guests to meet Dave, a celebrity * Jack has invited a number of fans to meet Dave, a celebrity. The fans arrive, but Dave doesn't ** (178 ch Jack to Dave) (1162 ch Burt to Dave) (1164)

703

(68) (96) (486a)
Jack is a gospel minister * Jack, a minister, commits an unethical act and becomes a victim of his conscience ** (279 tr Jack & Carol, ch "husband of Laura" to "wife of Eric") (348) (393) (951) (1461a)

704

(139) (601) (607) (716)
Loyalty to his friends makes Jack happy * Jack, because of a particular incident, is forced to turn against his friend, Pete ** (770b tr Jack & Pete) (790a) (840) (1227a) (1402) (1216 tr Jack & Pete)

705

(150) (248) (255) (288) (548b) (568c) (698)
Jack, unable to overcome his problems, commits suicide (868 tr Jack & Pete) (879)

706

(a) (115) (793a)
Engineer Jack has built a steel span across a mountain pass, gambling his reputation with a bridge in a place where other engineers said no bridge was possible * Jack's life work, nearing completion, is threatened with destruction by forces outside of Jack's control ** (546a) (603a) (726b) (779)

(b) (810) (898)
Scientist Jack has recorded a lifetime of research material * The priceless record of Jack's research is threatened by a disaster ** (918b)

(c) (959) (966-4)
Artist Jack has spent years painting a certain picture that he considers his masterpiece * Jack's masterpiece is threatened with destruction during a political protest ** (1233 ch Jack to Pete) (808a tr Jack & Carol)

707

(610) (866)
Jack asks a stranger, Dave, to remove handcuffs from his wrists (1066) (1311 ch Jack to Dave & Gary to Jack)

708

(770a) (797) (859) (918a) (952) (864) (611a)
After a long, mysterious absence, Jack returns to his home town * Jack, returning to his home town, discovers that no one recognizes him ** (1275) (1453)

709

(836) (1021a) (1058)
Jack takes charge of a valuable object, X, for a friend, Pete * Jack, custodian of a valuable object, X, mislays X and thinks it has been stolen ** (774) (807)

710

(130) (180) (726a) (1356)
Performer Jack is awaited by a large audience * Jack is forced by a sudden illness to drop out of a venture ** (757) (1162 ch Burt to Jack) (1163a) (1163a; 1163c)

711

(a) (130) (188a) (525)
Engaged in an important enterprise, Jack is suddenly confined because of a contagious disease (856) (875a tr Jack & Pete and eliminate "in prison")

712

(1248) (1282)
Doctor Jack is a fugitive * Jack, a doctor, is running from a law officer, Sam. Sam becomes temporarily blind, and Jack restores his sight ** (1011 ch Jack to Sam & Burt to Jack) (1013)

713

(662) (685) (692) (693)
Jack, deprived of food, faces slow death by starvation (878b) (878c) * Jack dies of starvation **

714

(650) (687) (863a; 690) (878a)
Entertainer Jack, a ventriloquist (an illusionist or escape artist?) is held captive and uses his talents to save his life; sudden loss of his voice (or amnesia) throws him back into danger (197) (244; 878c; 904)

715

(a) (661) (925-*)
Rich and influential Jack loses his clothes and all identification (658) * Wealthy Jack's claims of social status are ridiculed ** Jack is accused of being an impostor when he's unable to prove his identity *** (635) (963) (1348a; 1455b)

(b) (680b) (113; 257b)
Jack cripples himself rescuing a child, Lee, from death (842b) * Jack loses a fortune trying to help a friend, Pete (601) ** Destitute and ill, Jack reassesses his life *** (345) (690) (944)

(c) (212a) (1323b)
Jack is convicted of political conspiracy (793b) * Jack, convicted of betraying his country, is forced to live abroad ** (696) (826)

716

(830 tr Jack & Pete) (865 tr Jack & Pete)
Jack and Pete were the best of friends at a military academy (1021b) (662-*) * Jack is a captain in the army. His men capture his friend, Pete, now an enemy officer, and bring him to Jack ** (790a) (1016a ch Burt to Pete) (1016b)

717

(866) (1162 tr Jack & Pete & ch Burt to Sam) (1180 ch Dave to Sam)
Jack impersonates a law officer, Sam * Jack, impersonating Sam, encounters Sam's girlfriend, Carol, who recognizes him as an imposter ** (885a-*) (1173-*) (1176)

718

(a) (255) (257a)
Jack knows something others don't know, something that could prove an obstacle to his success (1061) * Jack knows he has a problem that could prove fatal ** (248) (657) (959)

(b) (800 ch Greg to Jack) (928b-* ch Greg to Jack & Jack to Eric)
Because youthful Jack was sheltered and pampered by his parents, he is ill-prepared to face the real world * Jack, immature and inefficient, learns about life through hard experience ** (759) (768) (769) (783) (918b)

719

(a) (130) (314-*) (430) (770a)
Jack disappears mysteriously * Jack, attacked by mysterious persons, Walt, Amy and Leo, in his high-rise office, is spirited away despite state-of-the-art security ** (540) (571)

(b) (690-*) (1116-*)
Jack, passenger on a ship at sea, is taken prisoner by terrorists Burt, Sally and Fred * Jack, captured at sea by terrorists Burt, Sally and Fred, is cast adrift in a small boat ** (692) (878b)

720

(288) (1061)
Jack is paralyzed by the fear that he has inherited the evil traits of an ancestor, Eric (862) (1374)

721

(706a, b, c) (903)
Jack's entire future hinges on a massive project that he has brought nearly to successful completion * Jack's life work is threatened with destruction ** (546a) (1256)

722

(833) (834) (1298 ch Jack to Burt)
Jack is a law officer pursuing a criminal, Burt * Jack, a law officer pursuing a criminal, Burt, runs into trouble ** (634) (664) (693) (711a) (712 ch Jack to Burt & Sam to Jack) (1013 ch Jack to Burt & Sam to Jack)

723

(998 ch Jack to Burt & Dave to Jack) (1016a-*)
Police officer Jack owes money to a criminal, Burt, but is unable to repay him (1011) (983 ch Jack to Burt & Eric to Jack)

724

(1227a-**) (1377a)
Jack recovers a stolen object, X, and sets out to return it to its owner * Jack, on his way to return a stolen object, X, to its owner, loses X and tries to recover it again ** (614) (711b)

725

(833) (1303 ch Carl to Burt)
Jack attempts to inform the authorities of the identity of a criminal, Burt, who, so far, is unsuspected * In trying to report a criminal, Burt, to the police, Jack runs into trouble ** (1228 ch Gary to Burt) (1232 ch Jack to Gary & Burt to Jack)

726

(a) (1060) (1082a)
Matador Jack is preparing for the bull ring * Jack, preparing for an endeavor, has his plans suddenly interrupted ** (710) (809-* tr Jack & Burt)

(b) (180) (782)
Jack, sick, is suddenly called upon to perform a difficult task (652a, b) (793a)

727

(3a) (297) (425; 813; 821) (800 ch Carol to Jack; 821)
Judge Jack, presiding at a murder trial, is unexpectedly confronted with an agonizing conflict (790b) (833)

728

(686) (687) (1319b-*)
Jack sets a trap for a large animal * Jack sets a concealed trap, and a loved one, Lee, falls into it (622 ch Greg to Lee) (591 ch Carol to Lee; 179a ch Carol to Lee) ** Jack constructs a deadly trap, and accidently falls into it himself *** (875b) (1319b ch Pete to Jack)

729

(601) (1334a) (1382b)
Desperately in need, Jack is offered a large payment for a diamond, X, that he knows is a fake * Jack, desperately in need of money, can pay off his debts at the expense of his integrity. He resists the temptation ** (778 ch Jack to Burt; 1144 ch Jack to Burt; 1166a ch Jack to Burt) (803b) (944)

730

(918a) (959) (1014 ch Burt to Gary)
Jack is the custodian of valuables, X, over which he fights with Gary * Gary kills Jack and takes valuables, X, that Jack was guarding ** Gary, having killed Jack, plants a gun in Jack's hand to make it appear that Jack committed suicide *** (569 ch Burt to Gary) (802b tr Jack & Carol) (977a)

731

(109) (608) (708) (808a)
Jack is an honest stranger regarded suspiciously * Jack is arrested as a suspect because he's in the vicinty when a crime is committed ** (695b) (815a ch Jack to Eric & Dave to Jack)

732

(288) (654) (683) (698)
Jack is convinced he is going insane, and that eventually he will be committed to a mental hospital (634) (638) (1365) (1374) (1375)

733

(718b) (723)
Jack finds a large-denomination bill * Jack finds a valuable paper, X, between the pages of an antique volume ** Jack finds a large-denomination bill. The banks are closed and he can't find anyone to change the bill *** (652a) (655) (731)

734

(222b) (315) (430)
Jack is mistakenly reported dead * Jack suffers combat fatigue and can't remember who he is ** Jack, victim of amnesia in a foreign land, finds his way back to his homeland *** (437) (548a) (1128a-*; 918b)

735

(912a ch Jack to Eric) (913 ch Jack to Eric & Pete to Jack)
Jack is annoyed by Eric, who constantly interferes with him * Jack deals harshly with meddlesome Eric, and later regrets his actions ** (762 tr Jack & Eric) (815a ch Jack to Eric & Dave to Jack) (822 ch Jack to Eric & Carol to Jack)

736

(322a) (737a) (740)
Carol inherits the trait of hiding her affections, a trait that hinders her success and happiness (162a) (594a) (742)

737

(a)　(12b) (36) (60) (62) (162a) (182a) (225) (226) (643)
Carol is discontented because of an unfortunate situation * Carol tries to overcome her discontentment, but the obstacles seem insurmountable ** (93a) (114) (346) (403) (785)

(b)　(470) (976)
At night in a motel, Carol, clad in her bathrobe, returns from the ice-maker and accidently enters the wrong room * Carol finds that the lock in a hotel room is broken and the door can't be opened ** (645) (885b) (890)

(c)　(470) (1154a)
Carol, tipsy with champagne, ties a ribbon to the doorknob of her big-city hotel room so she can find her way back * Lee, a child playing in the corridor of a big-city hotel, unties a ribbon from Carol's doorknob and reties it to Jack's door ** (645) (792b)

738

(60) (223) (397) (435a) (647) (665)
Carol, depressed, tries to escape her problems through self-destructive acts (879 ch Jack to Carol) (188b) (880a ch Jack to Carol & Pete to Annie)

739

(947) (1293b)
Owing to financial difficulties, Carol is forced to sell a greatly prized object, X * Carol is unable to repurchase an object she loves, X ** (806 ch Kate to Carol) (792a; 21) (1384 ch Carol to Jack)

740

(15a) (327a) (736) (848b ch Carol to Rita)
Carol's strange, wild traits are attributed to an event experienced by her mother, Rita while pregnant with Carol * Carol is ostracized because of a problem for which she isn't responsible ** (221a; 264) (221a) (738) (746) (872) (892 ch Laura to Jack)

741

(223) (676)
Carol is forced out of the house by her father, Frank (183) (743a) (869)

742

(57) (585a) (743a)
Carol writes a note that contains a vitally important secret * Carol writes a note that she inadvertently loses ** Carol writes an important note which, if read by anyone other than the addressee, will humiliate Carol *** (758) (955)

743

(a) (223) (435a) (676)
Overcome by desperate problems, Carol plans to commit suicide * Carol writes a letter explaining why she intends to kill herself ** (742) (673)

(b) (403) (594e) (646)
Carol commits a crime, and, to escape the consequences, secretly travels to a distant place and assumes an alias (750 ch Jack to Carol) (921)

744

(816b) (844a) (1105)
Carol goes to a restaurant to keep a date with Jack, who fails to show up (1240 ch Gary to Jack) (1391 ch Jack to Carol)

745

(947) (948)
Carol's father, Frank, pursuing thieves who have robbed him, is shot and killed * Frank's eldest daughter, Carol, has to support the family when Frank dies ** (14a) (1207)

746

(89) (212b) (649) (698 ch Jack to Carol) (740)
Believed by others to be eccentric, Carol truly has supernatural powers — fueled by tragic events in the past (766) (1328) (1441a ch Jack to Carol) (1373 ch Jack to Carol)

(21) Landing in Trouble Through Mistaken Judgment

747

(41a) (125a) (111)
Convinced of a certain stock's value, Jack invests in it himself and sells shares to his friends, Pete and Annie * Honest, principled Jack recommends a certain business proposition, then learns it's a swindle ** (604) (606) (619) (979)

748

(941) (958)
Jack is content, having taken a vow of poverty * Jack, believing wealth brings unhappiness, refuses to take advantage of personal resources that could make him rich ** (111) (700) (929)

749

(965) (966-1) (1074)
Writer Jack is fulfilled by his creativity * Writer Jack unconsciously plagiarizes another author's work ** (1238) (1357*-**) (1391; 1461b)

750

(224) (597)
Jack runs away to escape the consequences of a crime * Jack thinks he is guilty of a crime, but no crime has been committed ** (108) (237) (624)

751

(1061) (1210) (1102)
Informed that he only has a short time to live, Jack starts an unusual venture [1] Jack tries to spend all his money before he dies [2] Jack jumps into dangerous situations * Jack, told that he has only a short time to live, discovers that the doctor made a mistake ** (811) (918b) (1104) (1134*-**)

752

(113) (126) (923)
Jack is caught burglarizing a house * Jack, an intruder in a strange house, is discovered. He bolts through the nearest door — into another dimension ** (801 tr Jack & Carol) (856)

753

(484b) (524a)
Jack gambles with money that isn't his — and loses it (620) (638)

754

(380) (484b) (807)
Jack gambles with money he is holding in trust (829) (832) (865)

755

(49) (585a) (622)
Jack resigns himself to endure the loss of a loved one. But the loss is illusionary, not real (357) (576b)

756

(697a)
Although he wants a musical career, Jack complies with the wishes of his parents, Andy and Linda, and becomes a doctor; but he's plagued by feelings of unfulfillment (1153 ch Carol to Jack; 1248) (1388) (1434) (949a)

757

(114) (710) (176a, b)
Facing hard and dangerous duty, Jack is suddenly incapacitated by severe illness (1163a) (1163c) (1164 tr Jack & Dave)

758

(57) (742)
Wealthy Jack ruthlessly exploits the misfortunes of others * Jack finds a mysterious note containing Carol's ruinous secret ** Jack begins to exploit Carol's troubles for his own gain, but ends up offering Carol his sympathy and friendship *** (21) (817) (955)

CONFLICT SITUATIONS

759

(718b) (898)
Dude ranch guest Jack is ridiculed by tough ranch-hand, Eric * Jack and Eric settle their differences by a contest of skill ** (782) (820 ch Jack to Eric) (830 ch Pete to Eric)

760

(954) (925)
Jack achieves his aims so thoroughly that his success results in failure (1d, f, g) (231) (44b) (207) (377b) (595) (625) (751)

761

(a) (1126; 779) (793a) (836)
Jack, influenced by a reckless friend, Pete, is killed (601; 705) (793a; 603d tr Jack & Pete)

(b) (383) (837)
Cosmetic surgeon Jack attempts to remove a disfiguring mark from the exquisite face of his wife, Carol * Jack, trying to help Carol, makes a tragic mistake ** (385a) (416)

762

(735 tr Jack & Eric) (845 ch Pete to Gary) (1430a)
Jack tries vainly to win Eric's friendship *
Jack has a fatal accident (634) (705) ** After his death, Jack wins Eric's friendship — for which he had vainly struggled in life *** (868 ch Jack to Eric & Pete to Jack) (1423 ch Jack to Eric & Walt to Jack)

763

(1146) (1175a)
Wealthy criminal Jack returns to his home turf and the pals of his younger hoodlum days * Criminal Jack is depressed to discover that his old buddies are all married and straight-arrows ** (868 ch Jack to Eric & Pete to Jack) (963) (1087)

764

(671-**) (672)
In order to save his friend, Pete, Jack picks a fight with Pete's enemy, Gary, and kills him * Jack, in order to protect Pete, kills Gary, supposed enemy of Pete, unaware that Pete and Gary have made their peace (Or have they? Could Jack have been set up?) ** (671**-***) (1344 ch Pete to Gary) (1355)

765

(376 ch Carol to Annie; 414 tr Carol & Annie) (916)
Small town schoolteacher Carol unknowingly violates School Board regulations and opens a Pandora's Box of problems (31) (870a) (891)

766

(56) (1106) (1121)
Carol, a plain woman, believes she is gorgeous * Carol has a character weakness that deeply affects her life ** (642) (746) (893) (1067)

767

(1152 ch Carol to Annie; 642-**)
Impoverished Carol borrows a supposedly valuable object, X, and loses it * Carol, borrowing a supposedly valuable object, X, then losing it, sells her soul to replace it — only to find that X was a worthless fake ** (642**-***) (918b ch Jack to Carol)

(22) Misguided By Mistaken Judgment

768

(718b) (1060-*)
Nerd Jack deludes himself that he will be greatly missed if he drops out of society (617) (639)

769

(675) (718b) (1060-*)
Jack is mistakenly convinced that he is a great businessman * Jack tries to manage Pete's failing business and make it profitable ** (606 ch Jack to Pete; 1058) (672; 906)

770

(b) (490b) (601)
Jack, deeply in debt, tries to save himself from ruin by forging the name of a friend, Pete, on a loan (649 ch Tony to Jack) (704 tr Jack & Pete)

(c) (524a) (606)
Jack, deeply in debt, tries to save himself by misappropriating trust funds in his possession (701) (753) (754)

771

(a) (513) (614) (1337) (1386a)
Jack is convinced a certain crime has been committed and reports it to police officer Sam * Jack thinks a crime has been committed, but he is mistaken ** (780) (802a)

(b) (299) (657-**) (798)
Jack finds a top-secret Security Document * Jack finds and keeps an incriminating document, X, intending to return it at a later time ** Jack is accused of wrongdoing by his rival, Gary, and an incriminating paper, X, is found in Jack's possession *** (820 tr Jack & Pete) (657**-***) (829)

772

(600) (608) (612 ch Burt to Dave)
Jack befriends a needy stranger, Dave * Jack befriends a needy stranger, Dave, who turns out to be a criminal ** (613 ch Burt to Dave) (623) (635 ch Burt to Dave)

773

(817) (837) (1154a) (1159) (1173)
Jack, trying to be helpful, befriends Carol * Jack befriends Carol, who proves to be a criminal who has lied to Jack about her identity ** (828) (1171)

774

(513) (709) (772)
Jack pursues a stranger, Dave, to recover an object, X, that has been stolen * Jack pursues a stranger, Dave, taking from him a valuable object, X, that Jack thinks was stolen from him. Later, Jack discovers that X, which he believed was stolen, was in his possession all the time ** (780 ch Jack to Dave & Eric to Jack) (859)

775

(1144 ch Jack to Matt) (1212c ch Jack to Matt & Carl to Jack)
Jack trusts his assistant, Matt, and makes him his confidant * Jack discovers that his trusted assistant, Matt, is a thief ** (1166b ch Jack to Matt) (1008 ch Jack to Matt & Carl to Jack)

776

(732) (711b-*)
Jack is seriously injured by a horse * Jack is seriously injured by a horse and develops a paralyzing phobia toward horses ** (634) (1078)

777

(624) (783) (787) (1199-*) (1342a) (1389a)
Jack, though not a criminal, is convinced he is one * Jack conceals his identity, avoids people, and leads a furtive life ** (681b) (705) (1199)

778

(1143a ch Jack to Eric) (1152)
Thief Jack plans to steal a priceless gem, X * Jack, thinking that a fake gem, X, is genuine, plans to steal it ** (1144) (1217a)

779

(289) (840-*)
Jack's drunken friend, Pete, persuades Jack to take a drink, despite Pete's knowledge that Jack's doctor has warned Jack he mustn't drink (840*-**) (620) (761a)

CONFLICT SITUATIONS

780

(771a) (1317) (1386a)
Jack shows the police circumstantial evidence of a crime he's convinced Eric has committed * Eric, arrested on information supplied by Jack, proves that no crime has been committed ** (802a) (1340 ch Dave to Eric)

781

(898) (983)
Jack regards others as fair game for exploitation * Ruthless Jack has an experience that changes his character ** (377b) (639) (811)

782

(718b) (759)
Wealthy dilettante Jack clashes with street-smart, uneducated Eric in a mutual venture. Their differences result in a fist fight * Wealthy Jack and working-class Eric battle to a draw and as a result learn from each other and form a bond of respect and friendship ** (807 ch Pete to Eric) (830 ch Pete to Eric) (839 ch Pete to Eric)

783

(597) (718b) (777)
Jack lets himself be blackmailed by Matt because Jack is convinced that he unintentionally committed a crime * Jack, thinking he is a criminal, discovers that no crime has been committed ** (775) (1456 ch Burt to Matt)

784

(403) (669) (787 ch Jack to Carol)
Thinking that she is a criminal, Carol tries to evade the law * Carol discovers she isn't guilty of the crime she thought she had committed ** (468) (635 ch Jack to Carol) (870b)

785

(668; 33) (670; 33)
Carol's widowed mother, Rita, is in desperate trouble * Rita plans a course of action that Carol knows will result in unhappy consequences, but Carol's unable to dissuade her ** (420 ch Carol to Rita; 453 ch Carol to Rita) (892 ch Laura to Jack & Carol to Rita)

(23) Becoming Enmeshed in Mistaken Judgment and/or Suspicion

786

(598) (833) (1389a)
Jack, week-end guest at a country home, prowls about the place out of honest curiosity * Jack is mistaken for an intruder ** (664) (828) (1188-*)

787

(1291b) (1449)
Circumstantial evidence convinces Jack he is guilty of a crime he doesn't remember committing, and which in fact he never committed (296) (624) (695a, b) (1064)

788

(21) (1127 ch Ray to Carol)
Jack thinks Carol is an opportunist, attempting to obtain wealth by pretending she's the daughter of multi-millionaire Eric * Carol proves she's Eric's daughter ** (422b) (647 ch Burt to Jack)

789

(633) (1331-*)
Jack, lost, is convinced that everyone is trying to misdirect him (759) (1331*-**)

790

(a) (830) (865)
Before the war, Jack had a friend, Pete, who did him a great favor * During the war, Pete, is captured as an enemy agent and brought before Captain Jack ** Captain Jack lets enemy agent Pete escape and as a consequence Jack is branded a traitor *** (919a) (921 ch Carol to Jack) (1183)

CONFLICT SITUATIONS

790

(b) (838) (1115)
Judge Jack's childhood friend, Pete, is brought before him for trial * Without revealing their past relationship, and rather than disqualifying himself, Judge Jack presides at the trial of his friend, Pete, and manipulates the case so that Pete is acquitted ** Once revealed, Judge Jack's breach of ethics destroys his career *** (949b) (952)

791

(697a) (926)
Doctor Jack is married and has a growing family * Doctor Jack has dedicated himself to AIDS research and treatment ** Idealistic Doctor Jack's course of action places him in direct conflict with his wife, relatives and friends *** (1434) (1447)

792

(a) (642-**) (739; 1401)
When Jack returns an object, X, that Carol has lost, she mistakenly thinks Jack stole it * When Jack returns an object, X, that Carol has lost, Jack mistakenly thinks she is a thief because X seems too valuable to be owned by someone of Carol's modest circumstances ** (21) (822)

(b) (737c) (1154a) (1172 ch Sally to Irene)
Carol places an identifying mark on her hotel room door. The mark is transferred to another door; and Irene, occupant of the that room, is found murdered (645) (1204**-***)

(20) Getting Into a Sitauation From Which Difficult Problems are Likely to Result

793

(a) (599) (603c)
Jack is persuaded by his friend, Pete, to participate in a difficult venture * Jack is persuaded by friend, Pete, to begin a venture that Jack's judgment warns him to avoid ** (653) (761a)

(b) (79 ch Gary to Pete) (809 ch Burt to Pete)
Jack is persuaded by his friend, Pete, to hold some important papers * Jack obliges his friend, Pete, by holding Pete's important documents. Jack is arrested and, because he has the documents, is charged with a crime ** (108) (715c)

(24) Falling Victim to Mistaken Judgment in Carrying Out a Venture

794

(603d) (671) (1291b)
Jack thinks his friend, Pete, is dead * Jack is stunned when his friend, Pete, whom he thought dead, suddenly appears ** (1344) (1371)

795

(110-3) (182b) (431)
Jack is deceived into believing he has achieved a long-sought-after goal (313) (488a) (918b)

796

(687) (973) (976 ch Carol to Jack) (1038 ch Eric to Gary) (1274-*)
Through faith, Jack achieves success in a venture * Jack's success is mistakenly credited to Jack's enemy, Gary ** (1163c ch Dave to Gary) (1289b**-***) (1274*-**)

797

(930 ch Frank to Jack & Carol to Nina) (919b 1298)
Jack mysteriously disappeared long ago under suspicion of having committed a wrong (adultery, theft, murder, etc.) * Jack returns home, unrecognized by his daughter, Nina, who has glorified his memory ** (964b) (1461c ch Carol to Nina)

798

(1319a ch Jack to Eric & Gary to Jack) (1438b)
Jack finds a mysterious object, X, that is apparently priceless * Jack highly values a mysterious object, X, and is unaware that by having it in his possession, he is endangering his life ** (623) (711b) (1382a)

799

(24b) (58a ch Walt to Jack) (185) (737b ch Carol to Jack) (773) (786)
Jack behaves inappropriately * Jack forces his way into the room of a woman, Carol (766) ** Carol, to protect herself from Jack, summons a police officer, Sam *** (249) (347b) (658)

800

(514 ch Lee to Doug) (594c ch Lee to Doug) (551 ch Lee to Doug)
Carol deludes herself about her son, Doug * Carol is convinced her son, Doug, is brilliant and talented, although actually he's of less than average mentality ** (718b ch Jack to Doug) (821 ch Jack to Carol) (853 ch Jack to Doug) (896)

801

(24a, b, c, d, e) (27)
Carol earns Jack's respect and protection * Jack discovers that Carol has deceived him ** (45a) (61) (69) (147) (648) (665)

(61) Learning an Important Secret That Requires Decisive Action

802

(a) (771a) (780) (1444 ch Carol to Irene)
Jack learns that Carol, supposedly murdered, really committed suicide (669; 738) (741; 738) (324; 738)

(b) (833) (841 ch Pete to Carol) (1417)
Jack determines that Carol, who supposedly killed herself, was actually murdered (422b) (568a ch Jack to Eric) (1154a)

803

(a) (1337) (1444)
Jack learns that a coroner's verdict of "accidental death" should have been one of premeditated murder (79 ch Jack to Eric) (568c ch Jack to Eric) (568d ch Jack to Eric) (1456)

(b) (606) (729)
Desperately needy Jack learns that a gem, X, he thought worthless, is actually genuine and priceless (792a) (1166a ch Jack to Eric)

CONFLICT SITUATIONS

(21) Landing in Trouble Through Mistaken Judgment

804

(926) (928a) (709 ch Pete to Dave)
On a country road, Jack retrieves a suitcase, X, which has fallen from the roof-rack of a passing automobile * Jack, finding a suitcase, X, in the road, intends to return it to the stranger, Dave, who lost it ** Jack finds a bag, X, and, opening it, becomes aware that it contains incriminating evidence *** (608) (623) (808a)

805

(600) (613-* ch Burt to Dave) (772-*)
Jack tries to help Dave, an old man in trouble * Jack, trying to help a stranger, Dave, finds himself enmeshed in a difficult situation ** (613*-** ch Burt to Dave) (608) (623)

806

(162b) (1157 ch Carol to Kate & Jack to Burt) (1241a, b) (1244b) (1220b ch Jack to Eric)
In a crowded airport terminal, Jack sees a distraught stranger, Kate * Jack impulsively aids a stranger, Kate, and later regrets it ** (801) (152b) (1159) (1208 ch Carol to Kate)

807

(906-*) (913)
Jack, trying to help his friend, Pete, is suspected of treachery by Pete (906*-**) (603a, b, c, d) (867)

808

(a) (804-** ch Dave to Carol) (778-* ch Jack to Burt; 1214 ch Pete to Carol; 1227a ch Pete to Carol)
Jack assumes control over property of Carol's in order to save it for her * Jack, taking possession of Carol's property in order to save it for her, is wrongfully accused by Carol of attempting to steal it ** (21) (706c ch Jack to Carol)

(b) (747 ch Jack to Carol & Pete to Annie) (773) (766) (800)
Jack is older and more knowledgeable than Carol and attempts to counsel her so she'll avoid mistakes * Carol resents Jack's presumption ** (747*-** ch Jack to Carol) (799) (812a) (870a) (828)

809

(599 ch Pete to Burt) (612-*) (662-* ch Pete to Burt) (793b-* ch Pete to Burt)
Jack tries to help Burt in a certain venture * Jack, trying to help Burt, is unaware that Burt is a criminal ** (612*-**) (662-* ch Pete to Burt) (793b*-** ch Burt to Pete)

810

(461) (619) (695a) (929-*)
Jack is convinced he's slipping professionally and considers his life a failure * Jack's son, Greg, wins a difficult athletic competition; Greg tells despairing Jack, who considers himself a failure, that he was inspired by the knowledge that his father had never been defeated ** Jack regains his self-confidence because of his son, Greg's, faith in him *** (674) (729*-**)

811

(751-1) (781)
Tightwad, unloved Jack is talked into giving his millions to charity when he thinks he's about to die * Jack, giving away his fortune because he believes his death is imminent, regrets his generosity when he learns he still has a long life ahead of him ** Tightwad Jack wants to recover the fortune he gave to charity until he realizes how popular his generosity has made him. Pleased by his newfound popularity, he continues his generosity and is loved ***

812

(a) (646-* ch Walt to Dave) (808b)
Compassionate Carol befriends needy Dave * Carol, befriending needy Dave, finds herself drawn into a difficult complication ** (646*-** ch Walt to Dave) (669 ch Burt to Dave)

CONFLICT SITUATIONS

(b) (982a ch Jack to Frank & Jim to Jack)
(997a ch Jack to Frank)
Carol's father, Frank, unsuccessfully tries to
control Jack, a rebellious, unmanageable
young man left in his charge * When Carol's
father, Frank, fails in a venture, she takes
the project off his hands ** (22a) (115) (367a)

(50) Compelled by a Special Motive to Behave Underhandedly

813

(425) (551 ch Lee to Greg) (594c ch Lee to
Greg)
Jack attempts to protect his son, Greg, from
what he feels is his own disgrace and dishonor (821) (881)

814

(114) (176b) (225)
Jack succeeds in a venture which he is unaware that Carol has set up to test his abilities (281c) (367b)

(15) Finding the Power to Overcome Problems

815

(a) (598) (985; 623) (890 ch Carol to Dave &
Dave to Jack)
Jack encounters Dave, a fugitive pursued by
Sam, a law officer * Jack sympathizes with
Dave, a fugitive, and tries to help him **
(866) (998) (1161) (1163a tr Jack & Dave)

(b) (611b) (631)
Formerly rebellious Jack returns home to his
father, Andy, a subdued, wiser young man
* Jack, formerly rebellious, is forgiven his
past behavior by his father, Andy ** (821 ch
Jack to Andy & Greg to Jack) (1166b ch Carl
to Andy)

816

(a) (174) (834)
Jack is hurrying to an important meeting *
Enroute, Jack finds a stranger, Dave, ill and
unconscious ** Jack sacrifices his self-interest to help a sick stranger, Dave *** (772)
(1265b)

(b) (647) (669)
Jack's friend, Carol, is in a foreign country,
alone and homesick * Carol, abroad, unexpectedly meets Jack, a friend from home **
(744) (817) (850a)

817

(598) (610) (955)
Fugitive Jack is forced to stay on the move
to avoid capture * Jack, wanted by the law,
risks capture to help Carol (647) (57), a
stranger in desperate trouble ** (801) (837)
(870b ch Sam to Jack) (885a)

818

(a) (598) (610) (1169)
Jack, wealthy, from a socially prominent fam-
ily, pretends he's destitute * Jack is hired by
Dave to spread malicious gossip against
Carol (60 ch Jack to Dave) (339 ch Jack to
Dave) ** Jack is hired by Dave to harm Carol.
Jack meets Carol, feels sympathy for her and
rebels against Dave's scheme by warning
Carol *** (14a) (828) (870a; 870b ch Sam to
Jack & Burt to Dave)

(b) (887b) (1329)
Street-gang member Jack rescues Carol from
an attack by a rival gang * Carol befriends
Jack, takes him off the streets and reforms
him ** (837 tr Jack & Carol) (1075b) (850b)

(c) (905) (914)
Jack finds a small, abandoned child, Lee *
Jack takes Lee, an orphan, into his home and
raises him/her as his own child ** (305 ch
Carol to Lee) (1089)

(d) (898) (926)
Jack saves a baby, Lee, from death * Jack,
unable to determine the origins of abandoned
Lee, adopts the child ** (245 ch Jack to Lee)
(948 ch Carol to Lee) (1106 ch Carol to Lee)
(1458 ch Carol to Lee)

CONFLICT SITUATIONS

819

(646 ch Walt to Jack) (844a) (850a) (263 ch Gary to Burt)

Thief Jack tries to help Carol, a childhood friend * Carol's friend, Jack, breaks into a building to commit a robbery. He finds an employee, Burt, who is Carol's husband, dead at his desk, a note beside him explaining that he killed himself because he is guilty of embezzlement (753 ch Jack to Burt) ** Jack, trying to save his friend, Carol, from disgrace, destroys evidence that would prove Carol's husband, Burt, an embezzler and a suicide. Jack then ransacks the office, making it appear that Burt died trying to prevent a robbery *** (1075b; 918b) (922a) (952)

(25) Trying to Save Someone Accused of a Crime or Offense

820

(898) (913) (949b)

Jack's friend, Pete, is accused of a crime * Jack, learning that his friend, Pete, is accused of a crime, tries to prove his innocence ** (790b) (906)

821

(623 ch Jack to Greg) (628 ch Jack to Greg) (718b ch Jack to Greg; 770a ch Jack to Greg)

Jack's son, Greg, is arrested for a crime * Jack tries to save Greg from trouble and finds himself in equal jeopardy ** (1290b ch Jack to Greg & Andy to Jack) (601 ch Pete to Greg)

822

(648) (737b) (792a) (876a) (1172)

Jack thinks that Carol is a criminal * Honest Jack poses as a criminal to help Carol ** (1167) (1171) (1192)

823

(918a) (955) (972)

Jack, who considers himself a failure, admires his friend, Pete * Jack's friend, Pete, is unjustly sentenced to death (715c ch Jack to Pete) (793b ch Jack to Pete & Pete to Gary). Jack, deceiving the guards, takes Pete's place and is executed ** (875a)

(27) Refusing to Betray Another's Secret and Facing Persecution as a Result

824

(644; 147) (1016a-* ch Jack to Sam & Burt to Jack)

Sam tries to get his prisoner, Jack, to inform on Carol (878c) (943b)

(26) Secretly Trying to Save Another From Danger

825

(641 ch Carol to Nina & Frank to Jack) (1285a ch Jack to Jim)

Aware that he is dying, Jack makes a will in hope of protecting his adopted daughter, Nina (1041) (1270)

826

(793b) (1228) (1323b)

Jack is imprisoned on false evidence * Carol, covertly investigating, proves Jack's innocence and gains his release from prison ** (1244b ch Jack to Gary) (1278b ch Jack to Gary, Carol to Laura & Laura to Carol)

827

(711c) (603b, c d; 1334b) (855)

Sprinter Jack is about to lose a race because he thinks he hears the voice of a dead friend, Pete, calling for help (1160) * Jack, who is superstitious, is about to be beaten in an event because he thinks he hears the voice of a dead friend, Pete, calling to him. But he wins the event when his coach Eric, brings him to his senses ** (918b) (1365)

828

(16a) (818a-**)

Working undercover, Jack attempts to prove Carol's innocence of a crime (648) (1154a) (1172) * Jack, proving Carol innocent of a crime, proves that Sally, a criminal who resembles Carol, is the guilty party ** (818a**-***) (851-*)

829

(75a; 163) (663) (793b ch Pete to Gary) (1228)
(1323b)
Jack is arrested on charges concocted by a
jealous rival, Gary * Carol, secretly investigating, proves Jack didn't commit a certain
crime ** (352b tr Jack & Carol) (1244b ch Jack
to Gary)

830

(474 ch Jack to Pete) (1021b)
Pete's friend, Jack, exposes Burt, a spiritualist who is swindling Pete out of large sums
of money * Jack, threatening Burt with arrest, forces him to return the money to Jack's
friend, Pete ** (1323c ch Jack to Burt & Eric
to Jack) (1337 ch Eric to Burt)

**(16) Being Rescued From Trouble by One
Who Confesses a Guilty Secret**

831

(1024) (1027)
Jack, sick and hungry, receives food and
money from his friend, Pete * Pete confides
to his friend, Jack, that he is a criminal **
(815a-* ch Dave to Pete) (824 ch Carol to Pete)
(1269)

832

(754) (809 ch Burt to Pete) (1085)
Jack steals money from his employer, Carl,
to help his friend, Pete, overcome a financial
crisis (753 ch Jack to Pete). Jack intends to
make up the shortage when Pete can repay
the money * Jack admits to his friend, Pete,
that he has stolen money from Carl in order
to help Pete ** (601; 631) (601; 654; 628) (730
ch Gary to Pete)

(57) Trying to Solve a Puzzling Problem

833

(1334c) (1337)
Jack examines the circumstantial evidence of
a crime, hoping to discover the criminal
(1371) (1413a) (1449)

(53) Trying to Defeat a Devious Opponent

834

(1214) (837 ch Carol to Pete)
Secretly becoming aware of elaborate plans
for a major crime, Jack risks his life in an
attempt to prevent it (865 ch Jack to Eric &
Pete to Jack) (1227a)

**(43) Trying to Overcome Personal Limitations
in Carrying Out a Venture**

835

(115) (1074) (1090) (1096) (1111a)
Jack overhears a chance conversation and acquires very valuable information * Jack happens to overhear a conversation that gives
him material for a scandalous best seller **
(281c) (749)

**(28) Facing a Situation in Which the Problems
of Someone Highly Regarded Require Courage
and Wise Planning**

836

(601-*) (671-**) (716)
Jack runs into troubles of his own when
he tries to help his friend, Pete, who has
serious problems (601*-**) (671**-***) (704)
(764) (790a, b)

837

(179a b, c) (188b-*) (230-*) (382-*) (773-*)
(851-*)
Jack tries to help Carol — with unexpected
results (45a, b) (188b-**) (230*-**) (382*-**)
(773*-**) (851*-**)

838

(220 tr Jack & Pete) (716) (793a)
In order to help his friend, Pete, Jack discards his principles and embarks on a disagreeable venture (790a, b) (807) (840)

839

(1061 ch Jack to Pete) (1062 ch Jack to Pete) (1063 ch Jack to Pete)
Jack tries to correct a character flaw in his friend, Pete * Jack tries to correct a character flaw in his friend, Pete, by relating a story that subtly suggests a method of self-help ** ([Jack's story: 1082b]; 607) ([Jack's story: 1330]; 607) ([Jack's story: 1082b]; 918a ch Jack to Pete) ([Jack's story: 1330]; 918a ch Jack to Pete) ([Jack's story: 1082b]; 922a ch Jack to Pete) ([Jack's story: 1330]; 922a ch Jack to Pete) ([Jack's story: 1082b]; 1104 ch Jack to Pete) ([Jack's story: 1330]; 1104 ch Jack to Pete)

840

(126 ch Jack to Pete) (619 ch Jack to Pete) (1314 ch Jack to Pete)
Jack tries to stop his friend, Pete, from performing a reckless act that will have deadly consequences * Jack gets his friend, Pete, drunk to prevent him from committing a reckless act that would have deadly consequences ** (779 tr Jack & Pete) (880a tr Jack and Pete)

841

(313 ch Jack to Pete; 705 ch Jack to Pete) (720 ch Jack to Pete; 705 ch Jack to Pete)
Jack learns that his friend, Pete, has committed suicide * Jack tries to spare Pete's family the pain of public disclosure of Pete's actions ** (868) (1160)

842

(a)   (847) (911) (923) (963) (1061)
Jack makes a heroic attempt to rescue a child, Lee (842b-*), but both die

(b)   (847) (911) (923) (963) (1061)
Jack rescues a child, Lee, from [1] a burning house, [2] an airplane crash, [3] a sinking boat [4] or a near-fatal fall * Jack, in performing a rescue, permanently cripples himself ** (257b) (715b)

843

(59 ch Carol to Annie) (239 ch Carol to Annie)
Carol is convinced her friend, Annie, is making a mistake * Carol, certain that her friend, Annie, is making a mistake, decides to prevent Annie's actions ** (294b ch Jack to Carol, Pete to Annie & Carol to Jack) (849 ch Kate to Annie)

844

(a)   (850a, b) (1083)
Married Carol, attractive, clever and influential, finds amusement in helping her friend, Jack (17a, b) (257a)

(b)   (256) (324)
Carol's friend, Annie, tries to save Carol's fiance, Jack, from the clutches of a designing woman, Laura, and return him to Carol * Carol's friend, Annie, tries to save Carol's lover, Jack, from a designing woman, Laura, by convincing him that Laura is unprincipled ** (243 ch Annie to Laura) (24a, b ch Carol to Annie)

(30) Selflessly Aiding a Needy Person

845

(755 ch Jack to Pete; 922b ch Jack to Pete) (926)
Impoverished Jack, at great sacrifice, helps Pete, who is poorer than Jack * Jack restores Pete to friends and fortune ** (876a ch Carol to Pete; 850b ch Carol to Jack & Jack to Pete; 880b tr Jack & Pete; 601)

846

(710 ch Jack to Pete) (1145 ch Jack to Pete; 1161 ch Dave to Pete)
Jack's friend, Pete, collapses, exhausted, while engaged in a project * Jack completes a project for Pete, his friend, that Pete was unable to finish ** (662) (1058)

847

(911) (914)
Jack, a tough lumberman in a rough lumber camp, finds himself in charge of an abandoned baby, Lee (842a, b)

848

(a) (74b) (928a) (970)
Jack tries to help distressed Carol, and runs into disastrous complications (772 ch Dave to Carol) (773) (792a)

(b) (974) (1118)
Jack rescues Carol from an attack by a rattlesnake * Carol, attacked by a deadly snake, suffers delirium ** (505-*) (740 ch Carol to Vicki & Rita to Carol) (872) (1445)

849

(173) (1343 ch Jack to Carol)
Carol runs a booth at a charity bazaar, and tries to stop Kate from buying a certain object, X, that Kate wants very badly (1245) (839 ch Jack to Carol & Pete to Kate)

850

(a) (85a, b) (114) (115) (718b) (812a-* ch Dave to Jack)
Carol sees great promise in uncomplicated, naive Jack and tries to inspire him toward high ambitions (801 tr Jack & Carol) (814) (844a)

(b) (818b-*) (1075a) (1126) (1329)
Carol tries to save Jack from a wasted lifestyle * Carol rescues Jack from a life of dissipation and despair and employs him ** (818b*-**) (1075b)

(21) Landing in Trouble Through Mistaken Judgment

851

(87) (176b) (232) (375) (600)
Jack rescues Carol from imminent danger, but only by placing himself in equal jeopardy * Jack is unable to escape from the danger from which he rescues Carol ** Jack rescues Carol from [1] a ferocious animal, [2] a burning ship, [3] a murderous riptide, [4] an earthquake, [5] an automobile accident, or [6] a plummeting elevator (31) (367b) (500a) (885a)

852

(1366) (1428-*) (1433a, b, c)
Jack dreams he's in danger, but is convinced the danger is real (1428*-**) (1358) (1375)

853

(1374-*) (1377b) (1389b) (1418b-*)
Average Jack has a weird experience (1342a) (1082b) * Average Jack has an experience that convinces him that he possesses incredible powers ** (1418b*-**) (1374*-**) (1060) (1134) (1330)

854

(1346 ch Jack to Carl; 596 ch Burt to Carl) (1303) (1290a ch Jack to Carl; 596 ch Burt to Carl)
Jack discovers a deadly secret about his rich, powerful employer, Carl * Jack, because he knows Carl's secret, is harassed, spied upon and ultimately imprisoned on false charges ** (884a ch Burt to Carl) (887a ch Gary to Carl)

855

(661) (681a) (1347) (1391)
Jack fights an hallucinatory enemy, Walt, whose weapon is superstition (732) (1348a) (1375)

856

(690) (693) (1419b)
Jack, caught in a trap that makes him physically powerless but leaves his mind alert, attempts to break free (682) (1419a)

857

(858) (862) (1061) (1078) (1110)
Jack tries to rid himself of a fear that haunts every aspect of his life, and plunges him into serious problems (951) (1104) (1350) (1374) (1375)

858

(558 tr Jack & Gary) (1061)
Jack is tortured by the fear of death * Jack wants to overcome his fear ** (439 tr Jack & Gary) (1082a) (1104)

859

(249) (385a) (623) (786)
Jack, wrongly accused of a crime, tries to clear himself (828 tr Jack & Carol & ch Sally to Burt) (829) (1291a ch Jack to Burt) (1447)

860

(601) (606) (656)
Impoverished Jack tries to recoup his fortunes by marrying a wealthy woman (230) (378) (422b)

861

(718a) (332 tr Carol & Jack)
Alien Jack rescues Carol from an accident * When Jack rescues Carol, due to mistaken judgment he becomes the victim of an unwelcome complication ** (31) (282b)

862

(288) (937) (1064) (1075a)
Jack is afraid he will commit a crime * Fearing that he will commit a crime, Jack tries to overcome the fear, and the possibility of doing evil ** (963) (1075b)

(50) Compelled by a Special Motive to Behave Underhandedly

863

(a) (618) (726a) (954) (1071) (1094)
Jack's popularity becomes a burden to him * Jack wants total seclusion — to be isolated from all methods of communication ** (690) (719b) (897)

(b) (768) (965)
Jack tries to improve his social standing * Jack invites a celebrity, Dave, to be guest of honor at a reception in his home, and Dave accepts ** (702) (1164)

(c) (461) (606)
Owner of a summer resort hotel, Jack, faces ruin due to lack of business * Jack, a hotel owner facing ruin, invites a celebrity, Dave, to stay at his hotel and Dave accepts ** (1161 ch Jack to Eric) (1162 ch Burt to Dave)

864

(611a) (770a) (952)
Now rich and respected, Jack is haunted by a crime he committed in his youth * Jack returns incognito to his home town where he committed a youthful crime, and attempts to carry out a venture: [1] discover whether his youthful escapades have been forgotten and forgiven; [2] discover whether the person he victimized has suffered any lasting injury; and/or [3] to make anonymous restitution for the wrong that he committed. ** (708) (1199)

865

(216) (314-*) (619)
About to commit a foolish act, Jack is abducted and held prisoner by his friend, Pete, as the only means of restraining him (314*-**) (880a) (867 tr Jack & Pete)

866

(92) (637)
Jack is arrested by Sam * Jack's captor, law officer Sam, is killed in an accident. Sam's body is identified as that of Jack; as a result, Jack is set free ** (707) (717)

867

(807) (865 tr Jack & Pete) (808a ch Carol to Pete) (709) (1319a) (1214)
Jack, suspected of treachery by his friend, Pete, heroically saves Pete's life and property. Jack's heroism in the face of danger to which Pete was unknowingly exposed, proves Jack's loyalty (1227a) (839)

868

(601 ch Jack to Pete & Pete to Eric; 705 ch Jack to Pete) (838)
Jack destroys a suicide note written by his friend, Pete, and instead makes it appear that Pete is the victim of a crime (906) (944)

869

(949a) (955)
Fugitive Jack stops Carol from committing suicide (641; 743a) (647; 743a)

870

(a) (62) (134a) (220) (415) (447)
Carol, tortured by malicious gossip, attempts to clear her name (83) (86) (870b) (1151)

(b) (669) (784) (817 ch Jack to Sam) (818a ch Jack to Sam)
Carol, her integrity seriously questioned, is befriended by Sam, a detective * Sam proves that Carol's enemy, Burt, is a criminal, and brings him to justice **

871

(313) (676)
Carol's father, Frank, forces Carol to take an action that she knows will destroy her happiness * Carol, forced by her father, Frank, to take an action she knows will destroy her happiness, imaginatively avoids disaster ** (1241b) (1244b)

872

(740) (1334a ch Jack to Carol) (1342a ch Jack to Carol)
Carol is afraid she is going insane * Carol, afraid she is going insane, tries to break free of her demoralizing fear ** (1067) (1069) (1445)

873

(227) (305) (1458)
Carol discovers an evil secret in her past * Discovering an evil secret in her past, Carol contemplates suicide ** (802a) (870b) (893) (1051) (1055)

(15) Finding the Power to Overcome Problems

874

(430) (606) (680a)
Jack is deeply in debt and facing bankruptcy * Jack tries to get out of debt by undertaking an ultra-secret but honest venture (1394) (1399) (1408) that will earn enough money to pay off his creditors ** (540) (770a)

875

(a) (823-*) (824 ch Jack to Pete) (731 ch Jack to Pete)
Visiting Pete in prison, Jack swaps clothes with him and Pete leaves posing as Jack (823*-**) (1344 tr Jack & Pete)

(b) (233) (660a) (662) (664) (719a) (179b tr Jack & Carol)
Jack is rescued by Carol * Carol uses Jack's prize show dog in tracking Jack ** (367b) (850a)

876

(a) (3a) (949b; 801)
Jack spots a police officer, Sam, watching Carol, who is about to commit a theft (724 ch Jack to Carol) * Jack manages to warn Carol of the danger from Sam ** (69) (359)

(b) (85b) (97) (134b)
Jack and Carol find themselves imprisoned in an underwater research vessel * Jack and Carol, trapped in a submersible, desperately search for a method of escape (170). Jack squeezes himself into the damaged airlock, blasts himself to the surface, gets help and rescues Carol ** (140) (360a)

877

(895 ch Jack to Pete) (1070 ch Jack to Pete)
Sheriff Jack is duty-bound to hang a condemned friend, Pete * Sheriff Jack is convinced the man he is about to hang, Pete, didn't commit the crime for which he was sentenced ** Sheriff Jack delays hanging a condemned man, Pete, hoping that something or someone will intervene and save Pete *** (535 ch Jack to Eric & Gary to Pete) (826 ch Jack to Pete)

878

(a) (691) (687)
Amateur ventriloquist Jack is taken captive by a primitive tribe and is about to be executed * Amateur ventriloquist Jack, about to be executed, makes a water buffalo appear to talk — and is set free and elevated to a god ** (714) (714; 197)

(b) (692) (719b)
Adrift at sea in a small boat, Jack is near death from exposure when he lands on an uncharted coast (686) (690)

(c) (244) (331) (714)
Prisoner Jack, bound, helpless and facing death, is daringly rescued by resourceful Carol (347a) (901)

879

(188b ch Carol to Jack & Jack to Dave) (705)
Jack is prevented from committing suicide by Dave, who as fate would have it has come to the same place for the same reason (840 ch Pete to Dave) (850a ch Carol to Dave) (865 ch Pete to Dave)

880

(a) (216) (314) (840 tr Jack & Pete) (865)
Executive Jack's career is saved when his junior associate, Pete, employs deception to stop him from committing a foolhardy act * Jack, saved from a foolhardy act by Pete, comes to his senses, and rewards Pete **

(b) (805 ch Dave to Jack & Jack to Pete) (894 ch Burt to Jack & Jack to Pete)
Elderly Jack, a homeless outcast, is returned to family and self-respect by a friend, Pete (831; 1269) (1264)

881

(813) (928b-*)
Jack has sacrificed happiness because of an obligation he thinks he owes his son, Greg * Jack's son, Greg, discovers a long-hidden secret of Jack's (425), and persuades him to correct a mistake and regain lost happiness ** (928b*-**) (499a) (790b ch Pete to Greg)

882

(946 ch Carol to Jack) (914) (1239)
Jack's philanthropic venture is about to fail * Jack's philanthropic venture faces financial failure; Jack, a reformed racketeer, keeps the venture going by employing his former skills and rigging a horse race ** (665 ch Carol to Jack) (963)

883

(1209a) (1298) (955)
Jack, a hunted outlaw, hides with an enemy, Gary * Jack, a hunted outlaw, hides with an enemy, Gary; and Gary, feeling bound by the code of "honor among thieves," conceals Jack, saving him from pursuers, Sam and Faye ** (923 ch Burt to Gary) (1022)

884

(a) (136 ch Gary to Burt) (596) (660b)
Jack is bitterly harassed by a relentless enemy, Burt * Jack is bitterly harassed by a relentless enemy, Burt, who, in attempting to prevent Jack's escape — is accidentally killed ** (1344-* ch Pete to Burt) (1132)

(b) (579a) (976) (1427b) (1133)
Agnostic Jack is trapped by a devastating tropical storm * Jack is persuaded to a belief in God by Carol when her prayers enable them to escape from certain death ** (1375) (1128a-*) (922a)

885

(a) (666) (837) (879 ch Jack to Carol & Dave to Jack)
Faced with imminent danger while engaged in a venture, Carol is rescued by Jack * Jack, unable to save himself from danger incurred in rescuing Carol, is in turn saved by Carol ** (31) (191)

(b) (144) (146) (306) (483b) (737b)
Carol is trapped in an upper floor of a skyscraper * Carol, imprisoned in an upper floor of a skyscraper, saves herself by using her ingenuity (air-conditioning ducts, elevator cables, etc.) ** (31) (870a, b)

886

(676 ch Frank to Rita) (739) (741 ch Frank to Rita) (908) (996; 1105)
Carol's mother, Rita, is financially strapped and alienated from Carol * Carol's mother, Rita, unexpectedly inherits a fortune, sees Carol in a different light (or vice-versa) and they become reconciled ** (785) (1067) (1246)

(20) Getting Into a Situation From Which Difficult Problems are Likely to Result

887

(a) (677 ch Carol to Jack; 1309a ch Carol to Jack & Jack to Gary) (677 ch Carol to Jack; 568c)
Held on a murder charge, Jack is released on an unusual plea made by his attorney, Matt * Jack, held on a murder charge, is freed when his attorney, Matt, proves that Jack, under heavy medication, believed his victim, Gary, was trying to kill him ** (870a ch Carol to Jack) (695a)

887

(b) (682; 880b) (937)
Jack, who has "gone native," is rescued from a difficult situation by an old friend, Pete * Jack, having "gone native," returns to a way of life now alien to him ** (1093) (1132) (1291b; 1195) (1291b) (1345)

888

(1418a; 1427a) (1436; 1427a) (1441a; 1427a) (1426b-*)
Jack has a strange experience among a group which has been brainwashed * Jack has a strange experience among a brainwashed group, and finds the key to the brainwashing in a notebook belonging to Eric, one of the perpetrators. Using information obtained from the notebook, Jack rescues the victims ** (1366) (1368; 1061)

889

(115) (591) (633) (681a) (708) (1082b)
Jack, once again rational, relates a strange experience which his friends find impossible to believe (888) (1411) (1418a; 1422a)

890

(87; 1100) (470) (1154a) (1172)
While engaged in a clandestine venture, Carol finds herself in danger and asks a stranger, Dave, to help her (1025) (1417)

891

(32; 35 ch Jack to Gary) (765)
Carol's escort, Gary, gets into a fight with another man, Jack * Carol saves Jack from a weapon wielded by his enemy, Gary ** (31 tr Jack & Carol) (94a)

892

(220) (218a) (340) (946)
Carol dies of injuries sustained while rescuing Laura from an accident (53) (405 tr Carol & Laura)

893

(27) (124) (227) (514) (594c) (665) (800 ch Doug to Lee)
Carol heroically rescues a child, Lee, from death, but sacrifices her own life in the process

(25) Trying to Save Someone Accused of a Crime or Offense

894

(613) (926) (939)
Jack, robbed by Burt and wanting to save him from the law, tells the arresting officer, Sam, that he gave Burt the stolen property (918a ch Jack to Burt) (918b ch Jack to Burt) (923 ch Jack to Burt & Burt to Eric)

895

(568d ch Gary to Jack & Jack to Burt) (667) (1070)
Carol begs Carl, the governor of a state, to pardon condemned prisoner Jack * Carol knows that Jack isn't guilty of the crime for which he was convicted ** (108)

896

(467 ch Eric to Doug) (623 ch Jack to Doug)
Carol learns that her son, Doug, is suspected of a crime * Carol knows that her son, Doug, didn't commit the crime for which he is accused; she also knows who is guilty, but this knowledge makes it dangerous and difficult to protect Doug ** (516 ch Lee to Doug) (725 ch Jack to Carol & Burt to Jack) (1291a)

(21) Landing in Trouble Through Mistaken Judgment

897

(618) (954) (1094)
Jack's popularity so intrudes on his life that he seeks total seclusion (865; 664) (689) (690) * Jack, having sought seclusion because his popularity was a burden, realizes he misses the roar of the crowd ** (682) (900)

898

(106-*) (492a)
Selfish Jack is always looking out for "Number One" * Selfish, miserly Jack discovers his ways are wrong and that he isn't happy ** (106*-**) (307) (372) (597) (632) (661) (698) (918b)

899

(99) (902)
Rich, greedy Jack is only happy when adding to his fortune * Rich, greedy Jack loses everything by penny-pinching ** (322b) (377b) (747)

900

(1330) (1350)
Jack's imagination overtakes his sense of reality. Trying to rid himself of imagined problems, Jack lands in real trouble * Jack, possessing everything he thought necessary for happiness, discovers that he is the source of his unhappiness ** (150) (634) (1348a)

901

(687; 244) (878a) (937)
"Civilized" Jack attempts to impose his values on a primitive society * Jack "goes native" and marries Carol, a member of a primitive society ** (682) (922b)

902

(675) (718b) (913) (991) (1079) (1124) (1148a, b) (1150)
Jack is obsessed with a certain pastime: [1] gambling, [2] women, [3] sports, etc. He becomes so absorbed by his pastime that major issues demanding immediate attention are neglected with disastrous results (620) (629) (753) (957b)

903

(850a) (1143b)
Jack is a dedicated artist whose ideal is Truth * Jack, hired by Carol to paint her portrait, puts more character than beauty into his work, and Carol is deeply offended ** (1143b; 1386b; 1408) (1386b)

904

(197) (244)
Morally rigid Jack is stranded in a primitive environment where he is conquered by a "natural" native girl, Carol (347a) (901)

905

(656; 927) (768)
Despite Jack's lack of funds, his pride won't permit him to discontinue the large charity donations his family has always made, thus forcing him into trouble (628) (1213)

906

(157 ch Gary to Pete) (836) (838)
Jack learns that his partner, Pete, is unable to pay his bills * Pete has heavy personal responsibilities, and Jack doesn't — so Jack disappears, leaving false evidence that he is the guilty party ** (80a ch Gary to Pete) (603b, c, d) (807) (841)

907

(918a) (22a)
Jack dies, frustrated that he has fallen short of his high goals * Jack, after a lifetime spent seeking unattainable goals, dies unaware that it was the search itself that ennobled him ** (943a) (944)

908

(65-*) (372) (585b)
Carol is a selfish, bitter woman who lives only for herself, failing to recognize that she is the source of her unhappiness (65*-**) (310) (505)

909

(649) (628 ch Jack to Tony) (977a, b)
Carol indirectly causes the death of her brother, Tony, by opposing his questionable venture * Carol dies a broken-hearted victim of her own rigid ideals **

(31) Leading a Lonely, Unhappy Life and Looking for Companionship

910

(736 ch Carol to Nina) (1105 ch Carol to Nina)
Jack tries to maintain a close, fatherly relationship with his daughter, Nina * Jack is a free spirit, while his daughter, Nina, is uptight and reactionary ** (1067 ch Carol to Nina) (1151 ch Carol to Nina)

911

(698) (914) (914; 918a)
Jack looks for happiness in his love for a child, Lee, but for certain reasons he remains unfulfilled (912a) (842a, b) (922a; 923)

912

(a) (695a) (695b)
Desperately seeking companionship, Jack is thwarted by his appearance and/or personality (735 tr Jack & Eric) (762) (911) (1059)

(b) (1311) (1314)
Jack reconciles with an enemy, Gary, when Gary does him a service (815a ch Jack to Gary & Dave to Jack) (829 ch Gary to Eric & Carol to Gary)

913

(379) (457 ch Jack to Pete)
Jack has problems and looks for happiness in the companionship of Pete and/or in an avocation (157 ch Gary to Pete) (603b, c, d) (807) (820) (981) (1007) (1035)

914

(817 ch Carol to Lee) (911)
Jack is a professional gambler * Jack handicaps himself by looking after an abandoned baby, Lee ** (847) (963) (1087)

915

(623) (1186) (1282)
Jack takes refuge in a foreign country to escape the consequences of a crime * Jack, a fugitive in a foreign country, is driven by homesickness to return to his native land ** (237) (635) (635; 708) (864) (1199) (1209a)

916

(60) (816b)
Carol, who lives in a lonely place, craves excitement (88) (143) (414) (694) (765) (844a)

(32) Trying to Hide Identity Because of High Ideals

917

(512) (952) (971)
Jack mysteriously disappears. He resurfaces elsewhere, using an alias * Trying to promote a venture that associates would regard as foolhardy, Jack changes his name and goes to a place where he is unknown ** (259-3) (967)

918

(a) (80a) (150) (312-1) (602)
Jack tries to rebuild his wasted, dissipated life * Jack, pursuing a worthy venture, changes his identity and goes to a place where he isn't known ** (683) (708) (864)

(b) (718b) (898)
Jack experiences a tragedy that makes him a better person (639) (686) (751) (767 ch Carol to Jack) (819) (894 ch Jack to Eric & Burt to Jack)

919

(a) (940) (949a) (960a) (1082a)
Soldier Jack disappears from his unit * Soldier Jack disappears from his unit and dies while performing a heroic act; but he is reported to have deserted under fire ** (919c) (928b ch Jack to Andy & Greg to Jack)

(b) (930 ch Carol to Nina & Frank to Jack) (734) (967)
Soldier Jack deserted under fire but was incorrectly reported missing in action * Jack, after years of concealing his cowardice, returns to his home using an alias ** (548a) (550) (684 ch Frank to Jack) (797)

(c) (615) (1061)
Soldier Jack is listed a deserter under fire * Soldier Jack, facing a large enemy force, fights overwhelming odds until he is killed ** (930 ch Frank to Jack & eliminate "whom she mistakenly thinks is dead") (928b ch Jack to Andy & Greg to Jack) (958) (963)

920

Jack, an unsuccessful composer (718a) (748) (749-*), inadvertently loses his latest composition (709 tr Jack & Pete) (711b ch Jack to Pete) which bears no signature. Jack's music, X, is found and experts hail it as a work of genius. The news media urge the unknown composer to identify himself, but Jack has certain reasons for remaining anonymous (1275) (931 ch Carol to Jack & Rita to Andy)

921

(279-*) (435a)
Carol, who once committed a serious wrong, achieves happiness by assuming a new identity and way of life which enables her to right the wrong (279*-**) (743b) (665)

(35) Encountering a Problem That Challenges One's Ideals

922

(a) (578a) (819) (894 tr Jack & Burt) (918b)
Amoral Jack undergoes an abrupt change of heart * Jack's search for a hero-figure is unsuccessful ** (963) (964a)

(b) (158) (606)
On landing in trouble, Jack compromises his high moral standards * Jack becomes a social misfit ** (259-2) (263)

923

(224) (578a)
Criminal Jack is trying to go straight * Jack, a criminal trying to go straight, is forced by a former associate, Burt, to take part in a crime ** (894) (998 ch Jack to Burt & Dave to Jack)

924

(a) (700) (1062)
Wealthy Jack wants to get rid of his money * Wealthy Jack, who wants to get rid of his money, finds it impossible ** (431) (929)

(b) (898) (899)
Wealthy Jack leads a life of idle pleasure * Wealthy Jack's contentment with his lifestyle is challenged by an incident ** (322b) (751)

925

(139; 245 ch Jack to Pete & Gary to Jack) (433b ch Jack to Pete & Gary to Jack; 411b ch Jack to Pete, Gary to Jack)
Jack is a selfish man who has no regard for others * Jack seriously wrongs his friend, Pete, but learns a valuable lesson when Pete forgives him ** (922a) (963)

926

(954) (970)
Jack's goal is to help make a better world * Jack, trying to make the world better, encounters a disturbing experience ** (188b) (613) (791) (804)

927

(926) (928a)
Generous, sociable Jack wants to invite people into his home, but certain unpleasant conditions make it difficult (613) (905)

928

(a) (764-*) (769) (772-*) (773-*) (805)
Jack, in the spirit of charity, befriends all in need * Jack is never too busy to help others and, because of it, he has an unfortunate experience ** (764*-**) (772*-**) (773*-**) (807)

(b) (800 ch Carol to Jack)
Jack is proud of his son, Greg * Jack's son, Greg, dies shamefully and ingloriously, dishonoring and saddening Jack ** (568c ch Jack to Eric & Gary to Greg) (821) (919a)

929

(431; 488a) (924a)
Believing that money corrupts, Jack changes his mind when he becomes rich and is happier than he's ever been

930

(919b-* ch Jack to Frank) (1142b ch Jack to Frank)
Carol erects a monument to her father, Frank, whom she mistakenly thinks is dead, remembering him with pride and love (684) (797 ch Jack to Frank & Nina to Carol)

931

(65-*) (83) (143) (766) (1105) (1106)
Carol is happy in her mistaken ideals * When Carol's mother, Rita, adopts Carol's values, it causes Carol to question them ** (1246)

(50) Compelled by a Special Motive to Behave Underhandedly

932

(1111a) (1074)
Writer Jack plans to expand a favorite idea into a screenplay * Misguided writer Jack plans to test the commercial potential of a story idea before writing it ** (598) (835) (1460)

933

(104) (189)
Carol decides that she will gain more by losing in a venture than by winning (356) (931)

(17) Patiently Handling Problems and Trying to Honorably Achieve Goals

934

(181b-*) (425-*)
In an attempt to save his son, Greg, from disgrace, Greg's father, Jack, sacrifices his happiness out of a sense of duty (881) (181b*-**) (425*-***) (330b ch Andy to Jack & Jack to Greg)

935

(718b) (948 ch Carol to Jack)
Penniless Jack commits to ten years of servitude in exchange for a college education (595) (756) (918b)

936

(512) (513) (1006b) (1073)
Jack dreams of a life of adventure * Jack can't achieve his dream because he is the sole support of his family ** (991) (1148a)

937

(687) (689) (690)
Jack is morally rigid * Jack, morally rigid, is stranded in a savage, isolated environment where local customs challenge his morals ** (197) (244) (682) (901) (973)

938

(941) (1122)
Expert craftsman Jack struggles to earn a living while maintaining his integrity * If he chooses, Jack could become wealthy by compromising his principles ** (943a) (944)

939

(485) (922a) (926)
Rebel Jack, by associating with criminals hopes to prove that good can come out of evil (907) (772) (1167)

940

(939) (900-*)
Wealthy, influential Jack believes that his true worth is hidden by his riches * Jack enlists as a private in the army when he could easily have become a commissioned officer ** (918b) (919a, c)

941

(171) (748)
Victim of a martyr complex, Jack plucks failure from the jaws of success (942) (943a) (922b)

942

(903) (941)
Jack is having a hard time and bad luck awaits him at every turn * Jack clings to his principles despite incessant bad luck and troubles ** (601) (632) (944)

943

(a) (700) (715b) (729)
Jack gives up his life rather than compromise his sense of duty * Jack dies rather than becoming rich by violating his principles **

(b) (824) (987) (1014) (1022)
Prisoner Jack goes to his death rather than betray his sense of loyalty (80b) (136)

944

(171) (549) (715b) (729) (938) (942)
Jack lives a life of quiet desperation, enduring every kind of trouble. Clinging to what he believes are high ideals, Jack perversely counts his problems as blessings in disguise (907)

945

(121) (244) (279-*) (162b-*) (665)
Carol is regarded as immoral, but in her own estimation, Carol believes her goals transcend surface judgment * Regarded as immoral, the sincerity of Carol's convictions disarms criticism ** (211)

946

(162b) (211) (279) (403) (557a)
Criminal (or unethical) Carol tries to live down her unsavory past by exemplary conduct (665) (669) (892)

947

(96) (745) (647) (976)
Carol fights to maintain her standards in the face of challenges (242) (645)

948

(947) (978)
Carol, whose parents, Rita and Frank, are poor and uneducated, struggles to get an education that will allow her to escape a life of squalor (745) (935 ch Jack to Carol) (993)

(34) Starting a Rebellion to Improve Untenable Conditions

949

(a) (395) (420-*) (915)
Irresponsibly grasping for happiness, Jack loses sight of his moral duty (148) (155) (420) (628)

(b) (246b-*) (322b)
Judge Jack is a humanitarian * Judge Jack, in an effort to gain insight into the lives of those brought into his courtroom, assumes a disguise and immerses himself in their world ** (833) (834) (838) (876a) (1209b)

950

(1082b) (1090) (1111b) (1131)
Jack is handicapped by knowing little of the world * Jack believes he can be happier and more successful as an attorney than as a doctor, a general than as a private, an employer than as an employee ** Jack believes he can do more good outside the clergy than as a priest *** (900) (1091) (1098) (1104)

951

(68) (255) (703) (1304) (1306)
Jack's guilty conscience stands in the way of his happiness * Jack will be ruined and disgraced if he expiates his guilt ** (1295) (1461a)

952

(465) (601; 1277b) (606; 1277b)
Jack wants to vanish and start a new life * Jack leaves his coat on a seaside cliff, drops his hat on a bush below the edge, and vanishes ** (440) (864)

953

(74a-*) (604) (651)
Jack craves peace and quiet * Jack, wanting peace and quiet, assumes a false identity and finds a distant retreat ** (664) (719a) (1409) (1423) (1225)

954

(106-*) (539a) (863a)
Jack's imagination is the source of his discontent * Discontented Jack rebels against his surroundings in an effort to find contentment ** (106*-**) (391)

955

(1298) (1300)
Bandit Jack robs the mails * Bandit Jack, opening a letter from a mail sack, gains information (738) (742) (743a) that sends him on an altruistic mission — proving there is good in the worst of us ** (817) (869)

(20) Getting Into a Situation From Which Difficult Problems are Likely to Result

956

(279) (669 ch Burt to Eric) (557a) (377a ch Jack to Eric)
Carol volunteers to nurse a sick person, Eric, when no one else will do it * Eric has a deadly, contagious disease ** Carol, nursing Eric, contracts a deadly virus and dies ***

957

(a) (898-*) (899-*)
Jack becomes so rich and powerful that he loses perspective and believes he's omnipotent (517) (565) (661)

(b) (902)
Jack is an army general * Army general Jack is so distracted by an unimportant concern, he forgets about the attacking enemy. Jack's troops are defeated ** (919b, c)

(c) (692 ch Jack to Dave) (719b ch Jack to Dave)
Jack is captain of a ship, racing against the clock across the Atlantic * Jack won't delay his important venture long enough to rescue Dave, who is in distress and could die ** (632 tr Jack & Dave)

(33) Secretly Challenging a Questionable Convention for Honorable Reasons

958

(748) (918a)
Jack believes that poverty is the true source of happiness * Jack struggles to avoid wealth ** (127b) (311) (326-3) (700) (905)

959

(861) (954) (1088)
Possessing some minority blood, Jack wants all the opportunities given the predominant race (255) (271) (579b tr Carol & Jack) (919c)

960

(a) (922a-*) (928b ch Jack to Andy & Greg to Jack)
Soldier Jack, eager to fight, is ordered to retreat before superior enemy forces * Jack receives orders from his superiors that he feels are disgraceful ** (919b) (919c; 928b ch Jack to Andy & Greg to Jack)

(b) (902)
Jack is CEO of a giant corporation * During a hostile takeover attempt, top executive Jack is so absorbed in a trivial matter that he ignores the battle and his company is destroyed ** (705) (919b, c)

961

(606) (1079)
Jack's pride rebels when poverty costs him his family estate (628) (656)

962

(740) (946)
Carol, whose beautiful garden is the source of her happiness, learns that the garden is about to be destroyed (737a) (975) (848b; 1445)

(36) Having an Experience that Greatly Changes Character

963

(322b) (715a) (763) (862) (914) (922a)
Jack trades low ideals for high ideals * Jack, trading low ideals for high ideals, vainly struggles to achieve his high ideals. But, though unable to reach his goal, he becomes a better person ** (188b) (563c)

964

(a) (839 tr Jack & Pete) (888) (898) (1418b-*)
Learning of an old prophecy, Jack unconsciously tries to become the hero of the prophecy (963) (1418b*-**)

(b) (540) (797) (1209a)
Disgraced politician Jack, after a long absence, visits his daughter, Nina, incognito * Disgraced politician Jack learns that his daughter, Nina, thinks he's dead, and that he was an honorable man. By not revealing his identity, Jack leaves Nina happy in her mistaken beliefs ** (963) (964a)

(37) Fighting to Achieve a Cherished Ideal

965

(1060) (1088) (1091)
Jack is obsessed with achieving a high honor, albeit undeserved (749) (863b) (1101) (1103)

966

(539a) (965) (1150)
Jack, a wimp, is frustrated by dreams of accomplishments unimaginably beyond his abilities * Jack, a wimp, dreams of accomplishments unimaginably beyond his abilities: [1] being the first man on Mars, [2] performing the first brain transplant, [3] becoming the ultimate sex object, etc. ** (1058) (1065) (1075a)

967

(770a) (917) (919b) (864) (797) (763) (918a)
Jack mysteriously disappeared from his home years ago * Jack, for many years mysterious missing, tries to rekindle old ties when he suddenly reappears ** (869) (923) (1199)

968

(926) (939)
Young Jack is a romantic * Romantic young Jack samples a variety of experiences in his quest for a rich, noble life ** (773) (786) (937) (74a, b) (188b)

969

(620; 962 ch Carol to Jack) (620; 974 ch Carol to Jack)
Jack, a city person, longs for the great outdoors (608) (625) (683)

970

(922a-*) (926) (927) (928a)
Jack befriends and helps needy strangers, often neglecting his own family in the process (848a) (613) (612) (707 tr Jack & Dave) (772)

971

(322b) (577) (681a) (863a) (969)
Jack believes that solitude is the greatest of human blessings * Jack, valuing solitude above all else, has a difficult time finding it ** (664) (683) (686) (690)

972

(922b; 820) (922b; 859 ch Jack to Pete) (922b; 824 ch Carol to Pete)
Jack is a loser, while his friend, Pete, is a straight-arrow * Jack is determined, at any cost, to save his friend, Pete, from a menacing problem ** (823) (833) (836)

973

(650) (687) (689) (937)
Civilized outsider Jack fights the superstitions of a disease-ridden tribe of savages (888) (796)

974

(969 ch Jack to Carol) (921)
Reared in city poverty and hoping to find happiness in the great outdoors, Carol ends up living in a drab, bleak countryside (31) (31; 763) (563c) (848b) (916)

975

(741) (743b) (873)
Carol is terminally ill * Terminally ill Carol, convinced she can't die happy without a final look at her home town, revisits the fondly-remembered haunts of her childhood ** (893) (945)

976

(145) (268) (325) (372) (565)
TV evangelist Carol is determined to convince the world that it desperately needs her brand of religion and virtue, and tries to set an example with her lifestyle (242) (737b) (796 ch Jack to Carol & Gary to Laura)

977

(a) (992 ch Frank to Rita)
Carol is determined to protect her family's honor, but in so doing, her life is narrowly confined to duty (668) (649) (993)

(b) (977a) (976)
Carol's brother, Tony, is guilty of a crime * Carol, learning of the crime committed by her brother, Tony, tells the police and Tony is arrested ** (730 ch Jack to Tony) (909)

978

(668) (670) (948)
Carol's mother, Rita, is determined to give Carol a good education * Carol and her mother, Rita, are penniless, and Carol has to work to support them ** (647) (659) (935 ch Jack to Carol)

(21) Landing in Trouble Through Mistaken Judgment

979

(747; 606) (769) (898)
Jack innocently causes several people to invest money in a worthless venture * Having innocently caused several people to lose money in a venture, Jack cannot rest until he has recovered it for them ** (610) (635) (1148b)

980

(1382a ch Jack to Dave; 985) (718b)
Jack, by undertaking an obligation, is threatened by problems * Jack deviously shifts a dangerous obligation to a stranger, Eric ** (608 ch Jack to Eric) (623 ch Jack to Eric) (709 ch Jack to Eric & Pete to Jack) (1161 ch Jack to Eric)

981

(830 tr Jack & Pete) (865)
In return for a service Pete has performed for him, Jack agrees to grant any favor Pete wants that is within Jack's power (601) (836) (838)

982

(a) (611a ch Jack to Jim) (999 tr Jack & Pete)
Jack agrees to take charge of an incorrigible youth, Jim, who is too much of a hard-case for his uncle/guardian, Jack's friend, Pete (658) (701 ch Pete to Jim) (812b ch Jack to Jim & Frank to Jack)

(b) (193-*) (926)
Bachelor Jack agrees to care for Lee, the child of his married sister, Susan, while she's away on vacation (609) (193*-**) (639 ch Jack to Lee)

983

(433b ch Jack to Eric & Gary to Jack) (1251-*)
In order to control Eric, Jack deviously maneuvers him into heavy debt * Jack hopes to get Eric to help him in a venture by offering to pay off his debts ** (313 ch Frank to Eric, Jack to Pete & Gary to Jack) (380 ch Jack to Eric & Gary to Jack) (1251*-**)

984

(1001b-*)
After Carol dies, Jack honorably fulfills a distasteful obligation (1001b*-**) (1019) (1044a) (1001b-*; 1041 ch Jack to Milt)

985

(793b-* ch Pete to Dave) (805) (809 ch Burt to Dave)
Problems threaten Jack because of a mysterious package (1382b-* ch Jack to Dave), that Jack has obligingly taken from Dave, a stranger, and promised to deliver (608) (1438b) (793b*-**)

986

(16a) (1258) (1293a) (1293b) (1309b) (403 ch Jack to Eric; 468 ch Jack to Eric)
Detective Jack returns criminal Carol to the locale of her crime for trial * Criminal Carol, who has changed and become an honest woman, is tried by a jury who then set her free ** (363a) (359)

(38) Making a Serious Mistake and Secretly Trying to Live Down its Consequences

987

(1319a) (1214)
Influenced by compelling responsibility, Jack has to protect his friend, Pete, from danger * Jack indirectly endangers his friend — danger that Pete is unaware of and that Jack can't reveal ** (867) (1227a)

988

(1023) (1027)
Jack's friend, Pete, fathered Carol; and when Pete died, Jack promised to care for Carol as if she were his own child * Guardian Jack is disloyal to his ward, Carol ** (1211) (1285b)

(39) Giving Up Deeply Held Ambitions to Fulfill an Obligation

989

(697a) (990) (991) (996 ch Carol to Jack & Rita to Linda)
Jack's pledge to his mother, Linda, prevents him from pursuing a cherished venture (936) (1097a)

990

(258) (697a)
Jack's family sacrificed so that he could attain a college education * Jack feels duty-bound to work at a career he dislikes so that he can repay his family for their sacrifices ** (991) (1130) (1434)

991

(513) (990)
Unable to achieve his ambition because of family obligations, Jack comes as close as he can to realizing it * Unable to live an adventurous life, Jack seeks vicarious thrills ** (1433b; 719b; 878b; 650; 714; 197; 957a) (1433b; 1082b; 24a; 181c; 1363) (433b; 109)

992

(268-*) (976)
Carol makes a great personal sacrifice in fulfilling an obligation to live with and care for her father (368a) (641) (993)

993

(601 ch Jack to Frank; 705 ch Jack to Frank)
(606 ch Jack to Frank; 705 ch Jack to Frank)
Carol's father, Frank, dies heavily in debt * Frank's only child, Carol, considers herself honor bound to pay the debts of her dead father. She undertakes a strange venture in order to fulfill the obligation ** (88) (1032)

994

(574b ch Jack to Doug & Carol to Irene & Linda to Carol) (1009a)
Widow Carol is happy being independent * Widow Carol is forced by family obligations to live with a married son, Doug ** (543 ch Carol to Irene & Jack to Doug & Linda to Carol) (800) (1067)

995

(747 ch Jack to Frank; 705 ch Jack to Frank)
(770a ch Jack to Frank; 634 ch Jack to Frank)
Carol works for years on a lonely project * Carol spends years on a lonely project in order to clear her father, Frank, of dishonor ** (828 ch Jack to Carol, Carol to Frank & Sally to Burt) (993)

996

(285 ch Frank to Rita) (948)
Carol's mother, Rita, lives a life of self-denial in fulfilling her commitment to educate Carol (659) (670) (785) (1151 ch Carol to Rita & Vicki to Carol)

(20) Getting into a Situation From Which Difficult Problems are Likely to Result

997

(a)   (830 tr Jack & Pete) (865)
Jack gives his sacred oath to his friend, Pete, that he will do whatever Pete asks of him (139) (820) (846) (906) (1003) (1007)

(b)   (925-* ch Jack to Milt) (926) (958) (700)
Jack has $500,000. Jack's rich uncle Milt leaves a million dollars to Jack, provided Jack spends his half-million within a year * Jack, with a half-million dollars, must spend it all within a year, and he mustn't give any of it away or spend it foolishly ** (431) (865)

CONFLICT SITUATIONS

998

(613 ch Burt to Dave) (1277a ch Jack to Dave)
Jack discovers a crime Dave wants to hide *
Jack, aware of a crime Dave wants to hide,
threatens to tell the police unless Dave does
what Jack wants ** (923 ch Jack to Dave &
Burt to Jack) (1232 ch Jack to Dave & Gary
to Jack) (1267a ch Jack to Dave)

999

(611a ch Jack to Jim) (1024 ch Jack to Jim)
Jack is unable to control his recklessly wild
nephew and ward, Jim * Jack sends his unmanageable nephew and ward, Jim, to Pete,
his friend out West, who promises to tame
Jim no matter what it takes ** (793a tr Jack
& Pete) (982a tr Jack & Pete)

**(41) Finding an Obligation at Odds With Ambition,
Inclination or Necessity**

1000

(905) (925-*)
Jack is the heir of a proud old family whose
greatest pride has been to keep its holdings
intact * Desperately needy Jack ignores a family obligation ** (1260a tr Jack & Eric) (1291c)

1001

(a) (127a) (1123) (1127)
In order to become rich, Jack must perform
a distasteful task (1201) (1290b)

(b) (117 ch Andy to Milt) (1432 ch Jack to
Milt & Jim to Jack)
Jack will inherit a fortune from his uncle,
Milt, but only if Jack permits his life to be
controlled from the grave * Carol, who disliked Milt, who has left a fortune to Jack,
convinces Jack to violate certain conditions
of Milt's bequest ** (984) (116 ch Carol to
Irene)

1002

(106-*) (988-*)
Jack professes to hate women * Against his
wishes, Jack becomes guardian of a beautiful young woman, Carol ** (140) (106*-**)
(988*-**)

1003

(818a-**) (983 tr Jack & Eric) (997a)
Jack is obligated to commit a crime * Obligated to commit a crime, Jack isn't a criminal at heart and can't meet his obligation **
(818a**-***) (1014)

1004

(249) (263) (1194-*) (1248)
Jack, a young medical student who moonlights as a jewel thief, is in the midst of a
burglary when he is suddenly summoned to
minister to a sick man, Eric (1194*-**) (1196)
(1221)

1005

(913 ch Pete to Tom) (137a ch Gary to Tom)
(1021b ch Pete to Tom)
Jack and Tom are twin brothers with identical likes and dislikes * Brothers Jack and Tom
honor a distasteful obligation by living apart
** (157 ch Gary to Tom) (446a, b ch Pete to
Tom)

1006

(a) (446b ch Pete to Burt; 1291a ch Jack to
Burt) (1290b ch Jack to Burt)
Attorney Jack honors the distasteful duty of
defending a criminal, Burt (828 ch Carol to
Jack & Burt to Eric) (1311 ch Gary to Burt)

(b) (287) (334a) (756) (936)
In order to fulfill an obligation, Jack gives
up his chosen profession for another line of
work (900) (942) (950)

1007

(132) (607) (997a)
Jack honors the heart-breaking obligation of
performing euthanasia on his suffering, terminally ill friend, Pete * Pete begs Jack to be
merciful and kill him ** Pete is the brother
of Carol, whom Jack loves dearly *** (296 ch
Gary to Pete) (315)

CONFLICT SITUATIONS

1008

(775) (1212c) (775 ch Jack to Carl & Matt to Jack)

Jack, trusted servant in Carl's house, is really a criminal * Jack uses his trusted position in Carl's house as a cover to steal jewels belonging to Carl's wife, Carol ** (610) (614) (1209a)

1009

(a) (908) (574b ch Jack to Doug, Linda to Carol & Carol to Irene)

Widow Carol wants to be independent and have her own home; but there are certain obligations blocking her goal (384 ch Carol to Irene & Linda to Carol) (933) (1009b)

(b) (531 ch Carol to Irene & Linda to Carol & Jack to Doug) (994) (1009a)

Widow Carol has given all her assets to her son, Doug * Penniless Carol is forced to live with her son, Doug ** (543 ch Carol to Irene, Linda to Carol & Jack to Doug) (738)

1010

(152b) (666)

Thieves Burt, Sally and Fred order Carol to open a safe belonging to Jack. Carol refuses, despite threats that they'll kill her (144) (1309a ch Jack to Burt)

(40) Starting a Venture in Which One Obligation Conflicts With Another

1011

(723) (712 ch Jack to Burt & Sam to Jack)

Law officer Jack owes a personal obligation to a criminal, Burt * Law officer Jack is forced by duty to arrest a criminal, Burt, to whom he owes an obligation ** (1016a) (1284)

1012

(276 ch Jack to Terry & Andy to Jack) (288 ch Jack to Terry and "an ancestor" to Jack)

Jack's penniless grandchild, Terry, buys Jack a birthday gift, X, on credit * Birthday gift X won't be delivered until it is paid for ** Jack pays for a birthday gift, X, that his penniless grandchild, Terry, is giving him *** (118 ch Jack to Terry & Bill to Jack) (628 ch Jack to Terry & Carol to Jack)

1013

(722 ch Jack to Sam & Burt to Jack)

Jack, a fugitive in the desert, learns that a law officer, Sam, who is pursuing him, is sunblind and dying from thirst * Fugitive Jack will be arrested if he rescues Sam, the lawman pursuing him; and if Jack abandons Sam, the lawman will die ** (712) (817 ch Carol to Sam)

1014

(171 ch Gary to Burt) (959)

Jack, a payroll clerk responsible for his company's funds, is ordered by Burt (1079 ch Jack to Burt), a junior partner, to secretly give him a large amount of the company's money (730 ch Gary to Burt) (884a) (1003)

1015

(1174 ch Jack to Burt & Pete to Jack) (1175a ch Jack to Burt)

Jack is a United States consul in a third-world country * Jack lives in an area of a small third-world nation in which there are two other Americans, Pete and Burt, both friends of Jack ** Law officer Sam asks Jack to help him arrest Burt *** (1175b ch Jack to Burt) (1174 ch Jack to Burt; 1222a ch Jack to Sam & Gary to Burt) (1282 ch Jack to Burt)

CONFLICT SITUATIONS

1016

(a) (817 ch Jack to Burt & Carol to Jack; 1011) (1013 ch Jack to Burt & Sam to Jack; 1011)
Policeman Jack captures a criminal, Burt * Policeman Jack is duty-bound to arrest Burt, but he owes a personal obligation to help Burt escape ** Jack breaks a deadlock by killing himself ***

(b) (972 tr Jack & Pete) (1021b)
Army officer Jack has a friend, Pete, who is an enemy spy. Pete is brought before Jack for punishment * Jack's friend, Pete, rescues Jack from a gut-wrenching situation by taking his own life **

1017

(712 ch Jack to Burt & Sam to Jack) (816a ch Jack to Burt & Dave to Jack)
Law officer Jack and his prisoner, Burt, are lost in the desert, afoot, without food nor enough water for the two of them * Law officer Jack is old, and his prisoner, Burt, is young and there are extenuating circumstances in his case (1309b ch Carol to Burt) (1291b ch Jack to Burt) (747 ch Jack to Burt) ** Jack and Burt, lawman and prisoner, are lost in the desert with little water. They draw lots to see who will take the water and escape death. Jack deliberately loses the drawing so that Burt can win. Burt takes the water canteen and abandons Jack to die *** (713 ch Jack to Burt) (918b ch Jack to Burt)

(42) Landing in Trouble While Trying to Fulfill an Obligation

1018

(606 ch Jack to Andy; 705 ch Jack to Andy) (606 ch Jack to Andy; 638 ch Jack to Andy)
Andy's son, Jack, feels duty-bound to sell his property to help pay his dead father's debts (268 tr Carol & Jack) (943a) (944)

1019

(791) (1434)
Jack is anonymously threatened with violence if he tries to fulfill an obligation * Jack, anonymously threatened with violence if he fulfills an obligation, boldly goes ahead with what he feels is his duty ** (1287) (1351) (1414a) (1422a) (1424a) (1427a)

1020

(70) (445b) (1075a, b) (1125b)
Jack, vowing to die if Carol dies, learns that Carol has killed herself (576b) (802b)

1021

(a) (769) (836) (265b-*; 836)
Jack, as a favor to his friend, Pete, promises to embark on a certain venture * Jack promises his friend, Pete, that he'll undertake a certain venture, then reneges on his promise ** (603a tr Jack & Pete) (807) (744 ch Carol to Pete)

(b) (716) (782 ch Eric to Pete)
Jack and Pete are devoted friends * Jack and Pete's perfect friendship is challenged by an unusual experience ** (1016b) (1021a)

1022

(136-*) (883)
Jack's life is saved by his enemy, Gary * Jack's life is saved by his enemy, Gary; as a result, Jack agrees to do Gary's bidding ** (136*-**) (280a; 136*-**)

(21) Landing in Trouble Through Mistaken Judgment

1023

(113) (461) (606)
Jack desperately needs money * Jack, desperately needing money, does something rash and gets involved in an unpleasant complication ** (637) (753) (860) (1290a) (1373)

1024

(718b) (1297)
Youthful Jack was once rich, but a wild, reckless life has made him penniless * Jack finds it difficult to regain wealth ** (628) (1084) (1101) (1144) (1386a)

1025

(470) (890) (1033) (1100) (1154a) (1172)
Carol engages in a secret venture that endangers her * Carol, engaged in a secret venture and becoming endangered, asks for aid from a stranger, Dave; but Dave warily refuses ** (933) (1309a) (1417)

(20) Getting Into a Situation From Which Difficult Problems are Likely to Result

1026

(622 ch Jack to Andy & Greg to Jack) (1024) Jack is a disinherited son who desperately needs money * Jack tries to borrow money from Eric, a money-lender, on the chance that Jack will inherit the estate of his rich father, Andy ** (1217b) (1226 ch Jack to Eric & Burt to Jack)

1027

(770a) (1023)
Desperately needing money, Jack lets the devil tempt him into an unwise bargain (637) (1341) (1354a) (1373)

1028

(113) (114)
Out-of-work Jack performs a service for young millionaire, Carl * For his services, Jack is given the cast-off clothes of young millionaire, Carl, and discovers something of great value in a pocket ** (1146 ch Jack to Carl) (1163a ch Jack to Carl & Dave to Jack) (1168 ch Pete to Carl)

1029

(522) (523) (620) (656) (1257)
Capable Jack is almost bankrupt. While under pressure to recoup his fortune, he unexpectedly encounters additional difficulties (1217a) (1236) (1254) (1256)

1030

(608) (623)
Innocent Jack is held by the police on a groundless charge * Jack, held by the police, must be freed immediately in order to perform a certain task, but is unable to gain his release ** (73) (130) (174)

1031

(926) (1248)
Doctor Jack, while on an evening walk, is hurriedly summoned to attend a sick person. The experience turns into a nightmare for the doctor (1194) (1447)

1032

(745) (993)
Carol looks for work in a profession dominated by men, and is discriminated against * Carol, in order to carry out a venture, employs deception ** (1207) (1454)

1033

(532a) (659) (739)
Desperately needing money, Carol engages in an impulsive venture (368b) (1159) (1293a)

(21) Landing in Trouble Through Mistaken Judgment

1034

(957c ch Jack to Eric) (1107a ch Jack to Eric) Computer programmer Jack tests his new software * Computer hacker Jack inadvertently logs onto an international air-control grid, and creates worldwide chaos by grounding all commercial flights ** (1052b ch Jack to Eric) (1116 ch Jack to Eric)

1035

(139) (1021b) (1234 tr Jack & Pete) Thinking he is confronting a thief, Jack mistakenly shoots his friend, Pete (794) (786 ch Jack to Pete)

(20) Getting Into a Situation From Which Difficult Problems are Likely to Result

1036

(702 ch Jack to Eric) (1187) Jack is an ordinary man with average abilities * Ordinary Jack is mistaken for a celebrity, Dave ** (1161) (1173)

1037

(1146) (1164 ch Jack to Carl, Dave to Eric & Eric to Jack) (1224) Jack is impersonating Eric when he meets Eric in person (998 ch Dave to Eric) (1232 ch Gary to Eric)

1038

(1170) (1177) Wealthy and influential Jack, an executive, has the same name as ordinary, unimportant Eric, who lives in the same area (1146 ch Jack to Eric) (1448 ch Jack to Eric, Burt to Jack & Eric to Dave)

1039

(1314) (1316) Jack is trying to kill his enemy, Gary * Jack, trying to kill Gary, mistakes Dave for Gary because Dave happens to be wearing clothing identical to Gary's ** (1035 ch Pete to Dave) (1311 ch Gary to Dave)

1040

(130) (174) (599 tr Jack & Pete) Jack is enroute to an important meeting * Jack is injured in an accident and taken unconscious to a hospital ** (500a) (681b) (711b)

1041

(118 ch Jack to Eric & Bill to Jack) (825) (389-***) (899) (1433a) Jack is on his way to sign a new will disposing of his estate, but is killed in an accident (389***-*****) (1432)

1042

(a) (619) (1195) Jack carelessly leaves a door unlocked while involved in a task requiring secrecy * Jack, engaged in a secret task, is interrupted and his secret discovered ** (879) (1448 tr Jack & Burt)

(b) (153) (63 tr Jack & Carol) Married Jack has a merchant, Carl, send to his friend, Pete, monogrammed silk boxer shorts, and to Carol (976) an expensive charm bracelet * Jack's gifts to Pete and Carol are mis-delivered by Carl with calamitous results ** (321a) (635 ch Burt to Carl)

1043

(601) (606) (652a) Jack sells an almost valueless gold mine to Eric at a bargain price. Eric delays paying Jack, who in turn delays giving Eric the deed * Jack's gold mine, seemingly of little value, becomes a bonanza because of a lucky strike ** (1255b) (1255b; 1040) (1255b; 1040 ch Jack to Eric)

CONFLICT SITUATIONS

1044

(a) (513) (923) (1167) (1177) (1186)
As Jack gets off a plane, he mistakenly takes a suitcase belonging to a stranger, Dave, leaving his own bag in its place * Dave, a stranger, has Jack's suitcase. Dave meets with an accident and is killed. Because of items in the suitcase, Jack is reported dead ** (550) (608) (917)

(b) (370 ch Jack to Pete) (378 ch Jack to Pete)
Jack mistakenly takes an object, X-1, belonging to his friend, Pete. In its place Jack leaves a similar object, X-2. Close inspection is needed to differentiate X-1 and X-2 (390) (390-**; 594c ch Jack to Pete)

045

(1444; 1364a) (1444; 1384)
Jack, half-asleep, happens to overhear a conversation concerning a crime. But he can't decide if he heard a real conversation, or was dreaming (828) (1453)

1046

(677 ch Carol to Jack) (664 ch Jack to Dave) (1389b)
Jack walks along a city street late at night * Walking along a city street, an object, X, suddenly drops at Jack's feet from an upper window of a building ** (1364a ch Carol to Jack) (1369) (1394) (1400) (1425) (1435)

047

(666 ch Jack to Eric) (848a)
Blind man Jack makes his way along a city street * Blind man Jack responds to a cry for help, and blunders into a group of thieves, Burt, Sally and Fred, who are committing a robbery ** (27) (801) (1220b ch Jack to Burt) (1128a) (1253 ch Gary to Burt)

1048

(1304) (1296) (1298)
Years after stealing money from Pete, Jack by chance spends the night with Pete and his wife, Carol * Carol and her husband, Pete, happen to run into Jack and discover that Jack possesses a certain item of great value ** (1279b) (1291b) (1325) (1309a)

1049

(675) (747-*) (815a-*)
Whenever Jack has to make a decision, he decides by flipping a coin. He has done this all his life, and is invariably successful. But then, one day, he makes the wrong call (747*-**) (815a*-**) (836) (837) (848a)

1050

(3a) (524a)
Jack is shocked when, by chance, he finds stolen goods in Carol's possession (69) (566b) (623 ch Jack to Carol)

(15) Finding the Power to Overcome Problems

1051

(245) (364a,c-*) (697b) (1089)
Jack, by chance, encounters elderly nurse, Donna, who reveals a startling secret about his birth and parentage (364a,c*-**) (368b)

1052

(a) (1369 ch Dave to Eric) (1371) (1437)
Jack, by chance, meets Eric who drunkenly reveals an important secret * Jack gains a piece of information from Eric that can prove of great value — whether it was a man or his wife who died first in an accident ** (845 ch Pete to Eric) (1451b)

(b) (692) (719b) (1367b)
Jack is injured while on a dangerous expedition and is abandoned by expedition leader Carl, who refuses to sacrifice the group's safety by rescuing Jack * Badly injured Jack is rescued when a problem diverts an expedition led by Carl ** (1034) (1116 ch Jack to Eric)

CONFLICT SITUATIONS

1053

(622) (755) (1378 ch Jack to Greg & Andy to Jack)
Jack happens to hear a familiar name that solves a riddle of the past * Jack, happening to hear a familiar name, finds his long-lost son, Greg ** (928b) (1291a ch Jack to Greg; 1461c ch Jack to Greg & Carol to Jack; 928b)

1054

(245) (870a) (1089) (1458)
Jack solves a mystery involving his happiness * Jack solves a mystery when falling plaster reveals a hiding place containing old love letters ** (448) (1451c)

1055

(245; 1051) (245; 1054) (801; 828)
Jack and Carol find happiness when a certain assumption is proved to be false (366) (367b)

1056

(622; 674; 953) (759; 953*-**) (755) (1378)
Jack is hiding from a determined process-server, Dave * Dave, relentlessly searching for Jack, is almost convinced that Jack no longer exists ** Elusive Jack is finally trapped by Dave, who turns out to be Jack's long-missing son, Greg ***

(21) Landing in Trouble Through Mistaken Judgment

057

(a) (152a) (937-*)
Young, single Jack temporarily looks after an infant, Lee, for a female stranger, Kate * Jack, volunteering to look after an infant, Lee, for a female stranger, Kate, finds himself stuck with Lee when Kate fails to return ** (249) (914) (1229)

(b) (490b) (1224)
Jack borrows a baby, Lee, from its father, Pete (594c ch Jack to Pete) (1057a ch Jack to Pete), to help Jack succeed in an unusual venture (1218 ch Jack to Lee & Pete to Jack) (1289c)

058

(982a) (985 ch Dave to Pete)
Jack casually takes on a task to oblige his friend, Pete * Jack, taking on a task to oblige his friend, Pete, finds the task beyond his abilities ** (980) (812b ch Frank to Jack & Jack to Eric)

059

(912a) (177 ch Frank to Dave)
Simple, good-hearted Jack lacks all social graces * Jack befriends Dave, but because of his personality defects ends up alienating Dave ** (43 ch Frank to Dave) (762 ch Eric to Dave)

1060

(768) (1134-*) (1418b-*)
Jack, with average abilities, unrealistically views himself as being superior * Jack tries ambitious ventures, but loses confidence before finishing them ** (769) (1134*-**) (1187)

061

(115) (203) (436)
From early childhood, Jack has been programmed to believe that he lacks courage * Jack's belief that he lacks courage becomes a self-fulfilling prophecy ** (584b) (615) (839 tr Jack & Pete) (842a) (888) (919a)

1062

(115) (311) (1063)
Jack, happy with his life, sees no need for improvement (839 tr Jack & Pete) (1444; 1093)

1063

(311) (1131)
Jack's misguided values obstruct his advancement * Jack's concept of life is to do just enough to get by ** (595) (604) (620) (839 tr Jack & Pete)

1064

(787; 1461b) (1291b; 1291a ch Jack to Burt)
Jack mistakenly thinks he is a criminal, then learns he isn't * Jack has lived like a fugitive for so long, he is unable to accept freedom ** (952) (1075a) (1101) (1334a)

1065

(114) (235) (595)
Jack devotes ten years of service to his penurious uncle, Milt, in exchange for a promise of future security, and as a result loses his ambition and all sense of purpose * Jack's uncle, Milt, promises that Jack will inherit everything. But Milt dies bankrupt, leaving Jack with neither ability nor ambition ** (814) (839 tr Jack & Pete) (1354b) (1374)

1066

(610) (707)
Escaped prisoner Jack can't open his handcuffs. Desperate, he asks a stranger, Dave, to help him. But Dave notifies a policeman, Sam, and Jack is recaptured (866) (1309b ch Carol to Jack & Gary to Sam; 1142b)

1067

(384) (872) (908)
Carol fails to understand how her irritable disposition makes everyone around her unhappy * Carol, overhearing someone criticize her unpleasant personality, begins to face the truth about herself ** (921) (956) (976)

1068

(384) (908)
Carol realizes the consequences of her self-ishness when one of her children, Lee, dies (581) (1069 ch Nina to Lee) (1240)

1069

(378) (466a ch Lee to Vicki)
Carol, agonizing over the death (real or apparent) of her daughter, Vicki, (557b ch Carol to Vicki) (842a, b ch Lee to Vicki) (945 ch Carol to Vicki) experiences a personal revelation that alters her life (401) (410)

(29) Helping Another to Keep a Deadly Secret

1070

(371 ch Carol to Irene) (1163c)
On trial for murder, Jack could establish an alibi and prove his innocence — but only by a dishonorable act * Jack could save his own life by revealing a secret that would be ruinous to Carol ** (535 ch Jack to Eric & Gary to Jack) (877 tr Jack & Pete) (635)

(43) Trying to Overcome Personal Limitations While Carrying Out a Venture

1071

(1072) (1073) (1094) (1095)
Jack finds his workload overwhelming and cannot fulfill his responsibilities (863a) (1163a)

1072

(926) (963)
Jack's executive position makes it impossible for him to acquire certain important information (949b) (1167) (1170) (1184)

1073

(512) (991)
Jack is a successful businessman with an overwhelming desire to quit the commercial world and become a romantic adventurer * Only the fear of others' disapproval stops Jack ** (555b) (690) (917)

1074

(114) (258) (675)
Writer Jack finds that he is losing touch with his public, becoming unable to write salable material (598) (749) (835) (1103)

1075

(a) (850b) (902)
Struggling unsuccessfully against a character defect, Jack forms a platonic relationship with Carol (838 ch Jack to Carol & Pete to Jack) (850a, b) (1075b) (364d)

(b) (857) (862)
Jack's admiration for his friend, Carol, and his wish to please her, brings out the best in him (819) (844a)

1076

(837 tr Jack & Carol) (818b)
Loutish Jack is suddenly transformed into a gentleman * Transformed into a gentleman, Jack reveals the secret of his change to his friend, Carol ** (1209a) (1329)

1077

(1385) (1403, 1400) (1440 ch Jack to Pete) (1283)
Jack attempts to reclaim an object, X, pawned by his late friend, Pete * Jack loses the ticket to a pawned object, X, and the pawnbroker won't give him X without the ticket ** (1166b) (1384)

1078

(776) (857) (1111a) (1332)
Jack is obsessed with fear that he is being dogged by danger * Convinced that he's being pursued, Jack seeks peace of mind ** (888) (1350) (1351)

1079

(127a) (656)
Jack's weakness is gambling, and although he usually loses, he can't stop betting (367a) (524a) (902)

1080

(1092) (1101)
Reporter Jack, assigned to cover a certain story and finding it impossible, decides to write an imaginary interview and pass it off as the real thing (979 ch Jack to Dave) (1301 ch Jack to Dave; 1340)

1081

(1129c)
Jack finds himself unable, through normal channels, to find a man courageous enough to accept a dangerous mission * Jack uses subterfuge to locate a courageous man ** (1219) (1223a, b)

1082

(a) (115) (584b) (858)
Jack's cowardice inhibits his success * Cowardly Jack deliberately places himself in danger to develop his courage ** (918b) (1082b) (1104)

(b) (289) (1061)
Jack is trapped in a primitive society that worships a tyrannical god * Jack wants to escape from a community ruled by fear, but can't summon the courage ** (1082a) (181c)

1083

(114) (1075a)
Jack lacks initiative and the ability to succeed on his own * Jack enlists a friend, Carol, to help him in a difficult venture ** (225) (844a) (839 ch Jack to Carol & Pete to Jack) (850a) (963) (1278a)

1084

(113) (126)
Jack wants to engage in an honest venture but lacks the money to finance it * Jack, to finance an honest venture, temporarily turns to crime ** (92) (1309b ch Carol to Jack & Gary to Sam; 699a)

1085

(606 ch Jack to Pete) (639-* ch Jack to Pete)
Jack wants to save his friend, Pete, from disaster, but money is required and Jack has none (832) (1277b) (1281 tr Jack & Pete)

1086

(905) (914) (927)
Jack wants to achieve a difficult goal, but cannot finance the project (628) (1027) (1028)

1087

(763) (894 tr Jack & Burt) (898)
Criminal Jack wants to give back the money he stole without exposing his identity (923) (1097a) (1239)

1088

(959) (965)
Jack is a workaholic * Jack lacks the ability to take advantage of his opportunities ** (85a) (595)

1089

(914) (818c)
Jack tries to locate the family of Lee, an abandoned child he is looking after * Jack contacts authorities in an attempt to identify Lee, but is unsuccessful ** (818d) (697b ch Jack to Lee)

1090

(115) (950)
Lack of creativity is a handicap to Jack's work and limits his chances of success (598) (835)

1091

(950-*) (965)
Jack's knowledge of his chosen profession was obtained solely from watching TV (1111b) (1444)

1092

(1060) (1071) (1074)
Jack reaches a point in his profession where his ambition and creativity dry up (598) (1073) (1075a)

1093

(1444) (115) (887b) (1062)
Jack is not considered highly intelligent * Jack, not considered very bright, attempts to solve a complex problem that has baffled the experts (1076) (1174 ch Jack to Burt; 1282 ch Jack to Burt & Sam to Jack) (1283)

1094

(900) (1071)
Celebrity Jack discovering that the total loss of privacy is the price of fame, is unable to concentrate on his work (618) (863a)

1095

(71a-*) (101a) (1002) (1094)
Jack tries to get rid of certain meddlesome influences that interfere with his professional duties (71a*-**) (83 ch Carol to Jack; 207)

1096

(1074) (1090) (1092)
Experiencing writers-block, playwright Jack feels that real-world experiences will spark his creativity (598) (711a) (835)

1097

(a) (990) (991) (1018)
Jack, saddled with certain obligations, is unable to attain his cherished ambition * Jack no longer has the obligation which prevented him from attaining his cherished ambition, but discovers that he has become a confirmed procrastinator, his goals never achieved ** (1374) (1375)

(b) (1021b) (1376)
Jack poses as a criminal * Jack, posing as a criminal, discovers that several of his respectable friends, Pete, Annie and Larry are running a scam which is protected by the police ** (807) (834) (836)

1098

(115) (1396) (1444)
Mail room clerk Jack is held in low esteem * Mail room clerk Jack solves a problem that has baffled his superiors, and wins an executive position ** (1426b; 181c) (1376; 1097b) (1435) (1413a, b)

1099

(32) (102) (145) (325) (335)
Carol's youth, beauty and intellect threaten her success in her chosen career * Carol has to behave out-of-character to be successful at her job ** (818a) (358) (870a) (1154a)

1100

(82a) (87) (1207)
Carol's venture depends on her successful impersonation of a male * Carol, successfully impersonating a male, suffers by being treated as one of the boys ** (61) (1454)

(44) Using Radical Methods to Overcome Personal Limitations

1101

(111) (1024)
Jack attempts to overcome personal limitations by cheating (628) (1080) (1084)

1102

(751-1-*) (1024 ch Jack to Pete)
Wealthy Jack, who thinks he's too old to enjoy his money, gives a large sum to destitute young Pete * Jack hopes to enjoy Pete's spending spree vicariously ** (751*-**) (1023 ch Jack to Pete)

CONFLICT SITUATIONS

1103

(1074) (1090) (1092)
Scientist Jack plagiarizes research material created by his late friend, Pete (669 ch Carol to Jack) (1238)

1104

(584b) (615) (839 tr Jack & Pete) (857) (858) (1082a)
Investigative journalist Jack lacks the courage necessary for his work * Cowardly Jack, by forcing himself into dangerous situations to gain first-hand information, develops courage ** (1407) (1408) (1409)

1105

(910 ch Nina to Carol) (916)
Young, vibrant Carol is convinced that she can break the rules in her quest for self-expression (86) (182a) (252a) (310) (931)

1106

(740) (766) (948)
Carol yearns for social status * Yearning for social status, Carol throws a lavish party for alleged nobleman, Walt, whom she's never met ** (58a) (642) (931)

(37) Fighting to Achieve a Cherished Ideal
1107

(a) (117) (1432 ch Jack to Milt & Jim to Jack; 1201 ch Jack to Eric & Ray to Jack)
Jack must reach a distant city by a certain time or he will lose an important contract * In pursuit of an important goal, Jack takes outrageous, flamboyant measures — and succeeds ** (1034 ch Jack to Eric) (1414b)

(b) (606) (1129a ch Dave to Carl)
Jack applies for a job in the home of rich Carl * Jack, applying for a job, is asked for references by Carl. Jack uses rich Dave, whom he doesn't know, as a reference ** (805 tr Jack & Dave) (809 ch Jack to Dave & Burt to Jack)

1108

(675) (1149-* ch Jack to Greg)
Jack, consumed with his career, neglects his son (622; 674) (821) (1149*-** ch Jack to Greg)

1109

(1314) (1315)
Backwoodsman Jack pursues an enemy, Gary, to a large city * Jack, from a rural region, singlemindedly tracks his enemy, Gary, to a large city. Thrown into the unfamiliar, distracting environment, Jack quickly forgets his original goal ** (857) (831-* ch Jack to Gary & Pete to Jack) (832 ch Jack to Gary & Pete to Jack)

1110

(68) (1178) (1306)
Jack once committed a crime but was never suspected of it * Jack's guilty conscience prevents his happiness ** (857) (1291a, b) (1259)

1111

(a) (675) (749) (1074) (1090)
Author Jack suddenly becomes aware that he is losing his creativity (1391; 1455b) (1391; 1461b) (1103)

(b) (1091) (125a; 1444)
Reading medical novels makes Jack eager to become a doctor * Jack, confident of his ability, starts a new line of work despite having had no practical experience ** (1426a, b) (1435) (1418b; 1433b; 1330) (1397)

1112

(756) (1060) (1091)
Jack, practicing medicine without proper qualifications, finds himself in a desperate situation (605) (627) (1004) (1031)

1113

(934) (959) (966) 1389b)
Nobel Prize-winning scientist Jack secretly experiments with reanimating the dead (1333a) (1363) (1375) (1422b)

1114

(949a) (1060)
Jack, private secretary to Carl, is aware that Carl is jealously guarding a crucial secret * Jack's curiosity causes him to interfere with Carl's personal affairs ** (718a ch Jack to Carl; 596 ch Burt to Carl) (1194 ch Jack to Carl)

1115

(1021b)
Jack tries to be loyal to his friend, Pete, but certain conditions make it difficult (221a; 139) (601) (607) (662) (1269 tr Jack & Pete)

1116

(97) (100; 1209a) (1107a)
Jack is traveling a great distance to complete an important project * Jack, enroute to complete an important project, is unexpectedly delayed, placing the project in jeopardy ** (793a; 623) (1034 ch Jack to Eric)

1117

(1389a, b)
Novelist Jack, unaware that he's a sleepwalker, is baffled when, morning after morning, he discovers that the turgid novel he's writing by day has been, during the night, rewritten into a sophisticated comedy (562) (1111b) (1438a)

1118

(974) (1137b)
Sophisticated executive's wife Carol, finds it difficult to conform to the customs of a rural community (848b) (1151) (1172)

1119

(335) (676)
Carol lacks every qualification, yet still believes she is a highly gifted musician (364b) (743a) (749 ch Jack to Carol) (1153)

1120

(565) (1133)
Appalled by Jack's behavior, Carol prays to God on Jack's behalf (1353) (1433b; 1353) (918b)

1121

(766) (1099) (1119)
Carol, eager to advance her career, runs into demoralizing problems (679) (1067) (1100)

(20) Getting Into a Situation From Which Difficult Problems are Likely to Result

1122

(926) (941) (964a)
Jack constructs a handmade product of such character it can't be duplicated by machinery * Jack, by manufacturing a handmade product on a large scale to keep up with demand, will get rich but the quality of the product will suffer ** (938) (943a)

1123

(111) (31 ch Carol to Susan & Jack to Eric)
Unmarried Susan's brother, Jack, her only living relative, is poor, while Susan is rich * If Susan marries, Jack won't inherit her money ** (213 ch Jack to Eric, Carol to Susan & Matt to Jack) (892 ch Carol to Susan & Laura to Jack) (1001a)

1124

(1177) (1178) (1291a, b)
Jack absentmindedly doodles, unaware that he may be revealing important secrets (1289d) (1282)

1125

(a) (56) (61) (176a) (736) (744) (808a) (850a)
Jack coldly rejects Carol because he finds her irresponsible (261) (843 tr Carol & Annie) (893 ch Lee to Jack)

1125

(b) (73) (422b-****)
Driven by compelling motives, Jack and Carol enter into a suicide pact * Jack and Carol promise each other that they will die together ** (576b) (422b****-*****) (1020)

1126

(98) (289) (850b)
Jack, a heavy drinker, is given an ultimatum by his doctor: quit drinking or he'll die within a few months (761a) (779) (1326; 779) (364d)

1127

(1299) (1432 ch Jack to Eric & Jim to Ray)
Jack's cousin, Ray, is about to inherit the fortune of a deceased relative, Eric. If Ray were removed, Jack would be the legal heir (50) (1162 tr Jack & Pete & ch Burt to Ray) (1195)

1128

(a) (607) (446b)
Suffering a severe trauma, Jack is seemingly dead * Jack, apparently dead, is really in a cataleptic state, seeing and/or hearing everything around him but unable to speak or move ** (856; 878c) (1142a)

(b) (898) (1043)
Jack is in a mine when dynamite explodes prematurely * Jack is blinded by an explosion ** (918b) (1047)

1129

(a) (1217a) (1152 ch Carol to Kate)
Jack wants a certain object, X. But X is guarded carefully by Dave (1144) (1191) (1197 ch Eric to Dave) (1166a, b ch Carl to Dave)

(b) (1298 ch Jack to Burt) (1304 ch Jack to Burt & Pete to Jack)
Jack's priceless art collection is stolen by rival collector Burt * Jack attempts to find an adventurer who will recover Jack's stolen property for him ** (1081) (1219) (1129c)

(c) (1165) (1304 ch Pete to Burt)
Burt, a gentleman thief, steals valuable property, X, from Jack. Jack advertises to find another thief who will recover X for him (1081) (1219)

1130

(926) (1073)
Doctor Jack is about to leave his office one night on an emergency call, when mysterious strangers, Walt, Amy and Leo abduct him (660a ch Dave to Walt) (1447) (660b ch Burt to Walt)

1131

(158) (1062) (1063)
Jack, terminally laid-back, cheerfully welcomes his lack of ambition (114) (225)

1132

(887b) (1061)
Jack is superstitious * Jack's superstition prevents his success ** (1075a, b) (1332) (1334a, b) (1350)

1133

(565) (1120)
Agnostic Jack arrogantly professes his disbelief in a higher power (1353) (1443b) (1445 ch Carol to Jack)

1134

(1418b-*) (718b; 1061; 839 tr Jack & Pete)
Ordinary Jack suddenly acquires delusions of grandeur and turns into a megalomaniac * Jack, who was timid and lacked ambition, has a change of personality which causes him to behave brashly ** (111) (768) (769) (1418b*-**)

1135

(a) (737a) (1010)
Carol is held by criminals, Burt, Sally and Fred, who try to make her obey them by threatening the life of Jack, the man she loves (885a) (1309a ch Jack to Burt)

(b) (645) (1335 ch Jack to Carol)
Alone in a strange room, Carol discovers Walt, dead in the bed * When trapped in a room with Burt, Carol has to fight off his advances ** (885a, b) (1448 ch Jack to Carol, Eric to Walt)

1136

(41a, b, c) (335) (460)
Carol leaves an urgent message asking her employee, Donna's help (677) * Carol's message to her employee, Donna, is mistakenly received by Jack ** (499a, b)

1137

(a) (890 ch Dave to Jack) (1389b)
Carol is in a small sailboat, lost off a dangerous coast in a dense fog * Carol, alone and in great danger, attempts to summon distant Jack via ESP ** While swimming in the ocean, Carol is caught in the undertow and dragged out to sea *** (179a, c) (1433c) (1451c)

(b) (677) (872)
Ailing Carol's doctor orders her to leave the city and live in the country * City-bred Carol encounters unexpected problems when she moves to the country ** (916) (962) (1118)

(45) Trying to Forward a Project and Being Obstructed by Family Sentiment

1138

(1129a ch Dave to Carol) (1333b ch Jack to Eric & Carol to Frank)
Jack tries to acquire a desired object, X, from Carol * Jack, trying to acquire a desired object, X, from Carol, discovers that Carol prizes the object for sentimental reasons and won't part with it at any price ** (20a) (739) (1217c)

1139

(1023) (1026)
Irresponsible Jack tries to borrow money from Eric on the possibility of inheriting the estate of Jack's wealthy father, Andy. Eric doubts that Jack will inherit the estate (1162 ch Burt to Andy) (1226 ch Jack to Eric & Burt to Jack) (1217b)

1140

(898-*) (899-*)
Jack conceals his ruthless, unethical nature behind a respectable facade * Jack wants to acquire a tract of land belonging to Eric, a poor man whose family has owned the property for generations. Influenced by family sentiment, Eric refuses to sell ** (1220b ch Carol to Eric) (1260a)

(50) Compelled by a Special Motive to Behave Underhandedly

1141

(1095) (1133) (1427b-*)
Jack has terrifying, recurring nightmares * Jack, because of his terrifying nightmares, tries to avoid sleep ** (1427b*-**) (1343) (1360) (1365) (1366) (1375) (1377a) (830)

1142

(a)   (557a) (601; 638) (1128a; 1455a) (1128a)
Jack, presumed dead, is on the autopsy table when he awakens from a cataleptic trance * Jack, presumed dead and about to be buried at sea, awakens from a cataleptic trance, and secretly escapes **   (918a) (1313b)

(b)   (651) (699b)
Jack is believed to have died in a storm * Fugitive Jack, presumed dead, assumes an alias and vanishes ** (699a) (923) (930) (1066)

143

(a)   (778 ch Jack to Burt; 1217a ch Jack to Burt & Eric to Jack) (1144 ch Jack to Burt) Jack, dealer in precious stones, has a valuable collection * Jack, to protect his collection of valuable stones, displays fakes to would-be customers ** (729) (1166a ch Jack to Burt)

(b)   (903-*) (1370b ch Jack to Gene) (1370c ch Jack to Frank)
Carol hires artist Jack to paint a portrait into which he must render an intricate pattern which is in reality a treasure map (903*-**) (1444)

144

(778; 729 ch Jack to Eric) (1143a ch Jack to Eric)
In an effort to steal a carefully guarded object, criminal Jack tries to substitute a worthless counterfeit for the valuable original (1166a) (1217a)

1145

(1181)
Criminal Jack tries to sell Eric an object, X, that Eric already owns (1165 ch Jack to Eric & Burt to Jack)

1146

(59) (1152)
Criminal Jack disguises himself in order to carry out an illegal activity (763) (661 ch Walt to Jack) (1144) (1166a)

1147

(758-* ch Jack to Eric) (899-* ch Jack to Eric; 1129a ch Jack to Eric)
Jack, who has a valuable object, X, leaves it with Eric; Eric agrees to look after X for Jack * Jack attempts to reclaim a valuable object, X, that Jack had previously left with Eric. But Eric denies any knowledge of X ** (1433a ch Jack to Eric; 1443b ch Jack to Eric) (1439b)

1148

(a)   (486a) (1184-*) (1185)
Banker Jack likes to gamble in Las Vegas, but is afraid of causing gossip in his home community * Jack, wanting to do something that he fears will cause gossip, invents a fictitious relative, Walt, who requires frequent "visits" from Jack ** (1170) (1216 tr Jack & Pete)

(b)   (979) (770a) (1377b)
Innocent Jack, deeply in debt, is suspected of a crime * Fugitive Jack, assumes an alias and wins a fortune on a TV game show ** (1451a, b) (1408)

1149

(466a ch Lee to Jack, Carol to Linda & Jack to Andy) (1108 ch Jack to Andy)
Youthful, homesick Jack is unhappy because he doesn't receive any mail as do his young friends * Lonely Jack, never receiving mail from home, invents a family and writes letters to himself which he then shows to his friends ** (499a ch Lee to Jack, Jack to Andy & Carol to Linda) (622 ch Jack to Andy & Greg to Jack)

1150

(1061) (1132)
Cowardly Jack brags outrageously in hope of convincing others of his courage (615) (1433b; 1330) (1336) (1433b; 1363)

1151

(644) (669) (737b) (1240)
Carol pretends to be ignorant of a certain compromising event in her life * Carol, to avoid slanderous gossip and to protect her daughter, Vicki, who is about to marry a prominent man, tries to cover up a possible scandal in her own past ** (870a) (870b)

1152

(778) (1129a ch Dave to Carol)
Carol, owner of a priceless jewel that she is afraid to wear in public, keeps it in a safe and wears a replica. It is known that she owns the real stone, and no one suspects she's wearing a fake (767 ch Carol to Annie) (1144)

1153

(335) (413) (739) (850a tr Jack & Carol) (1099) (1119) (1121)
Carol fails to achieve a goal she prizes * Carol, failing to achieve a prized goal, attempts to make others think she succeeded ** (364b) (1203)

1154

(a) (179a, b, c) (470)
Carol, mistaken for another woman whose life has been threatened (1438b-1 ch Jack to Carol), attempts to elude her pursuers (792b) (1025) (1446b)

(b) (138;94a-*) (1229 ch Carol to Laura) (1265a ch Jack to Laura & Gary to Jack)
Carol assumes an alias in order to discover the accuracy of a slanderous story about Jack * Carol realizes that Laura has lied about Jack ** (844b) (944)

1155

(163) (606)
Jack's friend, Carol, learns that Jack is deeply in debt * Unknown to Jack, Carol pays off Jack's creditors ** (93a) (801) (850a, b)

1156

(645) (646) (647)
Carol accidently commits a crime * Carol keeps her inadvertent crime a secret ** (665) (669)

1157

(1159) (1220b)
Actress Carol is required to cry on cue. Jack, her leading man, uses force to make her grief more genuine (806 ch Kate to Carol) (1192)

1158

(766) (870a) (947) (1242a)
Traveling alone, Carol invents a non-existent aunt, Enid, as a chaperone (801) (1309b ch Gary to Enid)

1159

(1033) (1220b)
Carol fakes an injury from an automobile accident so she can collect damages from the car owner, Dave (801 ch Jack to Dave) (1192) (1192; 224)

(29) Helping Another to Keep a Deadly Secret
1160

(841) (1021b) (1291b)
Jack's friend, Pete, is the sole provider for his parents, Eric and Irene * Jack's friend, Pete, the sole provider for his parents, dies (603b, c, d). Jack withholds the news from Pete's parents, and continues sending money in Pete's name for their support ** (1461a) (1462)

1161

(724 ch Jack to Dave; 816a) (707 tr Jack & Dave) (787 ch Jack to Dave; 816a)
Jack, meeting Dave, a stranger who was injured in an accident, agrees to take over a project that the accident prevents Dave from completing * Jack, to help Dave, poses as Dave ** (711a, b, c) (1168 ch Pete to Dave)

1162

(793a tr Jack & Pete) (981 tr Jack & Pete)
Jack persuades a friend, Pete, to pretend to be Burt in order to complete a venture that requires Burt's presence (1148a ch Walt to Burt) (1164 ch Eric to Pete & Dave to Burt)

1163

(a) (615) (618)
Jack finds his "double" in Dave. Jack hires Dave to fulfill certain duties that require Jack's presence (1424b; 249) (639-* ch Burt to Dave) (1163b, c)

(b) (101a) (1095)
Jack, overloaded with romantic entanglements, enlists stranger Dave to help him out of an embarrassing situation (72 ch Jack to Dave & Pete to Jack) (101b ch Jack to Dave) (182a ch Gary to Dave)

(c) (1163a)
Jack's "double," Dave, completes a project posing as Jack that results in disaster for Jack (1180 tr Jack & Dave) (1192 ch Jack to Dave & Dave to Eric) (1197 ch Jack to Dave & Eric to Jack)

1164

(710 ch Jack to Dave) (711a ch Jack to Dave)
Jack invites friends to meet a celebrity, Dave, who fails to show. Jack persuades Eric to impersonate Dave so that the guests won't be disappointed (603a ch Pete to Eric) (610 ch Jack to Eric) (717 ch " law officer" to "celebrity" & Sam to Eric))

(47) Finding (Apparently) a Much-Desired Object, and Obtaining It (Apparently)

1165

(1145 ch Jack to Burt & Eric to Jack) (1161 ch Jack to Eric & Dave to Burt)
Jack is an art collector * X-1 and X-2 are priceless art objects, the only two in existence ** Jack owns an art object, X-1, which Burt steals. Jack, unaware that X-1 is missing, buys it back from Burt in the belief that he's purchasing X-2 *** (224 ch Jack to Burt) (1146 ch Jack to Burt)

1166

(a) (1129a) (1144)
Thief Jack steals a real gem, X-1, that he later believes is a fake * Thief Jack has a real gem, X-1, that he believes is a fake. Jack switches the real gem, X-1 for X-2, a fake that Jack believes to be genuine ** (614) (1166b)

(b) (1166a-*)
On a pretext, Jack obtains a much-desired object, X-2, from Carl, who has refused to sell it * Jack makes a replica, X-1, of a valuable original, X-2, then steals X-2, leaving X-1 in its place ** (1166a*-**) (1343)

(48) Pretending To Be a Criminal in an Honest Venture

1167

(598) (939)
Jack impersonates a criminal, Burt * Jack, impersonating a criminal, Burt, finds himself accused of a crime committed by the real Burt ** (249) (635) (1044a)

1168

(599) (1161 ch Dave to Pete)
Jack assumes Pete's identity and carries out a venture started by Pete * Posing as Pete, Jack doesn't know that Pete is a criminal ** (603a) (822 ch Carol to Pete) (1044a)

1169

(1073) (1096) (818a-*)
Jack wants to prove his ability to play a particular role in an upcoming play * To prove he has the talent to play a certain role in an upcoming play, Jack plays the role off-stage ** (818a*-***) (625)

1170

(485) (513) (949b) (1072) (1073) (1148a)
Dentist Jack, drowning in suburbia, is desperate for adventure * Dentist Jack, searching for adventure, inadvertently finds himself in the guise of an about-to-be deposed dictator ** (773) (786) (876a) (1148a*-**) (1209b)

171

(623 ch Jack to Frank) (773 ch Jack to Frank & Carol to Sally) (822)
Carol's father, Frank, is accused of a certain crime * Carol, to save her father, Frank, who is suspected of a crime, confesses that she is the perpetrator ** To save Carol, who is suspected of a crime, Carol's best friend, Jack, insists that he alone is guilty *** (635) (1291a ch Jack to Burt)

1172

(890) (1025) (1118)
Carol's striking resemblance to Sally, a criminal, causes her to be suspected of a crime (69) (792b) (822) (828) (1154a)

(49) Assuming a False Identity When Launching a Venture

173

(2b, c, d, e, g, h) (1187;2f)
Phony Jack meets phony Carol * Jack and Carol are phonies, but neither realizes the other isn't who he or she seems to be ** (773; 772 ch Jack to Carol & Dave Jack) (806 ch Kate to Carol) (1462)

1174

(1165 ch Jack to Eric, Burt to Jack & add Pete) (1311 add Pete)
Jack and Pete are criminals running from the law * Jack and Pete, criminals fleeing after pulling a successful job, slip past the police, Sam, Faye and Russ, when Jack disguises himself as a woman ** (603c, d) (1015 ch Jack to Eric & Burt to Jack) (1282)

1175

(a)　(59) (1146)
Stock speculator Jack assumes an alias in order to obtain insider information (69) (90a) (333) (338) (763)

(b)　(1021b) (1168)
Jack and Pete, close friends traveling together, are unaware that each has committed an act that will place them in jeopardy (1015 ch Jack to Eric & Burt to Jack) (1282 ch Jack to Burt)

1176

(610) (654)
Criminal Jack is surrounded by law officers, Sam, Faye and Russ * Jack, a criminal trapped by law officers, Sam, Faye and Russ, escapes by impersonating another cop and pretending to hunt for Jack ** (963) (1142b) (1209a)

1177

(263 ch Jack to Eric & Gary to Jack) (438) (658)
Banker Jack has embezzled the bank's funds * Jack conceals his criminal acts by framing a bank employee ** (1038) (1044a) (1124)

1178

(568c ch Gary to Eric) (1291b ch Pete to Eric) (1309b ch Carol to Jack & Gary to Eric)
Highly respected Jack has committed a murder * Jack buries his murdered victim, Eric, and continues to lead his life in a normal manner ** (1291a) (1302)

CONFLICT SITUATIONS

1179

(866) (1189) (1316 ch Gary to Burt)
Criminal Jack poses as a law officer hunting for another criminal * Criminal Jack poses as a policeman looking for another criminal, Burt. Burt is apprehended and turned over to Jack, who sets out with his prisoner for the scene of Burt's alleged crime — the crime Jack committed himself ** (923) (1209c ch Pete to Burt) (1309b ch Carol to Jack & Gary to Burt)

1180

(1146) (1181)
Jack, fleeing from his ex-wife's money-demands, poses as a famous novelist, Dave * Jack's impersonation of a famous novelist, Dave, backfires when the novelist's ex-wife has him served for non-payment of alimony ** (338) (717 ch Sam to Dave) (1163c) (1173 ch Jack to Dave) (1271)

1181

(126) (1146)
Criminal Jack poses as another criminal and commits a crime which will be attributed to that criminal (1145) (1180)

1182

(608) (611a) (623)
Jack is disowned by his parents, Andy and Linda * Jack, disowned by his parents, Andy and Linda, changes his name and makes a great success of his life. Andy and Linda, having admired Jack's accomplishments without realizing he's their son, reconcile with Jack when he reveals his true identity ** (830 ch Pete to Andy) (1199)

1183

(695a) (695b; 1160)
Jack is unjustly suspected of a certain action * Jack assumes the identity of a deceased friend, Pete ** Pete's sister, Carol, unaware of Pete's death, contacts Jack, thinking that he is her brother *** (31; 1461a) (1461a; 1461c)

1184

(420) (1072) (1073)
Jack's socially prominent position conflicts with a project he wants to begin * Jack, to proceed with certain plans, has to conceal his identity ** (917) (1181)

1185

(249) (1177) (1178)
Jack's family and friends believe he is an executive for a large multinational company, but in reality he is the CIA station chief in a foreign country (98) (438) (1148a)

1186

(249) (1184)
Jack tries to rebuild his life, which was ruined by substance abuse * Pursuing a worthy goal, Jack changes his name and goes to a place where he isn't known ** (152a) (818a)

1187

(513) (768)
Bank clerk Jack "borrows" bank funds for a weekend fling in Las Vegas (2a) (617) (1173)

1188

(680a) (1023) (1024)
To evade his problems, Jack fakes amnesia * Jack, faking amnesia, is mis-identified as an individual whom, Jack discovers, has as many problems Jack does; Jack finds himself between a rock and a hard place ** (1196) (1212b)

1189

(637) (664) (866)
When criminal Jack's captor, detective Sam, suddenly dies, Jack assumes his identity and tries to escape (717) (923) (1173) (1179)

1190

(1169) (1170)
Rock star Jack poses as one of his fans to find out how his staff treats the public (1053) (1147) (1161) (1196) (1199)

CONFLICT SITUATIONS

1191

(1129a) (1132)
Con man Jack targets a stranger, Dave, for a sting (1079 ch Jack to Dave) * Con man Jack pretends he's in trouble and needs Dave's help ** (1255a ch Jack to Dave & and Gary to Jack) (1276 ch Jack to Dave & Burt to Jack)

192

(1159) (1220b)
Con artist Carol's confederate, Jack, attempts to extort money from Dave, the driver of an automobile that allegedly injures Carol (338) (822)

1193

(1076 ch Jack to Gary) (70; 1459 ch Carol to Jack) (70; 1459 ch Carol to Jack & Gary to Frank)
Using a disguise, Jack gets a job with rival Gary for the purpose of obtaining certain information * Jack, his false identity unmasked, is placed in deadly jeopardy ** (1451b ch Eric to Gary) (1439a ch Pete to Gary)

194

(1004) (1031)
Thief Jack has an honest profession that he uses as a cover * Jack attempts to gain control of dying man, Eric's, fortune ** (338) (636)

1195

(887b) (1127) (1290b-*)
Murderer Jack tries to escape by impersonating the man he murdered (339) (1001a) (1290b*-**)

1196

(636) (1004 ch Eric to Carol) (1188) (1190)
Carol mistakes Jack for her son, Doug * Jack, mistaken by a dying woman, Carol, for her son, Doug, plays along with the misconception so Carol can die peacefully ** (1197 ch Eric to Doug) (1201 ch Ray to Doug)

1197

(1163c ch Jack to Eric & Dave to Jack) (1129a)
Jack greatly resembles Eric * Jack impersonates Eric for personal gain ** (1146) (1163a ch Jack to Eric & Dave to Jack)

1198

(598) (1167)
Police Commissioner Jack assumes the identity of a foot-patrolman to learn firsthand what problems the man on the beat faces (608) (717) (786)

1100

(205) (864) (915) (967)
Jack, in trouble as a youth, returns incognito to his home town * Jack, returning to his home town incognito, performs an heroic act ** (211) (1182)

1200

(59) (1194) (1196 ch Doug to Eric)
Jack, to escape his overwhelming problems pretends to be Eric, a man apparently free of problems * Problem-ridden Jack, pretending to be problem-free Eric, finds himself in even deeper trouble when he becomes the victim of Eric's secret life ** (236 tr Jack & Gary) (333)

1201

(1414a ch Jack to Ray) (1414b ch Jack to Ray)
Jack's cousin, Ray, has been mysteriously missing for a long time * Jack's uncle, Milt, dies and leaves Jack's missing cousin, Ray, a fortune. Jack impersonates Ray ** (95) (794 ch Pete to Ray)

1202

(a) (1168-*) (1169)
Jack, for laughs, pretends he's a doctor, and finds himself in deep trouble (625) (1168*-**)

202

(b) (926) (928a)
Wealthy Jack entertains lavishly; as a result, he has many friends * Wealthy Jack, to test his friends' loyalty, pretends to be broke and attempts to borrow money from them ** (681a) (922b)

1203

(335) (1153)
Carol tries to convince those in her home town that she's a success * Carol sends press clippings about a celebrity, Kate, back home, pretending that, under a stage or pen name, she is Kate ** (364b) (1208 ch Annie to Kate)

204

(450) (921) (1172) (1220b)
Carol desperately wants to change her life * Carol makes a deal with terminally ill Irene to take Carol's name ** Irene dies and is buried as Carol *** (435a) (1244b)

1205

(1160 ch Pete to Tony, "parents" to "sister" & Andy and Linda to Carol) (1168 ch Pete to Tony)
Carol, unaware that her brother, Tony, is dead, exchanges letters with Jack, who pretends to be Tony * Carol, after corresponding with Jack, whom she thinks is her brother, Tony, visits Jack unannounced and discovers the truth ** (21) (31)

1206

(784-*) (946)
Attempting to carry out a venture in a shopping mall, Carol finds her objective obstructed by detective Sam * Carol, fashionably dressed, escapes detective Sam by posing as a display mannequin ** (784*-**) (870a, b)

1207

(745) (1032) (1100-*)
Carol encounters sexual discrimination in the job market, so she disguises herself as a male (61) (1454) (1100*-**)

1208

(1172 ch Sally to Annie) (1203 ch Kate to Annie)
While Carol is impersonating Annie, the real Annie is, unbeknownst to Carol, injured in an accident and expected to die (1151) (1258)

(50) Compelled by a Special Motive to Behave Underhandedly

1209

(a) (100) (673-*)
Fugitive Jack disguises himself and risks arrest to carry out a romantic venture (52b) (673*-**) (684 ch Frank to Jack) (915) (964b)

(b) (420) (485) (949b) (1170) (1184)
Jack carries his suitcase into an airport restroom. He emerges in a totally different guise (681b) (711b)

(c) (820) (1212a)
Fugitive Jack disguises himself in order to save his friend, Pete, from the law (1179 ch Burt to Pete) (1174) (1216)

1210

(898) (925-*) (858-*)
Jack's doctor warns Jack that he only has three months to live * Wealthy Jack, whose doctor tells him he's got three months to live, decides to spend every penny so none will go to his worthless heirs ** (751) (865)

1211

(440-*) (988) (1087)
Jack, after pulling off a difficult jewel theft, has a change of heart and puts himself in jeopardy once again in order to replace the gems (440*-**) (422a) (1239)

1212

(a) (723 ch Jack to Pete & Burt to Jack) (981 tr Jack & Pete)
For selfish reasons, Jack helps his friend, Pete, who is in serious trouble (1218 tr Jack & Pete) (1209c) (1264)

(b) (622 ch Jack to Eric & Greg to Jack) (1188) (1414b ch Jack to Greg)
Jack pretends to be the long-lost son of wealthy Eric (1200 ch Eric to Greg) (1291a ch Jack to Greg)

(c) (1107b) (1181) (1146 ch Jack to Carl)
In an effort to get a job from Carl, Jack gives Dave as a character reference, telling Carl that Dave can be reached at an exclusive hotel at a certain hour by phone * When Dave is paged in an exclusive hotel, Jack answers the call, pretends he is Dave and gives himself an outstanding recommendation ** (1008) (352a-*)

1213

(905) (927)
Jack invents a fictitious servant, Matt * Jack invents a fictitious servant, Matt, whose unreliability seems to embarrass Jack, though in reality, it is a convenience for Jack ** (1423 ch Walt to Matt) (1424a ch Walt to Matt) (1216 tr Jack & Pete & ch Walt to Matt)

1214

(1129a ch Jack to Burt & Dave to Pete; 1268 ch Jack to Burt)
Pete's friend, Jack, learns that Pete is going to be the victim of a crime. Jack, discovering this too late to warn Pete, places himself in jeopardy to help Pete (834) (1227a)

1215

(1231) (1212a)
Jack tries to promote a fight between two boxers, Pete and Eric, who are good friends * Jack, for certain reasons, plots to make enemies of two friends, Pete and Eric ** (273 ch Jack to Eric; 230-*) (1278a)

1216

(86) (1148a ch Jack to Pete)
Jack's friend, Pete, invents a fictitious persona, Walt * Jack impersonates the fictitious character, Walt, invented by his friend, Pete ** (1146 ch Eric to Walt) (1184) (1187)

1217

(a) (778) (1129a ch Dave to Eric) (1144)
Thief Jack performs a daring robbery and then passes himself off as one of the victims * Criminal Jack gains access to Eric's collection of precious stones while pretending to be an appraiser ** (1143a ch Jack to Eric) (1166a)

(b) (1026) (1139)
Andy's disinherited son, Jack, tries to borrow money from Eric on the condition that Andy approve the loan * Jack, trying to borrow money from Eric with Andy's supposed approval, asks Eric to request Andy's approval ** (1195) (1290b)

(c) (1138) (1129a ch Dave to Carol)
Carol refuses to sell an object, X, to Jack. Burt, a criminal, steals X from Carol and offers to sell it to Jack (20a) (808a)

1218

(600) (639-*)
Jack is captured by a bandit, Burt, and held for ransom * Jack's friend, Pete, plans to rescue Jack from a bandit, Burt, who is holding Jack for ransom, and to do so without paying the ransom ** (653) (1281)

1219

(1081) (1129c)
Jack, searching for an adventurer, stages a test in order to find a man courageous enough to carry out a dangerous assignment (1287 ch Jack to Burt) (793a ch Jack to Burt & Pete to Jack)

1220

(a) (947) (1138) (1140 ch Eric to Carol)
In order to learn Carol's closely guarded secret, Jack makes her believe she's losing her mind (738) (951)

(b) (1157) (1220a)
Con man Jack forces Carol to participate in his scam * Jack forces Carol to become the bait for his scam ** (1159) (1192) (1204)

1221

(600) (652a)
Jack is captured by inept criminals, Burt, Sally and Fred, who attempt to drug him * Inept criminals Burt, Sally and Fred, attempt to drug Jack, but mistakenly administer a harmless fluid. Jack pretends to be unconscious ** (664) (834) (835)

1222

(a) (266) (657) (1175b ch Jack to Gary)
Jack thinks Gary is guilty of a crime * Jack, trying to force Gary to confess to a crime, places himself and Gary in a situation where both seemingly face imminent death ** (1461a ch Jack to Gary) (1456 ch Burt to Gary)

(b) (635-*) (833) (1222a)
Employing deception, Jack forces Gary to reveal a guilty secret, thus enabling Jack to succeed in a difficult venture (635*-** ch Burt to Gary) (894 ch Burt to Gary) (887a ch Jack to Gary)

1223

(a) (1090) (1102 ch Pete to Dave) (1111b)
Psychologist Jack, testing a theory about human behavior under pressure, places himself in difficult situations * Jack hires unsuspecting Dave and sends him into a potentially disastrous situation ** (1161 ch Jack to Eric) (1162 ch Pete to Dave) (1163a)

(b) (77 ch Jack to Dave, Gary to Eric & Frank to Jack) (1081)
Jack, needing people of unquestioned bravery for a certain venture, devises a test of excellence for two men, Dave and Eric * Jack, testing Dave and Eric, pretends to be in grave danger, and in their attempt to save him, Dave and Eric are plunged into real danger ** (295a ch Jack to Dave) (209 ch Jack to Dave & Gary to Eric)

1224

(1146) (1162 ch Jack to Pete, Pete to Jack & Burt to Eric)
For personal gain, Jack impersonates a widower, Eric, with a child, Lee. Jack doesn't have a child but overcomes this via deception (1075b) (1167 ch Burt to Eric) (1147-* ch Jack to Dave, "valuable object" to "child" & X to Lee)

1225

(429a) (734) (953) (1378 ch Andy to Jack & Jack to Greg)
Jack takes shelter in a vacant mansion (74a-*) * Jack, taking shelter in a vacant mansion and wishing to remain, secretly moves into the attic when the mansion becomes occupied ** (719a) (1056)

1226

(79 ch Gary to Burt) (600) (1275)
Jack finds out that Burt has made him the fall guy in a con game * Jack pretends to be duped in order to trap Burt in his own con game ** (630) (1193 ch Gary to Burt)

1227

(a) (252a) (704) (1214)
Jack's friend, Pete, is attacked and robbed by three people, one of whom is Jack * Jack's friend, Pete, is robbed by Jack and Burt; then Jack, in turn, robs Burt ** Jack robs Burt of valuables stolen from Pete, and returns them to Pete *** (867) (808a ch Carol to Pete)

(b) (234a) (252a)
In order to convince Carol that he's courageous, Jack gets Pete to help him stage a fake holdup of Carol * Jack shows up during a fake holdup and "rescues" Carol ** (234b) (367b)

(c) (234a) (252a)
Jack hires a friend, Pete, to abduct Carol * Jack hires Pete to kidnap Carol and pretend he's holding her for ransom ** Jack "rescues" Carol during a fake abduction *** (367b) (81)

1228

(725 ch Burt to Gary) (1447)
Jack has evidence that is potentially damaging to Gary * Jack is framed and jailed by politically powerful Gary, so that Jack's threatening information can't harm Gary (623) (826) (829)

1229

(1057a) (1430b)
Jack finds himself looking after an abandoned baby, Lee * Jack, looking after an abandoned baby, Lee, convinces Carol, who has other children, to take Lee off his hands ** (249 ch Carol to Irene) (1154b ch Carol to Irene)

1230

(1268 ch Jack to Burt) (1311 ch Gary to Burt)
Jack is obsessively fearful of burglars * Jack, obsessively fearful of burglars, installs a state-of-the-art security system so complex that he's unable to lead a normal life without setting it off ** (1252 ch Jack to Burt & "the body of his murdered victim, Eric" to X) (1313b ch Gary to Burt)

1231

(125a) (311)
Jack bets heavily on a sporting event * Jack, betting heavily on a sporting event between contestants Pete and Eric, learns that they are close friends, and suspects that each wants the other to win ** (606) (1215)

1232

(725 ch Jack to Gary & Burt to Jack) (998 ch Jack to Gary & Dave to Jack)
Jack learns that Gary knows a secret that will bring disaster to Jack if revealed * Jack decides it is necessary to kidnap Gary and hold him incommunicado ** (719a ch Jack to Gary) (875b ch Jack to Gary) (1130 ch Jack to Gary)

233

(79) (804) (980-*) (985) (1265a tr Jack & Gary)
Jack finds himself in jeopardy after innocently agreeing to look after a mysterious package, X * Jack, realizing he's in danger because of a mysterious package, X, in his possession, attempts to pass the package — and the danger — to another person ** (980*-**) (1226)

1234

(838) (1046) (1050)
Jack recovers property stolen from his friend, Pete * Jack, recovering property stolen from his friend, Pete, secretly tries to return it so Pete won't know it was stolen ** (786) (808a ch Carol to Pete) (1035 tr Jack & Pete) (1337)

235

(1216) (1227a-*)
Jack tries to profit by deceiving his friend, Pete, but fails — without Pete's knowledge * Jack's friend, Pete, is richly rewarded from a discovery he makes and offers to share with Jack. But Jack, knowing he tried to deceive Pete, refuses, thus arousing Pete's suspicions ** (1249) (1295)

1236

(213-* ch Jack to Eric, Carol to Susan & Matt to Jack) (1123; 126 ch Carol to Laura; 24a ch Jack to Eric & Carol to Susan; 262a ch Carol to Susan & Jack to Eric)
Employing subterfuge, Jack prevents his sister, Susan, from marrying Eric * Jack, through subterfuge involving his sister, Susan, inherits a fortune ** (1291a) (1295) (1443b)

1237

(a) (1314) (1316)
Jack pretends to lead the routine, unadventurous life of a middle-class commuter * Jack pretends that he is unadventurous and without courage in order to trick his enemy, Gary, into believing he isn't to be feared ** When Jack's deadly enemy, Gary, is lulled by a false sense of security, Jack kills him *** (1039) (1311)

(b) (484b) (606) (631)
Jack kills himself, but makes his death appear accidental * Jack kills himself so that his insurance money will pay off his overwhelming financial obligations ** (802a ch Jack to Sam & Carol to Jack) (952)

1238

(654) (839 tr Jack & Pete)
Writer Jack, decreasingly productive as he gets older, draws on long-forgotten incidents from his youth to generate new material. As he successfully uses the material, he ages, becoming weaker and weaker until finally, the material exhausted, Jack dies [Allegorical: Jack invents a robot, Walt * Jack, inventing a robot, Walt, is pursued and killed by Walt **] (868 tr Jack & Pete)

1239

(1087) (1211)
Jack forms a charitable foundation in an effort to make secret restitution of the wealth he gained illegally (882) (923)

1240

(449) (583b)
Carol goes with her friend, Gary, to spend a weekend at a country inn * Carol's friend, Gary, dies suddenly in their room in a country inn. Carol, first to find Gary dead, attempts to remove all traces of her presence before the body is discovered by others ** (410) (1151)

1241

(a) (916) (1033)
College student Carol is paid to confidentially gather seemingly innocent information (1267b, c, ch Jack to Eric) while assuming the role of a tour guide (677) (802b tr Jack & Carol) (890) (933)

(b) (284) (871) (1220b ch Jack to Frank)
Against Carol's will, her father, Frank, attempts to involve her in an action she wants no part of. She evades involvement by employing a deception (676) (741)

CONFLICT SITUATIONS

(c)　(664 ch Jack to Carol) (1135b)
Carol, involved in a situation which will result in embarrassment (or punishment) if she's discovered, uses her ingenuity in making her escape (669) (1151)

1242

(a)　(470) (1033)
Young Carol, involved in an action that might result in a lawsuit, takes the advice of others and, using a ploy, removes herself from the situation (84a) (86) (1025) (1158)

(b)　(117 ch Andy to Carol) (118 ch Bill to Carol & Carol to Irene)
Jack's rich relative, Carol, dies and leaves him a fortune provided that Jack fulfills a certain requirement * Jack gives up an inheritance because of a distasteful obligation attached to it ** (1041 ch Jack to Carol) (1462)

243

(125a) (189)
Carol, wanting Jack to develop some backbone, subtly places obstacles in his path; obstacles which, when overcome, will make Jack a stronger person (188a) (814)

1244

(a)　(241) (812b)
Carol plans to go forward with a venture which requires delicacy, so she resorts to deception (806 ch Kate to Carol) (1241a, b, c) (1242a) (1243)

(b)　(152b) (946) (1220b-*)
To advance a certain venture, Carol uses an alias and obtains a job as executive Jack's private secretary (666) (679) (826)

245

(849) (173) (1343 ch Jack to Carol)
Carol uses deception to prevent a stranger, Kate, from buying an article, X, about which Carol has just made a discovery (89) (1400)

1246

(766) (908) (1105)
Rita's daughter, Carol, behaves foolishly and rejects advice * Carol's mother, Rita, mimics Carol's conduct to show her daughter how foolishly she acted ** (931) (933)

(13) Trying by Deception to Escape Trouble

1247

(98) (658) (1177) (1185)
Jack shrewdly maintains his public image * Jack closely guards a secret that, if known, would ruin his reputation and destroy an important project ** (1084) (1101) (1103) (1110)

1248

(756) (925-*) (1146)
Jack uses his legitimate profession as a cover for illegal activities (660a) (712) (1031)

1249

(701) (1304)
Jack tries to clear himself of suspicion of theft * Jack explains that he invested money belonging to himself and Pete in a failed venture ** (1160) (1162) (1235)

1250

(280a) (655-*) (663) (607 ch Pete to Gary) (1255b ch Jack to Gary)
Jack is helpless against an armed enemy, Gary * Jack pretends to be defenseless in order to disarm his enemy, Gary ** (1222b) (1232) (1237a)

1251

(983) (998 ch Jack to Eric & Dave to Jack)
Jack realizes that Eric knows too much for Jack's good * Jack buys Eric's silence ** (1239) (1247)

CONFLICT SITUATIONS

1252

(1291b ch Pete to Eric) (1290a ch Pete to Eric) (1309b ch Carol to Jack & Gary to Eric)
Jack, to conceal the body of his murdered victim, Eric, and to escape suspicion, hides the corpse in a mortuary (1291a) (1302) (1344-* ch Pete to Eric)

1253

(1255a-**) (1265a)
Jack is tricked into a trap by Gary * Lured into a trap by Gary, Jack has set a counter-snare for Gary ** (1255a**-***) (1261) (1272 ch Carl to Gary)

1254

(1085) (1086) (1297)
Jack, while cleaning an office at night, accidentally discovers an electronic card-key * Jack finds the electronic key to Carol's safe ** Jack robs the safe of Carol, his employer, and returns the electronic card-key to her desk, unaware that he has left a telltale clue *** (1295) (1302) (1447 tr Jack & Eric) (1461a)

1255

(a) (75a) (1253) (1278a ch Eric to Gary)
Jack is lured by Gary into an illegal gambling club * Jack's enemy, Gary, lures Jack into an illegal casino and arranges for raid by bribed police officers ** Jack's enemy, Gary arranges a raid by corrupt policemen on a gambling casino, but Jack, learning of Gary's plan, summons honest cops for a genuine raid *** (236) (280b)

(b) (1029) (1043) (1128b)
Jack and Eric desperately compete for a large prize * Jack's fortunes depend upon getting his hands on a certain document, X, before Eric gets to it ** (711b-**) (685) (1250 ch Gary to Eric)

1256

(903) (1029) (1257)
Carol, in a rage, destroys Jack's valuable work of art * Celebrity Carol grabs Jack's crutch and clobbers him with it. Jack auctions off the crutch as a priceless collector's item ** (814)

1257

(721) (938)
Abstract sculptor Jack is commissioned to do a bust of Carol (908) (1067-*) * Carol, despising the work of abstract sculptor Jack, angrily destroys a bust. Without repairing the bust, Jack sells it as a self-portrait ** (1256) (1395)

1258

(448) (1309b)
Female terrorist Carol, tracked down by Federal agent Sam, takes a hostage to effect her escape (3b) (10a) (16a)

1259

(974) (1267a ch Jack to Burt)
Carol traps inept thief Burt by telling him her valuables are hidden in a closet — then locking him in the closet (1335 ch Jack to Burt) (850b)

(14) Getting into Trouble Because of a Clever Schemer

1260

(a) (1140) (1000-* ch Jack to Eric)
Rich Jack is determined to own a certain piece of property * Jack wants property that Eric refuses to sell. Jack ruins Eric financially and forces him to sell ** (1000*-**) (1443b) (1439b tr Jack & Eric)

(b) (380 ch Jack to Eric & Gary to Jack) (898-*)
Unscrupulous Jack maneuvers Eric into debt * Jack, maneuvering Eric into debt, offers to cancel the debt if Eric will agree to a certain proposition ** (48 tr Jack & Eric) (269 ch Gary to Eric)

CONFLICT SITUATIONS

1261

(280a tr Jack & Gary) (1191 ch Dave to Gary)
Jack's friend, Carol, uses her beauty to lure
Gary into a trap (1253 tr Jack & Gary) (1255a
tr Jack & Gary)

1262

(96) (98)
Jack is a sociopath, a compulsive liar * Compulsive liar Jack fabricates an elaborate story
which backfires, resulting in his prosecution
for a crime ** (753) (628) (1261 tr Jack & Gary)

263

(447 ch Jack to Eric) (1293a)
Jack discovers a dark secret in Carol's past
* Jack decides to use secret information in a
blackmail scheme ** (870b ch Burt to Jack)
(1309a)

1264

(1168-* tr Jack & Pete) (1277b ch Jack to Pete)
(1288-*)
Jack persuades his friend, Pete, to handle a
dangerous job — but doesn't tell Pete that
it's dangerous (1168 tr Jack & Pete) (1265a
ch Gary to Pete) (1288*-**) (1272 ch Jack to
Pete & Carl to Jack) (1275 ch Jack to Pete &
Burt to Jack)

265

(a) (75a tr Jack & Gary) (1264ch Pete to Gary)
Trying to take unfair advantage of Gary, Jack
persuades him to take possession of stolen
goods, knowing Gary will be arrested (623
ch Jack to Gary) (1154b ch Jack to Gary &
Laura to Jack)

(b) (174; 816a) (711a)
When Jack backs out of his agreement to join
Gary in a venture, Gary attempts to carry
out the venture alone (603a ch Pete to Gary)
(701 ch Jack to Gary & Pete to Jack)

1266

(98 ch Jack to Gary; 1326) (554)
Jack's enemy, Gary, is an authority on poisonous snakes * Jack, playing on Gary's ego
as an expert on poisonous snakes, lures Gary
into a life-threatening situation ** (1311-*)
(1311) (1325 ch Carol to Jack & Jack to Gary)

1267

(a) (409 tr Jack & Gary) (1314 tr Jack & Gary)
Persuaded to engage in an apparently honest venture, Jack discovers he is the victim
of a setup (1264 ch Jack to Eric & Pete to
Jack) (1265a ch Jack to Eric & Gary to Jack)
(1266 tr Jack & Gary)

(b) (1241a) (1267c)
Blind Jack is imprisoned in his home by Burt,
who attempts to force Jack to reveal where
he has hidden an item of great value (885a)
(890)

(c) (1278b ch Jack to Eric) (1438b)
Wealthy stroke victim Jack is dying. Priest
Eric is called in and suspects foul play. Eric
asks Doctor Carol to examine Jack (1432)
(1461b ch Jack to Carol & Walt to Jack)

1268

(1023) (1024)
Jack's plan to commit a robbery is discovered and a trap is set for him at the scene of
the intended crime (637) (664)

1269

(831) (832 tr Jack & Pete)
Jack discovers that his friend, Pete, has committed a crime or indiscretion * Jack notifies
the authorities about his friend, Pete's, crime
and is rewarded for Pete's capture ** (1039
ch Jack to Pete & Gary to Jack) (1313a tr Jack
& Pete) (1313b ch Jack to Pete & Gary to
Jack)

270

(825) (1024 ch Jack to Jim)
Jack disapproves of his nephew, Jim, whom Jack hasn't seen in years. Dying Jack calls in attorney Eric to draw up his will * Jack's nephew, Jim, poses as Eric, the attorney who has come to draw up Jack's will ** (117 ch Jack to Jim & Andy to Jack) (1432)

1271

(1180) (1184)
Jack poses as electronic security consultant, Dave * Jack, a criminal, pretends to be security consultant, Dave, designing a security system for wealthy art collector Eric (1177 ch Jack to Eric), who willingly supplies Jack with confidential information ** (1174) (1251 tr Jack & Eric) (1253 ch Gary to Eric)

272

(604 ch Eric to Carl) (1267a) (1264 ch Jack to Carl & Pete to Jack)
Jack is persuaded by Carl to unknowingly commit a crime * Innocent Jack is arrested for a crime, and his employer, Carl, testifies against him ** (866; 1322 ch Gary to Carl) (329 ch Pete to Carl; 850a)

1273

(922b) (1082b) (1389b)
Jack is a construction contractor who does substandard work * Dishonest contractor Jack fails to pay bribe money to building inspector Carl. Because Jack has failed to pay bribe money, Carl exposes Jack's crimes ** (1220a ch Carol to Carl) (1278e ch Eric to Carl)

1274

(689) (937) (1289b-*)
Missionary Jack tries to convert a primitive tribe, but his efforts are defeated by Gary, a witch doctor * Jack smashes an idol, X, that primitives believe is a god, and immediately good fortune comes to the tribe. Gary is discredited ** (973) (1289b*-***) (1319b tr Jack & Gary)

(52) Encountering a Would-Be Offender and Attempting to Prevent an Offense

1275

(572) (708)
Supposedly dead Jack uses an alias * Supposedly dead Jack discovers an imposter, Burt, using his name and pretending to be Jack ** (658) (1226)

1276

(612) (1191 ch Jack to Burt & Dave to Jack)
Jack catches Burt cheating at cards and denounces him; a fight follows and Burt is killed (750) (1017 ch Jack to Sam & Burt to Jack)

(51) Inventing a Clever Deception to Attain an Ambitious Goal

1277

(a) (568c) (1291b ch Pete to Gary) (1316) (1341 ch Dave to Gary)
Astronaut Jack ejects the corpse of the fellow crew member he has murdered, astronaut Gary, from their space capsule to make it appear that Gary died because of an equipment malfunction (1247) (1332)

(b) (952) (1085)
Jack fakes his own death * Jack, in the hope of collecting on his life insurance, fakes his own death ** (1211) (1222a tr Jack & Gary) (1239)

1278

(a) (125a) (126)
Carol deviously encourages Jack to make use of important papers belonging to Eric in order to advance a certain venture (1054) (110-2) (1278c)

(b) (153-*) (1461d)
Jack messengers a package to Carol * Laura, hiding in Carol's doorway, pretends to be Carol and signs for a package delivered by a messenger ** (218b) (153*-**) (826 ch Jack to Gary & Carol to Laura)

CONFLICT SITUATIONS

(c) (125a) (1278a)
Jack acquires confidential information sent by Dave to Eric * Jack doctors confidential information to convince Eric of Jack's qualifications and Jack wins a high-paying job ** (225) (367b)

(d) (1143a ch Jack to Dave;1144) (1188-*)
Jack, hungering for a taste of the good life, feigns an injury in a minor accident with wealthy Dave's Rolls Royce. Ensconced in Dave's palatial mansion, Jack contrives to have his own "Doctor," Eric, summoned by Dave * Jack conspires with "Doctor" Eric so that Dave covers all of Jack's expenses during Jack's lengthy recovery ** (698 ch Jack to Dave; 1378 ch Jack to Dave; 1212b ch Eric to Dave) (1166a)

(e) (1212a ch Jack to Eric & Pete to Jack) (1273 ch Carl to Eric)
Con artist Jack is selling worthless land. Threatened with exposure by influential Eric, Jack agrees to take Eric on as a silent partner as the price of continuing his scam * Jack and influential Eric become equal partners, Eric now publicly endorsing Jack's shady venture (1222a ch Gary to Eric) (1232 ch Gary to Eric)

1279

(a) (124-*) (135)
Middle-aged Carol's multiple cosmetic surgeries keep her looking as if she's in her early twenties (11b) (103) (124*-**)

(b) (1048) (1304)
Aware that Jack has stolen a valuable object from her, Carol uses deception in an attempt to recover her property * Carol deviously gains entrance to Jack's office and escapes with an object of great value ** Carol plants evidence that points to someone else *** (701) (1309b ch Gary to Jack) (1309a)

(53) Trying to Defeat a Devious Opponent

1280

(1254 ch Jack to Gary) (1303 ch Carl to Gary) (1305 ch Burt to Gary)
Jack catches his enemy, Gary, committing a crime * Jack catches Gary committing a crime, but instead of reporting him to the police, Jack blackmails Gary ** (1265a tr Jack & Gary) (1323b)

1281

(1218) (1085)
Burt kidnaps Jack, takes him to a secret place, and holds him for ransom * Jack's friend, Pete, kidnaps Burt's daughter, Carol, and offers to exchange her for Jack, whom Burt is holding for ransom ** (885a ch Jack to Pete) (3a-* ch Jack to Pete)

1282

(1093 ch Jack to Sam) (1174)
Female impersonator Jack commits a crime dressed as a woman, and removing his female attire, escapes dressed as a man * Female impersonator Jack, who committed a crime while in drag, is apprehended by detective Sam, who deduces the truth ** (651) (712)

1283

(1181) (1268) (1440 ch Jack to Pete; 1077)
Jack discovers where a certain small but immensely valuable object, X, has been hidden * In order to obtain a certain valuable object, X, Jack must operate in total secrecy ** (1146) (1166a,b)

1284

(983 ch Jack to Burt & Eric to Jack) (997a ch Pete to Burt) (1011)
Detective Jack captures a criminal, Burt, who was once his friend * Detective Jack owes criminal Burt a moral debt for having saved Jack's life. Burt hopes to collect on the debt by gaining his freedom ** Detective Jack, faced with a moral dilemma, decides to uphold the law *** (1209c ch Jack to Burt) (1319a ch Gary to Burt & tr Jack & Burt)

CONFLICT SITUATIONS

(20) Getting Into a Situation From Which Difficult Problems are Likely to Result

285

(a) (1123) (1127) (1289c-*)
Jack schemes to gain a rich inheritance (1289c*-**) (1197) (1201) (1285b) (1290a, b)

(b) (988) (1002)
Unknown to Carol, Jack holds a large sum of money in trust for her * Desperately needy Jack steals money belonging to Carol ** (422a) (1295) (647 ch Burt to Jack)

(c) (680a) (1248)
Thief Jack, in the guise of a repairman, gains entrance to wealthy Dave's mansion * Criminal Jack, posing as a repairman in Dave's mansion, claims that an emergency exists which requires an additional repairman, Eric ** (711c) (1278d)

286

(600) (1451d)
Jack finds a long-lost document belonging to his father, Andy * Jack finds evidence indicating the fate of his father, Andy ** (802b ch Carol to Andy) (1018)

1287

(1019) (1219ch Jack to Eric)
Investigative reporter Jack's life is threatened if he pursues a certain story * Jack, despite death threats, continues his venture ** (1006a) (1223b ch Jack to Carl & Dave to Jack)

1288

(245 ch Gary to Pete) (380 ch Gary to Pete) (1267a ch Jack to Pete)
Jack invites his friend, Pete, for drinks at his remote beach house * Jack, having committed a murder at his remote beach house, removes all traces of his presence, then summons the police. Pete arrives at the house, discovers the body, and moments later is accused by the police of having committed the murder ** (603a tr Jack & Pete) (624 ch Jack to Pete)

1289

(a) (830 ch Jack to Pete) (1199-* ch Jack to Greg)
Con artists Burt and Sally attempt to persuade wealthy Jack to disinherit his son, Greg (1199*-** ch Jack to Greg) (1432 ch Jim to Greg) (1432)

(b) (687) (689) (1274-*)
Missionary Jack, among primitives, tries to avert a disaster by using prayer * Jack's enemy, Gary, tries to prevent a disaster by an incantation ** Jack, by prayer, and Gary, by incantation, try to avert a disaster *** (1274*-**) (197)

(c) (490b ch Pete to Milt) (1057b) (1285a)
Jack's wealthy uncle, Milt, promises to leave his riches to Jack when Jack's wife, Carol, gives birth to a child * Jack, trying by deception to obtain a rich inheritance, loses out when his uncle, Milt, sees through the deception ** (781 ch Jack to Milt) (867 ch Pete to Milt)

(d) (1124) (1337 ch Jack to Sam & Pete to Jack) (1341)
Jack absently doodles diagrams that reveal clues to a confidential project * Sam, using clues unwittingly supplied by Jack, discovers the key to a secret project ** (1011 ch Jack to Sam & Burt to Jack) (1284 ch Jack to Sam & Burt to Jack)

(21) Landing in Trouble Through Mistaken Judgment

1290

(a) (1001a) (1285a)
Jack, slated to lose out on an inheritance if his sister, Susan, marries, murders her fiance, Pete (51a, b) (1252 ch Eric to Pete)

(b) (1195) (1217b)
Jack, disinherited son of Andy, murders Andy and conceals his death. Posing as Andy, Jack forges documents in an attempt to obtain Andy's property * Jack's scheme to obtain his father's property is exposed and Jack is apprehended for Andy's murder ** (705) (1006a ch Jack to Eric & Burt to Jack)

1291

(a) (1236) (1277a, b) (1278c) (1290a)
Jack commits a crime (or breach of morality) and escapes unsuspected * Jack, committing a crime and escaping unsuspected, is forced by his tortured conscience to confess ** (802b ch Jack to Sam) (803a ch Jack to Sam) (787 ch Jack to Eric)

(b) (1276 ch Burt to Pete) (1269)
Jack fights with Pete in a drunken brawl * Jack, sobering up after a drunken brawl, discovers Pete dead and believes he has killed him ** (1168) (1183) (1277a ch Gary to Pete)

(c) (1000) (1432 ch Jack to Andy & Jim to Jack)
Jack's estate has been in his family for generations, with the assumption that the land will never be sold * Jack breaks an unwritten family law when he sells a portion of his family estate ** (1353) (1358)

1292

(3a) (397) (448)
Reformed Carol tries to live down her past * Reformed Carol has her unsavory past exposed ** (359) (665) (669)

1293

(a) (179a, c) (532a)
Carol forges the signature of her father, Frank, on a note so she can acquire money for a certain purpose * Carol forges her father, Frank's, name to a note. Unknown to Carol, Frank unexpectedly dies prior to the date of the note ** (69) (410)

(b) (668) (993) (1033)
Carol unethically borrows money on property she is holding in trust in order to forward a certain venture (669) (743b) (801) (921) (946)

(c) (532a) (659) (1308)
To carry out a certain venture, Carol sells a valuable heirloom, X, entrusted to her care by Jack (1440 ch Jack to Carol; 1384 ch Carol to Kate) (1204)

1294

(446a) (448) (1309b)
Carol commits a crime in order to hide a smaller crime * Carol, committing one crime in order to hide another, is arrested for a crime she didn't commit ** (1308; 1309a) (1293c; 1309a)

(20) Getting Into a Situation From Which Difficult Problems are Likely to Result

1295

(1110) (1236) (1254) (1285b)
Jack, remorseful because he has committed a crime, tries to make restitution (422a) (842a) (1160) (1211)

1296

(1021b) (923)
Prospector Jack discovers gold * Prospector Jack makes a rich ore strike and hides the discovery from his partner, Pete ** (701) (1235) (1291b)

297

(111) (113) (484b-*) (723)
Debt-ridden but honest Jack is suddenly faced with the opportunity to illegally gain a large sum of money with no possibility of his being suspected of a crime * Jack struggles against temptation to make a fortune by illegal means ** (484b*-**) (1278c) (1254)

1298

(900; 31) (922b) (954)
Criminal Jack uses deception in an attempt to avoid capture (52b) (100) (651) (673) (699a) (722 ch Jack to Sam & Burt to Jack) (883)

299

(1123 ch Susan to Eric) (1127 ch Ray to Eric & Eric to Dave)
Jack attempts to take over a major corporation despite Eric's legal rights (1236 ch Susan to Irene) (1290a ch Pete to Eric & Susan to Irene)

1300

(1277b) (1291b)
Jack has committed a crime and fled to escape capture * It is important for Jack to appear at a particular time and place, but it's equally vital that he avoid capture ** (699a) (955) (1013)

301

(1277a) (1282) (1285a, b, c) (1289b-*)
Jack tries to avoid the consequences of a crime he has committed (866) (883) (887a) (923)

1302

(1291c) (1340) (1341)
An object, X, connected with a crime that Jack committed in his past, suddenly reappears. Jack becomes obsessed with memories he thought were long-buried (1344) (1355) (1360) (1365) (1366)

1303

(802b) (803a) (1114)
Jack discovers that his employer, Carl, is a murderer wanted by the police (725 ch Burt to Carl) (596 ch Burt to Carl) (854)

1304

(1079) (1085 ch Pete to Carol)
Jack and Pete are partners in a failing business * Jack, partner of Pete, steals the remaining assets of their business and accuses Pete of the crime ** (488b) (701) (1048) (1160)

1305

(968) (970) (1111b)
Jack captures a burglar, Burt, looting his house (1234) (1451b ch Eric to Burt) (1460 ch Dave to Burt)

1306

(68) (658)
Supreme Court Judge Jack secretly commits a breach of ethics * Universally respected Jack, in a high-profile position, attempts to conceal a dark secret (951) (1110) (1291a)

1307

(616) (898)
Jack's art collection is worth a fortune. While he is away, criminals, Burt, Sally and Fred unsuccessfully attempt to breach Jack's sophisticated security system * Carol, Jack's housekeeper, is taken prisoner by criminals, Burt, Sally and Fred when they fail to overcome Jack's security system ** (666) (152b) (921) (144) (801) (885b) (1010)

1308

(988) (1002)
Carol's attorney, Jack, misappropriates Carol's property * Carol is forced to give up a project for lack of funds when her attorney, Jack, misappropriates her money ** (642-*) (739) (812a) (850a ch Jack to Eric)

CONFLICT SITUATIONS

1309

(a) (407) (890) (947)
Carol, trying to protect herself from Jack, kills him (60) (887a ch Jack to Carol & Gary to Jack)

(b) (400) (483b) (495) (126 ch Jack to Gary)
Carol's friend, Gary, mysteriously vanishes (770a ch Jack to Gary) (1277b ch Jack to Gary) while in Carol's company * Carol is booked on suspicion of having murdered Gary ** (635 ch Jack to Carol) (648)

Art Center College of Design
Library
1700 Lida Street
Pasadena, Calif. 91103

(21) Landing in Trouble Through Mistaken Judgment

1310

(66a, b, c) (433a) (1320 tr Jack & Eric)
Jack uses deception in an attempt to get revenge on Carol * Jack tries to get revenge on Carol, but his plan backfires ** (647 ch Burt to Jack) (648) (669 ch Burt to Jack) (818a tr Jack & Dave)

1311

(1237a) (1317 ch Eric to Gary)
Jack revenges himself on his enemy, Gary * Jack revenges himself on his enemy, Gary, unaware that Gary is his brother ** (1039) (1319a)

(46) Attempting to Retaliate for a Serious Wrong, Either Real or Imagined

1312

(695b ch Jack to Eric) (696 ch Jack to Eric)
Jack's relative, Eric, feels he has been grievously wronged by a large corporation * Jack attempts to get revenge on a large corporation for a serious wrong ** (1372a, b)

1313

(a) (139) (446b) (601)
Jack seeks revenge on associate Pete * Jack, seeking revenge on his associate Pete, is forced by circumstances to conceal his true intent ** (1216) (1260a ch Eric to Pete) (1264) (1265a ch Gary to Pete) (1269) (1288)

(b) (79) (557a) (1142a) (1275 ch Burt to Gary) (1277b)
Jack, allegedly dead, pretends to be a ghost * Jack, thought to be dead, pretends to be a ghost and haunts his enemy, Gary ** (1291a ch Jack to Gary) (1334a ch Jack to Gary) (1332 ch Jack to Gary) (1344 ch Jack to Gary & Pete to Jack) (1358 ch Jack to Gary)

1314

(1003)
Jack has no personal quarrel with Gary, but because of his part in a family feud, he must kill Gary (1109) (1309a ch Carol to Jack & Jack to Gary) (912b)

1315

(123 ch Frank to Gary) (245) (1109-*)
Jack tries to get revenge on Gary for a slur against Jack's family (1109*-**) (840 tr Jack & Pete) (1222a)

1316

(1323c ch Jack to Gary & Eric to Jack) (1333a ch Jack to Gary)
Jack seeks revenge on Gary for a harassment that resulted in the death of Jack's parents and sisters (433a) (1039) (1237a) (1277a)

1317

(313 ch Frank to Eric) (171; 223 ch Frank to Eric)
For an imagined wrong, Jack seeks revenge on industrialist Eric (780) (1319a, b ch Gary to Eric)

1318

(79) (247 ch Jack to Gary) (411b) (567)
Jack wants to get revenge on Gary for a terrible wrong * Jack, wanting vengeance against Gary, discovers after a long search that Gary is dead ** (433a)

1319

(a) (567-*) (1269 ch Jack to Gary & Pete to Jack)
Jack, in order to get revenge on his enemy, Gary, assembles an explosive device, X * Jack sends an explosive device, X, to his enemy, Gary, but it ends up in the hands of Jack's friend, Pete ** (987) (1344)

(b) (887b) (300; 887b)
Jack sets a deadly trap for his enemy, Gary * Jack sets a deadly trap for Gary, but Pete is its victim ** (653 ch Jack to Pete & Burt to Jack) (728 ch Lee to Pete)

1320

(818a-*) (1138) (1310 ch Jack to Eric)
Innocent Jack is broke, but remarkably handsome * Jack, broke but handsome, is lured by wealthy Eric to become an unwitting pawn in Eric's revenge scheme ** (818a*-** ch Dave to Eric) (1217c ch Jack to Eric & Burt to Jack)

1321

(812a ch Carol to Susan) (1326 ch Carol to Susan)

Jack wants revenge for a wrong committed against his sister, Susan * Jack, wanting revenge for a wrong committed against his sister, Susan, finds people reluctant to name the perpetrator ** (737c ch Carol to Susan & Jack to Eric) (801 ch Carol to Susan)

1322

(567) (1228)

Jack tries to get revenge on Gary, but Gary is powerful and constantly on his guard against Jack (1222a) (1237a)

1323

(a) (433a) (662 ch Pete to Gary) (1323b)

Wanting revenge for a wrong committed by the late Gary, Jack chooses as his target Gary's widow, Laura * Wanting revenge against Laura for a wrong committed by her late husband, Gary, Jack discovers that Laura is unaware of Gary's offense ** Jack, about to take his revenge, realizes it would be an empty victory, its only result the destruction of an innocent person ***

(b) (157) (260a)

Prosperous Jack is hated by jealous rival, Gary * Jack's rival, Gary, maneuvers Jack into becoming a criminal suspect ** (715c) (829) (1280)

(c) (1310 ch Carol to Eric) (1317)

Jack's reprisal against Eric ends with more serious results than Jack intended (797) (1298) (817)

1324

(a) (1324b-*) (1299 ch Jack to Gary) (1261 tr Jack & Gary)

Jack's enemy, Gary, contrives to cause Jack's death without drawing suspicion to himself * By a subtle twist, Jack kills Gary instead of Gary killing him ** (1324b*-**) (1250) (1253) (1267a ch Jack to Gary)

(b) (1324a) (1310 ch Jack to Gary & Carol to Jack) (1313a ch Jack to Gary & Pete to Jack) Federal Witness Jack, protected by turncoat Agent Gary, is the target of hit-man Burt. Jack discovers that hit-man Burt was hired by Agent Gary, the man assigned to protect him * Jack, target of hired assassin Burt, contrives a situation in which Gary, the man who hired the assassin, becomes his victim ** (1262 ch Jack to Gary) (1313b ch Gary to Eric)

1325

(98) (605) (1422b)

Carol, maliciously slandered by Jack, becomes irrational and attempts to kill him (1268) (1445)

1326

(162b) (225 ch Jack to Eric)

Carol, wronged and unable to seek revenge herself, enlists the aid of her friend, Jack (188b) (294a; 294b)

1327

(1324b-*) (1323b)

Jack is condemned to death as a political conspirator * Jack learns of a conspiracy to kill him and narrowly escapes death ** (1324b*-**) (1329)

1328

(98) (246a)

Driven by revenge, Carol, in turn, is killed (746) (802b) (893)

1329

(777) (942) (1327)

Jack, an outspoken foe of religious fanatics, is tracked by assassins Gary, Laura and Stan * Jack, in the guise of a fanatic, rigs a trap in which his enemies, assassins Gary, Laura and Stan unwittingly destroy each other ** (1225) (1275) (1324a)

(21) Landing in Trouble Through Mistaken Judgment

1330

(853) (900-*) (1150)
Jack, a plunger with unrealistic expectations of success, impulsively takes over a business in which he has no experience * Jack, impulsively involving himself in matters he doesn't understand, constantly fails ** (231) (513) (900*-**) (1111b)

1331

(98) (565) (568b) (1342a)
Jack, refusing to acknowledge the severity of a storm, insists on driving home * Jack, insisting on driving through a severe storm, finds himself in serious trouble, his car half-buried in the snow ** (545) (789) (1345)

1332

(1061) (1078) (1132) (1344)
Jack runs from an imaginary pursuer (855) (857) (1104)

1333

(a) (96) (387-*) (1113) (1310)
Chemist Jack, experimenting with lethal chemicals, accidentally contaminates a bouquet of flowers * Carol, unaware that the flowers Jack gives her are contaminated with a deadly poison, lapses into a mysterious illness ** (387*-**) (371)

(b) (1410) (1384 ch Carol to Jack)
At an antique auction, Jack is outbid by Carol for an ancient locket * At an auction, Carol successfully bids for an antique locket which, unknown to Carol, conceals a poison-tipped needle ** (1461b) (1433c) (1438b ch Jack to Carol)

1334

(a) (475) (576a) (872 ch Carol to Jack) (1064) (1132)
Jack, obsessed by a superstitious fear, abandons a venture (1350) (1351) (1356)

(b) (603b, c, d)
Pete is killed in an accident while with his friend, Jack * Jack, who is superstitious, believes he is haunted by the ghost of his friend, Pete ** (827) (830 tr Jack and Pete) (839 tr Jack & Pete)

(c) (1277b ch Jack to Pete) (1348b ch Jack to Pete)
Jack's friend, Pete, is mysteriously murdered * Jack tries to solve the murder of his friend, Pete ** (1222a) (833)

1335

(74a) (513) (1248) (1283)
Long-distance trucker Jack, pulls into a freight depot, enters the deserted dispatcher's office to pick up a package, and finds himself in a bizarre trap from which there seems to be no escape (636) (1272)

1336

(922b) (1150)
Jack picks up the wrong pair of eyeglasses * Jack, picking up someone else's eyeglasses, looks in the mirror and is shocked to discover that he is seeing into his own future ** (1084) (1134) (1148a)

1337

(750) (1234)
Jack discovers the body of a murdered man, Eric * Jack, entering his friend Pete's home discovers the body of a murder victim, Eric ** (808a ch Carol to Eric) (807) (820) (833)

1338

(1215 ch Eric to Jack) (1344)
Pro football lineman Jack believes that quarterback Pete, a friend whom he accidentally killed during a practice scrimmage, is on the field with him during every game (602) (1357)

CONFLICT SITUATIONS

1339

(1129b ch Jack to Dave & Burt to Jack) (1129c ch Jack to Dave & Burt to Jack)
Thief Jack's cover is that of private investigator * Dave hires supposed private investigator Jack to recover stolen property that, unknown to Dave, was stolen by Jack ** (1193 ch Gary to Dave) (1209a)

1340

(623 ch Jack to Dave) (1080) (1301 ch Jack to Dave)
Reporter Jack, trying to beat a deadline, fabricates an interview in which Dave establishes that he was in a particular city on a certain day * Dave, accused of a crime, finds a fortunate alibi in a news story fabricated by reporter, Jack ** (635 ch Jack to Dave) (1302) (1203 ch Jack to Dave)

1341

(1027) (1277a ch Gary to Dave)
Jack murders a stranger, Dave, in a location which has an odd-colored soil, unique to the area. Jack returns home with traces of the soil clinging to his shoes (467) (1302)

1342

(a) (1357-*) (1374-*) (1389a)
Jack purchases a Victorian mansion and discovers X, an old Edison cylinder phonograph. Jack, listening to one of the cylinders, is stunned to hear voices and events from his past that portend events yet to come (265a) (633) (1358) (1361b) (1357*-**) (1374*-**) (1375)

(b) (1291a) (1301) (1311) (1324a) (1449 ch Pete to Gary)
Jack thinks he has murdered Gary. Then, suddenly, Gary appears before him (1366) (1375)

1343

(1380) (1382a-*) (1383)
Jack carries a mysterious object, X, in his pocket * Jack is unaware that carrying mysterious object, X, in his pocket is causing him to have inexplicable, bizarre experiences ** (595) (596) (597) (1352) (1377b) (1382a*-**)

1344

(683) (1291b)
Jack has delusions that he is haunted by Pete's spirit * Jack believes that he was the cause of Pete's death ** (633) (794)

1345

(53) (576a) (683) (887b) (681a)
Jack, suffering from acute depression, has a pessimistic view of life (1331) (1332) (1351)

1346

(723 ch Burt to Gary) (735-* ch Eric to Gary) (764) (775 ch Matt to Gary)
Respected Psychiatrist Jack, while still in his teens, accidentally killed Gary during a furious argument, and then fled. Gary's death has remained a mystery * Psychiatrist Jack finds himself increasingly haunted by his tragic secret ** (1263 ch Jack to Matt & Carol to Jack) (1269 ch Jack to Matt & Pete to Jack) (1114 ch Jack to Matt & Carl to Jack)

1347

(853) (855) (858)
Jack, investigating psychic phenomena, finds it increasingly difficult to separate truth from illusion (633) (1357) (1375)

1348

(a) (899) (925) (715a-*)
Jack has a split-personality: as Jack he is a respected college professor and family-man; as Walt, his alter-ego, he is a hard-drinking, inveterate womanizer * In a violent struggle between the personalities of Jack and his alter-ego, Walt, Walt emerges the victor and assumes control of Jack's life ** (681b) (715a*-***) (918a) (918b)

348

(b) (1387) (1389b) (1418a; 1433b)
Jack invents a robot, Walt * Jack, inventing a robot, Walt, is pursued and killed by Walt **

349

(98; 1326 ch Jack to Matt) (1177) (1178) (1262)
Famous film director Jack, although claiming innocence, is notorious for his romantic affairs * Film director Jack's agent, Matt, leads him into a trap that is intended to make Jack change his irresponsible ways ** (1266 ch Gary to Matt) (1267a) (1266 ch Jack to Matt & Gary to Jack)

350

(557b) (857)
Jogger Jack, obsessed with an irrational fear of dogs, is determined to overcome his phobia * Jack, obsessed with an irrational fear of dogs, dreams he's being attacked by a pack of wild dogs and is discovered the following morning, brutally savaged ** (634) (1375)

351

(1019) (1078) (1334a)
Jack comes to the realization that what he believes are real dangers are nothing more than figments of his imagination * Jack, to master his fears, exposes himself to what he believes is an illusionary danger — but it proves to be real ** (1350) (1367a) (1374)

1352

(1343) (1347) (1380)
Jack acquires mysterious object, X, from stranger Dave, who warns him that it carries a curse * Jack, possessing mysterious object, X, finds himself the victim of repeated misfortune and begins to believe that X is indeed cursed ** Jack tells Dave, from whom he acquired mysterious object, X, that the object's curse has come true. Dave admits that he invented the curse and the only thing Jack is a victim of is Jack's own gullibility *** (1375) (1400)

1353

(579a) (1120) (1134) (1291c)
Loner Jack, who believes he needs no one but himself, is lost in a wilderness * During a storm, Jack is struck by lightning and almost dies ** Recuperating in a hospital, Jack changes his views on certain important questions *** (918a, b)

1354

(a) (1027; 1421) (1441a) (1451b ch Eric to Walt) (1418b)
Jack makes a deal with the Devil; in exchange for each wish granted, the Devil extracts a number of years from Jack's life (1384 ch Carol to Jack) * Jack, thinking he can outsmart the Devil, makes a final wish that he will live forever, but the Devil reminds Jack that his account is already overdrawn ** (1432) (1433b)

(b) (1444; 1377b) (125a)
Carol encourages Jack to take an unaccustomed risk, and he gains a fortune (212b) (225) (307)

1355

(599; 1330) (830 tr Jack & Pete; 807) (1337; 820)
Jack is a captive of his superstitious beliefs * Jack is haunted by an act he committed in an effort to help a friend, Pete ** (732) (1302)

1356

(234a) (1344) (1352-*)
Risk-taker Jack is losing his confidence * Jack, whose career is dependent on his unwavering courage, begins to second-guess himself, aware that this condition can only lead to failure ** (633) (710) (1334a) (1334b tr Jack & Pete) (1352*-***) (1375)

1357

(541) (1343) (1344) (1347)
Jack is investigating psychic phenomena * Disaster hits Jack when he believes an illusion is real ** (1348a, b) (1351)

1358

(1433a, b) (1418a) (1427b)
Jack envisions his own death * Jack, taken ill, is haunted by a vision that foretells his death — and he dies **

1359

(1325) (1326 ch Jack to Eric) (1422b)
Jack associates a certain sound with a tragic experience from his past. The sound fills him with dread * Jack, dreading a certain sound, becomes a victim of his irrational fear **

1360

(586) (600) (1342a)
Jack has seemingly supernatural experiences that are related to an object, X * Jack has supernatural experiences that interfere with his ambitions ** (1354a) (1356) (1357)

1361

(a) (171; 1433b) (1366)
Jack dreams he sees his enemy, Gary, in his room * Jack has a nightmare that haunts his waking moments and affects his behavior ** (1311) (1317 ch Eric to Gary)

(b) (1142b; 1342a) (1377b; 1160)
Jack has an occult experience that predicts his success in a certain project * Jack is so sure of success in a certain project, that he reduces his effort and the project fails ** (836) (1166a)

1362

(1124 ch Jack to Burt) (1247 ch Jack to Burt; 1289d ch Jack to Burt)
Jack notices that Burt has developed an unconscious habit * Jack investigates a crime, and uncovers the criminal, Burt, through a unique clue ** (1284) (1222b ch Gary to Burt) (1289d*-** ch Jack to Burt & Sam to Jack)

1363

(1330) (1343) (1347)
Jack finds himself in serious difficulties because of his impulsiveness, and is rescued by a friend, Pete * Jack, experimenting with dangerous drugs, narrowly escapes from a life-threatening situation ** (1433b; 918b) (1375)

1364

(a) (1064 ch Jack to Carol) (1383 ch Jack to Carol)
Carol receives a photograph of someone who greatly resembles her * Carol receives a photograph, and a note warning that the person in the photograph is in great danger ** (328) (1154a)

(b) (461) (1424b)
Carol finds a note, apparently written by Jack, that greatly worries her * Annie plays a hoax by forging a note that concerns her friend, Carol, and Jack ** (1055) (1462)

(50) Compelled by a Special Motive to Behave Underhandedly

1365

(732) (827-*) (1361a) (1344)
Jack believes he hears strange voices * Jack, thinking he's hearing strange voices, convinces himself that they are a temporary hallucination ** (1357) (1374) (1375) (827*-**)

1366

(852) (1141) (1361a)
Jack is strongly influenced by his dreams * Jack, strongly influenced by his dreams, attempts to control them by will power ** (1374) (1387)

1367

(a) (1380) (1382a) (1383)
Annoyed by a certain object, X, Jack destroys it * Jack destroys a certain object, X, but it mysteriously reappears. Jack repeatedly destroys X, but it always reappears ** (1342a) (1375) (1381)

1367

(b) (1083) (1287)
Research scientist Jack develops a new serum which, if successful, will prove revolutionary * Researcher Jack, to test the serum
he has developed, uses himself as a guinea
pig ** (1414b) (1419b)

368

(231) (233)
Jack loses his memory * Jack, a victim of amnesia, assumes a new identity ** (7a, b) (437)

1369

(1382a) (1397) (1143b ch Jack to Eric & Carol
to Kate; 739 ch Carol to Kate; 1384 ch Carol
to Jack)
Jack receives half of an important message,
X, and searches for a stranger, Dave, who
has the other half. The message makes no
sense until both halves are joined (1286) (1436
ch Pete to Dave) (1451a)

370

(a) (793a) (1093) (1212a) (1427b)
Jack's friend, Pete, is unaware of a secret
connected with X, an object that has been
stolen from him * Jack knows the secret of
X, an object stolen from Pete, and using his
knowledge of X, attempts to recover it **
(833) (1234) (1453) (1456; 1377a)

(b) (1354b-2) (1374)
Jack, a prospector, is traveling with a fortune in gold dust * Prospector Jack and his
companions are attacked by bandits. Jack's
companions are killed and Jack is mortally
wounded ** Jack, alone and dying, buries
his gold dust and draws a map of the location on object X *** (1394 ch Jack to Eric)
(1369 ch Jack to Eric) (1401 ch Jack to Eric)

(c) (1298) (1358)
Discovering a rich vein of emeralds in the
Amazon, Jack dies before he can mine the
gems * Near death, Jack draws a cryptic map
showing the location of an emerald mine **
(1143b ch Jack to Eric) (1383 ch Jack to Eric)
(1384 ch Carol to Eric)

1371

(1290a ch Jack to Burt) (1334c)
Jack is convinced that his friend, Pete, has
been murdered by Burt * Jack suspects seemingly honest Burt, of a crime and attempts to
prove him guilty ** (1222a ch Gary to Burt)
(1413a) (1456) (1193 ch Gary to Burt)

1372

(a) (695b) (696) (1312) (1323b)
Disgruntled government employee Jack attempts to sell state secrets to a foreign power
(711c) (1372b)

(b) (1312) (696)
Jack turns traitor during wartime and joins
the enemy (919c) (1021b; 1016b tr Jack & Pete)

(13) Trying by Deception to Escape Trouble

1373

(1027) (1418a; 1433a, b)
Jack trades his dreams for a limitless fortune
(1354a) (1357)

1374

(475) (720) (857) (1064)
Jack's character defect prevents him from
achieving success * Jack has a psychic experience that enables him to overcome a character defect and become successful ** (853)
(1418b)

1375

(53) (475) (732) (853) (855)
Jack overcomes a superstitious obsession by
sheer will power (1141) (1365) (1366)

1376

(485) (598) (820) (822) (1098-*) (1161) (1209b)
Jack, convinced that his town's councilmen
and mayor, Burt, Sally and Fred, are corrupt, pretends to join them in order to prove
their guilt * Jack is wrongfully accused of a
crime by the public, which is unaware of his
true motives ** (635) (658) (854)

1377

(a) (1141; 1377b ch Jack to Pete) (1384 ch Carol to Jack) (1400) (1405 ch Dave to Burt) Mysterious object X is stolen from Jack's friend, Pete. Legend has it that X brings good luck to its owner, and Jack attempts to recover it for Pete * Down-and-out Burt, stealing X, finds himself suddenly showered with good fortune — which leads to his apprehension by Jack ** (724) (1425) (1427b)

(b) (1380) (1380; 114) (1075a; 1380) Carol gives underachiever Jack a lucky charm, X, which, she promises, will bring him success (1075b) (1098) (1104) (1354b)

1378

(681b) (1327) (1329) Jack has been missing for years and is presumed dead * Jack's father, Andy, has refused to give up hope that long-missing Jack is alive and will one day return ** (698 ch Jack to Andy & Lee to Jack) (1212b ch Jack to Dave & Eric to Andy)

(54) Involved in a Puzzling Complication that Concerns an Object with Mysterious Powers

1379

(259-3) (555b) Adventurer Jack is about to carry out a dangerous mission * Adventurer Jack, learning of a mysterious object, X, risks his life to obtain it ** (691) (693)

1380

(7a) (1377b) Jack, in possession of a certain object, X, that allegedly has good or evil powers, decides to test it (8a) (1134) (1330) (1343) (1352) (1354b) (1360)

1381

(562) (1211 ch Jack to Burt) (1387) (1389a, b) Jack is unable to explain to the Judge how he mysteriously acquired objects, X-1, X-2, X-3 * Jack, unable to explain certain events, attributes them to the supernatural ** (1400) (1424a) (1435)

1382

(a) (789) (980-*) (985) (1343) (1369) Jack innocently acquires lost or stolen object, X * Jack, innocently acquiring a lost or stolen object, X, suddenly finds himself plunged into terrible danger when strangers try to recover X ** (867 tr Jack & Pete) (980*-**) (1367a)

(b) (1384 ch Carol to Jack) (1401) (1400) Jack buys a small, decorative box, X, in an antique shop and is unable to open it * Jack owns a small, decorative antique box which he's unable to open. One night it mysteriously opens on its own, and Jack finds an object of great value inside ** (729) (1144 ch Jack to Burt) (803b)

1383

(1389b) (1427b) Jack, in the midst of a crowd, suddenly has a mysterious object, X, thrust into his hand by a strange woman, Amy, who, without a word, quickly disappears (541) (561) (1343) (1367a)

1384

(739 ch Carol to Irene) (1293c ch Carol to Irene & Jack to Eric) (1440) Carol purchases an object, X, in a shop * Carol wonders why shopkeeper, Carl, insists on buying back an object, X, which she bought in his shop ** (1444) (586) (1044b ch Jack to Carol & Pete to Annie)

(55) Involved in an Exotic Complication and Trying to Make the Best of a Bizarre Experience

1385

(603b, c, d; 168) (1160) (1334b, c) Jack is the only one who knows that his friend, Pete, has died suddenly * Jack is mistaken for his dead friend, Pete, and sees the opportunity to turn the situation to his advantage ** (5) (1275)

CONFLICT SITUATIONS

1386

(a) (1023) (1388 ch Dave to Eric)
Young photographer Jack is summoned to wealthy Eric's secluded estate where beautiful young Carol lies dead * Young photographer Jack is hired by Eric to photograph a bizarre subject ** (771a) (802a)

(b) (903) (1143b)
Art dealer Jack sells an antique tapestry to client Carol, who then insists on returning it * Art dealer Jack discovers that an antique tapestry contains a mysterious diagram ** (1394) (1399) (1403)

1387

(233) (1389a) (1400)
Timid tourist Jack takes part in a staged "native" ritual, and falls into a trance. Awakening from the trance, Jack is stunned to find his personality transformed (1381) (1418a)

1388

(111) (656) (1085)
Supermarket clerk Jack, is approached by a mysterious stranger, Dave * Stranger Dave offers clerk Jack a large sum of money to participate in an unspecified adventure ** (662 ch Pete to Dave) (1387) (1386a ch Eric to Dave)

1389

(a) (179a, c) (233) (265a) (572) (786)
Sleepwalker Jack has no recollection of his nocturnal adventures (1374) (1381) (1117)

(b) (586) (1113) (1137a)
Daydreamer Jack is fascinated by extraterrestrial phenomena * Daydreamer Jack, fascinated by UFOs, undergoes a shattering experience ** (541) (853) (1046)

1390

(548a) (681b) (734)
Amnesiac Jack, who has rebuilt his life and become a successful stockbroker, suffers a minor accident and is suddenly restored to his former identity as a bus driver, with no recollection of his second life (1036) (1124) (1128a)

1391

(749) (1061) (1074) (1111a)
Novelist Jack meets a character, Walt, whom he created in one of his stories (1451d) (1455b) (1461b)

1392

(110-3) (1401) (1441a)
Jack will learn an important secret if he is ingenious enough to decipher a riddle contained in an ancient document (1400) (1403) (1408)

1393

(1024) (1029)
Jack encounters a mysterious stranger, Walt, who seems to have supernatural powers * Jack attempts to learn the truth about a mysterious stranger, Walt ** (1388 ch Dave to Walt) (1404a ch Dave to Walt) (1405 ch Dave to Walt)

(56) Testing the Value of a Mysterious Communication and Being Drawn into Bizarre Complications

1394

(47a-*) (1384; 1444) (1386b) (874) (1046)
Jack discovers a mysterious document revealing the location of a fabled lost city (47a*-**) (662) (691)

1395

(419) (460)
Jack receives a strange communication from Carol, who is in a distant place (501) (1394)

1396

(1093) (1111b)
Embassy code-room clerk Jack, alone at his station, receives a garbled transmission from diplomat Eric, who is rumored to be in grave difficulties. Jack is forced to make a difficult decision. (1098) (1330)

1397

(513) (1111b)
Jack discovers that an object he uses every day contains an object, X, that is of great importance (541) (561) (1369) (1400)

1398

(1427b) (1444) (1459; 1444)
Investigating a psychic phenomenon, Jack finds it difficult to suspend his disbelief (1411) (1437)

(57) Trying to Solve a Puzzling Problem

1399

(110-3) (117) (1286)
Jack attempts to locate hidden wealth that is legitimately his * Jack attempts to locate an inheritance that his late father, Andy, concealed ** (1451b) (1452) (1461d tr Jack & Carol)

1400

(541) (1046) (1245) (1352-*) (1382a)
Jack tries to solve an enigma that concerns a mysterious object, X (1077) (1352*-**) (1392)

1401

(739) (1370b ch Jack to Eric)
Jack's curiosity is aroused by an object, X, which is being sold at auction * Jack buys a mysterious object, X, at an auction and attempts to learn its history ** (792a) (1384 ch Carol to Jack)

1402

(701 tr Jack & Pete) (705 ch Jack to Pete) (1021b)
Jack's curiosity is aroused by the mysterious actions of his friend, Pete, and he decides to investigate (704) (807) (841) (1334c)

1403

(109) (1392)
Jack inadvertently learns an important secret, and is drawn into a dark mystery (832 tr Jack & Pete) (1077)

1404

(a) (619 ch Jack to Dave) (1393 ch Walt to Dave)
Jack's curiosity is aroused by the odd behavior of a stranger, Dave * Jack, unsuccessful in preventing the suicide of stranger, Dave, finds himself embroiled in Dave's past ** (1391 ch Walt to Dave) (1461b ch Walt to Dave)

(b) (1111b) (1369) (1414a ch Jack to Dave) (1444)
Jack tries to find Dave, who has mysteriously disappeared * Jack's only clue in his search for Dave is the picture of a beautiful woman, X, left at the place where Dave disappeared ** (1400) (1143b ch Jack to Dave & Carol to Kate)

1405

(1175a ch Jack to Dave) (1194-* ch Jack to Dave)
Jack's curiosity is aroused by the odd behavior of a stranger, Dave * Jack, curiosity aroused, investigates Dave, who seems to have guilty knowledge of a crime that has just occurred ** (774) (1283) (1413a ch Burt to Dave) (1448 ch Burt to Dave) (1194*-**)

1406

(1372a ch Jack to Burt) (1437)
Jack sees a stranger, Burt, steal papers, X, from stranger Eric's attache case (1435) (1451b)

407

(675; 1080) (1080)
Reporter Jack is assigned to cover a story which involves a closely-guarded secret (596) (828) (1019) (1076 ch Jack to Eric)

1408

(109) (147) (874)
Jack learns of a closely-guarded secret * Jack, learning of a closely-guarded secret, investigates and finds himself in jeopardy ** (47a) (1148b)

1409

(147) (600) (953)
Jack attempts to uncover the mystery of a locked room (608) (623) (1414a)

410

(1403) (1414a ch Jack to Eric) (1414b ch Jack to Eric)
Trying to solve a mystery, Jack's only clue, X, is the portrait of a beautiful woman (1386b) (1404b)

1411

(1398) (1427b)
Scientist Jack investigates an alleged psychic communication. To his surprise, the communication proves accurate, except for X, a key element in the message * When Carol dies as predicted by a psychic communication, scientist Jack refuses to accept a supernatural explanation ** (1242b) (1328) (1355)

1412

(a) (1383) (1444 ch Carol to Amy)
On a city street, Jack glimpses Amy, a strange woman who has involved him in a puzzling mystery * Jack tries to overtake Amy to gain information regarding a certain mystery, but before he can reach her, she is killed by a car ** (1375) (1411)

(b) (816b; 744) (1360) (1433b ch Jack to Carol)
Carol meets Jack by chance in a foreign country * Carol meets Jack in a foreign country; then, returning home, Carol meets Jack and is stunned when Jack swears he hasn't left home ** (1387) (1389a)

1413

(a) (1302 ch Jack to Burt) (1305) (1334c)
Jack learns of criminal Burt's guilt via ESP (1451d) (1461b ch Walt to Burt)

(b) (1097b ch Pete to Burt) (1261 ch Gary to Burt)
Detective Jack discovers that Burt is key figure in a criminal activity, but the police refuse to arrest Burt * Jack discovers that suspect Burt is actually an undercover agent ** (1222a ch Gary to Burt) (1228 ch Gary to Burt)

(58) Taking Part in a Venture, Then Mysteriously Vanishing

1414

(a) (770a) (897) (953)
Jack mysteriously disappears, baffling all who attempt to locate him (917) (918a)

(b) (1347) (1367b-*)
Jack is engaged in an unusual venture * Jack mysteriously vanishes while working on a highly secret project ** (1367b*-**) (1357; 705)

1415

(837; 1446c) (1220b ch Jack to Burt; 806 ch Kate to Carol)
Bank messenger Jack mysteriously disappears with valuable securities * Messenger Jack vanishes with valuable bank securities; he is later discovered in jail, admitting his crime but accusing the police of stealing the securities from him ** (1447 ch Jack to Pete) (1456 ch Burt to Carol)

1416

(540 ch Carol to Irene & Laura to Carol) (977a) (1069)
Carol, waiting in a crowded airline terminal while her father, Frank, checks their luggage, mysteriously disappears (643) (743b) (1105) (1446c tr Jack & Carol)

1417

(470) (1025)
In desperate danger, Carol begs for help, is denied, and vanishes (802b) (1207) (1240)

(59) Taking Part in a Venture and Becoming Entangled With the Bizarre and the Supernatural

1418

(a) (922b) (925)
While engaged in an important venture, Jack inadvertently takes an hallucinogenic drug (918b) (1418b) (1419b) (1433b) (1438a)

(b) (853) (964a) (1374)
Wimpy, ineffectual Jack begins to believe he is the reincarnation of Walt, a powerful ancient ruler * Jack, because of a wild delusion, proves that he is to be reckoned with ** (1134) (1387)

1419

(a) (693) (856) (1379)
Caught in a deadly trap, Jack calls upon his psychic powers and teleports himself to safety (888) (918b) (1426a)

(b) (1367b) (1433b)
Out-of-work actor Jack, hired to portray a giant peanut for a promotional stunt, is witness to a robbery. Aware that he's a deadman if identified, and unable to remove the peanut costume without help, he is forced to flee, the bad guys giving chase (197) (713)

1420

(1330) (1342a) (1418a)
While eccentric, unsuccessful inventor Jack struggles to perfect a perpetual motion machine, he has a series of dreams which result in his inventing a practical, highly commercial device (1424b) (1455b) (1414b)

1421

(619) (1027)
Jack obtains a mysterious object, X, that grants wishes — which carry certain conditions (1330) (1354a)

1422

(a) (1421) (1423) (1427b)
Jack falls prey to an alien which invades his body (51a, b) (1019) (1424b) (1433a)

(b) (1113) (1353)
Jack, attempting to alter certain laws of nature, narrowly escapes death from an unexplained source * Jack, following a narrow escape from death, develops irrational fears ** (1325) (1333a) (1359)

1423

(1389b) (1422a)
Late at night, Jack enters his house and sees another man, Walt, sitting before the fireplace * Jack, thinking Walt is a friend, steps closer and suddenly Walt vanishes ** (1332) (1424a) (1455a,b)

CONFLICT SITUATIONS

1424

(a) (1334a) (1342a)
Jack mysteriously receives a warning of danger * Jack is unable to account for a mysterious stranger, Walt, who appears and warns Jack of peril, then vanishes ** (1347) (1348a)

(b) (540) (1414a)
Carol is told by an unquestionable authority that her friend, Jack, has been seen in two places, many miles apart, at the same time (249) (1163a)

1425

(541) (586)
Jack is frustrated by his inability to solve the mystery of a strange object, X * Jack, obsessed with a mysterious object, X, is close to solving its puzzle when it disappears and is replaced by another mystery ** (1054) (1075a)

426

(a) (74a, b) (953) (1409)
Jack tries to solve the mystery of a strange house * Jack, investigating a mysterious house, is caught in a violent electrical storm. When the storm clears, the house has vanished ** (54a) (1414a)

(b) (691) (1082b) (1404b)
Involved in a dangerous search for Dave, Jack finds himself cut off from the outside world * Jack is taken prisoner by an alien culture, and discovers that the man he has been seeking, Dave, is also a prisoner ** (181c) (888)

427

(a) (1061) (1082a, b)
Jack finds himself in an alien culture whose members are under the control of a charismatic leader (888) (1019)

(b) (898) (899)
Jack is skeptical about supernatural phenomena * Jack has a mystifying experience that causes him to re-examine his beliefs ** (1342a) (1343)

1428

(852) (1433a) (1443a)
Jack has a dream in which he falls from a great height * Jack dies of psychic trauma **

(60) Becoming Involved, Due to Curiosity, in a Mysterious Venture

1429

(730 ch Jack to Eric) (832 ch Jack to Eric; 705 ch Jack to Eric)
Thief Jack breaks into a building to commit a robbery, and finds a man, Eric, dead, a gun nearby (819 ch Burt to Eric) (906 ch Pete to Eric)

1430

(a) (245) (697b)
Applying for a job, Jack, is unable to supply information about his family background (1051) (1054) (1055)

(b) (898) (926)
Jack sees a stranger, Dave, abandon an infant, Lee, in a public place * Jack grabs infant Lee ** (911) (914) (1229)

1431

(1180) (1199-*)
Nearsighted Jack is mugged by bewigged, sunglassed Amy * Jack struggles with a female mugger, Amy, and comes away with her wig ** (801) (822) (828) (833)

1432

(1127 ch Jack to Eric & Ray to Jim) (1270)
Jack dies and leaves his estate to a nephew, Jim * Jack dies and leaves his estate to Jim, who hasn't been heard from in years ** (1001b ch Milt to Jack & Jack to Jim) (1107a ch Jack to Jim)

1433

(a) (51a) (852)
Jack, during a tennis match, has a vision of a grave being dug for himself (1040) (1358)

(b) (991) (1366)
The vividness of Jack's dream rivals reality * Jack confuses his dream with reality ** (1348a, b) (1433a)

(c) (1389b) (1433b)
Jack clairvoyantly becomes aware of grave danger threatening Carol (1137a) (1333b) (1446b)

1434

(756) (791)
Jack is warned anonymously that if he fulfills a certain obligation, it will cost him his life (1019) (1447)

1435

(985) (1111b) (1046) (1381) (1406)
Jack investigates a mysterious package, X, that has come into his possession * Jack discovers that a mysterious package, X, contains illicit goods. With X as a clue, Jack tracks down criminal Burt ** (596) (623) (1098)

1436

(1399) (1402)
Concerned about his friend, Pete's erratic behavior, Jack investigates * Jack discovers that his friend, Pete, is involved in a mysterious venture ** (662) (1369)

1437

(455b) (1024) (1041 ch Jack to Dave)
Jack's fortunes hinge on a legal technicality; both Dave and Kate, husband and wife, are killed in an accident; if Kate died first, Jack inherits, and if Dave died first, others inherit (1052a) (1398) (1406)

(20) Getting Into a Situation From Which Difficult Problems are Likely to Result

1438

(a) (677 ch Carol to Jack) (1117)
Jack, while on a drunken binge, buys an outlandishly expensive object, X, which he can ill afford. Sober, Jack has no recollection of the purchase (1451b ch Jack to Matt & Eric to Jack) (1457 tr Jack & Carl)

(b) (63) (798) (985) (1267c)
[1] Jack unknowingly possesses an object, X, which can cause his sudden death [2] Jack, unaware of his peril, places himself in circumstances that can prove disastrous (153) (1333a) (1333b)

(c) (339) (1310) (1313a)
Jack belongs to a secret society * Jack belongs to a secret society whose members have sworn vengeance against their enemies ** (1154a*-**) (1319a)

1439

(a) (1402) (1436) (1437 ch Jack to Pete)
Jack learns an important secret which, if revealed, will destroy Pete's career (1325) (1290a ch Jack to Pete & Pete to Eric)

(b) (1147) (1260a)
Jack is severely mistreated by Eric * Jack, severely mistreated by Eric, places a hex on Eric and his family ** (606 ch Jack to Eric) (619 ch Jack to Eric) (661 ch Jack to Eric)

(c) (1423) (1427b)
When it serves Jack's purposes, his alter-ego, Walt, materializes, unseen by others, in a menacing, demonic form (53) (552a, b) (606) (681a) (1424a)

CONFLICT SITUATIONS

1440

(1283 ch Jack to Eric) (1293b ch Carol to Jack)
College student Jack inherits an object which
he comes to believe is bringing him bad luck
* Jack, convinced that object X is bringing
him bad luck, rids himself of it ** Object X,
apparently leaving a trail of misfortune, finds
its way back to Jack *** (1384) (1384 ch Carol
to Eric; 1394 ch Jack to Eric) (1384 ch Carol
to Eric; 1400 ch Jack to Eric)

1441

(a) (1354a) (1392)
Young Jack studies philosophy in an attempt
to understand the meaning of life * Jack,
trying to unravel a great secret, encounters
an unexpected complication ** (746 ch Carol
to Jack) (888)

(b) (552b) (1311)
Jack has a psychological scar that results in
psychosomatic illnesses * Jack has a psychological scar, the result of a cruel act he committed long ago ** (1357) (1358)

1442

(1249) (1283) (1301) (1337) (1447)
Jack worries that Pete will unearth incriminating evidence that Jack has concealed
(1291a) (1461a)

1443

(a) (731) (1366)
Imprisoned criminal Jack experiences a vivid
dream in which he makes a successful escape (866) (875a tr Jack & Pete) (1428)

(b) (438) (1236) (1133) (1147 tr Jack & Eric)
(1260a)
Mountain climber Jack falls into a deep crevasse * Jack, trapped in a deep crevasse, is
unable to free himself, and he dies **

(c) (438) (1236) (1133) (1147 tr Jack & Eric)
(1260a)
Wealthy Jack returns to the dirt-farm where
he was raised and, forgetting the location of
an old well, falls into it * Jack, falling into a
well, can't get out, and dies of his injuries **

1444

(586) (1062) (1091) (1093)
Carol persuades Jack to attempt to solve a
mystery (802a, b, ch Carol to Irene) (1045)

1445

(1244a, b)
Carol is strongly influenced by a revelatory
vision in which her life unfolds before her *
Because of a revelatory vision, Carol redirects the course of her life ** (1245) (1258)

1446

(a) (850b; 1243) (1297)
Carol loses her purse, X, that contains the
key to her safe-deposit box * Carol finds her
lost purse, X, which still contains the safe-
deposit box key — but her safe-deposit box
has been looted ** (1254) (1284)

(b) (645) (647) (677) (1154a)
Carol flees from mysterious dangers * While
asleep, Carol is threatened by terrible danger ** (179a, b) (1433c)

(c) (383) (1279a) (1325)
Carol, while engaged in a venture, creates
an illusion which confuses Jack (471) (1206)
(1258 ch Sam to Jack) (1309b ch Gary to Jack)

**(61) Learning an Important Secret
That Requires Decisive Action**

1447

(791) (1019) (1031) (1130) (1434)
Doctor Jack, summoned to help a sick man, Eric, finds that Eric is dying * Jack learns the details of a crime from dying Eric ** (456 ch Jack to Eric) (1228)

1448

(1038 ch Eric to Burt) (1042a ch Jack to Burt) (1280 ch Gary to Burt) (1405 ch Dave to Burt) Jack observes Burt with valuables belonging to murdered Eric (828 ch Sally to Burt) (836 ch Pete to Burt)

1449

(1334c) (833) (1291b-*)
Jack investigates the murder of his friend, Pete * Jack, investigating the murder of a friend, Pete, is horrified to discover that the evidence targets Jack as the murderer ** (642) (732) (750) (787) (879) (951) (1291b*-**)

1450

(1220a, b) (1263)
Jack's plans take a sudden detour when he discovers he's the father of Carol's son, Doug (675) (945)

1451

(a) (1408) (1430a) (1437)
For years, Jack has been unable to solve a baffling mystery * Jack, trying to solve a baffling mystery, inadvertently discovers a clue in an object that has been in plain sight for years ** (1392) (1394)

(b) (1305 ch Burt to Eric) (1399)
Impoverished Jack receives information from Eric that earns him a fortune (1052a) (1408)

(c) (742) (743a) (870a)
Jack liberates Carol from an unpleasant situation (869) (876a) (870b ch Sam to Jack)

(d) (690 ch Jack to Andy) (1414a, b ch Jack to Andy)
Relying on supposedly valid information, Jack embarks on a dangerous mission * Jack engages in a dangerous search for his father, Andy, who vanished long ago ** (1286) (1404b ch Dave to Andy)

1452

(1387) (1395) (1399)
Jack searches in vain for the key to a seemingly insoluble mystery * Jack, escaping from danger, takes a wrong turn and falls into a chasm in which he inadvertently finds a clue to a baffling mystery ** (1398) (1403) (1409)

1453

(1369) (1389a)
Jack is about to give up trying to solve a puzzling riddle * Jack, by chance, overhears a scrap of conversation which reveals a clue to the whereabouts of missing property, X ** (1045) (1283)

1454

(61) (87) (1207)
Student Jack, during final exams, discovers that his new friend, Pete, is a girl student posing as her boyfriend * Jack, discovering that Pete is a girl posing as a boy, keeps her secret ** (837) (1100) (1451c)

1455

(a) (917) (1379)
Jack, receives information which causes him to abandon a favorite project (1432 ch Jack to Milt and Jim to Jack) (1433a)

(b) (715a) (1391)
Egotistical Jack is taught a lesson by Walt * Jack, rescued from a major problem by Walt, receives a surprising disclosure from Walt that results in a dramatic character change for Jack ** (918b) (922a)

CONFLICT SITUATIONS

456

(516 ch Jack to Burt) (624) (783 ch Matt to Burt)
By shrewd deduction, Jack proves Burt is a criminal (802b) (803a) (1222a ch Gary to Burt)

457

(1389a ch Jack to Carl) (1394 ch Jack to Carl) (1397 ch Jack to Carl) (1438a ch Jack to Carl)
Jack is accused of stealing a valuable document, X * Jack, accused of stealing a valuable document, X, is proved innocent when X is discovered in the possession of Carl ** (662 ch Pete to Carl) (1337 ch Eric to Carl)

458

(129) (331)
Snobbish Carol is proud of her patrician ancestry * Carol is shocked to learn that her ancestry is less patrician than she had assumed ** (23a, b) (873) (1054 ch Jack to Carol)

459

(1296) (1304) (1308)
Carol finds an old ledger, X, that contains records of dishonest dealings * Carol finds an old ledger, X, which contains information that has a major impact on her plans ** (1204) (1244b) (1279b)

(57) Trying to Solve a Puzzling Problem
1460

(932) (1074)
Insecure writer Jack doubts if a story he has in mind will appeal to his readers * Jack, attempting to discover if a story he has in mind will appeal to his readers, tests it on total strangers, Dave, Kate and Rick *** (598) (1305 ch Burt to Dave)

(20) Getting Into a Situation From Which Difficult Problems Are Likely to Result
1461

(a) (68) (456) (701) (703) (951)
Jack struggles with his conscience and makes an important decision in order to find peace of mind (51a, b) (358**-***) (952)

(b) (783) (1111a)
Jack receives an important message from a mysterious person, Walt, which enables him to correct a serious error (1064) (1333b)

(c) (797 ch Nina to Carol) (1183 ch) (1146; 29)
Jack discloses his true identity to Carol * By disclosing his true identity to Carol, Jack causes her great pain ** (53) (1187) (1188)

(d) (1461a, b)
Jack sends an important message to Carol that vitally concerns his welfare (1278b) (1461c)

(11) Facing a Situation in Which Only Courage and Devotion Can Save a Loved One
1462

(85a; 340) (540; 589)
Carol's friend, Annie, makes an important disclosure about Jack that causes Carol to correct a serious error (94a) (506a) (546b)

CONFLICT SITUATIONS

CHARACTER COMBINATIONS

CHARACTER COMBINATIONS

NOTE: In the following tables you will notice that toward the end of most sub-groups (Rejection, Vengeance, etc.) the Conflicts are preceded by numbers in parentheses. These are "final", or story-ending Conflicts, and the parenthetical numbers correspond to the 15 "C" Clauses in the MasterPlot Tables. For instance, under JACK and GARY, sub-group MYSTERY, you'll find

(10) Jack thinks he has murdered Gary. Then, suddenly,
Gary appears before him   1342b

(10) corresponds to "C" Clause #10: Encounters a situation whereby a wrong is righted.

Jack

ROMANCE'S BEGINNINGS

Politically conservative Jack pretends to be interested in social causes 1f

Bank clerk Jack crashes a high society party 2a

Wealthy, socially-conscious Jack, in an effort to understand inner-city problems, pretends to be one of its citizens 2c

Jack, trying to expose treachery, runs into the unexpected 4a

Jack unknowingly loses something of value in a public place 6a

Attorney Jack loses his briefcase 6b

Jack is crude and unattractive to women, although he wishes to be a ladies' man 7a

Bland, painfully dull Jack, rejected by women, shies away from them 8a

Jack's vows preclude romantic involvement with women 16b

ROMANTIC MISADVENTURES

Publisher Jack rejects a novel because of spite 44a

Confirmed bachelor Jack frantically tries to avoid marriage 71a

Jack, trying to avoid marriage, claims that he's homosexual 71a-2

Jack, trying to avoid marriage, claims that he's impotent 71a-3

Young romantic, Jack, sees a supposedly-deserted, rundown house on a city street 74a

Jack, curious, covertly watches the house; one day, he sees a young woman's hand emerge from behind a tattered curtain and place something on the window sill 74a

Jack, hearing a woman crying for help in a house he is passing, rushes through the door — into a complicated romance 74b

Jack is swamped by matching-making mothers; their meddling is ruining his business. He devises a plan to thwart them 101a

Jack is a sentimental, unattached man who longs for a relationship 101b

Jack is a poet, unattached, who is constantly on the alert for romance 101b

Mean-spirited Jack is unable to find pleasure in life 106

MARRIAGE PROPOSAL

Jack is absent-minded 204-265b

REJECTION

Jack is afraid he's inherited an ancestor's evil traits 288

Jack hopes that psychotherapy will cure his obsession with women 231

Though there are reasons why Jack shouldn't marry, he still plans to do so 258

Jack enters into a love affair at the same time that he is involved in a divorce proceeding as the "other man" 274

(1) Jack, overwhelmed by romantic problems, commits suicide 281b

(14) Jack, embittered by a hopeless love affair, throws himself into social causes 246b

(14) Jack, by his selfless acts, loses his bitterness 246b

(14) Jack undergoes a radical character-change 263

MARRIED LIFE

Jack foolishly starts gambling and loses money that isn't his 380

Jack, believed to be dead, returns mysteriously 402

Jack

MARRIED LIFE (cont'd.)

Jack's unhappy married life causes him to engage in reckless, destructive adventures 420

Jack indulges a taste for low-life friends and questionable adventures 485

Jack is prevented by family and business obligations from starting a new venture 512

Innocent Jack is arrested for murder 520

Jack mysteriously disappears, pretending he's dead 438

Jack moves away and struggles to overcome his problems 460

Jack faces a business failure — which he knows will destroy his happy marriage 461

Jack breaks the law in an effort to save himself from financial ruin 484b

MISFORTUNE

Jack exercises poor judgment in advancing a certain undertaking 595

Jack loses his initiative and his business and becomes a salaried worker 595

Jack learns a closely-guarded secret 596

Novelist Jack impersonates the criminal hero of a story he is writing and gets himself in trouble 598

Jack, in a foreign seaport, tries to return at night to his ship. He loses his way and ends up in a tough, sleazy neighborhood 600

Boxer Jack loses a fight and the money he bet on himself 602

Jack invests all his money in a certain venture 606

Jack, investing all his money in a certain venture, sees the venture collapse and himself plunged heavily into debt 606

Jack's youthful escapades, thoughtless and without malice, have given him a bad reputation in his home town 611a

Jack leaves home, squanders his money and, dead broke, he regrets his mistake 611b

Jack is a cowardly braggart. He is manipulated into a dangerous test and must either eat his words or prove himself 615

Jack, a coward who has been manipulated into a dangerous test of courage, is terrified as he confronts the test 615

Jack, embarrassed by his mistake, tries to save face but only makes matters worse 617

Jack is bored by certain duties he must perform 618

Jack, bored by certain duties he must perform, finds a way out — with disastrous results 618

Jack loses his life savings 619

Jack contemplates suicide, but fate intervenes 619

Jack loses his job 620

Jack lands in trouble because he deviates from a strict set of rules to pursue his own interests 620

Innocent Jack is thought to be a smuggler 623

Jack is thought to be a smuggler because he is caught holding contraband goods 623

Jack thinks he is a criminal until he discovers that his alleged criminal act was never committed 624

(4) Jack, needing money, hijacks a passenger jet 628

The line between reality and illusion blurs for Jack as he investigates a psychic phenomenon 633

(1) The mix of illusion and reality while investigating a psychic phenomenon drives Jack to the breaking point 633

(1) Jack, imagining that he sees a fast-moving car almost upon him, leaps out of its way and into the path of a real car which kills him 634

Jack is mistakenly accused of being a criminal 635

Jack is a burglar who becomes reckless in one of his robberies 636

Jack, a burglar, breaks into a research laboratory 636

Jack contracts a contagious disease 636

Jack robs an ancient temple of its priceless treasures 637

(1) Jack, committing a robbery, is caught and turned over to the law for punishment 637

(4) Jack, ruined financially, indulges in drugs and dies of an overdose 638

Jack is trapped in a deadly complication, and faces imminent disaster if he isn't inventive enough to save himself 652

In trouble, Jack tries desperately to avoid disaster 654

Jack's family estate is heavily mortgaged and he is about to lose the property 656

Jack, by any means, tries to save his family estate 656

Jack has great ability, but for whatever reason, he is perceived to be incapable (physical disability, ethnicity, etc.) 657

Jack is involved in an activity and is accused of treachery 657

Jack, innocent of treachery, attempts to prove his innocence 657

Jack, above reproach, fears that unusual conditions will discredit his reputation 658

Jack tries to protect his reputation which is being threatened by unusual conditions 658

Rich, powerful Jack is alone in an isolated location 661

Jack is unexpectedly locked in a room 664

Jack, suddenly finding himself a prisoner, attempts to remain calm and composed 664

Jack's sorrow is so overwhelming, it affects every area of his life 674

Jack's constant procrastination inhibits his business and restricts his abilities 675

Jack learns a lesson that shows how destructive a bad habit can become 675

Jack is a war veteran 680a

Before the war, Jack led a successful life; since returning he is physically and mentally incapable of leading a normal life 680a

Optimistic Jack suffers a critical illness that destroys his spirit 681a

Jack suffers a critical illness 681b

Jack recovers from a critical illness but is left with total amnesia 681b

Brilliant, capable Jack, fights for survival in a savage wilderness 682

Jack, fighting for survival in a wilderness, deteriorates in character until he sinks to the level of his primitive surroundings 682

Jack is a radar operator at a lonely post 683

Jack is an astronaut, the only survivor in a spaceship hurtling across the galaxies 683

Jack is a terrorist hostage in solitary confinement 683

Jack

MISFORTUNE (cont'd.)

Because of loneliness, Jack gradually loses his mind 683

Traveling alone, Jack is caught in a snowstorm 685

Jack, caught in a snowstorm in the mountains, becomes stranded, and can't reach safety 685

Gentleman Jack is stranded in a primitive, uninhabited wilderness, and forced to fight Nature to survive 686

Jack finds himself in a primitive, hostile culture 687

Jack, the only outsider in a primitive culture, finds himself a victim of local superstitions 687

Jack travels through a savage wilderness 689

Jack, traveling through a savage wilderness, is captured by natives who threaten to kill him 689

Jack takes an ocean cruise in the hope of recovering his health 690

Jack, taking an ocean cruise, is shipwrecked and stranded on an uncharted island 690

Explorer Jack is lost in a trackless wilderness 691

Jack, without food or water, is adrift in a small boat at sea 692

Wandering alone in the mountains, Jack is caught in a trapper's snare, unable to free himself 693

Jack, caught in a trap, faces death 693

Jack's neighbors think he is guilty of a crime for which he was tried and acquitted 695a

Jack, tried for a crime and acquitted, attempts to free himself of suspicion 695a

Jack is imprisoned for a crime he didn't commit 695b

Jack, completing a prison term for a crime he didn't commit, discovers that being an ex-con makes life on the outside extremely difficult 695b

Jack, a man without a country, is deprived of news of his homeland 696

Jack was an abandoned child who knows nothing of his parentage 697b

Jack knows nothing of his parentage, and finds it a handicap 697b

Jack is a fugitive who doesn't dare show up to claim his inheritance, knowing he will be arrested 699a

Trapped by pursuers, Jack hides in an old house 699b

Jack has taken a vow of poverty 700

Jack is a gospel minister 703

Jack, a minister commits an unethical act and becomes a victim of his conscience 703

Jack's life work, nearing completion, is threatened with destruction by forces out of Jack's control 706a, b or c

After a long, mysterious absence, Jack returns to his home town 708

Jack, returning to his home town, discovers that no one recognizes him 708

Performer Jack is awaited by a large audience 710

Jack is forced by a sudden illness to drop out of a venture 710

Engaged in an important enterprise, Jack is suddenly confined because of a contagious disease 711a

Engaged in an important venture, Jack is involved in an automobile accident 711b

CHARACTER COMBINATIONS

Jack is removed, unconscious, from an accident 711b

Jack, trying to carry out an important venture, runs into obstacles that defeat his plans 711c

Doctor Jack is a fugitive 712

Jack, deprived of food, faces slow death by starvation 713

Wealthy Jack's claims of social status are ridiculed 715a

Destitute and ill, Jack reassesses his life 715b

Jack is convicted of political conspiracy 715c

Jack knows something others don't know, something that could prove an obstacle to his success 718a

Because youthful Jack was sheltered and pampered by his parents, he is ill-prepared to face the real world 718b

Jack disappears mysteriously 719a

Jack's entire future hinges on a massive project that he has brought nearly to successful completion 721

Jack's life work is threatened with destruction 721

Matador Jack is preparing for the bullring 726a

Jack, preparing for an endeavor, has his plans suddenly interrupted 726a

Jack, sick, is suddenly called upon to perform a difficult task 726b

Judge Jack, presiding at a murder trial, is unexpectedly confronted with an agonizing conflict 727

Jack sets a trap for a large animal 728

Jack is an honest stranger regarded suspiciously 731

Jack is arrested as a suspect because he happens to be in the vicinity when a crime is committed 731

Jack is convinced he is going insane and that eventually he will be committed to a mental hospital 732

Jack finds a large-denomination bill 733

Jack finds a large-denomination bill. The banks are closed and he can't find anyone to change the bill 733

Jack is mistakenly reported dead 734

Jack, victim of amnesia in a foreign land, finds his way back to his homeland 734

(1) Jack dies of starvation 713

(1) Jack, convicted of betraying his country, is forced to live abroad 715c

(1) Jack starts a venture while he is prosperous; then, suffering financial loss and illness, his spirit is broken 680b

(1) Jack constructs a deadly trap, and accidently falls into it himself 728

(2) Jack, captive of a primitive, savage tribe, saves his life by convincing them he's a god 650

(5) Entertainer Jack, a ventriloquist (an illusionist or escape artist?) is held captive and uses his talents to save his life; sudden loss of his voice (or amnesia) throws him back into danger 714

(5) Rich and influential Jack loses his clothes and all identification 715a

(6) Jack, unable to overcome his problems, commits suicide 705

(8) Jack, desperately in need of money, can pay off his debts at the expense of his integrity. He resists the temptation 729

(11) Jack is accused of being an impostor when he's unable to prove his identity 715a

Jack

MISFORTUNE (cont'd.)

(11) Jack knows he has a problem that could prove fatal 718a

(13) Jack suffers combat-fatigue and can't remember who he is 734

(14) Jack, immature and inefficient, learns about life through hard experience 718b

MISTAKEN JUDGMENT

Jack is content, having taken a vow of poverty 748

Writer Jack is fulfilled by his creativity 749

Jack runs away to escape the consequences of a crime 750

Jack thinks he is guilty of a crime, but no crime has been committed 750

Informed that he only has a short time to live, Jack starts an unusual venture 751

Jack resigns himself to endure the loss of a loved one. But the loss is illusionary, not real 755

Facing hard and dangerous duty, Jack is suddenly incapacitated by severe illness 757

Wealthy Jack ruthlessly exploits the misfortunes of others 758

Wealthy criminal Jack returns to his home turf and the pals of his younger hoodlum days 763

Nerd Jack deludes himself that he will be greatly missed if he drops out of society 768

Jack is mistakenly convinced that he is a great businessman 769

Jack is deeply in debt 770a

Jack thinks a crime has been committed, but he is mistaken 771a

Jack finds a top-secret Security Document 771b

Jack is seriously injured by a horse 776

Jack, though not a criminal, is convinced he is one 777

Jack regards others as fair game for exploitation 781

Jack, week-end guest at a country home, prowls about the place out of honest curiosity 786

Circumstantial evidence convinces Jack he is guilty of a crime he doesn't remember committing, and which in fact he never committed 787

Jack, lost, is convinced that everyone is trying to misdirect him 789

Doctor Jack is married and has a growing family 791

Doctor Jack has dedicated himself to AIDS research and treatment 791

Jack is deceived into believing he has achieved a long-sought-after goal 795

Jack mysteriously disappeared long ago under suspicion of having committed a wrong 797

Jack behaves inappropriately 799

(1) Jack is caught burglarizing a house 752

(1) Jack, an intruder in a strange house, is discovered. He bolts through the nearest door — into another dimension 752

(1) Jack achieves his aims so thoroughly that his success results in failure 760

(1) Jack has a fatal accident 762

(1) Jack is mistaken for an intruder 786

(1) Once revealed, Judge Jack's breach of ethics destroys his career 790b

CHARACTER COMBINATIONS

(1) Idealistic Doctor Jack's course of action places him in direct conflict with his wife, relatives and friends 791

(4) Jack, believing wealth brings unhappiness, refuses to take advantage of personal resources that could make him rich 748

(4) Writer Jack unconsciously plagiarizes another author's work 749

(4) Jack gambles with money that isn't his — and loses it 753

(4) Jack gambles with money he is holding in trust 754

(4) Jack, to get money to pay off his pressing debts, leaves home to take a distant job; and he leaves without telling his creditors 770a

(4) Jack, deeply in debt, tries to save himself by misappropriating trust funds in his possession 770c

(4) Jack is seriously injured by a horse and develops a paralyzing phobia toward horses 776

(5) Jack conceals his identity, avoids people, and leads a furtive life 777

(7) Honest, principled Jack recommends a certain business proposition, then learns it's a swindle 747

(7) Jack, told that he has only a short time to live, discovers that the doctor made a mistake 751

(8) Through faith, Jack achieves success in a venture 796

(10) Criminal Jack is depressed to discover that his old buddies are all married and straight-arrows 763

(10) Jack, thinking he is a criminal, discovers that no crime has been committed 783

(10) Jack learns that a coroner's verdict of "accidental death" should have been one of premeditated murder 803a

(14) Ruthless Jack has an experience that changes his character 781

HELPFULNESS

Jack is convinced he's slipping professionally and considers his life a failure 810

Jack, giving away his fortune because he believes his death is imminent, regrets his generosity when he learns he still has a long life ahead of him 811

Jack is hurrying to an important meeting 816a

Fugitive Jack is forced to stay on the move to avoid capture 817

Jack, wealthy, from a socially prominent family, pretends he's destitute 818a

Jack examines the circumstantial evidence of a crime, hoping to discover the criminal 833

Secretly becoming aware of elaborate plans for a major crime, Jack risks his life in an attempt to prevent it 834

(1) Jack is imprisoned on false evidence 826

(7-12) Jack overhears a chance conversation and acquires very valuable information 835

(9) Jack happens to overhear a conversation that gives him material for a scandalous bestseller 835

(11) Tightwad, unloved Jack is talked into giving his millions to charity when he thinks he's about to die 811

(14) Tightwad Jack wants to recover the fortune he gave to charity until he realizes how popular his generosity has made him. Pleased by his newfound popularity, he continues his generosity and is loved 811

DELIVERANCE

Average Jack has a weird experience 853

Jack, caught in a trap that makes him physically powerless but leaves his mind alert, attempts to break free 856

CHARACTER COMBINATIONS

Jack

DELIVERANCE (cont'd.)

Jack tries to rid himself of a fear that haunts every aspect of his life, and plunges him into serious problems 857

Jack is tortured by the fear of death. Jack wants to overcome his fear 858

Jack, wrongly accused of a crime, tries to clear himself 859

Jack is afraid he will commit a crime 862

Jack's popularity becomes a burden to him 863a

Jack wants total seclusion — to be isolated from all methods of communication 863a

Jack tries to improve his social standing 863b

Owner of a summer resort hotel, Jack, faces ruin due to lack of business 863c

Now rich and respected, Jack is haunted by a crime he committed in his youth 864

Jack tries to get out of debt by undertaking an ultra-secret but honest venture that will earn enough money to pay off his creditors 874

Jack's philanthropic venture is about to fail 882

Agnostic Jack is trapped by a devastating tropical storm 884b

Jack, having "gone native," returns to a way of life now alien to him 887b

Jack has a strange experience among a group which has been brainwashed 888

(1) Jack is deeply in debt and facing bankruptcy 874

(1) Amateur ventriloquist Jack is taken captive by a primitive tribe and is about to be executed 878a

(2) Amateur ventriloquist Jack, about to be executed, makes a water buffalo appear to talk — and is set free and elevated to a god 878a

(2) Adrift at sea in a small boat, Jack is near death from exposure when he lands on an uncharted coast 878b

(2) Jack's philanthropic venture faces financial failure; Jack, a reformed racketeer, keeps the venture going by employing his former skills and rigging a horse race 882

(4) Jack dreams he's in danger, but is convinced the danger is real 852

(4) Impoverished Jack tries to recoup his fortunes by marrying a wealthy woman 860

(5) Jack, once again rational, relates a strange experience which his friends find impossible to believe 889

(12) Fearing that he will commit a crime, Jack tries to overcome the fear, and the possibility of doing evil 862

(12) Jack returns incognito to his home town where he committed a youthful crime, and attempts to carry out a venture 864

(14) Average Jack has an experience that convinces him that he possesses incredible powers 853

IDEALISM

Jack's popularity so intrudes on his life that he seeks total seclusion 897

Selfish Jack is always looking out for "Number One" 898

Selfish, miserly Jack finds that his ways are wrong and that he isn't unhappy 898

Rich, greedy Jack is only happy when adding to his fortune 899

"Civilized" Jack attempts to impose his values on a primitive society 901

Jack is a dedicated artist whose ideal is Truth 903

CHARACTER COMBINATIONS

Desperately seeking companionship, Jack is thwarted by his appearance and/or personality 912a

Jack is a professional gambler 914

Jack mysteriously disappears. He resurfaces elsewhere, using an alias 917

Jack, pursuing a worthy venture, changes his identity and goes to a place where is isn't known 918a

Soldier Jack disappears from his unit 919a

Soldier Jack deserted under fire but was incorrectly reported missing in action 919b

Jack, after years of concealing his cowardice, returns to his home using an alias 919b

Jack's search for a hero-figure is unsuccessful 922a

Jack becomes a social misfit 922b

Criminal Jack is trying to go straight 923

Wealthy Jack wants to get rid of his money 924a

Wealthy Jack leads a life of idle pleasure 924b

Wealthy Jack's contentment with his lifestyle is challenged by an incident 924b

Jack is a selfish man who has no regard for others 925

Jack, trying to make the world better, encounters a disturbing experience 926

Generous, sociable Jack wants to invite people into his home, but certain unpleasant conditions make it difficult 927

Jack, in the spirit of charity, befriends all in need 928a

Jack is never too busy to help others and, because of it, he has an unfortunate experience 928a

Writer Jack plans to expand a favorite idea into a screenplay 932

Misguided writer Jack plans to test the commercial potential of a story idea before writing it 932

Penniless Jack commits to ten years of servitude in exchange for a college education 935

Jack dreams of a life of adventure 936

Jack is morally rigid 937

Expert craftsman Jack struggles to earn a living while maintaining his integrity 938

If he chooses, Jack could become wealthy by compromising his principles 938

Rebel Jack, by associating with criminals hopes to prove that good can come out of evil 939

Jack enlists as a private in the army when he could easily have become a commissioned officer 940

Victim of a martyr complex, Jack plucks failure from the jaws of success 941

Judge Jack is a humanitarian 949b

Judge Jack, in an effort to gain insight the lives of those brought into his courtroom, assumes a disguise and immerses himself in their world 949b

Jack is handicapped by knowing little of the world 950

Jack believes he can be happier and more successful as an attorney than as a doctor, a general than as a private, an employer than as an employee 950

Jack feels he can do more good outside the clergy than as a priest 950

Jack's guilty conscience stands in the way of his happiness 951

Jack

IDEALISM (cont'd.)

Jack will be ruined and disgraced if he expiates his guilt 951

Jack wants to vanish and start a new life 952

Jack craves peace and quiet 953

Jack, wanting peace and quiet, assumes a false identity and finds a distant retreat 953

Jack's imagination is the source of his discontent 954

Discontented Jack rebels against his surroundings in an effort to find contentment 954

Bandit Jack robs the mails 955

Jack becomes so rich and powerful that he loses perspective and believes he's omnipotent 957a

Jack is an army general 957b

Jack is CEO of a giant corporation 960b

Jack is captain of a ship, racing against the clock across the Atlantic 957c

Jack believes that poverty is the true source of happiness 958

Jack struggles to avoid wealth 958

Soldier Jack, eager to fight, is ordered to retreat before superior enemy forces 960a

Jack receives orders from his superiors that he believes are disgraceful 960a

Jack's pride rebels when poverty costs him his family estate 961

Jack is obsessed with achieving a high honor, albeit undeserved 965

Jack, a wimp, is frustrated by dreams of accomplishments unimaginably beyond his abilities 966

Jack mysteriously disappeared from his home years ago 967

Jack, for many years mysteriously missing, tries to rekindle old ties when he suddenly reappears 967

Young Jack is a romantic 968

Romantic young Jack samples a variety of experiences in his quest for a rich, noble life 968

Jack, a city person, longs for the great outdoors 969

Jack befriends and helps needy strangers, often neglecting his own family in the process 970

Jack believes that solitude is the greatest of human blessings 971

(1) Rich, greedy Jack loses everything by penny-pinching 899

(1) Soldier Jack is listed a deserter under fire 919c

(1-12) Soldier Jack, facing a large enemy force, fights overwhelming odds until he is killed 919c

(1) Jack, morally rigid, is stranded in a savage, isolated environment where local customs challenge his values 937

(1) Jack is having a hard time and bad luck awaits him at every turn 942

(1) Army general Jack is so distracted by an unimportant concern, he forgets about the attacking enemy, and his troops are defeated 957b

During a hostile takeover attempt, top executive Jack is so absorbed in a trivial matter that he ignores the battle and his company is destroyed 960b

CHARACTER COMBINATIONS

(2) Jack takes refuge in a foreign country to escape the consequences of a crime 915

(4) Jack, a fugitive in a foreign country, is driven by homesickness to return to his native land 915

(4) Irresponsibly grasping for happiness, Jack loses sight of his moral duty 949a

(4) Possessing some minority blood, Jack wants all the opportunities given the predominant race 959

(6) Jack dies, frustrated that he has fallen short of his high goals 907

(6) Soldier Jack disappears from his unit and dies while performing a heroic act; but he is reported to have deserted under fire 919a

(7) Wealthy Jack, who wants to get rid of his money, finds it impossible 924a

(7) Believing that money corrupts, Jack changes his mind when he becomes rich and is happier than he's ever been 929

(8) Jack, possessing everything he thought necessary for happiness, discovers that he is the source of his unhappiness 900

(8) Jack, after a lifetime spent seeking unattainable goals, dies unaware that it was the search itself that ennobled him 907

(8) Jack tries to rebuild his wasted, dissipated life 918a

(8) Jack's goal is to help make a better world 926

(8) Jack clings to his principles despite incessant bad luck and troubles 942

(8) Jack gives up his life rather than compromise his sense of duty 943a

(8) Jack dies rather than becoming rich by violating his principles 943a

(8) Prisoner Jack goes to his death rather than betray his sense of loyalty 943b

(8) Jack lives a life of quiet desperation, enduring every kind of trouble. Clinging to what he believes are high ideals, Jack perversely counts his problems as blessings in disguise 944

(8) Bandit Jack, opening a letter from a stolen mail sack, gains information that sends him on an altruistic mission — proving there is good in the worst of us 955

(8-12) Jack trades low ideals for high ideals 963

(8) Civilized outsider Jack fights the superstitions of a disease-ridden tribe of savages 973

(10) Jack's imagination overtakes his sense of reality. Trying to rid himself of imagined problems, Jack lands in real trouble 900

(10) Jack is obsessed with a certain pastime: [1] gambling, [2] women, [3] sports, etc. He becomes so absorbed by his pastime that major issues demanding immediate attention are neglected with disastrous results 902

(10) Jack, valuing solitude above all else, has a difficult time finding it 971

(11) Despite Jack's lack of funds, his pride won't permit him to discontinue the large charity donations his family has always made, thus forcing him into trouble 905

(11) Jack can't achieve his dream because he is the sole support of his family 936

(12) Trying to promote a venture that associates would regard as foolhardy, Jack changes his name and goes to a place where he is unknown 917

(12) Amoral Jack undergoes an abrupt change of heart 922a

Jack

IDEALISM (cont'd.)

(12) Wealthy, influential Jack believes that his true worth is hidden by his riches 940

(12) Jack leaves his coat on a seaside cliff, drops his hat on a bush below the edge, and vanishes 952

(12) Learning of an old prophecy, Jack unconsciously tries to become the hero of the prophecy 964a

(14) Jack, having sought seclusion because his popularity was a burden, realizes he misses the roar of the crowd 897

(14) Jack experiences a tragedy that makes him a better person 918b

(14) On landing in trouble, Jack compromises his high moral standards 922b

(14) Jack, trading low ideals for high ideals, vainly struggles to achieve his high ideals. But, though unable to reach his goal, he becomes a better person 963

OBLIGATION

Jack innocently causes several people to invest money in a worthless venture 979

Jack, by undertaking an obligation, is threatened by problems 980

Jack's family sacrificed so that he could attain a college education 990

Jack feels duty-bound to work at a career he dislikes so that he can repay his family for their sacrifices 990

Unable to live an adventurous life, Jack seeks vicarious thrills 991

Jack, with a half-million dollars, must spend it all within a year, and he mustn't give any of it away or spend it foolishly 997b

Jack is the heir of a proud old family whose greatest pride has been to keep its holdings intact 1000

Desperately needy Jack ignores a family obligation 1000

In order to become rich, Jack must perform a distasteful task 1001a

Jack professes to hate women 1002

Jack is obligated to commit a crime 1003

Jack is a United States consul in a third-world country 1015

Jack is anonymously threatened with violence if he tries to fulfill an obligation 1019

(1) In order to fulfill an obligation, Jack gives up his chosen profession for another line of work 1006b

(8) Unable to achieve his ambition because of family obligations, Jack comes as close as he can to realizing it 991

(12) Having innocently caused several people to lose money in a venture, Jack cannot rest until he has recovered it for them 979

(12) Obligated to commit a crime, Jack isn't a criminal at heart and can't meet his obligation 1003

(12) Jack, anonymously threatened with violence if he fulfills an obligation, boldly goes ahead with what he feels is his duty 1019

(6) Jack breaks a deadlock by killing himself 1016a

NECESSITY

Jack desperately needs money 1023

Jack finds it difficult to regain wealth 1024

Jack is a disinherited son who desperately needs money 1026

Capable Jack is almost bankrupt. While under pressure to recoup his fortune, he unexpectedly encounters additional difficulties 1029

Innocent Jack is held by the police on a groundless charge 1030

Jack, held by the police, must be freed immediately in order to perform a certain task, but is unable to gain his release   1030

(1) Youthful Jack was once rich, but a wild, reckless life has made him penniless   1024

Doctor Jack, while on an evening walk, is hurriedly summoned to attend a sick person. The experience turns into a nightmare for the doctor   1031

(4) Jack, desperately needing money, does something rash and gets involved in an unpleasant complication   1023

(4) Desperately needing money, Jack lets the devil tempt him into an unwise bargain   1027

CHANCE
Computer programmer Jack tests his new software   1034

Jack is an ordinary man with average abilities   1036

Jack is enroute to an important meeting   1040

Jack is injured in an accident and taken unconscious to a hospital   1040

Jack, half-asleep, happens to overhear a conversation concerning a crime. But he can't decide if he heard a real conversation, or was dreaming   1045

Blind man Jack makes his way along a city street   1047

(1) Computer hacker Jack inadvertently logs onto an international air-control grid, and creates worldwide chaos by grounding all commercial flights   1034

(1) Jack is on his way to sign a new will disposing of his estate, but is killed in an accident   1041

(1) Jack, engaged in a secret task, is interrupted and his secret discovered   1042a

(4) Jack carelessly leaves a door unlocked while involved in a task requiring secrecy   1042a

(4) Whenever Jack has to make a decision, he decides by flipping a coin. He has done this all his life, and is invariably successful. But then, one day, he makes the wrong call   1049

(9) Jack's gold mine, seemingly of little value, becomes a bonanza because of a lucky strike   1043

(9) Jack happens to hear a familiar name that solves a riddle of the past   1053

(9) Jack solves a mystery involving his happiness   1054

(9) Jack solves a mystery when falling plaster reveals a hiding place containing old love letters   1054

PERSONAL LIMITATIONS
Simple, good-hearted Jack lacks all social graces   1059

Jack tries ambitious ventures, but loses confidence before finishing them   1060

From early childhood, Jack has been programmed to believe that he lacks courage   1061

Jack's belief that he lacks courage becomes a self-fulfilling prophecy   1061

Jack, happy with his life, sees no need for improvement   1062

Jack's misguided values obstruct his advancement   1063

On trial for murder, Jack could establish an alibi and prove his innocence — but only by a dishonorable act   1070

Jack finds his workload overwhelming and cannot fulfill his responsibilities   1071

Jack

PERSONAL LIMITATIONS (cont'd.)

Jack's executive position makes it impossible for him to acquire certain important information 1072

Jack is a successful businessman with an overwhelming desire to quit the commercial world and become a romantic adventurer 1073

Jack is obsessed with fear that he is being dogged by danger 1078

Convinced that he's being pursued, Jack seeks peace of mind 1078

Jack finds himself unable, through normal channels, to find a man courageous enough to accept a dangerous mission 1081

Jack uses subterfuge to locate a courageous man 1081

Jack's cowardice inhibits his success 1082a

Jack is trapped in a primitive society that worships a tyrannical god 1082b

Jack wants to escape from a community ruled by fear, but can't summon the courage 1082b

Jack lacks initiative and the ability to succeed on his own 1083

Jack wants to engage in an honest venture but lacks the money to finance it 1084

Jack wants to achieve a difficult goal, but cannot finance the project 1086

Criminal Jack wants to give back the money he stole without exposing his identity 1087

Jack is a workaholic 1088

Lack of creativity is a handicap to Jack's work and limits his chances of success 1090

Jack's knowledge of his chosen profession was obtained solely from watching TV 1091

Jack reaches a point in his profession where his ambition and creativity dry up 1092

Jack is not considered highly intelligent 1093

Jack, not considered very bright, attempts to solve a complex problem that has baffled the experts 1093

Celebrity Jack, discovering that the total loss of privacy is the price of fame, is unable to concentrate on his work 1094

Jack tries to get rid of certain meddlesome influences that interfere with his professional duties 1095

Experiencing writers-block, playwright Jack feels that real-world experiences will spark his creativity 1096

Jack, saddled with certain obligations, is unable to attain his cherished ambition 1097a

Mail room clerk Jack is held in low esteem 1098

Investigative journalist Jack lacks the courage necessary for his work 1104

Jack must reach a distant city by a certain time or he will lose an important contract 1107a

In pursuit of an important goal, Jack takes outrageous, flamboyant measures — and succeeds 1107a

Jack once committed a crime but was never suspected of it 1110

Author Jack suddenly becomes aware that he is losing his creativity 1111a

Jack, practicing medicine without proper qualifications, finds himself in a desperate situation 1112

Nobel Prize-winning scientist Jack secretly experiments with reanimating the dead 1113

Jack is traveling a great distance to complete an important project 1116

CHARACTER COMBINATIONS

Jack constructs a handmade product of such character it can't be duplicated by machinery 1122

Jack, by manufacturing a handmade product on a large scale to keep up with demand, will get rich but the quality of the product will suffer 1122

Jack, a heavy drinker, is given an ultimatum by his doctor: quit drinking or he'll die within a few months 1126

Jack, apparently dead, is really in a cataleptic state, seeing and/or hearing everything around him but unable to speak or move 1128a

Jack is in a mine when dynamite explodes prematurely 1128b

Jack is superstitious 1132

Jack attempts to find an adventurer who will recover Jack's stolen property for him 1129b

Jack conceals his ruthless, unethical nature behind a respectable facade 1140

(1) Jack has lived like a fugitive for so long, he is unable to accept freedom 1064

(1) Writer Jack finds that he is losing touch with his public, becoming unable to write salable material 1074

(1) Jack's weakness is gambling, and although he usually loses, he can't stop betting 1079

(1) Jack lacks the ability to take advantage of his opportunities 1088

(1) Jack no longer has the obligation which prevented him from attaining his cherished ambition, but discovers that he has become a confirmed procrastinator, his goals never achieved 1097a

(1) Jack's guilty conscience prevents his happiness 1110

(1) Jack, enroute to complete an important project, is unexpectedly delayed, placing the project in jeopardy 1116

(1) Jack absentmindedly doodles, unaware that he may be revealing important secrets 1124

(1) Suffering a severe trauma, Jack is seemingly dead 1128a

(1) Jack is blinded by an explosion 1128b

(1) Jack's superstition prevents his success 1132

(4) Young Jack, with less-than-average ability, deludes himself into thinking he's a genius 1060

(4) Jack's concept of life is to do just enough to get by 1063

(4) Reporter Jack, assigned to cover a certain story and finding it impossible, decides to write an imaginary interview and pass it off as the real thing 1080

(4) Jack, to finance an honest venture, temporarily turns to crime 1084

(4) Jack poses as a criminal 1097b

(4) Jack attempts to overcome personal limitations by cheating 1101

(4) Reading medical novels makes Jack eager to become a doctor 1111b

(4) Jack, confident of his ability, starts a new line of work despite having had no practical experience 1111b

(4) Jack, terminally laid-back, cheerfully welcomes his lack of ambition 1131

(4) Agnostic Jack arrogantly professes his disbelief in a higher power 1133

(9) Cowardly Jack deliberately places himself in danger to develop his courage 1082a

(9) Mail room clerk Jack solves a problem that has baffled his superiors, and wins an executive position 1098

Jack

PERSONAL LIMITATIONS (cont'd.)

(9-14) Cowardly Jack, by forcing himself into dangerous situations to gain first-hand information, develops courage 1104

(12) Jack mistakenly thinks he is a criminal, then learns he isn't 1064

(13) Novelist Jack, unaware that he's a sleepwalker, is baffled when, morning after morning, he discovers that the turgid novel he's writing by day has been, during the night, rewritten into a sophisticated comedy 1117

(14) Loutish Jack is suddenly transformed into a gentleman 1076

(14) Ordinary young Jack suddenly acquires delusions of grandeur and turns into a megalomaniac 1134

(14) Jack, who was timid and lacked ambition, has a change of personality which causes him to behave brashly 1134

PRETENSE

Jack has terrifying, recurring nightmares 1141

Jack, because of his terrifying nightmares, tries to avoid sleep 1141

Jack, presumed dead, is on the autopsy table when he awakens from a cataleptic trance 1142a

Jack is believed to have died in a storm 1142b

Jack, dealer in precious stones, has a valuable collection 1143a

In an effort to steal a carefully guarded object, criminal Jack tries to substitute a worthless counterfeit for the valuable original 1144

Criminal Jack disguises himself in order to carry out an illegal activity 1146

Banker Jack likes to gamble in Las Vegas, but is afraid of causing gossip in his home community 1148a

Jack, to protect his collection of valuable stones, displays fakes to would-be customers 1143a

Innocent Jack, deeply in debt, is suspected of a crime 1148b

Youthful, homesick Jack is unhappy because he doesn't receive any mail as do his young friends 1149

Lonely Jack, never receiving mail from home, invents a family and writes letters to himself which he then shows to his friends 1149

Jack is an art collector 1165

Jack wants to prove his ability to play a particular role in an upcoming play 1169

To prove he has the talent to play a certain role in an upcoming play, Jack plays the role off-stage 1169

Dentist Jack, drowning in suburbia, is desperate for adventure 1170

Stock speculator Jack assumes an alias in order to obtain insider information 1175a

Banker Jack has embezzled the bank's funds 1177

Jack conceals his criminal acts by framing a bank employee 1177

Highly respected Jack has committed a murder 1178

Criminal Jack poses as a law officer hunting for another criminal 1179

Criminal Jack poses as another criminal and commits a crime which will be attributed to that criminal 1181

Jack is unjustly suspected of a certain action 1183

Jack's socially prominent position conflicts with a project he wants to begin 1184

CHARACTER COMBINATIONS

Jack, to proceed with certain plans, has to conceal his identity 1184

Jack's family and friends believe he is an executive for a large multinational company, but in reality he is the CIA station chief in a foreign country 1185

Pursuing a worthy goal, Jack changes his name and goes to a place where he isn't known 1186

Rock star Jack poses as one of his fans to find out how his staff treats the public 1190

Thief Jack has an honest profession that he uses as a cover 1194

Jack, in trouble as a youth, returns incognito to his home town 1199

(2) Fugitive Jack, presumed dead, assumes an alias and vanishes 1142b

(3) Jack, presumed dead and about to be buried at sea, awakens from a cataleptic trance, and secretly escapes 1142a

(4) Cowardly Jack brags outrageously in hope of convincing others of his courage 1150

(4) Dentist Jack, searching for adventure, inadvertently finds himself in the guise of an about-to-be deposed dictator 1170

(4) Bank clerk Jack "borrows" bank funds for a weekend fling in Las Vegas 1187

(4) To evade his problems, Jack fakes amnesia 1188

(4) Jack, faking amnesia, is mis-identified as an individual whom, Jack discovers, has as many problems Jack does; Jack finds himself between a rock and a hard place 1188

(4) Murderer Jack tries to escape by impersonating the man he murdered 1195

(5-10) Jack, for laughs, pretends he's a doctor, and finds himself in deep trouble 1202a

(8) Jack tries to rebuild his life, which was ruined by substance abuse 1186

(9) Fugitive Jack assumes an alias and wins a fortune on a TV game show 1148b

(9) Jack, returning to his home town incognito, performs an heroic act 1199

(11) Jack, his false identity unmasked, is placed in deadly jeopardy 1193

(11) Police Commissioner Jack assumes the identity of a foot-patrolman to learn first-hand what problems the man on the beat faces 1198

DECEPTION
Fugitive Jack disguises himself and risks arrest to carry out a romantic venture 1209a

Jack's doctor warns Jack that he only has three months to live 1210

Jack, after pulling off a difficult jewel theft, has a change of heart and puts himself in jeopardy once again in order to replace the gems 1211

Thief Jack performs a daring robbery and then passes himself off as one of the victims 1217a

Jack, searching for an adventurer, stages a test in order to find a man courageous enough to carry out a dangerous assignment 1219

Psychologist Jack, testing a theory about human behavior under pressure, places himself in difficult situations 1223a

Jack takes shelter in a vacant mansion 1225

Jack is obsessively fearful of burglars 1230

Jack, obsessively fearful of burglars, installs a state-of-the-art security system so complex that he's unable to lead a normal life without setting it off 1230

Jack bets heavily on a sporting event 1231

Jack

DECEPTION (cont'd.)

Jack pretends to lead the routine, unadventurous life of a middle-class commuter 1237a

Jack forms a charitable foundation in an effort to make secret restitution of the wealth he gained illegally 1239

Jack shrewdly maintains his public image 1247

Jack closely guards a secret that, if known, would ruin his reputation and destroy an important project 1247

Jack uses his legitimate profession as a cover for illegal activities 1248

Jack tries to clear himself of suspicion of theft 1249

Rich Jack is determined to own a certain piece of property 1260a

Jack is a sociopath, a compulsive liar 1262

Jack decides to use secret information in a blackmail scheme 1263

Jack is a construction contractor who does substandard work 1273

Supposedly dead Jack uses an alias 1275

Female impersonator Jack commits a crime dressed as a woman, and removing his female attire, escapes dressed as a man 1282

Jack schemes to gain a rich inheritance 1285a

Investigative reporter Jack's life is threatened if he pursues a certain story 1287

Missionary Jack, among primitives, tries to avert a disaster by using prayer 1289b

(1) Writer Jack, decreasingly productive as he gets older, draws on long-forgotten incidents from his youth to generate new material. As he successfully uses the material, he ages, becoming weaker and weaker until finally, the material exhausted, Jack dies 1238

(1) Compulsive liar Jack fabricates an elaborate story which backfires, resulting in his prosecution for a crime 1262

(1) Persuaded to engage in an apparently honest venture, Jack discovers he is the victim of a setup 1267a

(1) Jack absently doodles diagrams that reveal clues to a confidential project 1289d

(4) Jack carries his suitcase into an airport restroom. He emerges in a totally different guise 1209b

(4) Wealthy Jack, whose doctor tells him he's got three months to live, decides to spend every penny so none will go to his worthless heirs 1210

(4) Jack, taking shelter in a vacant mansion and wishing to remain, secretly moves into the attic when the mansion becomes occupied 1225

(4) Jack's plan to commit a robbery is discovered and a trap is set for him at the scene of the intended crime 1268

(4) Jack, in the hope of collecting on his life insurance, fakes his own death 1277b

(6) Jack kills himself, but makes his death appear accidental 1237b

(6) Jack kills himself so that his insurance money will pay off his overwhelming financial obligations 1237b

(9) Jack gives up an inheritance because of a distasteful obligation attached to it 1242b

(9) Jack, despite death threats, continues his venture 1287

(12) Jack fakes his own death 1277b

CHARACTER COMBINATIONS

CRIME/IMMORALITY

Jack's estate has been in his family for generations, with the assumption that the land will never be sold 1291c

Debt-ridden but honest Jack is suddenly faced with the opportunity to illegally gain a large sum of money with no possibility of his being suspected of a crime 1297

Jack struggles against temptation to make a fortune by illegal means 1297

Criminal Jack uses deception in an attempt to avoid capture 1298

Jack has committed a crime and fled to escape capture 1300

Jack tries to avoid the consequences of a crime he has committed 1301

Supreme Court Judge Jack secretly commits a breach of ethics 1306

(4) Jack breaks an unwritten family law when he sells a portion of his family estate 1291c

(8) Jack, committing a crime and escaping unsuspected, is forced by his tortured conscience to confess 1291a

(8) Jack, remorseful because he has committed a crime, tries to make restitution 1295

(9) Prospector Jack discovers gold 1296

(12) Jack commits a crime (or breach of morality) and escapes unsuspected 1291a

(12) Universally respected Jack, in a high-profile position, attempts to conceal a dark secret 1306

(13) It is important for Jack to appear at a particular time and place, but it's equally vital that he avoid capture 1300

VENGEANCE

Innocent Jack is broke, but remarkably handsome 1320

(1) Jack is condemned to death as a political conspirator 1327

(2) Jack learns of a conspiracy to kill him and narrowly escapes death 1327

(3) Jack, allegedly dead, pretends to be a ghost 1313b

(4) Jack attempts to get revenge on a large corporation for a serious wrong 1312

(8) Jack, about to take his revenge, realizes it would be an empty victory, its only result the destruction of an innocent person 1323a

MYSTERY

Jack, a plunger with unrealistic expectations of success, impulsively takes over a business in which he has no experience 1330

Jack, refusing to acknowledge the severity of a storm, insists on driving home 1331

Jack runs from an imaginary pursuer 1332

Chemist Jack, experimenting with lethal chemicals, accidentally contaminates a bouquet of flowers 1333a

Jack picks up the wrong pair of eyeglasses 1336

Thief Jack's cover is that of private investigator 1339

Psychiatrist Jack finds himself increasingly haunted by his tragic secret 1346

Famous film director Jack, although claiming innocence, is notorious for his romantic affairs 1349

Jogger Jack, obsessed with an irrational fear of dogs, is determined to overcome his phobia 1350

Jack comes to the realization that what he believes are real dangers are nothing more than figments of his imagination 1351

Jack is a captive of his superstitious beliefs 1355

Jack

MYSTERY (cont'd.)
Risk-taker Jack is losing his confidence 1356

Jack is investigating psychic phenomena 1357

Jack envisions his own death 1358

Jack associates a certain sound with a tragic experience from his past. The sound fills him with dread 1359

Jack has a nightmare that haunts his waking moments and affects his behavior 1361a

Jack has an occult experience that predicts his success in a certain project 1361b

Jack believes he hears strange voices 1365

Jack, thinking he's hearing strange voices, convinces himself that they are a temporary hallucination 1365

Jack is strongly influenced by his dreams 1366

Jack, strongly influenced by his dreams, attempts to control them by will power 1366

Research scientist Jack develops a new serum which, if successful, will prove revolutionary 1367b

Jack loses his memory 1368

Jack, a prospector, is traveling with a fortune in gold dust 1370b

Jack's character defect prevents him from achieving success 1374

Jack has been missing for years and is presumed dead 1378

Adventurer Jack is about to carry out a dangerous mission 1379

Art dealer Jack discovers that an antique tapestry contains a mysterious diagram 1386b

Daydreamer Jack is fascinated by extraterrestrial phenomena 1389b

Daydreamer Jack, fascinated by UFOs, undergoes a shattering experience 1389b

Jack will learn an important secret if he is ingenious enough to decipher a riddle contained in an ancient document 1392

Investigating a psychic phenomenon, Jack finds it difficult to suspend his disbelief 1398

Jack attempts to locate hidden wealth that is legitimately his 1399

Jack inadvertently learns an important secret, and is drawn into a dark mystery 1403

Reporter Jack is assigned to cover a story which involves a closely-guarded secret 1407

Jack learns of a closely-guarded secret 1408

Jack, learning of a closely-guarded secret, investigates and finds himself in jeopardy 1408

Jack is engaged in an unusual venture 1414b

Jack mysteriously vanishes while working on a highly secret project 1414b

Bank messenger Jack mysteriously disappears with valuable securities 1415

While engaged in an important venture, Jack inadvertently takes an hallucinogenic drug 1418a

Jack, following a narrow escape from death, develops irrational fears 1422b

Jack tries to solve the mystery of a strange house 1426a

Jack finds himself in an alien culture whose members are under the control of a charismatic leader 1427a

Jack is skeptical about supernatural phenomena 1427b

CHARACTER COMBINATIONS

Jack has a mystifying experience that causes him to re-examine his beliefs 1427b

Jack has a dream in which he falls from a great height 1428

Applying for a job, Jack is unable to supply information about his family background 1430a

Jack, during a tennis match, has a vision of a grave being dug for himself 1433a

Jack is warned anonymously that if he fulfills a certain obligation, it will cost him his life 1434

Jack belongs to a secret society 1438c

Jack belongs to a secret society whose members have sworn vengeance against their enemies 1438c

College student Jack inherits an object which he comes to believe is bringing him bad luck 1440

Young Jack studies philosophy in an attempt to understand the meaning of life 1441a

Imprisoned criminal Jack experiences a vivid dream in which he makes a successful escape 1443a

Mountain climber Jack falls into a deep crevasse 1443b

Wealthy Jack returns to the dirt-farm where he was raised and, forgetting the location of an old well, falls into it 1443c

(1) Jack, impulsively involving himself in matters he doesn't understand, constantly fails 1330

(1) Jack, obsessed by a superstitious fear, abandons a venture 1334a

(1) Long-distance trucker Jack, pulls into a freight depot, enters the deserted dispatcher's office to pick up a package, and finds himself in a bizarre trap from which there seems to be no escape 1335

(1) During a storm, Jack is struck by lightning and almost dies 1353

(1) Jack, thinking he can outsmart the Devil, makes a final wish that he will live forever, but the Devil reminds Jack that his account is already overdrawn 1354a

(1) Disaster hits Jack when he believes an illusion is real 1357

(1) Jack, taken ill, is haunted by a vision that foretells his death — and he dies 1358

(1) Jack, dreading a certain sound, becomes a victim of his irrational fear 1359

(1) Jack has supernatural experiences that interfere with his ambitions 1360

(1) Jack is so sure of success in a certain project that he reduces his effort and the project fails 1361b

(1) Prospector Jack and his companions are attacked by bandits. Jack's companions are killed and Jack is mortally wounded 1370b

(1) Discovering a rich vein of emeralds in the Amazon, Jack dies before he can mine the gems 1370c

(1) Jack is wrongfully accused of a crime by the public, which is unaware of his true motives 1376

(1) Out-of-work actor Jack, hired to portray a giant peanut for a promotional stunt, is witness to a robbery. Aware that he's a deadman if identified, and unable to remove the peanut costume without help, he is forced to flee, the bad guys giving chase 1419b

(1) Jack falls prey to an alien which invades his body 1422a

(1) Jack, attempting to alter certain laws of nature, narrowly escapes death from an unexplained source 1422b

(1) Jack, trying to unravel a great secret, encounters an unexpected complication 1441a

Jack

MYSTERY (cont'd.)

(1) Jack has a psychological scar, the result of a cruel act he committed long ago 1441b

(1) Jack, trapped in a deep crevasse, is unable to free himself, and he dies 1443b

(1) Jack, falling into a well, can't get out, and dies of his injuries 1443c

(4) Jack, suffering from acute depression, has a pessimistic view of life 1345

(4) Jack, investigating psychic phenomena, finds it increasingly difficult to separate truth from illusion 1347

(4) Jack, obsessed with an irrational fear of dogs, dreams he's being attacked by a pack of wild dogs and is discovered the following morning, brutally savaged 1350

(4) Jack, to master his fears, exposes himself to what he believes is an illusionary danger — but it proves to be real 1351

(4) Loner Jack, who believes he needs no one but himself, is lost in a wilderness 1353

(4) Jack makes a deal with the Devil; in exchange for each wish granted, the Devil extracts a number of years from Jack's life 1354a

(4) Jack, whose career is dependent on his unwavering courage, begins to second-guess himself, aware that this condition can only lead to failure 1356

(4-12) Researcher Jack, to test the serum he has developed, uses himself as a guinea pig 1367b

(4) Disgruntled government employee Jack attempts to sell state secrets to a foreign power 1372a

(4) Jack turns traitor during wartime and joins the enemy 1372b

(4) Jack trades his dreams for a limitless fortune 1373

(4) Jack attempts to uncover the mystery of a locked room 1409

(5-10) Recuperating in a hospital, Jack changes his views on certain important questions 1353

(6) Near death, Jack draws a cryptic map showing the location of an emerald mine 1370c

(6) Jack dies of psychic trauma 1428

(9-14) Jack has a psychic experience that enables him to overcome a character defect and become successful 1374

(9) Jack overcomes a superstitious obsession by sheer will power 1375

(9) Jack discovers a mysterious document revealing the location of a fabled lost city 1394

(9) Caught in a deadly trap, Jack calls upon his psychic powers and teleports himself to safety 1419a

(10) The vividness of Jack's dream rivals reality 1433b

(11) Jack, picking up someone else's eyeglasses, looks in the mirror and is shocked to discover that he is seeing into his own future 1336

(12) Jack mysteriously receives a warning of danger 1424a

(13) Jack, insisting on driving through a severe storm, finds himself in serious trouble, his car half-buried in the snow 1331

(13) Jack, unable to explain certain events, attributes them to the supernatural 1381

(13) Timid tourist Jack takes part in a staged "native" ritual, and falls into a trance. Awakening from the trance, Jack is stunned to find his personality transformed 1387

(13) Sleepwalker Jack has no recollection of his nocturnal adventures 1389a

CHARACTER COMBINATIONS

(13) Jack mysteriously disappears, baffling all who attempt to locate him 1414a

(13) Jack, investigating a mysterious house, is caught in a violent electrical storm. When the storm clears, the house has vanished 1426a

(13) Jack confuses his dream with reality 1433b

(13) Jack has a psychological scar that results in psychosomatic illnesses 1441b

(14) Jack, a victim of amnesia, assumes a new identity 1368

(14) Amnesiac Jack, who has rebuilt his life and become a successful stockbroker, suffers a minor accident and is suddenly restored to his former identity as a bus driver, with no recollection of his second life 1390

(14) Messenger Jack vanishes with valuable bank securities; he is later discovered in jail, admitting his crime but accusing the police of stealing the securities from him 1415

REVELATION
For years, Jack has been unable to solve a baffling mystery 1451a

Relying on supposedly valid information, Jack embarks on a dangerous mission 1451d

Jack searches in vain for the key to a seemingly insoluble mystery 1452

Jack is about to give up trying to solve a puzzling riddle 1453

Insecure writer Jack doubts if a story he has in mind will appeal to his readers 1460

(8) Jack struggles with his conscience and makes an important decision in order to find peace of mind 1461a

(9-12) Jack, trying to solve a baffling mystery, inadvertently discovers a clue in an object that has been in plain sight for years 1451a

(9-12) Jack, escaping from danger, takes a wrong turn and falls into a chasm in which he inadvertently finds a clue to a baffling mystery 1452

(11) Jack receives information which causes him to abandon a favorite project 1455a

Jack and Pete

ROMANTIC MISADVENTURES
(4-5) Jack and Pete have an accident and Pete is killed 169

MARRIED LIFE
Jack visits his friend, Pete 446b

(12) Pete, wrongly suspected of crime/immorality, is in deep trouble until Jack clears him of suspicion 390

MISFORTUNE
Jack, trying to help his friend, Pete, lends him all his money 601

Jack and his friend, Pete, are attacked by thieves in a lonely place 603b

Jack's friend, Pete, is wounded and dies 603b

Jack and his friend, Pete, on horseback, try to cross a flooded river. Pete is hit by floating driftwood. Jack rescues him and gets him to the river bank 603c

Jack's friend, Pete, is so badly injured, he dies 603c

Jack and his friend, Pete, wander around in a desert. Pete is injured and they run out of water 603d

Jack's friend, Pete, dies 603d

Jack and his friend, Pete, are alone exploring a jungle 607

Jack's friend, Pete, berserk from eating the fruit a strange plant, attacks Jack and tries to kill him 607

Jack helps Pete hide treasure in a secret place 662

Jack and Pete

MISFORTUNE (cont'd.)

Jack's friend, Pete, kills himself before Jack can help him overcome his troubles 671

Jack forms a plan to help Pete 672

Jack tries to get rich by cheating Pete 701

Jack, because of a particular incident, is forced to turn against his friend, Pete 704

Jack and Pete were the best of friends at a military academy 716

Jack is a captain in the army. His men capture his friend, Pete, now an enemy officer, and bring him to Jack 716

(1) Jack's friend, Pete, fails to repay money loaned him by Jack, leaving Jack broke 601

(1) Jack loses out because his friend, Pete, fails to effectively carry out his part in a certain venture 603a

(1) Jack finds himself and his reputation ruined when his double, Pete, fouls up an important enterprise while posing as Jack 629

(1) Due to Pete, Jack's accomplice in a venture, Jack sustains a loss 630

(1) Jack is ruined when he asks his supposed friend, Pete, for money and is turned down 631

(1) Jack, helping Pete hide treasure in a secret place, is left to die by Pete who takes off alone with the treasure 662

(1) Jack, trying to get rich by cheating Pete, is tortured by his conscience 701

(1) Jack loses a fortune trying to help a friend, Pete 715b

(4) Jack, to help his friend, Pete, violates his own principles and suffers unpleasant results 599

(4) Jack and Pete are at a costume party. Pete, suddenly called away on urgent business, promises to return shortly; Jack agrees to wear Pete's mask and costume and take Pete's place. Pete fails to return, leaving Jack in a dilemma 599

(4) Jack has his double, Pete, replace him in an important venture 629

MISTAKEN JUDGMENT

Convinced of a certain stock's value, Jack invests in it himself and sells shares to his friends, Pete and Annie 747

Jack tries to manage Pete's failing business and make it profitable 769

Jack's drunken friend, Pete, persuades Jack to take a drink, despite Pete's knowledge that Jack's doctor has warned Jack he mustn't drink 779

Before the war, Jack had a friend, Pete, who did him a great favor 790a

During the war, Pete, is captured as an enemy agent and brought before Captain Jack 790a

Judge Jack's childhood friend, Pete, is brought before him for trial 790b

Jack is persuaded by his friend, Pete, to participate in a difficult venture 793a

Jack is persuaded by his friend, Pete, to hold some important papers 793b

Jack thinks his friend, Pete, is dead 794

(1) Jack, influenced by a reckless friend, Pete, is killed 761a

(1-5) Captain Jack lets enemy agent Pete escape and as a consequence Jack is branded a traitor 790a

(1-5) Without revealing their past relationship, and rather than disqualifying himself, Judge Jack presides at the trial of his friend, Pete, and manipulates the case so that Pete is acquitted 790b

CHARACTER COMBINATIONS

(1) Jack obliges his friend, Pete, by holding Pete's important documents. Jack is arrested and, because he has the documents, is charged with a crime 793b

(4) Jack, deeply in debt, tries to save himself from ruin by forging the name of a friend, Pete, on a loan 770b

(4) Jack is persuaded by friend, Pete, to begin a venture that Jack's judgment warns him to avoid 793a

(7) Jack is stunned when his friend, Pete, whom he thought dead, suddenly appears 794

HELPFULNESS
Jack's friend, Pete, is accused of a crime 820

Jack, learning that his friend, Pete, is accused of a crime, tries to prove his innocence 820

Jack, who considers himself a failure, admires his friend, Pete 823

Sprinter Jack is about to lose a race because he thinks he hears the voice of a dead friend, Pete, calling for help 827

Jack, sick and hungry, receives food and money from his friend, Pete 831

Pete confides to his friend, Jack, that he is a criminal 831

Jack runs into troubles of his own when he tries to help his friend, Pete, who has serious problems 836

In order to help his friend, Pete, Jack discards his principles and embarks on a disagreeable venture 838

Jack tries to correct a character flaw in his friend, Pete 839

Jack tries to stop his friend, Pete, from performing a reckless act that will have deadly consequences 840

Jack learns that his friend, Pete, has committed suicide 841

Jack tries to spare Pete's family the pain of public disclosure of Pete's actions 841

Impoverished Jack, at great sacrifice, helps Pete, who is poorer than Jack 845

Jack's friend, Pete, collapses, exhausted, while engaged in a project 846

Jack completes a project for Pete, his friend, that Pete was unable to finish 846

(1) Jack, trying to help his friend, Pete, is suspected of treachery by Pete 807

(6) Jack's friend, Pete, is unjustly sentenced to death. Jack, deceiving the guards, takes Pete's place and is executed 823

(9-12) Jack gets his friend, Pete, drunk to prevent him from committing a reckless act that would have deadly consequences 840

(9) Jack restores Pete to friends and fortune 845

(10) Jack tries to correct a character flaw in his friend, Pete, by relating a story that subtly suggests a method of self-help 839

DELIVERANCE
Sheriff Jack is convinced the man he is about to hang, Pete, didn't commit the crime for which he was sentenced 877

Sheriff Jack delays hanging a condemned man, Pete, hoping that something or someone will intervene and save Pete 877

(2) Executive Jack's career is saved when his junior associate, Pete, employs deception to stop him from committing a foolhardy act 880a

(2) Jack, saved from a foolhardy act by Pete, comes to his senses, and rewards Pete 880a

(5) About to commit a foolish act, Jack is abducted and held prisoner by his friend, Pete, as the only means of restraining him 865

Jack and Pete

DELIVERANCE (cont'd.)

(8-12) Jack destroys a suicide note written by his friend, Pete, and instead makes it appear that Pete is the victim of a crime 868

(9-12) Jack, suspected of treachery by his friend, Pete, heroically saves Pete's life and property. Jack's heroism in the face of danger to which Pete was unknowingly exposed, proves Jack's loyalty 867

(9) Elderly Jack, a homeless outcast, is returned to family and self-respect by a friend, Pete 880b

(9) Jack, who has "gone native," is rescued from a difficult situation by an old friend, Pete 887b

(9) Visiting Pete in prison, Jack swaps clothes with him and Pete leaves posing as Jack 875a

(14) Sheriff Jack is duty-bound to hang a condemned friend, Pete 877

IDEALISM

Jack learns that his partner, Pete, is unable to pay his bills 906

Jack has problems and looks for happiness in the companionship of Pete and/or in an avocation 913

Jack is a loser, while his friend, Pete, is a straight-arrow 972

Jack is determined, at any cost, to save his friend, Pete, from a menacing problem 972

(1-4-12) Pete has heavy personal responsibilities, and Jack doesn't — so Jack disappears, leaving false evidence that he is the guilty party 906

(14) Jack seriously wrongs his friend, Pete, but learns a valuable lesson when Pete forgives him 925

OBLIGATION

In return for a service Pete has performed for him, Jack agrees to grant any favor Pete wants that is within Jack's power 981

Jack indirectly endangers his friend, Pete — danger that Pete is unaware of and that Jack can't reveal 987

Jack gives his sacred oath to his friend, Pete, that he will do whatever Pete asks of him 997a

Pete begs Jack to be merciful and kill him 1007

Jack, as a favor to his friend, Pete, promises to embark on a certain venture 1021a

Jack promises his friend, Pete, that he'll undertake a certain venture, then reneges on his promise 1021a

Jack and Pete are devoted friends 1021b

(1) Jack honors the heart-breaking obligation of performing euthanasia on his suffering, terminally ill friend, Pete 1007

(1) Army officer Jack has a friend, Pete, who is an enemy spy. Pete is brought before Jack for punishment 1016b

(1) Jack and Pete's perfect friendship is challenged by an unusual experience 1021b

(6-12) Jack's friend, Pete, rescues Jack from a gut-wrenching situation by taking his own life 1016b

(12) Influenced by compelling responsibility, Jack has to protect his friend, Pete, from danger 987

CHANCE

(1) Thinking he is confronting a thief, Jack mistakenly shoots his friend, Pete 1035

PERSONAL LIMITATIONS

Jack casually takes on a task to oblige his friend, Pete 1058

Jack wants to save his friend, Pete, from disaster, but money is required and Jack has none 1085

Wealthy Jack, who thinks he's too old to enjoy his money, gives a large sum to destitute young Pete 1102

Jack hopes to enjoy Pete's spending spree vicariously 1102

Jack tries to be loyal to his friend, Pete, but certain conditions make it difficult 1115

(1) Jack, posing as a criminal, discovers that several of his respectable friends, Pete, Annie and Larry are running a scam which is protected by the police 1097b

(4) Scientist Jack plagiarizes research material created by his late friend, Pete 1103

(10) Jack, taking on a task to oblige his friend, Pete, finds the task beyond his abilities 1058

PRETENSE
Jack assumes Pete's identity and carries out a venture started by Pete 1168

Jack and Pete are criminals running from the law 1174

Jack assumes the identity of a deceased friend, Pete 1183

Wealthy Jack entertains lavishly; as a result, he has many friends 1202b

(1) Posing as Pete, Jack doesn't know that Pete is a criminal 1168

(10) Wealthy Jack, to test his friends' loyalty, pretends to be broke and attempts to borrow money from them 1202b

(13) Jack and Pete, close friends traveling together, are unaware that each has committed an act that will place them in jeopardy 1175b

DECEPTION
For selfish reasons, Jack helps his friend, Pete, who is in serious trouble 1212a

Pete's friend, Jack, learns that Pete is going to be the victim of a crime. Jack, discovering this too late to warn Pete, places himself in jeopardy to help Pete 1214

Jack recovers property stolen from his friend, Pete 1234

Jack explains that he invested money belonging to himself and Pete in a failed venture 1249

Jack persuades his friend, Pete, to handle a dangerous job — but doesn't tell Pete that it's dangerous 1264

Jack discovers that his friend, Pete, has committed a crime or indiscretion 1269

Jack invites his friend, Pete, for drinks at his remote beach house 1288

(3) Jack's friend, Pete, is attacked and robbed by three people, one of whom is Jack 1227a

(4) Jack notifies the authorities about his friend, Pete's, crime and is rewarded for Pete's capture 1269

(6) Jack, having committed a murder at his remote beach house, removes all traces of his presence, then summons the police. Pete arrives at the house, discovers the body, and moments later is accused by the police of having committed the murder 1288

(8) Jack's friend, Pete, is richly rewarded from a discovery he makes and offers to share with Jack. But Jack, knowing he tried to deceive Pete, refuses, thus arousing Pete's suspicions 1235

(9) Fugitive Jack disguises himself in order to save his friend, Pete, from the law 1209c

(9) Jack, recovering property stolen from his friend, Pete, secretly tries to return it so Pete won't know it was stolen 1234

(11) Jack tries to profit by deceiving his friend, Pete, but fails — without Pete's knowledge 1235

Jack and Pete

CRIME/IMMORALITY

Jack fights with Pete in a drunken brawl 1291b

Jack and Pete are partners in a failing business 1304

(1) Jack, sobering up after a drunken brawl, discovers Pete dead and believes he has killed him 1291b

(4) Prospector Jack makes a rich ore strike and hides the discovery from his partner, Pete 1296

(4) Jack, partner of Pete, steals the remaining assets of their business and accuses Pete of the crime 1304

VENGEANCE

Jack seeks revenge on associate Pete 1313a

Jack, seeking revenge on his associate Pete, is forced by circumstances to conceal his true intent 1313a

MYSTERY

Pete is killed in an accident while with his friend, Jack 1334b

Jack's friend, Pete, is mysteriously murdered 1334c

Jack tries to solve the murder of his friend, Pete 1334c

Jack has delusions that he is haunted by Pete's spirit 1344

Jack is the only one who knows that his friend, Pete, has died suddenly 1385

Jack's curiosity is aroused by the mysterious actions of his friend, Pete, and he decides to investigate 1402

Concerned about his friend, Pete's erratic behavior, Jack investigates 1436

Jack discovers that his friend, Pete, is involved in a mysterious venture 1436

Jack learns an important secret which, if revealed, will destroy Pete's career 1439a

Jack worries that Pete will unearth incriminating evidence that Jack has concealed 1442

(1) Jack believes that he was the cause of Pete's death 1344

(1) Jack is haunted by an act he committed in an effort to help a friend, Pete 1355

(5) Jack, experimenting with dangerous drugs, narrowly escapes from a life-threatening situation 1363

(5) Jack finds himself in serious difficulties because of his impulsiveness, and is rescued by a friend, Pete 1363

(12) Jack is mistaken for his dead friend, Pete, and sees the opportunity to turn the situation to his advantage 1385

(13) Jack, who is superstitious, believes he is haunted by the ghost of his friend, Pete 1334b

(13) Pro football lineman Jack believes that quarterback Pete, a friend whom he accidentally killed during a practice scrimmage, is on the field with him during every game 1338

REVELATION

Jack investigates the murder of his friend, Pete 1449

Student Jack, during final exams, discovers that his new friend, Pete, is a girl student posing as her boyfriend 1454

Jack, discovering that Pete is a girl posing as a boy, keeps her secret 1454

(1) Jack, investigating the murder of a friend, Pete, is horrified to discover that the evidence targets Jack as the murderer 1449

Jack and Gary

ROMANTIC MISADVENTURES

Pretending to be Jack's friend, his rival, Gary, sets a deadly trap for Jack 79

REJECTION
Jack is accused by Gary of having a secret past 245

MARRIED LIFE
Jack's enemy, Gary, who gravely victimized Jack, is dead 433a

(1) Jack is manipulated by Gary into speculating with money that isn't his, and losing it 434a

(1) Jack is maneuvered into trouble by Gary 434b

MISFORTUNE
Jack, is about to lose a physical contest to his rival, Gary 652b

(1) Jack's deadly enemy, Gary, has Jack at his mercy, and there is nothing for Jack to do but make the best of a bad situation 663

(1-12) Gary, having killed Jack, plants a gun in Jack's hand to make it appear that Jack committed suicide 730

(6) Jack, in an attempt to overcome his rival, Gary, meets with an accident and is killed 652b

MISTAKEN JUDGMENT
(1) Jack's success is mistakenly credited to Jack's enemy, Gary 796

HELPFULNESS
(1) Jack is arrested on charges concocted by a jealous rival, Gary 829

DELIVERANCE
Jack, a hunted outlaw, hides with an enemy, Gary 883

IDEALISM
(2) Jack reconciles with an enemy, Gary, when Gary does him a service 912b

OBLIGATION
Jack's life is saved by his enemy, Gary 1022

(1) Jack's life is saved by his enemy, Gary; as a result, Jack agrees to do Gary's bidding 1022

CHANCE
Jack is trying to kill his enemy, Gary 1039

PERSONAL LIMITATIONS
Backwoodsman Jack pursues an enemy, Gary, to a large city 1109

(8) Jack, from a rural region, singlemindedly tracks his enemy, Gary, to a large city. Thrown into the unfamiliar, distracting environment, Jack quickly forgets his original goal 1109

PRETENSE
(4) Using a disguise, Jack gets a job with rival Gary for the purpose of obtaining certain information 1193

DECEPTION
Jack thinks Gary is guilty of a crime 1222a

Jack, trying to force Gary to confess to a crime, places himself and Gary in a situation where both seemingly face imminent death 1222a

Jack has evidence that is potentially damaging to Gary 1228

Jack learns that Gary knows a secret that will bring disaster to Jack if revealed 1232

Jack decides it is necessary to kidnap Gary and hold him incommunicado 1232

Jack pretends that he is unadventurous and without courage in order to trick his enemy, Gary, into believing he isn't to be feared 1237a

Jack is defenseless against an armed enemy, Gary 1250

Jack pretends to be defenseless in order to disarm his enemy, Gary 1250

Jack is lured by Gary into an illegal gambling club 1255a

When Jack backs out of his agreement to join Gary in a venture, Gary attempts to carry out the venture alone 1265b

Jack and Gary

DECEPTION (cont'd.)

Jack's enemy, Gary, is an authority on poisonous snakes 1266

Jack's enemy, Gary, tries to prevent a disaster by an incantation 1289b

Jack, by prayer, and Gary, by incantation, try to avert a disaster 1289b

(1) Jack is framed and jailed by politically powerful Gary, so that Jack's threatening information can't harm Gary 1228

(1) Jack is tricked into a trap by Gary 1253

(1) Jack's enemy, Gary, lures Jack into an illegal casino and arranges for a raid by bribed police officers 1255a

(1) Trying to take unfair advantage of Gary, Jack persuades him to take possession of stolen goods, knowing Gary will be arrested 1265a

(3-9) Lured into a trap by Gary, Jack has set a counter-snare for Gary 1253

(3) Jack's enemy, Gary arranges a raid by corrupt policemen on a gambling casino, but Jack, learning of Gary's plan, summons honest cops for a genuine raid 1255a

(3) Jack catches his enemy, Gary, committing a crime 1280

(4-12) Astronaut Jack ejects the corpse of the fellow crew member he has murdered, astronaut Gary, from their space capsule to make it appear that Gary died because of an equipment malfunction 1277a

(5) Missionary Jack tries to convert a primitive tribe, but his efforts are defeated by Gary, a witch doctor 1274

(9) Employing deception, Jack forces Gary to reveal a guilty secret, thus enabling Jack to succeed in a difficult venture 1222b

(9) When Jack's deadly enemy, Gary, is lulled by a false sense of security, Jack kills him 1237a

(9) Jack, playing on Gary's ego as an expert on poisonous snakes, lures Gary into a life-threatening situation 1266

(9) Jack catches Gary committing a crime, but instead of reporting him to the police, Jack blackmails Gary 1280

VENGEANCE

Jack revenges himself on his enemy, Gary 1311

Jack tries to get revenge on Gary for a slur against Jack's family 1315

Jack seeks revenge on Gary for a harassment that resulted in the death of Jack's parents and sisters 1316

Jack wants to get revenge on Gary for a terrible wrong 1318

Jack sets a deadly trap for his enemy, Gary 1319b

Jack tries to get revenge on Gary, but Gary is powerful and constantly on his guard against Jack 1322

Prosperous Jack is hated by jealous rival, Gary 1323b

Jack's enemy, Gary, contrives to cause Jack's death without drawing suspicion to himself 1324a

(1-7) Jack revenges himself on his enemy, Gary, unaware that Gary is his brother 1311

(1) Jack has no personal quarrel with Gary, but because of his part in a family feud, he must kill Gary 1314

(1) Jack's rival, Gary, maneuvers Jack into becoming a criminal suspect 1323b

(1) Jack, an outspoken foe of religious fanatics, is tracked by assassins Gary, Laura and Stan 1329

(2) Jack, target of hired assassin Burt, contrives a situation in which Gary, the man who hired the assassin, becomes his victim 1324b

(2) Jack, in the guise of a fanatic, rigs a trap in which his enemies, assassins Gary, Laura and Stan, unwittingly destroy each other 1329

(3) By a subtle twist, Jack kills Gary instead of Gary killing him 1324a

(3) Jack, thought to be dead, pretends to be a ghost and haunts his enemy, Gary 1313b

(10) Jack, wanting vengeance against Gary, discovers after a long search that Gary is dead 1318

MYSTERY
Jack dreams he sees his enemy, Gary, in his room 1361a

(5) Respected Psychiatrist Jack, while still in his teens, accidentally killed Gary during a furious argument, and then fled. Gary's death has remained a mystery 1346

(10) Jack thinks he has murdered Gary. Then, suddenly, Gary appears before him 1342b

Jack and Dave

MISFORTUNE
In desperate danger, Jack asks a stranger, Dave for help 632

Jack appeals for help to selfish, powerful Dave, who refuses to endanger a major project in order to save Jack's life 632

Jack, a professional man, is kidnapped from his office at night by mysterious strangers, Dave, Kate & Rick. They blindfold him and take him to a secret place 660a

Jack, grabbed by Dave, Kate & Rick, is forced to perform a service that requires his expertise 660a

Jack invites a number of guests to meet Dave, a celebrity 702

Jack has invited a number of fans to meet Dave, a celebrity. The fans arrive, but Dave doesn't 702

(1) Dave leaves Jack to die 632

(4) Jack asks a stranger, Dave, to remove handcuffs from his wrists 707

MISTAKEN JUDGMENT
Jack befriends a needy stranger, Dave 772

(1-7) Jack befriends a needy stranger, Dave, who turns out to be a criminal 772

HELPFULNESS
Jack tries to help Dave, an old man in trouble 805

Enroute, Jack finds a stranger, Dave, ill and unconscious 816a

(1) Jack, trying to help a stranger, Dave, finds himself enmeshed in a difficult situation 805

(4) Jack sympathizes with Dave, a fugitive, and tries to help him 815a

(8) Jack sacrifices his self-interest to help a sick stranger, Dave 816a

DELIVERANCE
Jack invites a celebrity, Dave, to be guest of honor at a reception in his home, and Dave accepts 863b

Jack, a hotel owner facing ruin, invites a celebrity, Dave, to stay at his hotel and Dave accepts 863c

Jack won't delay his important venture long enough to rescue Dave, who is in distress and could die 957c

(7-10) Jack is prevented from committing suicide by Dave, who as fate would have it has come to the same place for the same reason 879

Jack and Dave

OBLIGATION

Problems threaten Jack because of a mysterious package that Jack has obligingly taken from Dave, a stranger, and promised to deliver 985

Jack discovers a crime Dave wants to hide 998

(3) Jack, aware of a crime Dave wants to hide, threatens to tell the police unless Dave does what Jack wants 998

CHANCE

Ordinary Jack is mistaken for a celebrity, Dave 1036

As Jack gets off a plane, he mistakenly takes a suitcase belonging to a stranger, Dave, leaving his own bag in its place 1044a

Jack is hiding from a determined process-server, Dave 1056

(2) Dave, a stranger, has Jack's suitcase. Dave meets with an accident and is killed. Because of items in the suitcase, Jack is reported dead 1044a

PERSONAL LIMITATIONS

(10) Jack befriends Dave, but because of his personality defects ends up alienating Dave 1059

PRETENSE

Jack, to help Dave, poses as Dave 1161

Jack, fleeing from his ex-wife's money-demands, poses as a famous novelist, Dave 1180

Con man Jack targets a stranger, Dave, for a sting 1191

Con man Jack pretends he's in trouble and needs Dave's help 1191

(1) Jack's "double," Dave, completes a project posing as Jack that results in disaster for Jack 1163c

(2) Jack, overloaded with romantic entanglements, enlists stranger Dave to help him out of an embarrassing situation 1163b

(4) Jack, meeting Dave, a stranger who was injured in an accident, agrees to take over a project that the accident prevents Dave from completing 1161

(4) Jack finds his "double" in Dave. Jack hires Dave to fulfill certain duties that require Jack's presence 1163a

(9) Jack's impersonation of a famous novelist, Dave, backfires when the novelist's ex-wife has him served for non-payment of alimony 1180

DECEPTION

Jack hires unsuspecting Dave and sends him into a potentially disastrous situation 1223a

Jack poses as electronic security consultant, Dave 1271

Thief Jack, in the guise of a repairman, gains entrance to wealthy Dave's mansion 1285c

MYSTERY

Reporter Jack, trying to beat a deadline, fabricates an interview in which Dave establishes that he was in a particular city on a certain day 1340

Supermarket clerk Jack is approached by a mysterious stranger, Dave 1388

Stranger Dave offers clerk Jack a large sum of money to participate in an unspecified adventure 1388

Jack's curiosity is aroused by the odd behavior of a stranger, Dave 1404a

Jack, unsuccessful in preventing the suicide of stranger, Dave, finds himself embroiled in Dave's past 1404a

Jack tries to find Dave, who has mysteriously disappeared 1404b

CHARACTER COMBINATIONS

Jack, curiosity aroused, investigates Dave, who seems to have guilty knowledge of a crime that has just occurred 1405

Involved in a dangerous search for Dave, Jack finds himself cut off from the outside world 1426b

Jack is taken prisoner by an alien culture, and discovers that the man he has been seeking, Dave, is also a prisoner 1426b

(2) Dave, accused of a crime, finds a fortunate alibi in a news story fabricated by reporter, Jack 1340

(2) Dave hires supposed private investigator Jack to recover stolen property that, unknown to Dave, was stolen by Jack 1339

(4) Jack murders a stranger, Dave, in a location which has an odd-colored soil, unique to the area. Jack returns home with traces of the soil clinging to his shoes 1341

REVELATION
(7) Jack, attempting to discover if a story he has in mind will appeal to his readers, tests it on total strangers, Dave, Kate & Rick 1460

Jack and Burt

MISFORTUNE
Jack tries to beat a con man, Burt, at his own game 630

Jack, kidnapped and held for ransom by Burt, is an officious, disagreeable man whose family and friends are glad to be rid of him and won't pay the ransom 639

Jack, held at gun point by a thief, Burt, tries to delay handing over his valuables 655

Jack, captured at sea by terrorists Burt, Sally and Fred, is cast adrift in a small boat 719b

Jack is a law officer pursuing a criminal, Burt 722

Police officer Jack owes money to a criminal, Burt, but is unable to repay him 723

Jack attempts to inform the authorities of the identity of a criminal, Burt, who, so far, is unsuspected 725

(1) Jack, learning a closely guarded secret, is hounded by a persecutor, Burt, who makes Jack's life miserable 596

(1) Jack, as Burt's sponsor, discovers that Burt is a con artist who uses Jack's sponsorship so he can cheat Jack's friends 612

(1) Jack befriends a drifter, Burt; and Burt, taking advantage of Jack, robs him 613

(1) Jack is cheated out of a large sum by Burt 621

(1) Jack is kidnapped by Burt and held for ransom 639

(1) Jack is held captive by Burt in a seemingly inescapable trap 653

(1) Jack is shot and seriously wounded by a thief, Burt 655

(1) Jack, passenger on a ship at sea, is taken prisoner by terrorists Burt, Sally and Fred 719b

(1) Jack, a law officer pursuing a criminal, Burt, runs into trouble 722

(1) In trying to report a criminal, Burt, to the police, Jack runs into trouble 725

(2-12) Jack, mistakenly accused of being a criminal, is finally cleared by the confession of the real criminal, Burt 635

(2) Jack, kidnapped and held for ransom by Burt, makes Burt's life so miserable that he pays to have Jack taken off his hands 639

(4) Jack, who enjoys helping the needy, befriends a drifter, Burt 613

HELPFULNESS
Jack tries to help Burt in a certain venture 809

(4) Jack, trying to help Burt, is unaware that Burt is a criminal 809

Jack and Burt

DELIVERANCE

(1) Jack is bitterly harassed by a relentless enemy, Burt 884a

(2) Jack, bitterly harassed by a relentless enemy, Burt, who, in attempting to prevent Jack's escape — is accidentally killed 884a

IDEALISM

(1) Jack, a criminal trying to go straight, is forced by a former associate, Burt, to take part in a crime 923

OBLIGATION

Attorney Jack honors the distasteful duty of defending a criminal, Burt 1006a

Law officer Jack owes a personal obligation to a criminal, Burt 1011

(1) Law officer Jack is forced by duty to arrest a criminal, Burt, to whom he owes an obligation 1011

Policeman Jack captures a criminal, Burt 1016a

Policeman Jack is duty-bound to arrest Burt, but he owes a personal obligation to help Burt escape 1016a

Law officer Jack is old, and his prisoner, Burt, is young and there are extenuating circumstances in his case 1017

(1) Jack, a payroll clerk responsible for his company's funds, is ordered by Burt, a junior partner, to secretly give him a large amount of the company's money 1014

(1) Law officer Jack and his prisoner, Burt, are lost in the desert, afoot, without food nor enough water for the two of them 1017

(6) Jack and Burt, lawman and prisoner, are lost in the desert with little water. They draw lots to see who will take the water and escape death. Jack deliberately loses the drawing so that Burt can win. Burt takes the water canteen and abandons Jack to die 1017

CHANCE

(1) Blind man Jack responds to a cry for help, and blunders into a group of thieves, Burt, Sally and Fred, who are committing a robbery 1047

PERSONAL LIMITATIONS

Jack's priceless art collection is stolen by rival collector Burt 1129b

PRETENSE

Jack impersonates a criminal, Burt 1167

(4) Jack, impersonating a criminal, Burt, finds himself accused of a crime committed by the real Burt 1167

(4) Criminal Jack poses as a policeman looking for another criminal, Burt. Burt is apprehended and turned over to Jack, who sets out with his prisoner for the scene of Burt's alleged crime — the crime Jack committed himself 1179

DECEPTION

Jack is captured by inept criminals, Burt, Sally and Fred, who attempt to drug him 1221

Jack finds out that Burt has made him the fall guy in a con game 1226

Detective Jack captures a criminal, Burt, who was once his friend 1284

Detective Jack owes criminal Burt a moral debt for having saved Jack's life. Burt hopes to collect on the debt by gaining his freedom 1284

(1) Jack is captured by a bandit, Burt, and held for ransom 1218

(1) Blind Jack is imprisoned in his home by Burt, who attempts to force Jack to reveal where he has hidden an item of great value 1267b

(1) Burt kidnaps Jack, takes him to a secret place, and holds him for ransom 1281

(3) Inept criminals Burt, Sally and Fred, attempt to drug Jack, but mistakenly administer a harmless fluid. Jack pretends to be unconscious 1221

(3) Jack pretends to be duped in order to trap Burt in his own con game 1226

(3) Jack catches Burt cheating at cards and denounces him; a fight follows and Burt is killed 1276

(3) Supposedly dead Jack discovers an imposter, Burt, using his name and pretending to be Jack 1275

(12) Detective Jack, faced with a moral dilemma, decides to uphold the law 1284

CRIME/IMMORALITY
Jack's art collection is worth a fortune. While he is away, criminals, Burt, Sally and Fred unsuccessfully attempt to breach Jack's sophisticated security system 1307

(2) Jack captures a burglar, Burt, looting his house 1305

MYSTERY
Jack notices that Burt, has developed an unconscious habit 1362

Jack suspects seemingly honest Burt of a crime and attempts to prove him guilty 1371

Jack, convinced that his town's councilmen and mayor, Burt, Sally and Fred, are corrupt, pretends to join them in order to prove their guilt 1376

(5) Detective Jack discovers that Burt is the key figure in a criminal activity, but the police refuse to arrest Burt 1413b

(9) Jack investigates a crime, and uncovers the criminal, Burt, through a unique clue 1362

(9) Jack learns of criminal Burt's guilt via ESP 1413a

(10) Jack discovers that suspect Burt is actually an undercover agent 1413b

REVELATION
(9) By shrewd deduction, Jack proves Burt is a criminal 1456

Jack and Sam

MISFORTUNE
Fugitive Jack is hunted by Sam, a law officer 610

Jack, a fugitive trapped by law officers, hides in an enclosure (house, cave, factory, etc.) 651

(1) Jack, in an airport in a strange city, is arrested as a criminal suspect 608

(1) Jack is trapped in town X. He can escape only by passing through towns Y or Z, and detectives Sam and Faye are watching for him in both places 610

(1) Fugitive Jack is surrounded by law officers Sam, Faye and Russ 651

(2) Trapped by pursuers Sam and Faye, Jack escapes when the house in which he's hiding catches fire 699b

(4) Jack impersonates a law officer, Sam 717

(8) Jack, a doctor, is running from a law officer, Sam. Sam becomes temporarily blind, and Jack restores his sight 712

MISTAKEN JUDGMENT
Jack is convinced a certain crime has been committed and reports it to police officer Sam 771a

DELIVERANCE
(1) Jack is arrested by Sam 866

(2) Jack's captor, law officer Sam, is killed in an accident. Sam's body is identified as that of Jack; as a result, Jack is set free 866

OBLIGATION
Fugitive Jack will be arrested if he rescues Sam, the lawman pursuing him; and if Jack abandons Sam, the lawman will die 1013

Jack and Sam

OBLIGATION (cont'd.)

(9) Jack, a fugitive in the desert, learns that a law officer, Sam, who is pursuing him, is sunblind and dying from thirst 1013

PRETENSE

(1) Criminal Jack is surrounded by law officers, Sam, Faye and Russ 1176

(2) Jack, a criminal trapped by law officers, Sam, Faye and Russ, escapes by impersonating another cop and pretending to hunt for Jack 1176

(2) When criminal Jack's captor, detective Sam, suddenly dies, Jack assumes his identity and tries to escape 1189

DECEPTION

(1) Female impersonator Jack, who committed a crime while in drag, is apprehended by detective Sam, who deduces the truth 1282

(1) Sam, using clues unwittingly supplied by Jack, discovers the key to a secret project 1289d

Jack and Matt

MISFORTUNE

Jack, out of ignorance of social graces, commits a gaffe before a servant, Matt, while a weekend guest at a country estate 617

MISTAKEN JUDGMENT

(1) Jack lets himself be blackmailed by Matt because Jack is convinced that he unintentionally committed a crime 783

(4) Jack trusts his assistant, Matt, and makes him his confidant 775

(10) Jack discovers that his trusted assistant, Matt, is a thief 775

DELIVERANCE

(2) Held on a murder charge, Jack is released on an unusual plea made by his attorney, Matt 887a

DECEPTION

Jack invents a fictitious servant, Matt 1213

(9) Jack invents a fictitious servant, Matt, whose unreliability seems to embarrass Jack, though in reality, it is a convenience for Jack 1213

MYSTERY

(1) Film director Jack's agent, Matt, leads him into a trap that is intended to make Jack change his irresponsible ways 1349

Jack and Eric

MARRIED LIFE

(4) Jack attempts to shift the blame for a crime onto innocent Eric 467

MISFORTUNE

Jack is employed by Eric, a man Jack admires 604

Jack, against his wishes, inherits a fortune from a relative, Eric 700

Jack is annoyed by Eric, who constantly interferes with him 735

(1) Jack is paralyzed by the fear that he has inherited the evil traits of an ancestor, Eric 720

(5) Jack's employer, Eric, is accused of a criminal act 604

(7) Jack deals harshly with meddlesome Eric, and later regrets his actions 735

(13) Fugitive Jack discovers that a relative, Eric, has died and left him a valuable estate 699a

MISTAKEN JUDGMENT

Dude ranch guest Jack is ridiculed by tough ranch-hand, Eric 759

Jack and Eric settle their difference by a contest of skill 759

Jack tries vainly to win Eric's friendship 762

CHARACTER COMBINATIONS

Wealthy dilettante Jack clashes with street-smart, uneducated Eric in a mutual venture. Their differences result in a fist fight 782

Jack shows the police circumstantial evidence of a crime he's convinced Eric has committed 780

(1) After his death, Jack wins Eric's friendship — for which he had vainly struggled in life 762

(5) Eric, arrested on information supplied by Jack, proves that no crime has been committed 780

(10) Wealthy Jack and working-class Eric battle to a draw and as a result learn from each other and form a bond of respect and friendship 782

DELIVERANCE
(9) Jack has a strange experience among a brainwashed group, and finds the key to the brainwashing in a notebook belonging to Eric, one of the perpetrators. Using information obtained from the notebook, Jack rescues the victims 888

OBLIGATION
In order to control Eric, Jack deviously maneuvers him into heavy debt 983

Jack hopes to get Eric to help him in a venture by offering to pay off his debts 983

Jack, a young medical student who moonlights as a jewel thief, is in the midst of a burglary when he is suddenly summoned to minister to a sick man, Eric 1004

(2) Jack deviously shifts a dangerous obligation to a stranger, Eric 980

CHANCE
Jack sells an almost valueless gold mine to Eric at a bargain price. Eric delays paying Jack, who in turn delays giving Eric the deed 1043

(1) Jack is impersonating Eric when he meets Eric in person 1037

(1) Wealthy and influential Jack, an executive, has the same name as ordinary, unimportant Eric, who lives in the same area 1038

(3-7-9) Jack, by chance, meets Eric who drunkenly reveals an important secret 1052a

(9) Jack gains piece of information from Eric that can prove of great value — whether it was a man or his wife who died first in an accident 1052a

PERSONAL LIMITATIONS
(10) Jack wants to acquire a tract of land belonging to Eric, a poor man whose family has owned the property for generations. Influenced by family sentiment, Eric refuses to sell 1140

PRETENSE
Jack attempts to gain control of dying man, Eric's, fortune 1194

Jack greatly resembles Eric 1197

Jack, to escape his overwhelming problems pretends to be Eric, a man apparently free of problems 1200

(4) Jack buries his murdered victim, Eric, and continues to lead his life in a normal manner 1178

(4) Jack impersonates Eric for personal gain 1197

(4) Problem-ridden Jack, pretending to be problem-free Eric, finds himself in even deeper trouble when he becomes the victim of Eric's secret life 1200

DECEPTION
Criminal Jack gains access to Eric's collection of precious stones while pretending to be an appraiser 1217a

Jack realizes that Eric knows too much for Jack's good 1251

Jack buys Eric's silence 1251

Jack and Eric

DECEPTION (cont'd.)
Jack and Eric desperately compete for a large prize 1255b

Jack's fortunes depend upon getting his hands on a certain document, X, before Eric gets to it 1255b

Unscrupulous Jack maneuvers Eric into debt 1260b

(1) Con artist Jack is selling worthless land. Threatened with exposure by influential Eric, Jack agrees to take Eric on as a silent partner as the price of continuing his scam 1278e

(4) Jack pretends to be the long-lost son of wealthy Eric 1212b

(4) Jack, to conceal the body of his murdered victim, Eric, and to escape suspicion, hides the corpse in a mortuary 1252

(9) Jack wants property that Eric refuses to sell. Jack ruins Eric financially and forces him to sell 1260a

(9) Jack doctors confidential information to convince Eric of Jack's qualifications and Jack wins a high-paying job 1278c

(9) Jack and influential Eric, become equal partners, Eric now publicly endorsing Jack's shady venture 1278e

(12) Jack, maneuvering Eric into debt, offers to cancel the debt if Eric will agree to a certain proposition 1260b

CRIME/IMMORALITY
(4) Jack attempts to take over a major corporation despite Eric's legal rights 1299

VENGEANCE
Jack's relative, Eric, feels he has been grievously wronged by a large corporation 1312

Jack, broke but handsome, is lured by wealthy Eric to become an unwitting pawn in Eric's revenge scheme 1320

(4) For an imagined wrong, Jack seeks revenge on industrialist Eric 1317

Jack's reprisal against Eric ends with more serious results than Jack intended 1323c

MYSTERY
Jack discovers the body of a murdered man, Eric 1337

Young photographer Jack is hired by Eric to photograph a bizarre subject 1386a

(1) Jack, severely mistreated by Eric, places a hex on Eric and his family 1439b

(5) Jack is severely mistreated by Eric 1439b

(13) Embassy code-room clerk Jack, alone at his station, receives a garbled transmission from diplomat Eric, who is rumored to be in grave difficulties. Jack is forced to make a difficult decision 1396

(13) Thief Jack breaks into a building to commit a robbery, and finds a man, Eric, dead, a gun nearby 1429

REVELATION
Doctor Jack, summoned to help a sick man, Eric, finds that Eric is dying 1447

Jack learns the details of a crime from dying Eric 1447

(9) Impoverished Jack receives information from Eric that earns him a fortune 1451b

Jack and Carl

DELIVERANCE
(1) Jack, because he knows Carl's secret, is harassed, spied upon and ultimately imprisoned on false charges 854

(3) Jack discovers a deadly secret about his rich, powerful employer Carl 854

OBLIGATION
Jack, trusted servant in Carl's house, is really a criminal 1008

CHARACTER COMBINATIONS

NECESSITY
For his services, Jack is given the cast-off clothes of young millionaire, Carl, and discovers something of great value in a pocket 1028

(2) Out-of-work Jack performs a service for young millionaire, Carl 1028

CHANCE
(1) Jack is injured while on a dangerous expedition and is abandoned by expedition leader Carl, who refuses to sacrifice the group's safety by rescuing Jack 1052b

(2) Badly injured Jack is rescued when a problem diverts an expedition led by Carl 1052b

PERSONAL LIMITATIONS
Jack applies for a job in the home of rich Carl 1107b

Jack, private secretary to Carl, is aware that Carl is jealously guarding a crucial secret 1114

(4) Jack's curiosity causes him to interfere with Carl's personal affairs 1114

DECEPTION
(1) Jack is persuaded by Carl to unknowingly commit a crime 1272

(1) Innocent Jack is arrested for a crime and his employer, Carl, testifies against him 1272

(1) Dishonest contractor Jack fails to pay bribe money to building inspector Carl. Because Jack has failed to pay bribe money, Carl exposes Jack's crimes 1273

CRIME/IMMORALITY
3) Jack discovers that his employer, Carl, is a murderer wanted by the police 1303

Jack, Pete and Gary

MISFORTUNE
Jack devises a plan to protect helpless Pete from a powerful enemy, Gary 671

(1) Jack's friend, Pete, is helpless against a powerful enemy, Gary 671

(1) Jack's friend, Pete, owns a flock of sheep. Gary is a rich, powerful cattle baron. Gary's men kill almost all Pete's sheep, and Gary schemes to take Pete's land from him. Pete, deep in debt, doesn't know where to turn 672

(4) In order to save his friend, Pete, Jack picks a fight with Pete's enemy, Gary, and kills him 764

(7) Jack, in order to protect Pete, kills Gary, supposed enemy of Pete, unaware that Pete and Gary have made their peace (Or have they? Could Jack have been set up?) 764

VENGEANCE
(1) Jack sets a deadly trap for Gary, but Pete is its victim 1319b

Jack, Pete and Burt

MISFORTUNE
(1) Jack, trying to beat the scam of a con man, Burt, is betrayed by an accomplice, Pete, whom Jack asks to help him 630

(4) Jack accepts Burt on a forged letter of introduction from a friend, Pete, and introduces Burt into his own social circle 612

HELPFULNESS
(3) Pete's friend, Jack, exposes Burt, a spiritualist who is swindling Pete out of large sums of money 830

(3) Jack, threatening Burt with arrest, forces him to return the money to Jack's friend, Pete 830

OBLIGATION
Jack lives in an area of a small third-world nation in which there are two other Americans, Pete and Burt, both friends of Jack 1015

PRETENSE
(4) Jack persuades a friend, Pete, to pretend to be Burt in order to complete a venture that requires Burt's presence 1162

CHARACTER COMBINATIONS

ack, Pete and Burt

DECEPTION
Jack's friend, Pete, plans to rescue Jack from a bandit, Burt, who is holding Jack for ransom, and to do so without paying the ransom 1218

(3) Jack's friend, Pete, is robbed by Jack and Burt; then Jack, in turn, robs Burt 1227a

(3) Jack robs Burt of valuables stolen from Pete, and returns them to Pete 1227a

MYSTERY
Jack is convinced that his friend, Pete, has been murdered by Burt 1371

ack, Pete and Sam

PRETENSE
(2) Jack and Pete, criminals fleeing after pulling a successful job, slip past the police, Sam, Faye and Russ, when Jack disguises himself as a woman 1174

Jack, Pete and Eric

HELPFULNESS
(2) Jack, who is superstitious, is about to be beaten in an event because he thinks he hears the voice of a dead friend, Pete, calling to him. But he wins the event when his coach Eric, brings him to his senses 827

DECEPTION
Jack tries to promote a fight between two boxers, Pete and Eric, who are good friends 1215

Jack, for certain reasons, plots to make enemies of two friends, Pete and Eric 1215

(7) Jack, betting heavily on a sporting event between contestants Pete and Eric, learns that they are close friends, and suspects that each wants the other to win 1231

MYSTERY
(13) Jack, entering his friend Pete's home, discovers the body of a murder victim, Eric 1337

Jack, Pete and Carl

HELPFULNESS
(4) Jack steals money from his employer, Carl, to help his friend, Pete, overcome a financial crisis. Jack intends to make up the shortage when Pete can repay the money 832

Jack admits to his friend, Pete, that he has stolen money from Carl in order to help Pete 832

Jack, Gary and Dave

CHANCE
(4) Jack, trying to kill Gary, mistakes Dave for Gary because Dave happens to be wearing clothing identical to Gary's 1039

Jack, Gary and Burt

VENGEANCE
(4) Federal Witness Jack, protected by turncoat Agent Gary, is the target of hit-man Burt. Jack discovers that hit-man Burt was hired by Agent Gary, the man assigned to protect him 1324b

Jack, Gary and Sam

DELIVERANCE
(2) Jack, a hunted outlaw, hides with an enemy, Gary; and Gary, feeling bound by the code of "honor among thieves," conceals Jack, saving him from pursuers, Sam and Faye 883

Jack, Gary and Matt

REJECTION
Matt is an agent of Gary, Jack's rival in love 213

DELIVERANCE
(2) Jack, held on a murder charge, is freed when his attorney, Matt, proves that Jack, under heavy medication, believed his victim, Gary, was trying to kill him 887a

Jack, Dave and Sam

HELPFULNESS
Jack encounters Dave, a fugitive pursued by Sam, a law officer 815a

CHARACTER COMBINATIONS

PERSONAL LIMITATIONS

(1) Escaped prisoner Jack can't open his handcuffs. Desperate, he asks a stranger, Dave, to help him. But Dave notifies a policeman, Sam, and Jack is recaptured 1066

Jack, Dave and Eric

PRETENSE

(4) Jack invites friends to meet a celebrity, Dave, who fails to show. Jack persuades Eric to impersonate Dave so that the guests won't be disappointed 1164

DECEPTION

Jack, needing people of unquestioned bravery for a certain venture, devises a test of excellence for two men, Dave and Eric 1223b

Jack acquires confidential information sent by Dave to Eric 1278c

Jack, hungering for a taste of the good life, feigns an injury in a minor accident with wealthy Dave's Rolls Royce. Ensconced in Dave's palatial mansion, Jack contrives to have his own "Doctor," Eric, summoned by Dave 1278d

Criminal Jack, posing as a repairman in Dave's mansion, claims that an emergency exists which requires an additional repairman, Eric 1285c

(9) Jack, a criminal, pretends to be security consultant, Dave, designing a security system for wealthy art collector Eric, who willingly supplies Jack with confidential information 1271

(9) Jack conspires with "Doctor" Eric so that Dave covers all of Jack's expenses during Jack's lengthy recovery 1278d

(14) Jack, testing Dave and Eric pretends to be in grave danger, and in their attempt to save him, Dave and Eric are plunged into real danger 1223b

Jack, Dave and Carl

PERSONAL LIMITATIONS

Jack, applying for a job, is asked for references by Carl. Jack uses rich Dave, whom he doesn't know, as a reference 1107b

DECEPTION

In an effort to get a job from Carl, Jack gives Dave as a character reference, telling Carl that Dave can be reached at an exclusive hotel at a certain hour by phone 1212c

(9) When Dave is paged in an exclusive hotel, Jack answers the call, pretends he is Dave and gives himself an outstanding recommendation 1212c

Jack, Burt and Sam

DELIVERANCE

(8) Jack, robbed by Burt and wanting to save him from the law, tells the arresting officer, Sam, that he gave Burt the stolen property 894

OBLIGATION

Law officer Sam asks Jack to help him arrest Burt 1015

Jack, Burt and Eric

REVELATION

(3) Jack observes Burt with valuables belonging to murdered Eric 1448

Jack, Sam and Eric

MISFORTUNE

(1) Jack, employed by Eric, arrives at work one morning and finds the office occupied by Federal Agents, Sam and Faye 604

Jack, Matt and Eric

MISFORTUNE

(1) Jack's chauffeur, Matt, is ordered by Jack to drive very fast. He apparently injures a pedestrian, Eric 597

(5) Jack, when his car apparently injures a pedestrian, tries to avoid consequences by telling his chauffeur, Matt, to drive on 597

Jack and Walt

MISFORTUNE
(1) Jack is robbed by Walt, who puts on Jack's clothes and drives off in Jack's car 661

(1) Jack, attacked by mysterious persons, Walt, Amy and Leo in his high-rise office, is spirited away despite state-of-the-art security 719a

DELIVERANCE
Jack fights a hallucinatory enemy, Walt, whose weapon is superstition 855

PERSONAL LIMITATIONS
(1) Doctor Jack is about to leave his office one night on an emergency call, when mysterious strangers, Walt, Amy and Leo abduct him 1130

PRETENSE
(4) Jack, wanting to do something that he fears will cause gossip, invents a fictitious relative, Walt, who requires frequent "visits" from Jack 1148a

MYSTERY
Jack encounters a mysterious stranger, Walt, who seems to have supernatural powers 1393

Jack attempts to learn the truth about a mysterious stranger, Walt 1393

Late at night, Jack enters his house and sees another man, Walt, sitting before the fireplace 1423

Jack, thinking Walt is a friend, steps closer and suddenly Walt vanishes 1423

(1) In a violent struggle between the personalities of Jack and his alter-ego, Walt, Walt emerges the victor and assumes control of Jack's life 1348a

(1) Jack, inventing a robot, Walt, is pursued and killed by Walt 1348b

(2) Jack is unable to account for a mysterious stranger, Walt, who appears and warns Jack of peril, then vanishes 1424a

(4) Jack has a split-personality: as Jack he is a respected college professor and family-man; as Walt, his alter-ego, he is a hard-drinking, inveterate womanizer 1348a

(4) Jack invents a robot, Walt 1348b

(9) Jack, because of a wild delusion, proves that he is to be reckoned with 1418b

(10) Novelist Jack meets a character, Walt, whom he created in one of his stories 1391

(10-11) When it serves Jack's purposes, his alter-ego, Walt, materializes, unseen by others, in a menacing, demonic form 1439c

(14) Wimpy, ineffectual Jack begins to believe he is the reincarnation of Walt, a powerful ancient ruler 1418b

REVELATION
Egotistical Jack is taught a lesson by Walt 1455b

(10) Jack receives an important message from a mysterious person, Walt, which enables him to correct a serious error 1461b

(14) Jack, rescued from a major problem by Walt, receives a surprising disclosure from Walt that results in a dramatic character change for Jack 1455b

Jack, Pete and Walt

DECEPTION
(4) Jack impersonates the fictitious character, Walt, invented by his friend, Pete 1216

Jack's friend, Pete, invents a fictitious persona, Walt 1216

Jack, Burt and Walt

MISFORTUNE
(2) Mysterious Walt forces Burt to hand over the money he swindled from Jack; Walt returns the money to Jack 621

(2) Jack, cheated out of a large sum by Burt, is on the verge of suicide when mysterious Walt returns his money 621

Jack and X

ROMANTIC MISADVENTURES
Shy, retiring Jack, acquiring a love charm, X, gains confidence and becomes attractive to women 8a

(4) Jack, trying to avoid marriage, claims that X, a department store mannequin, is his wife 71a-1

(7) Jack, believing that a certain "charm," X, has made him successful with women, learns that X has no magical powers; his newfound success was due solely to his increased self-confidence 161

MARRIED LIFE
(13) Whenever Jack shows X, a certain mysterious object, to anyone, he gets into trouble 541

MISFORTUNE
Inept Jack loses a priceless diamond, X, while at the zoo, and employs desperate measures to recover it 614

Desperately in need, Jack is offered a large payment for a diamond, X, that he knows is a fake 729

(1) Jack loses a priceless diamond, X 614

(1) Jack loses a priceless diamond, X, thinks he knows where it is, but he is wrong 614

(1) Jack, custodian of a valuable object, X, mislays X and thinks it has been stolen 709

(1) Jack loses an important object, X, at the scene of an accident 711b

(1) Jack, on his way to return a stolen object, X, to its owner, loses X and tries to recover it again 724

(2-12) Jack finds a valuable paper, X, between the pages of an antique volume 733

Jack recovers a stolen object, X, and sets out to return it to its owner 724

MISTAKEN JUDGMENT
Jack finds a mysterious object, X, that is apparently priceless 798

(4) Jack finds and keeps an incriminating document, X, intending to return it at a later time 771b

(4) Thief Jack plans to steal a priceless gem, X 778

(4) Jack, thinking that a fake gem, X, is genuine, plans to steal it 778

(4) Jack highly values a mysterious object, X, and is unaware that by having it in his possession, he is endangering his life 798

(9) Desperately needy Jack learns that a gem, X, he thought worthless, is actually genuine and priceless 803b

HELPFULNESS
(1) Jack finds a bag, X, and, opening it, becomes aware that it contains incriminating evidence 804

(4) On a country road, Jack retrieves a suitcase, X, which has fallen from the roof-rack of a passing automobile 804

IDEALISM
(8) Jack, an unsuccessful composer, inadvertently loses his latest composition, which bears no signature. Jack's music, X, is found and experts hail it as a work of genius. The news media urge the unknown composer to identify himself, but Jack has certain reasons for remaining anonymous 920

CHANCE
Walking along a city street, an object, X, suddenly drops at Jack's feet from an upper window of a building 1046

PERSONAL LIMITATIONS
(1) Jack loses the ticket to a pawned object, X, and the pawnbroker won't give him X without the ticket 1077

PRETENSE
Thief Jack steals a real gem, X-1, that he later believes is a fake 1166a

Jack and X

PRETENSE (cont'd.)

(5-7) Thief Jack has a real gem, X-1, that he believes is a fake. Jack switches the real gem, X-1 for X-2, a fake that Jack believes to be genuine 1166a

(9) Jack makes a replica, X-1, of a valuable original, X-2, then steals X-2, leaving X-1 in its place 1166b

DECEPTION

Jack discovers where a certain small but immensely valuable object, X, has been hidden 1283

In order to obtain a certain valuable object, X, Jack must operate in total secrecy 1283

(1) Jack finds himself in jeopardy after innocently agreeing to look after a mysterious package, X 1233

(2) Jack, realizing he's in danger because of a mysterious package, X, in his possession, attempts to pass the package — and the danger — to another person 1233

CRIME/IMMORALITY

(1) An object, X, connected with a crime that Jack committed in his past, suddenly reappears. Jack becomes obsessed with memories he thought were long-buried 1302

MYSTERY

Jack carries a mysterious object, X, in his pocket 1343

Jack, annoyed by a particular object, X, destroys it 1367a

Jack, in possession of an object, X, that allegedly has good or evil powers, decides to test it 1380

Jack innocently acquires lost or stolen object, X 1382a

Jack buys a small, decorative box, X, in an antique shop and is unable to open it 1382b

Jack tries to solve an enigma that concerns a mysterious object, X 1400

Jack's curiosity is aroused by an object, X, which is being sold at auction 1401

Trying to solve a mystery, Jack's only clue, X, is the portrait of a beautiful woman 1410

While eccentric, unsuccessful inventor Jack struggles to perfect a perpetual motion machine, he has a series of dreams which result in his inventing X, a practical, highly commercial device 1420

Jack is frustrated by his inability to solve the mystery of a strange object, X 1425

(1) Jack is unaware that carrying mysterious object, X, in his pocket is causing him to have inexplicable, bizarre experiences 1343

(1) Jack, possessing mysterious object, X, finds himself the victim of repeated misfortune and begins to believe that X is indeed cursed 1352

(1) Jack, innocently acquiring a lost or stolen object, X, suddenly finds himself plunged into terrible danger when strangers try to recover X 1382a

(3-4) Jack investigates a mysterious package, X, that has come into his possession 1435

(4) Jack purchases a Victorian mansion and discovers X, an old Edison cylinder phonograph. Jack, listening to one of the cylinders, is stunned to hear voices and events from his past that portend events yet to come 1342a

(4) Adventurer Jack, learning of a mysterious object, X, risks his life to obtain it 1379

(4) Jack buys a mysterious object, X, at an auction and attempts to learn its history 1401

(4) Jack unknowingly possesses an object, X, which can cause his sudden death 1438b-1

(6) Jack, alone and dying, buries his gold dust and draws a map of the location on object X 1370b

(6) Object X, apparently leaving a trail of misfortune, finds its way back to Jack 1440

(9) Jack obtains a mysterious object, X, that grants wishes — which carry certain conditions 1421

(10) Jack discovers that an object he uses every day contains an object, X, that is of great importance 1397

(13) Jack has seemingly supernatural experiences that are related to an object, X 1360

(13) Jack destroys a certain object, X, but it mysteriously reappears. Jack repeatedly destroys X, but it always reappears 1367a

(13) Jack is unable to explain to the Judge how he mysteriously acquired objects, X-1, X-2, X-3 1381

(13) Jack owns a small, decorative antique box which he's unable to open. One night it mysteriously opens on its own, and Jack finds an object of great value inside 1382b

(13) Scientist Jack investigates an alleged psychic communication. To his surprise, the communication proves accurate, except for X, a key element in the message 1411

(13) Jack, obsessed with a mysterious object, X, is close to solving its puzzle when it disappears and is replaced by another mystery 1425

(13) Jack, while on a drunken binge, buys an outlandishly expensive object, X, which he can ill afford. Sober, Jack has no recollection of the purchase 1438a

REVELATION
(1) Jack is accused of stealing a valuable document, X 1457

(9) Jack, by chance, overhears a scrap of conversation which reveals a clue to the whereabouts of missing property, X 1453

Jack, Pete and X

MARRIED LIFE
(4) While in a dubious situation, Jack accidently loses an object, X, that belongs to his friend, Pete 390

MISFORTUNE
(4) Jack takes charge of a valuable object, X, for a friend, Pete 709

CHANCE
(4) Jack mistakenly takes an object, X-1, belonging to his friend, Pete. In its place Jack leaves a similar object, X-2. Close inspection is needed to differentiate X-1 and X-2 1044b

PERSONAL LIMITATIONS
Jack attempts to reclaim an object, X, pawned by his late friend, Pete 1077

MYSTERY
Jack's friend, Pete, is unaware of a secret connected with X, an object that has been stolen from him 1370a

Jack knows the secret of X, an object stolen from Pete, and using his knowledge of X, attempts to recover it 1370a

Mysterious object X is stolen from Jack's friend, Pete. Legend has it that X brings good luck to its owner, and Jack attempts to recover it for Pete 1377a

Jack, Gary and X

MISFORTUNE
Jack is the custodian of valuables, X, over which he fights with Gary 730

(1-6) Gary kills Jack and takes valuables, X, that Jack was guarding 730

(1) Jack is accused of wrongdoing by his rival, Gary, and an incriminating paper, X, is found in Jack's possession 771b

DECEPTION
(2) Jack smashes an idol, X, that primitives believe is a god, and immediately good fortune comes to the tribe. Gary is discredited 1274

Jack, Gary and X

VENGEANCE
(4) Jack, in order to get revenge on his enemy, Gary, assembles an explosive device, X 1319a

Jack, Dave and X

MISTAKEN JUDGMENT
Jack pursues a stranger, Dave, to recover an object, X, that has been stolen 774

(1-4) Jack pursues a stranger, Dave, taking from him a valuable object, X, that Jack thinks was stolen from him. Later, Jack discovers that X, which he believed was stolen, was in his possession all the time 774

HELPFULNESS
Jack, finding a suitcase, X, in the road, intends to return it to the stranger, Dave, who lost it 804

PERSONAL LIMITATIONS
Jack wants a certain object, X. But X is guarded carefully by Dave 1129a

MYSTERY
Jack acquires mysterious object, X, from stranger Dave, who warns him that it carries a curse 1352

Jack receives half of an important message, X, and searches for a stranger, Dave, who has the other half. The message makes no sense until both halves are joined 1369

Jack's only clue in his search for Dave is the picture of a beautiful woman, X, left at the place where Dave disappeared 1404b

(10) Jack tells Dave, from whom he acquired mysterious object, X, that the object's curse has come true. Dave admits that he invented the curse and the only thing Jack is a victim of is Jack's own gullibility 1352

Jack, Burt and X

PERSONAL LIMITATIONS
Burt, a gentleman thief, steals valuable property, X, from Jack. Jack advertises to find another thief who will recover X for him 1129c

PRETENSE
(1-5) Jack owns an art object, X-1, which Burt steals. Jack, unaware that X-1 is missing, buys it back from Burt in the belief that he's purchasing X-2 1165

MYSTERY
(3) Down-and-out Burt, stealing X, finds himself suddenly showered with good fortune — which leads to his apprehension by Jack 1377a

(3) Jack discovers that a mysterious package, X, contains illicit goods. With X as a clue, Jack tracks down criminal Burt 1435

Jack, Sam and X

MISFORTUNE
(1) Jack, arrested at an airport, has innocently claimed a piece of luggage, X, staked out by the police. The bag, X, contains contraband 608

Jack, Matt and X

ROMANCE'S BEGINNINGS
An associate, Matt, offers Jack a mysterious object, X, that Matt insists will make Jack attractive to women. Jack accepts X and tries it out 7a

Jack, Eric and X

PRETENSE
Criminal Jack tries to sell Eric an object, X, that Eric already owns   1145

(1) Jack attempts to reclaim a valuable object, X, that Jack had previously left with Eric. But Eric denies any knowledge of X 1147

(4) Jack, who has a valuable object, X, leaves it with Eric; Eric agrees to look after X for Jack 1147

CHARACTER COMBINATIONS

Jack, Carl and X

PRETENSE
(9) On a pretext, Jack obtains a much-desired object, X2, from Carl, who has refused to sell it 1166b

REVELATION
(2) Jack, accused of stealing a valuable document, X, is proved innocent when X is discovered in the possession of Carl 1457

Jack, Burt, Eric and X

MYSTERY
(3) Jack sees a stranger, Burt, steal papers, X, from stranger Eric's attache case 1406

Jack, Pete, Gary and X

VENGEANCE
(1) Jack sends an explosive device, X, to his enemy, Gary, but it ends up in the hands of Jack's friend, Pete 1319a

Jack and Andy

MISFORTUNE
Jack persuades his father, Andy, to advance him his inheritance 611b

HELPFULNESS
(2) Jack, formerly rebellious, is forgiven his past behavior by his father, Andy 815b

(8) Formerly rebellious Jack returns home to his father, Andy, a subdued, wiser young man 815b

OBLIGATION
(12) Andy's son, Jack, feels duty-bound to sell his property to help pay his dead father's debts 1018

DECEPTION
Jack finds a long-lost document belonging to his father, Andy 1286

(10) Jack finds evidence indicating the fate of his father, Andy 1286

CRIME/IMMORALITY
(1) Jack's scheme to obtain his father's property is exposed and Jack is apprehended for Andy's murder 1290b

(4) Jack, disinherited son of Andy, murders Andy and conceals his death. Posing as Andy, Jack forges documents in an attempt to obtain Andy's property 1290b

MYSTERY
Jack's father, Andy, has refused to give up hope that long-missing Jack is alive and will one day return 1378

Jack attempts to locate an inheritance that his late father, Andy, concealed 1399

REVELATION
Jack engages in a dangerous search for his father, Andy, who vanished long ago 1451d

Jack, Eric and Andy

DECEPTION
Andy's disinherited son, Jack, tries to borrow money from Eric on the condition that Andy approve the loan 1217b

Jack, trying to borrow money from Eric with Andy's supposed approval, asks Eric to request Andy's approval 1217b

NECESSITY
Jack tries to borrow money from Eric, a money-lender, on the chance that Jack will inherit the estate of his rich father, Andy 1026

PERSONAL LIMITATIONS
Irresponsible Jack tries to borrow money from Eric on the possibility of inheriting the estate of Jack's wealthy father, Andy. Eric doubts that Jack will inherit the estate 1139

Jack and Tom

OBLIGATION
Jack and Tom are twin brothers with identical likes and dislikes 1005

(8) Brothers Jack and Tom honor a distasteful obligation by living apart 1005

Jack and Greg

MARRIED LIFE
(4) Jack keeps a family secret from his son, Greg 425

MISFORTUNE
Jack mistakenly thinks his son, Greg, died in a plane crash 622

(14) Jack loses his son, Greg, in whom all his ambitions were centered 674

HELPFULNESS
Jack attempts to protect his son, Greg, from what he feels is his own disgrace and dishonor 813

Jack's son, Greg, is arrested for a crime 821

Jack tries to save Greg from trouble and finds himself in equal jeopardy 821

(2) Jack regains his self-confidence because of his son, Greg's, faith in him 810

(10) Jack's son, Greg, wins a difficult athletic competition; Greg tells despairing Jack, who considers himself a failure, that he was inspired by the knowledge that his father had never been defeated 810

DELIVERANCE
Jack has sacrificed happiness because of an obligation he thinks he owes his son, Greg 881

(9) Jack's son, Greg, discovers a long-hidden secret of Jack's, and persuades him to correct a mistake and regain lost happiness 881

IDEALISM
Jack is proud of his son, Greg 928b

(5-10) Jack's son, Greg, dies shamefully and ingloriously, dishonoring and saddening Jack 928b

(8) In an attempt to save his son, Greg, from disgrace, Greg's father, Jack, sacrifices his happiness out of a sense of duty 934

CHANCE
(2) Jack, happening to hear a familiar name, finds his long-lost son, Greg 1053

PERSONAL LIMITATIONS
Jack, consumed with his career, neglects his son 1108

Jack, Dave and Greg

CHANCE
(2) Elusive Jack is finally trapped by Dave, who turns out to be Jack's long-missing son, Greg 1056

Jack, Burt and Greg

DECEPTION
Con artists Burt and Sally attempt to persuade wealthy Jack to disinherit his son, Greg 1289a

Jack and Jim

OBLIGATION
(1) Jack is unable to control his recklessly wild nephew and ward, Jim 999

MYSTERY
Jack dies and leaves his estate to a nephew, Jim 1432

Jack dies and leaves his estate to Jim, who hasn't been heard from in years 1432

Jack, Pete and Jim

OBLIGATION
(4) Jack agrees to take charge of an incorrigible youth, Jim, who is too much of a hardcase for his uncle/guardian, Jack's friend, Pete 982a

(5) Jack sends his unmanageable nephew and ward, Jim, to Pete, his friend out West, who promises to tame Jim no matter what it takes 999

Jack, Eric and Jim

DECEPTION
Jack disapproves of his nephew, Jim, whom Jack hasn't seen in years. Dying Jack calls in attorney Eric to draw up his will 1270

(1) Jack's nephew, Jim, poses as Eric, the attorney who has come to draw up Jack's will 1270

Jack and Milt

OBLIGATION
Jack has $500,000. Jack's rich relative, Milt, leaves a million dollars to Jack, provided Jack spends his half-million within a year 997b

Jack will inherit a fortune from his uncle, Milt, but only if Jack permits his life to be controlled from the grave 1001b

PERSONAL LIMITATIONS
(1) Jack devotes ten years of service to his penurious uncle, Milt, in exchange for a promise of future security, and as a result loses his ambition and all sense of purpose 1065

(1) Jack's uncle, Milt, promises that Jack will inherit everything. But Milt dies bankrupt, leaving Jack with neither ability nor ambition 1065

DECEPTION
(4) Jack, trying by deception to obtain a rich inheritance, loses out when his uncle, Milt, sees through the deception 1289c

Jack and Ray

PRETENSE
Jack's cousin, Ray, has been mysteriously missing for a long time 1201

Jack, Milt and Ray

PRETENSE
(4) Jack's uncle, Milt, dies and leaves Jack's missing cousin, Ray, a fortune. Jack impersonates Ray 1201

Art Center College of Design
Library
1700 Lida Street
Pasadena, Calif. 91103

Jack, Eric and Ray

PERSONAL LIMITATIONS
Jack's cousin, Ray, is about to inherit the fortune of a deceased relative, Eric. If Ray were removed, Jack would be the legal heir 1127

Jack, Terry and X

OBLIGATION
Jack's penniless grandchild, Terry, buys Jack a birthday gift, X, on credit 1012

(5) Jack pays for a birthday gift, X, that his penniless grandchild, Terry, is giving him 1012

Jack and Annie

MARRIED LIFE
Jack doesn't admire Annie or her ways 414

Jack and Laura

REJECTION
(4) By flattering Jack's vanity, Laura manipulates him into a wedding engagement 218a

MARRIAGE
(1) Laura leaves Jack when his fortunes decline 361a

MARRIED LIFE
Carol's husband, Jack, is haunted by idealized fantasies about a former love, Laura 393

Laura is a promiscuous tease whom Jack loves 421

Jack, while traveling abroad, marries Laura, a woman of another race, deserts her and returns to his own country 425

Jack has an alibi that can prove his innocence of a murder charge, but only by involving Laura, another man's wife 520

(1) Laura, for whom Jack got a divorce, marries another man 377b

(1) Laura is rich but shallow and Jack, following her advice, fails miserably in all his ventures 386

ack and Laura

MARRIED LIFE, (cont'd.)
(2) Jack seeks out Laura and realizes the folly of attempting to recapture the past 393

(4) After marrying Carol, Jack falls in love with Laura 382

(4) Jack assumes a false identity and marries Laura 437

(4) Carol's husband, Jack, falls in love with Laura 486a

(8) Jack's obligation to save himself is opposed by a need to protect Laura, another man's wife 520

ack and Kate

HELPFULNESS
In a crowded airport terminal, Jack sees a distraught stranger, Kate 806

(5) Jack impulsively aids a stranger, Kate, and later regrets it 806

Jack and Donna

CHANCE
(12) Jack, by chance, encounters elderly nurse, Donna, who reveals a startling secret about his birth and parentage 1051

Jack and Amy

ROMANTIC MISADVENTURES
(4) Jack, annoyed by sexually aggressive women, pretends he has an invalid wife, Amy 84b

REJECTION
Jack will inherit a fortune from a deceased relative, provided he marries Amy, a woman he doesn't know 298b

Amy, a woman Jack doesn't know, asks him for help 298c

(10) Jack, asked for help by a stranger, Amy, refuses her, but regrets doing so when Amy mysteriously disappears. Jack feels obligated to locate Amy 298c

Eligible young Jack is stunned by a newspaper announcement of his engagement to Amy, a woman he doesn't know 298a

MARRIAGE
Jack and Amy marry, then go their separate ways immediately after the wedding ceremony 365d

(4) Jack marries Amy, a total stranger 365d

MYSTERY
On a city street, Jack glimpses Amy, a strange woman who has involved him in a puzzling mystery 1412a

Nearsighted Jack is mugged by bewigged, sunglassed Amy 1431

(13) Jack tries to overtake Amy to gain information regarding a certain mystery, but before he can reach her, she is killed by a car 1412a

Jack, Amy and X

MYSTERY
Jack struggles with a female mugger, Amy, and comes away with her wig 1431

(13) Jack, in the midst of a crowd, suddenly has a mysterious object, X, thrust into his hand by a strange woman, Amy, who, without a word, quickly disappears 1383

Jack and Nina

MISFORTUNE
(1) While performing an experiment, scientist Jack inadvertently causes serious injury to his daughter, Nina 626

MISTAKEN JUDGMENT
(1) Jack returns home, unrecognized by his daughter, Nina, who has glorified his memory 797

HELPFULNESS
Aware that he is dying, Jack makes a will in hope of protecting his adopted daughter, Nina 825

IDEALISM

Jack tries to maintain a close, fatherly relationship with his daughter, Nina 910

Jack is a free spirit, while his daughter, Nina, is uptight and reactionary 910

Disgraced politician Jack, after a long absence, visits his daughter, Nina, incognito 964b

(8) Disgraced politician Jack learns that his daughter, Nina, thinks he's dead, and that he was an honorable man. By not revealing his identity, Jack leaves Nina happy in her mistaken beliefs 964b

Jack and Linda

OBLIGATION

(1) Jack's pledge to his mother, Linda, prevents him from pursuing a cherished venture 989

Jack and Lee

MISFORTUNE

Jack is temporarily in charge of two unruly children, Lee and Kenny, and is faced with more problems than he can handle 609

(1) Jack finds it impossible to get past his grief over the death of his only child, Lee 698

(1) Jack sets a concealed trap, and a loved one, Lee, falls into it 728

(14) Jack cripples himself rescuing a child, Lee, from death 715b

HELPFULNESS

Jack finds a small, abandoned child, Lee 818c

Jack takes Lee, an orphan, into his home and raises him/her as his own child 818c

Jack saves a baby, Lee, from death 818d

Jack, unable to determine the origins of abandoned Lee, adopts the child 818d

Jack, a tough lumberman in a rough lumber camp, finds himself in charge of an abandoned baby, Lee 847

(6) Jack makes a heroic attempt to rescue a child, Lee, but both die 842a

(9) Jack rescues a child, Lee 842b

IDEALISM

Jack handicaps himself by looking after an abandoned baby, Lee 914

(5) Jack looks for happiness in his love for a child, Lee, but for certain reasons he remains unfulfilled 911

PERSONAL LIMITATIONS

Jack tries to locate the family of Lee, an abandoned child he is looking after 1089

(13) Jack contacts authorities in an attempt to identify Lee, but is unsuccessful 1089

DECEPTION

Jack finds himself looking after an abandoned baby, Lee 1229

MYSTERY

Jack grabs infant Lee 1430b

Jack and Susan

PERSONAL LIMITATIONS

Unmarried Susan's brother, Jack, her only living relative, is poor, while Susan is rich 1123

(1) If Susan marries, Jack won't inherit her money 1123

DECEPTION

(4) Jack, through subterfuge involving his sister, Susan, inherits a fortune 1236

REVENGE

Jack wants revenge for a wrong committed against his sister, Susan 1321

(13) Jack, wanting revenge for a wrong committed against his sister, Susan, finds people reluctant to name the perpetrator 1321

Jack, Pete and Lee

PERSONAL LIMITATIONS
(4) Jack borrows a baby, Lee, from its father, Pete, to help Jack succeed in an unusual venture 1057b

ack, Pete and Susan

CRIME-IMMORALITY
(4) Jack, slated to lose out on an inheritance if his sister, Susan, marries, murders her fiance, Pete 1290a

ack, Pete, Eric and Irene

PRETENSE
Jack's friend, Pete, is the sole provider for his parents, Eric and Irene 1160

(8) Jack's friend, Pete, the sole provider for his parents, dies. Jack withholds the news from Pete's parents, and continues sending money in Pete's name for their support 1160

ack, Pete, Sally and X

MARRIED LIFE
(1) X, an object belonging to Pete, is lost by Jack in questionable surroundings. X is recovered and sent by a troublemaker, Sally, to Pete's wife with a note explaining where it was found 390

ack, Gary and Laura

VENGEANCE
Wanting revenge for a wrong committed by the late Gary, Jack chooses as his target Gary's widow, Laura 1323a

Wanting revenge against Laura for a wrong committed by her late husband, Gary, discovers that Laura is unaware of Gary's offense 1323a

Jack, Gary and Sally

ROMANTIC MISADVENTURES
(1) Deviously positioned by Gary, his rival in love, Jack is innocently drawn into a compromising situation with Sally, Gary's cohort 75b

Jack, Dave and Kate

MYSTERY
(13) Jack's fortunes hinge on a legal technicality; both Dave and Kate, husband and wife, are killed in an accident; if Kate died first, Jack inherits, and if Dave died first, others inherit 1437

Jack, Dave and Lee

MYSTERY
Jack sees a stranger, Dave, abandon an infant, Lee, in a public place 1430b

Jack, Eric and Susan

DECEPTION
(4) Employing subterfuge, Jack prevents his sister, Susan, from marrying Eric 1236

Jack, Eric and Lee

DECEPTION
(4) For personal gain, Jack impersonates a widower, Eric, with a child, Lee. Jack doesn't have a child but overcomes this via deception 1224

Jack, Eric and Nina

ROMANTIC MISADVENTURES
(1-5) Jack understood that he would have to live with his guilt when, to cancel a debt, he arranged for his daughter, Nina, to marry Eric, a man she didn't love 48

Jack, Kate and Lee

PERSONAL LIMITATIONS
(1) Jack, volunteering to look after an infant, Lee, for a female stranger, Kate, finds himself stuck with Lee when Kate fails to return 1057a

(4) Young, single Jack temporarily looks after an infant, Lee, for a female stranger, Kate 1057a

CHARACTER COMBINATIONS

Jack, Amy and Andy

ROMANTIC MISADVENTURES
Drifter Jack is left a fortune by his father, Andy, on condition that he can be located and marries Amy, a woman he's never seen 117

Jack, Amy and Eric

MARRIAGE
(1) In a prearranged marriage, Jack is wedded to Amy, a woman he doesn't know, by Eric 365c

Jack, Andy and Linda

MISFORTUNE
(1) Jack's parents, Andy and Linda, insist that he study medicine, while Jack longs to enter another profession 697a

MISTAKEN JUDGMENT
(1) Although he wants a musical career, Jack complies with the wishes of his parents, Andy, Linda, and becomes a doctor; but he's plagued by feelings of unfulfillment 756

PRETENSE
(1) Jack is disowned by his parents, Andy and Linda 1182

(9) Jack, disowned by his parents, Andy and Linda, changes his name and makes a great success of his life. Andy and Linda, having admired Jack's accomplishments without realizing he's their son, reconcile with Jack when he reveals his true identity 1182

Jack, Susan and Lee

OBLIGATION
(4) Bachelor Jack agrees to care for Lee, the child of his married sister, Susan, while she's away on vacation 982b

Carol

ROMANCE'S BEGINNINGS
Rich Carol devotes much time to charity work; and, in conducting her voluntary enterprises, she pretends to be a retail sales-clerk 2e

Carol is discouraged with her love-life 13a

Unmarried Carol dreams of motherhood 39

(1) Carol inherits her father's TV station. Each manager she hires comes on to her, and she fires him 9c

(1) Carol finds herself in a strange city, broke, victimized 14b

(1) Carol, desiring a relationship, has never had a lover 32

(1) Carol, pretty but dull, is unable to attract men 36

(4) Working girl Carol unexpectedly wins a small lottery jackpot; with it she briefly pretends to be wealthy 2f

(4) Carol, a maid, uses the wardrobe of her rich employer and poses as an important person 2g

(4) Carol, a criminal, assumes an alias and uses stolen funds to evade the law 2h

(4) Carol, discouraged by her lack of admirers, resorts to pretense 36

(4) Carol considers love and marriage the ultimate adventure, and eagerly pursues them 38

(10) Carol, discouraged with her love-life, receives a "sign" that predicts she'll be married within a year 13a

ROMANTIC MISADVENTURES
Carol is convinced that men are crazy about her 56

Carol is unaware that she is deluding herself 56

Carol, discouraged by a failed romance, plans suicide and writes a note explaining her motives 57

Carol is victimized by false gossip about her love-life 62

Carol

ROMANTIC MISADVENTURES (cont'd.)

Carol isn't sure which of her lovers love her for herself, rather than for her money; she devises a plan to find the answer 103

Unmarried, idealistic Carol, is determined to become a mother 121

Carol's time is totally consumed by her multiple romances 143

Attractive Carol is totally absorbed by her work; everything else, even love, is secondary to achieving her goals 145

Carol contemplates suicide 162b

Rich widow Carol has so many admirers she can't make a choice 164

(1) Carol, planning to take her own life, changes her mind — but inadvertently loses the suicide note 57

(1) Carol is falsely accused of being a homewrecker. She decides on a strategy to rid herself of suspicion 102

(1) Unmarried Carol is pregnant, deceived by her lover 162b

(2) Wealthy Carol pretends to lose all her money so she can discover which of her suitors loves her for herself 93a

(4) Carol, single, pretends she's married and calls herself "Mrs.—" 58c

(4) Narcissistic Carol believes herself irresistible to men 65

(4) Carol, in order to avoid the complications of romance, resorts to pretense 71b

(4) Carol pretends she's engaged to be married in order to avoid unwanted attentions 83

(4) Carol, in order to carry out a necessary venture, offers to sell herself in marriage to the highest bidder 88

MARRIAGE PROPOSAL

(1) Carol, in a storm at night, is proposed to. Unable to see her lover, and barely able to hear him, she still accepts — and faces an unpleasant surprise 195

REJECTION

Disapproving of men she meets in her own world, Carol envisions her ideal man and sets off to find him 242

Carol knows nothing of her birth or parents 305

(7) Carol dislikes the men in her own social and business world 242

(8) Carol, unsuccessful in love, attempts to find happiness in imagined romance 251

(8) Carol, disappointed in love, resigns herself to her loss 325

MARRIAGE

Carol must be married by a specific age in order to receive a large inheritance 354b

(1) Carol takes drastic measures when she discovers a skeleton in her family closet 364a

(2) Reformed delinquent Carol is rewarded with a happy marriage 359

(4) Carol pretends to be rich, and merely posing as a salesgirl 358

MARRIED LIFE

(4) Carol tries to save herself from the consequences of a crime by running away 453

(6) Carol dies in childbirth 515

Carol desperately wants a movie career 413

MISFORTUNE

Carol is unjustly accused of a crime 648

Carol leads an exemplary life, trying to live down a troubled past 665

Unless Carol hides a past indiscretion, she will seriously compromise herself 667

CHARACTER COMBINATIONS

Intellectual Carol has an artistic temperament 676

Carol is trying to make an important venture succeed 677

Carol fights anxiety 677

Carol drives a Land-Rover alone in the wilderness 694

Carol inherits the trait of hiding her affections, a trait that hinders her success and happiness 736

Carol is discontented because of an unfortunate situation 737a

Carol tries to overcome her discontentment, but the obstacles seem insurmountable 737a

Carol finds that the lock in a hotel room is broken and the door can't be opened 737b

Carol, tipsy with champagne, ties a ribbon to the doorknob of her big-city hotel room so she can find her way back 737c

Carol writes a note that contains a vitally important secret 742

(1) Late at night in a big city hotel, Carol enters what she thinks is her room. The following morning Carol awakens, horrified to find that she's sharing a strange man's bed in a city she's never before visited 643

(1) Carol finds herself imprisoned in a strange bedroom 645

(1) Carol, caught innocently in a compromising situation, discovers something that places her in serious jeopardy 645

(1) Carol is accused of being a criminal (or of an indiscretion) because she is apprehended in a high-crime area, or because she possesses evidence that indicates a crime (or indiscretion) has taken place 648

(1) Carol, driving alone in the wilds, crashes her vehicle and sustains injuries, leaving her helpless 694

(1) At night in a motel, Carol, clad in her bathrobe, returns from the ice-maker and accidently enters the wrong room 737b

(1) Carol is ostracized because of a problem for which she isn't responsible 740

(1) Carol writes a note that she inadvertently loses 742

(1) Carol writes an important note which, if read by anyone other than the addressee, will humiliate Carol 742

(1) Believed by others to be eccentric, Carol truly has supernatural powers — fueled by tragic events in the past 746

(4) Carol commits a secret offense 669

(4) Carol commits a crime, and, to escape the consequences, secretly travels to a distant place and assumes an alias 743b

(6) Carol, depressed, tries to escape her problems through self-destructive acts 738

(6) Overcome by desperate problems, Carol plans to commit suicide 743a

MISTAKEN JUDGMENT
Carol has a character weakness that deeply affects her life 766

(2-10) Thinking that she is a criminal, Carol tries to evade the law 784

(4) Small town schoolteacher Carol unknowingly violates School Board regulations and opens a Pandora's Box of problems 765

(4) Carol, a plain woman, believes she is gorgeous 766

(7) Carol discovers she isn't guilty of the crime she thought she had committed 784

HELPFULNESS
(1) Carol, attacked by a deadly snake, suffers delirium 848b

Carol

DELIVERANCE

Carol, tortured by malicious gossip, attempts to clear her name 870a

Carol, afraid she is going insane, tries to break free of her demoralizing fear 872

Carol discovers an evil secret in her past 873

Carol is trapped in an upper floor of a skyscraper 885b

(1) Carol is afraid she is going insane 872

(1) Discovering an evil secret in her past, Carol contemplates suicide 873

(2) Carol, imprisoned in an upper floor of a skyscraper, saves herself by using her ingenuity (air-conditioning ducts, elevator cables, etc.) 885b

IDEALISM

Carol, who lives in a lonely place, craves excitement 916

Carol is happy in her mistaken ideals 931

Carol is regarded as immoral, but in her own estimation, Carol believes her goals transcend surface judgement 945

Carol, whose beautiful garden is the source of her happiness, learns that the garden is about to be destroyed 962

Reared in city poverty and hoping to find happiness in the great outdoors, Carol ends up living in a drab, bleak countryside 974

Carol is terminally ill 975

Terminally ill Carol, convinced she can't die happy without a final look at her home town, revisits the fondly-remembered haunts of her childhood 975

Carol is determined to protect her family's honor, but in so doing, her life is narrowly confined to duty 977a

(1) Carol dies a broken-hearted victim of her own rigid ideals 909

(4) Carol is a selfish, bitter woman who lives only for herself, failing to recognize that she is the source of her unhappiness 908

(7) Carol decides that she will gain more by losing in a venture than by winning 933

(8) Carol, who once committed a serious wrong, achieves happiness by assuming a new identity and way of life which enables her to right the wrong 921

(8) Regarded as immoral, the sincerity of Carol's convictions disarms criticism 945

(8) Criminal (or unethical) Carol tries to live down her unsavory past by exemplary conduct 946

(8) Carol fights to maintain her standards in the face of challenges 947

(8) TV evangelist Carol is determined to convince the world that it desperately needs her brand of religion and virtue, and tries to set an example with her lifestyle 976

OBLIGATION

Widow Carol is happy being independent 994

Carol works for years on a lonely project 995

Widow Carol wants to be independent and have her own home; but there are certain obligations blocking her goal 1009a

NECESSITY

Carol looks for work in a profession dominated by men, and is discriminated against 1032

Carol, in order to carry out a venture, employs deception 1032

(1) Carol engages in a secret venture that endangers her 1025

(4) Desperately needing money, Carol engages in an impulsive venture 1033

CHARACTER COMBINATIONS

PERSONAL LIMITATIONS

Carol fails to understand how her irritable disposition makes everyone around her unhappy 1067

Carol's youth, beauty and intellect threaten her success in her chosen career 1099

Carol has to behave out-of-character to be successful at her job 1099

Carol's venture depends on her successful impersonation of a male 1100

Carol, eager to advance her career, runs into demoralizing problems 1121

Ailing Carol's doctor orders her to leave the city and live in the country 1137b

City-bred Carol encounters unexpected problems when she moves to the country 1137b

(1) Sophisticated executive's wife Carol, finds it difficult to conform to the customs of a rural community 1118

(1) Carol is in a small sailboat, lost off a dangerous coast in a dense fog 1137a

(1) While swimming in the ocean, Carol is caught in the undertow and dragged out to sea 1137a

(4) Carol, successfully impersonating a male, suffers by being treated as one of the boys 1100

(4) Young, vibrant Carol is convinced that she can break the rules in her quest for self-expression 1105

(4) Carol yearns for social status 1106

(4) Carol lacks every qualification, yet still believes she is a highly gifted musician 1119

(14) Carol, overhearing someone criticize her unpleasant personality, begins to face the truth about herself 1067

PRETENSE

Carol, owner of a priceless jewel that she is afraid to wear in public, keeps it in a safe and wears a replica. It is known that she owns the real stone, and no one suspects she's wearing a fake 1152

Carol accidently commits a crime 1156

Carol keeps her inadvertent crime a secret 1156

Carol desperately wants to change her life 1204

(1) Carol fails to achieve a goal she prizes 1153

(1) Carol, mistaken for another woman whose life has been threatened, attempts to elude her pursuers 1154a

(4) Carol pretends to be ignorant of a certain compromising event in her life 1151

(4) Carol, failing to achieve a prized goal, attempts to make others think she succeeded 1153

(4) Carol tries to convince those in her home town that she's a success 1203

(4) Carol encounters sexual discrimination in the job market, so she disguises herself as a male 1207

DECEPTION

College student Carol is paid to confidentially gather seemingly innocent information while assuming the role of a tour guide 1241a

Young Carol, involved in an action that might result in a lawsuit, takes the advice of others and, using a ploy, removes herself from the situation 1242a

Carol plans to go forward with a venture which requires delicacy, so she resorts to deception 1244a

Carol

DECEPTION (cont'd.)
(2) Carol, involved in a situation which will result in embarrassment (or punishment) if she's discovered, uses her ingenuity in making her escape   1241c

(4) Middle-aged Carol's multiple cosmetic surgeries keep her looking as if she's in her early twenties   1279a

(12) Carol plants evidence that points to someone else   1279b

CRIME-IMMORALITY
(1) Reformed Carol has her unsavory past exposed   1292

(1) Carol, committing one crime in order to hide another, is arrested for a crime she didn't commit   1294

(4) Carol unethically borrows money on property she is holding in trust in order to forward a certain venture   1293b

(4) Carol commits a crime in order to hide a smaller crime   1294

(8) Reformed Carol tries to live down her past 1292

VENGEANCE
(6) Driven by revenge, Carol, in turn, is killed 1328

MYSTERY
In desperate danger, Carol begs for help, is denied, and vanishes   1417

Carol flees from mysterious dangers   1446b

(1) Carol receives a photograph, and a note warning that the person in the photograph is in great danger   1364a

(1) While asleep, Carol is threatened by terrible danger   1446b

(10) Because of a revelatory vision, Carol redirects the course of her life   1445

(13) Carol receives a photograph of someone who greatly resembles her   1364a

(14) Carol is strongly influenced by a revelatory vision in which her life unfolds before her   1445

REVELATION
Snobbish Carol is proud of her patrician ancestry   1458

(1) Carol is shocked to learn that her ancestry is less patrician than she had assumed 1458

Carol and Annie

MISFORTUNE
(1-11) Carol loses a valuable ornament she borrowed from her friend, Annie   642

(4) Carol, to please her vanity, borrows a valuable ornament from her rich friend, Annie   642

HELPFULNESS
Carol is convinced her friend, Annie, is making a mistake   843

(4) Carol, certain that her friend, Annie, is making a mistake, decides to prevent Annie's actions   843

PRETENSE
(1) While Carol is impersonating Annie, the real Annie is, unbeknownst to Carol, injured in an accident and expected to die   1208

Carol and Laura

DELIVERANCE
(6) Carol dies of injuries sustained while rescuing Laura from an accident   892

DECEPTION
Laura, hiding in Carol's doorway, pretends to be Carol and signs for a package delivered by a messenger   1278b

Carol and Kate

PRETENSE
(4) Carol sends press clippings about a celebrity, Kate, back home, pretending that, under a stage or pen name, she is Kate   1203

Carol and Sally

PRETENSE
(12) Carol's striking resemblance to Sally, a criminal, causes her to be suspected of a crime 1172

Carol and Donna

PERSONAL LIMITATIONS
Carol leaves an urgent message asking her employee, Donna's help   1136

Carol and Irene

MARRIED LIFE
Carol closely resembles Irene   456

MISTAKEN JUDGMENT
(2-3) Carol places an identifying mark on her hotel room door. The mark is transferred to another door; and Irene, occupant of that room, is found murdered   792b

PRETENSE
(4) Carol makes a deal with terminally ill Irene to take Carol's name   1204

(9) Irene dies and is buried as Carol   1204

Carol and Enid

PRETENSE
(4) Traveling alone, Carol invents a non-existent aunt, Enid, as a chaperone   1158

Carol and X

ROMANTIC MISADVENTURES
Carol, convinced a keepsake of a lost love, X, has magical powers, tries to regain love by wearing the keepsake   89

(4) Unmarried scientist Carol, unable to find the man of her dreams, creates an android, X, as a substitute for a husband   84a

MISFORTUNE
(1) Owing to financial difficulties, Carol is forced to sell a greatly prized object, X   739

(1) Carol is unable to repurchase an object she loves, X   739

MISTAKEN JUDGMENT
(1) Impoverished Carol borrows a supposedly valuable object, X, and loses it   767

(5) Carol, borrowing a supposedly valuable object, X, then losing it, sells her soul to replace it — only to find that X was a worthless fake   767

MYSTERY
Carol purchases an object, X, in a shop   1384

(1) Carol loses her purse, X, that contains the key to her safe-deposit box   1446a

(13) Carol finds her lost purse, X, which still contains the safe-deposit box key — but her safe-deposit box has been looted   1446a

REVELATION
Carol finds an old ledger, X, that contains records of dishonest dealings   1459

(2-3-7) Carol finds an old ledger, X, which contains information that has a major impact on her plans   1459

Carol, Kate and X

HELPFULNESS
Carol runs a booth at a charity bazaar, and tries to stop Kate from buying a certain object, X, that Kate wants very badly   849

DECEPTION
(9) Carol uses deception to prevent a stranger, Kate, from buying an article, X, about which Carol has just made a discovery   1245

Carol and Rita

ROMANCE'S BEGINNINGS
Carol, daughter of Rita, a widow, has sound reasons for opposing Rita's intention to remarry   33

Carol and Rita

ROMANCE'S BEGINNINGS (cont'd.)
(1) Carol's mother, Rita, is determined that Carol marry wealth. Thus, Carol renounces the man she loves to marry the rich man she doesn't love, and finds herself miserable 341

MISFORTUNE
Carol's mother, Rita, is an ailing widow 659

Rita's life hangs on a change of climate, but she and her daughter, Carol, are broke 659

Carol is desperately determined to do anything necessary to raise the money to help her mother, Rita 659

Carol's mother, Rita, is a narcotics addict 668

Carol's mother, Rita, has periods of irrational behavior 670

(1) Carol makes a heavy personal sacrifice in order to help Rita keep a secret 668

(1) Carol's strange, wild traits are attributed to an event experienced by her mother, Rita, while pregnant with Carol 740

(4) Carol helps her mother, Rita, conceal Rita's problem 670

MISTAKEN JUDGMENT
Carol's widowed mother, Rita, is in desperate trouble 785

Rita plans a course of action that Carol knows will result in unhappy consequences, but Carol's unable to dissuade her 785

DELIVERANCE
Carol's mother, Rita, is financially strapped and alienated from Carol 886

(10) Carol's mother, Rita, unexpectedly inherits a fortune, sees Carol in a different light (or vice-versa) and they become reconciled 886

IDEALISM
Carol's mother, Rita, is determined to give Carol a good education 978

Carol and her mother, Rita, are penniless, and Carol has to work to support them 978

(7) When Carol's mother, Rita, adopts Carol's values, it causes Carol to question them 931

OBLIGATION
Carol's mother, Rita, lives a life of self-denial in fulfilling her commitment to educate Carol 996

DECEPTION
Rita's daughter, Carol, behaves foolishly and rejects advice 1246

Carol's mother, Rita, mimics Carol's conduct to show her daughter how foolishly she acted 1246

Carol and Frank

MISFORTUNE
Frank's eldest daughter, Carol, has to support the family when Frank dies 745

Carol rebels against her father, Frank, and his overly strict discipline 676

Carol's father, Frank, is a disreputable character who disappeared mysteriously long ago 684

(1) Carol tries to make a home for her widowed father, Frank, but he cruelly mistreats her 641

(1) Carol is forced out of the house by her father, Frank 741

(1) Carol's father, Frank, pursuing thieves who have robbed him, is shot and killed 745

(8) Frank changes his mind about identifying himself and leaves Carol content with her illusions 684

(11) Carol's father, Frank, long missing, returns home unrecognized and discovers that his daughter, Carol, thinks he is dead and has elevated him to sainthood 684

CHARACTER COMBINATIONS

HELPFULNESS
When Carol's father, Frank, fails in a venture, she takes the project off his hands 812b

DELIVERANCE
Carol's father, Frank, forces Carol to take an action that she knows will destroy her happiness 871

(2) Carol, forced by her father, Frank, to take an action she knows will destroy her happiness, imaginatively avoids disaster 871

IDEALISM
Carol erects a monument to her father, Frank, whom she mistakenly thinks is dead, remembering him with pride and love 930

OBLIGATION
Carol's father, Frank, dies heavily in debt 993

(1) Carol makes a great personal sacrifice in fulfilling an obligation to live with and care for her father 992

(4) Frank's only child, Carol, considers herself honor bound to pay the debts of her dead father. She undertakes a strange venture in order to fulfill the obligation 993

(9) Carol spends years on a lonely project in order to clear her father, Frank, of dishonor 995

PRETENSE
Carol's father, Frank, is accused of a certain crime 1171

(1) Carol, to save her father, Frank, who is suspected of a crime, confesses that she is the perpetrator 1171

DECEPTION
(12) Against Carol's will, her father, Frank, attempts to involve her in an action she wants no part of. She evades involvement by employing a deception 1241b

CRIME-IMMORALITY
(4) Carol forges the signature of her father, Frank, on a note so she can acquire money for a certain purpose 1293a

(5) Carol forges her father, Frank's, name to a note. Unknown to Carol, Frank unexpectedly dies prior to the date of the note 1293a

MYSTERY
(13) Carol, waiting in a crowded airline terminal while her father, Frank, checks their luggage, mysteriously disappears 1416

Carol and Tony

MISFORTUNE
(1) Carol, trying to prevent her brother, Tony, from dishonoring their family, unintentionally causes his death 649

IDEALISM
Carol indirectly causes the death of her brother, Tony, by opposing his questionable venture 909

Carol's brother, Tony, is guilty of a crime 977b

(12) Carol, learning of the crime committed by her brother, Tony, tells the police and Tony is arrested 977b

Carol and Judy

MISFORTUNE
Carol is forced to live with her sister, Judy 678

(9) Carol defies her bitchy, selfish sister, Judy, who makes Carol's life miserable 678

Carol and Doug

MISTAKEN JUDGMENT
Carol deludes herself about her son, Doug 800

Carol is convinced her son, Doug, is brilliant and talented, although actually he's of less than average mentality 800

DELIVERANCE
Carol learns that her son, Doug, is suspected of a crime 896

Carol and Doug

DELIVERANCE (cont'd.)
Carol knows that her son, Doug, didn't commit the crime for which he is accused; she also knows who is guilty, but this knowledge makes it dangerous and difficult to protect Doug 896

OBLIGATION
Widow Carol is forced by family obligations to live with a married son, Doug 994

Widow Carol has given all her assets to her son, Doug 1009b

(1) Penniless Carol is forced to live with her son, Doug 1009b

Carol and Lee

MARRIED LIFE
(10) Carol devotes herself to her children, Lee and Kenny, and emerges from her depression 505

DELIVERANCE
(6) Carol heroically rescues a child, Lee, from death, but sacrifices her own life in the process 893

PERSONAL LIMITATIONS
(5) Carol realizes the consequences of her selfishness when one of her children, Lee, dies 1068

Carol and Vicki

PERSONAL LIMITATIONS
(14) Carol, agonizing over the death (real or apparent) of her daughter, Vicki, experiences a personal revelation that alters her life 1069

PRETENSE
(4) Carol, to avoid slanderous gossip and protect her daughter, Vicki, who is about to marry a prominent man, tries to cover up a possible scandal in her own past 1151

Carol and Walt

ROMANTIC MISADVENTURES
(1) Walt, a handsome young man, arrives at an elegant estate where, to his surprise, he's greeted as a bridegroom, is hurried before the minister and hurriedly married to Carol, a beautiful young woman. After the ceremony she realizes he isn't the man she thought he was, but Walt has vanished 155

(4) Carol, single and driven by an unusual motive, pretends that she is engaged to marry an imaginary person, Walt, and has the announcement published in a newspaper 86

(11) Carol concocts an imaginary lover, Walt; and, to her surprise, a man with Walt's name and resembling him, enters her life 58a

MARRIAGE
Compelled by an unusual motive, Carol invents a fictitious man, Walt 354a

(9) Walt, a fictitious man invented by Carol, "comes to life," falls for Carol, and they marry 354a

MISFORTUNE
In an effort to be helpful, Carol befriends a stranger, Walt 646

(1) Carol discovers that Walt, the stranger she befriended, is a criminal on the run from the law 646

(4) Carol pretends that she's engaged to an imaginary lover, Walt, buys a ring, and has the engagement announced in a newspaper 58b

PERSONAL LIMITATIONS
Yearning for social status, Carol throws a lavish party for alleged nobleman, Walt, whom she's never met 1106

(1) Alone in a strange room, Carol discovers Walt dead in the bed 1135b

CHARACTER COMBINATIONS

Carol and Pete

MARRIED LIFE
(4) To avoid the consequences of her own indiscretion, Carol blames innocent Pete 446a

Carol and Gary

MARRIAGE PROPOSAL
(5) Impulsively, irresponsibly, Carol promises to marry Gary. Later, coming to her senses, she regrets the promise 183

Carol sends a message to Gary accepting his marriage proposal 194b

REJECTION
(4) Believing she's lost the man she loves, Carol decides to marry Gary, a man she doesn't love 261

MARRIED LIFE
Gary tries to use his power over Carol for his own selfish goals 411b

(4) Married Carol assumes a new identity and marries Gary 451

MISFORTUNE
(1) Reformed Carol has her troubled past revealed by Gary 665

DECEPTION
Carol goes with her friend, Gary, to spend a weekend at a country inn 1240

(12) Carol's friend, Gary, dies suddenly in their room in a country inn. Carol, first to find Gary dead, attempts to remove all traces of her presence before the body is discovered by others 1240

CRIME-IMMORALITY
Carol's friend, Gary, mysteriously vanishes while in Carol's company 1309b

(1) Carol is booked on suspicion of having murdered Gary 1309b

Carol and Dave

HELPFULNESS
Compassionate Carol befriends a needy stranger, Dave 812a

(1) Carol, befriending needy Dave, finds herself drawn into a difficult complication 812a

DELIVERANCE
While engaged in a clandestine venture, Carol finds herself in danger and asks a stranger, Dave, to help her 890

NECESSITY
(1) Carol, engaged in a secret venture and becoming endangered, asks for aid from a stranger, Dave, but Dave warily refuses 1025

PRETENSE
(4) Carol fakes an injury from an automobile accident so she can collect damages from the car owner, Dave 1159

Carol and Burt

MARRIED LIFE
(1) Carol finds herself in the clutches of Burt 410

Carol, in her teens, married a criminal, Burt 447

Criminal Burt is killed and Carol, his widow, tries a fresh start in a distant location 447

Carol's secret offense is discovered by Burt 669

Thieves, led by Burt, threaten deadly harm to Carol unless she opens the safe 666

(1) Respectable, straightlaced Carol, looking for employment, takes the advice of a supposed friend, Burt, and finds herself dancing in a topless bar 647

(1) Carol's secret crime or infidelity is discovered by Burt, who attempts to blackmail Carol 669

Carol and Burt

PERSONAL LIMITATIONS
When trapped in a room with Burt, Carol has to fight off his advances 1135b

DECEPTION
(2) Carol traps inept thief Burt by telling him her valuables are hidden in a closet — then locking him in the closet 1259

Carol and Sam

DELIVERANCE
Carol, her integrity seriously questioned, is befriended by Sam, a detective 870b

PRETENSE
Attempting to carry out a venture in a shopping mall, Carol finds her objective obstructed by detective Sam 1206

(2) Carol, fashionably dressed, escapes detective Sam by posing as a display mannequin 1206

DECEPTION
Female terrorist Carol, tracked down by Federal agent Sam, takes a hostage to effect her escape 1258

Carol and Eric

IDEALISM
Carol volunteers to nurse a sick person, Eric, when no one else will do it 956

(6) Carol, nursing Eric, contracts a deadly virus and dies 956

Carol, Dave and Sam

MISFORTUNE
(1) Carol innocently befriends a stranger, Dave. Later, it develops that Dave is a political radical wanted by government officials led by Sam 644

(5) If Sam knew that Carol had befriended Dave, she'd be labeled an accomplice and treated accordingly 644

Carol, Pete and Annie

MARRIED LIFE
Carol uses her telepathic powers to reshape the future of an unhappily married couple, Pete and Annie 594g

(1-5) Carol reconciles Pete and his alienated wife, Annie, only to realize she's in love with Pete 594g

Carol, Burt and Sam

DELIVERANCE
(3-12) Sam proves that Carol's enemy, Burt, is a criminal, and brings him to justice 870b

Carol, Carl and X

MYSTERY
(13) Carol wonders why shopkeeper, Carl, insists on buying back an object, X, which she bought in his shop 1384

Carol, Rita and Frank

IDEALISM
Carol, whose parents, Rita and Frank, are poor and uneducated, struggles to get an education that will allow her to escape a life of squalor 948

Carol, Frank and Gary

REJECTION
(2) Carol's bankrupt father, Frank, refuses to let Carol marry wealthy Gary, a man she doesn't love, despite the fact that it would solve Frank's financial problems 269

Jack and Carol

ROMANCE'S BEGINNINGS
Jack, poor, loves wealthy Carol 1a

Uneducated Jack falls in love with college professor Carol 1b

Jack, older, loves youthful Carol 1d

Politically conservative Jack loves passionately liberal Carol 1f

Stodgy Jack falls for Carol, a romantic 1g

Jack quarrels with his girlfriend, Carol, and is afraid he's losing her love 1h

Bank clerk Jack, taking a fling in high society, meets wealthy patrician Carol 2a

Fugitive Jack, using an alias, falls in love with Carol 2b

Jack, involved in a devious secret venture, falls in love with Carol who is also involved in a suspect venture 2b

Jack, posing as a citizen of the inner-city, meets Carol, and they fall in love 2c

Carol, while posing as a salesclerk, meets Jack, and they fall in love 2e

Carol, poor but pretending to be wealthy, meets rich, influential Jack, and they fall in love 2f

Carol, poor but pretending to be rich and important, meets apparently rich, influential Jack, and they fall in love 2g

Carol, a criminal in disguise, meets Jack and they fall in love 2h

Jack is a judge and Carol is a fugitive posing as a wealthy, fashionable woman 3a

Jack, trying to expose treachery, falls in love with Carol, suspected of the treachery 4a

Jack unselfishly returns property to a woman, Carol, whom he's never met — and falls in love with her 4b

Carol, who has been attempting to meet Jack, retrieves the item he lost and returns it to him. Jack and Carol fall in love 6a

Carol finds a mislaid briefcase belonging to Jack, an attorney, and returns it to him. Jack and Carol fall in love 6b

Jack loves Carol but worries that their affair has gone sour 7b

Jack, in an effort to help his romance with Carol, obtains a mail-order love potion 7b

Jack and Carol, young and single, become business partners 9b

Detective Jack arrests criminal Carol 10a

Carol, a criminal arrested by Jack, a detective, tries to seduce Jack in hope of escaping 10a

Carol, impoverished and in trouble, is befriended by wealthy Jack 10b

Carol, impoverished, tries to win the love of wealthy Jack 10b

Carol makes loves to Jack in an effort to escape from trouble 10c

Carol, who has a questionable past, discovers that she has won the love of straight-arrow Jack 11c

Jack and Carol each secretly believe themselves to be criminals 12a

Carol, inferior, falls in love with a superior person, Jack; and Jack's apparent love for Carol gives her the strength to endure her problems 13b

Carol, nearly overcome by troubles, meets Jack, and they fall in love 14a

Carol, helpless and in dire straits, meets a stranger, Jack, and they fall in love 14b

Carol, an attractive young widow, meets Jack, a handsome young widower 14c

Carol, a "plain Jane" working girl, falls in love with handsome, successful Jack 15a

Jack hasn't a clue that plain Carol is in love with him 15b

Jack, a detective, arrests Carol, a criminal, and is returning her to the crime locale 16a

Jack and Carol, while negotiating a commercial transaction, fall in love 20a

Jack and Carol

ROMANCE'S BEGINNINGS (cont'd.)

Jack and Carol, mutually involved in a devious venture, are attracted to one another and fall in love 20b

Jack and Carol, while meeting as attorney and client, fall in love 20c

Jack meets Carol and suspects she is dishonorable; Carol, in turn, thinks Jack is guilty of the same 21

Jack and Carol, despite mutual suspicions, fall in love 21

Woman-hater Jack falls in love with Carol 22a

Wealthy, sophisticated Jack falls in love with lower-class Carol 23d

Jack, attracted by Carol's beauty, falls in love with her 24b

Jack sees a photo of Carol, a woman he doesn't know 24c

Jack, hearing of the beauty and charms of Carol, a woman he's never met, falls in love and is determined to marry her 24d

Romantic Jack catches only a fleeting glimpse of Carol, and falls in love with her 24e

Jack, falling for Carol, whom he doesn't know, tries to get an introduction 25

Jack and Carol have never seen each other but they correspond, and through their letters become engaged 26b

Carol, from a questionable background, wins upstanding Jack's love, resulting in tense complications 27

Secretary Carol loves Jack, a junior partner of the company that employs her 30

Shy, insecure Carol worships Jack from afar 34

(1) Jack and Carol, believing themselves to be fugitives, meet while on the run, and fall in love 12a

(1) Jack, unmarried, and Carol, married, are stranded in an isolated area 12b

(1) Jack, under threat of disinheritance, is ordered to perform an act damaging to a near-relative of Carol, the woman he loves. Jack refuses 19b

(1) While running a con-game, Jack meets Carol, who astutely sees through his scheme; Carol is also involved in a scam, and Jack becomes suspicious 20b

(1) Jack has an experience with Carol that turns him into a woman-hater 22b

(4) Jack, in love with wealthy Carol, pretends to be rich 1a

(4) Uneducated Jack, in love with academic Carol, pretends to be part of her world 1b

(4) Jack, older, in love with young Carol, tries to enhance the relationship by pretending to be young 1d

(4) Criminal Jack pretends to be an honest man in order to enhance his romance with Carol 1e

(4) Stodgy Jack, in love with romantic Carol, tries to adopt an heroic facade 1g

(4) Jack, afraid he's losing Carol's love, pretends to attempt suicide 1h

(4) Jack, falling in love with Carol, pretends he's Eric 2d

(4) Jack, a judge, falls in love with Carol, a lawbreaker 3a

(4) Jack, a detective, falls in love with Carol, the criminal he has apprehended and is bringing back to the locale where the crime was committed 3b

(4) Jack and Carol, both single, vow to keep their relationship platonic 9a

(4) Jack and Carol, entering into a business partnership, try with every legal device to preclude romance — but in vain   9b

(4) Middle-aged Carol and youthful Jack love each other   11b   37

(4) Carol, a "plain Jane" servant, secretly adores Jack   15b

(4) Detective Jack falls for criminal Carol, whom he's arrested   16a

(4) Unmarried Jack and married Carol meet in an isolated environment, and fall in love 17a

(4) Marine Corporal Carol falls in love with Captain Jack, and tries to win him in marriage   23a

(4) Carol, a member of a racial minority, falls in love with Jack, a member of the racial majority   23b

(4) Jack, a member of a racial minority, falls in love with Carol, a member of the racial majority   23c

(4) Jack falls for Carol, a woman he doesn't know, and wants to marry her   24a

(4) Studying a photo of stranger Carol, Jack falls in love with her   24c

(4) Carol, critically ill, becomes convinced she's in love with Jack, her doctor   28a

(4) Carol, sharing troubles with Jack, thinks she's in love with him   28b

(4) Carol doesn't know Jack, but falls in love with him at first sight   29

(4) Carol, rescued from an accident by Jack, a stranger, falls in love with him   31

(7) Jack, unmarried, and Carol, married, fall in love. Then Carol makes a startling discovery   12b

(7) Carol, a widow, and Jack, a widower, meet in a cemetery while paying their respects to their deceased spouses — and they fall in love   14c

(7) Jack, although his vows forbid romance, falls in love with Carol   16b

(8) Carol wins the love of Jack, and finds the strength to endure her misfortune   14a

(9) Carol thinks her lover, Jack, too rigid for a happy marriage; so Jack, hoping to change Carol's mind, adopts a less daunting facade 1c

(9) Jack recovers property belonging to Carol, a woman he doesn't know   4b

(10) Jack, in love with Carol, finds that Carol thinks he's too rigid for a happy marriage   1c

(10) Jack and Carol, involved in a project, vow to keep their relationship platonic; but, despite their intentions, they fall in love   9a

(14) Carol hires Jack as manager of her TV station on the condition that he keep his distance; but Carol falls for him, and is pleased to learn that Jack's sole purpose in taking the job was to win her love   9c

(14) Jack devoutly dislikes women, but Carol's actions change his opinion   22a

ROMANTIC MISADVENTURES
Jack is crushed when Carol fails to respond to his message   40b

Jack promises Carol, the woman he loves, to give up a type of behavior that Carol finds unacceptable   41b

Jack meets Carol, a former love, and is disappointed to learn that his success abroad doesn't impress her; she believes success on one's home ground is what counts   46

Jack asks Carol to let herself be hypnotized so that he can learn a secret buried in her subconscious   47a

Jack and Carol

ROMANTIC MISADVENTURES (cont'd.)

Lovers Jack and Carol, narrowly escape tragedy 49

Jack, unable to accept the reality of Carol's death, spends years searching for her 53

Investigating a psychic phenomenon, Jack falls for Carol 54b

Jack, rejected by Carol, takes revenge by destroying something she values highly 66a

Rich, elderly Jack is in love with young Carol 67

Jack plans a test to find out if Carol really loves him 67

Jack's family hates Carol's family. Jack, in love with Carol, conceals his identity when calling on Carol 70

Carol disguises herself and meets Jack, the man she loves, without betraying her identity 82a

Carol tries to find out if Jack really loves her 82a

Carol resorts to pretense in order to find out if Jack, the man she loves, really loves her 82b

Carol uses deception to find out if Jack loves her 85b

Carol deliberately steers herself and Jack into a compromising situation and then blames Jack for it 85b

Carol, in love with Jack, tries to save Jack from disaster by an ingenious plan 91

Carol, trying to find out if Jack really loves her, resorts to a deception 93b

Jack betrays Carol by not marrying her as promised 96

Jack, in love with Carol, secretly uses any means to save Carol from an impending disaster 97

Jack is convinced that his lover, Carol, is dead; Carol, far away, learns of Jack's mistaken belief 105

Jack falls apart when he thinks his girlfriend, Carol, is unfaithful 107

Jack, Carol's lover, is condemned to die for a crime he didn't commit 108

Jack is in love with Carol, who will be permitted to marry him if Jack succeeds in a difficult venture 110

Jack, in love with Carol, struggles to acquire enough money to enable him to marry her 113

Carol informs Jack, the man she loves, that he will lose her unless he overcomes his lack of ambition 114

Carol loves Jack; but, before she will commit to marry him, she insists that he must perform heroic deeds 115

Carol, in love with unambitious Jack, influences him to take advantage of a certain opportunity 125a

Absent-minded Jack proposes to Carol, who loves him. Carol says she will give Jack her answer if he shows up at a specific date and time. If he remembers to come, she'll marry him 125b

Jack believes Carol won't marry him till he gets rich 127a

Jack believes Carol won't marry him till he overcomes his personal limitations 127b

Jack and Carol are in love, but certain conditions prevent their marriage 129

If Jack fulfills a certain obligation, he will be unfaithful to Carol and will lose her 132

CHARACTER COMBINATIONS

Jack loves Carol, but is helpless to stop her from embarking on a dangerous venture 133

Jack and Carol, the woman he loves, inadvertently find themselves in a compromising situation 134a

Carol loves Jack and has worn his engagement ring for years 141

Carol, held captive by enemies of Jack, is being forced to obey them by violent threats against Jack, the man she loves 144

Carol shares with her lover, Jack, a secret that, if revealed, would prove disastrous to Carol 147

Jack, in love with Carol, has a jeweler send Carol a valuable gift 153

Carol loves Jack, but isn't sure it's mutual 162a

Carol learns that her boyfriend, Jack, is in serious trouble 163

Carol loses a locket, and asks her suitors to look for it. Inside the locket is a photo of Jack, Carol's favorite suitor 165

Carol wore a certain ornament when her two timing lover, Jack, proposed. She is convinced that the same will happen to any other woman who wears the ornament 173

Carol promises to marry Jack if he succeeds in a difficult venture 176c

Jack, by ESP, learns of a terrible danger threatening Carol, the woman he loves 179a

Jack, in a distant country far from Carol, hears her cry of help over the telephone 179b

Jack has a telepathic vision warning him that danger threatens his lover, Carol 179c

(1) Jack gives his sweetheart, Carol, a novel. The book, unknown to Jack, includes passages that Carol interprets as uncomplimentary toward herself — and she assumes that Jack is sending her a not-so-subtle message 40a

(1) Jack is so wrapped up in his romance with Carol that it affects his business disastrously 44b

(1) Jack hypnotizes Carol, who dies while in a subconscious state 47a

(1) Lovers, Jack and Carol escape death in an accident, but each believes the other has died 49

(1) Jack impersonates another man who, it turns out, has a wife who insists Jack is her husband 50

(1) When Jack, who loves Carol, admits to Carol that he committed murder, Carol suffers a breakdown 51a

(1) Jack's confession to his lover, Carol, of a crime (or indiscretion), proves disastrous 51b

(1) Fugitive Jack hears someone approaching his hideout and mistakenly shoots and kills Carol, his girlfriend 52a

(1) Jack loves Carol despite his vows of celibacy. Jack comes to regret his vows 55

(1) Carol runs off with Jack, who later deserts her 60

(1) Jack, in love with Carol and thinking she's guilty of a crime, tells the police that he committed the crime 69

(1) Carol feels remorse after rejecting Jack 124

(1) Jack is enroute to marry Carol, when he runs into trouble 130

(1) Jack, and Carol whom Jack loves, are trapped in a burning house 134b

Jack and Carol

ROMANTIC MISADVENTURES (cont'd.)

1) Carol, in love with Jack, learns that Jack no longer loves her. Yet he is willing to stand by his promise to marry her 142

(1) Jack sends Carol a gift. By mistake, or by malicious intent, packages are switched; the gift Carol receives, supposedly from Jack, almost destroys their relationship 153

(1) Jack, planning to meet Carol at a rural church where they are to be secretly married, becomes lost in a storm and doesn't reach the church until Carol and all the others have left 154a

(1-7) Pretentious Jack, in love with Carol, learns that Carol has been ridiculing him; indignant, he leaves Carol 156

(2) Carol will lose her lover, Jack, if she lets Jack proceed with a venture that she instigated. To avoid losing Jack, Carol defeats the venture by making a confession 95

(2) Jack is attracted to Carol and asks for a date 181a

(4) Jack, in love with Carol, ignores Carol's astute business advice, and they break up 41a

(4) Yielding to temptation, Jack reneges on a promise he made to his girlfriend, Carol, and they split up 41b

(4) Despite his girlfriend Carol's protests, Jack persists in opposing a member of Carol's family. As a result, Jack and Carol split up 41c

(4) Jack learns that unhappily married Carol, with no encouragement from Jack, is in love with him 45a

(4) Jack persuades his girlfriend, Carol, to assume an alias and help him in a dishonest scheme — with unhappy results for both 47b

(4) Jack, in love with Carol, impersonates another man at her request 50

(4) Jack, trying to help Carol, undertakes a venture that ends in disaster 52b

(4) Jack loves Carol. Carol dies and Jack, grief-stricken, becomes mentally unbalanced 53

(4) Carol, a rich romantic, falls in love with Jack, a con-artist posing as a man of means 59

(4) Carol sends her lover, Jack, a gift she mistakenly thinks will promote their mutual happiness 63

(4) Jack persuades Carol to marry him in secrecy 64

(4) Jack, rejected by Carol, revenges himself by becoming a reckless womanizer 66b

(4) Jack, rejected by Carol, revenges himself by romancing wealthy women for their money 66c

(4) Carol, in love with Jack, uses harsh measures in an attempt to goad him into proving his abilities 85a

(4) Carol poses as a boy so she can be near Jack, whom she secretly adores 87

(4) Naive Carol, on the promise of a show-business career, runs off with Jack 90a

(4) Jack and Carol, both single, become business partners. They contract never to fall in love 99

(4) Jack, in love with Carol, is determined to be with her, knowing that he'll land in trouble unless he employs deception 100

(4) Jack's girlfriend, Carol, persuades him to commit a crime 126

(4) Jack is so consumed by his romance with Carol that his business suffers 131

(4) Jack, caught up in a romantic atmosphere, becomes convinced he's in love with Carol 148

(4) Elderly, wealthy widower Jack, swept up in the romance of Spring, imagines himself in love with Carol, one of his employees 149

(4) Carol, wanting to test her lover's devotion, impulsively places herself in danger to see if he will follow her 176b

(4) Carol, to test her lover's devotion, sends him into great danger 176a

(5) Jack loves Carol and dates her regularly. One night when he calls on her, he discovers her house has vanished and in its place stands a musty old tomb — the tomb of Carol, who, according to the inscription, died 100 years before Jack was born 54a

(5) Jack, believing that he loves Carol, changes his mind when he discovers a revealing truth about her 151

(7) Jack bluntly accuses Carol of narcissism 65

(8) Jack marries Carol against a rich relative's wishes, and is disinherited 116

(8) Carol, older than Jack, feels she would be doing Jack a disservice by marrying him, although she loves him deeply 124

(9) Adventurer Jack loses his girlfriend, Carol, and his freedom on a false charge, escapes captivity, survives a series of disasters, and finally reaches a location where something of great value is hidden. He finds the treasure 109

(9) Carol, alienated from Jack, a man she loves deeply, sends a message to another person and unconsciously addresses it to Jack 172

(9) Driving his Jeep across rugged terrain, Jack sees Carol on a runaway horse. Jack overtakes Carol, and rescues her 181a

(10) Jack is courteous to unassuming Carol, whom he considers merely an acquaintance. He's astonished to learn that she loves him 45b

(10) Carol, apparently in her early 20s, is gorgeous; but she's actually very old, and remained young-looking due to a psychic phenomenon. Jack's love breaks the spell; and, before his eyes, Carol ages grotesquely 54b

(10) Carol, impersonating a man, is suddenly discovered by Jack, whom she loves 61

(10) Platonic friends Jack and Carol unexpectedly fall in love 140

(12) Prominent Jack, once in love with Carol, secretly wronged her, then abandoned her to a life of pain and loneliness 68

(12) Wealthy playboy Jack turns his back on Carol, whom he secretly betrayed 98

(13) Carol, in love with Jack, learns that Jack is a narcissist and loves only himself 42b

(14) Mean-spirited Jack falls for Carol and, inspired by love, undergoes a personality-change 106

(14) Jack, learning that Carol is still true to him, reverts to his former self 107

(14) Jack is a wild, difficult youth; he falls in love with Carol and becomes a different person 152a

MARRIAGE PROPOSAL
Jack loves Carol and is determined to propose marriage. But Carol is so closely supervised that despairing Jack can't find an opportunity 185

Jack contrives to create an opportunity to propose to Carol 185

Frustrated Jack is unable to propose marriage because Carol is constantly on the run and never alone. He plans a deception to get her alone 187

Jack and Carol

MARRIAGE PROPOSAL (cont'd.)

Carol, compelled by an unusual motive, promises to marry Jack if she can defeat him in a certain test of skill 188a

Carol knows she can beat Jack in a contest of skill if she wants to 188a

Pregnant, unmarried Carol, having decided on an abortion, is stopped by a stranger, Jack 188b

Carol, asked by Jack to marry him, wants to know more about him before she decides 189

Carol challenges Jack to a contest of skill, her acceptance or rejection to be determined by the outcome 189

Jack's shyness prevents him from proposing marriage to Carol 196

Jack, fearing rejection, can't bring himself to propose to Carol 201

Jack loves Carol, but has reasons for not proposing to her 202

Both Jack and Carol are too shy to admit their love for one another 203

Jack forgets that he asked Carol to marry him 204

(1) Proud but poor Jack feels that he can't ask wealthy Carol to marry him 198

(1) Disabled Jack is too proud ask the woman he loves, Carol, to marry him 199

(4) Neither Jack nor Carol love each other. But Carol, for certain reasons, asks Jack to marry her 190

(4) Jack, lacking the nerve to propose to Carol directly, proposes via fax 192a

(4) Procrastinator Jack loves Carol and is eager to marry her. But, true to form, he puts off asking her 200

(5) Adventurer Jack's life is threatened by savages. Queen Carol, the 300 pound tribal leader, agrees to spare Jack if he'll marry her 197

(8) In order to help Carol, who is ill and destitute, Jack pretends to be in love with her and proposes marriage 186

(8) Jack, a stranger, offers to marry Carol 188b

(9) Witless Jack, desperate for an opportunity to propose to Carol, saves her from drowning and pops the question as they cling to an overturned boat 191

(9) Carol, thinking Jack loves her but lacks the courage to admit it, proposes to him after he's rescued her from almost certain death 194a

(10) Carol wrongly interprets Jack's ambiguous remark as a marriage proposal 184

REJECTION

Jack, winning Carol's love in his youth and throwing it away, tries to win it again when he's older 205

Conceited Jack loves Carol 218a

Jack loves Carol, but becomes alienated from her due to mistaken judgment 222a

Carol, the woman Jack loves, turns out to be unfaithful; Jack is afraid Carol will reveal a secret that will cause him trouble 224

At Jack's request, Carol wears a particular piece of jewelry to indicate that she loves him 228

Compelled by a special motive, Jack pretends to fall for Carol 230

Jack is upper class; the woman he loves, Carol, is from the working class and resents the wealthy 232

Jack loves Carol and wants to marry her, but Carol regards him as a wimp and keeps him dangling 234

Adventurer Jack loves Carol 234b

Carol and Jack meet in secret 240

Jack resists the advances of Carol, an unscrupulous woman who loves him 244

Jack loves Carol, a member of a minority, but gives her up because of misguided principles 246a

Carol loves Jack. But Jack avoids women, believing they're disciples of Satan 250

Carol turns down Jack's marriage proposal because she feels that Jack is too much of a perfectionist 252a

Carol refuses Jack's marriage offer because she feels Jack is irresponsible and likely to forget his vows 252b

Jack falls in love with Carol, which for Jack violates a moral standard 257a

Jack, terminally absent-minded, forgets that Carol has rejected him and continues to pursue her 265b

Struggling Jack, in love with Carol, suddenly strikes it rich 281c

Wealthy Carol and struggling Jack care deeply for each other, but Carol refuses to sacrifice luxury for love 291

Jack considers Carol the perfect woman 292

Jack believes Carol is perfect, seemingly unaware of her questionable character 292

Jack is upper class and Carol, the woman he loves, comes from the working class and resents the wealthy 293

If Jack marries Carol, the woman he loves, he'll be disinherited 302

Jack's love for Carol runs into obstacles 303

Jack is determined to marry Carol, but unavoidable duty stands in his way 304

Carol's rejected lover, Jack, spreads malicious rumors about Carol's past 305

Jack loves Carol and is about to marry her, but he's detained and fails to arrive in time for the wedding 314

When Carol fails to keep a date with Jack, he takes it as a rejection 316

Jack loves Carol, but suspects she's a confirmed tease who is toying with him 320

Jack loves Carol, but finds her cold, distant and inhibited 322a

Carol sends Jack away with the suggestion that he reassess his life 322b

Carol loves Jack, but apparently Jack doesn't love her 327a

Carol's lover, Jack, claims to be to be a working-stiff 336b

(1) Jack regrets telling Carol that he was married when he wasn't 207

(1) Jack didn't think he loved Carol, but later realizes he does 207

(1) Carol stirs her lover, Jack, out of his apathy by firing up his ambition to get ahead — with results disastrous to their relationship 225

(1) Carol wears a piece of jewelry to show her love for Jack; but, unnoticed by Carol, the jewelry is lost and when Jack sees her, he stalks off 228

(1-7) Carol, of a minority race, tries to win the love of Jack, of a majority race. She learns it's hopeless to challenge conventions 229

(1) Jack pretends to be in love with Carol, and eventually finds he has really fallen in love 230

(1) Jack loves Carol. They are to be married, but Jack mysteriously leaves town without saying where he's going, and doesn't return until after the date set for the wedding 233

Jack and Carol

REJECTION (cont'd.)

(1) Carol, in love with Jack, rejects him when she becomes aware of his evil character 249

(1) Only Jack knows he is of mixed race. He loves and is loved by Carol, a white woman 255

(1) Jack loves Carol, but he's alienated himself from her because he is overly absent-minded. Jack writes Carol a letter assuring her that he has reformed — and forgets to mail it 260b

(1) Carol, desperately in love, proposes to Jack and is rejected 264

(1) Jack and Carol are in love. But Jack, a member of a minority, realizes that if he marries Carol, of a majority race, it would bring great burdens to their lives 271

(1) Carol falls in love with Jack, who causes her great pain by keeping his marriage secret from her 278

(1) Jack discovers that his chosen career will suffer if he marries Carol, the woman he loves 287

(1) Jack is the judge at a murder trial in which the defendant is Carol, the woman Jack secretly loves 297

(1) Carol and Jack are in love. Jack is unaware that Carol is already married 309

(1) Carol rejects Jack. In an effort to forget Carol, Jack moves to an isolated region 315

(1) Jack tries to be philosophical when Carol, the woman he loves, rejects him 321a

(1) Carol tells Jack that she's rejecting him because he is selfish, cruel and obsessed with money 322b

(1) Carol, an alien, is deserted by Jack, whom she loves 323

(1) Carol loves Jack. Jack is kind to Carol but doesn't love her and is unaware that she loves him 327b

(1) Jack has a dangerous profession which Carol regards as an obstacle to their marriage 334a

(1) Jack, in love with Carol, realizes that Carol's career ambitions are an obstacle to their marriage 335

(1) Carol, who thought Jack poor, discovers that he's rich. Angered by his deception, Carol rejects him 336b

(4) Jack is committed by Carol, the woman he loves, to take part in a venture that will end disastrously for him 212a

(4) Carol commits Jack to a venture which, unknown to Carol, will end disastrously for Jack 212a

(4) Upper-class Jack, in love with working girl Carol, pretends to be of her class 232

(4) Jack, to prove his courage to Carol, stages a fake rescue 234a

(4) Carol, poor, doesn't love wealthy Jack, but would marry him to gain financial security 239

(4) Jack betrays Carol, mistakenly believing there is no one who will avenge the wrong he's committed 247

(4) Carol is loved by wealthy Jack. Carol doesn't love Jack, but for certain reasons, she marries him 253

(4) Despite his vows of celibacy, Jack falls in love with Carol 272

(4) Jack and Carol fall in love despite their feuding families 275

(4) Unmarried Carol falls in love with married Jack 279

(4) Carol, from another culture/planet, challenges convention by falling in love with Jack 331

(4) Carol, an alien, tries to marry Jack, whom she loves 332

(5) Jack loves Carol. When she refuses to marry him, Jack becomes aloof and cynical; reckless, unreliable, or irrational; or enters into a loveless affair 259

(5) Carol, swayed by an anonymous communication, severs her engagement to marry Jack 262a

(7) Carol thinks Jack is "Mr. Right" until she learns that he has clay feet like all other men 226

(7) Jack learns that he isn't a fugitive as he thought. He returns home, deserting Carol, the woman he had said he loved while believing he was a criminal 237

(8) Jack, having successfully concluded a venture instigated by unpredictable Carol, ends the relationship 212b

(8) Jack, facing an unavoidable obligation, gives up Carol, whom he loves deeply 248

(8) Carol, despite loving Jack, realizes she's not his intellectual equal, and that their marriage would handicap him 254

(8) Carol refuses to marry Jack, the man she loves, because of an obligation 268

(8) Carol sacrifices happiness when, true to an obligation, she refuses to marry Jack, the man she loves 268

(8) Jack, because he fears he's inherited his ancestor's evil traits, does not dare ask Carol, whom he loves, to marry him 288

(8) Jack is engaged to marry Carol, but feels he should give her up because of his weakness for drugs and alcohol 289

(10) Jack, in love with Carol, learns that Carol she's a dedicated flirt who is only toying with him 208

(10) Jack, under unusual conditions, falls in love with Carol; returning to normal conditions, Jack sees Carol as she really is and his love vanishes 210

(10) For a long time Jack thought Carol was his ideal woman. But when he returns home after a long absence, he finds that Carol has undergone a radical character-change 211

(10) Carol, in love with Jack, receives an anonymous letter that says the writer is secretly married to Jack, and asks Carol to influence Jack to return to her 262c

(10) Carol, in love with Jack, receives an anonymous letter that claims the writer is Jack's mistress and begs Carol not to take Jack from her 262b

(10) Carol, forced by circumstances to be with Jack in an isolated place, loses her romantic view of men 307

(10) Carol breaks her engagement to Jack because she doesn't feel up to the responsibilities of married life 310

(10) Jack, prevented from marrying Carol as planned, makes a discovery about Carol and decides not to marry her 314

(12) Carol loves Jack deeply but won't marry him 326

MARRIAGE
Carol and Jack, break up because of a lovers' spat 349

Jack, posing as a salesman, rescues Carol from an accident 352a

Working girl Carol learns that her lover, Jack, is wealthy and only pretending to be blue collar 358

Painfully shy Jack loves scatterbrained Carol, but he's unsure of her affections 360b

CHARACTER COMBINATIONS

Jack and Carol

MARRIAGE (cont'd.)
Teenager Jack is unfaithful to his girlfriend, Carol, and they break up 361b

Jack, middle-aged, searches for Carol, his childhood sweetheart 361b

Eloping lovers Jack and Carol are pursued by their feuding families 362

Carol, in love with Jack but alienated from him, discovers after several misadventures that Jack still loves her 364b

Jack, with Carol's help, overcomes a terrible weakness 364d

Jack passes up an inheritance because of a restriction that he must not marry, and marries Carol 366

Carol, an orphan, is told by Jack the secret of her lineage. Once Carol proves her parentage, she can claim a rich estate 368d

(1) Carol, capriciously placing her lover, Jack, in great jeopardy, bitterly regrets her impulsiveness 342

(1) Jack is alienated from Carol, the woman he loves, because of a trivial disagreement 343

(1) Jack breaks up with his girlfriend, Carol, who bitterly refuses to return valuables Jack had given her 344

(1) Jack and Carol are innocently plunged into a compromising situation 351b

(2) Jack realizes Carol was right, admits his error and they reconcile 343

2) Jack lands in trouble and Carol, from whom he's separated, rescues him by returning valuables he'd given her. They reconcile and marry 344

(2) To win Carol, Jack must confess his true status 358

(2) Jack and Carol, pursued by their feuding families, suddenly find themselves in terrible jeopardy. Jack heroically rescues Carol 362

(2) Jack, an alien, loves Carol, supposedly an earth girl. About to give Carol up, Jack finds that Carol is also an alien 364c

(4) On the eve of their marriage, Jack is placed in great jeopardy by unpredictable Carol 342

(4) Carol has no suitors, so a marriage of convenience is arranged with Jack, on the understanding that it's to remain secret, and that Jack and Carol will part after the ceremony 354b

(4) Jack and Carol, long-time friends, marry not for love but for companionship 365a

(4) Jack and Carol, strangers at a party, are married in a supposedly fake ceremony which later turns out to be legal 365b

(4) Carol offers to marry Jack and to help him rebuild his wasted life 367a

(4) Carol marries wealthy Jack, whom she doesn't love, so that she will have money to help a desperately ill parent 368b

(8) Jack cruelly abandons Carol, a woman he claimed to love deeply 347a

(8) Delinquent Carol wins the love of respectable Jack. By pretending to be respectable, Carol surprises even herself and eventually becomes respectable 359

(9) Carol, capable of besting her lover, Jack, in a contest, deliberately loses 355

(9) Carol loses a contest she could easily have won, sacrificing great financial gain so she can marry Jack, the man she loves 356

CHARACTER COMBINATIONS

(9) Carol, long lost and presumed killed in a jungle plane crash, returns incognito to spy on her former lover, Jack, a notorious womanizer. Much to Carol's surprise, she discovers that Jack has changed his ways. She reveals her true identity and they are reunited 357

(9) Carol, having given tit-for-tat, tells Jack the truth about herself 358

(9) Jack proposes to Carol and she accepts 360b

(9) Jack finds Carol and they realize they're still in love 361b

(9) Jack's rescue of Carol results in peace between their families, and marriage for Jack and Carol 362

(9) Jack rebels against restrictions and finds happiness by marrying Carol 363a

(9) Carol, still loyal, returns to Jack. They reconcile and marry 361a

(9) Jack, Carol's lover, obtains evidence that erases a shadow from Carol's past, and they marry 364a

(9) Jack and Carol, alienated, reconcile and marry 364b

(9) Jack marries Carol 364c

(9) Jack's gratitude to Carol turns into love; when Jack is sure he has reformed, he proposes and Carol accepts 364d

(9) Carol doubts Jack's love until, finally convincing herself of his sincerity, she accepts Jack and they marry 367b

(9) Though Jack loves Carol, he's poor and feels he isn't worthy of wealthy Carol; but Carol convinces him of her love, and they marry 368d

MARRIED LIFE
Jack and Carol, married and devoted to each other, are impulsive and intolerant 369

Carol grieves in the mistaken belief that she's lost Jack's love 370

Jack is suspected of murdering his wife, Carol 371

Jack and Carol are devoted to each other but because of their conflicting standards, their marriage begins to disintegrate 372

During their courtship, Jack finds Carol career-oriented and highly motivated 374

After their marriage, Jack is disappointed to discover that Carol has lost her ambition 374

Jack dominates his wife, Carol 376

Jack is a controlling individual who makes Carol miserable 376

Jack owes most of his financial success to his wife Carol's loyalty and shrewd advice 377a

Carol, recently divorced by Jack, inherits a large estate 377b

Jack is jealous of his wife, Carol 380

Jack's beautiful wife, Carol, has a minor physical flaw 383

Carol's insignificant physical imperfection is magnified out of all proportion in the mind of her husband, Jack; his love begins to fade 383

Jack and his wife, Carol, argue violently and often 385a

Jack gives his wife, Carol, a gift as a statement of his love 387

Jack divorces Carol, then tries to remarry her 388

At the time Jack divorced her, Carol's health and beauty were fading 388

Jack thinks he sees the ghost of his dead wife, Carol 392

Jack and Carol

MARRIED LIFE (cont'd.)

Jack's marriage to Carol is harmed by his fantasies 393

Jack, married to Carol, finds an excuse to be absent for a few days each month 394

Carol follows Jack and discovers he is merely trying to escape from her demanding nature 394

Jack's wife, Carol, is a nag, and they argue constantly 395

Carol feels she is neglected by her husband, Jack 398a, b

Carol is the sensible, loving wife of Jack 399

Jack, successful because of Carol's wise advice, deludes himself that Carol envies his considerable abilities 399

Jack and Carol become alienated 399

Carol worries when her husband, Jack, fails to return home 401

Carol's husband, Jack, is a brutal tyrant 403

Carol poisons her husband, Jack, and flees before the poison takes effect 403

Carol is widower Jack's second wife 405

Jack beats his wife, Carol, for an act she didn't commit 407

Carol, happily married to Jack, commits an indiscretion 411a

Jack's wife, Carol, finds his odd quirks annoying. These trivialities so aggravate Carol, that they cause bitter quarrels 412

Carol marries a much older man, Jack 413

To be happy, Jack needs to have his abilities acknowledged by his wife, Carol 419

Jack abandons Carol, leaving her to run their joint business alone, hoping his absence will make Carol appreciate his talents 419

Jack's wife, Carol, is a woman of mystery 432b

Jack, having acquired Carol's money, tires of her 422b

Jack tells Carol he is a criminal, about to be arrested by the police 422b

Jack persuades Carol to join him in a suicide pact 422b

Husband Jack and wife Carol each secretly leaves home on the same day 423a

Jack believes he has deserted Carol, and Carol thinks she has deserted Jack 423a

Husband Jack and wife Carol are rich and popular 423b

Jack and Carol are so occupied with social engagements, they have no time for each other 423b

Jack and Carol look for a place where they can be alone together 423b

Jack and Carol find the solitude they desire 423b

Artist Jack works secretly as a manual laborer so that he can help his wife, Carol, who is also an artist 424

Jack tells Carol his paintings are finally selling 424

Jack, married to Carol, is compelled by an unusual motive to surreptitiously lease a bachelor apartment in another town 427

Jack and his wife, Carol, are unsuccessful artists 428

Carol's husband, Jack, is heavily in debt 430

CHARACTER COMBINATIONS

Jack, rich and unhappy with his wealth, is determined to get rid of it by marrying notorious spendthrift Carol 431

Jack, married to Carol, devises a plan to change his unhappy marriage 432a

Jack doesn't know Carol, and hasn't seen her since the day they were married 432b

Jack, having pretended that his wife, Carol, is his sister, finds himself in jeopardy when Carol's new admirer turns out to be a notorious mob figure 436

Jack's wife, Carol, is a drug addict 441

Jack forbids his wife, Carol, to do a certain thing 442

Carol, forbidden by her husband, Jack, to do a certain thing, does it anyway when Jack is absent 442

Jack's wife, Carol, desperately tries to escape disaster 445b

Jack's wife, Carol, is guilty of an indiscretion 446a

Carol devises a plan to free herself from fear of her husband, Jack 452

Carol thinks she has killed her husband, Jack 453

Jack married Carol under false pretenses 454

Carol plots revenge against her husband, Jack 454

Carol marries Jack. Carol has property in her own name that, by a pre-nuptial agreement, will go to Jack if he outlives her 456

Jack and Carol, just married, board a plane to start their honeymoon 458a

Jack, realizing his wife, Carol's, beauty is a threat to himself, devises a self-serving plan to avoid the danger 458b

Carol's husband, Jack, is a tyrant 459

Jack deeply loves his wife, Carol 461

Jack deeply loves his wife, Carol, but rebels against the injustice she forces him to endure 463

Jack is sick and about to die; Carol, his wife, could save him, but she refuses 466b

Carol, attempting to poison her husband, Jack, mistakes a bottle of harmless white powder for the poison and gives Jack some of its contents 468

Carol tries to help her husband, Jack, with a secret venture, but lack of money stops her 469

Carol tries to run away from her bullying husband, Jack 470

Carol falsely accuses her husband, Jack, of a wrongdoing 478

Desperately ill Carol sends her husband, Jack, for a doctor 480

Jack, sent for a doctor by Carol, who is seriously ill, fails to return, nor does he send a doctor 480

Jack and Carol, married, struggle to achieve a long-desired goal 484a

Carol's husband, Jack, is rich, cultured and socially impeccable 485

Jack splits up with his wife, Carol 487

Jack marries Carol because he thinks she is poor 488a

Jack files for divorce from his wife, Carol 489

Jack's wife, Carol, loves him deeply 491a

Carol, through extravagant spending, almost ruins Jack 491b

Jack loves his wife, Carol, deeply 492a

Jack and Carol

MARRIED LIFE (cont'd.)

Carol's husband, Jack, is without funds 492b

Carol loves fine clothes and jewelry that her husband, Jack, can't afford 492b

Jack's wife, Carol, is an unfaithful bimbo 494

Jack's wife, Carol, has recently died 497

Jack tries to find his deceased wife, Carol 498

Jack and Carol, married, are alienated 499a

Jack is divorcing Carol 500a

Jack's business is almost bankrupt. He marries Carol, a shrewd, thrifty woman 500b

Jack receives a letter from Carol, asking him to come home 501

Carol thinks that her husband, Jack, is dead 502

Carol's husband, Jack, is a tyrant 503a

Carol tries to steer her husband, Jack, into a certain venture 504a

Carol is Jack's second wife 504b

Carol thinks her husband, Jack, has been unfaithful 506a

Carol, through unjust suspicion, breaks up with her husband, Jack 506b

Jack, married to Carol, finds that supporting his wife and family prevents him from pursuing his ambitions 511

Jack, married to dull Carol, is forced to lead a drab, monotonous, middle-class life 513

Jack, married to dull Carol, leads a "Walter Mitty" existence, fantasizing himself the star of daring exploits 513

Honest, idealistic Carol discovers that her corrupt husband, Jack, is planning a project that will severely harm the environment 517

Jack learns that his wife, Carol, is in grave danger 519a

If Jack leaves his post to save his wife, Carol, who is in mortal danger, he will sacrifice lives and property he is duty-bound to protect 519a

Jack receives a desperate phone call from his wife, begging for help. Carol is in terrible danger 519b

Jack and his wife, Carol, are faced with starvation 522

Because of extreme poverty, Jack can't buy his wife a Christmas gift (or birthday or anniversary) 523

Carol's husband, Jack, gambles recklessly in the stock market 524a

Jack, Carol's husband, is an attorney administering trust funds, and Carol is afraid he'll be tempted to gamble with them 524a

Jack, elderly husband of youthful Carol, will die unless he undergoes major surgery 524b

Jack struggles to fulfill an obligation to his deceased wife, Carol 526

Jack tries to be loyal to his wife, Carol 527

Jack's wife, Carol, is an alien (ethnic or planetary) 527

Jack doesn't love his wife, Carol 528

To overcome his wife, Carol's constant nagging, Jack assumes the unnatural role of minor tyrant 529b

Jack's wife, Carol, is reluctant to live in a house which has a mysterious past 530

Carol needs money in order to save her husband, Jack 532a

CHARACTER COMBINATIONS

Carol's husband, Jack, is desperately ill and will die unless he can move to a healthier climate 532a

Carol owns a family heirloom greatly admired by her husband, Jack 532b

Wimpy Jack's overbearing wife, Carol, goes out for the evening, ordering Jack to remain at home 533

Jack forbids his wife, Carol, to participate in a certain activity 534

Carol engages in a venture forbidden by her husband, Jack 534

Jack's wife, Carol, is murdered at a certain time of night 537

Carol's husband, Jack, returning to his country home, is caught in a storm that keeps him out all night 538

Jack, absent from his home all night, finds on arriving home in the morning that his wife, Carol, is missing 538

Carol's husband, Jack, has delusions of grandeur and thinks he is a great man 539a

Jack believes that the jealousy of his wife, Carol, prevents him from becoming famous 539a

Carol divorces Jack on the grounds of desertion 539b

Jack mistakenly believes that the generosity his wife, Carol, lavishes on others is motivated by selfishness 542

Carol believes that her husband, Jack, takes too much credit for her accomplishments 544

Carol's husband, Jack, doesn't return home. A blizzard rages. Carol is afraid Jack has run into trouble in the storm 545

Jack's wife, Carol, during his absence, sees Jack's life work threatened with destruction 546a

Unattractive Carol marries a blind man, Jack, who thinks she's incredibly beautiful 546b

Jack dearly loves his wife, Carol, but the fact that she doesn't love him causes Jack great unhappiness 547

Jack, married to Carol, believes in marital fidelity 549

Carol's husband, Jack, is a bully who enjoys persecuting his attractive wife 559

Jack finds that his apparent sighting of the ghost of his dead wife, Carol, contains a modicum of reality 560

Each day, Carol's husband, Jack, receives a mysterious letter or phone call regarding Carol 562

Jack, separated from Carol, the wife he dearly loves, works toward a reconciliation 563a

Jack marries Carol, a beauty notorious for her vicious temper and scathing sarcasm 563b

Jack deeply loves his wife, Carol, but not her bitchiness; he plans to change her personality 563b

Jack and Carol, married, despise the superficial, money-grabbing spirit of contemporary city life 563c

Jack and Carol, married, leave the city and explore rural areas for the ideal life 563c

Young, attractive Carol has just lost her husband, Jack 564a

Young, attractive widow, Carol, resolves to remain single 564a

Carol devoutly wishes for her husband, Jack, to become religious 565

Carol attempts to help her husband, Jack, overcome his depression and/or discontent 566a

Jack and Carol

MARRIED LIFE (cont'd.)

Carol pretends to be a thief, but has purchased the items that her husband, Jack, is horrified to find in her possession 566b

Jack discovers that his wife, Carol, has been unfaithful 568a 568c

Carol's husband, Jack, mysteriously disappears and is assumed dead; Carol mourns 572

Workman Jack tries to support his wife, Carol, and family by honest hard work; but he can't find a job, his wife is ill and his family in need 574a

Carol's husband, Jack, is flat broke 574b

Jack becomes aware that his wife, Carol, is dying 575

Jack is shattered by the death of his wife, Carol 576a

Carol, married to Jack, is convinced that their troubles stem from her husband's lack of religion 579a

Jack's wife, Carol, is of another culture, and is mentally Jack's inferior 579b

Carol feels she has lost her husband, Jack's love and consideration 581

If Carol is discovered doing something she has planned, she will be at odds with her husband, Jack 583a

Jack's wife, Carol, desperately needs money for a certain purpose 583b 583c

Carol, just married to Jack, finds in a hidden place her obituary notice (written by Jack?), with only the date of her death omitted 584a

Jack's wife, Carol, suddenly leaves home on important business while Jack is away 585a

Jack's wife, Carol, is a clotheshorse 585b

Jack's wife, Carol's happiness depends upon expensive clothes and luxurious surroundings 585b

Jack's fourth wife, Carol, discovers shortly after their marriage that Jack's former wives died suddenly and mysteriously 590

Carol rebels against certain unpleasant conditions involving her husband, Jack 592

Normally undemonstrative Carol arouses the suspicions of her husband, Jack, by her sudden display of affection and attention 594a

Jack's wife, Carol, innocently commits a crime 594d

(1) Jack and Carol, married, continually quarrel, and as a result, separate 369

(1) Jack is so much older than Carol that after they marry, the discrepancy in their ages becomes a problem and they separate 373

(1) Jack marries Carol, believing she is rich. After the marriage, Jack finds he was mistaken 377b

(1) Jack, marrying a widow, Carol, discovers that he has married a domestic tyrant 378

(1) Jack is forced by an agreement to divorce his wife, Carol 379

(1) Jack finds a note, worded somewhat ambiguously, that causes him to mistrust the conduct of his wife, Carol 381

(1) Carol is mysteriously murdered and Jack, innocent, is the suspect 385a

(1) Jack finds Carol dead, killed by the gift he gave her 387

(1) Due to mistaken judgment, Jack becomes alienated from his wife, Carol 391

(1) Jack attempts to catch Carol's apparition, falls from a cliff and is killed 392

(1) Carol discovers that her supposed legal marriage to Jack was a sham 415

CHARACTER COMBINATIONS

(1) Jack leaves Carol penniless and alone 415

(1) Jack's wife, Carol, dies as the result of a venture that was started supposedly for her benefit 416

(1) Carol, while raging at her husband, Jack, has a stroke and dies 417

(1) Jack is unhappily married to Carol 420

(1) Carol, in a suicide pact with Jack, kills herself; Jack reneges 422b

(1) Jack and Carol run into severe problems. Each tries a secret method of recouping their joint finances 428

(1) Jack, married to Carol, loses his memory 437

(1) Carol is happily married to Jack 449

(1) Carol and her husband, Jack, are experiencing hard times 455b

(1) Jack and Carol are married. Finding they are incompatible, they secretly agree to a separation without divorce 457

(1) Bride Carol, enroute to her honeymoon, encounters problems after the groom, Jack, gets off the plane to send a fax during a stopover, and is left behind 458a

(1) Jack and Carol, married, are stranded among a primitive people 458b

(1) Jack is separated from his wife, Carol, whom he loves deeply 460

(1) Jack is unhappily married to Carol 462

(1) Jack's wife, Carol, dies 474

(1) Yuppie Jack marries wild disco queen Carol, and with each full moon, finds himself the victim of bizarre, inexplicable experiences 475

(1) Carol is accidently killed due to a series of events initiated by her husband, Jack 479

(1) Carol is deserted by Jack, her husband by a secret marriage 481

(1) Carol is unable to prove she secretly married Jack 481

(1) Jack's loving, supportive wife, Carol, is devastated when Jack suddenly blames her for his problems 482

(1) Innocent Carol's world disintegrates when she is wrongfully accused of adultery by her husband, Jack 482

(1) Jack's wife, Carol, lands in trouble 483a

(1) Jack, who adores his wife, Carol, finds himself drowning in debt because of her extravagant spending 484b

(1) Jack, separated from his wife, Carol, wants to reconcile, but they quarrel over who caused the breakup and the separation continues 487

(1) Jack's wife, Carol, leaves him and gets a divorce 496b

(1) Jack deeply loves his wife, Carol, but she doesn't love him 499b

(1) Jack and Carol are separated, their marriage in disarray 501

(1) Jack's marriage to Carol stands in the way of his happiness 508

(1) Jack is unhappily married to Carol 510

(1) Jack and his wife, Carol, are unemployed 522

(1) Jack is deeply in love with his wife, Carol, who is suing him for divorce 529a

(1) Jack learns that his wife, Carol, is unfaithful 552a

(1) Carol's husband, Jack, vanishes mysteriously 572

(1) Jack's sorrow over the death of his wife, Carol, climaxes in hallucination 576a

Jack and Carol

MARRIED LIFE (cont'd.)

(1) Jack, mistakenly thinking his beloved wife is dead, kills himself 576b

(1) Carol, finding her husband dead, commits suicide 576b

(1) Jack suffers deep sorrow and remorse — sorrow over the death of his beloved wife, Carol, and remorse for his infidelities 577

(1) Mourning the death of his wife, Carol, Jack goes into seclusion 577

(1) Jack's wife, Carol, hinders him socially and in business 579b

(1) Carol, alone, helpless and in terrible danger, communicates with her husband, Jack, begging for help 591

(2) Jack, reformed by his experience, returns to his wife, Carol 391

(2) Jack deviously tries to escape problems, restore property and free himself from his wife, Carol 465

(2) Jack's wife, Carol, whom he is divorcing, nurses him back to health 496a

(2) Jack is reunited with Carol when she nurses him through a serious illness 500a

(2) Carol reorganizes and manages Jack's affairs so that he becomes prosperous 500b

(2) Carol loyally helps her husband, Jack, recover his financial losses 505

(2) Carol is reconciled with her husband, Jack, when her suspicion is proved unjust 506b

(2) Jack rescues Carol 519b

(2) Carol is subdued by Jack's pretense of power and she becomes docile and loving 529b

(2) Carol, involved in an activity forbidden by her husband, Jack, learns that he is also involved in the activity. Carol uses this knowledge to forge an understanding with Jack which respects the rights and privileges of each 534

(3) After marrying Carol, Jack discovers that she's still married to her previous husband 471

(3) Carol's husband, Jack, pretends to be innocent of a crime (or indiscretion) but she knows he's guilty 521

(3) Carol, afraid that her husband, Jack, will do something dishonest, attempts to discourage him from doing so 566b

(3) Jack, realizing that his wife, Carol, is unfaithful, kills her and himself 568a

(4) Jack is devoted to his wife, Carol, but is unable to demonstrate his true feelings, often expressing them in ways that suggest their exact opposite 370

(4) Jack is more capable than his wife, Carol, but she thoughtlessly treats him as her inferior 375

(4) Jack secretly cheated Carol out of money. In order to hide his crime, Jack marries Carol 382

(4) Carol, believing her husband, Jack, is in jeopardy, places herself in danger in hope of locating and rescuing him 401

(4) Goaded beyond her limit, Carol poisons Jack 403

(4) Carol's obsessive neatness makes her husband Jack's life miserable 408

(4) Carol commits a crime (or indiscretion) in order to help her husband, Jack 410

(4) Carol doesn't love Jack but thought when she married him that he would help her achieve her lifelong ambition 413

(4) After quarreling with her husband, Jack, Carol leaves him 418

(4) Jack secretly cheats Carol out of a fortune 422a

(4) Jack marries Carol so that he can surreptitiously replace the property he stole from her before their marriage 422a

(4) Jack married Carol for her money 422b

(4) Jack, wanting to get out of his marriage to Carol, resorts to deception 426

(4) Jack, married to Carol, is compelled by an unusual motive to vanish and assume a new identity 429a

(4) Jack and Carol, devotedly married, are propelled by an unusual motive to disappear, leave the life they know, and seek a fresh start 429b

(4) Jack, on the run from a relentless process-server, pretends that his showgirl wife, Carol, is his sister 436

(4) Jack searches for the cruelest way to hurt his wife, Carol 438

(4) Jack is compelled by an unusual motive to marry Carol, whom he doesn't love 440

(4) Carol conceals her drug addiction from her husband, Jack 441

(4) Carol drinks a potion that puts her into a deathlike state, but only after Jack's assurances that he'll revive her 445b

(4) Carol kills her husband, Jack, to stop him from revealing a dark secret 448

(4) Carol marries wealthy, prominent Jack and keeps her sordid past hidden 447

(4) Carol, married to Jack, pretends to be single 451

(4) Carol's husband, Jack, is compelled by an unusual motive to lead a double life 464

(4) Carol tries to poison her husband, Jack 468

(4) Carol, revealed as a vampire, draws innocent husband Jack into her demoniac world 475

(4) Jack marries Carol, a woman he doesn't love 488b

(4) Jack decides to divorce Carol, hoping to find happiness in a new relationship 489

(4) Jack and his wife, Carol, remain financially strapped because they place all their disposable income in their retirement plan 490a

(4) Carol dominates Jack in business matters 491a

(4) Jack's wife, Carol, insists on living above their means 491b

(4) Tightfisted Jack gives Carol very little money 492a

(4) Carol's husband, Jack, is affectionate and gentle in public but when he and Carol are alone, he is coarse, petty and abusive 493

(4) Jack, rich and powerful, is determined to use his wealth and influence to carry out a corrupt project. His wife, Carol, tries in vain to dissuade him 517

(4) Jack refuses to undergo major surgery. His wife, Carol, supports his wishes 524b

(4) Carol's husband, Jack, tries to carry out a shady venture despite family obligations 525

(4) Desperate Carol, refused a divorce by her husband, Jack, writes anonymous poison pen letters about herself, and sends them to Jack 564b

(4) Carol, wishing to divorce her husband and make him the heavy, writes anonymous poison pen letters about her husband, Jack, and sends them to herself 564b

Jack and Carol

MARRIED LIFE (cont'd.)

(4) Jack and Carol, for certain reasons, keep their marriage a secret 573a

(4) Carol steals money from her husband, Jack, for her own use 593

(4) Bitchy Carol, believing she's a widow, marries Jack 594b

(5) Jack divorces his wife, Carol 377a

(5) Jack, secretly married to Carol, betrays her 479

(5) Jack and Carol remain financially strapped, investing for their retirement — but the "safe" investments they've made vanish in a stock swindle 490a

(5) Carol stops loving her husband, Jack, when she realizes he's a coward 584b

(5) Carol, dying, tells her husband, Jack, a closely guarded secret that deeply disturbs him 588

(6) Carol dies in a storm while searching for her husband, Jack 545

(6) Carol is killed while heroically saving the life work of her husband, Jack, from destruction 546a

(6) Carol locates a noted eye-surgeon who succeeds in restoring the sight of her blind husband, Jack 546b

(7) Carol, recently married to Jack, tells Jack she doesn't love him 406

(7) Carol's husband, Jack, proves to be tyrannical and abusive 413

(7) After their marriage, Jack discovers Carol is wealthy 488a

(7) Carol opens a letter addressed to her husband, Jack, and discovers that he has lied to her 582

(8) Carol secretly sells a treasured possession so she can buy a gift for her husband, Jack 455a

(8) Jack finds inspiration and the will to go on in memories of his dead wife, Carol 497

(8) Jack wins his wife, Carol's love by patience, kindness and devotion 499b

(8) Jack, despite an unhappy marriage to Carol, and having to sacrifice his goals, continues to be a good father 510

(8) To finance a certain venture involving her husband, Jack, Carol sells an heirloom which he greatly admires 532b

(8) Jack, admiring his wife, Carol's courage in confessing her infidelity, tries to forgive her 535

(8) Jack, in order to save his wife, Carol, insists he's guilty of the crime she committed 594d

(9) Carol, with the help of a violent storm/flood/earthquake, etc., succeeds in guiding her husband, Jack, into a venture she has long advocated 504a

(9) Jack, by seeming to be cruel, secures happiness for himself and Carol 529b

(10) Carol, health restored, realizes she's well rid of Jack 388

(10) Suspicious Jack learns that his wife, Carol, has indeed been faithful 396

(10) Jack, desperately ill, incensed by his wife's infidelities, decides that living will be his ultimate revenge and undergoes the treatment that cures him 435b

(10) Jack and Carol discover that their goal is empty 484a

(10) Carol, watching TV, learns that her husband, Jack, whom she thought was dead, is alive 502

CHARACTER COMBINATIONS

(10) Jack finds a bundle of love letters locked in wife, Carol's, desk — letters written after Jack married Carol, but not by him 552b

(10) Jack and Carol discover they're pursuing an impossible dream 563c

(12) Carol, in order to pay the bills, finds menial work but tells Jack she has a responsible position 455b

(12) Jack has committed a crime; Carol knows of Jack's wrongdoing, and Jack marries her to keep her quiet 488b

(12) Jack, finding that his wife, Carol, is unfaithful, murders her 552b

(12) An apparition of Jack's dead wife, Carol, appears to a relative of Jack's and confides secrets of her relationship with Jack 587

(13) Unscrupulous so-called spiritualists pretend to materialize deceased Carol's spirit in order to persuade Jack to give them money 474

(13) Jack believes that his dead wife, Carol, has returned to earth to comfort him 498

(13) Carol's husband, Jack, mysteriously vanishes 540

(13) Jack hears the voice of his dead wife, Carol, and has no doubt that it's her voice 560

(13) Jack finds an anonymous message about Carol, his wife, on his computer screen 562

(13) Jack receives poison pen letters about his wife, Carol 562

(13) Jack, mysteriously absent, returns home to his wife, Carol, dazed and unable to offer an explanation 571 Jack and Carol

(13) Carol, leaving suddenly while Jack is away, writes a note to Jack explaining her departure. The maid inadvertently throws the note away. Carol's disappearance is considered a mystery 585a

(14) Jack learns from a newspaper story that his wife, Carol, has divorced him 539b

(14) Jack is so saddened by the death of his wife, Carol, that his personality changes 578a

(14) Carol, realizing that her behavior has hurt Jack, promises to change, and Jack returns home 394

MISFORTUNE

Jack, stricken with fever in the wilds, is looked after by an old woman, Carol 605

Carol tricks Jack in a certain venture 640

Carol knows the combination of Jack's safe, as well as the fact that it contains valuables 666

Unless Carol reveals a personal misdeed, she will cause Jack to pay for a crime he didn't commit 667

Fugitive Jack tries to rescue Carol from her troubles 673

Carol rebels when Jack takes credit for her achievements 679

Jack and Carol, strangers to each other, must join forces when their lives are threatened 688

Carol goes to a restaurant to keep a date with Jack, who fails to show up 744

(1) Jack, falling ill in the wilds, is looked after by an old woman, Carol, who, just Jack's luck, Jack had once taught a fake healing technique 605

(1) Jack inadvertently arouses a consuming desire in Carol to leave town, which is the opposite of what Jack wants; his impending business deal, which is of vital importance to Jack, requires Carol's presence 625

(1) Jack unintentionally causes Carol's death 627

Jack and Carol

MISFORTUNE (cont'd.)

(1) Jack, attempting to save Carol with an antidote for a poison, accidentally kills her 627

(1) Jack, hijacking a plane, is recognized by Carol, one of the passengers 628

(1) Jack, tricked by Carol in a venture, dies as a result of his involvement 640

(1) Carol is overshadowed and dominated by her less-competent employer, Jack 679

(1) Jack and Carol are stranded in a desolate, primitive environment where they must fight for their survival 688

MISTAKEN JUDGMENT

Jack finds a mysterious note containing Carol's ruinous secret 758

Cosmetic surgeon Jack attempts to remove a disfiguring mark from the exquisite face of his wife, Carol 761b

Jack, trying to be helpful, befriends Carol 773

Jack forces his way into the room of a woman, Carol 799

Carol earns Jack's respect and protection 801

(1) Jack befriends Carol, who proves to be a criminal who has lied to Jack about her identity 773

(4) Jack, trying to help Carol, makes a tragic mistake 761b

(5) Jack discovers that Carol has deceived him 801

(8) Jack begins to exploit Carol's troubles for his own gain, but ends up offering Carol his sympathy and friendship 758

(10) Jack learns that Carol, supposedly murdered, really committed suicide 802a

(10) Jack determines that Carol, who supposedly killed herself, was actually murdered 802b

HELPFULNESS

Jack is older and more knowledgeable than Carol and attempts to counsel her so she'll avoid mistakes 808b

Carol resents Jack's presumption 808b

Jack's friend, Carol, is in a foreign country, alone and homesick 816b

Carol, abroad, unexpectedly meets Jack, a friend from home 816b

Street-gang member Jack rescues Carol from an attack by a rival gang 818b

Carol befriends Jack, takes him off the streets and reforms him 818b

Jack thinks that Carol is a criminal 822

Married Carol, attractive, clever and influential, finds amusement in helping her friend, Jack 844a

Jack rescues Carol from an attack by a rattlesnake 848b

Carol sees great promise in uncomplicated, naive Jack and tries to inspire him toward high ambitions 850a

Carol tries to save Jack from a wasted lifestyle 850b

Carol rescues from Jack life of dissipation and despair and employs him 850b

(1) Jack, taking possession of Carol's property in order to save it for her, is wrongfully accused by Carol of attempting to steal it 808a

(1) Jack tries to help distressed Carol, and runs into disastrous complications 848a

(4) Jack assumes control over property of Carol's in order to save it for her 808a

(8) Jack, wanted by the law, risks capture to help Carol, a stranger in desperate trouble 817

(8) Thief Jack tries to help Carol, a childhood friend 819

(8) Honest Jack poses as a criminal to help Carol 822

(9) Jack succeeds in a venture which he is unaware that Carol has set up to test his abilities 814

(9) Carol, covertly investigating, proves Jack's innocence and gains his release from prison 826

(9) Working undercover, Jack attempts to prove Carol's innocence of a crime 828

(9) Carol, secretly investigating, proves Jack didn't commit a certain crime 829

DELIVERANCE
Alien Jack rescues Carol from an accident 861

Carol uses Jack's prize show dog in tracking Jack 875b

Jack and Carol find themselves imprisoned in an underwater research vessel 876b

Carol knows that Jack isn't guilty of the crime for which he was convicted 895

(1) Jack rescues Carol from imminent danger, but only by placing himself in equal jeopardy 851

(1) Jack is unable to escape from the danger from which he rescues Carol 851

(1) When Jack rescues Carol, due to mistaken judgment he becomes the victim of an unwelcome complication 861

(2) Jack is rescued by Carol 875b

(2) Jack and Carol, trapped in a submersible, desperately search for a method of escape. Jack squeezes himself into the damaged airlock, blasts himself to the surface, gets help and rescues Carol 876b

(2) Prisoner Jack, bound, helpless and facing death, is daringly rescued by resourceful Carol 878c

(2) Faced with imminent danger while engaged in a venture, Carol is rescued by Jack 885a

(2) Jack, unable to save himself from danger incurred in rescuing Carol, is in turn saved by Carol 885a

(8) Jack is persuaded to a belief in God by Carol when her prayers enable them to escape from certain death 884b

(9) Fugitive Jack stops Carol from committing suicide 869

IDEALISM
(1) Jack, hired by Carol to paint her portrait, puts more character than beauty into his work, and Carol is deeply offended 903

(4) Jack "goes native" and marries Carol, a member of a primitive society 901

(4) Morally rigid Jack is stranded in a primitive environment where he is conquered by a "natural" native girl, Carol 904

OBLIGATION
After Carol dies, Jack honorably fulfills a distasteful obligation 984

Detective Jack returns criminal Carol to the locale of her crime for trial 986

(1) Jack, vowing to die if Carol dies, learns that Carol has killed herself 1020

(4) Guardian Jack is disloyal to his ward, Carol 988

(4) Against his wishes, Jack becomes guardian of a beautiful young woman, Carol 1002

Jack and Carol

OBLIGATION (cont'd.)
(14) Criminal Carol, who has changed and become an honest woman, is tried by a jury who then set her free 986

CHANCE
(5) Jack is shocked when, by chance, he finds stolen goods in Carol's possession 1050

(9) Jack and Carol find happiness when a certain assumption is proved to be false 1055

PERSONAL LIMITATIONS
Jack could save his own life by revealing a secret that would be ruinous to Carol 1070

Struggling unsuccessfully against a character defect, Jack forms a platonic relationship with Carol 1075a

Transformed into a gentleman, Jack reveals the secret of his change to his friend, Carol 1076

Jack enlists a friend, Carol, to help him in a difficult venture 1083

Appalled by Jack's behavior, Carol prays to God on Jack's behalf 1120

Carol, alone and in great danger, attempts to summon distant Jack via ESP 1137a

(2) Jack coldly rejects Carol because he finds her irresponsible 1125a

(4) Driven by compelling motives, Jack and Carol enter into a suicide pact 1125b

(4) Jack and Carol promise each other that they will die together 1125b

(8) Jack's admiration for his friend, Carol, and his wish to please her, brings out the best in him 1075b

PRETENSE
Carol assumes an alias in order to discover the accuracy of a slanderous story about Jack 1154b

Jack's friend, Carol, learns that Jack is deeply in debt 1155

Actress Carol is required to cry on cue. Jack, her leading man, uses force to make her grief more genuine 1157

Jack and Carol are phonies, but neither realizes the other isn't who he or she seems to be 1173

Phony Jack meets phony Carol 1173

(2) Unknown to Jack, Carol pays off Jack's creditors 1155

(12) To save Carol, who is suspected of a crime, Carol's best friend, Jack, insists that he alone is guilty 1171

(13) Carol hires artist Jack to paint a portrait into which he must render an intricate pattern which is in reality a treasure map 1143b

DECEPTION
Con man Jack forces Carol to participate in his scam 1220b

Jack forces Carol to become the bait for his scam 1220b

Jack shows up during a phony holdup and "rescues" Carol 1227b

Jack "rescues" Carol during a fake abduction 1227c

Jack, while cleaning an office at night, accidentally discovers an electronic card-key 1254

Jack finds the electronic key to Carol's safe 1254

Abstract sculptor Jack is commissioned to do a bust of Carol 1257

Jack discovers a dark secret in Carol's past 1263

Jack messengers a package to Carol 1278b

CHARACTER COMBINATIONS

Aware that Jack has stolen a valuable object from her, Carol uses deception in an attempt to recover her property   1279b

Unknown to Carol, Jack holds a large sum of money in trust for her   1285b

(1) Jack robs the safe of Carol, his employer, and returns the electronic card-key to her desk, unaware that he has left a telltale clue 1254

(1) Carol, in a rage, destroys Jack's valuable work of art   1256

(1) Carol, despising the work of abstract sculptor Jack, angrily destroys a bust. Without repairing the bust, Jack sells it as a self-portrait   1257

(3) Carol deviously gains entrance to Jack's office and escapes with an object of great value   1279b

(4) In order to learn Carol's closely guarded secret, Jack makes her believe she's losing her mind   1220a

(4) To advance a certain venture, Carol uses an alias and obtains a job as executive Jack's private secretary   1244b

(4) Desperately needy Jack steals money belonging to Carol   1285b

(8) Carol, wanting Jack to develop some backbone, subtly places obstacles in his path; obstacles which, when overcome, will make Jack a stronger person   1243

(9) Celebrity Carol grabs Jack's crutch and clobbers him with it. Jack auctions off the crutch as a priceless collector's item   1256

CRIME-IMMORALITY
(1) Carol is forced to give up a project for lack of funds when her attorney, Jack, misappropriates her money   1308

(3) Carol, trying to protect herself from Jack, kills him   1309a

(4) Carol's attorney, Jack, misappropriates Carol's property   1308

VENGEANCE
Jack uses deception in an attempt to get revenge on Carol   1310

(4) Carol, maliciously slandered by Jack, becomes irrational and attempts to kill him 1325

Carol, wronged and unable to seek revenge herself, enlists the aid of her friend, Jack 1326

(4) Jack tries to get revenge on Carol, but his plan backfires   1310

MYSTERY
At an antique auction, Jack is outbid by Carol for an ancient locket   1333b

Carol finds a note, apparently written by Jack, that greatly worries her   1364b

Carol meets Jack by chance in a foreign country   1412b

Jack clairvoyantly becomes aware of grave danger threatening Carol   1433c

Carol persuades Jack to attempt to solve a mystery   1444

Carol, while engaged in a venture, creates an illusion which confuses Jack   1446c

(1) Carol, unaware that the flowers Jack gives her are contaminated with a deadly poison, lapses into a mysterious illness   1333a

(1) Art dealer Jack sells an antique tapestry to client Carol, who then insists on returning it   1386b

(9) Carol encourages Jack to take an unaccustomed risk, and he gains a fortune   1354b

(13) Jack receives a strange communication from Carol, who is in a distant place   1395

Jack and Carol

MYSTERY (cont'd.)

(13) Carol meets Jack in a foreign country; then, returning home, Carol meets Jack and is stunned when Jack swears he hasn't left home 1412b

(13) When Carol dies as predicted by a psychic communication, scientist Jack refuses to accept a supernatural explanation 1411

(13) Carol is told by an unquestionable authority that her friend, Jack, has been seen in two places, many miles apart, at the same time 1424b

REVELATION

Jack discloses his true identity to Carol 1461c

Jack sends an important message to Carol that vitally concerns his welfare 1461d

(1) By disclosing his true identity to Carol, Jack causes her great pain 1461c

(9) Jack liberates Carol from an unpleasant situation 1451c

Jack, Carol and Pete

ROMANCE'S BEGINNINGS

Jack, bringing news of the death of his friend, Pete, to Carol, the girl to whom Pete was engaged, is mistaken by Carol and her parents for Pete, who have never seen Jack or Pete 5

Jack, posing as dead Pete, falls in love with Carol and withholds mention of Pete's death 5

While traveling together, Jack and his friend, Pete, have an accident and Pete is killed. Before he dies, Pete asks Jack to tell his lover, Carol, of his death. Jack does as he is asked 168

Jack joins up with his friend, Pete, who is enroute to meet Carol, a girl he has never seen 169

(1) Jack learns that his best friend, Pete, loves Carol, the girl Jack wants to marry 139

(4) Jack runs off with Carol, the wife of his best friend, Pete 119

(13) Jack, in love with Carol, pretends to be his deceased friend, Pete who was engaged to Carol. Carol, finally learning of Pete's death, decides to keep it secret from her family 72

MARRIAGE PROPOSAL

Jack sends his friend, Pete, to propose marriage to Carol on his behalf 192b

(1) Pete proposes to Carol on behalf of Jack; Carol assumes Pete is speaking for himself and accepts 192b

REJECTION

Jack's friends, Pete and Annie, try to stop him from marrying Carol, whom they believe is unprincipled 220

Jack learns that his friend, Pete, is unfaithful in his relationship with Carol 294a

Jack strongly criticizes his friend, Pete, for his infidelity to Carol 294a

Jack falls for Carol despite the fact that his friend, Pete, has warned him against her 329

Wealthy Jack loves Carol. Jack's friends, Pete and Annie, believe Carol is unscrupulous and money-hungry 330a

(1) Jack, who loves Carol, secretly learns that she's about to marry his friend, Pete 319

(4) Jack falls in love with Carol, who is involved with his friend, Pete 273

(4) Angered by Pete's infidelities to his girlfriend, Carol, Jack decides to teach Pete a lesson, a course of action which places their friendship at risk 294b

(10) Jack loves Carol, but gives her up when his friend, Pete, convinces him the relationship is unwise 221a

CHARACTER COMBINATIONS

MARRIAGE

Jack and Carol's mutual friend, Pete, wanting to reunite them, arranges with each to meet him at a certain location 349

(10) Lovers Jack and Carol, at odds with each other, are reunited by Pete's surreptitious plan 349

MARRIED LIFE

Jack cons his friend, Pete, into running off with Carol 426

Jack is unaware that his wife, Carol, is cheating on him. Pete discovers Carol's infidelity and tells Jack, who is gravely ill but stubbornly refusing the treatment that might cure him 435b

Jack tells his wife, Carol, he's leaving town to meet a friend, Pete 443

Jack's friend, Pete, phones Jack, who is supposedly visiting him, and Carol finds the message on their answering machine 443

Jack's wife, Carol, visits her lover, Pete 446b

Pete hides Carol from Jack 446b

Jack and Carol, married, are to inherit money from a rich relative, Pete, when they have a child 490b

Carol is married to Jack, a friend of Pete's 580

Jack's friend, Pete, learns that Jack's wife, Carol, is promiscuous 580

(1) Pete, friend of Jack, is abroad and Carol conceals his message from Jack. The next time Jack leaves home "to meet Pete," Carol shadows him 443

(1) Jack finds his wife, Carol, hidden in Pete's apartment 446b

(4) Jack's wife, Carol, persuades his friend, Pete, to run off with her 477

(4) Jack's wife, Carol, has an affair with his friend, Pete, who is more successful in business than Jack 549

(4) Jack's wife, Carol, runs off with Jack's friend, Pete 557b

(6) Jack's wife, Carol, and Pete, with whom she is running off, are killed in a car accident 557b

OBLIGATION

Jack's friend, Pete, fathered Carol; and when Pete died, Jack promised to care for Carol as if she were his own child 988

Pete is the brother of Carol, whom Jack loves dearly 1007

CHANCE

Years after stealing money from Pete, Jack by chance spends the night with Pete and his wife, Carol 1048

Carol and her husband, Pete, happen to run into Jack and discover that Jack possesses a certain item of great value 1048

PRETENSE

Pete's sister, Carol, unaware of Pete's death, contacts Jack, thinking that he is her brother 1183

DECEPTION

(4) In order to convince Carol that he's courageous, Jack gets Pete to help him stage a fake holdup of Carol 1227b

(4) Jack hires a friend, Pete, to abduct Carol 1227c

(4) Jack hires Pete to kidnap Carol and pretend he's holding her for ransom 1227c

Jack, Carol and Gary

ROMANTIC MISADVENTURES

Jack and Gary both love Carol. Gary deviously tries to eliminate Jack 75a

Jack and Gary are rivals for the love of Carol. Gary plans to win at Jack's expense 76

Jack, Carol and Gary

ROMANTIC MISADVENTURES (cont'd.)

If Carol wins a certain competition, she also wins Gary, a wealthy admirer. Carol doesn't love Gary, but she does love money and social prominence. If she loses the contest, she wins Jack, a poor admirer whom she does love 104

Jack and Gary are in love with Carol 136

Twin brothers Jack and Gary both love Carol 137a

Jack's rival for Carol, Gary, has more on the ball than Jack and seems to be on the winning track 158

Jack loves Carol and is unaware that she prefers his rival, Gary 159

Jack has a rival/friend, Gary, whose self-confidence is the key to his extraordinary resourcefulness 160

Unsophisticated Jack has a rival, Gary, for the love of Carol. Gary is a cultured man of the world 171

Jack and Gary, rivals for Carol, confront her and demand that she choose between them 174

Carol tests the love of two admirers, Jack and Gary 175

(1) Jack, obliged to obey the orders of Gary, his rival for Carol's affections, is told to promote Gary's cause, or to disappear 136

(1) Carol loves Jack; but Jack's rival, Gary, kidnaps Carol and plans to make her marry him 146

(1) Jack and Gary, once buddies, become enemies because of their rivalry over Carol 157

(4) Jack and Gary, in love with Carol, are persuaded by impulsive Carol to expose themselves to danger to prove their love 78

(6) Elderly Jack and Gary both love Carol, but Jack learns that Carol prefers Gary. To insure the happiness of Carol and Gary, Jack kills himself and leaves them his estate 80b

(8) Jack wants to insure the happiness of Carol, who, he thinks, loves his rival, Gary; Jack vanishes so that he, rather than Gary, will appear guilty of a certain crime 80a

(8) Both Jack and Gary love Carol. Jack tries to protect Gary from arrest 122

(9) Jack abducts his sweetheart, Carol, while she is enroute to marry his rival, Gary 81

MARRIAGE PROPOSAL

(1) Carol thinks Jack has proposed to her, and she accepts. Later, she learns it was Gary who proposed 182a

(2) Carol, accepting Gary's marriage proposal, mistakenly sends the message to Jack, the lover she broke up with 194b

REJECTION

Jack loves Carol, and learns that his rival, Gary, has a dark secret. Carol apparently favors Gary 206

Jack's rival for Carol, Gary, tells her lies about Jack 217

Jack and Gary are rivals for Carol's hand. Carol secretly prefers Jack, but because Jack is shy and less ambitious than Gary, Carol pretends to prefer Gary, hoping to spur Jack into proving himself 235

Jack and Gary both love Carol. Carol is about to marry Gary, whom Jack knows is a criminal 236

Jack loves Carol but she rejects him in favor of Gary. Jack knows Gary is a liar/criminal, but Carol is unaware 260a

Jack loves Carol and wants to stop her from marrying Gary, whom Jack has learned is unscrupulous 266

Jack informs Carol, whom he loves, that he has killed Gary 296

CHARACTER COMBINATIONS

Jack loves Carol, but suddenly learns that Carol is engaged to Gary 300

(1) Jack's rival in love, Gary, kidnaps Jack and holds him prisoner to prevent him from marrying Carol 221b

(1) Jack loves Carol, but when Jack's fortunes decline, Carol switches her affections to his rival, Gary 257b

(1) Carol loves Jack, but her family disapproves of him and favors Gary, Jack's rival 290

(1) Jack and Carol were engaged. Jack, whom Carol thinks died in an accident, returns, finds Carol about to marry Gary, and attempts to prevent the marriage 328

(3) Carol has promised to marry Gary. But when Jack exposes Gary's infidelities, Carol agrees to marry Jack 267

(4) Carol rejects her straight-arrow lover, Jack, in favor of unscrupulous Gary 263

(5) Jack, who loves Carol, reads in the newspaper of her engagement to Gary 318

(6) Jack learns that Gary, his rival for Carol's love, has a guilty secret. To keep others from learning the truth, Gary murders Jack 280b

(8) Jack confesses to Carol that he has killed Gary, and asks her to call the police 296

(8) Social-climber Carol loves Jack but is about to marry celebrity Gary. Jack angrily accuses Carol of blatant shallowness, and a violent argument ensues 336a

(10) Under hypnosis, Jack envisions his romantic rival, Gary, being discredited while he, Jack, gets the girl 265a

(10) Jack learns that Gary, his rival for Carol's love, is unscrupulous 280a

MARRIAGE

Cruise-ship comic Jack is on the run from fat, ugly Carol, who desperately loves him and stows away on his ship. Mafia godfather Gary is a passenger on the ship and has taken a violent dislike to Jack's sense of humor 348

(1) Jack's enemy, Gary, forces Jack to marry Carol 347a

(1) Carol makes her plight known to Mafia don Gary, who makes Jack an offer he can't refuse: marry Carol or else 348

(1) Carol agrees to marry Jack, who gets the license; then, before Jack and Carol can marry, Carol suddenly marries his rival, Gary 368c

(3-9) Jack rescues Carol, the woman he loves, from Gary, a corrupt rival. Jack marries Carol 352b

(9) Jack and Gary are lured into an ordeal to prove themselves to Carol; Gary fails, and Jack succeeds but almost loses his life 350

(9) Jack kidnaps his sweetheart, Carol, as she's enroute to marry Gary 351a

MARRIED LIFE

Jack gambles with Gary, the man Jack thinks had an affair with his wife 380

Carol believes her husband, Jack, is dead and marries Gary 402

Jack tries to force Carol to give up her new husband, Gary 402

Carol, after a loveless marriage with Gary, gets a divorce and searches for Jack, the man she loved and broke up with 404

Jack sets out to revenge himself on Carol, Gary's widow, for a dreadful wrong committed by Gary 433a

Gary loves Jack's wife, Carol 433b

Gary deviously tries to win Carol, Jack's wife 433b

Jack, Carol and Gary

MARRIED LIFE (cont'd.)

Jack's wife, Carol, appears to be having an affair with Gary 434a

Carol's friend, Gary, tries to protect her from her brutal husband, Jack 439

Jack mistakenly assumes his wife, Carol, is having an affair with Gary 445a

Jack's wife, Carol, despises Gary, but visits him late at night at his apartment 445a

Jack plots to kill Gary, whom Carol loves 459

Jack learns that Carol has married Gary 472

Jack becomes Carol's second husband. Carol's first husband, Gary, vanished mysteriously and is supposedly dead 473

Gary threatens to tell Carol's husband, Jack, a deadly secret unless Carol agrees to a certain proposition 476b

Jack's wife, Carol, falls in love with youthful, reckless Gary 495

Jack, hen-pecked husband of Carol, discovers that Carol is still married to Gary 496c

Carol learns that her husband, Jack, wants to kill her lover, Gary 503b

Carol desperately tries to save her lover, Gary, from her husband, Jack's vengeance 503b

Carol runs off with Gary, a man who destroyed her faith in her husband, Jack 507a

Jack's wife, Carol, runs off with Gary 507b

Jack mistakenly assumes that his wife, Carol, has run off with Gary 538

Jack believes that his wife, Carol, loves Gary 553

Jack, unhappily married to Carol, falls for Laura, a girl much younger than himself 555b

Carol, wife of brutal, bullying Jack, has a loyal friend, Gary, who wants to help Carol escape from Jack 558

Carol's husband, Jack, is a huge, powerful, belligerent man — and Gary, though he wants to help Carol, is a coward 558

Carol's husband, Jack, receives anonymous calls and letters concerning Carol and Gary 561

Jack's wife, Carol, is raped and/or murdered by Gary 567

Jack tries to find Gary and avenge his wife, Carol 567

Jack attempts to get even with his wife, Carol, for falling in love with Gary 568b

Carol's husband, Jack, tries to kill Carol's lover, Gary 568d

Gary, to whom Carol is still married, approaches her new husband, Jack, and tries to extort money from him for keeping quiet 594b

(1) Married Carol is spending a romantic weekend with unmarried Gary when he suddenly dies 397

(1-10) Carol tells her husband, Jack, that she loves Gary 409

(1) Jack, influenced by Gary, is driven to divorce his wife, Carol 434b

(1-7) After Jack and Carol are married, Carol's first husband, Gary, secretly contacts Jack 473

(1) Jack's wife, Carol, finds herself in the power of a former lover, Gary 476b

(1) Gary drunkenly attempts to rape Jack's wife, Carol 483a

(1) Jack's wife, Carol, is tricked by Gary, a rejected lover, into becoming a prisoner in his apartment 483b

(1) Carol's husband, Jack, returns after a long mysterious absence to find that Carol has married Gary 550

(1) Jack discovers that his wife, Carol, is having an affair with Gary 554

(1) Jack dies because of a conspiracy between Carol and Gary, and Carol is remorseful 557a

(1) Carol, wife of brutal Jack, is loved by Gary. Although she loves Gary, Carol is too principled to run off with him 559

(1) Jack's wife, Carol, is raped and/or slain during a war (or in a foreign country — or while on holiday) by Gary 567

(1) Missing and assumed dead, Jack returns secretly and finds his wife, Carol, has married Gary 573b

(2) Jack happily leaves Carol to Gary, her legal husband 496c

(3) Jack murders Gary, his wife, Carol's lover 568c

(3) Attacked by Carol's husband, Jack, Gary kills Jack in self-defense 568d

(4) Carol, wife of Jack, flirts with unmarried Gary 397

(4) Gary, by flattering and sympathizing with Carol, makes her think she loves him 398a

(4) Carol, hoping to rekindle her husband, Jack's, passion by making him jealous, flirts with Gary 398b

(4) Carol leaves her husband, Jack, for another man, Gary 400

(4) Jack's wife, Carol, confidentially borrows money from a former lover, Gary 411b

(4) Jack marries Carol, unaware that she's still married to Gary 435a

(4) Carol runs off with Gary, who has underhandedly made Carol doubt her husband, Jack's loyalty 444

(4) Jack's wife, Carol, with an innocent motive, secretly meets with an old lover, Gary 449

(4) Carol secretly plans to free herself of Jack, her unsuccessful husband, so she can marry wealthy Gary 450

(4) Jack's wife, Carol, is deviously persuaded by Gary, the "other man," to run off with him 476a

(4) An old admirer, Gary, persuades Carol to accept a valuable piece of jewelry 492b

(4) Carol tells her husband, Jack, that the valuable piece of jewelry given her by Gary is a fake she bought herself 492b

(4) Carol, married to Jack, comes on to unmarried Gary 494

(4) Carol, wife of tyrant, Jack, loves Gary and he loves her 503a

(4) Carol's husband, Jack, has a weak heart. Carol allows him to be lured into over-exertion by Gary 557a

(4) Gary, Carol's rejected lover, promises to help Carol, wife of Jack, if she'll come to his home 583b

(4) Carol, wife of Jack, runs into an old lover, Gary, and has no choice but to borrow money from him 583c

(6) Carol's friend, Gary, concocts a plan whereby it will appear that Carol's brutal husband, Jack, has killed Gary, will be imprisoned and thus never harm Carol again. Gary either succeeds — or is killed — by Jack — or someone else 439

(7) Jack learns that Gary, the man Jack thought had run off with Carol, was in a distant city at the time of the alleged affair 396

Jack, Carol and Gary

MARRIED LIFE (cont'd.)
(8) Jack's wife, Carol, saves Gary, a suspected criminal, from the law by confessing her infidelity 535

(8) Jack, learning that his wife, Carol, deeply loves Gary, whom she married because she thought Jack was dead, quietly goes away and stays out of Carol's life 573b

(9) Carol forces Gary, at gun point, to return money he stole from Jack 445a

(10) Carol has an experience with Gary which convinces her that leaving her husband, Jack, was a mistake 418

DELIVERANCE
Carol's escort, Gary, gets into a fight with another man, Jack 891

(2) Carol saves Jack from a weapon wielded by his enemy, Gary 891

DECEPTION
(11) Jack's friend, Carol, uses her beauty to lure Gary into a trap 1261

ROMANTIC MISADVENTURES
Jack, a publisher in love with Carol, receives a fiction manuscript from Dave that describes in derogatory terms a character similar to Carol 44a

(2) Jack is in love with Carol; and Carol, rescuing Jack and Dave from their captors, escapes with them 181c

(9) Archaeologists Jack and Dave are prisoners in an ancient lost city. Carol, supposedly a goddess, helps them escape 181c

REJECTION
(1) Jack, in love with Carol, is devastated to find Carol in Dave's arms 222b

MISFORTUNE
Jack finds a U.S. Mail truck wrecked and its cargo scattered. The driver, Dave, has gone for help. Jack comes across a letter, and discovers that Carol is in trouble 673

Jack, Carol and Dave

HELPFULNESS
Jack is hired by Dave to spread malicious gossip against Carol 818a

(8) Jack is hired by Dave to harm Carol. Jack meets Carol, feels sympathy for her and rebels against Dave's scheme by warning Carol 818a

PRETENSE
Con artist Carol's confederate, Jack, attempts to extort money from Dave, the driver of an automobile that allegedly injures Carol 1192

Jack, Carol and Burt

ROMANTIC MISADVENTURES
Jack's secretary, Carol, is an accomplice planted in Jack's house by criminal Burt 152b

(1) Criminal Carol, accomplice of criminal Burt, falls in love with her employer, Jack 152b

MARRIED LIFE
Unscrupulous so-called spiritualists Burt and Sally pretend to materialize deceased Carol's spirit in order to persuade Jack to give them money 474

Carol's husband, Jack, dies at the hands of Burt 569

Carol's husband, Jack, is killed by Burt but due to legal delays and technicalities, Burt gets off with a light sentence 569

(9) Carol, wanting an eye for an eye, seeks revenge on Burt for murdering her husband, Jack 569

(9) Jack's widow, Carol, takes the law into her own hands and shoots her husband's murderer, Burt 594e

MISFORTUNE
Jack, captured by enemies of Carol, is threatened with death by Burt in an attempt to make him disclose a secret of Carol's 660b

CHARACTER COMBINATIONS

Jack, threatened with death by Burt in an attempt to force him to reveal a secret of Carol's, dares Burt to kill him   660b

HELPFULNESS
Carol's friend, Jack, breaks into a building to commit a robbery. He finds an employee, Burt, who is Carol's husband, dead at his desk, a note beside him explaining that he killed himself because he is guilty of embezzlement   819

(8-9) Jack, trying to save his friend, Carol, from disgrace, destroys evidence that would prove Carol's husband, Burt, an embezzler and a suicide. Jack then ransacks the office, making it appear that Burt died trying to prevent a robbery   819

OBLIGATION
Thieves Burt, Sally and Fred order Carol to open a safe belonging to Jack. Carol refuses, despite threats that they'll kill her   1010

PERSONAL LIMITATIONS
(1) Carol is held by criminals, Burt, Sally and Fred, who try to make her obey them by threatening the life of Jack, the man she loves   1135a

CRIME-IMMORALITY
Carol, Jack's housekeeper, is taken prisoner by criminals, Burt, Sally and Fred when they fail to overcome Jack's security system   1307

Jack, Carol and Sam

ROMANTIC MISADVENTURES
(1) Carol loves Jack, who has been arrested for a crime by Sam   92

(4) In order to help her lover, Jack, escape the law, Carol seduces the arresting officer, Sam   92

MISFORTUNE
(1) Jack, impersonating Sam, encounters Sam's girlfriend, Carol, who recognizes him as an imposter   717

MISTAKEN JUDGMENT
Carol, to protect herself from Jack, summons a police officer, Sam   799

HELPFULNESS
Sam tries to get his prisoner, Jack, to inform on Carol   824

DELIVERANCE
Jack spots a police officer, Sam, watching Carol, who is about to commit a theft   876a

Jack manages to warn Carol of the danger from Sam   876a

Jack, Carol and Matt

ROMANTIC MISADVENTURES
(1) Wealthy Carol invites her lover, Jack to her home so that he can meet her parents. Jack, arriving before Carol, is mistaken for Matt, a candidate for the position of family chauffeur   178

REJECTION
(10) Jack and Carol love each other; but Matt, an employee of Jack, tells Carol about an offense Jack has committed. Carol believes the story   213

MARRIED LIFE
(4) Young Carol, wife of elderly Jack, has an affair with Jack's servant, Matt   466b

Jack, Carol and Eric

ROMANCE'S BEGINNINGS
Jack is mistaken by Carol for another man, Eric, with whom she's communicated but never seen   2d

(4) Carol is unhappily married to brutal Eric. Out of sympathy for Carol, unmarried Jack falls in love with her   17b

ROMANTIC MISADVENTURES
(1) Unmarried Jack falls in love with married Carol. Carol's husband, Eric, won't divorce Carol; nor will she divorce him   120

(1) Jack, who loves Carol, learns that Carol is married to Eric   128

MARRIAGE
(2) Jack and Carol, in order to extricate themselves from a difficult situation, are hastily married by justice of the peace, Eric   351b

Jack, Carol and Eric

MARRIED LIFE
Unbeknownst to Jack, his wife, Carol, has seen him exchange a pair of muddy shoes for the clean shoes of Eric   467

MISTAKEN JUDGMENT
Jack thinks Carol is an opportunist, attempting to obtain wealth by pretending she's the daughter of multi-millionaire Eric   788

(12) Carol proves she's Eric's daughter 788

DECEPTION
Wealthy stroke victim Jack is dying. Priest Eric is called in and suspects foul play. Eric asks Doctor Carol to examine Jack   1267c

(9) Carol deviously encourages Jack to make use of important papers belonging to Eric in order to advance a certain venture   1278a

MYSTERY
(13) Young photographer Jack is summoned to wealthy Eric's secluded estate where beautiful young Carol lies dead   1386a

Jack, Carol and Carl

ROMANTIC MISADVENTURES
Unjustly imprisoned Jack is pardoned and released when Carol pleads with high authority, Carl   108

DELIVERANCE
Carol begs Carl, the governor of a state, to pardon condemned prisoner Jack   895

OBLIGATION
(9) Jack uses his trusted position in Carl's house as a cover to steal and run off with jewels belonging to Carl's wife, Carol   1008

Jack, Carol and Walt

ROMANTIC MISADVENTURES
(1) Carol, thinking she's marrying Jack, mistakenly marries Walt, his long-missing twin brother. When she attempts to rectify her mistake, Walt is nowhere to be found   166

REJECTION
(1) Jack, in love with Carol, is convinced by a spiritual advisor, Walt, to avoid romance at all costs   214

Jack, Carol and X

ROMANCE'S BEGINNINGS
Jack tries to buy an object, X, that he badly wants from Carol. Carol refuses to sell   20a

ROMANTIC MISADVENTURES
Lovers Jack and Carol argue violently and Carol returns a gift, X, given her by Jack   170

REJECTION
(1) Jack gives a valuable gift to Carol, the woman he wants to marry. The gift, X, turns out to have been stolen   333

MARRIAGE
(2) Jack finds an object, X, which Carol has lost, an object (love letter, poem, etc.) that proves she loves him   360b

MARRIED LIFE
Carol thinks that her husband, Jack, cares less about her than a certain small statue, X, to which he attributes special powers   586

(13) Jack shows X, a mysterious object, to his wife, Carol, and is astounded when she abruptly leaves him   541

MISFORTUNE
Jack gives Carol the combination of his safe, X   616

Jack, by giving Carol the combination to his safe, X, endangers her   616

MISTAKEN JUDGMENT
When Jack returns an object, X, that Carol has lost, she mistakenly thinks Jack stole it 792a

When Jack returns an object, X, that Carol has lost, Jack mistakenly thinks she is a thief because X seems too valuable to be owned by someone of Carol's modest circumstances 792a

CHARACTER COMBINATIONS

PERSONAL LIMITATIONS
Jack tries to acquire a desired object, X, from Carol   1138

Jack, trying to acquire a desired object, X, from Carol, discovers that Carol prizes the object for sentimental reasons and won't part with it at any price   1138

CRIME-IMMORALITY
(4) To carry out a certain venture, Carol sells a valuable heirloom, X, entrusted to her care by Jack   1293c

MYSTERY
(13) Carol gives underachiever Jack a lucky charm, X, which, she promises, will bring him success   1377b

Jack, Carol and Amy

ROMANCE'S BEGINNINGS
(2) Jack falls in love with Carol, and gives up the wealth he would have inherited if he'd married mysterious Amy   19a

Jack, Carol and Andy

ROMANTIC MISADVENTURES
Both Jack and his father, Andy, are in love with Carol and want to marry her   135

REJECTION
Carol loves Jack but she's disliked by Jack's father, Andy. Carol uses a third party to convince Andy of her grace and character   241

Jack's father, Andy, disapproves of Jack's girlfriend, Carol   330b

(1) Spineless Jack loves Carol but gives in to the objections of his strong-willed father, Andy, and decides not to marry her   282a

(1) Black Muslim Jack loves Carol, a white woman. He's ordered by his father, Andy, and by his religious leader to give up Carol   282b

(9) Carol, by an ingenious action, proves herself to Jack's father, Andy, and wins him over   330b

Jack, Carol and Frank

ROMANCE'S BEGINNINGS
Carol retains young attorney, Jack, to settle her the estate of her late father, Frank   20c

ROMANTIC MISADVENTURES
Jack, in love with Carol, is required by Carol's father, Frank, to amass a certain amount of money before he'll be seriously considered as a son-in-law   111

Jack loves Carol; and Carol's father, Frank, promises to allow him to marry Carol if Jack completes a dangerous venture   112

Carol is in love with Jack, who is settling the estate of Carol's deceased father, Frank   125c

Jack mistakenly believes that Frank, the father of Carol, whom he loves, is his enemy   177

(1) Frank, Carol's father, is mysteriously killed and innocent Jack is arrested for murder   43

(4) Jack, in love with Carol, quarrels with her father, Frank   43

(9) Carol's dead father, Frank, was deeply in debt and, unknown to Carol, wealthy Jack pays the debts   125c

REJECTION
Jack carries out a difficult venture so that Carol's father, Frank, will allow Jack to marry her   209

Jack loves Carol. He sues Carol's father, Frank, for damages sustained in a certain incident   295a

Jack loves Carol. Carol's father, Frank, disapproves of Jack and throws him out of Carol's home. Jack sues Frank for damages   295b

(1) Carol's father, religious fanatic Frank, throws Carol out of the house because she falls in love with Jack, who is not of their faith   223

Jack, Carol and Frank

REJECTION (cont'd.)

(1) Carol cannot marry Jack because her scientist father, Frank, working with Carol in an experiment, inadvertently infects her with a deadly bacteria 227

(1) Carol admits that she loves Jack, whose family is feuding with Carol's. As a result, Carol's father, Frank, stops her from seeing Jack 240

(1) Carol can't marry Jack, the man she loves, because she promised to care for her widowed father, Frank 285

(1) Jack loves Carol. But Carol's father, Frank, warns Jack to stay away from Carol 299

(1) Carol, who loves Jack, is detained by her father, Frank, when she tries to keep a date with Jack 306

(1) Carol is locked in her room by her father, Frank, to prevent her from meeting her boyfriend, Jack 308a

(1) Carol sends a letter to her boyfriend, Jack. The letter is intercepted by Carol's father, Frank, who disapproves of Jack 308b

MARRIAGE

Frank believes he is justified in forcing Jack to marry Carol 347b

Jack, posing as a salesman, calls at the home of Carol, the girl he loves, and her father Frank, who has forbidden him to see Carol 352a

(1) Carol rejects Jack, the man she loves, because she feels obligated to care for her father, Frank. Frank then gets married, and Carol finds herself alone in the world 368a

(2-9) Frank approves of Jack, who then marries Carol 350

(5) Jack is coerced by Frank, father of Carol, to marry Carol 347b

(9) Frank approves of Jack, and Jack and Carol marry 352a

(9) Frustrated Jack stops plotting against Frank, father of Carol, the girl he loves, when Frank drops his objections to Jack and allows him to marry Carol 363b

(9) Jack, in love with Carol but adamantly rejected by her tyrannical father, Frank, conspires to have Frank killed. Suddenly Carol calls Jack with the news that her father, Frank, has relented and now blesses their marriage. Jack must race to halt Frank's murder 360a

HELPFULNESS

Carol's father, Frank, unsuccessfully tries to control Jack, a rebellious, unmanageable young man left in his charge 812b

Jack, Carol and Greg

ROMANTIC MISADVENTURES

Jack's son, Greg, is determined to marry Carol, whom Jack thinks isn't the proper choice 181b

(4) Jack, trying to deter his son, Greg, from marrying Carol, seduces her 181b

Jack, Carol and Doug

PRETENSE

Carol mistakes Jack for her son, Doug 1196

Jack, mistaken by a dying woman, Carol, for her son, Doug, plays along with the misconception so Carol can die peacefully 1196

REVELATION

(10) Jack's plans take a sudden detour when he discovers he's the father of Carol's son, Doug 1450

Jack, Carol and Tony

PRETENSE

Carol, unaware that her brother, Tony, is dead, exchanges letters with Jack, who pretends to be Tony 1205

CHARACTER COMBINATIONS

(1) Carol, after corresponding with Jack, whom she thinks is her brother, Tony, visits Jack unannounced and discovers the truth 1205

Jack, Carol and Milt

OBLIGATION
(1) Carol, who disliked Milt, who has left a fortune to Jack, convinces Jack to violate certain conditions of Milt's bequest 1001b

DECEPTION
Jack's wealthy uncle, Milt, promises to leave his riches to Jack when Jack's wife, Carol, gives birth to a child 1289c

Jack, Carol and Annie

MISFORTUNE
(1) Carol and her husband, Jack, are financially ruined when forced to replace a valuable ornament that Carol borrowed from Annie, and lost 642

MYSTERY
Annie plays a hoax by forging a note that concerns her friend, Carol, and Jack 1364b

REVELATION
(10) Carol's friend, Annie, makes an important disclosure about Jack that causes Carol to correct a serious error 1462

ROMANCE'S BEGINNINGS
(4) Wallflower Carol is persuaded by her girlfriend, Annie, to go on a blind-date with Jack 35

ROMANTIC MISADVENTURES
(13) Jack, who loves Carol, learns that Carol loves her girlfriend, Annie 42a

REJECTION
Carol falls for Jack, who jilts her friend, Annie, in order to pursue Carol 277

Annie's distress over losing Jack causes Carol to feel torn 277

(1) Carol, in love with Jack, rejects him when she learns that he jilted her best friend, Annie, to pursue her 243

MARRIED LIFE
Jack is asked by Annie, a friend of his dead wife, Carol, for some love letters that Annie gave to Carol for safe-keeping 385b

Jack's wife, Carol, admires Annie's independence and wants to be like her 414

(5) Jack suspects his wife, Carol, of receiving love letters — but learns they belong to Annie and were being held by Carol for safe-keeping 385b

(7) Carol discovers through a friend, Annie, that the infidelity she accused her husband, Jack, of committing, never occurred 506a

Jack, Carol and Laura

ROMANCE'S BEGINNINGS
Because of her questionable past, Carol tries to persuade her lover, Jack, to transfer his affections to her rival, Laura 11c

(4) Jack falls for Carol, but he's already married to Laura, whom he's never loved but feels obligated to care for 18

(8) Carol, older, in love with young Jack, wants Jack to shift his affections to her rival, Laura, who is nearer Jack's age 11b

(1) Carol and Jack are in love. Laura underhandedly steals Jack away from Carol 94a

(3-9) Carol, forced to become devious, wins Jack back from Laura 94a

(4) Carol, determined to hurt Laura, runs off with Jack, Laura's fiance 90b

(4) Jack, engaged to marry Carol, receives an invitation from Laura, his former sweetheart 138

MARRIAGE PROPOSAL
(1) Jack loves Carol. Thinking that he has proposed to Carol, he later learns that it was Laura 182b

(1) Thinking he's proposed to Carol, Jack finds that he's mistakenly proposed to Laura, who accepts 182b

Jack, Carol and Laura

REJECTION
Jack loves Carol and Laura 215b

Jack is about to marry Laura, who has tricked him into believing his real love, Carol, is unfaithful 216

Jack wants to marry Carol, but is already secretly married to Laura 281a

Jack turns his back on Carol and goes after wealthy Laura 281c

Carol loves Jack. Laura, an alien, tries to lure Jack away from Carol 336c

Laura sues Jack for palimony 337b

(1) While Jack waffles over whether to propose marriage to Carol or Laura, Carol and Laura become engaged to others 215b

(1) Carol loses Jack's affections when Laura enters his life 324

(1) Jack, who loves Carol, runs into trouble when he leaves her for Laura, a woman who inflates his ego 337a

(1) Jack and Carol love each other, but Laura, through her machinations, wins him away from Carol 340

(4) Jack, as a result of seductive Laura coming on to him, breaks off his engagement to Carol, whom he loves 215a

(4) Jack sends a gift to Carol, whom he loves; Laura intercepts the gift and replaces it with a photo of Jack, lovingly inscribed to Laura 218b

(4) Jack, in love with "plain Jane" Carol, leaves her for Laura, a beautiful woman who massages his ego and turns him on 256

(8) Carol secretly loves unmarried Jack; when Jack vanishes and later reappears with a bride, Laura, Carol's love for Jack remains unchanged 270

(8) Unmarried Carol, falling in love with Jack, husband of Laura, is overcome with guilt. Carol leaves Jack and seeks solitude 279

(4) Jack, living with Laura, deserts her and marries Carol 337b

MARRIAGE
Carol, an alien, rescues Jack and falls in love with him, but Jack is engaged to marry a woman of his own people, Laura 346

Jack is unhappily married to Carol and in love with Laura, but he he doesn't believe in divorce 368e

(1) Laura, regretting her rejection of Jack, searches for him and learns he is about to marry Carol 345

(1) Jack leaves alien Carol, who loves him, promising to return. Instead, he marries one of his own people, Laura 346

(2) Jack's uncaring wife, Carol, is killed in an accident, leaving Jack free to marry his long-time love, Laura 368e

(4) Jack betrays Carol, whom he loves, and has a passionate affair with Laura 361a

(10) Jack, rejected by Laura, travels to a distant place where he meets Carol and falls for her 345

MARRIED LIFE
Bankrupt Jack divorces Carol and contrives to marry wealthy Laura 377b

Jack leaves his loving wife, Carol, and runs off with Laura, a woman who flatters him 386

Jack, feeling disloyal to his first wife, Laura, makes Carol miserable with his guilt 405

Jack becomes ill. Laura, who was in love with Jack before he married Carol, nurses him back to health 496b

Jack's grieving for his dead wife, Laura, causes his second wife, Carol, great unhappiness 504b

CHARACTER COMBINATIONS

Jack's marriage to Carol hinders his romance with Laura 509

Jack, married to Carol, whom he doesn't love, is haunted by memories of a former girl-friend, Laura, whom he still loves 528

Carol's husband, Jack, and Laura, both vanish mysteriously at the same time 540

Gossip says that Carol's husband, Jack, has run off with Laura 540

Jack is mistaken by Carol for another man, Eric, with whom she's communicated but never seen 2d

On her deathbed Jack's wife, Carol, makes Jack promise that he will marry Laura, her best friend 578b

Laura was in love with Jack before he married Carol 578b

Carol is certain that her husband, Jack, has run off with Laura 589

(1) Jack is suspected of murdering his wife, Carol; but, at the moment the murder was committed, Jack was with Laura 537

(1) Bigamist Jack's two wives, Carol and Laura, meet accidently and compare notes 548b

(1) Carol's husband, Jack, is killed in an accident while enroute to an assignation with Laura 556

(4) Jack has two wives, Carol and Laura, two homes several miles apart, two identities in two separate communities, two circles of friends, and practices two professions 486b

(4) Carol's husband, Jack, loses his memory and marries Laura 548a

(4) Jack marries Carol to free himself of the harmful influence of Laura 421

(4) Jack deserts his devoted wife, Carol, to run off with younger, prettier Laura 555a

(4) Leaving his wife, Carol, to run away with Laura, Jack becomes remorseful and unhappy 555a

(4) Carol's husband, Jack, pretends to be single while romancing Laura 556

(8) Jack, married to Carol but in love with Laura, takes a long journey to try and forget Laura 555b

(9) Free of his obsession with Laura, Jack returns to Carol 393

(9) Jack manages to find a way to leave his unloved wife, Carol, and, using an alias, marries the woman he loves, Laura 440

(9) Jack's second wife, Carol, discovers that his first wife, Laura, was unfaithful 504b

(10) Jack's wife, Carol, wears the mask and costume of Laura, Jack's lover, and meets him as Laura at a masquerade ball 594f

(13) Carol's husband, Jack, recovers his memory, forgets Laura and returns to Carol 548a

PRETENSE
(10) Carol realizes that Laura has lied about Jack 1154b

Jack, Carol and Sally

HELPFULNESS
(12) Jack, proving Carol innocent of a crime, proves that Sally, a criminal who resembles Carol, is the guilty party 828

Jack, Carol and Donna

REJECTION
(1) Donna, a maid in the home of Carol, Jack's girlfriend, warns Jack that Carol has informed the police of Jack's criminal activities, and that he's a former convict 338

Jack, Carol and Donna

PERSONAL LIMITATIONS
Carol's message to her employee, Donna, is mistakenly received by Jack 1136

Jack, Carol and Irene

MARRIED LIFE
(4) Irene dies, and Jack makes it appear that Carol died 456

(9) Carol, manipulated by Jack, is committed to an insane asylum as Irene, and Jack inherits Carol's money 456

Jack, Carol and Lee

MARRIAGE PROPOSAL
(9) Bumbling Jack loves Carol, but is too backward and shy to propose marriage. Jack is shocked when a child, Lee, who is aware of his shyness, proposes to Carol for him 193

MARRIED LIFE
Jack has a son, Lee, by his wife, Carol, who dies 425

Carol and her husband, Jack, have one child, Lee 466a

Carol loves her child, Lee, but not her husband, Jack 466a

Jack's wife, Carol, sacrifices her goals in order to give Jack the son, Lee, he wants 515

Carol divorces her husband, Jack, and wins custody of their child, Lee 594c

Jack steals their child, Lee, from his ex-wife, Carol 594c

(1) Carol's marriage to Jack, her second husband, is jeopardized by the presence of Lee, a child by her first husband 514

(5) Carol deserted her child, Lee, and her husband, Jack, but her love for the child causes her to return 507b

(5) Jack learns that his child, Lee, has been born since he and his wife, Carol, separated; they reconcile 501

(6) Jack tries to kill his son, Lee, whom he's framed for an offense that Jack, himself, has committed. Jack's wife, Carol, allows her husband to cause her death, sacrificing her life to save their son, Lee 516

(14) Jack and Carol, separated, become changed through love for their child, Lee, and are reconciled 499a

(14) Jack's wife, Carol, almost dies during childbirth and undergoes a complete personality change 505

MISFORTUNE
Lee, a child playing in the corridor of a big-city hotel, unties a ribbon from Carol's doorknob and reties it to Jack's door 737c

DECEPTION
(2) Jack, looking after an abandoned baby, Lee, convinces Carol, who has other children, to take Lee off his hands 1229

Jack finds himself looking after an abandoned baby, Lee 1229

Jack, Carol and Linda

MARRIED LIFE
Jack and his wife, Carol, live with Jack's mother, Linda 384

Carol battles with Linda, and with Jack over Linda 384

Jack's mother, Linda, lives with Jack and his wife, Carol 518

Jack's wife, Carol, is jealous of the attention Jack gives his mother, Linda 543

Carol mistakenly believes that her mother-in-law, Linda, is trying to come between her and Jack 543

Jack and his wife, Carol, are forced to live with Jack's mother, Linda, on her small income 574b

CHARACTER COMBINATIONS

(1) Jack and Carol quarrel over Linda, and Jack is forced to choose between Linda and Carol 518

Jack, Carol and Rita

ROMANCE'S BEGINNINGS

Carol's mother, Rita, a middle-aged widow, introduces her young lover, Jack, to Carol 11a

(8) Carol's mother, Rita, plans for her young lover, Jack, to transfer his affections to Carol. Rita's plan succeeds 11a

Jack, Carol and Betty

MARRIED LIFE

Carol is Jack's daughter and the step-daughter of Jack's wife, Betty 570

(4) Carol plans to get even with her stepmother, Betty, because she believes Betty stole her father, Jack's, affections 570

Jack, Carol and Judy

ROMANTIC MISADVENTURES

Twin sisters Carol and Judy both love Jack 137b

Jack, Carol and Susan

REJECTION

(1) Weak-willed Jack, under pressure from his unmarried sisters, Susan and Holly, gives up Carol, whom he loves 219

Jack, Carol, Pete and Gary

ROMANTIC MISADVENTURES

(1) Unmarried Jack runs off with Carol, the wife of his best friend, Pete; Carol then leaves Jack to run off with Gary 150

MARRIED LIFE

(3) Jack's friend, Pete, arranges for both of bigamist Carol's husbands, Gary and Jack, to meet, thus exposing the truth 435a

(9) Gary, running off with Jack's wife, Carol, encounters Jack's friend, Pete, who saves Carol from a foolish act 507a

Jack, Carol, Pete and Burt

DECEPTION

(9) Jack's friend, Pete, kidnaps Burt's daughter, Carol, and offers to exchange her for Jack, whom Burt is holding for ransom 1281

Jack, Carol, Pete and Carl

CHANCE

(1) Jack's gifts to Pete and Carol are misdelivered by Carl with calamitous results 1042b

(4) Married Jack has a merchant, Carl, send to his friend, Pete, monogrammed silk boxer shorts, and to Carol (976) an expensive charm bracelet 1042b

Jack, Carol, Pete and Lee

MARRIED LIFE

Jack and Carol, married, are to inherit money from a rich relative, Pete, when they have a child 490b

Pete informs Jack and Carol that he's coming to see their child, Lee. Jack and Carol find it necessary to employ further deception 490b

Jack, Carol, Pete and Lee

MARRIED LIFE (cont'd.)

(4) Jack and Carol, childless, notify a wealthy relative, Pete, that they have had a son, Lee 490b

(12) Jack learns that his wife, Carol, has borne Pete's son, Lee 551

Jack, Carol, Gary and Burt

ROMANTIC MISADVENTURES

(4) Jack's rival for Carol, Gary, learning of Jack and Carol's abrupt decision to marry, sends an ally, Burt, who lures Carol away by saying Jack sent for her 154b

Jack, Carol, Gary and Laura

MARRIED LIFE

(1-10) Carol leaves her husband, Jack, for Gary, only to discover that Gary is involved with another married woman, Laura   400

(1-5) Carol admits to tells her husband, Jack, that she married him out of resentment toward Gary, the man she loved, for having married Laura   406

Jack, Carol, Gary and Lee

MARRIED LIFE

(4) Carol loves Gary and runs off with him, leaving her child, Lee, with her husband, Jack   466a

Jack, Carol, Gary and X

REJECTION

Jack's rival, Gary, finds an object that Carol has lost. The object, X, symbolizes Carol's love for Jack. Gary keeps X and says nothing about it   301b

(3) Jack persuades his rival, Gary to send Carol a certain gift, X. Then, after X is sent, Jack proves Gary stole it   236

Jack, Carol, Dave and Tony

REJECTION

(1) Jack, finding his girl, Carol, in Dave's arms, storms out, unaware that Dave is Carol's brother, Tony   222b

Jack, Carol, Frank and Gary

ROMANTIC MISADVENTURES

Struggling sculptor Jack and Carol are in love. Carol's wealthy father, Frank, wants his daughter to marry his protege, Gary. Frank suggests a contest between Jack and Gary, the winner to marry Carol   180

REJECTION

Jack's rival, Gary, is preferred by Carol's father, Frank   301a

(1) Jack is promised Carol in marriage by her father, Frank. But Frank reneges and forces Carol to marry wealthy Gary   313

(8) Jack, learning secretly that Carol loves a rival, Gary, refuses to hold Carol to Frank's promise of marriage   209

Both Jack and Gary love Carol. Her father, Frank, secretly attempts to determine which suitor is more deserving   77

MARRIAGE

Jack and Gary, rivals for Carol's affections, are put to a severe test by Carol's father, Frank   350

MARRIED LIFE

(1) Carol's father, Frank, unaware that Jack and Carol are secretly married, insists Carol marry Jack's rival, Gary   573a

Jack, Carol, Frank, Rita and Pete

MARRIAGE

(4) Carol's parents, Frank and Rita, mistake Jack for Pete, the man to whom Carol is engaged   353

(9) Jack runs off with Carol and marries her   353

Jack, Carol, Frank, Rita and Gary

REJECTION

(4) Carol loves Jack but is forced by her parents, Frank and Rita, to marry Gary   284

(4) Carol, believing the man she loves, Jack, is dead, obeys the wishes of her parents, Frank and Rita, and agrees to marry Gary   339

CHARACTER COMBINATIONS

Jack, Carol, Pete, Gary and Walt

MARRIED LIFE
(3-9) Jack's wife, Carol, is running off with large, physically menacing Gary when they're surreptitiously spotted in an airport terminal by slightly built Pete. While Carol is in the ladies room, Pete approaches Gary and points out a large traveler, Walt, (actually a total stranger) as his hit-man buddy; unless Gary walks out of Carol's life immediately, Pete will turn Walt loose on him. It works, though Carol remains unaware of Pete's role 53

Jack, Carol, Annie and Laura

ROMANTIC MISADVENTURES
(3) Carol's friend, attractive, married Annie, tries to save Carol's fiance, Jack, from a conniving woman, Laura, and restore him to Carol. Annie hopes to accomplish this by winning Jack away from Laura 94b

REJECTION
(3) Seductive Laura tries to compromise Jack so his fiance, Carol will leave him. Generous Annie attempts to rescue Jack from Laura's clutches and return him to Carol 238

HELPFULNESS
Carol's friend, Annie, tries to save Carol's fiance, Jack, from the clutches of a designing woman, Laura, and return him to Carol 844b

Carol's friend, Annie, tries to save Carol's lover, Jack, from a designing woman, Laura, by convincing him that Laura is unprincipled 844b

Jack, Carol, Laura and Lee

MARRIED LIFE
Jack, thinking his first wife is dead, remarries and has children by his second wife 389

Jack learns that his first wife was still alive when he remarried, but that she has since died 389

(1) Jack's second marriage is unwittingly invalidated 389

(1) Jack decides to make a new will and have another wedding ceremony with his second wife, but he's killed in an accident enroute to his attorney 389

(1) The children of Jack's second marriage are illegitimate, so Jack's property goes to the relatives of Jack's dead first wife 389

Jack, Carol, Andy and Linda

REJECTION
(10) Jack falls in love with Carol and plans to marry her. Jack's parents, Andy and Linda, disapprove of Carol, and send Jack to a distant location 321b

Jack, Carol, Frank and Rita

ROMANTIC MISADVENTURES
Jack and Carol are in love but Carol's parents, Frank and Rita, dislike Jack, so Jack and Carol decide to run off and get married 73

REJECTION
Carol's parents, Frank and Rita, insist she have nothing to do with Jack 286

Carol's parents, Frank and Rita, dislike Carol's boyfriend, Jack, because he lacks ambition 311

Carol's parents, Frank and Rita, are obstacles to her romance with Jack 312

(1) Carol lets herself be governed by parental duty when Frank and Rita order her not to see Jack, the man she loves 286

Jack, Carol, Frank and Rita

REJECTION (cont'd.)
(1) Jack loves Carol, but he's divorced and Carol's parents, Frank and Rita, are opposed on religious grounds to Carol marrying a divorced man 334b

(9) Adventurer Jack, in love with Carol and disliked by her parents, Frank and Rita, runs off with Carol 234b

aak, Carol, Andy and Frank

ROMANCE'S BEGINNINGS
(4) Jack and Carol have never seen each other but their fathers, Andy and Frank, arrange for them to marry 26a

ROMANTIC MISADVENTURES
(1) To protect his father, Andy, Jack is forced to take action against Frank, father of Carol, the girl Jack loves 123

REJECTION
(1) Jack and Carol fall in love, but their fathers, Andy and Frank, are bitter foes 276

(5) Carol loves Jack, but rejects him because of her father, Frank's feud with Jack's father, Andy 283

ack, Carol, Bill and Frank

ROMANTIC MISADVENTURES
Jack will be disinherited by his wealthy grandfather, Bill, if he refuses to carry out an act that will seriously harm Frank, father of Carol, the woman Jack loves 118

Jack, Carol and Nancy

ROMANCE'S BEGINNINGS
(1) Jack's romance with Carol is going nowhere, so Jack buys an aphrodisiac and mixes it secretly in a cup of tea — which Carol's maiden aunt, Nancy, mistakenly drinks 8b

REJECTION
(1) Carol sends a gift to Jack, but her aunt, Nancy, who dislikes Jack, secretly alters the gift in such a way that Jack will be offended by it; or she exchanges it for an item that will offend him 308c

Jack, Carol, Walt and Amy

ROMANTIC MISADVENTURES
(2) Jack is married to Amy, a woman he doesn't know. Carol is married to Walt, a man she's never seen 167a

(2) Jack and Carol meet, fall in love, whereupon Jack discovers Amy is Carol, and Carol discovers Walt is Jack, the people to whom they're married but have never seen 167a

Jack, Carol, Burt and X

DECEPTION
Carol refuses to sell an object, X, to Jack. Burt, a criminal, steals X from Carol and offers to sell it to Jack 1217c

THE END

CHARACTER COMBINATIONS

DID YOU KNOW

PLOTS®

Unlimited

IS ALSO AVAILABLE AS
A COMPUTER PROGRAM?*

Acclaimed by experts, regarded as indispensable by thousands
of enthusiastic professionals and soon-to-be professionals
throughout the world, the fast, powerful, easy-to-use,
imagination-jogging Plots Unlimited software program contains
all of the Conflict Situations found in this book, *plus* dozens of
exciting features that are *only* possible on a computer:

★ Generate plot outlines and story ideas in minutes
★ Easy printing of your plots
★ Simple exporting to your word-processor
★ Speedy viewing of alternate Conflict choices
★ Preview Conflict choices two steps ahead
★ Instant global character-name changes
★ A Notepad, where you can edit your plot-in-progress,
   or make random story-notes
★ And many, many more, including numerous additional,
   imaginative, writer-friendly ways to access this huge database
   of plot segments - and stimulate your own creativity!

**Put this remarkable tool for fiction writers
and educators at *your* fingertips.
To learn more, call 1-800-833-PLOT**,
or inquire at your software dealer.**

* Available for PC or Macintosh® computers.

**From outside the U.S. call (310) 456-1277

5137

II0688717

Career Counseling and Development in a Global Economy

PATRICIA ANDERSEN
Midwestern State University

MICHAEL VANDEHEY
Midwestern State University

Lahaska Press
Houghton Mifflin Company
Boston • New York

Publisher, Lahaska Press: Barry Fetterolf
Senior Editor, Lahaska Press: Mary Falcon
Editorial Assistant: Lindsey Gentel
Project Editor: Kerry Doyle
Executive Marketing Manager: Brenda L. Bravener-Greville
Marketing Manager: Barbara LeBuhn
Manufacturing Manager: Karen Banks

Cover image: Mark Weber, Lone Figure on Road © Images.com/CORBIS

Lahaska Press was established as an imprint of Houghton Mifflin
Company in 1999. It is dedicated to publishing textbooks and
instructional media for counseling and the helping professions.
The editorial offices of the imprint are located in the small town
of Lahaska, Pennsylvania. *Lahaska* is a Native American Lenape word
meaning "source of much writing."

Copyright © 2006 by Houghton Mifflin Company. All rights reserved.

No part of this work may be reproduced or transmitted in any form or by
any means, electronic or mechanical, including photocopying and recording, or by any information storage or retrieval system without the prior
written permission of Houghton Mifflin Company unless such copying is
expressly permitted by federal copyright law. Address inquiries to College
Permissions, Houghton Mifflin Company, 222 Berkeley Street, Boston, MA
02116-3764.

Printed in the U.S.A.

Library of Congress Control Number: 2003110161

ISBN: 0-618-42634-5

3456789-DOC-09

Contents

PART **III**   **Career Counseling Skills**   165

Preface

Like other instructors who have taught career counseling to graduate students for many years, we came to the realization that our teaching goals would be more readily achieved if only we could find a textbook that worked with us rather than against us. We wanted to bridge the gap between textbook material and counseling practice, but we realized, as Savakis and Lent (1994) point out, that career theory is *not* career counseling theory. It also occurred to us that the traditional test-and-tell dilemma may exist precisely because textbooks do not describe the process of career counseling. We wanted a text that would integrate standard therapy techniques with information processing and decision-making skills. We found that our students didn't apply listening skills with career clients because they had learned from their textbook that career counseling is different and separate from other forms of counseling. We wanted support from a textbook that would describe both traditional theories and new concepts that stress adaptability to constant change while showing how to apply these ideas in practice. Finally, in our lectures we felt compelled to elaborate on the pressures of the global economy, and we wanted a text that would support that emphasis.

Several factors moved us toward the conclusion that it would indeed be possible to translate our teaching approach into a textbook that would support our own courses and those of other instructors with similar commitments to career counseling. First, it occurred to us that the Career Diamond, a pedagogical tool we use throughout our course, could be a visual aid throughout the textbook to demonstrate the application of theory. We had found, for example, that the Career Diamond helped students grasp the need for client exploration prior to decision making because they recognized the flow of the process. By inverting the Career Diamond, we were better able to illustrate how external pressures, such as social constructs and limited economic resources, can weigh down and flatten out personal preferences (Chapter 7).

Second, we discovered that career information could be presented from a practitioner's viewpoint as we shared our experiences in developing and managing a career resource center (Chapter 11). We could also emphasize the importance of career education both in the public schools and, increasingly, in the private sector with examples from our consulting work. Finally, we wanted to attend to the neglected area of spirituality—of helping clients who find that career transitions often become the vehicle for examining life's meaning (Chapter 16).

The Organization of This Book

We begin this book with a thematic overview of the history of career counseling—moving from Parsons (1909) to the developmental theory of Super (1957) to more current cognitive constructivists such as Krumboltz, Mitchel, and Jones (1976), Lent, Brown, and Hackett (2000), and Gottfredson (1981). Our goal is to enable students to see theory as having actual application in client sessions. We stress the competencies needed by career counselors as provided by NCDA (Chapter 2). When the Career Diamond (Chapter 3) is introduced, the figure is shown as a tool for representing counseling concepts and also as a simple diagram for use with clients. We describe the clinical decisions important to career counseling, such as providing enough structure to facilitate client development while resisting the pull for too much counselor intervention so the client remains the center of the counseling process.

In the chapter dealing with current trends in the world of work (Chapter 6), we offer specific strategies for helping clients succeed in a global economy while also explaining theoretical concepts such as positive uncertainty by Gelatt (1991). In the interest of applying theory to practice, we place some theories where the concepts are most applicable to the topics discussed. In the chapter describing today's multicultural workforce (Chapter 7), we discuss Brown's (1996) values approach as well as the stages of acculturation for members of marginalized groups and those from the dominant group who accept the diversification. We include an extensive section on gender issues, for heterosexual men and women and for same sex orientations. We discuss public policies that affect all workers, from the middle class to participants in welfare-to-work programs to the working poor. Our intent is to encourage career counselors to see career issues as relevant to those marginalized in an exclusionary economy and to recognize the impact of political issues on career clients.

We placed our full description of the career counseling process about midway through the textbook (Chapter 8) so that previously explained concepts enhance students' understanding of working with clients. We follow up the process chapter by presenting many career counseling techniques we have used with our clients over the years (Chapter 9). At this point, we expect that students are ready to learn specific strategies with an informed sense of how to select and time use techniques depending on the client's need. We deliberately save the discussion of assessment until Chapter 10, embedding the use of instruments in the body of the text so that testing can be seen as a tool, not the focus of counseling.

Chapter 11 describes the career resource center developed and directed by the first author. Application of theory comes through in small details such as organizing library material by Holland (1997) codes and in the bigger picture of developing different services for clients just starting career exploration compared to clients fully examining their career identities.

Chapters 12, 13, and 14, which describe the career development of school-age children, are an integration of Gysbers and Henderson's (2000) work and theories of psychological development. These three chapters are written specifically for graduate students who are planning counseling careers in educational settings; career counselors who plan to work in the community will be more interested in Chapter 15, which describes working with the whole range of adults coping with the current working conditions.

In Chapter 15, work adjustment theory is presented as applicable to adult workers who are hired and rewarded for traits and behaviors that serve the working environment and where workers influence the environment. We also include ideas from writers not typically found in career textbooks when the ideas are useful to career counselors—Branden's (1998) application of self-esteem issues for organizations and Prochaska, Norcross, and Declemente's (1994) concepts of readiness for psychological change.

Finally, our inclusion of a discussion of spirituality in Chapter 16 recognizes that career choices can express the deepest sense of what is worthwhile in life.

Pedagogical Features

As a book designed to meet the needs of practitioners-in-training, most chapters contain skill exercises and case studies that illustrate the concepts discussed. The goal is to build skills and understanding of ideas so that both come together in ways that make the practice of career counseling come alive for the learner. Most of the case studies came from experiences with actual clients. After each case study, in "How Would You Conceptualize this Client," we provide two or three questions as prompts to help students envision what they would do if they were counseling the client described. The questions are followed by a section, "What Actually Happened," in which students can view the real resolution of the case. At the end of each chapter, students find two additional learning aids: a Study Outline and Exercises designed to be executed individually or in small groups. The Study Outline contains terms that are bolded both in the text and in the outline. These terms are defined in the outline and are often words students would find on professional tests for licensing or credentialing.

Encouraging Career Counseling Discussions in Class

We encourage students and instructors to tell their career stories and freely exchange their experiential reactions to the book's material. As educators, many career counselors struggle with common issues, such as how to assist clients who may have unrealistic career goals, how to draw out clients to a full identity exploration, and how to account for the "chance factor" affecting most careers. We have found that class discussions model weighing ethical concerns so students learn to weigh professional judgments and to trust their subjective experience. Students also learn how to prevent the projection of their fears onto clients and to develop a humanistic, holistic, professional, and thoughtful approach to career counseling practice.

In this book, we freely share our clinical experience, giving examples of integrating external requirements with the client's personal soul searching and telling how we deal with the personal connections we make with clients. Much can be learned from the stories of professionals—organizing concepts and experience, offering pictures of cases resolved, and creating visions of what career counseling can be.

Finally, our hope in writing this text is that it will enable career counselors-in-training to see the field in all its complexity and to realize that facilitating career development is itself a meaningful gift to students, clients, and society at large. We encourage the counseling educators and counselors-in-training who use our book to visit the Lahaska Press website (http://www.lahaskapress.com) and share with us their reactions to the material and their suggestions for improving future editions.

Acknowledgements

I (Patricia Andersen) would like to acknowledge the students and clients at Iowa State University who invited me to share their personal and career concerns and allowed me to witness their growth. I appreciate in particular the efforts of Amy Vybiral, who served as a graduate assistant directing the Career Exploration Program at the Student Counseling Service. I am also grateful to the faculty of the West College of Education at Midwestern University who gave so much support in the final stages of this project. Co-authors do not ordinarily thank one another, but I want to say here that I am forever indebted to Michael Vandehey, co-author and friend, who believed in the conceptualization of this book before a word was written and who has shared the research and writing process from start to finish.

I (Michael Vandehey) would like to give my thanks to my wife Torry and my sons Brennan and Riley for their loving support and playful diversions during the writing of this text; to Michael Shuff, whose friendship spans many facets of my personal and professional development; to the many faculty and administrators at Midwestern State University who took a chance on a young kid—I hope there are no regrets; and finally, Patricia Andersen, co-author and mentor, who allowed a career specialization during my internship year to turn into this text and a wonderful friendship.

We also thank Susie Day who referred the book to Lahaska Press and offered advice and Barry Fetterolf, publisher of Lahaska Press, for his willingness to consider new authors and a new approach. We are tremendously grateful to Mary Falcon for her tireless editing of several drafts and to Merrill Peterson for catching the details needing correction in production.

Finally, we want to thank the following counseling educators who reviewed the various drafts of the book: LuAnnette T. Butler, Austin Peay State University; Kathy M. Evans, University of South Carolina; Francesca G. Giordano, Northern Illinois University; Aaron P. Jackson, Brigham Young University; and Beverly A. Snyder, University of Colorado–Colorado Springs. Special thanks to counseling educator Eleanor Weber at Johnson State College in Vermont for going over the first draft with a fine-tooth comb and making detailed suggestions for improvement.

PART I

Background for Understanding Career Services

CHAPTER 1

Importance of Career Services

Though a little one, the master-word (work) looms large in meaning. It is the open sesame to every portal, the great equalizer in the world, the true philosopher's stone that transmutes all the base metal of humanity into gold.

Sir Edmund Osler

Career plays a significant role in the identity, life-style, and sense of well-being for most adults in today's world. Work is the major venue for adults to develop mastery for tasks, knowledge, and expertise, as they earn competency and self-efficacy. A choice made to develop one's abilities in a specified work area is simultaneously a choice regarding one's identity. The centrality of career identity is also shown by how people describe themselves and by reactions to occupational titles. When making introductions, people do not use adjectives such as, "Hi, my name is John, and I'm a caring, intelligent, extroverted, and middle class man." Instead, people say, "Hi, my name is John, and I'm an engineer (or teacher or janitor)."

Knowing a person's occupation brings to mind other personality characteristics. Intelligence is associated with occupations requiring higher levels of education. Economic class is connected to job titles and to where one works. Within a societal context, a person's place is partly determined by occupation. The social standing of some jobs so permeates the social consciousness that even kindergarten children know which occupations have higher status and which have lower standing. Furthermore, the status of career affects not only individuals but also relatives. Parents and other family members exhibit pride for someone whose career brings positive attributions whereas a family may show shame or embarrassment for kin who are not seen as successful. In other words, work is a source of internal self-esteem and a means to integrate individuals into society.

Work is so important that unemployment is associated with psychological and physical disorders. In regards to mental and emotional states, increases in depressive affect, negative mood, and hopelessness were reported for both men and women (Winefield, Tiggemann, & Winefield, 1991). Theodossiou (1998) found that the unemployed have increases in anxiety, depression, and a loss of confidence. On the physical side, Brenner and Mooney (1983) reported increases in heart disease, stroke, and liver cirrhosis after a peak in unemployment, and these findings were supported by international data. It is important to note that a lag occurs between the actual peak of unemployment and the observed physical effects (typically 0–5 years; Brenner & Mooney, 1983). The lag occurs because the behaviors that lead to heart disease, stroke, and liver cirrhosis do not lead to immediate death; there is a cumulative effect. Suicide, on the other hand, is immediate, and spikes in unemployment have a direct relationship to increases in suicide (Brenner & Mooney, 1983). Finally, longitudinal research found a clear connection between unemployment rates and homicide (Brenner & Swank, 1986).

Economic stress, be it due to underemployment or unemployment, has a negative impact on couples and children. Couples experiencing economic loss demonstrate withdrawal of social support by one or both spouses (Vinokur, Price, & Caplan, 1996) and increased hostility with decreased supportiveness and warmth by husbands (Conger et al., 1990). Children living in economically stressed families have been found to receive lower levels of maternal warmth and social support (Klebanov, Brooks-Gunn, & Duncan, 1994). In addition, the children demonstrated higher levels of depression, impulsivity, and antisocial acts (Takeuchi, Williams, & Adair, 1991). Finally, adolescents who are aware of and worry about their parents' financial situation report somatic complaints such as stomachaches, loss of appetite, sleep disturbances, and psychological complaints such as depression and inability to concentrate (Hagquist, 1998).

Given the pivotal nature of career to individuals' lives, it is no wonder that career services are frequently the presenting concern of counseling clients. Career issues are easier for clients to name than many other psychological difficulties. Often, clients enter counseling saying they need help with career issues, and later other problems are raised as well. Counselors are the major practitioners offering the services of career education and career counseling. Because career issues are of such importance in the lives of clients, career development is an important area of expertise for the entire profession.

For society, a healthy economy and full employment channels wealth and human resources. In a stagnant economy with high unemployment, social problems increase, placing pressure on limited resources. A strong, growing economic base is needed to create job openings. The very morale of the populace and the people's confidence in government are affected by employment rates and the presence of occupational opportunities.

Indeed, throughout the history of the United States, career development issues have emerged and reemerged in response to historical events and changes in the economy. Changes in the economic structure have required adaptations by workers to meet the demands of the workplace. At the same time, theoretical concepts have evolved to enhance our understanding of career development.

HISTORICAL PERSPECTIVES

Work Values

In colonial times and in the early days of the nation, the Protestant work ethic prevailed for self-employed farmers, craftsmen, laborers, and small business owners. Thomas Jefferson, in his first inaugural address, envisioned an agrarian economy that supported the ideals of independence and freedom. Government would be limited in power, providing services to citizens and the "encouragement of agriculture, and of commerce as its handmaid" (Coates, n.d.a). Jefferson, who organized the Louisiana Purchase, noted the new nation had the advantage of enough land to make individual property ownership possible for many citizens. "I think our governments will remain virtuous for many centuries as long as they are chiefly agricultural; and this will be as long as there shall be vacant lands in any part of America" (Coates, n.d.b). In an agrarian nation, hard work by individuals was the key to success. "A prosperity built on the basis of agriculture is that which is most desirable to us, because to the efforts of labor it adds the efforts of a greater proportion of soil" (Coates, n.d.c). Independent citizens working hard to develop land resources was the basis for economic expansion and human values.

After industrialization, much of the economy moved to an organizational base, and individuals gained success through efforts within the structure of companies. As the country experienced the growth of industry, public education was needed to train workers in the attitudes and behavior expected in the working environment. In 1859, the Massachusetts Secretary of Education explained how mill owners supported educating future workers:

> The owners of factories are more concerned than other classes and interests in the intelligence of their laborers. When the latter are well educated and the former are disposed to deal justly, controversies and strikes can never occur, nor can the minds of the masses be prejudiced by demagogues and controlled by temporary and factious considerations. (Zinn, 1995, p. 257)

Classroom management with structured tasks requiring obedience to authority mimicked the routine of workers in the factories (Spring, 1973). In this way, public education had its beginnings as training for the basic skills and deportment expected at work.

Horatio Alger

To uphold the historical image of the individual working hard to gain success after industrialization and through the end of the 19th century, Horatio Alger, Jr., wrote popular dime novels describing young male heroes who overcame poor backgrounds to gain success. Through good character and hard work, the fictional idols went from "rags to riches" and carried the American work ethic into the new industrial economy (http://www.horatioalger.com).

Early Professional Standards

By the turn of the century, the sophisticated variety of the economy and the world of work required new professionals to assist people in choosing occupations. In 1909, Frank Parsons published *Choosing a Vocation,* which described the decision-making process. The first step would be to analyze the person's traits, such as abilities, skills, and temperament. The second step was to analyze the characteristics of a job: the work activities required, the location and work atmosphere, and credentials needed for success. The third and final step was to apply "true reasoning." Parsons' method has been named the trait-factor approach, or the matching of the person's traits with the factors of the job. The trait-factor method matches the personal characteristics of the person to the external requirements of an occupation (Parsons, 1909).

Government Initiatives: DOT

With the advent of the Great Depression, the Department of Labor began to analyze jobs and to classify them in an effort to facilitate the employment of workers. In 1929, the *Dictionary of Occupational Titles (DOT)* was first published, and revisions have continued to classify occupations until today (Gysbers et al., 1984). By 1950, Fine divided work "orientations" into the standard three categories of things, data, or people, later used by the *DOT* in the 1965 edition (Figler & Bolles, 1999).

Measurement of Traits

The beginning of the 20th century was a period when considerable strides were made in measuring human traits, from intelligence to interests. Simon and Binet, Cattell, and Terman made progressive improvements in measuring basic IQ (Hunt, 1993). By 1939, Hall developed aptitude tests predicting the capacity to learn specific fields (Crites, 1981). The Strong Interest Inventory, published in 1927, measured interests related to occupational categories. By 1938, the *Mental Measurement Yearbook* began reviewing a variety of tests (Hunt, 1993).

The availability of tests to measure human traits and the availability of job classification systems to codify occupational factors continuously provided the expectancy that career counseling could be based on matching clients with jobs. However, given the complexity and ever-changing nature of both the job market and of human beings, a simple matching method is less and less viable. Although career counselors may still use interest inventories and ability testing, choosing occupations and dealing with the world of work has become more sophisticated.

MATCHING APPROACH VERSUS CAREER IDENTITY AND DEVELOPMENT

In 1939, Williamson wrote about directive and structured methods solidifying the trait-factor approach and offering a step-by-step counseling procedure that matched worker traits with job factors. By comparison, in 1957, Donald Super published the results of a longitudinal study describing career as a developmental process. The Super model suggested that career identity developed over time and involved more than a one-time, lifelong decision based on a definitive match. Super also introduced the concept of career identity, suggesting a person's general self-concept included an identity specific to career.

About the same time, Carl Rogers (1961, 1965) introduced a humanistic counseling process in which clients were encouraged to express their feelings and to gain self-awareness. Rogerian counseling distrusted the use of tests and structure and instead insisted that individuals could take responsibility for their own career choices, rather than make decisions based on the advice of an expert (Crites, 1981).

The dilemmas of career counseling were set: job requirements and other external factors create demand characteristics whereas the psychological dynamics of individual self-concepts require fluid self-expression to gain personal satisfaction. The counselor can facilitate self-awareness, yet the external demands must also be taken into account. The field adapted matching methods that linked stagnant job factors to the person's qualifications and a dynamic approach focusing on the psychological process of the individual who could integrate both the external and personal characteristics.

FROM VOCATION TO CAREER, FROM SINGLE CHOICE TO DEVELOPMENT

McDaniels and Gysbers (1992) demonstrated the progress of the career field through the use of language in the literature. Parsons and others used vocation and occupation interchangeably and saw counseling as helping clients select a field and adapt to its requirements. The use of the word *career* began to increase in the 1950s as Super's research regarding development across the life-span was introduced. Suggesting a change from *vocation* to *career* was a part of the profession's redefinition. Career decision making changed from a one-time choice to a holistic consideration of multiple roles and all the factors that influenced self-concepts and development. By the 1980s, Carlson (1988, p. 186) defined career as "not … just a job … [but] … a guiding image or a concept of a personal path, a personal significance, a personal continuity and meaning in the order of things." *Career* became the preferred term, replacing vocation and broadening the profession's view of its purposes. To underscore the changing professional image, on July 1, 1985, the National Vocational Guidance Association (NVGA), changed its name to the National Career Development Association (NCDA) Removing the term *guidance* could also be seen as significant. No longer were counselors "guiding" clients to a career choice; instead, they were facilitating the clients' career development.

CAREER ISSUES IN THE NEW MILLENNIUM

Philosophical and Theoretical Changes

Today career educators and counselors deliver services within the context of a new era characterized by constant change. Innovative theoretical concepts capture new societal perspectives to account for the impact of technological advances and the greater dispersal of increasing amounts of information. Attitudes toward work are changing also as careerists integrate the values of diverse cultural backgrounds and cope with a fluid job market. The vision of a stable fit between the person and one occupation performed in similar settings no longer describes careerists who adapt their multiple talents and skills to make varying contributions through ever-changing work roles.

Current research and clinical practice are often guided by theories dating back to the 1950s, when occupational segregation based on race and gender and stability in work patterns and family life were the norm (Barnett

& Hyde, 2001). Postmodern philosophy is an attempt to describe broad shifting social views affected by the proliferation of information, increasing technology, and changes in scientific thinking. Much of the career literature describes the modern use of scientific, objective empiricism (logical positivism) to predict occupational choice, behavior, and satisfaction. Postmodern approaches point out that scientific studies describe only one view of reality when life actually presents multiple realities that are subjectively interpreted by individuals. Logical positivism often runs the risk of reducing "rich relationships and complex developmental processes to such micro levels that the meaning of the results becomes ambiguous at best" (Blustein, 2003, p. 22).

The context of human experience represents a multiplicity and complexity of variables that cannot be isolated and described as *a single* phenomenon. Career development theories cannot fully describe the career life as the individual experiences it. Since the 1960s, counselors have recognized that interest inventories and values surveys do not fully capture a client's career self-concept, and these isolated measured factors could not possibly predict lifetime matches between an individual and an occupation (Calia, 1966). Nor can satisfaction measures describe the joy of work from a holistic view of work behavior. For the 21st century, career counselors will need to approach clients as unique and complex individuals with their own subjective experience and in the context of an ever-changing work environment. However, the scientific system has provided tools such as psychometric instruments and linear decision-making models that are also useful to clients. Blustein (2003) recommended that the vocational field move forward by integrating both modern and postmodern approaches. Counselors need to be trained in the skills of both and apply them to career services in a flexible manner.

Gergen (1991a, 1991b) extended the description of postmodern experience by describing the pressures created by the multiplicity of technological communication devices. From electronic mail to cell phones, people are caught up in an accelerated pace of socially connecting to more and more people from many more areas of life. The individual is split with communicating from many different sides of one's self to a state of social saturation. Many of these communications may be superficial, relating to only a shallow level of self. A coherent sense of identity becomes difficult to maintain as the person relates to others from multiple viewpoints and roles. Social saturation in the workplace occurs when customers, supervisors, subordinates, and colleagues can all leave messages and expect responses (e.g., voice mail, pagers, e-mail). An individual's priorities must be clear when spontaneous reactions are demanded from all sides. An individual's sense of meaning must be well grounded when multiple subjective viewpoints are constantly heard.

Counseling may become one of the few places where clients can sort through their values and meaning and where individuals can regain their own private sense of reality.

A Changing Work Ethic

As was mentioned, the Protestant work ethic once dominated the picture of individuals pursuing independent work lives. American vocational attitudes defined a view that meaning resided within the person who gained success through self-expression and individual effort. After industrialization, meaning resided within a context of organizations, and individuals gained success by using facts and rational thought to determine the appropriate behavior in the external world. Postmodern interpretations of current economic changes suggest attitudes will change: as people no longer work within one organization but within constantly changing contexts, success will be gained by workers interpreting differing environments, coping with a diversity of values and world views, and working cooperatively in teams to make contributions for all (Peterson & Gonzales, 2000). Table 1.1 summarizes changes in work ethics across historical and future time periods.

Changes in the work ethic in a postmodern era coincide with economic changes. Career counselors must draw from a variety of fields as they recognize the interdependence of the economic system, individual career development, social systems, and training/school environments. The historic goal of counseling, finding a fit between an individual and a stable occupation

Table 1.1 Comparisons of Work Ethics

19th Century Vocational Ethic	20th Century Career Ethic	21st Century Development Ethic
Self-employed farmers	Employed by organizations	Work in teams and craftspeople
Romantic conceptualism (Meaning in the person)	Logical positivism (Meaning in the world)	Postmodern interpretivism (Meaning in the word)
Value feelings	Value facts	Value perspectives
Be creative	Be rational	Actively participate in the community
Success through self-expression & individual effort	Success through moving up someone else's ladder	Success through cooperation & contribution

Source: Savickas (1993), p. 210. Reprinted by permission of Springer Publishing Company.

within a stable organization and with consistency for family life, is no longer reasonable. Attitudes toward work have changed because people and the world of work have changed.

Globalization

Since the 1980s, the economy has demonstrated steady change, with industrial jobs decreasing and service jobs increasing and with the newer jobs paying less and having fewer benefits. Layoffs, downsizing, corporate mergers, outsourcing, and job exporting are everyday news. Corporations restructure themselves regularly, creating what Dent (1995) called "job shock," variations on the psychological reactions to job loss identified since the Great Depression.

Berger (1990) reported that all workers are expected to make major job changes at least seven times over a lifetime. Career counselors will need to offer life and transition planning that will continually reorient clients to new fields. Feller (1996) said career counselors need to:

> Integrate new rules, consider new foundations, and constantly assess the gaps between what is needed and what is available. Only then will a client's employment and career development be better served in a world of change. (p. 19)

The individual's career self-concept will be the major factor under a person's control; and although changes in career identity may be regularly needed, the careerist can establish some consistency by holding onto some critical self-defining priorities. Career development has always required the integration between the external demands and the internal self, but regular change requires such adaptations be made over and over again. Career counseling for the new millennium requires skillful therapy interventions that facilitate an increasingly complex process.

SUMMARY

The recent past allowed for matching a worker's skills and traits to specific jobs. If the match was satisfying, the worker could count on a lifetime of employment. Today's reality is quite different. Flexibility and being a "free agent" are today's reality. Career counselors and educators can no longer ask, "What do you want to be for the rest of your life?" Instead, they need to ask, "Who are you as a complex human being?" "How is your current job/degree preparing you for the next job?" "What do you observe as the next trend in the job market?" "What personal priorities must be met in whatever job you choose?"

STUDY OUTLINE: KEY TERMS AND CONCEPTS

I. Importance of Career Counseling
   A. For the individual
      1. Important identity factor for adults
      2. Major source for building and maintaining self-esteem
      3. Critical avenue for belonging in society
      4. Influential in position in family
   B. For counseling profession
      1. A frequently requested service
      2. An easy means for clients to enter counseling
      3. Related to many other psychological issues
      4. Important specialty for counseling psychology
   C. For society
      1. Major means to channel human resources
      2. Primary method for renewing and building goods and services
      3. Full employment could prevent many other social problems
      4. Affects the morale and sense of common good
II. Career Services and Theory Affected by:
   A. Historical societal influences
      1. Protestant work ethic
      2. Horatio Alger myth
      3. Measurement of traits
   B. Concepts from career psychology
      1. Trait-factor matching
      2. Career identity as a psychological and developmental process
      3. Change from NVGA to NCDA
   C. Current external pressures of economy
      1. Globalization
      2. Communication advances
   D. Postmodernism
      1. Changing work ethic
      2. Globalization

EXERCISES

1. The following questions encourage examining your personal history and its impact on your career path, as well as your thoughts about recent events that are impacting the career paths of students and workers. They can be answered privately or in group discussions.
   a. How have your past, current, and future *career* choices influenced your life?

    b. How have careers influenced your family's life?

    c. What family, social, or historical events in your lifetime have affected the careers of people in your life?

    d. How important do you think career development is for young people? Middle aged? Older adults?

    e. What are the developmental, psychological, and educational needs of young, middle aged, and older people that are related to their future/current careers?

    f. What are recent events that are changing the career landscape for you?

2. Use the above questions and the following ones to begin writing a paper examining your personal career development. What major historical events affected your career or the careers of members of your family (history may be within your family or have impacted society at large)? For example, after the Sputnik was launched and NDEA loans became available, the first author was able to use the federal funding to finance college. Also, the author was encouraged to gain an education and a career because her mother told stories about the freedom and enjoyment of working outside of the home during World War II.

3. What current societal events are affecting your career and the careers of your family and friends? After reading each chapter in the text, continue your writing by applying the concepts to your own career development. Expanding your own sense of your career and all the factors affecting your life experiences will help you expand those considerations affecting students and clients.

4. Begin thinking about career education programs that would meet professional standards (beginning in Chapter 2). As you read about theoretical concepts and research, take notes about factors that would be important to consider in a program you might develop. Try to adjust your program after each chapter. Date this work and look back to see how your program has changed as you learned more about the career development field.

REFERENCES

Alger, Horatio. Retrieved from http:www.horatioalger.com on September 5, 2004.

Barnett, R. C., & Hyde, J. S. (2001). Women, men, work and family: An expansionist theory. *American Psychologist, 56*(10), 781–796.

Berger, P. (1990). *The human shape of work.* New York: Macmillan.

Blustein, D. L. (2003). When the trees obscure the forest—Modern and postmodern approaches to the study of work and relationships: Comment on Tokar et al. (2003). *Journal of Counseling Psychology, 50*(1), 20–23.

Brenner, M. H., & Mooney, A. (1983). Unemployment and health in the context of economic change. *Social Science & Medicine, 17*(16), 1125–1138.

Brenner, M. H., & Swank, R. T. (1986). Homicide and economic change: recent analyses of the joint committee report of 1984. *Journal of Quantitative Criminology, 2*(1), 81–103.

Calia, V. F. (1966). Vocational guidance: After the fall. *Personnel and Guidance Journal, 45,* 320–327.

Carlson, M. B. (1988). *Meaning-making: Therapeutic processes in adult development.* New York: Norton.

Coates, E. R., Sr., a. Thomas Jefferson on Politics & Government: Quotations from the Writings of Thomas Jefferson. 1st Inaugural, 1801. ME 3:322. Retrieved from http://etext.Virginia.edu/jefferson/quotations on September 10, 2004.

Coates, E. R., Sr., b. Thomas Jefferson on Politics & Government: Quotations from the Writings of Thomas Jefferson. Letter to James Madison, 1787. Papers 12:442. Retrieved from

http://etext.Virginia.edu/jefferson/quotations on September 10, 2004.

Coates, E. R., Sr., c. Thomas Jefferson on Politics & Government: Quotations from the Writings of Thomas Jefferson. Circular to Consuls, 1792. ME 8:352. Retrieved from http://etext.Virginia.edu/jefferson/quotations on September 10, 2004.

Conger, R. D., Elder, G. H., Lorenz, R. O., Conger, K. J., Simons, R. L., Whitbeck, et al. (1990). Linking economic hardship to marital quality and instability. *Journal of Marriage and the Family, 52,* 643–656.

Crites, J. O. (1981). *Career counseling: Models, methods, and materials.* New York: McGraw-Hill.

Dent, H. (1995). *Job shock.* New York: St. Martin's Press.

Feller, R. (1996). Redefining 'career' during the work revolution. In R. Feller & G. Walz (Eds.), *Career transitions in turbulent times: Exploring work, learning, and careers* (pp. 143–161). Greensboro, NC: ERIC Counseling and Student Services Clearinghouse.

Figler, H., & Bolles, R. N. (1999). *The career counselor's handbook.* Berkeley, CA: Ten Speed Press.

Gergen, K. J. (1991a). The saturated family. *Family therapy networks, 15*(5), 27–35.

Gergen, K. J. (1991b). *The saturated self: Dilemmas of identity in contemporary life.* New York: Basic Books.

Gysbers, N. C., & Associates. (1984). *Designing careers.* San Francisco: Jossey-Bass.

Hagquist, C. E. I. (1998). Economic stress and perceived health among adolescents in Sweden. *Journal of Adolescent Health, 22,* 250–257.

Hunt, M. (1993). *The story of psychology.* New York: Anchor Books.

Klebanov, P. K., Brooks-Gunn, J., & Duncan, G. J. (1994). Does neighborhood and family poverty affect mothers' parenting, mental health, and social support? *Journal of Marriage and the Family*, 56, 441–455.

Lyon, R. (1965). Beyond the conventional career: Some speculations. *Journal of Counseling Psychology, 12*, 153–158.

McDaniels, C., & Gysbers, N. C. (1992). *Counseling for career development.* (1992). San Francisco, CA: Jossey-Bass.

Parsons, R. (1909). *Choosing a vocation.* Boston: Houghton Mifflin.

Peterson, N., & Gonzalez, R. C. (2000). *The role of work in people's lives.* Pacific Grove, CA: Brooks/Cole.

Rogers, C. R. (1961). *On becoming a person.* Boston: Houghton Mifflin.

Rogers, C. R. (1965). *Client-centered therapy.* Boston: Houghton Mifflin.

Savickas, M. L. (1989). Annual review: Practice and research in career counseling and development, 1988. *Career Development Quarterly*, 45, 54–62.

Savickas, M. L. (1993). Career counseling in the post-modern era. *Journal of Cognitive Psychotherapy: An International Quarterly, 7,* 205–215.

Savickas, M. L., and Lent, R. W. (1994). *Convergence in career development theories.* Palo Alto, CA: Consulting Psychologist Press.

Spring, J. H. (1973). *Education and the rise of the corporate state.* Boston: Beacon Press.

Super, D. E. (1957). *The psychology of careers.* New York: Harper & Row.

Takeuchi, D. T., Williams, D. R., & S Adair, R. K. (1991). Economic stress in the family and children's emotional and behavioral problems. *Journal of Marriage and Family Therapy* 53(4), 1031–1041.

Theodossiou, I. (1998). The effect of low-pay and unemployment on psychological well-being: a logistic regression approach. *Journal of Health Economics, 17*, 85–104.

Vinokur, A. D., Price, R. H., & Caplan, R. D. (1996). Hard times and hurtful partners: How financial strain affects depression and relationship satisfaction of unemployed persons and their spouses. *Journal of Health and Social Behavior, 71*, 166–179.

Williamson, E. G. (1939). *How to counsel students.* New York: McGraw-Hill.

Winefield, A. H., Tiggemann, M., & Winefield, H. R. (1991). The psychological impact of unemployment and unsatisfactory employment in young men and women: Longitudinal and cross-sectional data. *British Journal of Psychology, 82*(4), 473–486.

Zinn, H. (1995). *A people's history of the United States: 1492–present.* New York: Harper Perennial.

CHAPTER 2

Career Counseling: Structure and Competencies

We have too many people who live without working, and we have altogether too many people who work without living.

Charles Reynolds Brown

In the historical review in Chapter 1, we looked at ways in which career issues have been viewed across time. It is obvious that external factors such as changes in the economy, education, technological advancements, and government programs have had an impact on career opportunities. At the same time, the source for making career choices is the internal self that is the person. The trait-factor approach (Parsons, 1909; Williamson, 1939) dealt with both internal and external career influences by proposing that job factors be matched with an individual's personality characteristics. The matching method has been maintained by the development of assessment instruments measuring a variety of personality characteristics and by the creation of increasingly sophisticated methods to construct job analyses and occupational categorizing systems. This matching mindset created many structured and directive counseling models to "fit" the client into the occupational system, a mindset that overly simplifies a complex identity process (Lyon, 1965).

In the 1950s, however, career research and theory expanded to include personal influences. Super's (1957) developmental stages and the concept of career identity and Rogers' (1951) client-centered focus made it conceivable that career counselors could focus on the client's internal dynamics, encouraging self-exploration and the discovery of the client's career identity.

Of course, a dilemma is created when using only an individualistic, growth orientation for career concerns. External factors are so primary for career choices that a purely client-centered view does not give enough weight to the realistic matters that impinge on career decisions. Such a social-psychological area has a context that is not quite the same as that of many other personal concerns. It is difficult to integrate internal and external factors. Finding a balance between the internal and external influences requires additional theoretical development and forces counselors to be very adaptive.

Career counseling is the same as counseling for other personal issues in that the counselor attends to the client's presenting concern as well as the related feelings and cognitions. However, the history of the practice of career counseling has confused implementation of the service. Career counseling has been dominated by an overreliance on measurement instruments and by structured interventions, such as step-by-step decision-making models. When counselors allow structured techniques to dominate the counseling interaction, the best outcome becomes a learning experience for the client without tapping into the client's internal process. Such structured sessions may serve some clients appropriately but may not serve other clients well.

Career counseling creates an interaction process between the client and the counselor similar to counseling for other major psychological concerns. A career counselor pays full attention to a holistic view of the client as the client creates a picture of his/her identity. During counseling, career clients gain personal insight, and they integrate such increased self-understanding with career information. A career client may take an assessment instrument that is chosen for the particular client and for a specified purpose. The interpretation of the instrument's results also encourages career identity development. Ultimately, career counseling facilitates self-awareness and the integration of information so the client has a realistic view of options available in the **world of work**. The client explores occupational information and defines how work can bring self-satisfaction and how the client can make contributions to society.

CAREER DEVELOPMENT

One key to providing quality career counseling is the counselor's determination of the client's developmental need. Some clients are not developmentally prepared to take advantage of exploring and developing a complete picture of their career identities. Instead, they are ready to learn the basics involved in making career choices. The role of the career counselor may then resemble that of a teacher tutoring the client in the lessons needed to advance the career development process. Clients may end the individualized sessions with the understanding that their **career identity** process will gradually ripen over time as they continue exploring personal preferences and occupational information.

It takes considerable counseling skills to determine the developmental level of the client and to decide if the client is ready to expand the counseling process toward a full identity search. The readiness and willingness on the part of the client to engage in an identity quest depends partly on the counselor's skill in facilitating such a process. On one side, career counselors and clients examine personal considerations such as values and interests, personality traits, family of origin issues, and personal needs. On the other side, clients examine occupational information describing career activities, training, and personnel interactions. The integration of both sides allows a client to develop a **career identity.**

EMOTIONAL PROCESSING

Career counselors facilitate the client's career identity search by noting the client's emotions and cognitive patterns. As the client hears the counselor's reflections, the client can view his/her own internal process and determine the unique meaning he/she brings to career considerations. Figler (1989) eloquently describes the personal-emotional process.

> Emotions are the genie in the bottle of career development, the winds whipping around inside a client, while s/he wears the polite mask of reasonableness. For career counselors to be fully effective, they must unbottle the emotions that often accompany clients' struggles toward career goals. (p. 1)

The counselor may also introduce structured techniques and assessment instruments as tools for exploring the client's identity needs. The structured interventions become talking points to assist in creating a picture of the client's identity. The career counselor may also interpret client behavior by drawing ideas from career theory, personality theory, counseling theory, and developmental theory. As the counseling interaction continues, the client's picture of self becomes clearer, and priorities for career choices are determined.

It is this art of facilitating identity exploration along with the integration of occupational information that distinguishes career counseling from counseling for other client concerns. Providing information and teaching basic concepts are components of many counseling issues. With career concerns, the educational approach can easily dominate the counselor-client interaction. The vision of this book is to describe career counseling and to demonstrate approaches and techniques that expand the process to one of facilitating identity development.

To summarize, career counseling fosters the integration of the whole person into the career development process. This includes personal experiences, family and work history, as well as private and professional values, interests, and skills. Educational and structured interventions are used, but as with other forms of counseling, such interventions are intended to further the client's internal exploration by exposing the meanings and priorities the client brings to the issues.

BLOCKS TO CAREER COUNSELING

Career counselors usually take only one career course emphasizing theory and test interpretation, and career courses typically ignore the development of the counseling skills needed to facilitate the process of career identity exploration. Clients often come to career counseling with the expectation that an expert will administer some test that tells the client "the answer" as to what occupation is "the right one." The client's expectation for "test and tell" and the limits of the counselor's training set the stage for the client and the career counselor to depend on a limited, structured approach.

Counselors are taught the concept that, "Career counseling is the same as other forms of counseling." But how such counseling is implemented is not always fully explicated to trainees. Counselors may not assume the need to spend time exploring the client's description of self because counselors may, in fact, see career counseling as distinct from other types of counseling. Career counseling may be too rigidly associated with structured activities that match client characteristics with occupations.

Another major block to effective career counseling is failing to differentiate the career counseling process and a structured, teaching interaction. As was noted, sometimes the appropriate intervention for clients who are not ready to explore career identity is to teach some basic concepts and to encourage them to spend time exploring interests and information. However, the client's anxiety promotes a need for "the answer" and may prompt the counselor to inappropriately follow the client's lead. Trying to make the client feel more comfortable, the counselor can move too quickly to assign a test, such as an interest inventory, colluding with the client to use a quick solution. The counselor has not had time to know the client as a unique individual. What is even more critical is that the client has not been given the space to bring into being a picture of self for use as career choices present themselves. As with other counseling concerns, clients need to come to their own psychological insights before they can integrate what they have discovered or recognized.

Once counselors assign an instrument, they can again move too quickly by fully interpreting the instrument in only one counseling session. Without having identified the client's unique needs, the test becomes the focus of the counseling process rather than a tool for self-examination. Clients expect the test to "tell them what to do," and the counselor's test interpretation, however skillfully expressed, meets clients' simplistic expectations. Competent career counseling avoids this trap and facilitates self-exploration to the degree that the client is able to participate in interpreting career inventories.

Up to this point, the discussion of career-counseling barriers has been about clients who are developmentally unprepared to participate in identity exploration. Career counseling does not develop into an identity search for other reasons as well. Progress building career self-concepts can be impeded by personal issues that range from typical concerns to severe mental health diagnoses. For some clients, psychological patterns block the resolution of career concerns. A common psychological barrier is low self-esteem; another common area can be family patterns impeding career growth. When a counselor identifies a client's personal blocks, the counselor can explain to the client that progress in the career area may not be forthcoming until the psychological pattern is changed. Crites (1981) calls for "renegotiating the contract." Because the client came with an expectation that career would be the focus of counseling, an implicit contract is assumed. As the counselor redirects the emphasis of the counseling, the change to emphasizing personal problems is discussed with the client. Examples of interweaving psychological and career issues will be described in later chapters.

Other clients, such as those with diagnoses of mental illness, present more serious psychological impediments. Brown and Brooks (1996) recommend that if the career counselor is not trained to deal with the psychological diagnosis, a referral should be made to an appropriate therapist.

Another block to career counseling is the confusion surrounding what career counseling is and how it is distinguished from other career services. Many professional and nonprofessional services similar to and overlapping with career counseling exist. Educational advisors help students choose courses and may discuss how the courses are related to different occupations. Placement administrators may perform services that help people find jobs. Teachers may offer information and advice about careers. Personnel officers may give information about jobs and determine the qualifications required for specific positions. Career counseling is not always easily defined as distinct from these services provided by other professionals. What is unique about the services offered by career counseling is that counselors can facilitate a psychological identity process when it is appropriate for the client.

Career counselors need training in the therapeutic skills used in all counseling. They must have the skills to determine what career intervention is appropriate for individual clients. They need to know when to detour from career considerations and deal with other related psychological issues. Career counselors are aware of their counseling competencies and when to refer clients to other professionals. And finally, career counselors need to be able to describe the professional help they offer as distinguished from other career services.

COMPETENCY REQUIREMENTS FOR CAREER COUNSELORS

The following list has been taken from the NCDA (1997) description found in Appendix A.

Basic Counseling Skills and Therapeutic Stance

When clients seek the services of a counselor, basic listening and responding skills promote the development of a relationship. During the early sessions, clients are encouraged to fully explain their concerns as a counselor adds little to the content of the dyadic exchange. For example, a client describes a conflict between her and her parents and the counselor paraphrases or clarifies what the client has said, adding only some emotional reflections to let the client know she has been heard and understood. The client may ask the counselor what to do or what the answer would be for such a dilemma. However, the counselor would avoid giving a solution and encourage the client to explore her own thoughts and feelings as to what to do. Likewise, when clients seek help with career considerations, counselors use basic counseling skills to build a relationship with the client and to encourage the client to examine her own thoughts and feelings.

The most basic competency requirement for career counselors is to attend to the client's description of presenting concerns. Counselors manage the communication in a way that says to the client, "This is your personal need that we can examine together so you can determine for yourself what you want to do." Admittedly, career clients often come with strong expectations that a career counselor has answers and will quickly solve questions such as what career would be best for the client. However, competent career counselors can deal with client expectations that place the counselor in the role of an expert rather than the position of a facilitating counselor. Career counselors help clients understand that career development requires the self-exploration of personal factors such as values, interests, and aptitudes. They also have the patience to encourage the client in describing her thoughts and feelings, to clarify client statements, and to reflect feelings. It is through self-exploration that a client grows into an awareness of self and to a place where career choices can be made. It is the same process as when a counselor encourages a client to determine her own choices for dealing with a family conflict or another psychological concern.

Counseling Theory

Professional career counselors need training in concepts from the various schools of psychological theory. Theoretical orientations offer explanations of human personality and behavior that are also applicable to career issues. For example, psychodynamic concepts of defense mechanisms could give insights into how particular job activities or interpersonal interactions at work affect a client (Strupp & Binder, 1984). Adlerian concepts regarding the sibling array can explain why an adult, who was a middle child, chooses one career when his brother, the oldest child, chose another (Carlson & Slavik, 1997). Maslow's (1962) hierarchy of human needs describes what conditions prompt the striving for mastery in career, whereas Rogerian theory elucidates the nature of client-centered counseling (Rogers, 1961). Existential theories can be helpful when a client is searching for meaning in his life and work (Schneider & May, 1995). Cognitive-behaviorists offer techniques to help clients change negative thinking and dysfunctional behavior that block career development or lead to poor performance on the job (Meichenbaum, 1977).

Theoretical Models for Career Development

Career development theorists focus their thinking on the nature of developing career maturity, choosing occupations, acquiring competency in a field, and changing fields. Super (1957) offers a theory describing career development across the life-span. Holland (1997) describes a person-environment fit between the characteristics of occupations and the people who are found in various categories of occupations. Krumboltz (1979) adapts the social learning theory to career behavior. Tiedeman (1961) and his wife (Tiedeman & Miller-Tiedeman, 1984), and Gelatt (1989) have investigated the characteristics of career decision making.

Professional career counselors draw on these and other ideas and use the concepts when applicable in the career counseling session. Having a framework for understanding clients' issues and development makes counseling an in-depth activity informed by an understanding of human nature.

Theory and empirical studies also add to career counselors' ability to adapt to the individual styles of clients and to craft interventions that recognize the differing values of diverse populations. For example, crosscultural differences may affect clients' decisions and work habits, and gender differences affect the stereotypes people hold of different occupations (Astin, 1984; Brown, 1995; Gottfredson, 1996; Hackett & Betz, 1981; Lent, Brown, & Hackett, 1995).

Utilizing Career Assessment Methods and Instruments

Competent career counselors have the skill to effectively assess through a variety of methods the client's developmental interests, values, abilities, and personality patterns. To use the same techniques for every client in a routine way does not encourage adapting to unique identities. Counseling cannot be reduced to a formula of procedures assuming one-size-fits-all.

Assessment begins with the first counseling session as the counselor interviews the client to determine the client's strengths and weaknesses. Numerous personality and interest inventories are available. Though the tests have similar qualities, they also have different attributes and purposes, and are developed with different norming groups. Competent counselors determine which instrument would best meet the particular goals of each client. Other assessment methods can be used for a specific purpose, such as determining motivating skills. Card sorts can be used to assess interests, values, or other characteristics, in addition to determining how the client sets priorities. Counselors also assess clients' backgrounds, examining educational achievements or limitations, and work experience. Assessing family system themes may be useful in understanding the career influences of parental models or from the sibling array. Decision-making skills can be determined through interviews and/or by using one of many decision scales. Finally, career counselors may need to be familiar with personnel evaluation methods to assist clients with worker adjustment needs.

Assessment offers the counselor and the client a picture of the client and the client's fit in the world of work. Certainly, counselors need to be professionally skilled in choosing the right assessment techniques and interpreting the results. However, career counselors also integrate the assessment within the ongoing process of counseling. Interest inventories are not simply interpreted but are used to help the client explore possible occupations. Because any assessment method may generate a number of possible occupations for the client, the client will not find the answer or the perfect choice. It is in the process of sorting out possible choices that the client grows in awareness of self and of potential occupations. For some clients, assessment tools will not generate choices the client wants to consider. In these circumstances, the counselor and client need to examine the client's approach and determine what is blocking the exploration. In other words, assessment is not an end in and of itself. Though laypeople may come to counseling believing there is a test that can tell them what to do, professional counselors know the fallacy of trusting assessment tools over and above the client's own internal evaluation.

Information Resources

There is a current common phrase that states we live in an age of information. The proliferation of career information follows the prevailing pattern of an increasing quantity of material available for review by clients. However, the presence of an enormous amount of information also increases the pressure to locate what is truly needed and to integrate the information with the client's needs. An extremely useful service is to help clients sort out the benefits and requirements for numerous occupations as they begin to determine what the information means to them. Counselors can also support clients using a number of computer-assisted programs and structured self-help books.

Career counselors are often responsible for organizing libraries containing sets of books written for clients with different reading abilities. National and state government offices provide labor market information that may require interpretation for the lay public. Professional associations have brochures and pamphlets describing occupations. With appropriate preparation, often facilitated by counselors, clients can gain useful knowledge by speaking directly with workers for informational interviews. Professional counselors know what information might be beneficial to clients at different stages of career development and can assist clients in merging self-knowledge with descriptive material.

SUMMARY

Career counseling includes forming a supportive relationship where the client's concerns predominate. The counselor follows the client's internal process and facilitates the client's discovery and insight into personal issues related to career pursuits. Career counselors use techniques similar to interventions used in counseling for other client concerns, including reflections and open-ended questions. Career counseling takes into account the client's developmental level and the client's readiness for counseling and self-examination. Career counseling assessment can include determining the client's motivation for change, cognitive clarity, and personality characteristics such as interests, style, and values, as well as work adjustment factors. Integrating information is another career counseling function. Sometimes, but not always, career counseling facilitates complex decision making for major life career choices. Ultimately, the goal of career counseling is to foster self-awareness, personality integration, and a realistic picture of occupational opportunities and demands.

STUDY OUTLINE: KEY TERMS AND CONCEPTS

I. **Career Counseling** (A process of exploring career-related issues that reveals the internal psychological dynamics involved with the whole of an individual's identity)
   A. Creates a therapeutic relationship
   B. Draws from career, personality, counseling, and developmental theory
   C. Helps the client integrate personal values, interests, and skills with occupational requirements
   D. Helps the client create a picture of **career identity** (The person's self-concept, or the way a person thinks about himself as related to career across the life-span. Termed "occupational identity" by Super (1957).
   E. Integration of information
      1. Information about the **world of work** (The job market, employment trends, labor market, occupations available in the current economy [Seligman, 1994])
      2. Information about occupations (Demand characteristics of occupations such as work activities, job requirements, salary, evaluation standards, etc.)

II. Career Counseling Competency Requirements
   A. Counseling skills
      1. Basic listening and responding
      2. Relationship building
      3. Clarification of feelings and thoughts
      4. Conceptualizations that expand the presenting concern
      5. Facilitating client's career identity search
   B. Using psychological and career theory
      1. Personality, counseling, and developmental theory
      2. Career theory
      3. Multicultural theory
      4. Able to integrate and use different aspects of theories to match the client's need and promote growth
   C. Career assessment
      1. Skill of obtaining client information from the clinical interview
      2. Knowledge of a variety of career interest inventories
      3. Capacity to use personality instruments for career interpretations
      4. Ability to determine the best assessment device to a particular client

III. Blocks to Career Counseling
  A. Not differentiating between career education and career counseling
    1. Simplistic client expectations and counselor interventions collude
      a. Tests are assigned and interpreted too quickly.
      b. Building of relationship is ignored.
      c. Full understanding of client problem is not pursued.
    2. Counselors' inability to distinguish counseling from career education services offered by other professionals (advisors, placement officers, etc.)
  B. Typical psychological factors
    1. Low self-esteem
    2. Family pressure
  C. Atypical client factors
    1. Mental illness
    2. Physical impairment

EXERCISES

1. In dyads, role-play a client seeing a counselor. The client presents with a career concern such as "I need to choose a college major" or "I need to find a better job." The counselor can only reflect content or feelings and can use no other interventions. Proceed for 5–10 minutes. As a counselor, how does it feel to use only reflections? Does using reflections feel different when a client presents with concerns other than career topics? What other kind of interventions would you naturally want to use? As a client, how does it feel to have the counselor use only reflections? How did you react to the counselor using only reflections? What do you want to share with the counselor with this kind of interaction?

2. Again in dyads, role-play a client seeing a counselor, switching the roles if you so choose. This time the counselor may also use open-ended questions and follow up with reflections or requests for further information. Try not to use close-ended questions at all or very few if absolutely necessary. Do not use too many questions in a sequence and get into a pattern of question–answer but instead use reflections in between. As a counselor, how does this type of interaction feel? Is this type of interaction similar to interactions with clients presenting concerns other than career issues? As a client, how does this interaction feel? Would you want any other types of interactions with the counselor?

REFERENCES

Astin, H. S. (1984). The meaning of work in women's lives: A sociopsychological perspective. *Counseling Psychologist, 12,* 117–126.

Brown, D. (1995). A values-based approach to facilitating career transitions. *Career Development Quarterly, 44,* 3–11.

Brown, D., & Brooks, L. (1996). *Career choice and development.* San Francisco: Jossey-Bass.

Carlson, J., & Slavik, S. (1997). *Techniques in Adlerian psychology.* Washington, DC: Accelerated Development.

Crites, J. O. (1981). *Career counseling: Models, methods and materials.* New York: McGraw-Hill.

Figler, H. (1989). The emotional dimension of career counseling. *Career Waves, 2*(2), 1–11.

Gelatt, H. B. (1989). Positive Uncertainty: A new decision-making framework for Counseling. *Journal of Counseling Psychology, 36*(2), 252–256.

Gottfredson, L. S. (1996). Circumscription and compromise: A developmental theory of occupational aspirations (Monograph). *Journal of Counseling Psychologist, 28,* 545–579.

Hackett, B., & Betz, N. E. (1981). A self-efficacy approach to the career development of women. *Journal of Vocational Behavior, 24,* 326–339.

Holland, J. L. (1997). *Making vocational choices.* Odessa, FL: Psychological Assessment Resources.

Krumboltz, J. D. (1979). A social learning theory of career choice. In A. M. Mitchell, G. B. Jones, & J. D. Krumboltz (Eds.), *Social learning theory and career decision making* (pp. 19–49). Cranston, RI: Carroll Press.

Lent, R. W., Brown, S. D., & Hackett, G. (1995). Toward a unifying social cognitive theory of career and academic interest, choice and performance. *Journal of Vocational Behavior, 45,* 79–122.

Lyon, R. (1965). Beyond the conventional career: Some speculations. *Journal of Counseling Psychology, 12,* 153–158.

Maslow, A. H. (1962). *Toward a psychology of being.* Princeton, NJ: Van Nostrand.

Meichenbaum, D. M. (1977). *Cognitive-behavior modification: An integrative approach.* New York: Plenum Press.

Miller-Tiedeman, A., & Tiedeman, D. V. (1984). Career decision making: An individual perspective. In D. Brown & L. Brooks, (Eds.) *Career choice and development* (2nd ed., pp.308–337). San Francisco: Jossey-Bass.

National Career Development Association (1997). *Career counseling competencies.* Retrieved May, 23, 2003 from http://www.ncda.org/pdf/counselingcompetencies.pdf.

Parsons, F. (1909). *Choosing a vocation.* Boston: Houghton Mifflin.

Rogers, C. R. (1951). *Client-centered therapy.* Boston: Houghton Mifflin.

Rogers, C. R. (1961) *On becoming a person.* Boston: Houghton Mifflin.

Schneider, K. J., & May, R. (1995). *The psychology of existence: An integrative, clinical perspective.* New York: McGraw-Hill.

Seligman, L. (1994) *Developmental career counseling and assessment.* Thousand Oaks, CA: Sage.

Strupp, H. H., & Binder, J. L. (1984). *Psychotherapy in a new key: A guide to time-limited dynamic psychotherapy.* New York: Basic Books.

Super, D. (1957). *The psychology of careers.* New York: Harper & Row.

Tiedeman, D. V. (1961). Decision and vocational development: A paradigm and its implications. *Personnel and Guidance Journal, 40,* 15–20.

Williamson, E. G. (1939). *Vocational counseling.* New York: McGraw-Hill.

PART II

Career Counseling Theory and the Global Economy

CHAPTER 3

The Career Diamond:
A Teaching Tool

I look on that man as happy, who, when there is question of success,
looks into his work for a reply.

Ralph Waldo Emerson

The use of pictorial models to envision concepts is common in the career field. As we shall see later in the text, there are models for showing categories of occupations with similar characteristics (e.g., Holland's hexagon; DISCOVER'S world of work map) (Holland, 1997). Super illustrates life roles with a rainbow, career development with a ladder, and personal and social determinants for career identity with an arch (Super, Savickas, & Super, 1996). Lent, Brown, and Hackett (1994) use a model to show the development of career interests over time. Genograms are also used to explore intergenerational careers in families.

We have found that clients and students respond well to pictorial models illustrating psychological constructs. The Career Diamond is an easily understood image that shows the basic movement of the career development process. In this book, the diamond figure will also be used to describe different stages of career counseling in order to explain basic concepts of career theory and to demonstrate the use of career instruments for different stages of career growth. Figures 3.1–3.7 are each partial depictions describing parts of the complete representation of the Career Diamond, which is shown in full as Figure 3.8.

UNDERSTANDING THE CAREER DIAMOND

Figure 3.1 is a simplified version of the Career Diamond that shows the two basic factors that must come together when people deal with career issues. One factor is the self that represents the career identity of the human being. The dimension of the self is placed along the top lines of the diamond and indicates the primary task of realizing aspects of one's self as related to career development. For example, finding a satisfying career requires an

Figure 3.1   A represents an awareness of the need to make a career decision. The Career Diamond process begins with awareness of Self and of the World of Work expanding to create a Vision for the Self in the World of Work. The second half of the Career Diamond shows a contracting movement while the Self integrates personal priorities with the requirements of the World of Work until the two sides come together at point D, where a current decision is made.

understanding of one's personality. Clients need to know if they are extroverted—enjoying interactions with others at work—or introverted—becoming tired when interacting with others too often. A person who dislikes a competitive atmosphere and values working with others as a team may want to avoid a sales position in which each employee is rewarded for doing better than anyone else. Knowing one's interests and values can serve as important indicators for finding work expressive of one's career self-concept. The self can also find outlets for abilities through work and can use career performance for achievement motivation.

The second factor for all careers is the world of work, which is placed along the bottom lines of the diamond. The world of work includes all the external factors that must be taken into account when making career decisions; it is the context for career choices and behaviors. External factors might be the requirements and specifications of occupations, economic realities, new career opportunities, or any other demand characteristic of a career decision. The realistic facts provide the context within which careers operate.

External factors are the practical considerations. They include factors such as the salary paid for a job. Each factor may have weight in the making of career decisions, but such facts must also be contingent upon other situational determinants. For example, a low-salaried position that opens doors to opportunities for making more money in the future would be considered differently than a low-paying job that was described as a permanent dead end.

Often, career decisions are justified as rational conclusions where the external factors give the decider no other choice. Although some career decisions may seem to be dictated by realistic facts, the self determines the weight given to all the factors in making choices. The self is placed at the top of the diamond to indicate the primacy of the person making career decisions. External factors must be thoroughly considered, but only the careerist can determine how to deal with the realities presented.

Letters are placed at two points of the diamond, with A on the left point and D on the right point. A is the starting point for a particular phase of career development and signifies Awareness—when a person recognizes the need to start making a career decision. D is placed on the end of the diamond designating the Decision made at the final point of this particular phase of career development.

Throughout the process of career development or decision making, the person determines the movement and so the self is placed on top of the model. However, external factors related to the world of work are critically important and must be taken into account.

The Exploring Phase

The first part of the Career Diamond starting at point A and moving toward the middle, or peak, is called the Exploring Phase (Figure 3.2). In order to move away from the starting point, a person has to increase self-awareness and must expand knowledge of external factors that will impact the decision. The first half of the diamond opens up in an expansive way and depicts an exploration process.

Expanding Self-Awareness

Self-awareness for a career requires the identity development that defines the self as a worker or careerist. The most common personal areas for career exploration are abilities, interests, and values. However, career identity encompasses the whole of a person, including spirituality, early family experiences,

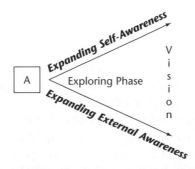

Figure 3.2   The first half of the Career Diamond represents the Exploring Phase. The Self expands an awareness of career identity issues while also expanding awareness of the external World of Work. A Vision of the Self becomes a picture of a careerist meeting external demands. Such an expansive process is necessary before career decision making is possible.

role models, personality, work experiences, and social influences. Self-esteem is always a primary issue for career counseling because making quality life choices can rarely work well when a person is coming from a negative self-concept or low self-esteem. Until a person is grounded in a solid sense of self and her relationship to the world, knowing how she wants to participate in the world of work is unclear.

An example may illustrate how values impact career choices. Person A may value a good paying job, but does not care for the taste of alcohol. Person A can work as a bartender without any problems. Person B may like the taste of alcohol and a good paying job, but views alcohol as sinful. Person B working as a bartender may create internal turmoil because she would be participating in the sins of the customers. To conclude, some preferences (e.g., material goods, prestige) may not interfere with career choices whereas strongly held values or spiritual morals might.

Expanding External Awareness

Clients need information regarding external factors in order to begin to integrate their career identity with the realities of the world of work. Broad-based correspondence between the characteristics of an occupation and the career self-concept is the simplest starting point in exploring the vast array of opportunities available. In a modern economy, occupations are not easily visible in daily life, and exploring often requires searching through a variety of informational sources. With regular changes in the global economy, work roles may often change. Even after one enters into a career, the careerist may be required to be aware of and continually reintegrate external factors into a renewed vision of his career identity.

The Peak of the Diamond

As the client experiences the process of self-exploration and a search for relevant external factors, the client can begin to envision the future. Personal characteristics and needs begin to come together into a vision of "Who I want to be," and a career identity is formed. External requirements take form as an image of the working environment or the context where the career self-concept can develop, contribute, and achieve. With a vision of self along with a realistic picture of work, the client is prepared to begin sorting out the factors for the integration of self into the external world. This process of integration requires a narrowing of career options, setting priorities, and moving toward deciding. Changes in self may be required, but with a motivating vision, such change is seen as, "What I need to do to move toward what I want." The vision creates motivation to continue efforts toward making difficult choices and preparing to take the actions a decision will require.

The Deciding Phase

The second half of the diamond is called the Deciding Phase (Figure 3.3). After expanding knowledge of self and realistic considerations in the exploring phase, a person starts to focus on a few occupations or new work roles and determines what choices will best meet personal needs. The movement for the deciding phase has a narrowing or contracting feel, so the diamond narrows to a point where a decision is made at D.

Applying Career Self-Concept

By the time a person enters the deciding phase, she is truly ready to begin a more sophisticated, dynamic process of applying career identity to realistic requirements of occupations. Envisioning the environment for an occupation and actually seeing one's self in the role is now possible. Clients are advised to rate the importance of the different factors for the self. Specific occupational tasks may tap into a person's temperament and preferences whereas other occupational activities may not be favorites. The goal is to find enough positive outlets in an occupation to maintain motivation and satisfaction.

While integrating personal priorities and external demands, there may be recognition that an occupation requires changes in some aspects of the self. Other difficult choices may also be factored in, accepting some conditions that arc less than personally ideal in order to gain some other positive aspects, which are a priority for the person. For some, high income may be ranked high; for others, the working environment reflecting a personal value system is more critical than salary (e.g., youth minister). After rank-ordering needs and desires for the self, the client determines which ones are "have to haves" and/or what others are "wishes." Finding

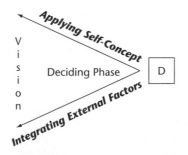

Figure 3.3   The second half of the Career Diamond shows the Vision of the careerist coming to point D, deciding. To come together, the Career Self-Concept, or career identity, is applied by integrating personal priorities to demands of the external requirements of the World of Work.

the external opportunity that provides the most factors closest to personal requirements moves the self to a decision.

New experiences (e.g., birth of a child, dying parent) may result in new "have to haves" and new "wishes" and may create some "don't cares." When new self-awareness occurs, clients may realize it is time to start again at the beginning of a new diamond in their career development.

Integrating External Factors

Integrating external factors means gaining a fully realistic picture of job rewards and demands. The deciding phase entails in-depth understanding of a specific work environment, gaining commitment to a field, and seeing the occupation as making an important contribution to self and society. Several occupations might well be weighed in determining which one meets the most needs of the self at this particular time.

After a choice is made to work in an occupation and the diamond closes, experience will bring a greater awareness of what the job entails and what doing this job is like for the client. A current job prepares an individual for the next job. Each diamond process of expanding and deciding determines choices for a period of time, not a lifetime, and most careers will entail many choices over the years.

A Career Decision-Making No-No

The most important concept depicted by the Career Diamond is that a person cannot move from point A to point D without experiencing the process of expanding in the exploring phase and contracting in the deciding phase. A client who comes for career services seeking "an answer" is saying, "I'm at the starting point in considering my career development or decision making. Now, tell me what to do." The Career Diamond illustrates that moving directly from A to D is NOT possible (Figure 3.4). An intervening process of exploring and prioritizing is necessary.

If a client pursues a straight-line move from A to D, truncating the process without fully exploring and integrating personal and external fac-

Figure 3.4   The straight arrow moves between A, awareness, and D, deciding, without the expanding/contracting process of the Career Diamond. Such a leap does not work. The expanding of the Exploring Phase and the contracting of the Deciding Phase is needed to inform the integration of the Self and the World of Work.

Figure 3.5   As one Career Diamond closes a decision-making process, another Career Diamond opens for another phase of career exploration, until a new vision creates a need for another decision to be made, and the process begins again. The Career Diamond process repeats itself numerous times over the course of a lifetime (e.g. High School; College; First Job, Second Job ...; Mid-Career; Another Career; Retirement; Part-Time Job after Retirement; ...).

tors, future dissatisfaction is likely to occur. The short-term release of anxiety gained by making a premature decision is replaced with a long-term feeling of being trapped and/or mismatched.

Career Development Includes Multiple Diamonds

Although a single diamond illustrates the movement for determining a decision at one particular point in the client's life, the career development process is not finished when one choice is made. Another expanding and integrating process will occur when the client is ready or needs to make a new decision at a different point in life. As shown in Figure 3.5, a chain of diamonds might better represent the repetition of decisions across a lifetime.

The simple diagram of the Career Diamond is a useful picture illustrating the steps a client goes through from the point of approaching a career decision to the point of making a decision. The career counseling process matches these steps if the client is ready to proceed through all the stages. Career education programs also stimulate the developmental process by increasing students' self-awareness and knowledge of the world of work. Both students and career counselors benefit from a practical guide to what can be expected in career services.

USING THE CAREER DIAMOND WITH CLIENTS

Showing a simple, plain diagram of the Career Diamond to a client is a way of making the abstract ideas of the career development process concrete. The shape of the diamond can be described to help the client understand the expanding and contracting movement of career decision making. The client needs to increase his knowledge of occupations while also increasing self-awareness and determining related occupations. With the diamond shape as an image, the client can concretely see the need for exploring before deciding.

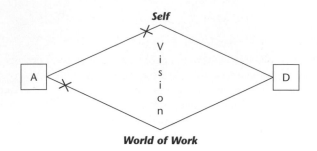

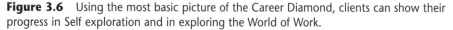

Figure 3.6   Using the most basic picture of the Career Diamond, clients can show their progress in Self exploration and in exploring the World of Work.

Counselors ask the client to place an X on the bottom of the diagram to show how much occupational information the client has. The client is then asked to rate the completeness of her identity awareness by placing an X on the top of the diamond picture. One client may say she thinks she has a pretty good picture of herself and places an X near the top crest of the diamond shape. She may recognize, however, she knows very little about occupations and places herself close to A on the bottom half of the diagram (see Figure 3.6 for an example). Hence, it is easily shown that the client may need to spend time researching occupational information before beginning a decision mode.

Another client may say he knows a great deal about a variety of occupations, naming several and citing information about the activities of several jobs. However, he may recognize that he does not have much insight regarding his career self-concept and he needs to expand his self-knowledge. The latter client could place an X near the peak of the bottom line of the diamond, but close to A on the top half of the diagram. The picture of the diamond may help this client better understand that he needs to spend time determining his career identity. Just hearing the counselor say the same words may not make as clear an impression.

The career counselor can deal with the typical client expectation of seeking "an answer" with the Career Diamond depiction of how progress is made in moving toward career choices. The process shown by the diamond picture demonstrates that time and effort is required for the client to examine information and self. The diamond picture could be reexamined from time to time to reveal client progress (e.g., placing a new X on the diamond). A picture showing the need to advance along the lines of the diagram shows the client that proceeding in the process is appropriate and decisions are not usually made quickly in one or two counseling sessions. Some clients may be better able to accept that they are not yet ready to make a decision and that they can return to counseling when ready to continue considering their choices.

The diamond demystifies the process that is often described through intangible abstractions. It gives the client permission to follow a natural developmental pace. Readiness to make a decision becomes more easily understood when the simple picture becomes a figure where the client can place herself. The client's anxiety can be reduced when the diamond picture is presented as the *usual* process for everyone and the client is not behind others, failing, or lacking in any way. Although the diamond can be seen as normalizing the developmental time frame, it also helps to define clear activities that encourage exploration and movement for career development. In short, the diamond illustrates the need to explore first. The diamond also identifies both self-exploration and awareness of external factors as necessary and defines vocational decisions as integrating both career information and identity needs.

Using the Career Diamond to Conceptualize Clients' Needs

The career counselor usually forms impressions of the client that are not exactly the same as the client's own view of self. The client may present with strong emotion saying that a decision must be made very soon when the counselor understands that deciding is not immediately mandatory. The counselor may hypothesize privately, without sharing thoughts with the client, that the pressing need expressed by the client is indicative of the client's anxiety. Clients may say they know quite a lot about occupations while the counselor finds some clients' descriptions of occupational activities as limited in realistic detail. The Career Diamond can serve as a tool for determining where the client is in the career development process or how close the client is to actual readiness to explore or decide. Different points on the diagram suggest what the client needs at the moment and what the next step in the developmental process will be.

It is helpful, when considering an approach to use with a client, to frame internal questions that guide the counselor to a decision about the client's place in the process. First, does the client say she wants to start considering career options? Then, the client is at point A. However, another more demanding question important for making progress in career considerations would be, "How ready is the client to engage in some effort to make headway in defining a career self-concept and researching information?" The client's description of pressure from others does not necessarily mean the client is committed to working on the issue. For clients to be ready for career counseling, they usually need to have spent some time thinking about options and to say convincingly that they want to learn more about themselves and occupations that might interest them.

Assuming the client is ready to start career counseling, the counselor can begin to visualize at what point in the exploring phase the client might be.

The counseling question for this determination might be:"How extensive and sophisticated is the client's current knowledge of occupations?" Likewise, "How self-aware does the client seem to be?" "Does the client know the strengths, interests, and values relevant to the occupations in question?" Although the Career Diamond is not a sophisticated measure with refined calibrations, the basic sections do suggest content areas to think about in considering client needs. With general occupational information and a basic sense of personal characteristics, clients can begin to make broad matches between the two dimensions of World of Work and Self. In the middle of the exploring phase, a client can say, "These occupations have characteristics that are like my interests; these careers express this value of mine; these occupations require this ability of mine." Broad matching does not require knowing if any one or several occupations fit holistically with the client's self-concept; instead, matching general characteristics is a way to identify occupations for further investigation.

A career counselor could begin to see a client at the end point of the exploring phase when the client seems able to describe a realistic vision of herself in the future. At the peak of the diamond, clients tend to slow down the exploring process, and realistic factors begin to be the focus of attention. The client is able to articulate costs and benefits for occupations and identify relevant personal preferences for the occupations' primary characteristics. The client could say, in some detail, "These occupations have attributes that I can see as important to who I am as a person."

As a client moves to a capacity for integrating occupational information with characteristics of self with increasing specificity, the client enters the deciding phase. The important question for the career counselor to determine if a client is ready to approach decision making is, "How ready is the client to set priorities and eliminate some choices in order to examine a few occupations in greater depth?" Setting priorities requires the client to picture a self-image in an occupational role. Or, stated in another way, the client can identify self-characteristics, set personal priorities, and apply those criteria to determine if the characteristics of a few occupations can meet personal needs.

It is important to note that at any time during career services, the client and career counselor can decide that the client is not ready to move forward in the process. The value of the Career Diamond is that it visually depicts where the client is and how the client can focus energy to move forward. However, the client does not necessarily need to press forward prematurely toward making a decision. If it makes sense to the client and the career counselor, a decision could be put on hold for a break, for further exploration, for reality testing, for gradual maturing, or for a change in circumstances.

The final point in a single episode of the Career Diamond process is point D. At this time, the career counselor considers the question, "Is the client able to begin to commit to a choice, willing to make the necessary accommodations the choice requires, and able to evaluate the choice for personal satisfaction?" If the client is ready for a realistic commitment, the client is approaching an end to the current growth process. Another growth point could begin later, when the client determines that new considerations indicate reopening the expanding and contracting movement for another decision.

The expanding exploration process on the left side of the diamond and the narrowing decision-making right side depict both the career counselor's choice of interventions and the client's movement in dealing with a career transition. Clients in the exploring phase may benefit from nondirective techniques that increase introspection and from specific directions for developing information-gathering skills. By comparison, in the deciding phase, the client may need encouragement to use both intuitive and analytical skills to determine priorities and to apply personal criteria to career options. The career counselor may return to using reflections as clients show affective reactions to letting go of personal priorities in order to meet external demands. Finally, the counselor might validate a client's budding decisions and reinforce the client's steps toward making choices and acknowledging the hard work and strengths the client has shown.

When the External Dominates

The diagram in Figure 3.7 reverses the Career Diamond and shows the external factors weighing down heavily over the self. The self does not expand to fully explore personal preferences and an individual career identity may not develop. The self is shown as flattened with the external dominating the picture.

There are times when the external dominates a client's career experience, sometimes because the client makes implicit choices, sometimes

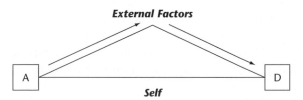

Figure 3.7   The external factors are reversed from the bottom lines to the top of the Career Diamond, dominating the Self. Self expansion is limited and the bottom line is flattened.

because the client's choices are limited by external factors. For example, clients may come from families who require adherence to family tradition or adherence to specific cultural values. The families may be wealthy and/or famous and may have socialized the client to believe that upholding the family name is of more importance than individual preferences. Or, clients may be so committed to finding a career that produces a high income or high status that they cancel out any other expressions of self. In these two examples, clients do have other choices; they are choosing to let the external factors dominate all other personal considerations.

Other situations, however, may realistically limit choices severely. If economic needs are very great, being aware of internal preferences may be considered a waste of time and may be truly impossible due to the press to make enough money to live. Discrimination in employment practices may also realistically limit personal choices. Finally, for some cultures, collective values emphasize the needs of the group over the needs of the individual and the primacy of personal choice is not present. An obvious example of external pressures dominating would be a client who chose a paid apprenticeship program for training as a machinist rather than pursue a college degree in engineering because the low economic status of her family required more immediate relief than academic pursuits would allow.

When clients show such a press of external pressures, the career counselor has to determine whether it is in the best interest of the client to confront the realities of the situation. Most often, following the client's lead will build a picture of how the client views the circumstances, and the counselor can decide how to proceed. An example illustrating external pressures would be the consultation of two parents with one of the authors. Their son had changed his major to philosophy and announced his intention to pursue a Ph.D. The parents were concerned that an academic career would not supply enough income for the son to maintain the high economic status of the family. Consequently, the parents were considering reducing economic support for the son's tuition and living expenses so he could learn what it meant to live with less income. The withdrawal of financial resources for the son was clearly designed to send a message that it was unacceptable to major in a field that did not reproduce an income considered worthy of the family's status. A high income and social prominence can create external expectations for children. In this situation, the external dominates by enforcing the value that a Ph.D. in the wrong area would be an embarrassment.

Describing the Career Diamond

The Career Diamond, shown in its entirety in Figure 3.8, depicts the career development process of beginning awareness, exploring–expanding, creating a vision, integrating, and deciding. Such a process occurs gradually

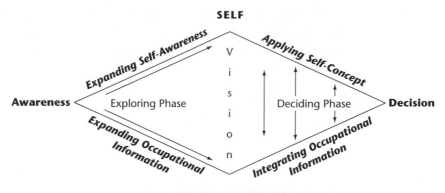

Figure 3.8 The Career Diamond depicts the Exploring Phase where the Self expands personal awareness (A) and awareness of the World of Work coming to a Vision of the Self in the World of Work. In the Deciding Phase, the vision of career identity is refined as the Self's personal priorities are integrated with the external requirements of the World of Work to come to a current decision.

in developmental stages as young people move toward a maturity level at which they can envision their career identity. Once a basic career identity is established, the very same process recurs periodically when it is time for career renewal. The diamond shape also illustrates the career counseling process as counselors facilitate the client's movement through self-development.

The diamond shape illustrates the feel of movement through the processes of identity development. It is a visual attempt to bring a visceral sense of the experience of a career change. Clients feel expansive when exploring. When the feel of contracting or narrowing occurs, clients are pulling things together and experiencing a sense of integration, a sense that "this feels right." The Career Diamond sets a tone for considering career issues holistically as a part of clients' overall sense of self and all of life's experiences.

SUMMARY

The Career Diamond is a visual image that demonstrates the need to expand self-awareness and information regarding relevant external factors before narrowing the field of choices for a decision. Expansive exploration allows identification of many occupations that loosely relate to self-characteristics. The contraction of setting personal priorities and determining the fit of a specific occupation creates a choice that is the current decision for a unique person.

In the exploring phase, the interaction between self and external factors is based on broad matches. The goal of expansion is to provide multiple options; however, exploration also encourages the client to create a vision of the self in the working world. Such a vision provides motivation to move toward a realistic decision. Personal priorities that are in keeping with the newly formed career identity are determined. Changes for the self and the elimination of some options may occur before the integration process is complete.

The converging movement in narrowing choices for a decision entails the integration of both professional and personal awareness in the deciding phase. Occupational information must be sorted out and the necessity for determining the differences among the possibilities begins to become apparent. Ranking the occupations by standards set by the self is needed. Priority is given to positions whose characteristics are in line with the self-concept. Finally, one occupation or career choice is determined to be the best in meeting personal standards. The movement ends for the time being as the process comes to a point of convergence between occupational information and the career self-concept.

STUDY OUTLINE: KEY TERMS AND CONCEPTS

I. Understanding the Career Diamond
  A. Visually depicts the influence of both internal and external factors that impact career movement and decisions
    1. First half involves expanding one's understanding of self and external factors.
    2. Second half involves integrating of knowledge about self and external factors.
    3. A straight line from awareness to decision-making is not recommended. Clients must expand before contracting.
    4. Expanding and contracting occur with every major decision, ranging from pursuing more training to accepting a promotion, to changing companies, to retiring.
  B. The personal or self overrides the external influences and is depicted on the top half of the diamond.
    1. Expanding consists of thinking and learning about the self. May include formalized personality tests, identifying interests, abilities and values, considering family needs, desired income, geographical concerns, etc.
    2. Contracting consists of applying knowledge of the self to different career options and looking for an optimal fit between interests, values, morals, etc.

    C. External factors, which are secondary to the self, are on the bottom half of the diamond.

       1. Expanding consists of learning occupation specifics such as job availability, training requirements, licensure/certification, etc.

       2. Contracting consists of continually narrowing the field of choices based upon external factors and needs of the self. The goal is the overlap of "have to haves" and "wishes."

    D. When the external dominates

       1. Very Rich: family name, status requirements, etc.

       2. Poor: Economic needs so great that gaining money as quickly as possible is critical. Being aware of internal needs is either a waste of time or impossible due to external pressures.

       3. Minorities: Discrimination is a primary consideration; collective values dominate over individual values.

       4. External values are primary: dollars or high status cancel out internal needs.

II. Using the Career Diamond

    A. To help clients visualize the career development or transition process

    B. As a format for counselors to conceptualize client needs

    C. As a format for educators to determine students needs

    D. As a means to determine appropriate assessment tools

    E. As a means to determine the appropriate counseling techniques

EXERCISES

1. Think back to your undergraduate days. How did you make a decision to go to graduate school? Did you go straight from A to D? Use the Career Diamond to assess your self retrospectively.

    a. How well did you know your self; how well developed was your career identity?

    b. How much information did you have about external factors?

    c. If you were making the same decision today, what would you want to know now, that you did not know then?

    d. How would you have gone about learning more about your self and the external?

When marking your X on the Career Diamond, try to mark it as if you were still an undergraduate. If you took time off before returning to school, pick the time where you started to seriously consider graduate school. (Some hints: You may find it helpful to think of yourself as the career counselor helping a client. Use the outline of themes in the Study Outline to help organize your information.)

2. Do a role play in dyads with one person playing the career counselor and the other playing the client. Use the Career Diamond to define career counseling to the client and to explain what the career counseling experience will be like. Next, ask the client to place an X on the two lines of the exploring or deciding phases of the diamond to depict where he is in the process and to describe why the X's were placed where they are. Switch roles.

3. Consider planning a career education program for high school students or adults. How could you use the Career Diamond to describe career development? Jot down the major points you would want to make. How could you involve participants in learning activities other than lecturing methods?

REFERENCES

Andersen, P., Worthen, V., Fink, R. A., & Sharp, P. (1991, March). *The diamond model: Conceptualizing the career counseling process*. Paper presented at the meeting of the American Counseling and Personnel Association, Atlanta, GA.

Andersen, P., Worthen, V., Fink, R. A., & Sharp, P. (1993, March). *Conceptualizing differentially in developmental career counseling: The diamond model*. Paper presented at the meeting of the American Counseling Association, Atlanta, GA.

Holland, J. L. (1997). *Making vocational choice.* Odessa, FL: Psychological Assessment Resources.

Lent, R. W., Brown, S. D., & Hackett, G. (1994). Toward a unifying social cognitive theory of career and academic interest, choice, and performance. *Journal of Vocational Behavior, 45*, 79–122.

Peterson, G. W., Sampson, J. P., & Reardon, R. C. (1991). *Career development and services: A cognitive approach*. Pacific Grove, CA: Brooks/Cole.

Super, D. E., Savickas, M. L., & Super, C. M. (1996). The life-span, life-space approach to career. In D. Brown, L. Brooks & Associates (Eds.), *Career choice and development* (pp. 121–178). San Francisco: Jossey-Bass.

Tokar, D. M., Hall, R. J., & Moradi, B. (2003). Planting a tree while envisioning the forest—The recursive relation between theory and research: Reply to Blustein (2003). *Journal of Counseling Psychology, 50*(1), 24–27.

CHAPTER 4

Career Theory: Holland Super

True individual freedom cannot exist without economic security and independence. People who are hungry and out of a job are the stuff of
which dictatorships are made.

Franklin Delano Roosevelt, message to Congress, 1944

The description of theories related to the psychology of career choice
and development begin with two foundational theories related to the
most basic counseling interactions. John Holland's theory of person-
environment fit is a sophisticated form of Parson's earlier trait-factor approach.
This elegant, simple theory allows counselors and clients to match personality characteristics to occupational categories. Super's career development the
ory describes psychological stages culminating to form **career identity** as a
person seeks career self-expression. Career identity, from a developmental perspective, matures over time and changes throughout life. Career identity is
never stagnant but is psychologically dynamic. To capture a client's career experience, the counselor facilitates self-exploration through active listening
skills and by forming a relationship with the client where self-expression becomes explicit.

HOLLAND'S THEORY OF PERSON-ENVIRONMENT FIT

John Holland (1973) presents a career theory that is exceptionally useful for
career counselors. The basic model is easily understood and offers a simple
means for clients to match self-characteristics and occupational attributes.

Holland's basic thesis is that an individual's personality is better suited to
some work environments and poorly matched to other work environments.
His early writings did not focus on how individuals develop self-concepts,
though he did suggest that personalities grow through exposure to experiences, by reinforcement from parents and others, and by individual choices

Box 4.1   RIASEC Personality Patterns

Realistic people prefer activities that entail the explicit, order, or systematic manipulation of objects, tools, machines, and animals. They avoid goals and tasks that demand subjectivity, intellectual or artistic expressions, or social abilities. These individuals are described as practical, persistent, natural, and materialistic. Preferences include agricultural, technical, skilled-trade, and engineering vocations. Common activities involve motor skills, equipment, machines, tools, and structure, such as athletics, scouting, crafts, and shop work.

Investigative people prefer activities that entail intelligence, manipulating ideas, words, and symbols. They prefer scientific vocations that involve observation and the creative investigation of physical, biological, and cultural phenomena. These individuals enjoy theoretical concepts, reading, collecting, mathematics, and foreign languages. Self-descriptions include being scholarly, broad minded, and able to solve problems. Achievement, independence, logic, and ambition are valued. Preferences include scientific and academic careers as they are described as being curious, intellectual, analytical, and complex.

Artistic individuals prefer ambiguous, free, nonsystematic activities that entail using physical, verbal, or human materials to create art forms and products. They rely on subjective impressions and fantasies in seeking solutions to problems. These individuals prefer musical, artistic, literary, and dramatic vocations and activities that are creative in nature. Personal descriptions include being imaginative, introspective, sensitive, impulsive, and flexible. Other descriptions include being complicated, emotional, expressive, idealistic, intuitive, original, and open to feelings and new ideas.

Social people prefer activities related to interacting with people by informing, train-

over time. Later writings by Holland and his colleagues describe the gradual development of specific personality dispositions or preferences (Holland, 1997). By adolescence, individual personalities can be divided into six types. See Box 4.1 for a description of the six types using Holland's mnemonic, RIASEC (realistic, investigative, artistic, social, enterprising, and convention).

People may be categorized as "pure" types when one category appears to be truly descriptive of their personality but, more commonly, people tend to have characteristics from two or three of the six types. If two or three of the Holland personality areas are applicable, a person usually prefers one area over the others, with the second category being preferred over the third.

Holland's (1997) research has created an image showing the interrelationships between six personality categories (Figure 4.1).

The first category R, or realistic, is placed in the upper left point of the hexagon. Holland "codes" are depicted by the first letter for the title of each

ing, developing, curing, or inspiring. They typically demonstrate strong social skills and the need for social activities. These individuals prefer educational, therapeutic, and religious vocations and such activities as church, community services, music, reading, and dramatics. They want to serve others and to participate in reciprocal supportive relationships. Other descriptors include being sociable, cooperative, empathic, responsible, accepting, persuasive, warm, and generous.

Enterprising people prefer activities that entail leadership, striving for organizational goals, public speaking, and economic gain. They value expressing adventurous, dominant, and enthusiastic qualities. These individuals aspire to become influential and known for their leadership. Characteristics include being persuasive, self-confident, optimistic, ener-

getic, popular, and resourceful. Preferences lie in sales, supervisory, managerial, and leadership vocations and activities that satisfy needs for recognition and power.

Conventional people prefer activities that entail the explicit, orderly, and systematic manipulation of data. They choose goals and activities that carry social approval. Their approach to problems is consistent, and they correctly follow set procedures. These individuals create a good impression by being neat, sociable, and conservative. Preferences include clerical, organizational, and computational tasks. They identify with business, look to authority figures for advice, and place a high value on economic matters. Other descriptors include being careful, controlled, conscientious, obedient, orderly, thorough, and efficient.

Descriptions adapted from Holland (1997), pp.21–28.

of the personality categories. Other categories follow around the model in the following order: R, I, A, S, E, C. Career counselors often refer to the Holland categories with the mnemonic of RIASEC.

If a person's first, most obvious personality descriptor is S, for social characteristics, and she enjoys elements of creativity, or A for artistic, her code could be SA. If the person also has characteristics within the enterprising area with some leadership characteristics, the person's code could be SAE. Holland personality types can be determined by taking the instrument *Self-Directed Search (SDS)*.

Holland writes that **consistent** personality types have letters that are adjacent to each other on the hexagon model. SAE in the previous example is consistent because the letters are next to each other on the diagram. A person who demonstrates inconsistency in personality characteristics would have letters farther apart on the hexagon, such as SRC. This means the personality characteristics for the Realistic categories are quite different than those for the Social category, showing "inconsistencies" between the individual's preferences.

A person is said to be **differentiated** if the interests are well defined with higher scores on the first category (showing strong preference), lower scores on the second category, and even lower scores for the third category. If the scores for the top three categories are similar, there is less differentiation among the areas. This may mean the person is able to work in multiple work environments (flexibility) or is unable to commit to one type of work environment.

Holland's research also categorizes six different occupational environments that parallel the six personality areas previously described. The descriptions for these work settings are shown in Box 4.2.

An occupational environment that has attributes mostly characterized by realistic qualities would be labeled R. If other qualities of the occupation were similar to conventional descriptors, the occupation would be RC. Finally, if there were a few occupational factors that would be categorized as E for enterprising, the Holland code is RCE.

According to Holland, people seek compatible work environments occupied by other people of similar personality types (**congruence**). The more a person's personality matches his occupational environment, the more congruent the match. For maximum job satisfaction, individuals need to be participating in occupations where the people milieu and environmental activities are congruent to their personality

The *Self-Directed Search* (Holland, 1994a) is accompanied with a booklet entitled *The Occupations Finder* (4th ed.) and a *Dictionary of Holland Codes* (Gottfredson & Holland, 1996) with extensive lists of occupations classified by code letters. In addition, another publication by Holland (1994b), *You and Your Career,* introduces clients to the theory and the *SDS.* Rosen, Holmberg, and Holland (1997) also created *The Educational Opportunities Finder,* listing college majors related to RIASEC codes. Finally, Holmberg, Rosen, and Holland (1997) prepared *The Leisure Activities Finder* associating nonwork activities to RIASEC codes.

The elegance of Holland's theory is that with relative ease, clients can gain a list of occupations that fall within their major areas of interest. Furthermore, occupations from nonmatching personality categories are eliminated, allowing for greater focus in career exploration. However, the simplicity of the theory rarely leads to a definitive choice of a specific occupation. Therefore, the match between an individual and several broad categories of occupations is related to the first half of the Career Diamond where a person is exploring many potential choices of occupations based on broad matches to self-characteristics.

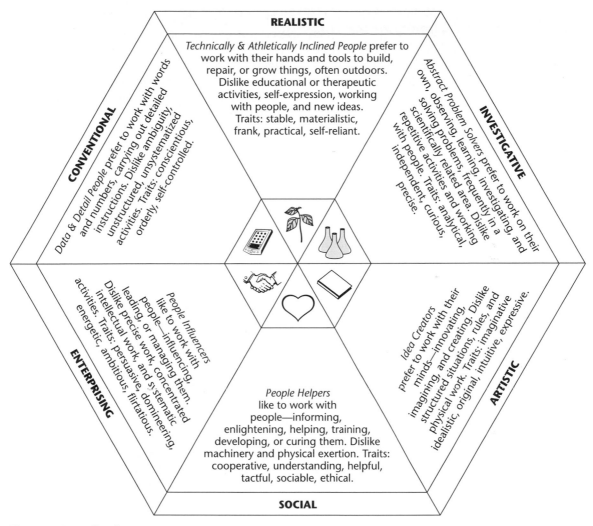

Figure 4.1   Holland's Hexagon

Practical Use via the Career Diamond

The use of Holland's theory is best for clients at the beginning of the exploring phase (Figure 4.2). This includes young clients who lack experience in the world of work and who do not have a sophisticated understanding of how occupational choices are self-expressive.

The RIASEC categories introduce the client to the concept of broad matches between the individual's personality and the characteristics of the work environment. Many clients recognize their interests and abilities are

Box 4.2   RIASEC Work Environments

The *Realistic* environment involves concrete, physical tasks requiring mechanical skill, technical competencies, persistence, and physical movement. People in realistic environments have direct coping methods and deal with problems pragmatically. Typical realistic settings include a filling station, a machine shop, a farm, a construction site, and a barbershop.

The *Investigative* environment requires the use of abstract and creative abilities. Satisfactory performance demands intelligence and analytical skills. The work is with ideas and things rather than people. Interactions between workers are rational, analytical, and indirect. Typical settings include a research laboratory, a library, or a work group of scientists, mathematicians, or research engineers.

The *Artistic* environment requires the creative and interpretive use of artistic forms. Workers draw on knowledge, intuition, and emotional life in solving typical problems. Information is judged against aesthetic, subjective criteria. The work usually requires intense involvement for prolonged periods. Typical settings include a theatre, a concert hall, a dance studio, a library, and an art or music studio.

The *Social* environment demands the ability to interpret and modify human behavior and an interest in caring for and dealing with others. The work requires frequent and prolonged personal relationships, emotionally laden interactions, and flexibility. Typical work situations include school and college classrooms, counseling offices, mental hospitals, churches, educational offices, and recreational centers.

The *Enterprising* environment requires verbal skill in directing or persuading other people. The work requires directing, controlling, or planning activities of others, and social contact that is often brief and friendly in nature. Enterprising workers are viewed as self-confident and use speaking and leadership skills. Typical settings include a car lot, a real estate office, a political rally, and an advertising agency.

The *Conventional* environment involves the systematic, concrete, routine processing of verbal and mathematical information. The tasks frequently call for repetitive, short-cycle operations performed according to an established procedure. Work is often clerical in nature, requiring the use of office equipment. Typical settings include a bank, an accounting firm, a post office, a file room, and a business office.

Descriptions adapted from Holland (1997) pp. 43–48.

expressed in work activities. However, they tend to see work environments as a set of skills and miss the nuances of similar environments populated with other workers who share basic skills and personality characteristics.

Holland's theory is best suited for suggesting fields the client can further explore (broad matching) to identify specific careers or occupations. Using the RIASEC personality categories and matching the related RIASEC occupational categories creates a teaching interaction between the client and the

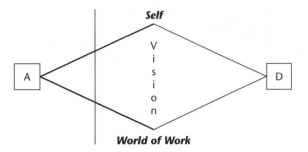

Figure 4.2   Holland's theory is particularly relevant at the beginning of the Exploring phase where clients are starting their explorations and where matches between Self and the World of Work are broad and not yet refined for the integration of the Deciding Phase.

counselor. The client learns about the world of work and how differing personalities fit in specific categories. This elegant but simple model is great for starting a journey, but lacks the sophistication for making career decisions based on a full identity search. Finally, occupational titles and descriptions of work activities are introduced in an easy to understand manner. Career clients can use this language as an aid for information searches or to add sophistication to their interview skills.

Expanding Occupational Categories

A group of researchers extended Holland's hexagon model to include the twenty-three job families from the World-of-Work Map (Figure 4.3) by ACT (Prediger, Swaney, & Mau, 1993). Its authors point out that using the three-letter Holland codes could eliminate occupations that are similar to a person's first letter if those occupations do not have matching second or third letters. For example, a person with an SAE code is not instructed by the *Self-Directed Search*'s *(SDS)* instructions to look up in *The Occupations Finder* occupations categorized as SCI or SIR, eliminating some appropriate possibilities. By superimposing the World-of-Work Map onto the RIASEC hexagon, clients and counselors can transfer Holland codes to World-of-Work job.

The American College Testing (ACT) company took the idea of transposing the World-of-Work Map onto the RIASEC categories and included the joint classification system in its DISCOVER computer-based exploration program. Prediger (1981) added the *Dictionary of Occupational Titles (DOT)* categories. The *DOT* categories of data, people, things, and ideas were developed by Fine in 1950 and have been used by the Department of Labor since the 1965 edition (Figler & Bolles, 1999). RIASEC categories provide an overlay to the previous two classification systems. Data encompasses the Holland codes E and C, People focuses on S, Things includes R, and Ideas has both A and I

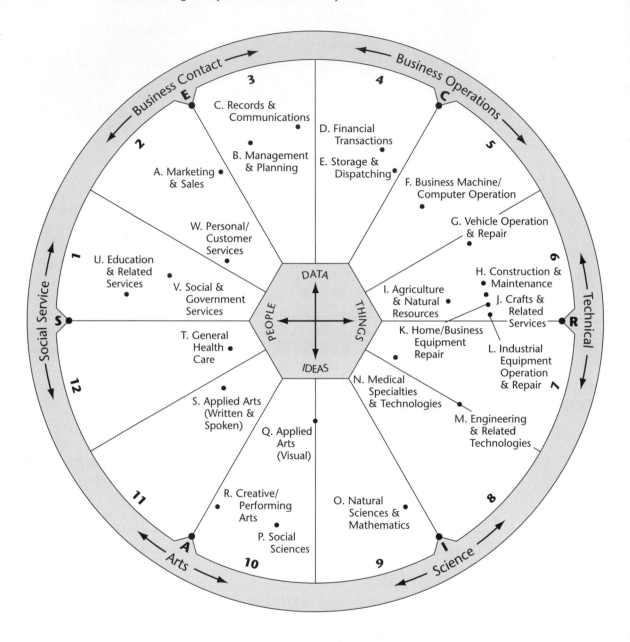

About the Map

- The World-of-Work Map arranges job families (groups of similar jobs) into 12 regions. Together, the job families cover all U.S. jobs. Although the jobs in a family differ in their locations, most are located near the point shown.
- A job family's location is based on its primary work tasks—working with DATA, IDEAS, PEOPLE, and THINGS.
- Six general areas of the work world and related Holland (1985) types are indicated around the edge of the map.

Figure 4.3   The World-of-Work Map (Note: Copyright 1990 by American College Testing. Used by permission.)

within it (Prediger, 1982). Thus, the six Holland types are placed on two foundational dimensions (Prediger, 1982).

DISCOVER has adopted a model combining all three systems, which allows counselors to create activities that include any or all of the major classifications. Figure 4.3 presents the model showing the four DOT categories in the center, the World-of-Work Map in a circle with lines drawn to dark dots on the outside of the circle labeled RIASEC letters.

Although the World-of-Work Map extends the number of occupations explored with Holland codes, the critique of the matching method remains the same. Basic matching to many occupations is useful in the exploration stage of career development, but it does not encourage a full integration of personal and external factors. More occupations do, however, extend exploring when the client remains motivated to continue searching. Appropriate clients can begin their exploration with a RIASEC code and a search for occupations with the code letters. Then, after the clients examine personal reactions to the occupations found in the first search, another search using the World-of-Work job families extends exploration. For clients at the early exploring level, continued searching offers additional opportunities to move toward creating a vision of self and the world of work.

CAREER DEVELOPMENT AND SUPER'S SELF-EXPRESSION THEORY

Donald Super has provided the most notable contribution to the field of career development of any theorist (1957; 1994; Super, Savickas, & Super, 1996). His writing spans nearly half a century, and his ideas offer a significant departure from trait-factor theories. His original research for the *Career Pattern Study* (1957) followed the work history of a number of men for 25 years and determined a series of life stages for career development. In 1996, Super et al. updated the career stages with a pictorial diagram of steps representing the broad changes experienced over time by many careerists (Figure 4.4).

Each step in the ladder represents a stage of development. As with most theories of development, each preceding stage must be completed before the next stage can take place. Descriptions of the stages are in Box 4.3.

Super's description of the stages of career development presents a view of psychological movement over the course of a lifetime. Whereas trait-factor theories match people with work environments in a static way, Super's developmental model suggests an evolving process.

The Career Diamond incorporates Super's concepts of development by picturing the process that occurs as people change from one stage to

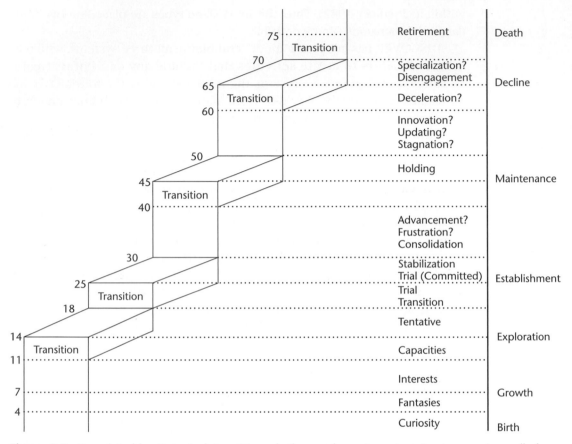

Figure 4.4   Super's Ladder. Note: Each transition, whether psychogenic, sociogenic, econogenic, or all of these, has its own minicycle of growth, exploration, establishment, maintenance, and decline: it's recycling. (*Source:* Super, Savickas, & Super, 1996.)

another (Figure 4.5). We could add a diamond turned upward between each step on Super's stairway. This visually demonstrates the opening and narrowing process that occurs as an individual rises from one stage of development to the next.

Super's writing also presents other critically important concepts that suggest a dynamic course to career growth. Super offers the following fourteen propositions, only one of which describes the career development stages. The other proposals entail concepts of career identity, career maturity, and the implementation of self-concepts through occupational roles. Super paints a picture truly psychological in nature, where people with individual differences grow and learn to meet occupational demands while gaining awareness of their unique nature as human beings.

Box 4.3   **Super's Career Developmental Stages**

The first step is called the *Growth stage,* and it represents the early development of childhood. During this earliest phase, individuals form physical abilities and learn skills that are the basis of a unique self-concept. Attitudes toward work and images of work roles are also formed.

The *Exploratory stage* is represented on the second step. Here the individual becomes aware of occupations. At first, adult roles are a part of fantasies enacted during play. Next, young people enter a period of tentative choices of occupation that are somewhat more realistic. Eventually, a choice is made.

The third step represents the *Establishment stage.* During this phase, a person enters the job market by actually choosing to work at a particular occupation. Trial-and-error experiences allow the person to determine if first choices are or are not a valid outlet for the individual's self-concept. With further experience, most people stabilize by finding and adapting to a field that "fits" their personalities and engenders satisfaction.

The *Maintenance stage* is the next step in career development. During this phase, individuals adapt and continue to develop skills and interests, which will lead to success and satisfaction. Their participation *could* become stale and require renewal in the same field or a change to another field.

The final step is the *Disengagement stage* occurring prior to retirement. Workers retain satisfactory performance, but their focus on their work has diminished. Eventually, people choose to leave the work force.

Stage descriptions adapted from Super, Savickas, and Super, 1996.

Super's Theoretical Propositions

The following are Super's propositions regarding career development with explanatory comments (Super et al., 1996, pp. 123–125).

1. *People differ in their abilities and personalities, needs, values, interests, traits, and self-concepts.*
   Super starts with the unique individual differences of each person. People all have strengths and areas of greater and lesser ability. Each individual forms a view of self to include likes and dislikes, and personal requirements. Individuals are able to define what activities serve a meaningful purpose in life. Finally, each person has an internal view comprising a constellation of personal attributes that describe the person's self-concept. When the self-description is defining the self at work, it is termed *career self-concept* or *career identity*.

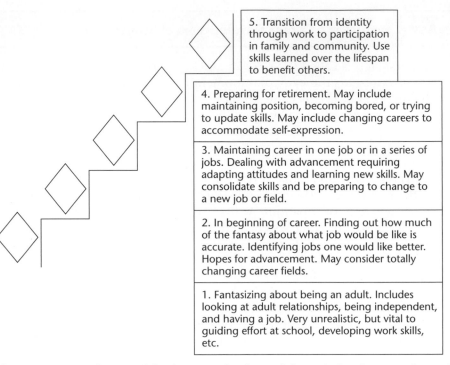

5. Transition from identity through work to participation in family and community. Use skills learned over the lifespan to benefit others.

4. Preparing for retirement. May include maintaining position, becoming bored, or trying to update skills. May include changing careers to accommodate self-expression.

3. Maintaining career in one job or in a series of jobs. Dealing with advancement requiring adapting attitudes and learning new skills. May consolidate skills and be preparing to change to a new job or field.

2. In beginning of career. Finding out how much of the fantasy about what job would be like is accurate. Identifying jobs one would like better. Hopes for advancement. May consider totally changing career fields.

1. Fantasizing about being an adult. Includes looking at adult relationships, being independent, and having a job. Very unrealistic, but vital to guiding effort at school, developing work skills, etc.

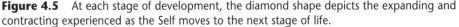

Figure 4.5   At each stage of development, the diamond shape depicts the expanding and contracting experienced as the Self moves to the next stage of life.

2. *People are qualified, by virtue of these characteristics, for a number of occupations.*
   Individual difference does not require finding one specific occupation to match self-characteristics. Instead, many occupations will meet individual needs and abilities to varying degrees and in various combinations.

3. *Each occupation requires a characteristic pattern of abilities and personality traits, with tolerances wide enough to allow some variety of occupations for each individual as well as some variety of individuals in each occupation.*
   In every field, there will be people who are similar and dissimilar in various ways. To perform the responsibilities of a job, there are particular abilities and personality attributes needed to meet the *minimum* job responsibilities. However, there will also be room in any occupation for a variety of people with a whole host of personal characteristics.

4. *Vocational preferences and competencies, the situations in which people live and work, and hence their self-concepts change, with time and experience, although self-concepts as products of social learning are increasingly stable from late adolescence until late maturity, providing some continuity in choice and adjustment.*

By the time a person develops an adult identity, she gains a sense of self that is somewhat stable though there will be some change as she gains experience and ages. Therefore, changes in the self-concept take place within a range that expresses the stable core identity of the person as well as reflects new insights and adaptations made over time. With changes in self-concept, a person may choose to change her working or living situation. Or, a change in working or living situation may require some change in self-concept.

5. *This process of change may be summed up in a series of life stages (a "maxicycle") characterized as a sequence of Growth, Exploration, Establishment, Maintenance, and Disengagement, and these stages may in turn be subdivided into periods characterized by developmental tasks. A small (mini) cycle takes place during career transitions from one stage to the next or each time an individual's career is destabilized by illness or injury, employer's reduction in force, social changes in human resource needs, or other socioeconomic or personal events. Such unstable or multiple-trial careers involve the recycling of new growth, reexploration, and reestablishment.*

This is the full statement of the developmental pattern Super found in his research. The references to a maxicycle and minicycle suggest an overall pattern for a lifetime. Specifically, economic forces and/or changes in personal needs result in periods of smaller transitions to the new requirements. Each change, either in a stage of development or to new occupational choices, requires the person to explore and reestablish the self to new conditions.

As depicted in Figure 4.6, the Career Diamond depicts the exploring stage as the opening up of the diamond and the reestablishment stage as the closing of the diamond when a person comes to terms

(e.g., High School: College/Training: Early Career: Mid-Career: Retirement)

Figure 4.6   The sequence of diamonds illustrate that as one decision is made, closing one stage of development, another stage begins. The process of expanding and contracting reoccurs.

with a new situation. Given that change is expected over time, the recycling has been shown as a string of diamonds periodically opening and closing.

6. *The nature of the career pattern—that is, the occupational level attained and the sequence, frequency, and duration of trial and stable jobs—is determined by the individual's parental socioeconomic level, mental ability, education, skills, personality characteristics (needs, values, interests, and self-concepts), and career maturity and by the opportunities to which he or she is exposed.*

Super recognizes the powerful influences of the family of origin on career development. The socioeconomic level of an individual's family determines what exposure is gained to various occupations. Parents and other family members influence young people through encouragement and by providing resources to develop abilities and skills and to obtain a formal education. Parents also affect the development of personality and career maturity both by direct teaching and by role modeling.

Super further demonstrates the influence of the wider community supporting the family. He created a picture called "The Archway of Career Determinants" that displays the factors of both the self and the outside world as playing a part in career development.

The left side of the arch in Figure 4.7 shows a biological base with needs, values, and interests beside several forms of abilities (i.e., intelligence, aptitudes, and special aptitudes). The integration of this pillar leads to personality, which is the upper cornerstone of the arch; all of these personal factors also lead to achievement. On the right column, the environmental area is shown. A geographical base supports the community, family, school, and peer groups along side the economy, society, and the labor market. All of the named environmental areas support the right upper cornerstone of social policy that influences employment practices. The self, pictured at the top of the arch, goes through the developmental stages creating role self-concepts, which translate the influences of the self factors and the environmental influences from the two columns.

7. *Success in coping with the demands of the environment and of the organism in that context at any given life-career stage depends on the readiness of the individual to cope with these demands (that is, on his or her career maturity).*

Super defined **career maturity** as the ability to deal with the requirements of the particular situation within the context of a person's stage of development. For a child, capacity to observe adult behavior

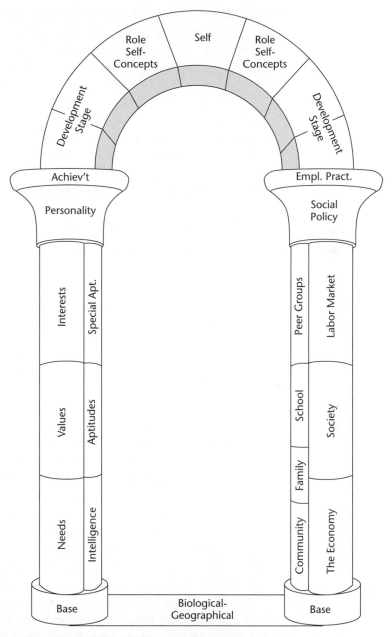

Figure 4.7   The Archway of Career Determinants

and fantasize the taking on of adult roles is the maturity expected for
the growth stage. For adolescents, exploring multiple occupational
paths and making tentative choices that fit the developing self-
concept is the psychological task needed. For adults, continued

refinement of self-concepts in light of experience and insights gained as well as adapting to the changes required by the marketplace is expected. Age or developmental stage determines career maturity, and like personal development, meeting the demands of previous levels of development is necessary before one can move to the next stage.

Readiness is a psychological concept suggesting that time is needed for a person to develop and to be ready to move between stages of development. Teaching children to read before they are ready is known to be useless and frustrating. Likewise, attempting to force young people to make a choice of occupation before they are ready is a mistake, and as adults, people need time to emotionally process the loss of one job (e.g., grieve) before they are ready to face choosing and finding another job.

8. *Career maturity is a psychosocial construct that denotes an individual's degree of vocational development along the continuum of life stages and substages from Growth through Disengagement. From a social or societal perspective, career maturity can be operationally defined by comparing the developmental tasks being encountered to those expected based on the individual's chronological age. From a psychological perspective, career maturity can be operationally defined by comparing an individual's resources, both cognitive and affective, for coping with a current task to the resources needed to master that task.*

Ever the research scientist, Super consistently worked to construct definitions that could be empirically validated. He developed the instrument *Career Development Inventory* to serve as a survey of factors considered to be a part of career maturity. Later, his students (Crites & Savickas, 1995) also developed the instrument *Career Maturity Inventory (CMI)* to determine areas of career maturity. The *CMI* can be use for planning career education interventions for groups. Factors identified as a part of career maturity include planfulness, exploration, information, decision making, and reality orientation. See Table 4.1 for Super's (1990) outline defining each of these areas.

Super's outline illustrates topics a counselor can use to assess career maturity, adapting the complexity to the stage of development. For example, a younger client would be expected to demonstrate less complexity in the reflection of experience or anticipation of the future. Role relationships may not be fully apparent to adolescents, but a basic awareness of multiple roles may be expected. Young adults would not yet have a great deal of work experience nor would they be expected to have stabilized in implementing their career plans.

Table 4.1   Career Maturity: A Basic Assessment

I. Planfulness
  A. Autonomy
  B. Time Perspective
    1. Reflection upon experience
    2. Anticipation of the future
    3. Concepts of life stages
  C. Concepts of Self
    1. Role self-concepts
    2. Self-esteem
    3. Cognitive complexity

II. Exploration
  A. Querying: self, situations, roles
  B. Resources: awareness of, use
  C. Participation in school, college, community

III. Information
  A. The world of education
  B. The world of work
    1. Career stages and tasks
    2. Coping behaviors
    3. Occupational structure
    4. Typical occupations
    5. Access and entry
    6. Rewards and drawbacks
    7. Trends and changes
  C. The preferred occupational group
    1. Education and training needed
    2. Entry requirements and routes
    3. Duties, methods, materials, tools
    4. Advancement, transfer, stability
    5. Conditions and rewards of work
    6. Life-style
    7. Future prospects
  D. Life-Career Roles
    1. Work, homemaking, leisure, etc.
    2. Role relationships and effects
      a. Supplementary
      b. Complementary
      c. Conflicting
    3. Multiple role self-realizations
  E. Decision Making
    1. Principle
    2. Applications to people and situations
    3. Style: rational, impulsive, intuitive, conforming
  F. Reality Orientation
    1. Self-knowledge
    2. Realism as to outlets
    3. Consistency of preferences (exploratory and definitive)
    4. Crystallization of self-concepts, values, interests, and objectives
    5. Work experience: exploratory, instrumental, implementing, stabilizing

9. *Development through the life stages can be guided, partly by facilitating the maturing of abilities, interests, and coping resources and partly by aiding in reality testing and in the development of self-concepts.*

Super proposes that progress through the career developmental stages can be encouraged by the gradual enhancement of abilities and interests, which is what education is about. In addition to education, the person matures by determining realistic choices and by gaining an awareness of the self.

The Career Diamond takes Super's description of the interchange between information about the world of work and the person's awareness of self and creates the two sides of the diamond. The career professional determines the current needs of clients as either an indication for education or counseling. Career education facilitates growth by teaching a model of career development so the client can continue developing abilities and interests until there is a readiness to make choices. Career counseling prompts the client toward gaining insights into self-concepts and helps the client deal with reality factors, both of which lead to making choices.

10. *The process of career development is essentially that of developing and implementing occupational self-concepts. It is the synthesizing and compromising process in which the self-concept is a product of the interaction of inherited aptitudes, physical makeup, opportunity to observe and play various roles, and evaluations of the extent to which the results of role-playing meet the approval of superiors and peers.*

Here Super summarizes the basic concept that each person develops career self-concepts and then implements her self-view through occupational choice and behavior. The process requires an awareness of personal characteristics and the readiness to adapt to reality factors realized through feedback from supervisors and others. Super uses the term *interactive learning* to describe the ever-changing nature of career development. As a person interacts with others and the environment, new information is taken in and the person learns to make adjustments both in thinking and in behavior.

The **implementation of self-concepts** is a growth-filled model that depicts the psychological nature of career development. Career issues must be individualized and personal if they reflect each person's unique self-concept. Career choice is more than a broad match between occupational categories and basic personality characteristics. A full career self-concept contains the unique, complex, and ever-evolving nature of being human. People and their self-concepts change over time, suggesting that broad basic matches could not fully account for all of career movement over the lifetime.

11. *The process of synthesis of and compromise between individual and social factors, between self-concepts and reality, is one of role-playing and of learning from feedback, whether the role is played in fantasy, in the counseling interview, or in such real-life activities as classes, clubs, part-time work, and entry jobs.*

Super offers examples of ways people learn and grow by "trying on" different career roles. To come to a realization that an occupation can express an individual's career identity, the person needs to imagine the self in the work-role by creating a holistic picture of what it would be like. Parts of the self-concept need to coalesce into a frame that would be appropriate for a particular job or work activity. The career role will demand specific requirements and responsibilities, and compromises may be needed to create the integration needed between the person and the role.

Gaining such a view of the self and occupation is a complex process not fully explicated by any theorist. It is presumed that experiences replicating work activity or stimulating the imaginary picture of the work induce the synthesis and compromising needed. Counseling is one activity that encourages the thoughtful integration of the self and work, and counselors can aid clients further by recommending some of the other activities Super suggests.

12. *Work satisfactions and life satisfactions depend on the extent to which an individual finds adequate outlets for abilities, needs, values, interests, personality traits, and self-concepts. They depend on establishment in a type of work, a work situation, and a way of life in which one can play the kind of role that growth and exploratory experiences have led one to consider congenial and appropriate.*

If a person is in a role that encourages the use of the individual's abilities, interests, or personality, then the worker will be satisfied. If the occupation is not reflective of the individual's self-concepts, then the person will be unsatisfied. Again, it takes more than broad matches between the person and the specific work activities to gain satisfaction. Super states it is not only the type of occupation that leads to maximum satisfaction, but also the particular situation where that occupation is performed and the life-style related to the occupational position. Give and take between the work environment and self-constructs is also suggested. With experience, a worker may adapt expectations and personal needs to match more closely the work roles and by doing so may gain satisfaction.

13. *The degree of satisfaction people attain from work is proportional to the degree to which they have been able to implement self-concepts.*

Super takes the construct of implementing self-concepts to the maximum level by suggesting that work satisfaction depends on the individual's capacity to find or create a work role that allows for such implementation. Variations in **work satisfaction** are dependent on the degree of self-expression found in the demands of the work. The greater the time spent performing activities seen as reflective of the person's view of the self, the greater the work satisfaction. The more an individual is required to do work not expressive of the self, the less satisfaction is experienced.

14. *Work and occupation provide a focus for personality organization for most men and women, although for some individuals this focus is peripheral, incidental, or even nonexistent. Then, other foci, such as leisure activities and homemaking, may be central. Social traditions, such as sex-role stereotyping and modeling, racial and ethnic biases, and the opportunity structure, as well as individual differences are important determinants of preferences for such roles as worker, student, leisurite, homemaker, and citizen. (See Career Rainbow.)*

Super recognizes that occupational roles are a major identity factor for many people; for others, career titles and activity might be less important as a statement of who they are. Super's original longitudinal study of career patterns did not include women. When more women began careers outside the home, some writers in the career literature suggested Super's developmental stages might be different for women than for men. Super answered by stating that women, whose identity focus was career, would follow patterns similar to men, but others might combine homemaking and work. For variations of ethnic, racial, and cultural influences, Super stated that differences of opportunity or group values may affect individual priorities. Career issues may be of greater or lesser importance depending on the salience of work role for individual identity.

Super (Super et al., 1996) created another picture—that of the Life Career Rainbow—to demonstrate the most common roles played across the life-span.

The rainbow in Figure 4.8 displays multiple roles and can be used as an educational tool to illustrate the impact of different roles across the life-span. A larger picture of the rainbow labeled with several roles can also be used for clients to color, showing the amount of time or importance each role has in their lives at a particular point in time. (Have the client color the amount of importance each role has. Length of line and color are important. Have the client explain both.)

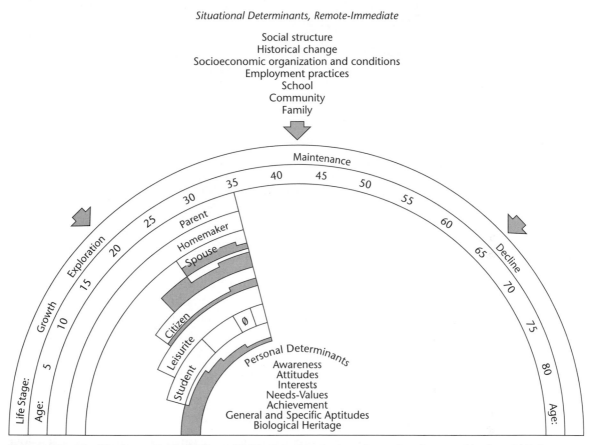

Figure 4.8   The Life Career Rainbow (From "A Life-Span Approach to Career Development" by Donald E. Super, 1990, *Career Choice and Development: Applying Contemporary Theories to Practice,* p. 200. Copyright 1990 by Jossey-Bass. Reprinted by permission.)

Practical Use via the Career Diamond

Borgen (1991) noted that Super "has splendidly stood the test of time" (p. 278). Super introduced the concept of first conducting self-exploration and exploring the world of work before the deciding phase. Within this approach, career exploration included a broad life view that was developmental in nature. That is, career exploration changed depending upon the developmental stage of the client. The overall development of career identity and career experiences over time is called a "maxi-cycle." In addition, mini-cycles repeat the process of exploring, fantasizing, making tentative choices before setting priorities, and deciding. Mini-cycles represent

Figure 4.9   The Career Diamond illustrates Super's stages of first exploring to create a broad vision or basic career identity. After the broad matches of the Exploring stage, a narrowing or contracting stage follows where the Self and external realities are integrated to make a decision.

transitions made within a lifetime, suggesting career decisions are not final, but can be made over and over.

In Figure 4.9, the Career Diamond illustrates the process Super describes—with an exploring phase first, coming to a vision of a career choice, and integrating the interaction between the self and the world of work realities in the deciding phase. Active listening is an important skill that enables the career counselor to hear the entirety of the client's exploring experience and to help the client explore the needs of the self prior to making career decisions.

Although Super's developmental model is quite general, developmental theories from general psychology can be used to supplement the broad concept that career identity develops over time. Also, Super's theory does not make specific recommendations for career counseling techniques that facilitate client exploration and decision making. Again, the career literature and other theories can supplement the broad concept of exploring prior to deciding.

Super's archway introduces the concepts of both individual influences and external factors affecting career identity. The Career Diamond pictures Super's description of mini- and maxi-cycles. Exploration is shown within the expansion of the diamond, and decision making pictures contracting priorities in a process that repeats itself with each new diamond.

Super himself was influenced by the work of Ginzberg and his colleagues (Ginzberg, 1952, 1972; Ginzberg et al., 1951). Ginzberg introduced the three stages of exploration, crystallization, and specification as tied to an adolescent's development and experience. Super's original theory retained the developmental, age-related concepts, but his later theory suggested the stages were more flexible. The exploration, crystallization, and specification became a natural sequence of career growth not necessarily tied only to a young adult's development, but also as repetitive patterns occurring throughout life during career transitions. The implications of continual growth, rather than stage growth, are extremely relevant as career theory and practice changes to help clients adapt to the fluidity of the modern job market.

SUMMARY

Holland's typology for personalities and for work environments offers a simple, elegant method for helping clients identify broad interest areas. Clients designate their personality types by choosing several categories describing six different dispositions (RIASEC). Then, the personality types are matched with occupational categories using the same letters. The broad matches are helpful in eliminating those categories that are not of interest and by prioritizing the categories that are of interest. The client learns how occupations are distributed in the world of work and how personal attributes are expressed in occupations. For unsophisticated clients, such a teaching/learning process is appropriate.

Super provides a developmental description for how career identity gradually matures and changes. Experienced career counselors will often rediscover constructs from developmental theory, as clients share their experiences and the abstract notions come alive. Developmental guidelines provide excellent snapshots of the sequential challenges most individuals experience. An understanding of developmental constructs is useful for understanding the direction of psychological growth. A sophisticated understanding of client development enhances the counselor's capacity to choose appropriate techniques to meet client's needs. It is critical to understand, however, that though career identity develops in stages, growth and change is a lifelong process and gaining initial **career maturity** is not an ending point but the beginning of additional changes that continue in a recycling pattern. Super's general description of expansive exploring prior to the contracting of options in deciding illustrates the movement of the career development process. In the next chapter, other theorists add further concepts that suggest counseling interventions to help clients broaden their self-concepts, their understanding of occupational requirements, and the integration of both.

STUDY OUTLINE: KEY TERMS AND CONCEPTS

I. Holland: Trait-Factor
    A. Match personality of person with demands of job (**congruence**).
        1. Individuals' personalities can be categorized into types combining one, two, or three of the RIASEC personality areas.

2. Jobs entail specific behaviors characterized by providing specific services or products produced. Job environments can be classified by RIASEC categories.
3. People seek out people with similar codes and congregate in like occupations.
4. Career choice and other occupational behavior equals the interaction between the person and the environment.

II. Holland: Important Concepts
  A. Personality types match job characteristics.
    1. The more a person's personality matches the job environment, the more congruent the occupational choice is.
    2. **Consistent**: When the letters of the two or three letter code fall next to each other on the hexagon
    3. **Differentiated**: When there is a clear preference for one letter as indicated by a higher score

III. Career Diamond Application of Holland's Theory
  A. Very useful for the beginning of exploration phase. Creates a process where the counselor serves as a teaching guide, explaining the career choice process.
  B. Holland's research is easy to understand and helpful in categorizing occupations in career libraries.

IV. Super's Developmental Theory
  A. The individual and the workplace change and evolve over time.
    1. There are a variety of jobs that can suit every client (no perfect match).
    2. Jobs need to be flexible enough to allow for worker variability.
    3. There is a major developmental movement (maxi-cycle) made up of five stages:
       Growth, Exploration, Establishment, Maintenance, and Decline
    4. Each major stage contains a mini-cycle within it:
       New growth, Reexploration, and Reestablishment
    5. Transitions include an exploratory phase (fantasy, tentative choice) and an establishment stage (trial behavior; stabilizing).
    6. Career determinants include personal and social influences with the self bridging and overriding the two.

V. The Individual Is More than Traits and Abilities.
  A. Satisfied workers are able to express a career identity and demonstrate career maturity (**work satisfaction**).
  B. Career self-concepts (**career identity**) grow and develop and change with experience.

    C. **Implementation of self-concept** is an interplay between the self and external realities.

    D. Individuals must become aware of the self and be able to articulate a self-concept.

    E. **Career maturity** defined as an individual's capacity to meet demands of age-appropriate developmental tasks. **Readiness** is the person's capacity to learn career-related concepts or skills.

        1. Career maturity requires planfulness; exploring self and resource information (e.g., world of work, occupations, and personal roles)

        2. If work conditions do not meet the needs of the self, then other roles can meet those needs (e.g., family roles, hobbies, volunteer work, etc.).

VI. Career Diamond Application of Super's Theory

    A. Each major stage consists of at least one diamond.

    B. Suggests to clients that the current need is one in a chain of decisions yet to be made.

    C. Takes into account internal and external factors affecting career development.

    D. Pictures the process of expanding for exploration and contracting for making choice or deciding.

EXERCISES

1. Super says career development is the implementation of self-concept. How would you describe your career self-concept? How would you facilitate a process where a client articulates his self-concept? Remember basic counseling skills such as active listening and reflecting feelings. Practice in dyads playing the roles of counselor and client.

2. Use the RIASEC personality descriptions or the *Self-Directed Search* to determine your Holland Code of two or three letters. What occupations are suggested by your code? What common characteristics of the occupational categories are particularly relevant to you as a unique human being?

    Although you may use the personality descriptors or the occupational characteristics, are there other factors about the occupations or unique qualities descriptive of you that are not captured by the RIASEC definitions? Role play in dyads as counselor and client. How can the counselor use the Holland Codes to facilitate career exploration? Does the matching method curtail the counseling dialogue or exploration? What kind of clients would find the RIASEC method useful? How would the RIASEC matching method be useful for career education programs?

REFERENCES

Borgen, F. H. (1991). Megatrends and milestones in vocational behavior: A twenty-year counseling psychology retrospective, *Journal of Vocational Behavior, 39,* 263–90.

Crites, J. O. (1969). *Vocational psychology: The study of vocational behavior and development*. New York: McGraw-Hill.

Crites, J. O., & Savickas, M. L. (1995). *Career maturity inventory*. Odessa, FL: Psychological Assessment Resources.

Figler, H., & Bolles, R. N. (1999). *The career counselor's handbook*. Berkeley, CA: Ten Speed Press.

Ginzberg, E. (1952). Toward a theory of occupational choice. *Occupations, 30*, 491–494.

Ginzberg, E. (1972). Toward a theory of occupational choice: A restatement. *Vocational Guidance Quarterly, 20*(3), 169–176.

Ginzberg, E., Ginsburg, S. W., Axelrad, S., & Herman, J. L. (1951). *Occupational choice: An approach to a general theory*. New York: Columbia Univ. Press.

Gottfredson, G. D., & Holland, J. L. (1996). *Dictionary of Holland occupational codes* (3rd ed.). Odessa, FL: Psychological Assessment Resources.

Holland, J. L. (1973). *Making vocational choices: A theory of career*. Englewood Cliffs, NJ: Prentice-Hall.

Holland, J. L. (1994a). *Self-directed search*. Odessa, FL: Psychological Assessment Resources.

Holland, J. L. (1994b). *You and your career*. Odessa, FL: Psychological Assessment Resources.

Holland, J. L. (1996). *The occupations finder* (4th ed.). Odessa, FL: Psychological Assessment Resources.

Holland, J. L. (1997) *Making vocational choices* (3rd ed.). Odessa, FL: Psychological Assessment Resources.

Holmberg, K., Rosen, D., and Holland, J. L. (1997). *The leisure activities finder*. Odessa, FL: Psychological Assessment Resources.

Osipow, S. H. (1968). *Theories of career development*. New York: Appleton-Century-Crofts.

Prediger, D. J. (1981). Getting ideas out of DOT and into vocational guidance. *Vocational Guidance Quarterly, 29,* 293–305.

Prediger, D. J. (1982). Dimensions underlying Holland's hexagon: Missing link between interests and occupations? *Journal of Vocational Behavior, 21,* 259–287.

Prediger, D., Swaney, K., & Mau, W. C. (1993). Extending Holland's hexagon: Procedures, counseling applications, and research. *Journal of counseling and development, 71,* 422–428.

Rosen, D., Holmberg, K., & Holland, J. L. (1997). *The educational opportunities finder*. Odessa, FL: Psychological Assessment Resources.

Seligman, L. (1994). *Developmental career counseling and assessment.* Thousand Oaks, CA: Sage.

Super, D. E. (1957). *The psychology of careers.* NY: Harper & Row.

Super, D. E. (1990, March). *Career counseling and assessment.* Paper presented at the annual convention for the American Counseling and Personnel Association, Atlanta, GA.

Super. D. E. (1994). A life span, life space perspective on convergence. In M. L. Savikas & R. W. Lent (Eds.), *Convergence in career development theories: Implications for science and practice* (pp. 63–74)). Palo Alto, CA: Consulting Psychologist Press.

Super, D. E., Savickas, M. L., & Super, C. M. (1996). The life-span, life-space approach to careers. In D. Brown, L. Brooks, and Associates (Eds.), *Career choice and development* (3rd ed., pp.121–177). San Francisco: Jossey-Bass.

CHAPTER 5

Career Theory: Krumboltz Gottfredson

I do the thing which my own nature drives me to do.

Albert Einstein

The theories of Krumboltz, Gottfredson, and Lent, Brown, and Hackett consider the influences of learning and cognitive constructs, including the impact of social messages. Such concepts expand a holistic understanding of career behavior and can be integrated with the theories previously described. Krumboltz suggests attitudes and beliefs, learned within a social context, can either facilitate or retard career behavior. Gottfredson explains how career options are based upon social constructs that narrow potential choices before personal interests are explored. Lent, Brown, and Hackett show how broad self-evaluations influence an individual's choices. All these theories offer a rich source of ideas for potential counseling interventions. Counselors can encourage clients to reconsider basic thinking patterns that have limited self-concepts and eliminated some of the occupations considered.

KRUMBOLTZ—SOCIAL LEARNING THEORY AND CAREER DEVELOPMENT

John Krumboltz (1976, 1994) applies the social learning theory developed by Bandura to career behavior and makes specific recommendations for practice. In fact, he critiques most career theories as being "largely irrelevant to practice because they have focused on career development, not counselor intervention" (Krumboltz, 1996, p. 55). Krumboltz (1993) critiques trait-factor theory as being unrealistically simplistic, overfocusing on cognitive matches between the individual and the work environment, failing to acknowledge the emotional components of career problems, and boring for new career counselors. Interest inventories are seen as nonsensical because many clients have little or no experience with many of the items they mark as like, dislike, or indifferent. Krumboltz (1996) suggests changing interest inventory answers to, "I don't know yet," "I haven't tried that yet," or "I'd like to learn more about that before I answer" (p. 57).

Krumbotz's theory offers concepts that describe how individuals learn crucial career constructs that affect career attitudes and behavior. Although the theorist acknowledges genetic and cultural influences, he places all career development in the context of a learning model.

> People with differing genetic characteristics are exposed to infinitely varied learning opportunities (or lack thereof) as a result of the social, cultural, and economic circumstances that exist at the time and place where they live. The consequences of these learning experiences are synthesized by each individual …(to) guide each person's thinking about appropriate career decisions and actions. (1996, p. 60)

Career counseling can aid clients in identifying, developing, or learning skills, interests, beliefs, values, work habits, and other personal qualities that will allow clients to achieve a satisfying life within an ever-changing workplace (Krumboltz, 1996). New learning can take place at any point in an individual's life so career behavior *cannot* be predicted, and career movement can change at any time. Each individual is unique because each person has different experiences and different perceptions of experience based upon previous learning.

The counselor facilitates client change by helping the client learn what behaviors, attitudes, and beliefs are effective in gaining self-determined goals. Personal constructs subject to learning, and hence to change, can be cognitive, emotional, and behavioral. Ineffective personal patterns are learned because learning has been affected by a lack of social support, emotional deprivation, traumatic events, inaccurate ideas, or poor role models.

Once learning has taken place, the person may be closed to further evidence that the original learning was faulty (**confirmatory bias**). The person only pays attention to ideas or observations that confirm an original learning and does not pay attention to any evidence to the contrary (Krumboltz, 1991). For example, the lion in the movie *The Wizard of Oz* could have observed his own behaviors and determine that he was courageous. However, the lion was convinced he was a coward and only paid attention to behaviors showing he was afraid, denying the acts of courage he demonstrated.

Self-Observation Generalities, Task Approach Skills, and Areas of Change

Individuals gain a sense of self by observing their behavior, attitudes, beliefs, and feelings. Over time, an individual forms generalizations about the self (**self-observation generalities**). People also learn in gradations, first learning small pieces of behavior that eventually combine into larger skills. Such small skills are called **task approach skills**. Finally, a major form of learning occurs through **modeling**. People duplicate the behaviors of an admired person who demonstrates qualities desired by the learner.

Krumboltz (1996) criticizes other career theories for assuming that the career counselor and client are stuck with the current skills, interests, beliefs, values, and even personality. From this stuck perspective, the counselor helps the client find a career match, retaining the client's limited viewpoints rather than extending career vision.

Skills can be developed; clients just need to know how much time and money it will take to acquire the new learning (Krumboltz, 1996). A client can rule out an occupational choice because the effort or cost is prohibitive rather than accepting a limited self-concept saying, "I can't; I'm incompetent." Interests develop via exposure. If matches are solely based upon similar interests, then clients born to families or attending school systems that fail to provide exposure restrict the individual's options. Career counseling can help clients expand their experiential background, thus opening them up to new interests. Beliefs are both logical/illogical and emotional. Illogical beliefs may be fervently held by clients who attach strong emotions to the concepts. These emotions can override logic and trap a client. If career counselors deal with the emotion as well as the logic, erroneous or false beliefs can be exposed and changed.

Even values change, according to Krumboltz. He offers the example of priests becoming agnostics, and agnostics becoming priests. In fact, Krumboltz notes that it is not uncommon for people to hold contradictory values. Career counselors need to bring conflicting values into the open so clients can fully examine their beliefs. Finally, personality can be adjusted. Krumboltz states that career services can aid clients in changing their personality styles and strategies. Assertiveness training for introverts is an example. Although a person may remain an introvert, assertiveness training may expand career options. As new perspectives are established, the clients may actually change some of their personality preferences, affecting not only their career outlook but their personal lives as well.

Krumboltz's perspective values the impact of sophisticated career services.

Career counseling is the most complex type of counseling because the counselor must possess all the skills of other counselors; and, in addition, know employment trends, methods of preparing for various work roles, career assessment techniques, and methods for changing work-related behavior, emotions, and cognitions. (1996, p. 59)

What to Listen for in Career Counseling

Krumboltz's (1994) research has identified attitudes and beliefs that restrict successful career behavior. A client's perspective that goal attainment must proceed in a specific sequence is restrictive; whereas a perspective suggesting several routes to success opens possibilities. Another example is a strong need for privacy in dealing with others, which is less successful than a preference for open communication. Attitudes such as recognizing the need for hard work, flexibility, self-responsibility, and conscientious behavior promote career success unless such attitudes are taken to unnatural extremes. Personal characterizations can also sabotage career behavior. For example, clinging to a self-description such as "I'm a night person" can lead to an inability to get enough sleep. Krumboltz (1994) describes the night person as afflicted with a personal ism called *diurnalism*. Other isms could be *maritalism*, "I can't because I'm married"; or *characterism*, "I'm stubborn; that's the kind of person I am."

Clients often express self-statements that could limit their career development. Krumboltz (1994) lists the following self-defeating cognitive constructs:

1. A lack of recognition that changes could happen
2. Eliminating alternatives for inappropriate reasons
3. Viewing life in negative terms
4. Blaming others
5. Repeatedly saying "I can't," sometimes accompanied by negative feelings of depression and/or anxiety

Counselors can detect such self-statements and encourage clients to reconsider the validity of such self-limiting remarks. One of Krumboltz's contributions to career theory is his recognition that cognitive constructs often seen as detrimental to personal development also have a negative impact on career movement.

Krumboltz (1991) extends the application of cognitive therapy to career counseling and lists several characteristics of faulty reasoning affecting career decision making.

1. Overgeneralizations
2. Self-evaluations with unreasonable standards or, often, a single standard

3. Exaggerating the impact of an outcome (sometimes labeled as failure)
4. Overemphasizing a single or narrow focus
5. Undue weight given to a low probability outcome

His *Career Beliefs Inventory (CBI)* was developed to identify and measure cognitions that block career development (Krumboltz, 1991). However, counselors can often identify those attitudes and beliefs held by a client while interacting in counseling sessions. The *CBI* may be most useful in identifying ineffective constructs held by a group of clients in planning career education programs.

Changes in Career Planning to Awareness of Serendipity

In the '70s through the mid-'80s, Krumboltz described a rational decision-making model that provided linear steps for processing career choices based on traditional problem-solving methods: define problem, determine alternatives, determine consequences, choose alternative, take action, evaluate (Krumboltz & Baker, 1973; Krumboltz & Hamel, 1977). However, by the late '90s Krumboltz and his colleagues amended his theory, changing from a static, rational approach to a dynamic, adaptive approach where the unexpected happenstance is taken into account (Mitchell, Levin, & Krumboltz, 1999). Krumboltz described traditional decision making as obsolete (personal communication, January 14, 2005). Following the outdated model of applying *true reasoning* as per Parsons (1909) resulted in structured counseling in a step-by-step format. If clients "sensibly resist our efforts to get them to predict their own futures, we label them as undecided, or even indecisive, and feel that our counseling has failed" (Krumboltz, 1998, p. 391). Krumboltz and his colleagues go on to say that the global economy has changed client needs:

> Rational planning alone would serve its purpose if career were to follow a simple, straightforward, and logical path. Unfortunately, due to major technological advances, the world of work today is not what it used to be. In virtually every employment sector, job descriptions are changing, some occupations are becoming obsolete, and unforeseen occupations are being created. (Mitchell, Levin, & Krumboltz, 1999, p. 116)

Happenstance suggests career choices require planning but are also adaptive to new circumstances that happen along the way. Rather than planning that remains stagnate, the term captures persistence and flexibility, as well as an optimistic attitude toward change and a capacity for risk taking.

The four steps in Box 5.1 describe the process for preparing clients to remain open to change.

Box 5.1   Serendipity Mindfulness

Step 1: Normalize happenstance in the client's history.

    A. Identify actual happenstance events in client's history and how the client made choices that enabled them to benefit from chance occurrences.

Step 2: Help clients transform curiosity into opportunities for learning and exploration.

    A. Unexpected events are opportunities to explore and be curious. For example, missing a flight may be a frustrating 4-hour delay or an opportunity to find out about the person sitting in the next seat. Through that conversation, information is garnered and a relationship that may make a future difference could be formed.

Step 3: Teach clients to produce desirable chance events.

    A. Yes, chance events tend to come out of the blue (e.g., a vice president of a big company shops at a store and ends up offering a young salesperson a job of a lifetime). However, clients can create chance events by visiting places or people of interest or communicating via e-mail, phone calls, or networking with someone who knows someone. Information is learned and relationships are formed.

Step 4: Teach clients to overcome blocks to action.

    A. Develop skills in curiosity, persistence, flexibility, optimism, and risk taking.

    B. Assess deeply held beliefs that interfere with taking action, being curious, or identifying unexpected opportunities.

    C. Deal with negative chance events such as illness, accidents, rejection, etc. Which of these types of events demoralize the client, and which ones could serve as a motivator or challenge to overcome?

Mitchell, Levin, & Krumboltz (1999), pp. 121–122.

Practical Use via the Career Diamond

Krumboltz made a major contribution in applying social learning theory to career development. It is useful for counselors to note clients' faulty cognitions and to facilitate changing thinking patterns that block career growth. In essence, this theory recognizes that the self can be truncated and cognitive techniques are useful for expanding the self (Figure 5.1). Furthermore, Krumboltz offers specific attitudes useful for career movement over time. On the other hand, he seems to pay attention to learning and thinking without much attention to feelings. Although he acknowledges the importance of

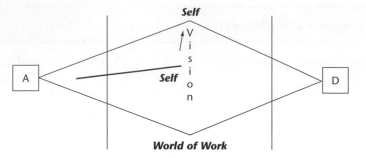

Figure 5.1   Krumboltz's concepts suggesting the Self can learn attitudes to enhance career movement are shown by arrows that widen the Self. Broadening the Self in the Exploring Phase allows clients to be open to more options in the World of Work. Broadening the Self in the Deciding Phase encourages greater integration with changes in the World of Work.

emotions, the theory focuses on techniques that are cognitive in nature, and the implied assumption is that feelings follow thoughts.

Krumboltz's embrace of happenstance demonstrates his ability to update theory to remain current with changing economic conditions in the world of work. The concept of planning ahead while remaining aware of new opportunities follows the Career Diamond process of integrating external factors with new visions of the self and being open to change. As one diamond closes, another exploring phase opens up. Happenstance also demonstrates that the cognitive sets of the self can either limit or broaden the self's ability to take advantage of external changes.

The techniques chapter (Chapter 9) has an outline using a linear decision-making format by providing questions the counselor can use to stimulate client thinking. Throughout the decision outline, however, are questions asking the client to apply information to personal criteria important to the self. With any structured approach in counseling, it is important to reflect client content and feelings and to ask the client to summarize intermittently. Otherwise, the client may simply go through the motions without internalizing the process. Such issues are more thoroughly examined in the counseling process chapter (Chapter 8), where happenstance and other similar concepts are discussed.

GOTTFREDSON—CIRCUMSCRIPTION AND COMPROMISE

Gottfredson (1981, 1996) extends the developmental literature by looking at the early experiences of children from preschool through adolescence. Specifically, she determined that values and interests are weak predictors (but popular in the career literature) whereas social class, intelligence, and the individual's sex are much better predictors (but largely ignored in the career literature) of career choice. Gottfredson and Lapan (1997) accurately criticize career counseling for concentrating on adolescents' and adults' career development, without paying enough attention to important career milestones that occur in the years before adolescence. Their second critique is on the profession's overfocus on the career choices of college students, who are in the minority and likely to be more intelligent and have more options. Finally, they view career development not as career selection but as career *rejection*. "Early vocational choice is the rejection of unacceptable alternatives, of identifying what is most repellent and threatening to the self, not what is most attractive. In short, it is deciding what one wants to avoid" (Gottfredson & Lapan, 1997, p. 429). This is a conceptual shift that can inform many career counselors. Gottfredson elucidates a career development process that begins at a very early age, and this process should be of particular interest to those career counselors who work with grade and middle school-aged youth.

First and foremost for Gottfredson is the concept that young children begin to narrow their acceptable career options in a process referred to as **circumscription**. Her second major tenet emphasizes **compromise**, when individuals are required to modify ideals and make adaptations to the real world of work. Unfortunately, many young children artificially rule out careers, and many adults fail to consider a full range of realistic career options. This theory posits that **gender** is the first element of self-concept and is the least likely to be violated when making compromises. Regrettably, gender stereotypes and career limits are inculcated at an early age, well before an understanding of the complex adult world exists (Gottfredson, 1981; Gottfredson & Lapan, 1997).

Some additional important principles describe the progression of children eliminating career options (Gottfredson, 1981). First, young children think at an intuitive level; older children think concretely; and adolescents are capable of abstract thought. Hence, career rejection follows a similar pattern. As children become aware of the self, they begin to create visions about the self in the future. Jobs are obvious distinguishers among people, and children can use stereotypes about work to describe the self (e.g., "When I grow up, I'm going to be ..." tells us about the child's view of the self). Each stage of career awareness includes an addition of a more complex concept of the self. Stages do not replace each other, they add to each other.

The Four Stages

The following four stages for developing career awareness begin in the preschool years and end in adolescence. The impact of completing each stage lasts throughout life (i.e., the boundaries set in each stage), and each stage builds upon the last. Due to varying rates of development, younger children are expected to be more similar to each other, and older adolescents will demonstrate more variety in their development. Finally, the age ranges are "fuzzy because they represent the ages at which children first enter the stage in any sizable proportion" (Gottfredson, 1981, p. 555).

Stage 1: Orientation to Size and Power

Preschool-aged children (3–5 years) are very concrete in their classification of people and the world. There is a shift from seeing power as magical to power as a part of adulthood. At this age, children have a simple and crude understanding of people and jobs. Big is connected to power, and big people work. Finally, the world is divided into dichotomous distinctions of big–little and good–bad (Gottfredson, 1981; Gottfredson & Lapan, 1997).

Stage 2: Orientation to Sex Roles

Roughly from 6–8 years of age (Gottfredson, 1981), children know about and use sex roles to guide behavior; however, their focus is primarily on visible gender indicators such as clothing, or masculine or feminine activities (dichotomous, inflexible thinking). Also, children in this stage view the adherence to sex roles as "a moral imperative" (Gottfredson, 1981, p. 559; Gottfredson & Lapan, 1997, p. 421). Career decisions are made considering whether more men or more women work in a particular profession. "[T]hey tend to view same-sex behavior as obligatory and cross-sex behavior as wrong or morally deficient" (Gottfredson & Lapan, 1997, p. 421).

Stage 3: Orientation to Social Valuation

Children, typically 9–13, develop the social views of various careers including peer group evaluations. With the onset of abstract thinking comes an understanding that different individuals, regardless of gender, have different levels of prestige; the child becomes aware of prestige and how prestige is very important to adults. Another example of developing abstract and complex thought is the understanding that society connects higher education, and higher intelligence, to careers with more prestige. Those careers come with rewards that lower prestige careers do not (e.g., nice clothes, big office) (Gottfredson, 1981; Gottfredson & Lapan, 1997).

Stage 4: Orientation to the Internal, Unique Self

Stage 4 begins roughly around age 14, although it can begin later for some adolescents. Even though a keen awareness for the public world exists, teenagers can also apply their understanding of personal interests, personality, aptitudes, and morals/values to career choice. This is the process of creating a personal identity via individual uniqueness. The ability to understand

Table 5.1   Summary of Four Stages in the Development of Self-Concept and Occupational Preferences

| Characteristic | *Stage* | | | |
	1. Orientation to Size and Power	*2. Orientation to Sex Roles*	*3. Orientation to Social Valuation*	*4. Orientation to Internal Unique Self*
Ages (years)	3–5	6–8	9–13	14 and over
Grades	Nursery school and kindergarten	1–3	4–8	9 and over
Thought processes	Intuitive	Concrete	Less concrete	Abstract
Ability to classify objects, people occupations	Has not achieved object constancy	Simple groupings	Two-factor groupings	Complex groupings
New elements in perceptions of self and others	Little vs. big	Gender	Social class and intelligence	Personal interests, values, and competencies
New elements in occupational perceptions and preferences	Occupations as adult roles	Sextype	Prestige level	Field of work

and use abstract concepts of the self, adult roles, and work roles makes a career identity possible; however, this budding awareness also brings uncertainty and instability. Table 5.1 presents a summary of Gottfredson's four stages (Gottfredson, 1981; Gottfredson & Lapan, 1997).

Images

For Gottfredson, as with Super, career choice is an attempt to implement one's self-concepts. However, unlike other theories, the primary focus is on the social self. The psychological self is implemented after the public self has been established (Gottfredson & Lapan, 1997). Essentially, a person's concern about how others will view "my image" is primary. Internal thoughts and feelings are secondary. On the other hand, if a career choice is publicly supported, then psychological issues can become more important. A very public characteristic is gender; and humans are, according to this theory, very sensitive to gender issues and violations of gender roles.

A second element of career image is prestige. Prestige of various careers is quite universal in our culture, and by adolescence, most individuals agree on prestige ranking of various careers (Gottfredson & Lapan, 1997).

Circumscription

Starting in stage 1, children begin to eliminate unacceptable or incompatible career options. At first, fantasy fades away. Stage 1 children stop wanting to grow up and be a tiger or knight and begin to identify with actual adult careers. Stage 2 finds the child setting a **tolerable-sextype boundary**. This boundary eliminates unacceptable feminine jobs for men and unacceptable masculine jobs for women (Gottfredson & Lapan, 1997). The environment sends young children important messages about what is unacceptable, and high socioeconomic status (SES) families have different tolerable-sextype boundaries as compared to low SES families.

Stage 3, as mentioned earlier, is the budding awareness of prestige. According to Gottfredson, children at this stage set a tolerable-level boundary. Any vocation that is considered beneath the family's social status is eliminated and will not be pursued unless there are dire circumstances (Gottfredson & Lapan, 1997). By stage 4, enough internal awareness exists that the adolescent can semirealistically assess whether or not he has the ability or skill to be successful. Furthermore, the adolescent may accurately assess that he could be successful, but that the effort it would take to be trained/educated or successful is just too much. In either case, the adolescent sets a tolerable-effort boundary (Gottfredson & Lapan, 1997). Jobs above this boundary will not be pursued, and jobs just below the boundary may fall into the ideal category.

The Zone of Acceptable Alternatives (Figure 5.2) includes jobs that do not violate acceptable sex roles, have enough prestige, but are not beyond personal skills or willingness to invest effort. The goal for career counselors is to help young people have as large a zone as possible. Counselors may help older clients reassess their three boundaries and hopefully expand their acceptable zone. Finally, clients may be taught that most people are "multipotential" (Gottfredson & Lapan, 1997, p. 426). So, a goal of narrowing options to a single occupation forever limits most people unnecessarily.

Compromise

Compromise "is the process by which individuals relinquish their most preferred futures" (Gottfredson & Lapan, 1997, p. 426) and is "changing one's goals to accommodate to uncontrollable circumstances" (Gottfredson, 1981, p. 569). Various factors moderate young people's career decisions. For example, how accessible is the profession? As a teacher of undergraduate psychology students, the second author regularly sees students who want to work in forensics for the FBI. Given the limited number of available jobs in this area, the dream for students at 18 is rarely a realistic choice by the time the students graduate. Compromise can also be impacted by perceived dis-

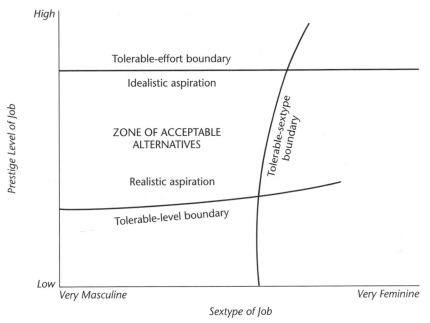

Figure 5.2   Zone of Acceptable Alternatives

crimination or family constraints. The goal is to compromise and to gain a "good enough" career (Gottfredson & Lapan, 1997, p. 427).

In a departure from her earlier work, which postulated that compromise occurs first for vocational interests, second for level of prestige, and third at sextype, more recently, Gottfredson (1996) has suggested that the degree of compromise is indicated by levels of change required: major, moderate, and minor. Initially, young people may have idealistic career choices that are solely based upon preference and do not include real world moderators (e.g., accessibility, discrimination, etc.). Compromise is the process by which young people shift from idealistic careers to realistic careers.

Major compromises occur when a choice clearly violates one of the boundaries. This type of career choice is highly threatening to the self-concept, and individuals, especially boys, will sacrifice prestige as long as the job does not violate sextype. Moderate compromises are tolerable across all three boundaries. Although not ideal by any stretch of the imagination, the choice clearly does not threaten self-concept. In this case, sextype will be "good enough," and the focus will be on prestige. That is, the individual will purse higher prestige jobs even if the jobs are not good matches with the psychological self. In the event that the compromises are considered minor, the individual views a variety of career options as good. In this case, sextype and prestige are "good enough," and the individual can focus on the best match for internal preferences, such as interests, values, etc. (Gottfredson & Lapan, 1997).

On a final note, not all change in adolescence is compromise (Gottfredson & Lapan, 1997). Young people have new experiences that correct errors in perceptions of the world of work or the self. These new experiences may also adjust the various boundaries. Compromise only occurs when an individual feels *forced* to avoid or give up a preferred career choice(s).

Practical Use via the Career Diamond

According to Gottfredson's theory of circumscription, self-interests are not developed because individuals limit their awareness to what is socially acceptable for people in their groups, be it gender, SES, or race. Because the career identity of the self is underdeveloped, the world of work dominates and people fit themselves into external demand characteristics.

Gottfredson has made a valuable contribution to career development literature by exposing societal influences that limit personal choices. Specifically, the Career Diamond is flipped when a client presents career concerns that are in line with Gottfredson (Figure 5.3). The self is truncated, and the external world dominates. Counselors may introduce the concept of family and/or cultural background to encourage the client to tell the story of how interests developed and choices were eliminated. Career counselors can identify the boundaries and zone of acceptable occupational alternatives to facilitate clients' awareness of the limits set by social constructs of gender-type, prestige, and self-concept. Specifically, the counselor explores with the client what cognitive restrictions the client has inculcated based upon social messages regarding gender; what social value the client attributes to careers under consideration; and how the client's self-image is in line with such social constructs or not. Hence, the self has an arrow indicating the need to expand so that it becomes equal to the external width. If the self

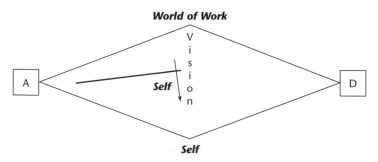

Figure 5.3   The Career Diamond is turned upside down in Gottfredson's theory, with the World of Work on top, dominating the Self on the bottom.

can expand to full self-expression, free of limiting social constructs, the diamond can reverse with the self in control.

The zone implies that multiple jobs can be acceptable. The responsibility for narrowing choices is the individual. Compromise also implies that the current decision does not have to be a final decision. The career counselor can listen to the "have to haves," "wishes," and "don't cares." Client themes may include one or more of Gottfredson's three boundaries and may reveal what issues are most important to the client.

If one is working with grade school- to middle school-aged children, the development of career boundaries has direct implications for career services in the school. This theory could be used as a psychoeducational presentation for teachers. Finally, Gottfredson offers interesting insight as to why a client might purposely ignore personal interests when choosing a career (Remember Super's 14th proposition?).

LENT, BROWN, AND HACKETT—SOCIAL COGNITIVE CAREER THEORY

Social cognitive career theory (SCCT) is based upon Bandura's (1986) social cognitive theory. SCCT applies learning principles to describe the development of an individual's career interests, choices, and performance efforts (Lent, Brown, & Hackett, 1994; Lent & Brown, 1996). The empirical support found for SCCT constructs (Brown & Lent, 1996; Swanson & Gore, 2000) suggests the theory may replace Krumboltz's original as Super replaced Ginzberg.

SCCT describes career development as a complex interaction between an individual, her behavior, and the environment (Lent & Brown, 1996; Lent & Hackett, 1987). The interactive factors are directly related to Bandura's (1986) **triadic reciprocal model of causality**. Basically, an individual has unique internal cognitive and affective states. These internal states may or may not be connected to overt behavior (think about a time you were embarrassed, but pretended not to care), but they are connected to an external environmental cue that anticipates rewards and punishments for behavior (Lent & Brown, 1996). Thus, the internal self responds to external cues with specific behaviors. Overt behavior (e.g., spilling coffee on one's shirt) can influence internal states as well as creating responses (e.g., spilling coffee on a co-worker). At the same time, the external environment sends cues that may or may not change internal states and overt behavior. Plus, the individual sends cues to the external environment. Needless to say, all three domains interact and influence each other. Add some more people to the mix, and one can see how complex this can get! In career development, SCCT defines

CASE STUDY 5.1   But You Could Be a...

Sherry was struggling with her motivation to do as well academically as she knew she could. As a 19-year-old sophomore, she had recently won the Outstanding Chemistry Student award at the university honors banquet. Her freshmen-year GPA as a pre-med major was 3.625. Sherry was active in the community, including participating in chemistry fairs and serving as a counselor for the high school chemistry camp. Though clearly she was a talented science student, she began to dread attending class and could not bear the thought of participating in another chemistry camp. The dream of becoming a physician with many more years of science courses was becoming a nightmare. An even bigger problem was the sequential nature of the courses she was scheduled to take. If she took a semester to try other, nonmajor courses, she would effectively lose a year. Because her family was struggling to afford college, Sherry could not bring herself to ask for financial assistance for an extra year. Her advisor, the one who recommended her for the chemistry award, strongly suggested she keep taking the science sequence. He assured her that her doubts were common and the exciting courses were just around the corner.

How Would You Conceptualize This Case?

1. What developmental tasks do Sherry and most adolescents Sherry's age face?
2. How would you conceptualize Sherry's situation using concepts from theories by Super or Gottfredson?
3. Would the family's financial situation change your counseling approach? (That is, if the client could easily afford

another year, would you make different recommendations?)
4. As a counselor, would you worry that Sherry is "supposed" to become a physician to increase the family's social respect (i.e. Sherry as the "hero" of the family)? How would this situation affect your career counseling approach?

What Actually Happened?

Sherry sought counseling at the university counseling center. The counselor labeled Sherry's struggle as her search for identity. Counseling became the space where she could examine what she truly wanted and how she would deal with the pressures she felt. Over time, Sherry recognized she had circumscribed her choices by her economic fears and family pressure. She determined that she had the right and the opportunity to explore her interests.

Sherry told everyone she was still a pre-med major, but she decided to take a year off from the science courses. She spent a year taking introductory classes in almost every college on the university campus (business, liberal arts, etc.) and made an interesting discovery—students can enjoy what they are studying! Sherry finally decided to major in political science and minor in theater and psychology. She rarely missed class and graduated with a 3.821 GPA. Her final struggle became which area of graduate study she wanted to pursue. There were just too many exciting options across a variety of fields where she could gain adequate financial aid! After the initial shock, her family supported her decision when they saw how much happier she was.

the three primary domains as self-efficacy beliefs, outcome expectations, and personal goals (Lent et al., 1994; Lent & Brown, 1996).

Self-efficacy is defined as an individual's evaluation of her own abilities to plan and institute the correct action(s), which will lead to successful performance and goal attainment (Lent & Brown, 1996; also see Bandura 1986). It is important to remember that self-efficacy is based upon actions a person knows she can accomplish as well as an awareness of the consequences for taking or not taking said actions (Osborne, 1996). Self-efficacy is also based upon past experience and not potential. There is a difference between *knowing* what one can do and *hoping* one can be successful.

Self-efficacy is believed to "determine one's choice of activities and environments, as well as one's effort expenditure, persistence, thought patterns, and emotional reactions when confronted by obstacles" (Lent et al., 1994, p. 83). A person's self-efficacy can be positively or negatively impacted by: (a) actual personal accomplishments, (b) internal states (e.g., feel good/bad about actions), (c) observational or vicarious learning, and (d) responses from the social environment (can impact view of personal accomplishments and/or internal states) (Lent & Brown, 1996). Obviously, positive experiences are expected to enhance self-efficacy while negative experiences have the opposite impact.

Outcome expectations are, as one would expect, a person's beliefs about how something will turn out (Lent et al., 1994; Lent & Brown, 1996). Outcome expectations are based upon past experiences (being successful or unsuccessful) as well as observing others in a similar situation. If a highly skilled individual fails, an observer is unlikely to have positive expectations. On the other hand, if a less-skilled individual is successful, then the more-skilled observer might assume success even if she has little to no experience in that particular domain (e.g., a teenager watches a 10-year-old do something on a skateboard).

In regard to career, high outcome expectations will motivate a person to continue trying even with minor setbacks, whereas low outcome expectations lead to little effort, giving up quickly, or avoiding the task altogether (Lent et al., 1994). It is also important to note the impact outcome expectations have upon internal states. Just because a person has high expectations for success does not mean the person will pursue that type of work. For example, a person may expect a Ph.D. in physics to lead to a lucrative career; however, if that person has low self-efficacy in science, then a career in physics will be avoided. In addition, a person may consider chances for success high as a mechanic (e.g., a parent owns a shop and has taught the child for the last 10 years), but hate that type of work. In that case, the inner state has a stronger influence, and the person avoids the career even though high expectations exist. To sum it up, outcome expectations are important, but they do not hold the strongest influence for behavior (Lent & Brown, 1996).

Personal goals come into play via organization and guidance. Namely, a person organizes behavior in the direction of achieving one's goals (Lent & Brown, 1996). Goals are important because they represent a desired future, a set of internal standards for performance, and links to self-satisfaction by successfully meeting set goals (Lent et al., 1994). Organizing and directing behavior may include specialized training or education, internships/apprenticeships, or just plain practice. In addition, many goals are long-term and require repeated attempts before success occurs. Personal goals help provide the direction and motivation to persist despite setbacks or periods of no rewards (Lent & Brown, 1996). Personal goals are impacted by self-efficacy in that one typically chooses a domain where skills exist. Career counselors regularly tune in to client descriptions of personal goals that are not based upon self-efficacy. Such unrealistic personal goals may set up a client for disappointment. Finally, failure to meet personal goals could be expected to have deleterious effects for inner states whereas success has the opposite effect. Thus, career counselors need to pay attention to the inner world of the client as well as presenting concerns.

SCCT (Lent & Brown, 1996) emphasizes two additional concepts: (a) level of attainment and (b) persistence. Self-efficacy, outcome expectations, and personal goals impact and are impacted by level of attainment and persistence. Self-efficacy and outcome expectations combine to influence personal goals. If goals are set high, then one is expected to have a higher level of attainment and be able to perform job tasks at a superior level. If self-efficacy or outcome expectations are low, then level of attainment will follow suit. Persistence leads to self-efficacy (repeated practice of the skills) and positive outcome expectations (over time, rewards are expected or the person will give up and make a different career choice). Consequently, there is a feedback loop that mutually influences self-efficacy, outcome expectations, personal goals, level of attainment, and persistence. Career counselors can help clients identify each area and assess what psychological work is needed. In addition, understanding the feedback loop between external demands and self-evaluations can help clients discriminate between "I'm totally wrong for this field" and "Oh, if I work in this one area, I could be successful in this field."

Barriers, whether environmental or intrapersonal, truncate career development (Lent, Brown, & Hackett, 2000). Historically, barriers have been considered external to the individual. Lent et al. (2000) add *intra*personal barriers as an important factor to consider, and they emphasize the point that environmental and intrapersonal barriers typically co-occur. Thus, career counselors should: (a) assess environmental barriers (e.g., discrimination), (b) assess intrapersonal barriers (e.g., self-concept—how one thinks about himself), and (c) assess the interplay between the two barriers. By removing barriers, career interests can grow. Interests are expected to lead to career goals, and goals are expected to lead to action (Lent et al., 2000).

Finally, other theories postulate that aptitudes (abilities) and values are important predictors of career satisfaction and success. SCCT captures those concepts within self-efficacy and outcome expectations. Specifically, the development of self-efficacy is the development of abilities, and values are expressed through outcome expectations (Lent et al., 1994; Lent & Brown, 1996). If a person values helping others, then the outcome expectations of "doing a good job" would include benefiting others. Although other theories may describe values differently, it is heartening to know that so many great minds agree that values are an important factor for career identity.

Vocational Interests

The developmental process is expected to repeat itself over the life-span; however, SCCT describes vocational interest development as most flexible during childhood and adolescence (Lent et al., 1994; Lent & Brown, 1996). In addition, SCCT recognizes changes in the work environment (e.g., a career field becomes static, exposure to a new field of work) or special events (e.g., birth of a child) as creating opportunities for clients to expand self-efficacy (i.e., grow in new skills) and pursue new personal goals (i.e., change careers).

According to Lent and Brown (1996), the environment exposes individuals vicariously, as well as directly, to a whole host of activities that are connected to various careers. Young people hear parents and other adults talk about their jobs; school presents information and skill-building activities (e.g., band, athletics); and TV and literature open windows to the entire world. With all of this information available, individuals focus on some careers while ignoring others because the social environment provides selective reinforcement. Parents, teachers, and other adults provide reinforcement and punishment for various careers. As a child ages, peers and eventually one's own internal states reward and punish the pursuit of different careers. In addition, self-efficacy is developing during this time. As an individual practices various skills (e.g., public speaking), a feedback loop is created. If positive feedback occurs, the individual will persist in developing those skills and have positive internal states. Later, these experiences can positively influence outcome expectations and personal goals. Of course, negative feedback would be expected to have the opposite effect.

Box 5.2   Social Cognitive Career Counseling Goals

According to Brown and Lent (1996), the above tenets relate to career counseling. The following is a short description of SCCT therapy goals:

1. **Self-efficacy** beliefs and **outcome expectations** are the foundation for occupational and academic interest development. Clients often present with faulty self-efficacy beliefs and outcome expectations. Counselors assess both domains and look for differences between observable or historical information and current client evaluations. Career counselors then focus on helping the client develop accurate perceptions. One technique is to have a client's family member(s) or close friend(s) fill out an aptitude test for the client. (There is a variety to choose from.) Then compare the client's scores to those of the family member(s). If discrepancies exist, a thorough exploration is warranted. (Typically, clients will be harder on themselves.)

2. Perceptions of barriers to accessing education/training or being hired may limit a person's choices, even if he has high self-efficacy. Counselors assess the accuracy of the client's perceived barriers. If accurate, the client can form plans for overcoming or living with said barriers. If inaccurate, developing corrective experiences can be implemented. Also, counselors identify barriers the client may have missed and help the client prepare to deal with obstacles before the barriers materialize. This can aid in self-efficacy development while avoiding a punishing experience.

3. Positive **self-efficacy** and **outcome expectations** are reinforced through personal accomplishments. Clients require help identifying and persisting in acquiring new skills (this may include finding a model to observe). Reinforcement of those efforts is paramount either in counseling or in their

It is important to note that vocational interests can be unnecessarily narrowed (Lent & Brown, 1996). First, individuals miss opportunities when they are not exposed to a full range of activities or cannot observe positive models that can build self-efficacy. So, some people may avoid career options because they have little or no experience in certain domains and consequently have low outcome expectations (Lent & Brown, 1996; Lent & Hackett, 1987). Second, individuals may have unrealistic or inappropriate perceptions about the outcome expectations or their self-efficacy (e.g., math is too hard for girls; boys cannot be good cooks). Third, social expectations of gender may limit a person (Lent & Brown, 1996; Lent & Hackett, 1987). Males and females experience negative inner states (punishment) if they violate gender stereotypes. The environment may provide cues about what males and females should and should not do. Fourth, social norms may limit career choices for people of different races (Lent & Brown, 1996; Lent & Hackett,

environment. Counselors remind clients how much improvement they have made. This self-comparison can help a client adjust how he thinks about himself. In addition, old experiences that led to low self-efficacy beliefs and negative outcome expectations may have been inaccurately interpreted. Environmental context, age at the time of the experience, personal skills at that time, etc. may have led to a faulty generalization to the present day. Reprocessing old experiences may also be beneficial.

Lent et al. (1994) suggest that increased vocational interest development may take time. Specifically, newly acquired self-efficacy may not lead to immediate change. Repeated successful experiences that demonstrate mastery need to occur before a person is willing to consider new opportunities.

Clients and career counselors need to be aware of this very possible temporal lag.

4. Analyzing occupations of little interest is very useful. It provides a client an opportunity to discuss past negative experiences and beliefs that may have led inaccurately to low self-efficacy. In addition, incorrect information about various occupations can be identified and corrected.

5. Differences between stated interests and demonstrated skills are fertile ground. Whether it be high interest and low skill or low interest and high skill, the client provides the career counselor with a window into self-efficacy beliefs, outcome expectations, and personal goals. Exploration of these differences can help a client to expand options (if skills are high) or identify barriers (if skills are low).

1987). SCCT understands that race and sex may have some physiological impact, but primary impact for race and sex are psychological and social. When working with clients, SCCT theorists suggest expanding career options and using "expert" opinions to describe how racial and gender barriers can interfere with career satisfaction and success.

Occupational Choice

SCCT recognizes that in an ideal situation, individuals would pursue careers that interest them and work with people who have similar interests and values (a la Holland). However, the realities of economics, family dictates, educational/training background, and discrimination can override personal interests and narrow choices (and these can combine with unrealistic evaluations of self-efficacy and outcome expectations) (Lent & Brown, 1996).

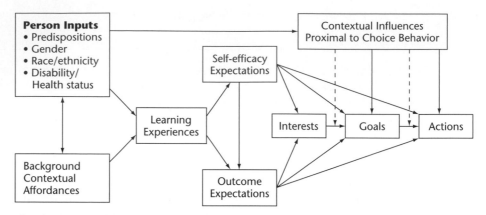

Figure 5.4   Model of Social Cognitive Influences on Career Choice Behavior

Important environmental factors can be objective (e.g., access to education, financial support) or perceived (e.g., how the individual appraises and responds to the environment) (Lent et al., 2000). Career choice is not directed solely by environmental factors. However, as in the Career Diamond, SCCT describes an interplay between the individual and the environment—present objective environmental influences and "how individuals make sense of, and respond to, what their environment provides" (Lent et al., 2000, p. 37).

When helping clients identify their career interests and make choices, career counselors may want to consider two levels (Lent et al., 1994; Lent & Brown, 1996). First, there are the distal background influences (e.g., family, available role models) that have influenced various learning experiences connected to current self-efficacy beliefs, outcome expectations, and personal goals. Second, there are current environmental factors (e.g., discrimination, financial support) that expand or limit current career choice. SCCT hypothesizes that career interests will be broader and that clients will be more likely to form and pursue their goals if the environment is supportive. Nonsupportive or hostile environments will limit career interests and reduce the likelihood of forming and achieving goals (Lent & Brown, 1996; Lent et al., 2000). Career services may include helping clients assess and leave nonsupportive environments and enter supportive environments. Figure 5.4 is a graphic representation of SCCT.

Practical Use via the Career Diamond

SCCT does a nice job of capturing the limits imposed by internal dynamics such as self-esteem and self-efficacy, as well as the restrictive influences of external factors. Hence, both the self and the world of work require greater

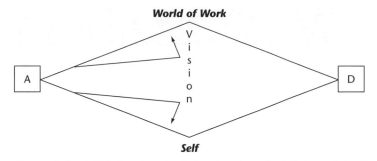

Figure 5.5   SCCT describes the limits placed on the Self through ineffective attitudes and beliefs. Personal restrictions are learned in an external environment that confines learning, so the Self is not only restricted but the view of the World of Work is also limited.

exploration to expand factors used for building a vision and before setting priorities in the Deciding Phase (Figure 5.5). This theory can be used to help clients recognize where external demands have limited their career choices, to identify self-given limits according to social constructs, and to question their acceptance of either limit.

As with Krumboltz, SCCT theory may be criticized for appearing to focus on logic and rational interpretation of external and internal cues while minimizing affect. SCCT does recognize "inner states," which include emotions as motivators and punishers for choosing a direction and maintaining persistence. However, there is a definite "think before you feel" sense to this theory. Finally, there is the lack of a thorough application to practice. SCCT is a newer theory, and it attempts to correct some of the gaps in previous career theory by explaining how career interests and choices are made (Lent et al., 2000). Career counselors may need to be creative in applying this theory to actual practice or look to related literature for application strategies.

SUMMARY

Although no one theory fully describes all career behavior and its antecedents, counselors draw from each theory what is applicable to each individual client. The Career Diamond offers the counselor a means to picture the client's needs and to choose the concepts and techniques that apply to the client's situation. In this way, the Career Diamond serves as generic diagram that can adapt to many theoretical ideas within the framework of a basic exploring and deciding process. The strength of a generic picture is not in what it adds to the body of knowledge but in how it directs the use of existing ideas. For example, all of the theories in Chapter 5 suggest some

CASE STUDY 5.2   What Happened to My Career?

Luis (who has an undergraduate degree) worked as a contractor for 15 plus years. After constructing new homes and small commercial buildings, remodeling, and running subcontracting crews, he decided to leave the field. His business had not grown enough to allow him to work only as a foreman, so he was still involved in manual labor. But, due to health changes, he found it more and more difficult to do such physical labor. He also consistently had difficulties collecting all of the money owed to him. Reasons ranged from poor record keeping to customers purposely failing to pay. Due to his expertise, Luis was able to secure excellent employment as a retail manager for a major home repair store. After gaining several promotions in the company, a political incident with a district manager resulted in a demotion. Luis applied to a different company that promised him a store manager position within one to three months. Six months later, he was still making $8 an hour as a swing manager. Finally, after changing companies again, Luis was rapidly promoted into a position in which he was making a good salary.

Luis comes to counseling presenting his current problem. His new company just declared bankruptcy; he has three months to liquidate the inventory and is then out of work. There are no other local companies in need of his expertise, and he will not move because his youngest child is still in high school. Also, he and his wife just built a new home. Luis is very discouraged and unsure of what his options are "at my age."

How Would You Conceptualize This Case?

1. Which theories do and do not apply to this client (include theories from this and the previous chapters)?
2. If the client changed careers, he would probably earn a lot less than his last salary. How would you help him with this reality?
3. How important do you think the new home and/or keeping his child in the local high school is in regard to making career decisions? Are these

form of cognitive restructuring to encourage the client's full exploration and discerning decision making. Krumboltz's concepts describe limited thinking patterns that narrow the number of occupational options. Gottfredson shows how cognitive limits stem from the social constructs related to gender and prestige. Lent and colleagues explain how people weigh alternatives based upon self-evaluations and social influences. Counselors can use these theoretical concepts to create interventions that encourage clients to reframe their thinking.

The Career Diamond also notes adaptations that career clients and counselors must make in regard to external factors affecting career behavior. The next chapter describes changes in career concepts that are required to adapt to a fluid global economy.

examples of an "ism," a la Krumboltz, or something else?

4. Would you invite his spouse to come for counseling, too? Should his child come in? If yes, would you conduct individual or family sessions?

5. Would you ask the client about his spouse's career? If she had a career, what would your approach be? If she did not work outside the home, what would your approach be?

What Actually Happened?

Early in counseling, the client needed to work through feelings of anger against employers and fears that age would limit his job opportunities. He also examined his embedded construct of masculinity. Accepting less salary would reduce his sense of worth as a breadwinner and could mean, he feared, lesser status in the eyes of his wife and son. His wife was invited to counseling sessions and reminded the client that a stable income, even if less, would probably meet their expenses and might give him time to build rental prop-

erty, a dream they shared years earlier. The wife was very fulfilled as a swimming instructor at the local YWCA and coached a girls' swim team. Her salary was low, but she felt her enjoyment of her work made the job worth it. She saw no reason why her husband could not find satisfying work without feeling pressured to bring in a high salary. The client expressed his gratitude for his wife's understanding.

The counselor connected the client to a state program for displaced workers. The program paid for him to return to school where he earned a master's degree and sought employment in the state transportation agency as an administrator for highway building and maintenance. Even though the salary was much less than his previous earnings, job security was a priority for the client, who was committed to staying in the area. He also used his contractor knowledge to build a rental, in his spare time, for supplemental income. During termination, the client remarked that he felt he had moved through a crisis to a more meaningful part of his life.

STUDY OUTLINE: KEY TERMS AND CONCEPTS

I. Social Learning Theory and Krumboltz

A. Learning is important to the ever-changing workplace.

1. Learning can be behavioral, emotional, or cognitive in nature.

2. Career development occurs through learning concepts, attitudes, personal constructs, work habits, and role modeling.

a. **Task approach skills**: To learn a new skill, a person gradually tries new behaviors with each attempt progressively approximating the final goal. Behavior is slowly shaped by doing small actions first and then trying more encompassing behaviors.

      b. Learning is positively and negatively impacted by **role models** (other people who demonstrate desired traits and behavior patterns to be imitated).

      c. **Self Observation Generalities (SOG)**: The person observes herself and constructs general concepts defining her self concept.

    3. Once something is learned, even if unhelpful, the individual may be closed to new learning.

      a. Attitudes and concepts conform to **confirmatory bias** (The person denies evidence that contradicts previously held attitudes or biases or SOGs.)

    4. Work habits include a series of learning units such as task approach skills.

  B. Attitudes and reasoning

    1. Positive work attitudes include hard work as necessary, flexibility, acceptance of change, self-responsibility versus blame, and conscientious behavior.

    2. Personal constructs: self-observation generalities, personal "isms," and importance of assessing positive/negative attitudes ("I can't).

    3. Ineffective reasoning includes overgeneralizations, unreasonably high standards, exaggerated fears or consequences, inflexibility, narrow goals or focus, and fighting versus all odds.

  C. Changing Rigid Career Planning to Awareness of Serendipity

    1. Needed for constant change in world of work

    2. **Happenstance**

      a. Surprise events can represent opportunity.

      b. Positive attitude to change helpful for career adaptations

  D. Career Diamond application

    1. Focuses on some aspects of the self (thinking, internalized messages)

    2. Provides guidelines for expanding external awareness

    3. Recognition of adapting to change

    4. Little emphasis on feeling

II. Gottfredson—Circumscription and Compromise

  A. Early career development involves "rejection" of options as opposed to "choosing" options.

    1. **Circumscription**: Process of narrowing adult work roles into acceptable and unacceptable categories

      a. **Tolerable-sextype boundary**: What can I do given I'm a male or female?

      b. Tolerable-level boundary: What jobs are beneath my family?

      c. Tolerable-effort boundary: What is within my skill level? Does the training/education go beyond my willingness to invest into it (e.g., time, effort)?

      d. Zone of acceptable occupational alternatives: jobs that do not violate the three boundaries.

  2. **Compromise**: Process of giving up ideal careers for more realistic ones

      a. Major: Clear violation of a boundary. Will sacrifice prestige in order to maintain sextype.

      b. Moderate: Tolerable across all three domains. Sextype is "good enough," so will now focus on prestige.

      c. Minor: Good match with each domain. Sextype and prestige are "good enough." Will now focus on personal issues (e.g., interests, values).

  3. **Gender**: The first element of self-concept. Used by younger children to eliminate future career options. Based upon not violating gender-based norms and very important to career development.

C. Stages of development of career awareness

  1. **Orientation to size and power**: Ages 3–5. Shift from magical thinking to size equals power. Dichotomous thinkers: good–bad, big–little.

  2. **Orientation to sex roles**: Ages 6–8. Moral imperative to adhere to sex roles. Male jobs versus female jobs.

  3. **Orientation to social valuation**: Ages 9–13. Develop an awareness of prestige—what does society think about different jobs.

  4. **Orientation to the internal, unique self:** Age 14+. Personal interests and values can be matched with different work environments.

D. Career Diamond application

  1. Gender stereotypes and prestige are useful topics to help clients examine how occupational exploration has been restricted or not.

  2. Clear implications for career services in grade and middle schools.

  3. Offers a rationale for why some clients may sacrifice personal interests.

  4. Deals with both the internal and external factors of career choice.

  5. Explains why some individuals have very narrow career options.

III. Lent, Brown, and Hackett—Social Cognitive Career Theory
   A. Based upon Bandura's (1986) **Triadic Reciprocal Model of Causality**
      1. A complex interaction exists between the individual, behavior, and the environment.
      2. **Self-efficacy** beliefs: A person's appraisal of their abilities. Based upon past experience. Contains the concept "aptitude" from other theories.
      3. **Outcome expectations**: Person's beliefs about how effort and persistence will turn out (successful/unsuccessful). Perceived barriers and unsupportive environments can limit a person despite high self-efficacy. Contains the concept "values" from other theories.
      4. **Personal Goals**: Symbolic of future. Organize and direct behavior.
      5. Level of attainment and persistence are influenced by self-efficacy beliefs and outcome expectations.
   B. Vocational interests
      1. Development of interests repeats itself over the life-span, but is most flexible in adolescence and early adulthood.
      2. Environment exposes individual to new career options.
      3. Environment rewards and punishes individuals for pursuing various careers. This may follow gender stereotypes.
      4. Development of self-efficacy influences what a person will and will not be interested in.
      5. Limited environmental exposure leads to limited interest development.
      6. Gender and race are social constructs. Limits placed on various groups of people are more environmental than physical.
   C. Occupational choice
      1. Ideally, people will pursue careers that match their personality and work with people with similar interests.
      2. Reality finds the environment limiting career choice (regional layoffs, financial restraints, family dictates).
      3. First, look at the background of client that has helped form self-efficacy beliefs, outcome expectations, and personal goals.
      4. Second, look at current environment for barriers and nonsupportive or hostile friends/family.
      5. Interaction of points c and d may expand or narrow occupational choices as well as effort put forth to commit and follow through.

D. Career Diamond application
   1. Cognitions dominate affect.
   2. Theory well developed, needs more application to practice.

EXERCISES

1. Consider Gottfredson's concepts of circumscription and compromise. Try to recall your early ideas regarding appropriate occupations as a member of your race and gender. When you were a child what occupations were considered to be prestigious by your family? In what ways does your experience validate Gottfredson's hypotheses or not? Do you think eliminating occupations is as important a factor in career development as projecting fantasies about possible occupations?

2. Krumboltz describes isms, self-observation generalities, and negative attitudes that impede career development. As a group, brainstorm examples of statements a client could make that reveal negative constructs that need to be examined and reframed in counseling. In dyads, role-play the client using the statements and consequent counselor interventions. How would Krumboltz's application of social learning theory apply to career education programs?

3. How does self-efficacy differ from self-concept? Describe the impact of self-efficacy for career choices from an example in your life or the life of someone you know.

REFERENCES

Bandura, A. (1986). *Social foundations of thought and action: A social cognitive theory*. Englewood Cliffs, NJ: Prentice-Hall.

Brown, S. D., & Lent, R. W. (1996). A social cognitive framework for career counseling. *Career Development Quarterly, 44*(4), 354–366.

Gottfredson, L. S. (1981). Circumscription and compromise: A developmental theory of occupational aspirations. *Journal of Counseling Psychology, 28*(6), 545–579.

Gottfredson, L. S. (1996). Gottfredson's theory of circumscription and compromise. In D. Brown & L. Brooks (Eds.), *Career choice and development* (3rd ed., pp. 179–232). San Francisco: Jossey-Bass.

Gottfredson, L. S., & Lapan, R. T. (1997). Assessing gender-based circumscription of occupational aspirations. *Journal of Career Assessment, 5*(4), 419–441.

Hackett, G., & Lent, R. W. (1991). Advances in vocational theory and re-search: A 20-year retrospective. *Journal of Vocational Behavior, 38*(1), 3–38.

Holland, J. L. (1976). A new synthesis for an old method and a new analysis of some old phenomena. *The Counseling Psychologist, 6*(3), 12–15.

Krumboltz, J. D. (1976). This Chevrolet can't float or fly. *The Counseling Psychologist, 6*(3), 17–19.

Krumboltz, J. D. (1983). Private rules for career decision-making. (Special Publications Series No. 38). Columbus: National Center for Research in Vocational Education, Advanced Study Center, Ohio State University. (ERIC Document Reproduction Service No. ED 229 608).

Krumboltz, J. D. (1991). *Career Beliefs Inventory.* Palo Alto, CA: Consulting Psychology Press.

Krumboltz, J. D. (1993). Integrating career and personal counseling. *Career Development Quarterly, 42*(2), 143–148.

Krumboltz, J. D. (1994). Improving career development theory from a so-cial learning perspective. In M. L. Savickas & R. W. Lent (Eds.), *Convergence in career theories: Implications for science and prac-tice* (pp. 9–31). Palo Alto, CA: Davies-Black.

Krumboltz, J. D. (1996). A learning theory of career counseling. In M. L. Savickas & W. B. Walsh (Eds.), *Handbook of career counseling theory and practice* (pp. 55–80). Palo Alto, CA: Davies-Black.

Krumboltz, J. D., & Hamel, D. (1977). *Guide to decision-making skills.* New York: Psychological Assessment Resources.

Krumboltz, J. D., Mitchell, A. M., & Jones, G. B. (1976). A social learning the-ory of career selection. *Counseling Psychologist, 6*(1), 71–81.

Lent, R. W., & Brown, S. D. (1996). Social cognitive approach to career de-velopment: An overview. *Career Development Quarterly, 44*(4), 310–321.

Lent, R. W., Brown, S. D., & Hackett, G. (1994). Toward a unifying social cognitive theory of career and academic interest, choice, and perform-ance. *Journal of Vocational Behavior, 45*(1), 79–122.

Lent, R. W., Brown, S. D., & Hackett, G. (2000). Contextual supports and barriers to career choice: A social cognitive analysis. *Journal of Counseling Psychology, 47*(1), 36–49.

Lent, R. W., & Hackett, G. (1987). Career self-efficacy: Empirical status and future directions. *Journal of Vocational Behavior, 30*(3), 347–382.

Mitchell, K. E., Levin, A. S., & Krumboltz, J. D. (1999). Planned happen-stance: Constructing unexpected career opportunities. *Journal of Counseling and Development, 77,* 115–125.

Osborne, R. E. (1996). *Self: An eclectic approach.* Boston: Allyn & Bacon.

Sharf, R. (1997). *Applying career development theory to counseling* (2nd ed.). Pacific Grove, CA: Brooks/Cole.

Swanson, J. L., & Gore, P. A., Jr. (2000). Advances in vocational psychology theory and practice. In S. D. Brown and R. W. Lent (Eds.), *Handbook of counseling psychology* (3rd ed., pp. 233–269). New York: John Wiley.

CHAPTER 6

Career Counseling for the Global Economy

We believe that if men have the talent to invent new machines that put men out of work, they have the talent to put those men back to work.

John F. Kennedy, speech, Wheeling, West Virginia, September 27, 1962

The economy of recent years has seen such rapid changes that new challenges are presented for the career field. Some occupations have become obsolete, and new, unforeseen occupations have been created. Job descriptions change so expeditiously that job titles lose any consistency of meaning. Career information has proliferated and is readily available in multiple formats. Such rapid change makes it obvious to anyone who is paying attention that predicting the future with certainty is unlikely. Constant transformations in the world of work seem to invalidate a traditional sense of career planning and goal-setting.

Bingham and Ward (1994) remind us that a new millennium will call for change in the practice of career services.

> If vocational counseling was born from the changing demographics and economic needs of this century, then clearly career counseling will need to change in response to the changing needs of the coming century. (p. 168)

Several authors propose career concepts designed to deal with the fluidity of the modern economy. Worldwide, corporations have streamlined operations to adapt to constantly changing conditions. Workplace locations are moved from country to country, and products are produced as they are ordered to save costs on warehousing inventories. Within such an inconstant milieu, employees are hired and fired; and small business suppliers start up and go out of business as large corporations downsize and then hire again. To meet the demands of changing working conditions, workers must also adapt regularly.

GLOBAL ECONOMY'S IMPACT ON CAREER

Miller-Tiedeman (1999) describes the modern workplace as experienced today by many career clients. Frequent changes in employment force individuals to be responsible for their own careers in almost every respect. Because organizations have downsized and flattened the hierarchies of chains of command, people work in self-managed teams that replace the supervisory roles of middle management (Keeley, 2003). As a result of the streamlined management, workers are responsible for their own work and the rate of production. They do not have supervisors advising them on what they need to learn to remain competitive. Reductions in budgets also mean reduced in-house training. However, outdated work skills place workers at a risk of losing their jobs, so people need to continually upgrade their training. New learning is both mandatory and another area of self-responsibility. Even if a worker can maintain excellent performance and high-level skills, the worker will still probably experience many job changes and even multiple changes of career fields (Berger, 1990). **Careerists** are wise to continually maintain dependable support networks and mentoring resources for advice and emotional encouragement. (A *careerist* is a person who views work life across the life-span.)

Lean, cost-effective budgets also set up a structure where workers are hired for increasingly specialized fields that fulfill specific contracts and are needed for periods of time. When the company's needs change, the current specialists are let go, and new specialists are hired. Employees are responsible for showing how they add value to the company, and they are expected to learn, on their own, what is required to demonstrate ever-increasing contributions. If young people who are educated in the latest skills are readily available, companies may prefer to hire a young person for less money than they are paying the established worker. With job security for the long term becoming obsolete, age discrimination is more likely and even retirement saving becomes another area of responsibility for the individual.

Self-employment is the fastest growing alternative for many careerists who have learned to be self-sufficient and adaptable in creating their own places in the new economy (Levy & Murnane, 1992; Mishel, Bernstein, & Schmitt, 2000; Pink, 2001). Even as employees, careerists need to consider themselves as self-employed because in reality, companies actually rent a worker's contributions for only as long as the worker serves a purpose. The wise careerist bears the responsibility of managing the ever-present possibility of downsizing and is ever observant of the signs of potential layoffs and/or other opportunities.

As the work force grows and shrinks, companies maintain profits by retaining a small core of critical employees while saving the costs of salaries, benefits, and retirement contributions for a larger workforce. Even when a business is profitable, the company may decrease its workforce to please stockholders who prefer increasing profits each financial quarter. All employees must be responsible for maintaining their own health and other insurance and for monitoring retirement investments.

Another way for companies to reduce costs is to hire many part-time employees, saving not only benefits costs, but also reducing adherence to legislated obligations, such as unemployment payments and affirmative action guidelines. Many highly trained technicians, such as computer consultants, make excellent hourly wages, but many are also only hired on a temporary or "long-term temporary" basis. Educated workers may combine two or more part-time jobs not only to gain income, but also to hope for a semblance of security. The hope is that if one job is lost, the second job may be maintained for a while and full unemployment will be avoided.

Careering

Miller-Tiedeman (1999) writes that new approaches to career management are needed to respond to the changing economy. Because the external pressures are capricious, she centers her approach on the person and the person's ability to determine her unique intentions while also managing life as it is.

To create a new prototype for career, she uses new language and terminology to express her ideas. Miller-Tiedeman (1999) says that many traditional theories and practices of career development are too obsolete to deal with current economic conditions. Instead of separating career as only part of the person, this theorist describes each person as an individual system, creating and organizing life, and forever evolving with experience. She portrays individuals as acting in accordance with the drift of life, taking advantage of opportunities for personal growth, and maintaining equilibrium during restful periods.

Accordingly, in the careering model, career counselors respect the unique insight of clients and the clients' ability to determine their own intentions for organizing their lives. Adherence to formal decision models or directive methods, seen as typical for career counseling, only interferes with the natural process of life and disempowers the client. Theories of career developmental stages create cumbersome fabrications that are not an accurate account of the fluctuations of life. Likewise, counselors who encourage clients to set concrete goals are setting up artificial designations that are not in keeping with the realistic forces affecting clients (i.e., chance and change).

Instead of goals, the careering model encourages clients to determine their **intentions** and to patiently wait until life presents the avenues for action. Within this model, there are no right or wrong career moves, only turns of events that are given meaning according to the interpretations of the careerist. Decision making is unique to each individual, and each individual creates a private career orientation. Counselors help clients stay calm within the context of dealing with career pressures, and counseling becomes an atmosphere where individuals can hear their own signals for creating new possibilities.

An overall picture of one's life is the appropriate lens for career considerations ("careering as living"), according to Miller-Tiedeman (1999). Rather than viewing career as separate from other areas of life, the client herself becomes the central focus of counseling, and counselors use techniques such as reflecting inner meanings to determine career identity. The basis of Miller-Tiedeman's approach is philosophical. It suggests both clients and counselors realize new paradigms to understand career as a growing experience, rather than a linear contrivance separate from life. Counselors can assist clients in maintaining a positive attitude, trusting themselves and life. Counseling teaches clients to eliminate fear and distrust, eliminate negative self-talk, and identify personal themes and values. Clients are also taught to broaden their perspectives of career and to pay attention to their own readings of the flux of their lives.

Miller-Tiedeman (1999) offers realistic advice for people managing their lives in the current economy. All individuals need a vision of their own lives and an awareness of what they need to learn to stay marketable. She suggests that each person save enough money to sustain themselves during periods of unemployment. Miller-Tiedeman also recommends self-responsible workers learn techniques to deal with stress and to maintain health. She advises reducing life-style requirements to manage economic pressure and building social support networks that can provide assistance during times of unemployment or related changes.

Counseling in the Miller-Tiedeman model focuses on the individual and on attitudes that prepare one for constant change and self-responsibility. The rationale of sustaining one's self by relying on inner signals, however, is too vague to meet the psychological needs of many clients. Keeping an open mind, observing workplace requirements, and constantly upgrading qualifications are the hard-core necessities for surviving in the current working world. Counselors may help clients ferret out inner signals and wait for the right life context, but career counseling also requires some structure to provide safe vehicles for clients facing harsh realities.

STRATEGIES FOR DEALING WITH THE GLOBAL ECONOMY

> It's a recession when your neighbor loses his job, it's a depression when you lose your own.
>
> *Harry S. Truman*

Accepting Change—Challenging Paradoxes

Other theorists have offered concepts that help careerists cope with the fluctuations of the global economy. Gelatt (1991) describes a term for psychological flexibility, labeled "positive uncertainty," that helps workers accept change as they manage their careers and promotes new decision-making attitudes. Gelatt writes that careerists must realize that more information can equal more uncertainty and that knowing personal desires and beliefs can be more informative than known facts. Traditionally, the career literature has stressed the importance of information. Careerists are left with the mistaken impression that enough information will clearly delineate what occupations will be like in the future. Understanding what is commonly known actually requires some critical evaluations of the information because all information has been subjectively arranged. The objective approach needs to be balanced with a subjective optimism, accepting that the future will never truly be known. The careerist is a captain of a ship maneuvering in a sea that can never be fully charted.

Positive Uncertainty

Gelatt's (1991) writing is filled with paradoxes that startle the reader. He urges careerists to be focused and flexible as well as goal-guided, not goal-governed. His advice is often ambiguous: Know what you want, but don't be too sure. Avoid unreasonable risks, but move into the unknown. Seek comfort, but be willing to confront life as contradictory. Be sure, but ask questions and learn. Honor tradition, but be open to surprise and possibilities. Goals are to be treated as hypotheses. A balance is sought between achieving goals and discovering them. A balance of logic (a left-brain function) and intuition (a right-brain function) is encouraged. Gelatt wants the careerist to think critically *and* playfully consider ideas outside the box. Like Miller-Tiedeman, he disputes rigid planning, firm deciding, and overdependence on external criteria. Yet Gelatt attempts to retain the positive aspects of a traditional, linear, fact-based approach along with its opposites. He challenges the reader to keep both approaches operating simultaneously.

Planned Happenstance

The career literature has often alluded to the obvious, that chance plays a part in careers (Bandura, 1982; Hart, Rayner, & Christensen, 1971; Miller, 1983;

Salomone & Slaney, 1981). Although acknowledging that chance events do impact careers, writers are still reluctant to include such randomness in a system of counseling. Cabral and Salomone (1990) say that counseling models cannot incorporate chance, but career counselors are still expected to help clients deal with effects of chance. Scott and Hatalla (1990) express the perceived threat of trying to theorize about chance's effects on careers:"The thought of including chance factors such as unexpected personal events into the theory and practice of career counseling is disconcerting because it is, by its very definition, unpredictable and untidy" (p. 28).

The idea of telling clients to pay attention to chance happenings started in the last decade. Some writers (Cabral & Salomone, 1990; Miller, 1995) describe chance events as unique opportunities. The term **planned happenstance** expresses the concept that being open to serendipity can open doors to new career paths or can alter career self-concepts (Miller, 1995; Mitchell, Levin, & Krumboltz, 1999; Williams et al., 1998). Keeping an eye on developing events can present opportunities for the successful worker. Serendipitous occurrences can create new possibilities and positive turns for careers. Examples of chance include: early retirement of a superior; the opening of a new management slot; new customers needing the client's specialty; a new company hiring; changes in licensure laws; a new employee introducing a new specialty area and teaching experienced employees; the introduction of new technology that changes how services are delivered; etc.

To deal with changing career conditions, counselors need to support the client's movement toward establishing a direction, yet remind the client that current decisions are temporary ones that will likely change in the future. As Tiedeman-Miller (1999) and Gelatt (1991) suggest, an increasing number of writers in the career field recommend that careerists maintain a positive attitude toward chance occurrences.

Timely decisions include being prepared for chance occurrences that may present new choices. To be prepared for chance, clients stay in touch with their sense of career identity and the personal values that have top priority. With a thoroughly grounded sense of self, careerists can adapt to chance well. Rather than planning as though the future can be known, the plan is to be open to the unpredictable. On the other hand, some career events can be predicted. Clients can learn to forge their careers in a process where conditions and their interests are expected to change. Career counseling need not be seen as an attempt to decrease uncertainty, but as the means for teaching clients how to cope with the inevitable change of circumstances that frequently occur.

The concept of learning to accept the unexpected can be seen as an extension of the social learning theory of career development (Krumboltz, 1996). Continual learning occurs throughout the course of each lifetime, and some of the learning occurs through chance events. Counselors teach clients the cognitive frames or attitudes that are effective for dealing with change.

Adlerian counseling theory suggests ways to facilitate healthy reactions to deal with the unpredictable. Adler (Ansbacher & Ansbacher, 1956) emphasizes the need for courage in facing life's contingencies and points to the positive effect of encouraging clients to meet demands. Young and Robert (1997) describe examples of encouragement and the effects of encouragement for successful careerists in building positive self-esteem and reducing fears of ambiguity. What is most important is that counselors teach a proactive attitude where clients see themselves as capable of adapting to changes because they are open to new experiences. Clients can gain a positive encounter with change through career counseling that treats chance as a natural phenomenon.

Watts (1996) suggests that career counseling may reoccur many times over the course of clients' lives. Career counseling interventions may be needed periodically to offer encouragement to clients to let go of one career and open up to a new one. Counseling can be the venue for helping clients deal with the anxiety that very well might accompany change. Clients can learn that stress reactions are normal and can be worked through.

Expecting change is not a rationale for blowing off required planning or searching for information. Instead, preparing for eventual change requires thoughtful awareness of personal purpose and careful observation of external signals that indicate new chances may be available soon. Counselors can assist clients in developing such an awareness. Neither the client nor the counselor relies on luck or blind faith. Client and counselor depend on the counseling process to create a safe zone where ambiguities can be tolerated and preparations are made to construct a personally determined and realistic future. The Career Diamond's picture showing a process of exploring and integrating both personal and external considerations offers clients the perspective of change that can be used to their advantage.

Planned happenstance requires an exploratory attitude and a readiness for accepting each new situation as a means for growth. An attitude of curiosity is continually maintained, as one is forever active in a search for whatever life has to offer. Career counselors are responsible for maintaining such a tone in sessions with clients and would, therefore, not usually approach a client's presenting concern as in need of a concrete solution. Clients may need to learn to be still and patient in the face of not knowing what will happen next and with being undecided. Valuable lessons are to be gained in the milieu of trusting the stream of life and the internal wisdom of the client to know when and how to change. Faith in the process is rewarded when the next stage of life becomes known and appreciated.

CASE STUDY 6.1   *Once an Entrepreneur, Always an Entrepreneur*

A former Internet entrepreneur, Tom, seeks career counseling after his company has failed. He is depressed, saying he has just lived through both the best of times and worst of times. His original concept for his dot-com business was exciting, and the initial success was phenomenal. However, with a changing economic cycle, bankruptcy came. His career motivation now is to find a secure position where he will never have to reexperience failure.

How Would You Conceptualize This Case?

1. As a career counselor, how would you assist Tom in dealing with his depression?
2. What was Tom's internal construct for failure? How could a counselor inoculate Tom against failure forever?
3. Did Tom need to explore interests and values? How did his previous experience affect his reopening of the Career Diamond?

What Actually Happened?

The counselor encourages Tom to review his life to determine career activities that express his strengths, values, and interests. As a child, he wanted to be a racecar driver who experiences excitement and is the center of attention. In middle school, he became enamored with the Discovery Channel and strategy games using metal character models he painted himself and collected. He loved learning new things and impressing others with unique pieces of knowledge. Tom enjoyed competition that requires thoughtfulness, planning, and "psyching out" his adversaries. In high school, he was a debater and a computer whiz, and in college, he majored in information systems. Ever since he has enjoyed trouble shooting for computer networks and data bank operations. Tom's company devised a method for testing potential hacking methods and built safety walls for preventing break-ins to various computer systems used by a variety of organizations.

In counseling, Tom is encouraged to examine his values. He recognizes his priority for winning and achieving, but he also notes that he has made important contributions to his field. He values being on the cutting edge of technology, having variety in his work environment, and competence. Tom's family is also valued, and he has provided his wife and child a comfortable life-style, though his absorption in his work has meant he has spent little leisure time with them. He tearfully acknowledges that without the family base, he would not have the stability they offer in his current crisis. Tom fears his extended family—parents, grandparents, and cousins—will not respect him if he cannot renew his success. Tom spends some time considering the meaning of his life and explores several spiritual avenues.

The counselor suggests that the client spend some time researching places where he could apply his knowledge of computers, and he finds several government departments that have positions related to his qualifications. The security of government work appeals to him, given regular paychecks and benefits, though the salaries offered are considerably lower than his company earnings. He does a number of interviews while still attending regular counseling sessions, weighing his options, and relating job characteristics to his interests and values.

(continued)

(Case Study 6.1 continued)

For the last counseling session, Tom enters the counselor's office laughing. He has found a perfect job, setting up a new security systems network for several governmental agencies. His laughter recurs when he says that this job will be eliminated within three to four years. Tom exclaims, "I thought I was looking for a job for 20 years; and here I am again, going for the latest system and setting myself up for short-term tenure." Then he winked, explaining that within several years, he will have established contacts within the organizations using the system he is setting up. Then, he can start a consulting firm assisting the agencies he is now serving and adding private sector organizations who will need compatible systems to implement government contracts.

Self-Esteem at Work

Nathaniel Branden (1998), in *Self-Esteem at Work*, explicates how positive and resilient careerists need high self-esteem to compete in a fast-paced, technologically oriented society. Managing change and keeping up with fast-moving demands may require more sophisticated methods than downsizing and rehiring, according to a company's latest profit report.

In previous stages of history, such as the agricultural and industrial ages, when major changes did not occur in a worker's lifetime, the majority of employees were rewarded for obedience and reliability, not independent thought (Zinn, 1995). Industry built huge bureaucratic organizations that dominated market shares for their products. Hierarchical management systems maintained company social norms by rewarding employees who fit into the system, not employees who questioned current methods and offered innovations. In the past, production workers and management's organizational man needed only enough self-esteem to demonstrate basic competence within the defined structure (Brandon, 1998).

In the current information age, there is an increasing need for workers with advanced verbal and mathematical knowledge, as well as sophisticated social skills. According to Branden (1998), employees have specialized expertise unknown to many other employees and to the boss. Collegial relationships maintain the organizational structure within a flattened hierarchy. The nature of employees' contributions and changing relationships, as well as continual adaptation to constant competition, requires higher levels of autonomy and self-esteem for all members of the work culture. Production workers now monitor sophisticated equipment and are required to understand the technology in order to anticipate needed repairs and solve production problems.

Managers and workers consult regularly and understand that intersecting functions require both independent action and cooperation to fulfill the overall purpose of the company. In short, high levels of self-esteem are needed by all employees, who carry independent responsibilities, must work in teams, and must be ready to adapt to ever-changing conditions. Low self-esteem hinders ready adaptations and is susceptible to impulsive action, both reactions that can be economically disastrous. Branden's (1998) analysis of the global economy leads to the bold statement that "high self-esteem is a competitive edge" (p. 21).

Branden (1998) describes the defensive reactions of low self-esteem employees as damaging both their careers and the company's performance. Anxiety stemming from fear of low performance evaluations leads to self-sabotaging behaviors and possibly the loss of a valuable employee. High-performing employees with low self-esteem may perceive criticism when none is intended. Managers with low self-esteem may feel threatened by the new ideas of subordinates and may hide valuable contributions or maneuver to claim credit for another's work. In fact, when ideas and analyses are primary economic vehicles and roles are more equal, there may be more room for more people to act out psychological problems. A worker with healthy self-esteem comes to work ready to make a contribution whereas a low self-esteem worker is concerned with keeping up appearances, self-aggrandizement, and limiting self-responsibility.

Branden (1998) calls for management methods that enhance the self-esteem of all working colleagues. He makes the point that the behaviors that generate self-esteem are also the expressions of self-esteem. A system that encourages the enhancement of self-esteem creates a working atmosphere where people feel safe, accepted, challenged, and recognized. In return, people gain self-esteem and are able to interact with others in the same respectful, accepting way without feeling threatened by challenges or the recognition of others. Self-esteem promotes honest feedback for workers regarding areas in need of improvement and for areas of accomplishment, with clear noncontradictory messages. When high self-esteem is operating as the norm, people have access to information, encouragement for learning, and the appropriate power needed to perform their jobs.

Finally, a system that enhances self-esteem and demonstrates integrity is of primary importance. High self-esteem companies demonstrate congruence between their public relations messages regarding their purpose and philosophy and the actual behavior of the management. A system of integrity strengthens the employees' sense of purpose by sharing the sense of accomplishment for what is produced and the experience of earning self-esteem through worthwhile activity.

To rise to the challenge of accelerating global competition, businesses have an incentive to value employees who value themselves. Only within a cooperative and respectful atmosphere can innovation and creative adaptability be fully achieved. There may be pressures to hire and fire specialists as they are needed. But valued employees have the power to create new solutions for new problems, and they may become indispensable to the organizations. The global economy also offers opportunities for entrepreneurs who can quickly create cost-effective products and services to meet changing needs. Within such an atmosphere, there are also new opportunities for career counselors who can facilitate the growth of careerists responding to the pressures and challenges of companies. Attention to the clients' self-esteem is an important factor in helping careerists deal with external demands (Branden, 1998).

Mihaly Csikszentmihalyi and the Concept of Flow

Mihaly Csikszentmihalyi (pronounced "ME-high CHICK-sent-me-high-ee," Santrock, 2002, p. 433) employs concepts that can increase job and life satisfaction. Although his overarching concept of flow seems like a rather esoteric way to describe the mundane activity of working to earn a living, Csikszentmihalyi (1993) has done research using the term to describe the ultimate satisfaction derived from sustained activity. Rather than a vague description, the researcher defines factors that literally create a transcendent experience.

Two factors of flow are clear: goals and constant concrete feedback. People know what they are doing, where they are going, and how well they are doing in achieving their goals. Other factors include conditions where a person can act decisively and with control, performing a task that is somewhat difficult but no more difficult than what is possible for the individual to do.

Some work activities meet the Csikszentmihalyi (1993) criteria. As a person concentrates on the task, irrelevant stimuli are ignored, and the person becomes aware only of the flow of the action. Personal concerns disappear, and a consciousness of time is absent. As the work continues, the person feels a sense of growth and a purpose beyond one's self. The experience is felt to be worthwhile for its own sake, regardless of external rewards. The deep concentration on the task creates an intense focus on the moment in time, as all energy is committed to continuing the flow of what is happening.

Emergence in such activity, whether at work or elsewhere, brings such satisfaction that doing the complex tasks over time brings more and more enjoyment as skills improve. Flow experiences enhance creativity, peak performance, talent, productivity, self-esteem, and stress reduction. Without experiencing flow and the beneficial cycle of meeting the challenges of complex activities, people become bored and seek enjoyment through leisure activities that are less productive. Eventually, if unchallenging activity becomes the norm for one's life, the capacity to rise to challenges begins to atrophy.

Csikszentmihalyi (1993) believes that engaging people in the creative zest of performing challenging tasks not only ensures lives of satisfaction and enjoyment, but also guarantees the betterment of society. He argues that when work depends solely on economic rewards, materialism is fostered, and the planet's resources are overused. He also explains that evolutionary progress for society requires all the talent the human race can muster. The society that socializes its citizens to believe that enjoyment comes only from nonproductive relaxation and collecting material goods is misusing human resources. An economy fostering deadening work for money fails to achieve the possibilities that fully challenged human beings have to offer.

Csikszentmihalyi (1993) also comments on the effect of current attitudes toward work as leading to a disinterested generation of workers. The current focus on materialism and the willingness of adults to tolerate drudgery is sending the wrong message to children. Instead of young people learning that work is something that can be enjoyed and can have intrinsic value, they are learning that work is only as good as the items it affords a person to buy. In reaction, Csikszentmihalyi suggests that the youth will reject a work ethic and instead focus on leisure and pleasure.

According to Csikszentmihalyi's (1993) research, many people experience flow through their jobs, and when people report feeling happy and satisfied, they are usually working. However, when there are few opportunities for people to engage in tasks commensurate with their abilities, people lose the motivation to put forth effort in challenging tasks. The improvement of society is dependent on creating work opportunities that encourage everyone to meet challenges and gain satisfaction.

Csikszentmihalyi (1993) suggests that counselors can help clients identify those situations in their lives that increase the quality of experience. By understanding the enjoyment of challenging activities, people can create feelings of satisfaction and a sense of self that is in control of their own happiness.

Certainly the flow concept is applicable to career issues. If clients can learn to identify work activities that create the experience of flow, they can gain satisfaction. Continuing to enjoy work activities will require continuing to find challenging experiences either through doing tasks of increasing complexity or by finding new tasks. Although many jobs don't entail flow encounters all the time, careerists can increase satisfaction by locating as many of these activities in a job as possible. Career counselors can teach clients the characteristics of flow activities. Management and job analysts could certainly do as much as possible to design jobs that create flow according to the abilities of the workers assigned to the tasks.

Csikszentmihalyi (1993) uses surgery as an example of work that induces satisfaction and a sense of flow where time and personal perspective are transcended. Surgeons perform specific tasks and receive concrete feedback when the tasks are successfully completed. Surgery is challenging and requires high levels of skills that can be consistently improved. While performing surgery, doctors reported being so involved with doing the task that they are oblivious to all outside influences. Concentration is so focused, doctors are aware only of what they are doing in the moment. Even routine surgeries are challenging enough to be called relaxing and worthwhile endeavors. Every surgeon interviewed reported they would never consider another profession, and they would do surgery without pay or recognition if that were the only way they could do it. Surgeons are not interested in other medical specialties because they would not see the same results as easily and quickly. The only negative described by the doctors is their dependence on the enjoyment they gain from doing their work. The surgeons in the study described their work as almost addictive, and when they are not able to do it, the loss is psychologically felt.

Certainly surgery is a highly specialized career, and only a few can gain such a position. However, other occupations can be viewed as including activities with the characteristics that produce flow. If a worker sets out to define activities from the perspective of finding flow, satisfactions can be found. The supermarket checker interviewed by Studs Terkel (1974) described creating a rhythm with the cash register, becoming engrossed in conversations with customers, and creating relationships with regular patrons.

Leisure activities provide the intrinsic enjoyment producing the flow activities as well. Csikszentmihalyi (1993) studied rock climbing, chess, and other activities demonstrating the demand characteristics of flow: control, challenge, use of skills, and immediate feedback determining success. Counselors can help clients create challenging leisure activities that will bring enjoyment into people's lives.

Also studied by Csikszentmihalyi were microflow activities that fill time without offering much challenge, such as socializing and physical activities. Physical activities offered enjoyment and increased self-esteem; but solitary exercise and competitive sports also added feelings of alienation from others. Social activities offered enjoyment without alienation but also brought doubts about one's self, lowering self-esteem. Most counselors have helped clients increase social activities when clients report leisure time filled only with solitary pursuits and have recommended fitness activities for increasing a sense of self-improvement. Flow studies offer concrete factors for designing the healthy use of free time and for balancing activities so positive feelings are created without the negative side effects of overemphasizing any one type of activity.

Sociopolitical Issues: A Critique of the Global Economy

Csikszentmihalyi (1993) recommends that counselors be aware of how society distributes enjoyable activities. On the one hand, it may be a challenge to set up an efficient assembly line (e.g., an engineer finds great satisfaction in improving worker efficiency or using space in a more effective manner). On the other hand, assembly-line work removes the challenge and control needed for workers to find enjoyment in the work activities (e.g., the worker repeats the same activities all day).

When opportunities for education and training are not equally available to all citizens, a society is literally limiting the pursuit of happiness for many alienated groups. Counselors may be able to help clients see what they are missing if their lives have little control or challenge. However, counselors must realize there are also limits to how much education and training are available for many clients. Counselors may need to help some clients learn how to tolerate boring work and add flow activities in other areas of life through hobbies or volunteer work.

A. G. Watts (1996) writes about the career choices available to groups underrepresented in higher-paying occupations. He states that the underemployed and underchallenged are bound by the norms of the majority. Societies control who has maximum opportunities and who does not through various means. Educational, licensure, and certification requirements serve gate-keeping functions and often go beyond the actual criteria of what is needed to do some jobs. Counselors can serve as enforcers of the status quo by discouraging clients who seem unlikely to meet the established criteria for some careers. On the other hand, not relaying established criteria could set the clients up for disappointment. Watts raises an ethical question by asking if counselors should be social activists advocating for social changes that would create true equal opportunities. Another possible ethical concern is how appropriate is it for counselors to educate clients about the systemic constraints that limit opportunities for some groups of people?

Ethical concerns regarding career issues are raised when it becomes obvious that every one of the writers making recommendations for dealing with the rapid change in the economy lays full responsibility for adapting to the changes on the individual careerist. Self-responsibility for career decisions is certainly a healthy attitude, but the amount of change described hardly seems fully manageable for all individuals over time. Recommending that careerists be positive about change and constantly monitor the work environment for signs of pending downsizing may be normalizing an economy that treats workers as interchangeable parts. Economists report unemployment as simply a statistic to manipulate for holding down inflation and stimulating investment. What is not controlled is the human impact of certain percentages of people out of work or underemployed, paying the sacrifice for a "healthy" economy.

It may be considered radical and naïve, but the concept that a nation's economy exists to provide work and income to all its citizens is hardly unreasonable. Certainly, counselors may prefer to work with individuals and help them cope with the career world. However, all those concerned with career issues, counselors and clients alike, might also consider the political implications of expecting workers to adapt to an economy designed only for material gain and not for developing all human potential.

SUMMARY

Counselors and clients need to be aware of the influences of the global economy for individuals managing careers across time. Clients might best make short-term decisions that fit into a long-term career outline. The term *outline* suggests a direction, but allows for chance and change to alter specific short-term decisions. In addition, an outline suggests there are multiple steps. A career is a collection of steps that move toward goals fitting into an overall picture of personal intentions.

The global economy includes many specialized careerists in the workforce. Clients will benefit by having a marketable specialty. Developing and maintaining a specialty also requires that careerists constantly update skills. However, too much attention to specialization entails risk because some specialties are very marketable for a time and then later eliminated. Clients also need to remain flexible enough that they can work across specialties.

Periods of unemployment or partial employment are becoming commonplace as people move through their careers. Clients need to purchase homes, vehicles, vacations, etc. with the assumption that unemployment is around the corner. Having a savings account to cover expenses during career transitions becomes vital. Social support not dependent on the current workplace is also important in dealing with times between jobs. A mentoring and collegial network for employment contacts may also offer invaluable assistance in seeking a new job.

Due to the ambiguous and unpredictable nature of the global economy, clients need to have strong career self-concepts that go beyond the current job. Healthy careerists also develop an identity broader than career alone and find value in life that is not based upon work. In addition, healthy stress management skills are a must. Clients need to be able to manage stress during periods of unemployment and when coworkers are downsized.

Companies will benefit by creating an environment that encourages employees to maintain high self-esteem and be capable of independent actions. In order to attract such employees, work environments will need to manage competitive pressures, infused with power dynamics and judgmental attitudes, and replace them with a tone that is collaborative, egalitarian, and supportive. Such a major shift for some companies requires the services of career consultants or coaches.

A society might do well to consider the impact of limiting access to challenging work roles in a competitive global economy. Expanding the number of careerists who can live up to their potential would expand the creative and productive progress of the financial system. The world of work is the external structure providing the stage where careerists act in their roles to make a contribution for the common good. Career counselors can facilitate the expansion of career roles by facilitating the personal growth of clients and by interpreting the influences of the system. The professionals providing career services are creative consultants helping clients act effectively on the world of work stage.

STUDY OUTLINE: KEY TERMS AND CONCEPTS

I. Impact of Globalization
   A. Rapid change
       1. Predicting future with certainty is impossible
   B. Work force grows and shrinks according to the needs of the company/economy
       1. Flattened hierarchies
       2. Removal of middle management
   C. Self-responsibility for career
       1. **Careerist**—a person who recognizes that she will have many jobs, either within or between companies, and actively prepares herself for continued employment via continual training within field or retraining into another specialty.
       2. Professional development now the individual's responsibility
       3. Adding value to organizations is expected
       4. Individual responsible to market herself

     5. Savings account needed to support individual when unem-
ployed/underemployed

     6. Life-style choices need to take into account variable income.

     7. Proactive preventative health habits needed to deal with
stress.

  D. All employees are self-employed

     1. Never knowing when the current job will end

     2. May combine part-time jobs into some semblance of full-time
work

       a. May lack health and retirement benefits

II. New Concepts for Career

  A. Careering

     1. Personal process in tune with flexible approach to life

     2. Empowerment comes with listening to inner signals versus
linear decision making.

     3. Growth model continuously redefining identity versus fitting
into external paradigms

     4. People set **intentions**, their personal goals for their lives and
careers, and wait for opportunities to serve as vehicles for individually determined goals.

     5. Careerist interprets changing external factors.

  B. Positive uncertainty

     1. Current choices are temporary

     2. Positive attitude, appreciating chance

     3. Information fluid and subjective

     4. Grounded values and personal priorities, though adaptable, are
the most dependable stability available.

  C. **Planned happenstance**

     1. Openness to the unexpected

     2. Career planning includes coping with inevitable change

  D. Appropriate career attitudes

     1. Curiosity: exploring new opportunities

     2. Persistence: exerting effort despite setbacks

     3. Flexibility: changing attitudes and circumstances

     4. Optimism: viewing new opportunities as possible and
attainable

     5. Risk taking: taking action in the face of uncertain outcomes

  E. Self-esteem

     1. Information age requires higher self-esteem than previous his-
torical periods.

     2. Advanced levels of expertise required for all levels of
employees.

3. Consultation and teamwork required between all levels of employees.
4. Self-esteem encourages communication, autonomous responsibility, cooperation, and adaptation to change.
5. Workplace atmosphere creating self-esteem: safe, accepting, challenging, and recognizing contributions
6. People working in respectful atmosphere interact with others with same respect: honest feedback, dealing with mistakes, and giving clear messages.
7. High self-esteem employees need information, encouragement, continual learning, and appropriate power.
8. High self-esteem organization needs integrity, real public relation messages, mission, and behavior consistent with values.

F. Flow
1. Clear goals: task clearly defined
2. Concrete feedback
    a. How well task is being done.
    b. How well is task moving toward goal.
3. Decisive action under person's control
4. Task difficulty is a challenge but not beyond possibility.
5. Task is defined as important in and of itself despite external rewards.
6. Transcendental experience:
    a. Concentration on task
    b. Focus intense: irrelevant stimuli disappear from awareness. Personal factors are not in awareness.
    c. Sense of personal growth, purpose, satisfaction
    d. Felt sense of flow of energy
    e. Skill improvement creates more satisfaction.
7. Peak experiences
    a   Talent expressed
    b. Self-esteem enhanced
    c. Stress released
8. Without flow
    a. Boredom
    b. People seek pleasure, not productivity.
    c. Person's ability to rise to challenges is diminished.
9. With flow
    a. Creative zest; satisfying life
    b. A society fostering mostly pleasure seeking rather than creative contributions will gradually deteriorate.

EXERCISES

1. In dyads, describe significant changes that have occurred in your life, and how you handled the situation. What did you learn from making the change? Describe changes you might want to make in the future. Use the terms "positive uncertainty" and "planned happenstance" in approaching future changes.

2. Again in dyads, describe times when you have experienced "flow." Then make a list of personal satisfiers. Brainstorm with your partner activities, work related or other, where you could experience flow and/or gain personal satisfaction.

REFERENCES

Ansbacher, H. L., & Ansbacher, R. R. (1956). *The individual psychology of Alfred Adler.* New York: Harper & Row.

Bandura, A. (1982). The psychology of chance encounters and life paths. *American Psychologist, 37,* 747–755.

Berger, P. (1990). *The human shape of work.* New York: Macmillan.

Bingham, R. P., & Ward, C. M. (1994). Career counseling with ethnic minority women. In W. B. Walsh & S. H. Osipow (Eds.), *Career counseling for women* (pp. 331–365). Hillsdale, NJ: Erlbaum.

Branden, N. (1998). *Self-esteem at work: How confident people make powerful companies.* San Francisco: Jossey-Bass.

Cabral, A. C., & Salomone, P. R. (1990). Chance and careers: Normative versus contextual development. *Career Development Quarterly, 39,* 5–17.

Csikszentmihalyi, M. (1993). *The evolving self: A psychology for the third millennium.* New York: HarperCollins.

Gelatt, H. B. (1991). *Creative decision making: Using positive uncertainty.* Lanham, MD: National Book Network.

Hart, D. H., Rayner, K., & Christensen, E. R. (1971). Planning, preparation, and chance in occupational entry. *Journal of Vocational Behavior, 1,* 279–285.

Keeley, E. S. (2003). From vocational decision making to career building: Blueprint, real games and school counseling. *Professional School Counseling, 6*(4), 244–251.

Krumboltz, J. D. (1996). Improving career development theory from a social learning perspective. In M. L. Savikas & R. W. Lent (Eds.), *Convergence in career development theories* (pp. 9–31). Palo Alto, CA: Consulting Psychologist Press.

Levy, F., & Murnane, R. J. (1992). U.S. earnings levels and earnings inequality; A review of recent trends and proposed explanations. *Journal of Economic Literature, 30,* 1333-1381.

Miller, M. J. (1993). The role of happenstance in career choice. *Vocational Guidance Quarterly, 32, 16-20.*

Miller, M. J. (1995). A case for uncertainty in career counseling. *Counseling and Values, 39,* 162-168.

Miller-Tiedeman, A., & Associates (1999). *Learning, practicing and living the new careering.* Philadelphia: Accelerated Development.

Mishel, L., Bernstein, J., & Schmitt, J. (2000). *The state of working America, 2000-2001.* Ithaca, NY: Cornell Univ. Press.

Mitchell, K. E., Levin, A. S., & Krumboltz, J. D. (1999). Planned happenstance: Constructing unexpected career opportunities. *Journal of Counseling and Development, 77,* 115-125.

Pink, D. H. (2001). *Free agent nation: How America's new independent workers are transforming the way we live.* New York: Warner.

Salomone, P. R., & Slaney, R. B. (1981). The influence of chance and contingency factors on the vocational choice process of nonprofessional workers. *Journal of Vocational Behavior, 19,* 25-35.

Santrock, J. W. (2002) *Life-span development* (8th ed.). Boston: McGraw Hill.

Scott, J., & Hatalla, J. (1990). The influence of chance and contingency factors on career patterns of college-educated women. *Career Development Quarterly, 39,* 18-30.

Turkel, S. (1974). *Working.* New York: The New York Press.

Watts, A. G. (1996). Toward a policy for lifelong career development: A transatlantic perspective. *Career Development Quarterly, 45,* 41-53.

Williams, E. N., Soeprapto, E., Like, K., Touradji, P., Hess, S., & Hill, C. E. (1998). Perceptions of Serendipity: Career paths of prominent academic women in counseling psychology. *Journal of Counseling Psychology, 4,* 379-389.

Young, J. B., & Robert, R. F. (1997). A model of radical career change in the context of psychosocial development. *Journal of Career Assessment, 5,* 267-182.

Zinn, H. (1995). *A people's history of the United States: 1492-present.* New York: Harper Perennial.

CHAPTER 7

Career Issues for a Diverse Work Force

We will never congratulate the laborer, not talk of the dignity of labor. It is work that dignifies. Labor wears, kills, destroys: that is the meaning of the word. We will show the laborer how to cease from his labors, as he comes up on that other level where his works shall be sure to follow him, where mind controls matter, and the spirit rules the thing.

Edward Everett Hale, 1885

Career matters are inextricably bound to multiple psychosocial factors such as age, gender, socioeconomic status (SES), race, ethnicity, cultural background, and family influences. The identity of each individual includes internalized messages affected by societal factors. Human beings, as members of a social species, develop within a context where societal demands are inculcated as internal facets of a person's identity (Gollnick & Chinn, 2002).

The Career Diamond shows one side representing the self (or internal factors) and the other side corresponding to external factors. Both sides come together through a process of integration. However, a more realistic depiction might show multiple facets on both sides. The internal side's multifaceted lines would show the characteristics of age, gender, race, ethnicity, SES, and cultural background while the external side would show the societal norms related to the same factors. For example, the author could list female as a personal characteristic and U.S. social constraints for women on the external side. The constraints might include the social practice of women typically earning less or the social stereotyping of behaviors and traits associated with being female. The stereotype could suggest nurturance as acceptable for women; and if a woman displayed such behavior, or internalized such a characteristic as a part of her identity, there could be congruence between societal influence and personality. Similar societal influences and personal characteristics for the author could be the race label *Caucasian*, with an internal personal message related to the self's White identity development, such as, "As a White person, I have had privileges and opportunities and am working to expand my limited awareness of cross-cultural values." It is the work of career counselors to bring into the open internal attributions and to explore the external influences affecting career concerns.

This chapter begins by identifying specific background factors that affect all individuals and encourages career counselors to look at their own embedded societal influences. Then, the most basic identity factor of gender and sexual orientation is examined. Next, values are considered, i.e., those characteristic of the majority culture and crosscultural values that affect career choices and behavior. Finally, the career issues related to marginalized workers will be examined by describing economic and political influences. Most workers balance various background factors within the context of workplace requirements. The climate of diversity in the work force is a reality, and acclimatizing to the multiplicity of values is a necessity. Career counselors use their sophisticated skills to bring into awareness the variety of cultural influences, internalized characteristics, and external pressures affecting all clients and students.

INCREASING CULTURAL SENSITIVITY: EXAMINING PERSONAL–SOCIETAL BACKGROUNDS

Counselors as a group typically value education and hard work. Most hold onto the hope that career services will contribute to work satisfaction and success for clients and students. These values alone will influence career programming and counseling interactions. Recognizing the effect of personal and professional values can alleviate a tendency for professionals to assume their clients' values are the same.

Career counselors and clients alike have internalized background experiences that form basic orientations to life and work. Sensitivity to differing attitudes increases awareness of how embedded mindsets express the limits of individual experience. With self-understanding, career counselors can be open to the variety of intercultural differences and recognize that one's individual context is only one of a limitless variety. The first step in learning about crosscultural differences is for counselors to explicate the influences of their own cultural background so potential biases are identified. Everyone has a **background view**, a perspective shaped by age, socioeconomic level, culture, gender, sexual orientation, family roles, and other factors. Everyone forms socially influenced cognitive sets. As a career counselor, self-understanding helps determine areas where a client's different outlook may influence the counseling relationship. Without self-examination, a

CASE STUDY 7.1   Missed the Message

Esther, a 19-year-old African-American woman, was referred to counseling by her advisor. Esther informed the counselor that there were six children in her family—two older and three younger than Esther. The two oldest siblings had long since left home to make their own way in the world. Esther, now the oldest in the house, seemed depressed and said she was unable to successfully move out and live on her own. She had begun college, but was considering dropping out. The counselor began by asking Esther how she felt about living at home. She replied that it was hard, because the girls in her family had a much stricter rule regime than the boys. For example, her 13-year-old brother did not have a curfew and was able to ride a motorcycle around town despite his being too young to have a driver's license. She indicated that as the boys in the family grew older, they became even more uncontrollable. By comparison, she still had a curfew at the age of 19. On the other hand, Esther did not want to follow her older sister who moved out, was now using drugs, and was pregnant but unmarried. Her older brother was working as a bouncer in a bar. Esther's parents said the strong brother could handle himself, but "good" girls had to stay away from all that partying.

How Would You Conceptualize This Case?

1. As Esther's counselor, what further information would you need to gather?
2. What possible impact did Esther's gender or race have for her issues?
3. Would it be appropriate to offer a motivational talk encouraging her to move out of her family home and/or to stay in college?

What Actually Happened?

The counselor inappropriately concluded that the gender issue was the predominant problem for Esther and validated her con-

counselor's values could create blind spots, missing important aspects of a client's identity; or values conflicts between counselors and clients could affect the therapeutic interaction. Similarly, crossed interactions could impact career education programs. The following are topics that tap into background issues to explicate individual world views.

Many Americans have family histories that include someone from a previous generation immigrating to the United States. Sometimes, people from another country live in the same neighborhoods for at least a generation and can maintain customs from their homeland, handing them down to the next generation. Other families integrate quickly into the American culture, leaving their original customs behind. Either way, the cultural values brought to America can be a part of a family's stories and heritage. Identifying values originating in a family's history is important for career counselors and clients, because these cultural values represent a core of considerations for career identity. Some families describe themselves as American with little emphasis on a background related to immigration. Again the ownership of American

cerns that she was more restricted than the brothers. The counselor announced a counseling goal of helping the client separate from her family of origin and become an independent adult.

However, had the counselor dug a little deeper, he would have learned that Esther did not want to separate from her family. She was committed to helping her younger siblings and trying to keep them out of trouble. Moving out had a negative connotation for her (partying and getting into trouble like her older sister). Had the counselor grasped the values of the client, the most important values (family, not partying) would have been clear to him. Yes, it meant that the client put her life on hold until her younger siblings were older, but these were her values.

By comparison, the White middle-class counselor had left his home at age 17 to study abroad. Upon return to the United States, he immediately applied to a college that was a distance from his home. His academic focus and privileged background impacted what he heard from the client, so he heard her complaining about her restraints, not describing her family situation.

The counselor could have facilitated the client's exploration of further education/training while she continued to live with her family. Although her parents restricted her social life, Esther wanted to help with her siblings. The parents and daughter actually shared the value of family members helping and protecting each other. The differential treatment between Esther and her younger brother could also be examined, allowing Esther to express her primary concern, her brother's safety or her restrictions. Once Esther was clear as to her choices, a family session might have been suggested.

citizenship, whether associated with immigration or not, involves a set of values and attitudes that are basic to how a person views life and others.

Socioeconomic level is another important determinant of career values and motivation. U.S. citizens have for most of history prized upward mobility. Each generation has been expected to increase socioeconomic status beyond the level of the last generation. Increasing the next generation's educational level is one way to foster increased earning power. Listening to the client's family stories describing economic circumstances for great-grandparents, grandparents, and parents convey themes for family expectations. In addition, both the client's experience of generational socioeconomic levels and the counselor's SES background might highlight differences that could affect interactions between the two.

Gender identity often determines many career considerations. As women's roles have expanded, many women are aware of traditionally feminine occupations and those fields occupied by few women. Men, too, are cognizant of the occupations considered to be masculine. Achievement expectations set by family members are also influenced by gender. Sexual orientation affects basic career choices and work behavior. Clients and career counselors will relate to each other with cognitive sets affected by both gender and sexual orientation (Fitzgerald, Fassinger, & Betz, 1995).

Every family determines specific roles, characterizations, and expectations for each member. Psychological placement in the sibling array (birth order) sets up each brother and sister with family expectations. The psychological oldest (may be chosen by age or gender—e.g., girls have more responsibility to care for others) is expected to do more and to be more responsible than other siblings, and the psychological youngest (intellectual ability may be more important than age for some families—lowest ability becomes psychological youngest) may be taken less seriously than others and may be considered unable to take care of himself. Middle children may feel a solid place is not available for them. Often, brothers and sisters develop interests in fields not similar to other siblings so they will not have to compete. Determining the counselor's and the client's family roles may offer clues to the interaction of the counseling dyad. Other family situations may have had an impact, such as an intelligent or gifted child being identified as the hero of the family or another child designated as the family black sheep. Exploring basic family roles will provide much information regarding influences for career identity. These family systems issues are inextricably intertwined with other background issues, and sorting out the influences frees people to understand their personal preferences and to determine unique core identity priorities (Adler, 1931, 1937; Carlson & Slavik, 1997; Sweeney, 1981).

GENDER ISSUES AND CAREER

One of the most obvious and pervasive social changes in the last several decades has been the ever-increasing numbers of women entering the work force (Barnett & Hyde, 2001). Over the last three decades, more and more women have worked outside the home. The literature is replete with books and articles related to the gender issues (Bardwick, Douvan, Horner, & Gutmann, 1970; Bernard, 1972; Holm, 1970; Jordan, Kaplin, Baker-Miller, Striver, & Surrey, 1991; Matthews, 1972, 1989, 1990; Nieva & Gutek, 1981; Tannen, 1994; Williams, 1977). As the previous section described, gender socialization affects family expectations for individuals. In this section, the continuing influence of gender for adults in the workplace will be examined.

Female Gender Issues

Although women have integrated the work force and are present in most career fields, gender bias continues as a pervasive factor in the world of work. Glass ceiling effects limit women to fewer positions of leadership and dis-

tribute many women workers into jobs with lower pay and fewer opportunities for advancement. Fitzgerald and Betz (1994) have explicated the struc-
tural factors in the work environment that affect women. Using the Theory
of Work Adjustment, where work is conceptualized as an interaction between the worker and the work environment, the two researchers describe
job satisfaction as based on matching abilities and job requirements. The
work environment encourages productivity and length of service in a job by
placing workers in jobs that promote the use of their skills. The pervasive
underutilization of women's abilities means such matching is less likely for
women than for men and suggests less work adjustment for women. Sexual
harassment, particularly in male dominated fields (e.g., science, blue-collar
trades) is another factor by which women are routinely "driven out" or made
uncomfortable in workplaces (Fitzgerald & Rounds, 1993).

Some gender social constructions define women in negative terms or
with characteristics that are not adaptive to the world of work. Feminine
stereotypes are social constructions (conceptual labels accepted by a society) that describe women in specific roles such as mothers, lovers, or help-
mate wives. Historically, these roles defined the appropriate place for
women, with most people assuming that women belonged in the home,
kitchen, and nursery. The characteristics for such roles overemphasize
women in relation to others, do not view women as unique individuals, and
the roles imply servitude, passive acquiescence to others, or pervasive attempts to please others (Jordan et al., 1991).

Women have challenged limiting **social constructs** by visibly taking
on career roles. In actuality, women have worked outside the home throughout history. But in recent times, greater numbers of women have entered
the marketplace, and some now work in fields previously closed to women
(Barnett & Hyde, 2001). Of course, regardless of roles, not all women have
displayed temperaments of serving others or accepting others' opinions
without expressing opinions of their own. In any case, the traditional
models for women are no longer reflective of the breadth of women's experience today.

Consequently, social constructs of stereotypic feminine behavior are no
longer practicable, particularly in the workplace. But there is still considerable
conflict over how women should behave. For instance, the traditional moth-
ering stereotype depicts women as nurturing, which may be a positive attrib-
ute unless assertiveness is required on the job. On the other hand, if a woman
is seen as too assertive or demanding, she can be characterized as the witch,
the antitheses of a nurturing person. Women cannot successfully adopt male
behavioral constructs without being denigrated as unfeminine; nor can they
be "too much like a girl," if they are to be taken seriously (Tannen, 1994).
Sexual harassment can be seen as actions depicting women as sex objects;
and women who complain about inappropriate gestures or sexual innuendo

can be accused of being too sensitive or of dressing provocatively (Gutek, 1985; Maremont & Sassen, 1996; Webb, 1991).

Traditional role stereotypes and the characteristics and behaviors ascribed to women do not work well in the work environment. Yet for generations women have been inculcated about the attributes society dictated as feminine, and many built defensive behaviors or rationalizations to justify individual differences (Baker-Miller, 1976). With expanding roles, women deal with the external pressures of socialized attributes and the demands to perform differently at work than at home. Such a process requires sorting out the mixed messages as well as personal preferences. The psychology of women provides an example of the mixture of individual dynamics in the contexts of social influences.

The Stone Center at Wellesley College produced theoretical writings that pointed out the strengths of the feminine social constructions (Jordan et al., 1991). The emphasis on relationships ascribed to women has encouraged them to develop social skills such as collateral relating and caring. Indeed, such sophisticated social skills are valued in the workplace. And, although the culture has given greater status to the individualistic male stereotype, both men and women live in the context of relating to others. Psychology has defined health in individualistic terms, following the societal overemphasis, but in reality both men and women need a balance of individualism and relating. *Self-in-Connection* is the term the Stone Center theorists use as a label for that part of identity that includes relating to others (Jordan et al., 1991).

Although the inclusion of women has not yet developed into fully egalitarian roles, women have demonstrated remarkable adaptability. They have found ways to show leadership without appearing too male or female. Women have gained expertise to gain respect, and they have demonstrated they can get the job done. While adapting to workplace requirements, women have juggled family roles and have created flexible work patterns that could serve as a model for all workers dealing with frequent change in the future. Women have combined social and psychological factors, changing their own experience while also changing both the workplace and family patterns (Ulrich & Dunne, 1986).

The Excelsior Model

A group of women career counselors discussing gender issues at a regional career conference created the Excelsior Model to picture societal influences promoting male and female stereotypes (Andersen, Wickwire, Lewis, Vetter, & Hansen, 1992). Figure 7.1 denotes the compromises continually made by men and women inheriting stereotyped roles.

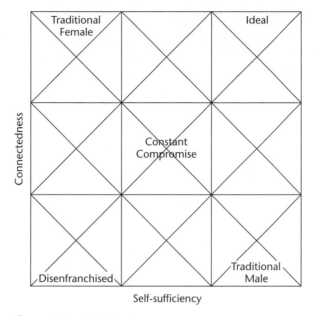

Figure 7.1 Excelsior Box

In the left and right corners of the box in Figure 7.1 are the traditional female and male stereotypes. The sides of the box represent connectedness, or the relationship-oriented identity (self-in-connection) traditionally assigned to women. The top and bottom lines of the box represent the self-sufficiency, or the independence mode of the male stereotype. An emphasis on a relationship orientation without self-sufficiency shown in the bottom left corner results in a lack of status, or a marginal state of being disenfranchised from the mainstream of society. An ideal state for both men and women would be to combine the relational with independence, shown in the upper right-hand corner. However, the career educators found that in society today, the androgynous ideal is not readily found for either men or women. Instead, the career professionals determined that men and women must constantly make compromises between traditional roles and the attempt to gain an integration of both. Thus, the label of constant compromise between the gender stereotypes is found in the middle of the box. Career counselors can be helpful in encouraging the development of **androgyny,** combining traits of male and female stereotypes. Still, the theorists felt that there were many environmental influences in the workplace and elsewhere in society that prevented the ideal integration for men and women. The Excelsior Model was developed to represent societal influences that encourage or discourage gender integration.

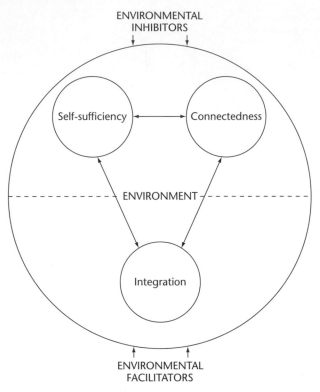

Figure 7.2   Excelsior Model

Figure 7.2 is titled the Excelsior Model because it depicts a hopeful picture, showing both the positive and the negative influences prompting change and suggesting the integration of male and female strengths. Self-sufficiency and connectedness are represented in small circles enclosed by a larger circle depicting the environment surrounding everyone. The goal of integration is represented in the lower half of the larger circle showing the two broad stereotypes coming together. At the top of the large circle, arrows are pressing down and splitting the two smaller circles, preventing the movement toward integration. Examples of inhibitors to integration are stereotypes, discrimination, and rigid policies in work environments (e.g., preventing job sharing or flextime). At the bottom of the circle are influences that facilitate androgynous integration such as affirmative action and egalitarian schools.

The Excelsior Model pictures the societal pressures that reinforce negative social constructs of gender. Career counselors can facilitate the goal of career self-expression by refusing to fit individuals into stereotyped, hence restrictive, roles that limit the contributions men and women can make to society. This can be accomplished, in part, by helping individuals recognize that some internalized attributes may have been influenced more by social constructs than by personal preference or choice.

At the same time that women may need to separate personal choices from the messages received via societal pressure, they may also need to recognize the benefits of the relating skills they possess. Because the social structure has overemphasized individualism, rather than supporting collateral relating, women may not value the interaction skills they can offer. Career counselors can facilitate a more balanced view of personal identity by valuing the individual both as self-sufficient and as connected to others. The Excelsior Model is also used to describe issues specific to male gender identity.

Male Gender Issues

Much of the traditional career literature contains explanations based on men's experiences. In fact, Tyler (1977) describes career theory as the patterns applicable to White males, and Barnett and Hyde (2001) point out that most career theories date back to the 1950s, when gender roles were strict and work patterns were stable. The traditional society disseminated a construct of the male breadwinner who provided income for families. The stereotyped social contract presumed men were defined by work roles and that career success was the primary vehicle for earning self-esteem and respect by others (Skovholt & Morgan, 1981). Limited opportunities for some men, including racial and ethnic minority men, excluded them from the stereotypical pattern of social respect and rewards for career achievement.

Other sources for making social contributions and personal growth were negated as of less value. Consequently, the rigid sex role limited male participation in the family and demanded a highly competitive achievement orientation. An overemphasis on power and winning the success symbols required restrictive emotional, sexual, and affectional behaviors that lead to health problems (O'Neil, 1987). One study by Robertson and Fitzgerald (1990) found even counselors were influenced by societal male role stereotypes. Nontraditional men who were not devoted to being the *provider* were seen as having greater pathology caused by socially inappropriate choices, and counselors designed their interventions to change the nontraditional behavior.

Some literature has explored male gender issues, with Pleck (1981) and others challenging "the myth of masculinity." Male writers have exposed the rigid limits of narrow emotional expression and restrictive attention to relationships, including relating to women and children and interactions between fathers and sons (Kimmel, 1987). The external presses prevent an integration of relationships as a part of the male identity, which leads to an overemphasis on individuality and self-sufficiency, which is shown in the Excelsior Model.

Male career clients often demonstrate adherence to the male role by seeing career choices as bounded by economic and achievement gains only. The meaning of work as an expression of personal values can seem irrelevant when getting ahead and making money is the major criteria for judging success. The assumption that others will judge men only in economic terms supports the Excelsior Model's focus on self-sufficiency. O'Neil and Fishman (1986) described male clients as struggling with concerns of self-devaluation for any discrepancy in the prescribed formula for success, threatening men with the extremes of self-hatred and exaggerated fears. Career counselors can help male clients examine the validity of a restrictive male identity and open views to other sources of satisfaction.

Both men and women benefit from career counseling that explores the topics of gender role identity issues. Traditional social constructs for both masculinity and femininity confine people to stereotypes in terms of choice of occupations and career behavior. Teasing out the social directives and determining those that serve the client well and those that do not expands career counseling into an arena that allows for individual preferences not bounded by stereotypes.

The Excelsior Model demonstrates the external pressure that social constructs represent for gender issues. Society's institutions maintain the values seen as appropriate over time. Changing attitudes means challenging the pervasive influence maintained by the complex web of social constructs that are inculcated by members of society. The social and psychological nature of gender issues demonstrates the interweaving of personal and external factors that is the pattern of all diversity issues.

SEXUAL ORIENTATION

Many negative consequences result when a person identifies with a sexual orientation that does not follow traditional male or female constructs. There may be no positive social constructs for same sex or transgender orientations, and many shaming approbations may be a part of identity development. Some Middle Eastern countries do not even recognize the existence of differing sexual orientations (Gollnick & Chinn, 2002). Other countries, like the United States, barely acknowledge homosexuality as legitimate, with few laws conferring basic human rights in regards to discrimination for housing, employment, and marital status. Some religions react to diversity in sexual orientation with judgmental attitudes. Permanent partnership arrangements for gay couples do not have legal status in most places. Societal

CASE STUDY 7.2   Real Men Support the Family

The story of Phil and Barbara, clients seen by the first author at a mental health center, is a good example of the psychological power of the breadwinner role. Phil came for counseling first. He presented as experiencing panic attacks each and every time he sat down to a meal with family members. His first attack occurred during a celebratory dinner for his in-laws' anniversary, shortly after he had been laid off from his factory job for the sixth time. His job as an apprentice machinist paid very well, but layoffs were frequent in a volatile economy. The job fulfilled his lifelong dream of working with his hands and tinkering with equipment while earning a good living to support his wife and son. During layoffs, he would seek other temporary jobs where he earned much less and where he felt demeaned.

He knew other jobs might offer more consistent money and even more total yearly income if the loss of salary during layoffs were factored in. Yet earning the higher hourly rate meant to him that he was valued and a good provider. In describing his first panic attack, he revealed his shame that the extended family would see him as less than a real man, a bum who could not earn enough for his family. He felt undeserving of a place at the table or a portion of food. His wife, Barbara, wanted to become a hairdresser and set up a shop in their home so she could balance work and her homemaker/mother role. However, each time she started cosmetology school, she couldn't finish because the family resources were restricted by another layoff. It was important to both the husband and wife that she be at home caring for their son as much as possible.

How Would You Conceptualize This Case?

1. How were the panic attacks connected to eating family meals? How would such a connection be useful in therapy for Phil and Barbara?
2. What do you make of Phil's career goals? Of Barbara's career goals? As a career counselor, would you validate their career behaviors or would you insist they deal with realistic considerations?
3. What role did the extended family play in Phil's career identity? How did Phil and Barbara value their roles as parents?

What Actually Happened?

Once the obvious symbolic nature of the panic attacks was explored in therapy, couples counseling ensued to further examine the gender roles and to bolster problem solving in partnership. When Phil realized that Barbara saw his masculinity as more complex than his paycheck and as the two learned to support each other in their common family goals, the panic attacks decreased. He could eat with his wife and child but not with extended family. Eventually, he was able to learn construction skills with a male mentor and was able to supplement his income and buffer the effects of layoffs. Barbara was eventually able to open a hair salon at home.

Phil was not able to let go of the machinist trade, though the changing economy could mean that his chances of completing the apprenticeship were slim.

(continued)

(Case Study 7.2 continued)

With income supplements in place, however, he was able to host a dinner for the extended family and to occasionally eat with in-laws, though never without some discomfort. The breadwinner role re-mained primary, but the expanded view of masculinity and the partnership communication with Barbara enriched his identity and his life satisfaction.

attitudes encourage gays to hide their orientation and an open, healthy adolescent sexual development is almost impossible (Gollnick & Chinn, 2002).

In terms of career identity, few occupational models are easily seen as fully supporting of an openly gay lifestyle. The few that are identified as occupational homes for gays, creative fields in the arts and fashion for example, depict the gay professionals as caricatures, openly ridiculed for amusement rather than respected. In the workplace, gays and lesbians struggle to assess the consequences of openly sharing sexual orientation. The social constructs of masculinity and femininity encourage denigration of gay men and women, so keeping sexual orientation a secret might require quietly accepting mockery. "Coming out" may lead to victimization by serious discriminatory practices in terms of hiring and advancement, and such practices are not universally prohibited by law (Gollnick & Chinn, 2002).

Career counselors must not only understand the realities faced by individuals with diverse sexual orientations but must also deal with their own comfort level in discussing the range of professional and relevant lifestyle issues. Homophobic attitudes for career counselors range from subtle assumptions to major blind spots.

FAMILY ISSUES AND CAREER

The combination of work and family roles are interrelated with gender issues, and the variety of family forms constitutes a diversity issue. Couples and parents who work must agree on the delegation of family tasks, as was seen in the previous case study. Dual career couples have to determine whose career choices will take precedence at different times. Also, the variety of family forms are not fully recognized. Gay families do not fit with the social construct of an *Ozzie and Harriet* sitcom. Women's greater participation in work outside the home has changed the nature of the family. The traditional nuclear family with a male breadwinner and stay-at-home mother is not representative of the majority of households. The traditional model corresponds to only 11 percent of all families. Dual career families are 40 percent of the work force, and single parents account for 6 percent (Fredriksen-Goldsen & Scharlach, 2000). In addition, caring for elderly parents as well as children is the responsibility of one fifth of workers, those dubbed the *sandwich generation*.

Career counselors need to bring family issues into the mix of relevant considerations in counseling and educational programs. Recognizing societal changes and the necessity for clients to negotiate uncharted terrain where there is no standard way to deal with multiple roles (e.g., caring for elderly parents, dealing with divorce and remarriage) brings career services into the realm of assisting with the whole range of lifestyle choices.

In the previous case history, the effect of the gender roles and the family adaptation required the participation of both parents as a couple. Years later, the family sought counseling again.

As seen in the case study, counselors can facilitate a process where families can retain the bonds of caring even if crossgenerational experiences and values clash.

BOUNDARY ISSUES

Both genders maintain individual separate identities, yet must negotiate relationships with others. How this is done can impact one's life and career, and is often quite different for men and for women. The concept of oscillating self (Jordan et al., 1991) discusses how these relationships can be handled.

The diagram in Figure 7.3 (developed by Andersen and Vandehey) shows three circles along a continuum. The first circles are formed out of a solid line and represent closed **boundaries**. Individuals with closed boundaries are islands. Bridges can be built to others, but a strong sense of individualism, hence isolation, remains paramount (stereotypical male identity). This leads to a restricted social and emotional life. At the other end of the continuum is a barely discernable circle. The boundaries are so open that the individual lives life by reacting to others (stereotypical female identity). No separate identity exists. The middle of the continuum shows a clear circle

Bridge Isolation   Mutual Influence   Who's Who?

Figure 7.3   Oscillating Self: Open and Closed Circles

CASE STUDY 7.2   Real Men Support the Family, continued years later

Phil and Barbara returned to counseling. Phil was sullen, saying nothing. Barbara finally described a recent family dinner, when their son Steven, now a teenager, announced to his stunned parents that he was gay. Both parents followed the community standard and tried to argue that his orientation could be changed. Phil broke his silence and forcefully stated that his son could not be gay; he was confused, mixed up. He had even recommended that Steven join a military service where he could reform his sexuality. The counselor listened, allowing the venting of emotion, and then asked the parents, "What if it's true; what if Steven is gay, then what?" Barbara started to cry, and Phil returned to a sullen stare. Barbara expressed her fear that Phil and Steven would stop speaking to each other and the family would fall apart. Finally, at the counselor's urging, Phil admitted he did not want to lose his son, and he needed help trying to discuss the issue with Steven.

The counselor suggested a family session, and the three returned the following week. The counselor asked Steven to explain the situation. The son was exceptionally patient for his developmental stage and insisted that his parents accept his identity. The counselor asked Phil to describe to his son the struggle to define his masculinity in previous counseling. Phil did remember his own pain in trying to conform to a rigid model of masculinity but was completely at a loss as to how to deal with his son's sexual orientation. When the counselor asked Barbara to offer her input, Barbara said she would accept Steven no matter what. She just wanted the family to remain intact. She was fearful that her son would become estranged from his father and would leave the small conservative community. At the counselor's urging, Phil looked Steven in the eye and said, "I don't want to lose you; I love you."

Over the next few years, this loving family struggled to understand each other. Phil and Barbara eventually came to an understanding, if not a full acceptance, of Steven's gay lifestyle. Steven left town after graduating from high school, and the grandparents were never told of his "difference," as Phil phrased it. Yet father and mother visit their son regularly, and communication remains open between parents and son.

with open boundaries (formed by a dotted line). The metaphor here is a patchwork quilt. The individual is a separate piece of cloth, but is connected to others. Clients at either end of the continuum are hampered in their career development and life satisfaction.

The openings for the center circle can open or oscillate by creating wider openings to some people and closed boundaries to others. For clients who struggle with being separate, the middle circle suggests that relating to another person is an important part of one's identity; however, an individual identity is important too. The openings can also retract to limit flow between oneself and another to force greater separation. In this way, identity can be defined as separate from others and as open to various degrees of sharing where the influence of another is a part of the self. By honoring both openness and individualism, the career counselor avoids sending clients the message that they must give up who they are and become someone else. Either a man or a woman can keep the strengths of traditional stereotypes, the strong, boundaried self (men) or open boundaries responding to others (women) for those situations where boundaries or openness are appropriate. However, both men and women can also choose when to be more open or more closed, allowing the self to be more flexible in engaging the world.

The image of a self defined both by personal space and responding to others allows the self to be a defined identity that is both individual and social. Many cultures assume a collective identity in which individual preferences are subordinated to the needs of the social group and asserting individual needs is not primary (Gollnick & Chinn, 2002). Although an emphasis on social identity rather than individualism seems contradictory, the oscillating self concept demonstrates that both approaches to identity can be held without negating one over the other. Keeping an open mind to accepting values and ideas that may seem contradictory at first allows individuals to grow personally and socially. Career counselors may want to help clients identify those individuals (e.g., coworkers, boss) with whom more separation is appropriate and those people where more openness may be beneficial.

CAREER AND CROSSCULTURAL ISSUES

Career counselors attend to the needs of a diverse work force. The 1996 Census showed 30 percent of the population as nonwhite, with growing numbers for African Americans, Hispanic Americans, and Asian/Pacific Island Americans (U.S. Bureau of Census, 1998). Women have been entering the job market at an increasing rate for several decades and are expected to increase to 48 percent of the work force (U.S. Department of Labor, 1997). The diversifying demographics in the census are reflected in the labor market and in the clients seeking career services. For career counselors, adapting career services to the diversity present in the work force has been a priority issue in recent times. Theoreticians have broadened traditional theoretical concepts to include a view of cultural influences for diverse groups and have attempted to conceptualize the impact of differing values and concerns for career issues (Brown, 1996). The work of career counselors and educators is dramatically affected by the changing demographics. Career practices that assume a standard set of values and points of view as a one-size-fits-all will not work for a multicultural society.

The social structure that existed for only part of the population decades ago is outdated not only in terms of a changing economy, but also in terms of the diverse groups participating in the world of work. Career counselors need to be cognizant of the differing needs of people with widely differing economic status, cultural backgrounds, values, and multiple noncareer roles. However, just noting differences between different ethnic groups does not fully express the pluralistic impact of crosscultural, gender, and socioeconomic issues for counseling and in the world of work.

EMBEDDED ASSUMPTIONS FOR THE CAREER COUNSELOR

Career counselors who grow up as part of the mainstream middle class culture typically adhere to some basic values that directly affect their interactions with clients. One of the most basic mainstream cultural beliefs is an emphasis on the individual. The individual is responsible for the shape of a life, with all major choices being made by the individual. Most psychological theory starts with the individual, and healthy development to maturity is seen as creating an independent self, separate from others. Career counselors assess the individual's interests and abilities and reflect the meanings and values expressed by the person as a unique being.

Career theories and practices also start with an attitude that paid employment is central in everyone's life. Choices that limit participation in career activities are seen as a lack of motivation or lack of effort to gain what is supposed to be primary in life. Doing well is often defined as making money, attaining recognition for one's achievements, or being respected for what one does.

Such attitudes may be projected onto clients who may have differing experiences or backgrounds and who approach life with different attitudes. The profession of career counseling has its own context with tools and concepts influenced by the majority culture. It is important that career counselors recognize a diversity of attitudes, both their own and those of their clients. Recognizing the limitations of a single viewpoint allows the counselor to be open to differing attitudes and to assist clients in broadening their perspectives. Exposure to descriptions of cultural norms offer topics for counselors to explore during counseling or clues as to what interactive approaches may work well. Although a client may not view life from an individualistic framework, the client's self-description will create the picture of relevant external and internal factors. In the counseling room, the client and counselor work together to understand the client's world.

BROWN'S THEORY OF CROSSCULTURAL VALUES

Brown's (1996) theory involves the influence of values on career choice and satisfaction. The theorist delineates differences in cultural values among many groups. Career counselors need to recognize the value orientations of clients as a part of career identity. Respecting differences in values is critical, as is interpreting the impact of values in the workplace.

Career counselors can offer respect and understanding for these and other cultural values in helping clients deal with career issues. It may also be a useful service to interpret values that dominate the workplace for clients whose world views may be incongruent with the dominant culture. Depending on the acculturation process, many clients may very well understand the differences in the values of their communities and those of the workplace. Counselors can offer respectful comparisons that suggest differences in values do not entail superiority of one value system over another.

Brown (1996) offers several propositions regarding the influence of crosscultural values. He states that prioritized values are the most important determinants of career choice. However, values are not fully implemented when there are the constraints of different cultural values, gender, and socioeconomic pressures preventing some choices. Consequently, women, the poor, racial/ethnic groups, and those with same-sex orientation are constrained in choosing occupations reflective of their values. The values of collateral, or collective relationships, lengthy problem solving, and past orientations are not compatible with the current American workplace. Individuals who have these as high priority values must recognize that their mores conflict with external demands. Important aspects of their identities are denied. They cannot execute all their values, but must compromise with the expectations of the dominant culture.

Brown describes specific ways in which career behavior is affected by values not shared with the dominant culture. The process of choosing a career includes estimating one's ability and values, and the availability of occupational choices. **Collective values** may impede an individual's capacity to make estimations of ability because the person's natural inclination is to emphasize the group rather than the self, particularly if humility is an integral part of identity. Consequently, career instruments dependent on self-report may be less accurate.

Collective values also make dealing with conflict difficult and participating in competitive achievement activities problematic. An orientation of collective relationships makes the evaluations of others more important than self-evaluation, and asserting an opinion different than others is strenuous. Motivation is drained by the pressure of environments attuned to values incongruent with personal values. Success in the working world requires a

Box 7.1   Brown's Diversity Values

Time orientation is an area of difference for various cultures. Asians demonstrate a respect for the past, and some subgroups prize the influence of ancestors, elders, and traditional values and rituals. Many Spanish cultures live in a present-time orientation where the here-and-now is more important than yesterday or tomorrow. Native Americans have a time orientation based on the cycles of nature. Individuals from mainstream American culture, particularly in the workplace, expect a future orientation where people continually strive toward a better tomorrow. Educational environments are also future oriented as students are expected to delay gratification, working in the present for rewards in the future.

Problem-solving approaches may vary across cultures. Spanish cultures often take a slow, not very active, approach to problem solving. The expectation for this cultural perspective is that often solutions come in time. Asian cultures work toward a consensus in problem solving and spend much time consulting with everyone concerned. An American approach, again stressed in the workplace, is to solve problems actively and quickly. The expectation for a U.S. cultural perspective is to do something and to get the job done.

Social relationships are determined by cultural values. In most northern European democracies and in the United States, value is placed on individualism. For many other cultures, in-cluding African American, Spanish American, Native American, and Asian American, collective or collateral relationships are valued. In the U.S. workplace, hierarchical structures dominate; and each individual is judged separately, even when teams of workers work together. Cooperation between workers may be expected, but a higher value is generally attached to individual achievement.

Self-expression is viewed differently by various cultures. Spanish cultures and some segments of the African-American community value spontaneous self-expression, particularly within the family. Asian cultures value limited self-expression. Native Americans often demonstrate nonverbal, action-oriented self-expression. The American workplace places value on controlled self-expression and considers carefully planned strategies of interaction important to influence others and to manage career reputations.

Emotional self-control varies among cultures. Asian cultures demand very restrictive emotional self-control, as do Native American. African Americans and Spanish descendents allow open emotional self-expression particularly within their own communities, as in church and at home. The American workplace expects emotional self-control, and emotional release can be considered a weakness. Manipulating emotional responses is considered a legitimate means to influence others in some areas such as marketing.

future orientation because tenure and performance require looking ahead and adjusting to tomorrow's expectations as well as to present demands. In addition, success is affected by performance evaluations that are made by others who judge with differing cultural values.

Predictions for the future suggest employers may need to offer more accommodations for personnel, given a shortage of workers with some skills and the increasing diversity of the work force. There may be bottom-line reasons to adapt the values of the work environment. Polarized values that prevent accommodating collective relationships, different time orientations, or various problem-solving attitudes make work environments less compatible for some workers. Maybe work environments could integrate values for the benefit of all workers rather than creating demands that negate the values of diverse groups. Certainly, promoting true collateral relationships could enhance productivity in some situations. Maybe a variety of problem-solving orientations could create differing solutions and possibly, the pressurized time orientation of the workplace could be more adaptable.

Career counselors can be instrumental in facilitating a client's recognition of how personal values conflict with the demands of the workplace. Sophisticated skill and compassionate respect are required to help clients retain their dignity and to carefully deal with the values choices required to cope with the dominant workplace attitudes.

ACCULTURATION AND RACIAL IDENTITY DEVELOPMENT

Dealing with ethnicity and related racial issues also requires an understanding of research regarding the **acculturation** process and racial identity development. Several descriptions have been proposed by researchers (Gottfredson, 1992; Helms, 1984; Pederson, 1991), but all versions share a common progression of awareness and integration. All members of society deal with actual or perceived discrimination. White males, in reaction to affirmative action, may feel as if they do not have a chance if a minority applies for the same position. A woman may walk into an all-male workplace and question its openness to having a female coworker. People of color may be treated with disrespect in an attempt to discourage their applications and, if hired, made to feel like the tokens, not valued employees.

Being aware of typical reactions to difference can aid the career practitioner in helping the client manage his reactions to the world of work. There are, in fact, five stages in acculturation and racial development, which we summarize below. The process begins with individuals recognizing differences between groups and defending their own group to the detriment of others. With psychological growth, people gradually acknowledge differences as nonthreatening. Eventually, they can appreciate the variety.

Combining models of acculturation and racial development for minorities as well as the White majority is intended to relay a process of awareness for everyone (see Box 7.2). When awareness first opens to a sense of differences in values, experience, and social justice, polarized psychological reactions occur. In essence, the issues of difference become personal, and the common reaction is to assert one's own group as superior and blame other groups as of less value. Over time, an integration process occurs where the individual becomes less personally defensive and more accepting of differences in values and more honest in regard to historical social privilege.

Career counselors need to take into account not only differences in values and background but also variation in the client's acceptance of differences. The work of career counselors is to facilitate the client's process of coming to terms with both personal and external factors as the client gains a mature acceptance of reality and of the responsibility to make choices. Career counselors and educators must be prepared to encourage and deal with the range of emotions that are a part of identity development for clients, including indifference, anger, blame, and guilt. At the same time, career counselors themselves can expect to feel a similar range of emotions in reactions to their clients' feelings. The skill of awareness of such an internal and interactive process and dealing with it effectively is the mark of a true professional.

Racial identity development is related to career development (Carter & Constantine, 2000). Students may lack confidence or believe that interests and values differing from the majority culture put them at a disadvantage in making decisions reflective of their personal selves. Minority members who are unaware of distinctly racial identity issues may not recognize discriminatory practices at work whereas others with greater awareness may lack trust in dealing with White supervisors or colleagues (Helms, 1984). Career counselors must be skilled in assessing and drawing out potential blocks to individuated career identity. Such topics as race and economic constraints are necessarily breeched within a respectful, trusted, and safe relationship. It is important to make assessments of the client's needs on an individual basis and not to assume the client will demonstrate conformity with textbook models or descriptions of the characteristics for particular groups.

Culturally specific values and personal characteristics can be seen as valuable strengths the client can bring to career planning and to career performance. Some theorists who write about cultural differences state that some groups prefer a more directive approach rather than the counselor reflecting feelings and facilitating an introspective process (Sue & Sue, 1999). Career counselors must be aware of the timing for interventions with clients

---

Box 7.2   Cultural Identity & the Process of Accepting Differences

1. Lack of awareness of differences characterized by assuming that the standards of the majority are applicable to all people from all groups, which in effect devalues the principles of any subgroup and suggests the majority group is superior.

2. Dissonance occurs when differences are acknowledged. For Whites, confusion abounds when initially recognizing societal racism and feeling twinges of shame and guilt or resisting such feelings. For minorities, acknowledging discrimination and devaluing subgroup values disrupts acceptance of majority group viewpoints.

3. Idealizing one's own group while denigrating other groups or the White majority. White majority members may rationalize reasons for inequality and, in effect, blame the victims or be angry with the concept of accepting individ-

ual responsibility for inequities. Minorities may reject the values of the dominant culture while valuing their own.

4. Introspective processing of the over-idealization of any group and the denigration of other groups. For minorities, positive valuing of own group but letting go of denigration. For Whites, intellectual acceptance of racism without admitting privilege and unearned superior status.

5. Integration of multiplicity while valuing one's own group and retaining respect for other groups. For Whites, it is admitting privilege and demonstrating an understanding and valuing of differences. For minorities, it is understanding the oppression of some other groups and selectively appreciating some values of the White majority.

---

who are acculturating to a system defined by the White majority. What is crucial is to remain client-centered even if the interaction is more directive and to be sure the client is in charge of the choices to be made. Given values such as a collective orientation, it may be appropriate to consider techniques such as group career counseling or the inclusion of the family. The career practitioner who is aware of cultural interaction styles and values as well as the impact of individual differences can create innovative approaches to suit the needs of clients at all stages of the counseling or education process.

Economic Issues and Career Practice

Understanding the diverse experiences of all people requires recognizing the social and economic influences impacting different groups living in our own country and those from other nations. Thinking globally means understanding the different contexts for the lives of diverse peoples, not only in our own country, but throughout the world as a whole. To help readers gain a broader world view, Smith (2002) described an imaginary village populated proportionately by people from around the globe. Of the 1,000 village inhabitants, there are only 50 North Americans, Asians total nearly 600, and Africans number 124. There are 95 Europeans in the village, 85 Latin Americans, and 52 Russians. More than 200 languages are spoken by different groups in the village. Approximately 90 religions would be represented by different groups. Two hundred of the 1,000 inhabitants, or one fifth of the total, receive 75 percent of the total income, and half of the adults are illiterate. Clean water is available to only a third of the population. Imagining such a village emphasizes socioeconomic, religious, language, and demographic differences. Hansen (1997) used such a description to suggest that career counselors adopt a world view that integrates a sense of what work needs to be done for a planet characterized by a multiplicity of changing contexts.

As corporations spread over the globe, workers will be exposed to conditions present on different continents. Making decisions regarding exchanges between such dramatically different contexts requires stretching our minds to recognize everyone has very different privileges and opportunities. Even the distribution of wealth and opportunity within one country can show disparities if most of the resources are controlled by a small percentage of the population. How can career services meet the varying needs of multiple backgrounds and varying economic resources? How do the actions of career counselors affect the peoples of the planet and diverse groups within one country? Gaining the perspective of recognizing multiple variations in external demands and the diversity of contexts for people's lives is essential before career counselors can determine the needs of their clients.

In truth, the focus of career services as a means for self-expression rather than an economic necessity is a privilege many people of the world could not afford. For many in economically developed countries, thinking globally means dealing with increased competition and changing jobs frequently as companies and institutions adapt to changing conditions. Yet the global economy also means increasing technology and greater stratification of economic classes because some groups lack the societal conditions that create complex economies and varieties of jobs. Professional career counselors possess the capacity to see multiple contexts, both economic and cultural, and to recognize differing needs of diverse clients. Although all the world's peoples deal with external conditions, only a few have the privilege to consider personal preferences. Career counselors have the sophistication to tease out the impact of external pressures while respecting cultural variations, including the determination of how much each client can accommodate personal preferences within career choices.

Case Study 7.3 demonstrates the struggle with crosscultural concerns and the influence of economic constraints. Both money and cultural values were relevant, and both were primary in the client's internal struggle and his decisions.

Wealth Distribution

American society has strong cultural values that are reinforced in the workplace. One historically significant value for the dominant culture has been a strong work ethic. In the period of industrialization, Horatio Alger was a character in stories that demonstrated that through hard work even a poor lad could rise in the occupational structure and make a fortune. Future predictions and current economic conditions suggest that the Horatio career pattern is becoming a relic of an earlier time. Still, the dominant culture stresses hard work as a primary value, though compensatory rewards are clearly not available for all.

An analysis of recent trends in the economy suggests that external adaptations have accommodated some groups more than others (Ellwood et al., 2000). Understanding the changes in the economy is a must for career counselors because career choices are strongly affected by how workers are compensated. The impact of socioeconomic status requires a review of how the economy operates. Economic differences between various groups can be revealed by showing the effect of recent economic changes on families with different income levels.

Research describing changes in the American economy have found some consistent patterns for change in income levels over the last 25 years. From 1973 to 1996, the top one third of earners increased their average income by 43 percent, the middle one third gained 9 percent, and the bottom one third lost 16 percent (Ellwood et al., 2000). The middle one third of earners experienced this much smaller gain in income, compared to the top one, despite an increase in the number of two working parent families.

Women's individual income has gone up over the last two decades as more women work, as they work longer hours, and as they gain experience. Women's salaries are still not on parity with men's, but the gap is lessoning. Men's salaries in the middle one third of earners have not increased (Ellwood et al., 2000). Most of the income gained through capital investments added to the top one third of earners' income. Corporate earnings for executives have increased about the same amount as the wealthy earners, but corporate profits have not increased in the percentage of all income (Ellwood et al., 2000).

CASE STUDY 7.3   My Selfish Interests

This story of a client who sought counseling at a university counseling center demonstrates the intertwining of cultural and economic issues. The client was a student from an underdeveloped African country. He was studying engineering agriculture and had a 3.8 grade point after two years of study. However, he reported to the counselor that he spent every free moment in the library reading psychology and counseling books. Fascinated by the field that described human experience from an individual's perspective, he spent some time in sessions describing the more collective approach of his culture. It was difficult for him to understand how a country could take care of the common needs of all its citizens if each person made decisions based on individual preferences. He said his reading had given him a better understanding of his own experience, and he could recognize some of the difficulties and emotions of members of his family. But using an individual psychological perspective as an overall approach to living or to

working was too "selfish." That said, he began to express his secret fantasy that he would leave the engineering field and formally study psychology. However, his government was paying for his education and his country needed engineers, not counselors. He had even fantasized that he could abandon his country's sponsorship, find a way to major in psychology, and create a "selfish" life.

How Would You Conceptualize This Case?

1. What values of collective identity are threatened by psychology's emphasis on individual identity? How does this client fit or not fit with Super's concept of "implementing self-concept"? Or Holland's matching of personal and environmental characteristics? Or Krumboltz's learning theory model?
2. Given the crosscultural nature of this career counseling, how would you adapt your interventions to the client's values? How would counseling this client be different than how you

Clearly, the changes in the distribution of money have dramatically hurt those categorized in the lowest one third of income level. The shift in earnings favored those with more skills and education, and the gap in wages between those with more education and those with less widened considerably (Ellwood et al., 2000).

The assumption that career choices and economic success is based on individual effort assumes that each individual has the economic base to afford multiple choices. Another assumption is that there will be the opportunities available to the individual as long as the person is willing to work hard to gain the chosen goal. If basic income is limited, one attitude is that one can "suck it up" and "pull one's self up by the bootstraps." Working hard is assumed to be enough to demonstrate anyone's ability to gain opportunities based on merit. It may be difficult for novice counselors to understand that many people have contexts where choices are limited by economic

would approach a client from the United States?

3. What are your feelings about the client's need to study a field his country needed? Would your values and feeling affect your counseling?

What Actually Happened?

The client was not fully acculturated to ways of the United States, and he was struggling with the clash of values he was experiencing. Then, he expressed his pain that in truth he had no choice because he had no economic resources of his own and could never afford to study a field not financed by his government. From his perspective, the clash of values was real but secondary to the money issue. The client experienced therapy as a truly unique experience. In his country, people consulted elders when they had concerns but rarely was the emotional component of issues primary. Indeed, the counselor was cautious about labeling feelings and allowed

the process to move very slowly to be sure the client was sharing and examining only what he chose. At times, when the client started to tear up, he was given a choice as to whether he wanted to continue or not. Eventually, the client fully examined the issues on several levels: philosophical ideas; societal implications; application to his own life, and finally with deeply felt emotion.

With the help of his counselor, he did resolve his situation to his satisfaction. He recognized that he would bring back to his country the learning he gained from his extracurricular reading and his experience in counseling as well as his engineering skills. As he gained experience in the workplace, he would try to gain an administrative post in the government and supervise others. As a respected leader and private consultant, he would be able to use his understanding of individual dynamics to help others who sought his counsel.

realities, where opportunities are limited by discrimination, and where differing values are misunderstood as not worthy of respect. It is sometimes easier to believe that the world is just and that hard work and merit override racial, ethnic, and economic differences rather than struggle with the complications of varying societal contexts. In other words, a limited perspective could blame the victim rather than deal with the complexities of differing contexts for people who live within a context of little hope for upward mobility.

The Underclass

Much of the data regarding the lowest income earners has been collected by the *Multi-City Study of Urban Inequality* (Holzer, 1999). This study was designed to describe the impact of economic restructuring on ethnic and minority groups living in the inner cities where workers compete for a diminishing number of unskilled jobs and also experience discrimination in hiring. The intersection between minority group standing and poverty is tangled with variables difficult to separate and interpret.

There is a documented shortage of available jobs for unemployed workers in the inner cities, and yet there is also some difficulty filling some jobs that are available. Many inner city jobs are filled by more educated, skilled workers who have more experience and who commute from the suburbs. Jobs that could be filled by less skilled, less educated workers (e.g., jobs in the retail stores and service industries) are mostly located in the suburbs. Transportation difficulties are an obstacle for the urban poor commuting to the suburbs. Blue-collar jobs such as factory work and construction positions are diminishing, and only about 20 percent of such jobs are located in the center city (Holzer, 1999).

Most employers hiring unskilled workers require a high school diploma, specific experience, references, and/or some training. Most jobs require basic skills in reading, writing, and arithmetic, and many require some basic skills in the use of computers or other business machines. Most retail and service jobs require social skills for dealing with customers, skills subjectively assessed during interviews. Skill requirements for many jobs limit the hiring of inner city minorities, most of whom are Hispanic or Black (Holzer, 1999). Finally, many jobs are filled through word of mouth to friends of current employees, and this further restricts the hiring of certain populations.

Minority women are more likely than minority men to be hired for the clerical and service jobs prevalent in the unskilled category. Sadly, the average pay of employed minority women is lower than the average pay of employed minority males who, in turn, earn less on average than White males with similar jobs. Discrimination can be easily revealed in the hiring practices of employers in the suburbs. Studies have found that suburban employers demonstrate their biases when they are asked to explain why minorities are less represented in the applicant pools and in the hired group. Employers describe applicants from inner cities as products of poorer schools, crime, and the prevalence of single-parent households. Minority workers who have overcome the conditions employers describe still have difficulty convincing employers that they are capable and motivated to meet job requirements (Holzer, 1999).

Political Issues and Public Policy

Political proposals to deal with unemployment and poverty rarely suggest that the distribution of wealth created by the structure of the economy is so disparate that basic changes are needed. Yet the gap in income gains has continued for decades. A few economists suggest that such conditions devalue employment, marginalize specific groups of citizens, increase child poverty, increase crime, and create such a chasm between groups that civil conversations regarding our nation's well-being become difficult. Political debates that support the work ethic may omit the related issue of an economy that excludes many.

Career counselors have an ethical issue to consider when serving disenfranchised clients. Does the counselor say to clients that job losses have been created by an economy designed to increase profits regardless of the effect on workers? That profits for the few are supported by government policies that accept that a large percentage of people will rarely work and many will work intermittently? By ignoring descriptions of the economy, are counselors reinforcing low self-efficacy for those clients who have been excluded? Are middle and lower class White men justified in resenting an economy that has been structured so that their incomes have not risen in decades? Are minorities and the handicapped justified in feeling excluded? How do these issues play out in career counseling and education (Ellwood et al., 2000)?

The primary ethic required of all counselors by the ACA Code of Ethics is client welfare, respecting the dignity of clients and encouraging client growth as well as paying attention to diversity issues (Martinez, 2003). Such respect can include an understanding of the difficulties of marginalized groups who have not benefited from public economic policy. On the other hand, using external restraints as a reason for not trying or for not encouraging self-growth is not in the client's interests. The career counselor determines the appropriate balance between justifying the client's situation and the need for the client to assert independent actions regardless of external circumstances.

When working for agencies associated with public policy, counselors must also determine their responsibilities to both clients and to the institution in which services are performed. Counselors strive to be influential in creating changes in institutional policies supportive of the growth and development of clients (Martinez, 2003). Professional ethics could suggest a need for career counselors to advocate for changes in national economic practices.

Welfare to Work

The most obviously disenfranchised groups within economically developed countries are the working poor and those people on welfare. In the United States and Western Europe, a debate titled *30 Year Tug of War* (Berlin, 2001) has posited two positions. One argument is that basic subsistence welfare is needed for those in poverty, particularly for women and children. The opposing opinion is that public assistance should be time limited and that the poor should work at whatever jobs they can get. In the last decade, political programs have emphasized the welfare-to-work approach. National governments have funded block grants to states or local municipalities that link benefits to programs that put participants to work within a specified time. Welfare recipients lose economic assistance if they do not show progress toward getting a job. The literature (see Finn, 2000; Freidlander & Burtless, 1995; King & Wickham-Jones, 1999; O'Neil & O'Neil, 1997; Stolsen, 1997) describes programs that assist people in obtaining work, with arguments as to whether it is appropriate to provide education or training in the process. Whether or not programs include education or training, most programs provide life-skills instruction with job search methods (Hyland & Musson, 2001; Neenan & Orthner, 1996; Ricco & Orenstein, 1996; Weaver & Hasenfeld, 1997).

These programs are organized in a variety of ways. Some show gains in employment with social support provided through job clubs and other methods. A few programs provide education, some through junior colleges (Allen, 2002; Katsinas, Banachowski, Bliss, Timm & Short, 1999; Thompson, 1993); other programs have specific training for specific jobs in specific companies (Glazer, 2000; Herzenberg, Alic, & Wial, 2000). Sadly, most programs are administered by case workers with no specific training in career education or counseling.

One proposal suggested is a tiered system starting with entry level jobs and then progressing to jobs of increasing skill difficulty and increasing pay (Herzenberg et al., 2000). Such a plan would create training to increase worker skills and improve customer services. For example, home health care workers would be trained to learn how to paraphrase what a home patient requested and how to interpret care-giving methods to the incoming home health care worker on the next shift. Caregivers can eventually be promoted to coaches who teach skills to entry level workers, instruct others on how to interpret differing situations, teach trainees how to handle the variety of patient requests, and develop learning contracts devised to help workers identify and define those skills that need improvement. This promotion comes with more dignity, self-efficacy, and pay.

Another strategy would set up informal but powerful groups of similar workers. Worker associations in health care, construction and janitorial service, childcare, and retail clerks could provide skill development training that offers advancements beyond entry level jobs. Such groups would operate like worker guilds so members would be less isolated. The worker groups would assist members in finding employment when laid off and help in finding better jobs (Herzenberg et al., 2000).

Traditional career counseling textbooks have not dealt with issues affecting people chronically unemployed or the working poor. However, the most successful welfare-to-work programs do incorporate concepts supported by career counseling. Specifically, such programs provide interventions to assist participants increase self-esteem and self-efficacy; provide social networks offering advice, support, and information about job openings; and access progressively more complex training (Allen, 2002; Ricco & Orenstein, 1996). Career counselors could supply consultation services to community and worker associations and aid in creating new worker programs (Hagen, 1997). Finally, career counselors could make proactive contributions to society by using professional expertise to analyze legislative initiatives and advocate for programs that emphasize career development.

Career Clients with Disabilities

In 1990, Congress passed the Americans with Disabilities Act, prohibiting discrimination against qualified workers with impairments that require reasonable accommodations (CGP, 2001). The act provides that if an employee or potential employee could perform the essential tasks of a job, it is discriminatory for the employer to refuse to make simple, inexpensive accommodations that do not cause undue hardship on the organization.

Career counselors can also provide services for clients with minor disabilities or clients who have completed rehabilitation for their impairment. The basic accommodation needed to help those with restricted abilities is to emphasize what the client can do and to de-emphasize what the client can't do (Prachyl, 1998). Attention to self-esteem and self-efficacy is also a must. Reviewing the rules regarding what the law defines as reasonable adaptations in the workplace may also be a part of career services (Kissane, 1997).

Mental illness is considered a disability and is included as an area with legal protection against discrimination. Typically, clients with physical disabilities receive counseling as a part of rehabilitation services, and few physically handicapped clients request services of career counselors who are not trained in the specialty of rehabilitation. However, career counselors are the standard providers for those with a psychological diagnosis because many mental health clinicians are not trained in dealing with career issues.

Most psychological disorders are treated prior to dealing with career concerns. For example, a depressed client would deal with the mood disorder and when the feelings were managed well, career issues would follow in a therapeutic sequence. The client would learn what habits would predispose a recurrence of depression and would hopefully make changes to prevent further episodes. The client would also learn what signals might indicate a recurrence, and how to cope and prevent another episode from becoming severe. Career issues would be taken in context, that is, whether particular work encourages behaviors and attitudes that lead to depression. Other psychological symptoms, such as anxiety, might use the same therapy sequence, dealing with the symptoms and then integrating the coping mechanisms with career issues.

Personality disorders would be the more common diagnoses associated with disabilities because full change may not be possible for such clients. For an Axis II diagnosis, the counselor would need to integrate dealing with problematic behaviors along with career issues. Personality disorders entail a cluster of problematic behaviors that can interfere with occupational functioning. However, if the work requirements do not emphasize the particular dysfunctional characteristics, job performance may not be affected.

Counseling clients with personality disorders usually requires the counselor to take a particular stance while interacting with the client. The following are examples of more common personality disorders and areas of special concern to the counselor. For the dependent personality disorders, the counselor usually follows a set procedure that the client understands and can expect. With such structure, the client can manage the anxiety prevalent in making decisions associated with a dependent personality. The client would need a job where independent thinking was not required. Job loss would trigger great stress for those with dependent personalities because low self-esteem is characteristic and the loss would be interpreted as indicating low self-worth.

A borderline personality client might show extremes on interest inventories because these clients waver between positive idealism and negative devaluation. Jobs for borderlines must not require sophisticated problem solving, but a borderline can perform well enough on jobs with variety, flexible supervision, and clear directions. Working with borderlines requires counselors to be clear, caring, and consistent to prevent prompting intense interactions. Assessing for periodic psychological crises including suicidality is also necessary with borderlines.

Obsessive-compulsive personalities (OCPD) are often workaholics who are dependable, precise, and able to maintain high standards on the job. However, individuals with OCPD have difficulty coping with colleagues who are less concerned with perfectionism. They tend to do most of the work because delegating is not an easily learned behavior. In career counseling, OCPDs may weigh each and every item of an interest survey and may want to carefully check out the reliability of instruments. Decisions take an excessive amount of careful consideration given a fear that the outcome may not be controlled. Counselors patiently allow enough time, not pressing an anxious

CASE STUDY 7.4   Computer Whiz

Robert, a 32-year-old client seen by the first author, serves as an example of career work with a mentally ill and disabled client. Robert had been diagnosed as schizophrenic when he was 23 years old. He lived in a partial care community home and was medicated so his intrusive thoughts did not interfere with his daily functioning. He was intellectually bright, though his social interactions were very restrained and he rarely said anything beyond terse answers to questions. He was working as a dishwasher in a restaurant where he functioned well, with regular attendance, coming to work on time, and completing assigned tasks as directed. In counseling, however, Robert expressed dissatisfaction with his job.

An interest survey was administered verbally over several sessions, and the results showed similar interests with computer programmers. Discussing these results encouraged Robert to share that he had been a student at the United States Military Academy at West Point where he had training in computer programming. There was no record of such an education. However, when it was arranged for him to have access to a computer, he demonstrated considerable skills.

How Would You Conceptualize This Case?

1. What are the limits of career counseling with clients who have been diagnosed with a mental illness? Would you have helped Robert accept his illness and the obvious limits to his occupational endeavors?
2. Would interest surveys or personality instruments have been appropriate for Robert? What adaptations could make some career tools useful?
3. How could a career counselor deal with the self-esteem issues for a client like Robert or others with disabilities? How could a counselor have helped Robert recognize and build on his strengths?

What Actually Happened?

A volunteer mentor brought Robert to a computer facility on a university campus, and the two worked on programs, solving some glitches that had presented great difficulties for the technical staff. Eventually Rob obtained a job working nights in a private, quiet area of the university computer lab. Program difficulties were left for him to solve and invariably he was able to do so. He did not have to interact with the rest of the staff, and he was quite content to spend hours working out solutions to programming problems.

reaction but also gently encouraging the client to become aware of feelings that can be better managed (Kjos, 1995).

For clients with physical or mental disabilities, effective career counselors focus their efforts on determining how each client can make his or her contribution in the working world. As clients learn to internalize a similar attitude, that they have something to offer on the job, they can perform well and gain satisfaction in their work.

SUMMARY

The diversity of clients in today's work force requires career counselors to know their own backgrounds and to be aware of their reactions to the variety of interactions and values clients may present. Counselors and educators need to be sensitive to all the variations of race, ethnicity, and SES represented by clients. The personal impact of psychosocial factors affects career choices and experiences at work. External presses will create different reactions for different people. Differences within the societal structure will create different experiences for people from different backgrounds. Career counselors must demonstrate clinical and educational sophistication to adapt teaching and counseling according to the needs of those who use career services.

STUDY OUTLINE: KEY TERMS AND CONCEPTS

I. Increasing Cultural Sensitivity
   A. Career counselors must become aware of their own values and cultural background.
   B. **Background view**: Lens of values, attitudes that shade how a person sees the world, life, dominant culture and other groups. A perspective shaped by age, socioeconomic level, culture, gender, sexual orientation, family roles, and other factors.
   C. Many clients have family values that date back to immigration and may form important parts of career identity.
   D. Family constellation: Psychological role in family can impact career choices
      1. Actual birth order may influence psychological role in family.
      2. Family-assigned roles and their expectations influence career identity.
II. Gender: Women
   A. **Gender**: Attributions given to women and to men according to societal stereotypes
   B. **Social constructs**: Conceptual labels accepted by a society
   C. Women's talents are routinely underutilized leading to lower satisfaction, and male-dominated professions may be hostile toward women
   D. Historical roles placed women in care-giving roles, and many of the expected societal behaviors do not easily transfer into the world of work.

III. Excelsior Model
  A. Environment impacts the integration of self-sufficiency and connectedness. The environment can both inhibit and facilitate integration.
  B. Examples of inhibitors: Stereotypes; discrimination; rigid policies that minimize certain groups from accessing resources (e.g., not allowing flextime or job sharing for single parents).
  C. Examples of facilitators: affirmative action; egalitarian schools; role models of androgynous individuals.
IV. Gender: Men
  A. Theories for career development are based on the White majority and are heavily influenced by 1950s social constructs that stereotype men as breadwinners only.
  B. Men may assume that they are judged by how much money they make.
V. Sexual orientation
  A. If a social construct exists, it is typically negative and does not allow for normal, healthy development of identity.
  B. Concerns of being hired/fired and promoted are connected to being "out."
  C. Career counselors need to be aware of their own attitudes toward homosexuality.
VI. Family Issues and Career
  A. Traditional career model only accounts for 11 percent of families.
  B. Some families also struggle with caring for elderly parents.
VII. Individual Boundary Issues and Career
  A. **Boundary**: The dividing line representing the separation between people in relationships.
  B. Oscillating self: People contain both a separate identity and are impacted by relationships with others.
  C. Clients who try to be totally self-sufficient live restricted lives and need help to become more open to important relationships whereas clients who live life in reaction to others lack a direction for growth. They need help in restricting their openness
  D. It is possible to hold both an individual focus and a social focus at the same time. One need not dominate the other.
  E. **Androgyny**: Men and women who are able to combine traits stereotypically assigned to only men or women.
VIII. Career and Crosscultural Issues
  A. Growing minority populations bring a wider range for values, identities, and concerns.

B. One-size-fits-all theories or practices do not work.

C. Embedded assumptions for the American career practitioner

IX. Brown's Theory

    A. Values impact career choice and satisfaction

    B. Time orientation:

        1. Past orientation: Honoring tradition and elders

        2. Here-and-now orientation: The moment is what matters.

        3. Future orientation: Delay gratification in hopes of a better tomorrow.

    C. Problem solving:

        1. Slow, nonactive versus quick and active

        2. Group consensus versus individual decisiveness

    D. Social relationships:

        1. Individual success versus group success

        2. Cooperation versus clearly delineated hierarchy

        3. **Collective values** (the good of the group is favored over individual gain) from some cultures contrary to American individualism

    E. Self-expression:

        1. Spontaneous (genuine) versus carefully planned (strategic)

        2. Limited (quiet) versus quite expressive (loud, obvious) versus verbal and controlled

    F. Emotional self-control

        1. Restricted versus open

        2. Controlled versus uncontrolled

X. Acculturation and Racial Identity Development

    A. **Acculturation**: The degree to which a person has adopted the cultural habits and attitudes of the dominant culture

    B. Stages of cultural awareness

    Stage 1: Believing that standards of the majority apply to all; subgroups devalued and majority group seen as superior

    Stage 2: Acknowledging that differences exist and experiencing dissonance

        a. Minorities: Acknowledge discrimination; question majority group standards

        b. Majority: Recognize racism and feel twinges of shame and guilt

    Stage 3: Idealizing one's own group while devaluing other groups

        a. Minorities: Reject values of dominant group

        b. Majority: Rationalize inequality and blame victim

Stage 4: Thinking about overidealization of one group and the denigration of other groups
  a. Minorities: Value own group, starting to let go of rejecting the dominant group
  b. Majority: Intellectual acceptance of racism without admitting privilege

Stage 5: Valuing one's own group while retaining respect for other groups
  a. Minorities: Understanding the oppression of one's own and other groups, but appreciating some of the values of the dominant culture
  b. Majority: Admitting privilege and valuing differences

XI. Economic Issues and Career Practice
  A. In many countries, work is an economic necessity. Americans are fortunate to have work be an expression of the self.
  B. Even though many Americans are fortunate, many are not. Class stratification results in some Americans being unable to achieve in the sense of the traditional American dream.

XII. Wealth Distribution
  A. The American dream: Anyone can make it if they work hard enough. The reality is that a variety of forces (e.g., amount of resources, education, discrimination) trap some individuals in poverty no matter how hard they work.
  B. In recent years, the top one third of earners enjoyed a huge increase in income. The middle one third enjoyed a small increase, and the bottom one third saw a decrease.

XIII. The Underclass
  A. Skilled, higher-paying jobs located in cities are often filled by more educated, experienced people who commute from the suburbs while less-skilled jobs are often located in the suburbs and commuting is an obstacle for the poor.
  B. Unskilled workers are expected to have a high school diploma, experience, references, and/or some training, and many do not.
  C. Minority women make less than minority men. Minority men make less than White males.

XIV. Welfare to Work
  A. Subsistence welfare limited to specified time limits; benefits are contingent upon making progress toward getting a job
  B. A variety of programs exist. Some focus on getting jobs; others focus on education; but many are staffed by individuals with no training in career education or counseling.

C. Programs are needed that go beyond helping clients gain an entry level job, aiding individuals to move into higher positions.

XV. Career Clients with Disabilities

A. The Americans with Disabilities Act (1990) states that reasonable accommodations must be made for qualified workers with impairments.

B. Career counselors can help clients emphasize abilities and deemphasize disabilities, and become knowledgeable about what the law considers reasonable accommodations.

C. Mental illness is disability protected by the ADA.

1. Mental illness should be dealt with first, then integrate career issues later.

2. Personality disorders may never be corrected. Integrate career issues earlier in the treatment.

3. Whether working with depression, anxiety, or a personality disorder, look for work environments that do not exacerbate the condition.

EXERCISES

1. In a class group with all students sitting in a circle, each student shares background issues: family immigration culture; SES; gender; sibling position/family roles described on pages 5–7. Students can share spontaneously or can prepare a week ahead. Counselors in training are to consider what factors might set viewpoints or bias that could affect relationships with students or clients. Themes for individuals and the group are discussed.

2. Have the class budget for a lower class life-style for a person who is a young, single, childless adult. Research the typical amount of money a person in poverty receives each month through a minimum wage job without benefits or full-time hours. Students are to find out the typical costs of: rent, car payment/insurance, groceries, utilities, slowly adding furniture, buying clothes, etc. Discuss how this fits with the American dream.

REFERENCES

Adler, A. (1931). *The Case of Mrs. A: The diagnosis of a life-style.* Chicago: Alfred Adler Institute.

Adler, A. (1937). Position in family constellation influences life-style. *International Journal of Individual Psychology, 3,* 211–227.

Allen, M. (2002). OLC welfare to work named exceptional. *Tribal College, 12*(4), 26–29.

Andersen, P., Wickwire, P., Lewis, E., Vetter, L., & Hansen, S. (1992 December). *Connectedness and Self-sufficiency: Helping counselors increase sensitivity to gender issues.* Presentation for the annual meeting of the American Counseling Educators Society, San Antonio, TX.

Baker-Miller, J. (1976). *Toward a new psychology of women.* Boston: Beacon Press.

Bardwick, J. M., Douvan, D., Horner, M., & Gutmann, D. (1970). *Feminine personality and conflict.* Belmont, CA: Brooks/Cole.

Barnett, R. C., & Hyde, J. H. (2001). Women, men, work, and family: An expansionist theory. *American Psychologist, 56*(10), 781–796.

Berlin, G. (2001). The 30-year tug-of-war. *Brookings Review, 19*(3): 34–39.

Bernard, J. (1972). Roles of modern women. *Sociological resources for the social studies.* Washington, DC: American Sociological Association.

Brown, D. (1996). Brown's values-based, holistic model of career and life-role choices and satisfaction. In D. Brown, L. Brooks, & Associates (Eds.), *Career choice and development* (pp. 337–372). San Francisco: Jossey-Bass.

Carlson, J., & Slavik, S. (1997). *Techniques in Adlerian psychology.* Washington, DC: Accelerated Development.

Carter, R. T., & Constantine, M. G. (2000). Career maturity, life role salience, and racial/ethnic identity among Black and Asian American college students. *Journal of Career Assessment, 8,* 173–187.

CGP. (2001). *Americans with Disability Act: A monograph.* Moravia, NY: Chronicle Guidance Publications (Reprint R-199).

Ellwood, D. T., Blank, R. M., Blasi, J., Kruse, D., Niskanen, W. A., & Lynn-Dyson, K. (2000). *A working nation: Workers, work, and government in the new economy.* New York: Russell Sage Foundation.

Finn, D. (2000). Welfare to work: The local dimension. *Journal of European Social Policy, 10*(1), 40–58.

Fitzgerald, L. F., & Betz, N. E. (1994). Career development in cultural context: The role of gender, race, class and sexual orientation. In M. L. Savickas & R. W. Lent (Eds.), *Convergence in career development theories: Implications for science and practice* (pp. 103–117). Palo Alto, CA: Consulting Psychologist Press.

Fitzgerald, L. F., Fassinger, R. E. & Betz, N.E. (1995). Theoretical advances in the study of women's career development. In W. B. Walsh & S. H. Osipow (Eds.), *Handbook of vocational psychology: Theory, research and practice* (2nd ed., pp. 67–109). Mahwah, NJ: Erlbaum.

Fitzgerald, L. F., & Rounds, J. (1993). Women driven out of the workplace: Theory encounters reality. In W. Walsh & S. Osipow (Eds.), *Career counseling for women* (pp. 327–354). Hillsdale, NJ: Erlbaum.

Fredriksen-Goldsen, K. K., & Scharlach, A. E. (2000). *Families and work: New directions in the twenty-first century.* New York: Oxford Univ. Press.

Freidlander, D., & Burtless, G. ((1995). *Five years after: The long-term effects of welfare to work programs.* New York: Russell Sage Foundation.

Glazer, J. W. (2000). The Sprint model: Private and public sectors working together to make welfare to work a success. *Economic Development Review, 17,* 41–46.

Gollnick, D. M., & Chinn, P. C. (2002). *Multicultural Education in a Pluralistic Society.* Upper Saddle River, NJ: Merrill, Prentice-Hall.

Gottfredson, L. S. (1992). Dilemmas in developing diversity programs. In S. E. Jackson & Associates (Eds.), *Diversity in the workplace human resource initiatives* (pp. 279–305). New York: Guilford Press.

Gutek, B. A. (1985). *Sex and the workplace: The impact of sexual behavior and harassment on women, men and organizations.* San Francisco: Jossey-Bass.

Hagen, J. L. (1997). Women, work and welfare: Is there a role for social work? *Social Work, 37*(1), 9–15.

Hansen, L. S. (1997). *Integrative life planning: Critical tasks for career development and changing life patterns.* San Francisco: Jossey-Bass.

Helms, J. E. (1984). Toward a theoretical explanation of the effects of race on counseling: A Black and White model. *Counseling Psychologist, 1,* 153–165.

Herzenberg, S. S., Alic, J.A., & Wial, H. (2000). A new deal for a learning economy: Jobs and careers in postindustrial society. In J. M. Kummerow (Ed.), *New directions in career planning and the workplace: Practical strategies for career management,career planning and the workplace: Practical strategies for career management professionals* (pp.77–122). Palo Alto, CA: Davies-Black.

Holm, J. M. (1970). Employment and women: Cinderella is dead! *Journal of the National Association of Women, Deans and Counselors, 34*(1), 6–12.

Holzer, H. J., (1999). *What employers want: Job prospects for less educated workers.* New York: Russell Sage Foundation.

Hyland, T., & Musson, D. (2001). Unpacking the new deal for young people: Promise and problems. *Educational Studies, 27*(1), 55–68.

Jorden, J. V., Kaplin, A. G., Baker-Miller, J. Striver, I. P., & Surrey, J. L. (1991). *Women's growth in connection.* New York: Guilford Press.

Katsinas, S. F., Banachowski, G., Bliss, H., Timm, J., & Short, J. (1999). Community college involvement in welfare to work programs. *Journal of Research & Practice, 23*(4), 401–422.

Kimmel, M. S. (Ed.). (1987). *Changing men: New directions in research on men and masculinity.* Thousand Oak, CA: Sage.

King, D., & Wickham-Jones, M. (1999). From Clinton to Blair: The Democratic (party) origins of welfare to work. *Political Quarterly, 70*(1), 62–75.

Kissane, S. F. (1997). *Career success for people with physical disabilities.* Lincolnwood, IL: VGM Career Horizons.

Kjos, D. (1995). Linking career counseling to personality disorder. *Journal of Counseling & Development, 73*(6), 592–597.

Maremont, M., & Sassen, J. A. (1996, May 13). Abuse of power: The astonishing tale of sexual harassment at Astra U.S.A. *Business Week,* 86ff.

Martinez, J. (Ed.). (2003). *Codes of ethics for the helping professions.* Pacific Grove, CA: Brooks/Cole.

Matthews, E. (1972). *Counseling girls and women over the life span.* Washington, DC: American Personnel and Guidance Association.

Matthews, E. (1989). Perspectives: Occupational status of women—1968–1988. Invited Program: National Career Development Association, AACD Convention, Boston, MA.

Matthews, E. (1990). Stability and change in women's lives: 1940–1990. Marguerite C. McKelligett Memorial Lecture, Worcester State College, Worcester, MA.

Moss, P., & Till, C. (2001). *Stories employers tell: Race, skill, and hiring in America.* New York: Russell Sage Foundation.

Neenan, P. A., & Orthner, D. K. (1996). Predictors of employment and earnings among job participants. *Social Work Research, 20*(4), 228–238.

Nieva, V. F., & Gutek, B. A. (1981). *Women and work: A psychological perspective.* New York: Praeger.

O'Neil, D. M., & O'Neill, J. E. (1997). *Lessons for welfare reform: An analysis of the AFDC caseload and practices in welfare to work programs.* Kalamazoo, MI: W. E. Upjohn Institute for Employment Research.

O'Neil, J. (1987). Male sex role conflicts, sexism and masculinity: Psychological implications for men, women and the counseling psychologist. *Counseling Psychologist, 9*(2), 61–80.

O'Neil, J., & Fishman, D. M. (1986). Adult men's career transitions and gender-role themes. In Z. Leibowitz & D. Lea (Eds.), *Adult career development: Concepts, issues and practices.* (pp. 132–162). Alexandria, VA: National Career Development Association.

Pederson, P. B. (Ed.). (1991). Multiculturalism as a fourth force in counseling. [Special issue.] *Journal of Counseling and Development, 70.*

Pleck, J. H. (1981). Two worlds in one: Work and family. *Journal of Social History, 10*(2), 178–195.

Prachyl, P. (1998). Career counseling for people with disabilities. *Journal of Rehabilitation, 64*(3), 56–57.

Riccio, J. A., & Orenstein, A. (1996). Understanding best practices for operating welfare to work programs. *Evaluation Review, 20*(1), 3–29.

Robertson, J., & Fitzgerald, L. F. (1990). The (mis) treatment of men: Effects of client gender roles and life-style on diagnosis and attribution of pathology. *Journal of Counseling Psychology, 37,* 3–9.

Skovholt, T. M., & Morgan, J. I. (1981). Career development: An outline of issues with men. *Personnel and Guidance Journal, 60*(4), 231–237.

Smith, D. (2002). *If the world were a village.* Tonowanda, NY: Kids Can Press.

Stolsen, D. (1997). Welfare behaviorism. *Society, 34*(3), 68–78.

Sue, D. W., & Sue, D. (1999). *Counseling the culturally different: Theory and practice* (3rd ed.). New York: Wiley.

Sweeney, T. J. (1981). *Adlerian counseling: Proven concepts and strategies.* Muncie, IN: Accelerated Development.

Tannen, D. (1994). *Talking from 9 to 5.* New York: Morrow.

Thompson, J. J. (1993). Women, welfare and college: The impact of higher education on economic well-being. *Affilia: Journal of Women & Social Work, 8*(4), 425–442.

Tyler, L. (1977). *Individuality.* San Francisco: Jossey-Bass.

Ulrich, D. N., & Dunne, H. P., Jr. (1986). *To love & work: A systemic interlocking of family, workplace, and career.* New York: Brunner/Mazel.

U.S. Bureau of the Census (1998). 1996 Census Bureau report. *Career Opportunities News, 15,* 7.

U.S. Department of Labor (1997). *News.* Washington, DC: U.S. Department of Labor, Bureau of Labor Statistics.

Weaver, D., & Hasenfeld, Y. (1997). Case management practices, participants responses, and compliance in welfare to work programs. *Social Work Research, 21*(2), 92–99.

Webb, S. L. (1991). *Step forward: Sexual harassment in the workplace.* New York: Master Media.

Williams, J. H. (1977). *Psychology of women: Behavior in a biosocial context.* New York: Norton.

PART III

Career Counseling Skills

CHAPTER 8

Career Counseling Process

> The single most important realization I hope you will get ... is that this metaphysical business called psychotherapy, this "talking cure," has to be comprehended ultimately as a powerful, distinctly personal relationship between two essentially similar human beings. (p. xxvii)
>
> *C. Peter Bankart, 1997,* Talking Cures: A History of Western and Eastern Psychotherapies

The process of career counseling mirrors both the pattern of career development and the course of career decision making. The goal of career counseling is to advance the client's awareness of self-identity and to create the readiness for internal psychological movement. Because the choices made are the client's responsibility, the counselor's role is to create conditions that facilitate the process of the client's psychological growth and the attainment of career identity.

CLASSIC CAREER COUNSELING INTERACTION

Most clients come to career counseling expecting to find the decision that will finalize career goals, at least for the time being. Although clients expect to decide something, most have only a minimal knowledge of what is involved in determining career choices. To the counselor, it seems the client wants to be told what to do. Although many clients will admit that they would like the counselor to provide an answer, most also accept that they have to make decisions themselves. Usually, clients will cooperatively participate in activities initiated by the counselor. However, many clients are impatient with taking too much time to come to a choice. The time involved to gradually create psychological movement does not fit with the client's image of decisively determining an answer. It may appear to the counselor that a client's tacit cooperation is limited to superficial self-examination at best. This is the classic frustration for both client and career counselor. The master career counselor is aware of this basic overlay to career counseling but is skilled in turning the career counseling process into a substantive psychological experience for the client.

The Career Diamond depicts the career counseling process. As described in Chapter 3, the process assumed by some clients would be a quick jump from the starting point to the end point of the diamond without experiencing the expanding and contracting process the diagram depicts. The career counselor's goal is to encourage the client's understanding and openness to the exploring and deciding process according to the client's needs and stage of development.

Exploring Phase

Self-Exploration

In practical terms, the effective counselor engages the client in an exploration process through which the client becomes aware of personal characteristics that can be expressed through related career activities. Only after clients become open to the possibilities of individualized career identity and the relationship of identity to occupational factors can they begin to set priorities for the decision-making phase.

With this sequence in mind, the career counselor focuses first on facilitating the client's self-awareness. Many clients do not truly understand that career decisions proceed from self-awareness; therefore, the first step of career counseling is sometimes difficult. The effective counselor introduces open-ended interventions to lead the client toward examining embedded personal constructs such as life experiences, values, and vague visions for the future. Such interventions offer some **structure** to the counseling interaction so the client can gradually become aware of what is needed.

A counselor's attempts to introduce self-exploration without some structure does not always meet the client's needed assurance that progress will be made toward making a career decision. The client needs some defined structure to start a process fraught with doubts and unknowns. The client's subliminal need for structure in counseling may be a difference between career counseling and counseling for other personal concerns. Many clients may enter noncareer counseling immediately releasing emotion as a first step in coming to terms with issues. In career counseling, clients are reluctant to display emotions that reveal insecurities because a determined, self-confident attitude promotes hope that the answer will be found.

In fact, one of the counselor's functions in facilitating career development is enhancing self-esteem so a client can project a vision of success in the future. Some form of structure directs clients toward a positive self-evaluation, which in turn motivates clients to continue self-examination and, indeed, counseling itself. Clients are drawn into the process of identity exploration and begin to experience the self as providing direction for career considerations.

The underlying pull for some structure to meet client emotional needs does not mean the counseling interaction becomes counselor directed or that the counselor's voice dominates. However, introducing a structure, including interest inventories, value checklists, or personality surveys, serves to stimulate client self-exploration and can provide a reasonable starting point. The key to the counselor's management of the counseling interaction is focusing on the client's **content**, on the client's voice, or on the client's description of self-discovery.

Because structure is used to assist the client in coming to terms with personal considerations, it is appropriate to consider structured interventions as client-centered. Interventions that dominate the counseling interaction and close down the client's internal process are inappropriate even if the client wants a directive format. A client's initial presenting request may imply that a test or an expert career counselor could provide an answer perfectly suited to the client's needs. Such a client is not prepared for an open-ended discussion examining personal career identity. Instead, career counselors infer clients' need for structure and use the structure to open clients' self-awareness to a point where they can participate in unique career deliberations by providing content.

The first goal of career counseling is to promote an expanded awareness of self and to facilitate the attainment of career identity. Underlying all life choices, including one's choice of work, are more existential questions such as, "Who am I?" "What is the meaning of my life?" "What contribution can I make?" Yet with the pressures of gaining knowledge, skills, credentials, and of finding income-producing work, it feels impractical to be focusing on esoteric questions that do not offer solid progress toward getting a job and paying the bills. Even when career decisions need to be pragmatic, choosing one's life's work still evokes value-laden issues of life's meaning. As Howard Figler writes, "Choosing a career is giving yourself permission to be who you are ... [against] competing forces" (1999, p. 39).

Clients will vary in their desire to consider values and other abstractions within their career decisions. Some clients are quite concrete and materialistic whereas others ponder their capacity to let go of ideals in order to do the work that provides necessary income. Counselors may need to facilitate a balancing of idealism and practicalities and/or encourage thinking beyond the paycheck according to the client's cues and underlying needs.

Exploration: Counseling Movement

Career counseling is often brief, from five to ten sessions. Thus counselor interventions are designed to broaden the topic of career decision making to include the client's full view of self within a five- to ten-session time frame. The counselor's slowing-down pace is designed to give time for the client's self-reflection. When a client feels the urgency of pending deadlines and expresses discomfort with the ambiguity of not knowing, the struggle between internal growth needs and external pressures can be reflected back to the client with phrases such as, "It's hard to give yourself the time and space to determine what you want when you feel outside pressures."

The counselor's role is to separate the internal and external pressures so the client can put distance between personal needs and external demands. The two sides of the Career Diamond will come together in due time, but during exploration, the client needs the counselor's understanding support as well as firm patience with the process. The movement of exploration is similar to the diamond's shape, expanding both a sense of self and external requirements but with the self dominating. Information about the external world of work is also expanding, but exploring information is done to inform self-exploration, checking out what is available that is relevant to the self, keeping information somewhat at a distance, while the self grows in strength.

Information is grist for the mill that is proceeding toward a vision where the client can find self-expression in an occupation or work goal. When the client brings information to the counseling session, the counselor consistently brings up the issue of, "How does this possibility fit with how you see yourself?" Such a question and other similar leads make information gathering a tool for self-exploration, rather than a cue for choosing too quickly.

Identity Exploration

"Tell me about yourself" is a general counselor lead to introduce self-exploration, but many, if not most, clients usually respond with blank stares or confusion that suggest, "What do you want to know?" It is important that the counselor encourage client self-description by introducing topical leads that require extensive narration. Opening up identity themes is another type of structure provided by the counselor. For this type of counselor intervention, clients are afforded the opportunity to examine their sense of self. The various client stories can be pulled together into themes that weave together the descriptors of self into meaningful patterns that begin to define a personally owned self-concept. As in counseling for other issues, sometimes ferreting out themes from the stories of life's experiences can provide a picture of self that provides a sense of wholeness.

Adler created the original concept that human beings create semi-conscious life fictions containing thematic issues that require resolution. Individuals then construct their life goals as purposeful movements toward resolving such themes and defining their self-concepts (Ansbacher & Ansbacher, 1956).

A postmodern counseling theory, called narrative therapy, has extended the idea that individuals are authors of their own lives. Howard (1989) describes effect of psychological life stories:

> People tell themselves stories that infuse certain parts of their lives and actions with great meaning and deemphasize other aspects. But had any of them chosen to tell himself or herself a somewhat different story, the resulting pattern of more meaningful and less meaningful aspects of his or her life would have been quite different. (p. 168)

It is the self-constructed meaning of the person's life story that the counselor is drawing out into the counseling atmosphere. Cochran (1997) points to those private narratives as providing continuity to lives, and the stories as creating an individual's meaning structure that organizes experience into a holistic framework. The plot(s) of individuals' stories contain the problems and the actions that attempt, at varying levels of success, to solve different dilemmas.

Career choices are a major vehicle for people acting out the story of their lives, and career counseling can be a vehicle for reflecting on the meanings created by the client's interpretations of life's experiences. By exploring the stories, clients learn that career choices are life choices. Life choices determine the answer to the question, "Who am I?" When clients tell the stories of self and career, they recognize their current self-knowledge. Present career self-concepts can move into projected visions of a future self in new working environments. The counselor opens counseling to topics that encourage the client to explore life's experiences, including experiences that are not, on the surface, related to career directly. As with all counseling, meaningful material can sometimes come from childhood experiences.

Life Themes

Adler wrote that life themes can be discerned by analyzing a person's place within the family of origin and early recollections from childhood (Nikelly & Verger, 1971). Values held by parents may or may not be ideals retained by the person. Adler postulates that the values representing agreement between both parents are usually retained in some form or another.

For values where parents disagree, the child often chooses to align with one parent or find a compromise. Encouraging the client to describe what priorities parents taught and the client's reaction to the teachings can open the door to meaningful stories revealing aspects of the individual's core identity.

Adler also contended that a person's psychological place in the order of siblings is more important than the actual physical birth order. In 1937, Adler wrote, "It is not, of course, the child's number in the order of successive births which influences his character but the situation into which he is born and the way in which he interprets it" (p. 211).

An only child grows up in the company of adults and may then develop a feeling of being taken care of without developing self-reliance. The oldest child is often the most achievement oriented because she has a view of being first, and she works to stay ahead of younger children. The middle child may feel lost in the array of other brothers and sisters. Finally, the youngest child may be taken care of by all the family members and may not feel as though he is taken seriously (Carlson & Slavik, 1997). Further reading regarding psychological birth order effects can expand a counselor's perception of such themes. What is most important is that the client relays the story of a life lived in a unique family context, and these contextual factors create influences for the client's sense of self and his purpose for the future.

Here are some questions that may be useful when trying to understand birth-order effects (Patterson & Watkins, 1996):

A. How did the child fit into the family?
B. How many siblings? What is the birth order?
C. What are the client's siblings' attitudes toward her?
D. How have family members succeeded in life? Do they have any problems?
E. What is the state of parents' character and mental health?
F. If the parent(s) are dead, what happened?
G. How did the parents treat the client?
H. Who was the mother's favorite? Who was the father's favorite?
I. How would the client describe her upbringing?

These and other leads encourage clients to describe their place in the social structure of the family, a place in relation to others that can be of long-lasting importance. "Who was known for what in the family?" "What was the primary strength for you and each of your brothers and sisters?" Often, siblings carve out separate areas of achievement or recognition within the family. Such areas may be cues for satisfying adult activities, or they may point to areas that were discarded too early and may offer areas of interest later in life.

Another source of life themes are early recollections (ER). Gysbers & Moore (1987) list a number of life-style themes demonstrated by the client's behavior across time and by memories of an early life experience. These terms become labels for identity descriptions: the getter; driver; controller; person who must be right, or liked, or good; superiority striver; person who always opposes everything; the victim; martyr; baby; inadequate person; feeling avoider; excitement seeker. Again, reading psychological descriptions of identity themes can help counselors become aware of common patterns. However, with experience, counselors can become skilled in perceiving and labeling unique themes for each client.

Soliciting early childhood memories can be done with the question, "What is your earliest memory of what you wanted to be when you grew up?" One of the authors answered this question in counseling with an admiring description of the cowgirl Dale Evans who rode across the silver screen, singing with Roy Rogers. The memory elicited the author's desire to gain recognition, to be respected, and to gain a partnership relationship. These themes fit, in the author's view, with becoming a teacher, a profession recognized in the community, respected by others, and offering a life-style accommodating marriage and family. To continue early fantasies about future careers, the counselor can ask, "As you became older, how did your idea of what you would be change?" The client's description of a childhood vision sets one view of early expectations that change over time and will continue to change in the future.

Counselors seek themes by looking for patterns in client interpretations of experiences that repeat themselves in the client's stories. Contradictions in which a client expresses a preference or value but later describes a choice or experience that suggests something different are also noted.

For example, a client named Marissa described childhood activities of writing and reading and the encouragement of instructors from elementary school through undergraduate college to pursue a profession doing scholarly research. Marissa had recently found she was unable to sit still and concentrate on her studies. Instead, she spent time talking to strangers and friends, "wasting time" in ways she thought irresponsible. "Working through" her seemingly contradictory impulses, to study versus socializing, she became aware of values expressed in talking to others. She found that reading was separate from life; though enjoyable, it seemed of less value if not directly related to people's lives. She became quite passionate in describing conversations in which she could express an idea that someone could actually use. She still did not know of any occupations where she could enact her ideal exactly, but teaching came to mind, if it were the right kind of teaching. Eventually, she changed her major from physics to literature and became a teacher in a home for single, pregnant women. She also writes short stories filled with hope and lessons learned through life experiences.

Career Identity

Themes from a client's life can be infused with career content and can become labels useful for melding the personal and the career self. Everyday examples could be describing the client as creative, active, or handy. An important factor is to positively frame the identified attributes, reinforcing positive self-esteem and creating an encouraging atmosphere for counseling and for the client's positive view of self. Crosscultural themes are significantly relevant as with Marissa, who said, "I'm a Hispanic woman who loves ideas that come to life in conversations with other people."

Career theory offers terms and concepts that the counselor can use to summarize potential career identity characteristics. For example, the counselor is familiar with RIASEC categories and can look for personality characteristics and values associated with the Holland Codes (see Chapter 5). If a client talks about getting things in order, this can suggest organizational skills or enjoyment of data manipulation, an R category characteristic. The *Myers-Briggs Type Indicator*® (CPP, 2005) offers descriptors that can be often identified as themes within the context of client descriptions (e.g., extroverted, intuition, etc.). Marissa, for example, used the term "people ideas" to summarize the type of knowledge she preferred. She found physics as more purely I as per the Holland Code and she needed more A and S.

The use of descriptors from assessment instruments does not mean that the tests even have to be given. Counselors can use the classification systems to reflect a theme for the client's consideration. Even more important to the process is encouraging the client to discover personal trends for himself. The experience of realizing identity factors will be an activity the client can continue to refine throughout life. If the client can learn to associate personal characteristics to career choices, future decisions will be easier to make and the natural development of career will occur with greater clarity.

Another thematic area for exploration can be client achievements, which suggest skills relevant to careers. The effective counselor is also familiar with the *Dictionary of Occupational Titles* (1991) categories and can use the related descriptors of people, ideas, and things to reflect related aspects of career identity. For example, a people orientation may suggest that the client could enjoy selling or teaching. Several techniques for ferreting out career skills and interests will be described in the techniques chapter (Chapter 9).

It is important to note that emphasizing skills too early in counseling can move the client toward consideration of occupational titles before a full exploration of self has been completed. The task in early counseling sessions is to create a holistic narration of the client's life and to seek or define the embedded career identity within the personal context. Pointing to skills demonstrated by the client's experience is a counselor intervention that builds self-efficacy. The client's career identity begins to include constructs that say, "I'm a person who can do (name skill)."

Use of Questions

The beginning sessions for career counseling may differ from counseling for other concerns in the use of questions. To encourage self-exploration, an important structuring tool can be questions that stimulate a review of the person, the life lived up to this point, and projections of the life envisioned for the future. Because the purpose of the questioning structure is to expand awareness of self, these interventions need to be general, drawing a description from the client rather than one- or two-word answers or brief phrases. "Can you type?" doesn't usually bring out full personality descriptions from the client. To stimulate greater client self-description, open-ended questions should be constructed within a general topic. For example, "What professional skills do you bring to a job, and which ones do you like performing and which ones do you dislike doing?"

Questions regarding the family of origin can reveal not only long-term themes but also basic perceptions of the world of work. "Tell me about what you have observed from the careers of your family members" is an intervention leading the client to recognize occupations they may know something about. Following up on family job descriptions could be asking the client how he would see himself in such jobs.

Experiences in school direct students to potential fields of interests and abilities. An obvious request to describe such experiences is, "Tell me about your experience in school, what subjects have you liked the most and the least?" It is important to use follow-up questions that imply that getting a grade of an A in a subject is not the single criteria for finding possible interests. Students may have liked one part of a subject but not others. Interests may be related to distinct activities within a subject even if the overall subject would not be described as a favorite. The social interactions at school are also indicative of potential career behavior. "How would teachers and other students describe you?" may draw out worthwhile material to examine in counseling. Extracurricular activities may also have provided motivating, skill-building experiences.

Other questions specific to occupational history and future projections are of value if they are not used too early in the exploratory process. At the beginning of counseling, asking questions that lead to a description of jobs held currently or in the past does not open up the self-exploratory process and often misses how an occupation reflects self-concept and has meaning for the overall life pattern.

Asking a client to describe present and previous jobs within the context of all of life's experiences allows potential themes of interests to develop. It is important to follow up job descriptions by asking what parts of the job the client liked the most and what parts were disliked. Interest patterns and areas of satisfaction begin to form when work history is delineated in detail and put into the greater context of the client's life.

Another note of primary importance is for the counselor to use work history and other descriptions of life experiences to validate client strengths and contributions made by the client. Remember, praise grounded with actual behavior helps build the client's self-esteem and self-efficacy. An example could be, "The care you took writing reports for your company demonstrates not only writing skill but your ability to work with data and your capacity for analyzing the production results." Again, underscoring the multiple skills shown by the client builds self-efficacy for the client's career identity.

Questions asking the client to project an image of an ideal future also offer themes and hints of possible career areas for further investigation. "If you imagine yourself working, what is your favorite fantasy of yourself in the perfect job?" can be used with or without the variation of the image of using a crystal ball. However, such a question takes on more substance if it can be tied to a previously developed picture of the client's life of work experiences *and* activities other than work (e.g., "What is your favorite fantasy of the perfect life, including work, family, fun, etc.?").

Once the mode of fully examining the self is established, direct questions regarding the meaning of activities for the worker make sense to clients. The following questions may encourage considerations of meaning and purpose to career: "How would you describe your primary values for your life? What do you believe in, and how do you want your life to demonstrate your beliefs? How does your work fulfill the meanings of life that are important to you?" Other techniques for exploring values are described in the techniques chapter (Chapter 9). However, the best values clarification can occur by noting implicit values heard within counseling sessions.

Finally, it is important to open career counseling to the domain of balance between the work and nonwork areas that make up clients' lives. "How do you picture your family when it is established? How will (or do) your family life and your career relate to each other?" Such questions put career in perspective and introduce a topic that either is or will be of major consideration for most clients. Without carefully dealing with issues of balance between major areas of life, dissatisfaction may develop regardless of the gratification brought by work.

Blocks and Detours to Self-Exploration

Throughout the self-exploration phase, the counselor uses counseling techniques appropriate for all forms of counseling: reflecting content, addressing feelings, identifying implied meaning, providing counselor's summaries, reframing, and providing encouragement. All the interaction tools appropriate for counseling are used in career counseling!

There are, however, unique qualities to career counseling. Counselor interventions follow the client's lead but also bring into focus career-relevant factors such as interests, personality style, values, work skills, work history, and schooling. When considering the whole of the client's life, some issues, such as family dynamics and other background influences, may detour around career identity. Career counselors become adept in determining when client content is wandering in areas that might become relevant to client growth and when the story telling is meandering in ways that only fill time. Sometimes issues are meaningful but not directly related to career and sometimes a focus on personal concerns is needed to remove a block to career identity. Fears, low self-esteem, or self-efficacy deficits may stem from client experiences that require full examination, reexperiencing and reinterpreting the event(s) with the goal of building new cognitive sets. Interweaving personal and career concerns represents the richness of the client's self-exploration and the personal social context for career.

Exploring Information

While engaging the client in self-exploration, the early and middle phases of career counseling also include encouraging the client to seek information. As was mentioned earlier, early information gathering can be general and can be a tool for self-examination. However, coming to terms with career identity issues is determined in part by the client facing realistic provisions of occupational conditions. Some of a client's indecision can be caused by a general recognition that prerequisites are likely, but the client is not sure what the qualifying factors are or if he can meet them. In the face of a demanding world of work, lack of information can be frightening. It can be a way to avoid coming to terms with personal limitations and/or making a decision. Not knowing where to fit in as a worker can be felt as a near failure for the client before he has even begun to explore the possibilities. A mind-set of underlying insecurity could be a part of the unspoken plea, "Tell me what to do!"

A grounded picture of realistic possibilities for an individual requires both factual information and an honest assessment of the person's capacity to meet the demands of work. The second goal of career counseling is to encourage clients to seek additional information to expand their knowledge of what is actually available in the world of work. Many clients are reluctant to search extensively for information. Though a judgment of laziness is the easiest explanation for not finding information, most often clients do not pursue information because although not knowing is difficult to handle, the actual facts are seen as even more difficult to face. Indecision keeps possibilities open and does not require actually coming to terms with honest self-assessment. Encouraging clients to diligently seek information is part of the counselor's role. To serve such a function, the counselor has to establish a truly collaborative tone so the client maintains a personal motivation for the information search, rather than feeling like a student with an assignment guided by an evaluator.

Another obstacle for clients searching for information is the overwhelming amount of material available. The Internet has expanded access to information, but it has not provided the means to determine the quality of information or its relevancy to the client. Clients often do not know how to use the information or know what is pertinent at different points in the career choice process. A valuable and often neglected function of career counseling is to listen to clients struggling to determine what exactly the career information means to them individually. Regularly asking questions to clarify what some tidbit means or how a piece of information applies to the client's career identity is important for the client to progress toward realistically founded choices. Clients will gain the essence of the career choice process if they can begin to establish personal criteria for determining what information is useful and learn how to apply the facts they find to their career goals.

It is not the counselor's responsibility to research information for the client. Although counselors can easily clarify general misconceptions, often very specific information about particular fields requires consulting with someone or several someones in the field. For example, a counselor might succinctly explain that a liberal arts degree may apply to many jobs in the business field as well as a business degree. A counselor might also briefly define a field, such as, "Public relations is managing a company's image for customers or the general public. The image may be represented in writing, speaking, or managing social interactions." However, the client will benefit from interviewing several people in the field who could give specific information about their positions. Sometimes clients need encouragement to approach others to interview for information. The authors often tell clients that people enjoy being interviewed because it allows them to brag about their work and to explain why their work is important. Helping clients determine what to ask during informational interviews helps allay fears.

It is important to recognize that much of the labor market information about the expected availability of jobs and entry-level requirements is regularly changing. Clients need to follow their personal priorities before allowing concrete information to eliminate possibilities. By interviewing people in the field who have current information, the client can learn about realistic ways to enter the field, regardless of market conditions.

Managing the amount of information within the counseling hour can be critical. Keeping the client focused on small amounts of information will encourage a client-centered interaction as opposed to an information-centered interaction. Each piece of information has relevance to the client's needs, and it is those needs that direct the client's personal process. The counselor keeps the attention on the client and relays the message that external information is used within the context of client self-expression.

Creating the Vision

The exploration of self and general occupational information comes to a point where the client can begin to imagine a vision of the future. The counselor's efforts to draw out client self-description begin to take hold, and the client begins to define personal intentions. Different clients approach their goals in different ways. An imaginative client may describe a well-drawn picture; a more concrete thinker might give a specific job description. This is one of those moments in counseling that is not to be rushed. Clients and counselors need to connect personal themes and to explicate the purposes and meaning of the client's aims. Themes are meaningful expressions of the client's career identity, distinct from some personal areas, but interrelated to a holistic view of identity of self and one's place in the world.

Having a complete vision allows the client to look ahead and face the difficult choices that more detailed external requirements entail. The future pulls the client forward when the picture of an ultimate position is at least moderately clear. One mistake clients and counselors make is to let specific requirements of occupations block the vision. Spending the time to create meaningful mental images and articulating intentions has a motivating effect in which difficult external demands become less important. Visualizations can also create excitement that the future is bright, and personal contributions will be made while the client expresses his self-concept in a satisfying way.

Decision-Making Phase

When clients can describe their own career identity, they can begin the process of integrating internal and external factors. The vision of the future is complete in that the client can identify his self-concept within several options that are basically realistic. The career counselor serves another function in helping the client recognize that coming to terms with current choices is necessary and that continuing to search for additional career possibilities will be unproductive for the time being.

This is a place where the client begins to narrow his choices. The client has to accept the need to eliminate some possibilities and to begin investigating a few options in more detail. Personal criterion for evaluating information is primary. The information is less critical than the client's acceptance of some choices and the letting go of others. Setting personal priorities determines what to investigate further and what to eliminate. Any career choice will require overcoming some obstacles, so a final decision may depend on what option seems worth the price when compared to other options. Sometimes one choice does not seem to fit any better than any other, so the client simply has to choose, at least temporarily. It is easy, at times, to stay in the swirl of more and more information, fearful that eliminating anything will close down possibilities that could have been the right choice.

Counselors can reinforce the client's capacity to determine current choices and to know when to make new choices in the future if one choice requires change. Encouragement to move on in the career choice process eases the stress for the client, enhances the client's resolution to make personal choices, and serves as validation of the client's career identity.

Using personal needs as the criteria for evaluating information reinforces the nature of career development as a process of expanding self-awareness while delineating career identity more and more clearly. Seeking career information entails not only collecting the facts but also relating the information to one's unique characteristics. As the client considers new information, she also makes new self-discoveries, solidifying a picture of self as a careerist. A skilled counselor provides interventions to create an intricate process of integrating information with the client's priorities and continually reexamining those priorities as a deeper, more sophisticated sense of self develops. The result is the client learning what is required to enhance the career development process and the nature of career decision making for use throughout life.

Decision-Making Theory

Many career materials, ranging from graduate school textbooks to self-help books, offer a traditional model for the decision-making process. The standard format is: defining the decision to be made; determining criteria; finding alternatives; finding information regarding alternatives; ranking alternatives; and choosing the best alternative. Such a mold duplicates a linear problem-solving process.

H. B. Gelatt (1962) originally described decision theory as the rational format extending the scientific method as the appropriate means of determining life choices. More recently, Gelatt (1991) wrote in a different vein.

> Like other "decision experts," I have developed rational models, invented logical formulas and prescribed scientific techniques for decision-making.... I am aware that everyone didn't always decide by rational logic, even when I was preaching it and when it was considered conventional wisdom.... We need some decision advice that is more closely related to what people do than what experts say they should do. (p. i)

Gelatt recognizes the restrictions felt by many career counselors and clients when bound by the customary correct way to make decisions: logic and objective analysis. A career counseling structure that walks a client through a rational step-by-step procedure only works some of the time and for only some clients. Even when the standard decision-making formula does work, often it works because some light bulb of insight goes off for the client, and neither counselor nor client can describe what really happened. What Gelatt suggests is a decision-making method that balances traditional concepts with more creative ones.

Searching for career information and analyzing various reports requires the arrangement and rearrangement of the facts. It is the procedure of rearranging facts that brings a subjective element to all information. The client is only one of the many information processors to take information and turn it into a usable form. Many previous information analyzers have performed their shaping of the data, too. Treating facts as objective reality when all information is, to a degree, subjective reinforces an attitude that there is a right answer.

Gelatt (1991) suggests information be treated as open to the subjective reality of intermixing the client's inner reality with the pictures presented by descriptions of external reality. Adding the client's intuitive responses brings in the personal qualities that are unique to the client. Personal intuition is held to be as valid as objective, reasoned analysis. In previous models of career decision making, the career counseling profession gave little encouragement to intuitive leaps, even though creative risk takers such as Bill Gates obviously used intuition to open new career possibilities and gain great success.

Logical and Intuitive Decision Making

Gelatt (1991) correctly points out that some of the standard attitudes recommended for career decision making are limited. He offers continuums of attitudes that seem to be contradictory but offer versatility. An example is a continuum of focus and flexibility. Certainly, clients need to focus attention on goals and to carefully gather information. However, information quickly becomes obsolete. Flexibility could encourage openness to new information. Setting goals focuses efforts, and yet flexibility could adapt goals for greater success and satisfaction. Likewise, objectivity creates the realism to face relevant facts, but there is also the need to dream and view possibilities with optimism. Practicality can block intuition; important hunches can bring success even if logical considerations might suggest otherwise.

As Gelatt (1989) argues, it may be good counseling practice to revitalize information seeking by focusing on the internal process within the client. Clients can set goals but also need to be ready for new opportunities that may present themselves at any time. Clients can determine values and priorities and still be open to reevaluation. Surprise discoveries can enliven a systematic approach to planning and information gathering. Approaches to career and life can even be playful, mysterious, and open to ever-changing perspectives. Although clients may fear that changing attitudes, interests, and values will lead to unknown consequences, rigid avoidance to change can hinder success. Gelatt (1991) challenges counselors and clients to use both sides of the brain, the left half, using logic and analysis, and the right half, using creativity and intuition. A holistic approach to decision making can not only prepare for the future but also invent one.

Facilitating decision making that provides a planful attitude and an openness to change requires a sophisticated approach on the part of career counselors. Heppner (1989) agrees with Gelatt (1989) in saying counselors need to use more complex models for decision making and change. Heppner states that clients should apply their thoughts, feelings, and behavior to career information as they also struggle with current concerns in other areas of life. Counselors can help in processing the wide array of information, experiences, and meaning making. Processing in counseling requires sifting through the client's reactions as information is applied to personal priorities and experiences. Clients are encouraged to keep their desires and values in awareness but also to develop new interests and be aware that adjustments in personality naturally occur over time. As Gelatt (1989) says, counselors need to continue to help clients make up their minds as in traditional decision making, but they should also assist clients in keeping their minds open.

As clients begin to set personal priorities to integrate external realities with career identity, counselors need to be supportive and challenging. When clients appear to be emphasizing one facet of their personalities and neglecting a holistic view that includes other factors, counselors need to bring the overlooked components back into the picture. When clients present a logical thinking pattern for making a rational choice, counselors can introduce a metaphor or a creative exercise to introduce an intuitive perspective. When clients seem to intuitively describe a vague picture of a career choice, counselors can help the client delineate the abstract into a more realistic possibility, rather than dismissing the ideas as completely irrelevant.

Clinical judgment is critical for determining when to introduce an intervention outside the context of what the client is saying in the moment. Sometimes, clients offer nonverbal or implied clues when there is openness to a new idea or approach. Other times, the counselor decides the client would benefit by a gentle push to look at a new perspective outside the box. In general, the counselor is prepared to interject something new into the interaction process and is in tune with the overall balance of the logical and the intuitive of the client's approach.

Another consideration for clinical determination is the client's maturity and ego strength. Does the client have the capacity to participate in an approach that may be different than the typical decision-making style she usually uses? When an intervention creates an emotional reaction for the client, the counselor needs to allow the client the space to experience the feelings and the time to discuss what the emotional reaction means to her. Decision making that encourages reactions on a deep emotional level brings career counseling clearly into the realm of other personal counseling. The Career Diamond may open and close several times for each decision made in the here-and-now as well as opening and closing each time a new decision is made now and in the future (Figure 8.1).

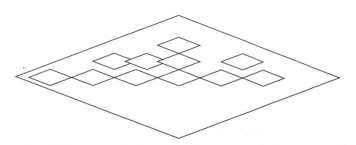

Figure 8.1 The smaller diamonds represent different career development phases within the context of a large diamond representing a lifetime career. Across a life-span, many career diamond experiences take place. The whole of a lifetime can be envisioned as a process of exploring and deciding. Yet within the overall lifetime experience, many smaller expanding and contracting experiences have taken place.

CASE STUDY 8.1   Real Women Aren't Bosses

A young woman, Sally, was an ongoing client seeing the school counselor several times a year from the tenth grade through her senior year. She was a good student, though she described herself as "not brilliant; I just work hard and like to study." Active in extracurricular clubs, she was often elected to leadership roles and was president of several groups her senior year. Her organizational skills and time management were quite good. With the counselor, she discussed her interests, saying she wanted to work with people and liked social studies, math, and biology. She investigated nursing, teaching, and accounting. Her father was an accountant, and her mother was a homemaker active in community volunteer work. Sally decided accounting would allow her to combine homemaking and a career because she could have an office in her home. The counselor noted Sally's strengths and complimented her on the exploration she had accomplished. The counselor also described the career development process as ongoing and suggested Sally could continue to explore in college.

How Would You Conceptualize This Case?

1. Why do you think the counselor encouraged Sally to continue to explore careers in college?
2. What developmental changes might the counselor have expected for Sally as she attended college? Would Sally have faced changes specific to her gender?
3. Sally was a successful high school student who would have been expected to have a successful college experience. What role do counselors serve for students who don't have serious personal, social, or academic problems?

What Actually Happened?

After her freshman year, Sally came back to see the school counselor. She had done well academically, but she expressed dissatisfaction with her major. Accounting was boring to her. She had also taken college biology and found it interesting but in examining the required courses for a major in biology, she didn't think she would like that either. Discouraged and somewhat depressed, Sally

CLIENT CHANGE

The client's experience of career counseling is one of growing career maturity. The client learns to let go of a limited sense of career development, to personalize the process as a complicated journey using individual characteristics and priorities as criteria, and to investigate and come to terms with the external demands of reality. Moving through this terrain of the personal and external also teaches the client to manage feelings of doubt and to tolerate ambiguity while the process is occurring. Tolerating ambiguity is a key skill that is used over the course of the life-span.

The counselor, who is seen at first as an expert who can provide an answer to the difficult enigma of finding a place in a complicated world of

felt all her exploration had been fruitless because she felt she was now back to square one. The counselor normalized changing interests and encouraged Sally to trust her reactions, saying Sally's efforts were worthwhile.

As Sally described college, the counselor noticed there was no mention of clubs or other nonacademic activities. Sally said she had been to some club meetings, but she was not comfortable participating as she had in high school. As Sally's social life and descriptions of her impressions of college continued, the counselor reflected that Sally sounded much less active than in high school. The counselor wondered aloud what made it so Sally didn't speak up as much or why she sounded so much in the background when she had been so different in high school. Finally, Sally said she knew she could be the leader in college that she had been in high school. Yet she was certain that the young men at college didn't like girls who were too forceful.

Later, Sally mentioned she had found one major in the college offerings that she found interesting, but it would not work for her. The major was business management. Her reasoning against majoring in management paralleled her fear of becoming a forceful woman who would be socially rejected by men. Sally blurted out, "I just couldn't be a boss. I couldn't fire anyone or tell them what they did wrong." The counselor reflected that it was as difficult for Sally to imagine herself a leader in a tough business world as it was for her to know what men might find attractive about a leader.

Once Sally shared her fears, she was open to new possibilities. She read some material on team leadership and broadened her view of what bosses might do. As she and the counselor talked about Sally's leadership style, using the *MBTI*, Sally decided to try a management course. She also agreed to talk to some high school buddies, young men she trusted, and hear their opinions as to how they felt about women leaders. She agreed to let the counselor know what she found out.

work, becomes a resource person who encourages choices that only the client can make. The client is empowered by recognizing self-responsibility for career development and by developing self-efficacy in knowing how to make choices.

The client's identity is firmer and personally owned with recognition that there will be identity changes throughout life, and new decisions can be made to accommodate any personal changes. At the same time, external conditions can and likely will change, and the client can have the confidence that whatever change occurs, a similar process will work again. Clients also gain confidence in knowing that when new choices need to be made, they can trust their abilities to remain open to personal signals that indicate their priorities for making changes.

For the client to gain the special empowerment that comes from career counseling, a delicate relationship between the counselor and client is maintained. The counselor is warm and understanding, encouraging the client to feel safe to explore new and unknown territory. However, the counselor is sensitive to the client's need to limit expression of self-doubt and fear. The counselor looks for opportunities to enhance the client's self-esteem and encourages the client to approach activities that build the his self-efficacy. The counselor can easily slip into the role of educator who determines the client's readiness for identity exploration and who points to the next step for the client to explore. The client and counselor are aligned for the common goal of enhancing the client's awareness of career identity. The counselor creates an atmosphere in which the client is encouraged and accepted at any level of development and it is appropriate to tolerate the uneasiness of not being ready to move ahead to other levels until the client is ready.

The client learns to be more open and honest. Often, in later counseling sessions, career counseling becomes very personal as clients admit self-doubts and describe the psychological growth that has occurred over the course of the counseling experience. The counselor encourages the client to take credit for personal gains and to feel grounded in a sense of self-knowing with the realization that looking to other experts cannot provide the confidence that comes from self-examination. The counselor's validation of the client's movement is no longer needed when the client has learned to trust self-validation.

SUMMARY

Career counseling requires the very same skills as counseling for other psychosocial issues. Career counselors must be able to identify and bring into the open emotions and self-constructs that are motivating or blocking psychological movement toward creating or reinventing a career identity. At the same time, external environmental factors must be taken into account to establish a place in the world of work. Skilled counselors help clients integrate their personal priorities with external information. The result is a temporary decision that furthers the client's career identity and sets the stage for future success. Finally, the client has learned how to make successful decisions and can apply the process to the next diamond that presents itself.

STUDY OUTLINE: KEY TERMS AND CONCEPTS

    I. Classic Career Counseling Interaction
        A. Clients may not expect to discuss emotions.
        B. Clients may expect quick interaction with an expert.

    C. Counselor goal: Create expansive exploring before contractive deciding

    D. Process as in exploring/deciding phases of Career Diamond

II. Exploring Phase

    A. Self-exploration

        1. Personal characteristics are expressed through career(s).

        2. Counselor facilitates structure to promote exploration; client provides content.

            a. **Structure**: Counselor interventions such as questions, information, exercises, reflections of cognitions/affect/behavior, general observations, and test interpretation

            b. **Content**: Client provides a personal sense of direction, the purpose of the journey, the expectations for the destination. The client describes thoughts, feelings, and experiences of a life's journey or the story of a life lived, being lived, and to be lived. The client's story; the client's interpretations of life's experiences; the client's self-description.

        3. Need to expand self-understanding, "Who am I?" "What is the meaning of life?" "How will my career contribute to the world?"

    B. Exploration: Counseling movement

        1. Career counseling is brief; typically 5–10 sessions.

        2. Client sense of urgency; counselor slows process

        3. Separate internal versus external pressure

        4. Career information used for self-exploration

    C. Identity exploration

        1. Themes for client's self-exploration

        2. Family roles, themes

        3. Encouraging client narratives

        4. Meaning structure

    D. Life themes

        1. Birth order and family atmosphere impact career aspirations

        2. Early recollections help identify themes in client's life.

    E. Career identity

        1. Use vocabulary of assessment devices to indicate themes

        2. Client achievements illustrate motivated skills.

        3. Use of *DOT*: people, ideas, things

    F. Use of questions

        1. Look for themes across areas discussed.

        2. Have client provide a person review.

        3. Have client provide a life-lived review.

    4. Have client discuss hopes for future.
    5. Avoid yes–no and factual questions.
    6. Ask about lessons from family/friends' careers.
    7. Integrate family, leisure, and career into a picture of the future.
  G. Exploring information
    1. Quantity of information can be overwhelming
    2. Counselor supports information search and helps client to filter out unhelpful information.
    3. Client is responsible for actual search, but counselor can aid in developing search skills.
    4. May need to refer client to actual expert in a field. Counselor may only know basic information.
    5. Important question: how does information relate to the client's specific personality or situation?
    6. There may be ways to enter a field even if the market is tight (good reason to ask expert within the field).
  H. Creating a vision
    1. Holistic view of career identity and one's place in the world
    2. Motivates the decision-making phase; encourages overcoming obstacles

III. Decision-Making Phase
  A. Integrating personal priorities with realistic information
    1. There comes a time when gathering more information becomes counterproductive.
    2. Use personal criteria to eliminate some information.
    3. Choices are temporary and can be undone.
    4. Client's lack of personal fit to some choices should eliminate those choices.
  B. Decision-making theory
    1. Historically a logical process that is linear in implementation.
    2. Information must be interpreted and therefore goes from being objective to subjective.
    3. The "right answer" is subjective and can only be "right" if it meets the client's personal criteria.
    4. Creativity, intuition, and insight need to be added to decision-making theory.
  C. Logical and intuitive decision making
    1. Logic provides one basis for determining outcome.
    2. Intuition is to be respected as another source of judging potential decisions.
    3. Adjust the amount of logic and intuition to match the needs of the current situation.

4. Learn how to make decisions while remaining open to new information.

5. Emotions, thoughts, and behaviors hold equal importance.

IV. Client Change

   A. Client begins to learn to tolerate doubt and ambiguity.

   B. Client practices making choices and experiences effective decision making (builds self-efficacy).

   C. Client understands and expects to have adjustments in personality over time.

EXERCISES

1. In dyads, role-play the interaction between a counselor and a client who asks, "What is career counseling?" The counselor practices describing the career counseling process. Try using the Career Diamond in the explanation. Ask the client to draw an X on the top and bottom of the diamond to indicate self-exploration and occupational awareness.

2. In dyads, role-play the interaction between the counselor and the client in the Case Study 8.1. Be able to describe the counselor's interventions and the counseling process purpose for the interventions.

3. Discuss how the case study demonstrates the client's developmental movement according to the Career Diamond.

REFERENCES

Adler, A. (1937). Position in family constellation influences life style. *International Journal of Individual Psychology, 3*, 211–227.

Ansbacher, H. L., & Ansbacher, R. R. (1956). *The individual psychology of Alfred Adler.* New York: Harper & Row.

Bankart, C. P. (1997). *Talking cures: A history of western and eastern psychotherapies.* Belmont, CA: Brooks/Cole.

Bolles, N. B. (1995). *What color is your parachute?* Berkeley, CA: Ten Speed Press.

Briggs, K. C., & Briggs-Myers, I. (1998). *Myers-Briggs Type Indicator* (Form M). Palo Alto, CA: Consulting Psychologists Press.

Carlson, J., & Slavik, S. (1997) *Techniques of Adlerian therapy.* New York: Brunner Routledge.

Cochran, L. T. (1997). *The sense of vocation: A study of career and life development.* Albany: State Univ. of New York Press.

Figler, H. (1999). *The complete job search handbook.* New York: Holt, Rinehart &Winston.

Gelatt, H. B. (1962). Decision-making: A conceptual frame of reference for counseling. *Journal of Counseling, 9*(3), 240–245.

Gelatt, H. B. (1989). Positive uncertainty: A new decision-making framework for counseling. *Journal of Counseling Psychology, 36*(2), 252–256.

Gelatt, H. B. (1991). *Creative decision making: Using positive uncertainty.* Lanham, MD: National Book Network.

Gysbers, N. C., & Moore, E. J. (1987). *Career counseling: Skills and techniques for practitioners.* Englewood Cliffs, NJ: Prentice-Hall.

Heppner, P. P. (1989). Identifying the complexities within clients' thinking and decision making. *Journal of Counseling Psychology, 36*(2), 257–259.

Howard, G. S. (1989). *A tale of two stories: Excursions into a narrative approach to psychology.* Notre Dame, IN: Academic Publications.

Myers-Briggs Type Indicator. (1995) Palo Alto, CA: Davies Black.

Nikelly, A. G., & Verger, D. (1971). Early recollections. In A. Adler & R. Dreikurs (Eds.), Application of Adlerian theory: Techniques for behavior change (pp. 55–60). Springfield, IL: Charles C. Thomas.

Patterson, C. H., & Watkins, C. E., Jr. (1996). *Theories of psychotherapy* (5th ed.). New York: Harper Collins.

U.S. Department of Labor Employment and Training Administration (1991). *Dictionary of occupational titles,* Vol. I (4th ed.). Lincolnway, IL: VGM Career Horizons, NTC Publishing Group.

CHAPTER 9

Career Counseling Techniques

For a while, it seemed that The Technique had been found. But with the passage of time, the excitement wore off. Patients and therapists became less enthusiastic, and ultimately bored. Each technique was useful as long as it produced excitement and curiosity in the therapist. Like the Wizard of Oz's medal, which gave courage only to the courageous, technique is only a vehicle for the therapist's creative exploration.

Minuchin & Fishman, 1981, pp. 286–287

Although beginning students consider counseling techniques to be important to learn, experienced counselors view specific methods as secondary to the interaction process between client and counselor. It cannot be stressed enough that the primary career counseling techniques are communication interventions such as reflecting, open-ended questioning, tracking, redirecting, reframing, encouraging, etc. The effectiveness of the techniques described in this chapter is determined by the client's receptivity and the contextual timing within the counseling relationship.

The Career Diamond can be used to determine when particular techniques are appropriate. Interventions that encourage clients to open up to exploring new possibilities are used early in the counseling process, in the first half of the diamond. Interventions that engage the client in setting personal priorities are used during the second half of the counseling process when counseling focuses on narrowing the choices (in the second half as the diamond closes).

TECHNIQUES FOR EXPANDING SELF-AWARENESS

Career Genogram

Several authors have presented the family genogram in a form adapted for career counseling (Brooks & Brown, 1991; Gysbers & Moore, 1987; Issacson & Brown, 1997; Okiishi, 1987). The purpose of the genogram is to explore

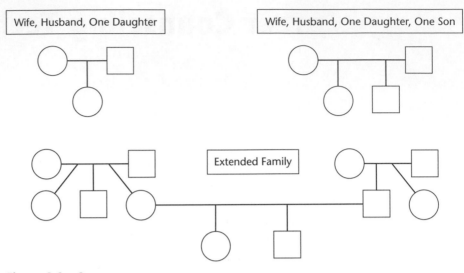

Figure 9.1   Genogram

family influences on the client's career identity. Client expectations, motivations, sex-role stereotypes, values, and views of the working world can become apparent as the rich story of the client's background is revealed.

Clients are asked to name members of their families and to tell each relative's occupation. A diagram using symbols taken from family therapy is used to gain a picture of the relationships. Figure 9.1 shows an example of a family layout.

Typically, the client starts by naming the father (shown by a square) and the mother (shown by a circle). A vertical line drawn between mother and father shows them to be a couple. Horizontal lines drawn down from the original line connect to the siblings in birth order. Circles are used for girls and squares are used for boys. After the circles and squares are named, numbers that indicate ages are written inside. Under the names, occupations are indicated. After the family of origin is finished, lines are drawn above mother and father respectively to connect them to their parents and in a line of their siblings. Stretching out the lines to include aunts and uncles, their spouses, and their children can take up quite a bit of space, so multiple pages or a blackboard works best.

As the client tells about the family members and their occupations, the counselor encourages some storytelling and reflects the values, feelings, and meanings conveyed. Or, the counselor asks open-ended questions to gain more complete descriptions for adjectives, meanings, values, and expectations. Roles, secrets, traditions, memories, myths, and misperceptions can be examined. Career patterns and overt or covert messages regarding education and success criteria are worth discussing as well as encouraging or discouraging experiences.

The disadvantages of career genograms include the lengthy amount of time required and the fact that some clients may not know their extended family well or what occupations relatives have. Start with the family of origin, but end the exercise if it does not bring forth much worthwhile information. Occasionally, clients can give vague descriptions of work roles for family members, and discussing the client's lack of exposure to the world of work may be helpful.

Life Reviews

Several techniques suggested by Savakis (1997) are used to elicit personal themes implanted through childhood early recollections (ER). Savakis begins by asking clients to tell three childhood memories. He believes such memories are blueprints for the individual's future strivings and for preoccupations that sensitize individuals to particular struggles that motivate the individuals to consummate particular projects. People pursue their strivings to gain a sense of completeness, and the movement toward wholeness provides direction to one's life. In keeping with Adlerian theory, Savakis sees the individual's psychological undertaking as part of a social whole and the means for the people to belong to and advance the social order.

Once early recollections are described, Savakis (1997) asks clients to write a headline distilling the essence of the experience of the memory. Headlines are described as requiring a verb, a behavioral word that summarizes the action of the memory. By emphasizing action, Savakis encourages the client to describe the psychological movement of the memory. Several headlines suggest a life direction. The goal is to take the thematic life preoccupation and determine how such a natural endeavor could become an occupational activity contributing to society. To move from the personal theme to a social theme, Savakis then asks the client to name and describe three role models she admires. Role models are seen as examples of others that have solved a life dilemma in a commendable way.

The counselor interprets the role model description in several ways. First, the traits attributed are seen as those characteristics the client believes will be needed to solve her personal preoccupation. Second, the role models will have descriptors in common, and these descriptors are the goal that the client is seeking. Finally, the counselor notes those traits the client ignores in the description because these are not seen as important or as much of a priority. Values and embedded goals come through in the analysis of the admired figures.

To connect the themes from ERs and the role models, the counselor asks the client to identify the career interests that might be suggested by the session's activities. According to Savakis (1997), occupational interests connect the individual's private needs to the external contributions needed by society. In other words, career interests express the means for a person to contribute to the social benefit for all. As the person develops himself in a movement toward self-actualization, society also benefits through the contributions made by the individual.

Savakis (1997) suggests that interest themes can be determined by writing the ERs and client needs on one side of a paper and role model descriptors and goals on the other side. In the middle of the paper, client and counselor brainstorm what career interests, themes, or goals are indicated.

Career Imaginings

The simplest career fantasy encouraging client self-exploration is the *Occupational Daydreams* included in the original *Self Directed Search (SDS)*. By determining the RIASEC categories associated with daydreams, clients are led to occupational interest categories. It is recommended that daydreams be thoroughly discussed before using Holland codes. Other important themes may be garnered before the occupational structure becomes the overlay.

On the one hand, some clients act surprised when asked about their daydreams, as if career counselors should require much more serious approaches. On the other hand, some clients are eager to share their private musings and seem relieved when given permission to do so. Lest professionals consider daydreams irrelevant, one study suggests daydreams are as rich a source of client material as guided fantasies (Skovholt, Morgan, & Negron-Cunningham, 1989).

Career fantasy exercises are commonly included in workbooks and counseling texts. Descriptions of **guided imagery** techniques can be as simple as directly asking the client to imagine a future career (as shown in Chapter 8) or as elaborate as the mental imagery exercises described in this section. Part of the rationale for creating imaginary pictures is to engage the intuitive left-brain hemisphere and to eliminate the critical thinking that often discounts possibilities before they are fully examined. Some clients need encouragement to dream a little and to trust embedded leanings that point to worthwhile prospects.

Typical guided fantasies use relaxation techniques to ease the client into a meditative state. Instructions include sitting comfortably, breathing deeply, and closing eyes until breathing naturally slows and the client is relaxed. Relaxation is continued with statements such as, "Just relax for a few minutes." Then the client is asked to imagine a day in the future, usually speci-

---

Box 9.1   Example: Future Career Fantasy

Imagine it is morning and you are waking up. Where are you? What is your living space like? Who is there with you or are you alone?

You begin to prepare for your day. You get up, shower, and dress. As you look at yourself in the mirror to check your appearance, what will you be wearing?

After breakfast you prepare to go to work. If you are leaving your living space, obtain an outside wrap to suit the weather. What is the weather like? What form of transportation will you use to get to work? Imagine yourself going to work.

You arrive at work. Where are you? What are your surroundings like? Look around and picture your workplace. What do you see?

Who is at your workplace with you or do you work alone? Greet coworkers. Imagine a conversation you may have, and then let the talking gradually finish.

Who are the people you work with? How do you feel around them? Will other people, not coworkers, be there? Who are they, and what do they look like? How do you react to these people?

Imagine the tasks you plan to do today. Organize your schedule in your mind.

What will you do first? What will you do second? What tools will you need for your work? Picture the objects you will use. Imagine yourself getting into the work you will do.

It is time for lunch. Imagine getting ready to eat. Where do you eat? Who do you eat with? Visualize eating comfortably and enjoying your lunchtime. Then refocus on returning to work and the afternoon tasks you will complete.

On returning to work, you note that the afternoon will be different than the morning. Imagine other activities you will do at work. Picture yourself doing the work for the afternoon.

It is time to finish your work. As you leave the workplace, think about what you will be doing this evening. You will be having a meal. What else might you be doing?

It is soon bedtime. Think about your day. Experience your feelings as you reflect on what the day was like. You will be going to work tomorrow. What is your reaction to the next day?

Our fantasy trip is ending. Slowly open your eyes and notice you have returned to the present day. Let's begin to share what your fantasy was like.

---

fied as five or six years (far enough away that current life-style conditions could be different). The counselor continues to guide the client to picture what the day will look like.

Discussing reactions to the fantasy are as important as the imaginary experience. Clients are encouraged to describe what the experience was like and the insights they have gained about their future careers. Reflecting client content and affect is an important validation. Counselor invitations for clients to expand their fantasy description also promote awareness.

Some scripts for future day fantasies offer more examples in each segment. For example, in the transportation section, a script could read, "Are you in a car? Are you on a train? What other mode of transport might you use?" The author prefers to keep the fantasy description general, allowing clients to fill in the specifics. Adult clients have given feedback that several suggestions for the same scene can interrupt their private imaginings. However, counselors might evaluate the developmental level and the cognitive style of the clients to determine the number of choices to offer and the amount of detail most appropriate.

Skovholt et al. (1989), in describing career fantasies, suggest other possible scripts:

> *An award ceremony:* A scene where the client receives recognition for work well done.
>
> *The opposite sex:* Where clients imagine growing up as the opposite sex and/or having jobs usually held by the opposite sex.
>
> *Another race:* Where participants imagine job experiences and prospects if they were another race or ethnicity.
>
> *Career change* or *retirement:* Fantasy exercises create future visions for appropriate clients.

Counselors can create scripts uniquely appealing to any client or any group depending on the vision desired. With the counselor leading the fantasy, the client is freed up to allow scenes to present themselves without self-censorship or interruption. Fantasies appeal to the holistic intuitive possibilities, creating pictures in the mind's eye and managing multiple stimuli. The client is given permission to be creative and innovative and to use intuition to increase the chances that an integrative view may come to fruition. Emotional, value-laden, symbolic, and spiritual insights can occur with any exercise that is designed to use the right brain. So, clients could draw or use music to gain access to deep-seated signals that have never been fully articulated. Dail (1983) has clients draw several pictures for: "What I am? What I would like to be? What hinders me? What will overcome the obstacles?" She has the client free associate after each drawing. Such an exercise encourages the client to expand career identity facilitating a process where clients seek new realms beyond concrete and practical solutions.

Metaphors

Metaphors are stories that offer a point of view that may be helpful in dealing with life. Usually metaphors imply an indirect meaning that softens a lesson or reframes issues for a client. Clients can take the message and apply it to their lives even when an exact correlation does not exist. Counselors can learn the story analogies and use them spontaneously in session. The lesson of the metaphor need not be explained concretely. In fact, allowing the client to draw the meaning is probably more effective for the client's learning. Often, the story is never fully discussed but a telling change in attitude or approach occurs for the client. Sometimes the counselor can facilitate a process in which clients create their own meaningful stories.

Common experiences from everyday life can be the basis for such stories. For example, a tale of discovery for a child who accidentally mixes white paint with red paint and creates pink paint can relay the joy of the serendipitous discovery. Any story of first-time experiences—learning to tie shoestrings, the first day of school, or meeting in-laws for the first time—can evoke the emotions of facing new experiences and remind clients that original struggles do not last.

Mental images for career movement in one's life are common. Career itself originally meant road or street (Bloch & Richmond, 1997) and has been adapted to suggest path or passage. Accordingly, metaphors can easily be made up to describe a person's journey through life. A compass can be used as a symbol for the values that guide a person's career choices. A map can be the plan showing the way to a career destination. A crystal ball or a time tunnel can be added to the future day fantasies to suggest imagining another time or place.

A garden requiring care and where plants are subject to unpredictable elements is a very adaptable metaphor. Transplanting so plants can flourish provides a parallel for career change and moving to new places. Of course, sports provide many metaphors regarding team building, responsibility to others, and dealing with winning and losing. An athlete who second-guesses herself and thereby undermines her performance can suggest the impact of such a practice on career performance. One career counseling text describes a baseball player who broke his leg and recovered but forever after limped when he was called out sliding into first base. The subtle message not only implies the power of a mindset to undermine performance but also a refusal to accept the accident (Gysbers, Heppner, & Johnson, 1998). Careerists, as well as athletes, may benefit from a metaphor implying the need to take responsibility for performance and to keep trying, even in the face of painful previous experiences.

Likewise, spiritual traditions use story metaphors to make a point or deliver a message. The story of Ruth in the Bible can be described as an example of the willingness to leave an established life to seek a new one when she left home to accompany her mother-in-law Naomi (Rayburn, 1997). Or, Lot's wife who turned to look back against instructions to the contrary and turned into a pillar of salt is an example of staying stuck in the past rather than looking forward to the future. Lao Tsu, a Buddhist poet-philosopher, is quoted as saying, "Shape the clay into a vessel. It is the space within that makes it useful" (Richmond, 1997). Such is a metaphor for creating a life and paying attention to the context.

Children's stories and fairy tales are a rich source of metaphors. The three little pigs can serve as examples of building a solid future or not. Little Red Riding Hood or Sleeping Beauty can be seen as being overly trusting or waiting for another person to awaken identity before fully participating in life.

Castle Metaphor

One very adaptable metaphor uses the image of a castle to represent aspects of a person or of problems (Martin, 1987). For career purposes, the castle can be the home of the knight on his quest pursuing personal honor and serving the people of the kingdom. Or the castle can be the home of the king or queen determining the best means to govern the kingdom and to serve as models of behavior and ethics. The main character of the metaphor has built the castle to represent himself. A coat of arms representing the hero's true identity is displayed on the front wall of the castle. However, aspects of the primary character or client are symbolically visible throughout the architecture of the castle.

The moat around a castle can be described as beautiful with water lilies or as dangerous with sharks. As such, moats may be representative of the person's appearance as inviting or as signaling a need for a zone for personal space. The outer wall of a castle is a protection and can be built with only spaces for guns and cannons or with large windows letting in the sunshine. Likewise, the person's social mask can hide and protect or be open to the warmth and beauty of the externals potentially influencing his life.

The drawbridge can be opened or closed suggesting a person has control over those who are allowed into or out of her life. A castle is manned with guards representing how well guarded a person is. The inner courtyard of the castle can be the private, personal space where others are or are not allowed. The castle may have a library for storing important documents or learning, just as a person has important memories and mementos or trusted books. The dungeon can represent painful memories that torture a person. Secret passages may be avenues of forgotten experiences. The castle chapel can represent a person's spiritual life. The well can suggest inner resources to assist a person in times of crisis.

The people in the castle can suggest aspects of personality. The jester represents a sense of humor. The court magician can be seen as magical thinking creating illusions. Witches casting spells can be irrational thoughts or self-defeating behavior. The royal cook or attorney can be called upon

Box 9.2   One More Metaphor

The following is a story that suggests the dependence on another's wisdom does not work very well. The story was presented by Schulman and Mozak (1967) as an Adlerian technique.

The Search for the Lama

A man was unhappy because he was searching for the meaning of life and could not find it. He went from one wise man to another but was never satisfied. He finally heard about a lama who lived in the moun-tains of Tibet and he undertook an expedi-tion. For many months he traveled over mountains, across rivers, and finally he found the lama and obtained an audience. He asked the wise man, "Please, tell me, what is the meaning of life?"

The lama answered, "Life is a fountain."

The man was puzzled and said, "Life is a fountain?"

The lama shrugged his shoulders and said, "So, life isn't a fountain."

---

to offer nourishment or to present the case for a person's misunderstood behavior. The local town near the castle can be a support system.

The wise advisor to the king or queen in the castle can be the per-sonal wisdom that can be trusted. White knights and black knights can offer symbols for the strengths and weaknesses each person has. Battles between good and evil can show that a person's values can win in life.

The counselor can choose to adapt or elaborate the castle metaphor ac-cording to the needs of the client. It is important to note that metaphors are effective only with people who can imagine the picture and access the im-plied meanings. The counselor can tell the metaphor and interpret it (in this case, the counselor has analyzed the client and builds a castle that would be meaningful to the client), or the counselor can outline the castle metaphor and let the client build the metaphor as well as explain the symbolism.

The first author used the castle metaphor with a client who had spent most of her life creating a lovely home, entertaining guests for her husband's clients, and raising several accomplished children. As the queen of the beau-tiful castle, the client demonstrated many skills that benefited her family and the village outside the castle. The client enjoyed hearing herself described as a queen, and she elaborated the script by telling of the interior design for the ballroom, the gourmet dining, the lesson provided for the royal children, and the conferences between the king and queen to determine important decisions for the kingdom. Her homework between sessions was to continue the narrative describing the castle and the queen's leadership. The only requirement for the continued story was to make sure the queen was accurately described as having accomplished a great deal. In the next session, the client readily described the queen's many achievements, noting only that the queen could do more if she used her strengths outside the castle as well as inside. The stage was set to explore how the client's creativity, social and organizational skills, and intelligence had been useful in taking care of her family and could also be used as valuable contributions for endeavors outside the home. The playful use of imagination translated into a career exercise in transferable skills (see skills section below).

The advantage of telling such stories is that the parallel meaning applicable to the client's life does not have to be made explicit. A client could be amused with the old man in the above story (Box 9.2) and may not have to admit that he was looking to the counselor as the expert who would solve all career problems. In this way, the lesson is brought into the counseling session without confronting the client or by engaging the client's self-critical judgment. The imagination and possibly the affective area can be the vehicle for the client's absorption of the message.

IDENTIFYING SKILLS

Skill identification methods have helped clients determine appropriate career venues for the past several decades. Bolles, in *What Color Is Your Parachute* (1995), popularized one approach. First, he recommends writing an autobiography or a number of notable memories describing satisfying achievements. Such achievements represent activities in which an individual felt she was doing her best and was pleased with the efforts and results. The accomplishment could be any activity in any situation (e.g., school, home, on vacation, hobby, volunteer activity). The major criteria are the sense of satisfaction and meeting her own standards. No recognition by others is necessary.

After the achievements are identified, the person describes, in detail, exactly what she did to accomplish the task. Each and every step that was required to complete the accomplishment is explicated. The actions or behaviors required to complete the project are emphasized. What goals were reached, what obstacles were overcome, and how the success of the mission was measured can be included to fully describe the achievement.

Third, from the full accounting, the **motivated skills** are identified. Some skills are seen as traits (extroversion) and others as abilities (social skills) that point to other tasks and other jobs where similar traits/abilities might be used. As such, skills are **functional** when used in a specific occupation and **transferable** between occupations where the context or the field where the skills are applied may be different. Liberal arts majors use such a process to demonstrate proficiencies not obviously shown on a transcript of content courses taken (Figler, 1979). Career-searchers of any age can build self-efficacy by recognizing traits/abilities already demonstrated. A client can also identify skills from a list provided by the counselor and then describe the situations where these skills have been used and the resulting achievements—reversing the order from the previous paragraph.

What is most useful about the skill identification method is that specific occupations are not the focus. Skills are seen as the basic elements that motivate the worker and what he has to sell to an employer or to customers. Given the changing economy, such a method is most likely to meet the demands of the workplace in the future. Indeed, for job-changers, Bolles (1995) states that demonstrating the usefulness of transferable skills to solve a company's problems is the most successful way to create a position. Career counselors might consider teaching skills identification methods to students and clients as part of the career development process rather than overemphasizing occupational titles.

The client handout in Box 9.3 lists some skills and offers space for identifying experiences where skills are demonstrated.

Values

In addition to reflecting values embedded in the context of what clients say or values listed on a checklist or a measurement instrument, discussions can be opened to reveal important priorities. Clients can be asked what they did during the last week that reflected the kind of person they are. Inviting clients to describe an experience where they had to consider moral or ethical choices along with a follow-up question asking how such values could be expressed at work. Values can be defined as personal constructs that involve both thoughtful and affective components.

So, values could be expressed as actions a person would feel good about and be described as acting in accordance with important ideals that could be explained to others. Or, seen another way, values might be expressed when someone does something she doesn't feel good about. Asking how the client's values differ from other people or family members is sometimes fruitful. Counselors might ask what values the client would want to teach a sibling or a child. Some clients can describe one personal value that conflicts with another, creating the need to weigh or rank choices.

Values card sorts, described in Box 9.5, are a semistructured method to flesh out life-style or career-related priorities. Time spent examining values puts career counseling into the appropriate realm of considering how a life reflects personal ideals and how a client can use choice as a source of self-respect.

Box 9.3   Skills Clusters

Communication
Persuasion (selling products or ideas)
Public speaking
Dramatic ability
Oral clarity
Effective writing skills
Promotion writing
Technical writing
Conceptual writing
Writing instructions
Letter writing
Speech writing/presentations
General conversational skills
Translating
Foreign language usage
Listening skills
Creativity
Inventing new ideas (conceptual)
Presenting new ideas (concrete, manual)
Creating works of art (music, visual, written)
Applying creative ideas—drawing charts, performing, editing

People Contact
Teaching
Helping others
Interviewing
Negotiating
Coaching for performance
Supervising
Managing
Training
Establishing rapport
Counseling
Confronting
Entertaining
Committee participation, leadership
Meeting the public
Fund-raising
Treating ailments
Following directions
Leading others

Research
Scientific investigation
Library research
Internet research
Laboratory research
Detective work
Gathering information systematically
Synthesizing information
Analyzing information according to criteria

Managerial
Coordinating administrative tasks/events
Decision making
Attending to details
Financial transactions/budgeting
Scheduling
Time management
Working under time pressures
Coping with competitive pressures
Formulating policies and procedures
Problem identification/problem solving
Retaining memory of facts, figures, people
Orderly record keeping
Establishing priorities
Planning programs
Arranging social events
Organizing committees
Delegating

Manual/Physical
Building, constructing
Manual dexterity
Physical stamina
Outdoor work skills
Eye/hand coordination

Technical/Computational
Data processing
Accurate, efficient use of scientific equipment
Spatial perception
Machinery operations
Comprehending technical manuals
Computing quantitative data
Synthesizing data
Data interpretation and analysis
Solving quantitative problems

Box 9.4   Identify Your Skills

Try identifying your own skills in the Table 9.1. Choose three or four experiences that you enjoyed and that you regard as achievements, and write each in a separate box in the left column (see example). Consider work, academic, leisure, extracurricular, volunteer, and unstructured experiences. Then identify what tasks you performed, that is, what you did and what your responsibilities were for the experience and write them into the second column. Then, using available listings of skills, compile a list of skills developed and demonstrated in the third column.

Table 9.1   Identifying Skills

Experiences	Tasks Performed	Skills Developed/Demonstrated
Example 1. Summer Camp Counselor	Supervised cabin of 10 boys, ages 11–14	Formed supportive relationships Enforced discipline Teaching Leadership
1.		
2.		
3.		
4.		

Occupational Card Sorts

Another card sort method involves creating categories for occupations. Typically three rows are designated as Like, Dislike, and Indifferent. Then, the client places cards each labeled with an occupational title in one of the rows. The client explains why a particular occupation was put in the Like row or the Dislike row. The counselor encourages the client's explanations and may take notes. Writing down client statements and noting patterns of interests and preferences can provide a record that can be used in the here-and-now or in future sessions.

Box 9.5   Values Card Sort

Use the following list to create a values card sort. (Feel free to change the definitions to match your clientele or region of the world.)

A comfortable life (enough money to do most things, minimizing really difficult tasks)

Ambitious (motivated, earning promotions, merit raises, awards, becoming well known)

An exciting life (being on the cutting edge of culture—daring, taking the unknown road, and not knowing what will happen)

Assertiveness (standing up for one's self, getting one's needs met)

Athletic (exercise, being physically active, physical competition)

Belonging (being a part of a group)

Competent (being an expert, effective, and efficient)

Happiness (lighthearted, joyful)

Clean (neat, tidy)

Community involvement (volunteering, giving back to the community)

Deep friendship (share most everything, a lot of trust, emotional intimacy)

Environmentally minded (nonpolluting, healthy air and water)

Equality (equal opportunity for all)

Flexibility (have options or different ways of doing things. No set way. Comfortable in new situations)

Forgiving (not holding negative emotions or thoughts against others)

Healthy habits (absence of illness, eating well, and exercising)

Honesty (being sincere and truthful)

Humor (seeing the light side of things, being able to laugh)

Imaginative (creative, being novel)

Independence (freedom to make choices on one's own, not responsible to a group)

Inner harmony (being true to one's self/one's beliefs, no inner conflicts)

Intellectual pursuits (abstract thinking, reflective, induction, deduction)

Justice (fairness, due process)

Logic (consistent, rational, emotions under control)

Loyal (committed to other people and vice versa, protective, trustworthy)

Loving (affectionate, tender)

Mature love (spiritual intimacy, deep trust)

Multicultural awareness (aware of and values other cultures and people)

Nurturance (giving to others without self reward)

Obedient (follow the rules, dutiful, respectful)

Open-minded (nonjudgmental, accepting, try new things)

Outdoorsy (be outside, avoid being confined, nature)

Patience (being able to wait, not rushed)

Pleasure (minimizing discomfort, enjoying almost every moment)

Polite (courteous, well-mannered)

Religious (Bible study, prayer, worship, church activities)

Responsible (dependable, reliable)

Salvation (saved, eternal life)

Safety (limiting risks to self, family, and friends

Security (Knowing what to expect)

Sucurance (Receiving love or care from others without having to give back)

(continued)

(Box 9.5 continued)

Structure (having rules or guidelines to operate by. Knowing the right way to do things)

Self-control (dependable, reliable)

Self-respect (mostly feel and think good thoughts about one's self)

Social recognition (famous [may only be locally], admired/respected by others)

Spiritual (connected to a higher power)

Wisdom (knowing via experience, not books; seeing the big picture)

World peace (free from war and terror)

Other (create your own and/or have client create at least 3 cards)

Here are some activities using the cards:

1. Choosing one's worst
   A. Pick the 10 that least describe you. Discuss why.
   B. Discuss the worst 3 (who you are not and never will be).
   C. Who is the closest person to you? What would his top 10 and top 3 be?
2. Choosing one's best
   A. Pick the 10 that most describe you. Discuss why.
   B. Discuss and rank the top 3.
   C. Which cards should be in the top 3 but are not, why?
   D. Who is the closest person to you? What would his top 10 and top 3 be?
   E. If you could pick your ideal self, what would be your top 10, top 3?
3. The neutral middle
   A. How important are these traits when making decisions, being satisfied in life, relationships, etc.
   B. Which ones do not apply at all?

As you do the values card sort activities with a client, be on the lookout for inconsistencies between the client's best and worst list. Sometimes the client has different definitions than the counselor, and there isn't an inconsistency. Other times a client's past experience or observation will come to light and a hidden value or motivator is discovered. Discuss how easy/difficult it is to limit the list to 10 and then 3. A client cried once when turning a top 10 to a top 3. She had chosen personal desires over family and friends, and it hurt to say that out loud. Yet it was important to acknowledge if making important decisions. Ask if there are specific areas where these values are more or less important. For example, a person may be flexible in work, but not in spiritual matters.

The flexibility of card sorts offers many possibilities. Categories can be tailored for specific client needs, such as occupations gaining others' approval or occupations the client respects. The major advantages of the card sort are the client's reactions and reasoning for labeling occupations is spoken, and the client's statements offer much material for discussion. Occupational stereotypes are readily apparent and misperceptions can be identified. Client motivations are verbalized, and sometimes insights come into awareness that were previously unrecognized.

The *Missouri Occupational Card Sort (MOCS),* developed at the University of Missouri by Norman Gysbers, is widely used, and there are other sets available commercially. However, in a workshop given by Gysbers and attended by the first author, he suggested that the card sets can be easily made. Index cards are labeled with one occupation, and other cards contain the word for the categories (such as Like, Dislike, Indifferent). It is also useful to put some information regarding the occupation on the opposite side of the card. Such information could be a Holland Code, description of the work activities for the occupation, education, or training requirements, etc.

Student Card Sort

Below are some cards that can be made for working with students in middle school through college. (Use the directions from the values card sort.) The goal is to understand, from the student's perspective, why they aren't doing well in school. The concepts can easily be modified for work (e.g., "problem with instructors" is turned into "problem with managers"). This card sort was designed in a college counseling center and refers to college students. Again, feel free to modify it to match your clientele.

Work so many hours that it interferes with studying
Do not understand the university's procedures (e.g., when to drop a
    class)
Poor note-taking skills
Health problems
Financial problems
Difficulty only on certain courses (list which ones)
Family problems
Emotional problems
Goof off too often
Lack motivation
Can't concentrate
Been out of school too long
High school did not prepare me for college
Adjusting to college is difficult
Problems with instructors
Often do not attend class
Not sure about educational goals
Poor study habits
Lack basic skills in some areas
Lonely
Poor advising
Problems taking tests

Don't remember what I read
Don't understand what I read
No time for studying due to family, athletics, commuting, hobbies, etc.
Poor time management
Wrong major
Other _____

(Developed by Midwestern State University, Counseling and Disabilities Service, Wichita Falls, TX. Used with permission.)

Defining Success

Helping clients define their personal criteria for success offers an inoculation against the middle age disease of "Is that all there is?" Careers cannot be self-expressive if "making it" is defined solely by external sources. Although values clarification is usually included as a part of career counseling, clients can state values such as good parenting or helping people, and still not fully envision the future they will eventually hold in high regard. Counselors need to take time to examine the basic question of how does the client define success. Simply ask the impolite question of how money fits in with the client's picture of having arrived. Confronting obvious discrepancies is appropriate when, for example, a client says family is the first priority but also expects to spend 60 plus hours a week to become a law partner.

Exploring how the client views success, as compared to peers or family members, builds a language to answer other people's inquiries and encourages the client to be self-determined. Even asking clients to describe how they view the media's picture of success brings out the client's capacity to resist subtle or not-so-subtle external pressures. Some clients may mention the pressure they feel from others, especially coworkers who question a client who makes choices outside group norms. A sensitive counselor will communicate to the client that counseling is a safe place to examine personal choices regardless of the judgments of others.

NARROWING AND PRIORITIZING

Decision Making

Although adherence to a uniform, rational decision-making model does not respect individual personality differences or styles, counselors can offer leading questions that encourage a thought process that considers many aspects of making a choice. The counselor is cautioned not to force the interaction by following a rigid structure and considering each component of rational deciding, but to regularly check out client feelings and reactions.

Another caution is to set a tentative tone so clients feel allowed to change the process and to avoid a staccato beat of asking a question, waiting for a short answer, and asking another question. Introducing questions intermittently and encouraging the client to determine counseling content is most important. The following are only suggestions of possible questions that can be asked at different points in the decision-making process.

Questions for Facilitating the Process

I. Objective, goal
   A. Definition
      1. What are you trying to figure out?
      2. Is there more than one part to what you want to decide, and what are those parts?
   B. Importance
      1. Which part is most important for you to decide first, and why is it important to you?
      2. What will it do for you to figure this out?
      3. How will it affect your life to make this decision and act on it?
   C. Significant others
      1. What have other important people in your life said about this decision?
      2. What do you think about their ideas?
      3. Of what importance is what others have said to you?
   D. Past experience
      1. How have you made similar decisions in the past?
      2. In what ways would the process you have used in the past be applicable for your current situation?
      3. In what ways would the process you have used in the past not be applicable for your current situation?
      4. What other considerations, which you may not have considered before, do you need to take into account now?
   E. Planning
      1. How can you plan a step-by-step procedure for making this decision?
      2. What is the first step for you to take?
      3. What would you do next?
II. Information
   A. First search
      1. What kind of information is important for you to find?
      2. Where can you find such information?
      3. Of what use will such information be to you?

B. Using information
   1. What information have you found that is important to you?
   2. What are you going to do with this information?

C. Second search
   1. What additional information on what you have already found might you need to view?
   2. Of what use would such information be to you now? In the future?

III. Alternatives, Obstacles, Outcomes, and Probabilities

A. Alternatives
   1. Name the alternatives available to you in view of the information you have found and in view of your own thinking.
   2. Describe a picture of yourself living out each alternative.
   3. What are the characteristics of each alternative? Which are most important to you?
   4. What important characteristics from the alternatives would you be unwilling to give up?
   5. How could you combine alternatives in a way that would give you the most of what you want?

B. Obstacles
   1. What alternatives are not available to you in view of the realities of your situation?
   2. What are any possible obstacles for obtaining each of the alternatives?
   3. What would it take to overcome each of the obstacles?
   4. What would you be willing to do to overcome a given obstacle?

C. Outcomes
   1. What are the possible outcomes inherent in each of the alternatives?
   2. What would be the effect of such outcomes for you and for other important people in your life?

D. Probabilities
   1. What is the probability (on a scale from 0–100) of the possible outcomes occurring?
   2. What does such a probability rating mean for you in carrying out a decision for and in acting on each alternative?

IV. Values

A. Rating
   1. Which of the alternatives seems most desirable to you and why?

2. Which of the alternatives seems least desirable to you and why?
3. Rate the alternatives on a priority list with the most desirable first and the least desirable last.
4. If your top choice were eliminated, what would you do?
5. How would you feel if your top choice were eliminated? On a scale from 0–100, how badly would you feel?

V. Choice
  A. Choosing
    1. If you had to make a choice, right now, on the spot, which alternative would you choose?
    2. What criteria would you use in making a choice?
  B. Timing
    1. When does it make sense for you to make your choice and to begin acting on that choice?
    2. What reasons would you have for making your choice at the time specified?

VI. Acting
  A. Information
    1. What information will you need to plan a step-by-step procedure for reaching your goal?
  B. Planning—See I. E.

Career Portfolio

The portfolio is a notebook collection of career-related information describing a variety of the owner's qualifications, goals, work samples, reflections, educational plans, daily logs, test results, etc. The concept is to expand a traditional resume and to provide a self-portrait with a variety of materials. The portfolio can be an educational tool as a career counselor facilitates a process in which a student recognizes the value and implications of many work efforts. Some career counselors report successful group sessions using the portfolio, career fairs where employers view portfolio displays, family discussion reviewing student efforts, and job site visits when students leave their portfolios for employers to review and return with comments (Drummond & Ryan, 1995).

Career Support Groups/Psychoeducational Groups

In addition to classroom educational units, other formats for the delivery of career services are support groups and psychoeducational groups. **Support groups** are often formed for job seekers who meet regularly and share information with and understanding for each other. Emotional support allays the strains of the job search. Similar groups are also effective for high school seniors awaiting college admissions and others in transition.

Psychoeducational groups have educational goals and affective components. Group facilitators create sequential exercises designed to teach career concepts and to promote personal growth. Rather than merely explain the career development process or provide methods to delineate cognitive ideas, group leaders also facilitate awareness of the psychological aspects of career development. The validation experienced as group members share with each other is invaluable in building and maintaining self-esteem. As participants listen to each other, cohesion between the members grows and the stages of the group proceed to unfold.

The demand for frequent job changes in the global economy may increase the need for such group work. Introducing such experiences to young people would teach them interaction skills for future use. The ever-changing economy requires that all groups, be they in the classroom or in the community, create experiences for members to learn how to cope with change and how to use change to advantage. Many of the concepts delineated by authors describing the global economy are related to change, depicted by the Career Diamond's string of diamond shapes where one choice soon opens up to further career exploration.

SUMMARY

Counseling techniques are useful tools only because they offer vehicles for clients to do the work of exploration or decision making. Career counselors use such methods as talking points where the structure of the technique is of less importance than the interaction the tools created. Techniques can be chosen by considering the type of conversation the counselor is trying to promote. Consequently, some techniques are introduced when the counseling goal is to encourage clients to talk about themselves, and other exercises are used to open a dialogue regarding the priorities that will determine clients' choices.

STUDY OUTLINE: KEY TERMS AND CONCEPTS

    I. Techniques for Expanding Self-Awareness
       A. Career genogram: Look for patterns of:
          1. Career status
          2. Education requirements
          3. Willingness to move
          4. Gender roles

B. Life Reviews
   1. Early memories give insight into personal motivation.
   2. Use headlines technique to distill the essence of the messages.
   3. Look for three role models.
   4. Common themes across these areas offer insight into how a client wants to fit into the world.
C. Career imaginings
   1. **Guided imagery:** The use of mental images to encourage fleshing out a full picture of the client's goals for the future. Visual imaginings increase motivation and allow the client to believe in changes in attitudes and behavior.
   2. Look for themes in career daydreams (may listen for RIASEC codes).
   3. Goal is to avoid logic from dominating creativity.
   4. Discuss insights from the fantasy.
   5. Use role changes (e.g., sex, race) in a fantasy.
D. Metaphors
   1. Stories provide a different interpretation or solution to a situation.
      a. Does not need to directly correlate to the problem at hand.
      b. Ideally, the client will draw out the meaning.
   2. Culture is ripe with metaphors (e.g., sports, children's stories)
E. Skill identification methods
   1. Write an achievement autobiography.
   2. Identify traits and abilities.
   3. **Motivated skills**: Skills or abilities that the client judges he does well and enjoys doing.
   4. **Transferable skills**: Skills that are useful in one job that could also be used for other jobs or in different work contexts. An example would be supervising others, a skill needed in various occupations.
   5. **Functional skills**: Skills that serve specific functions that may be needed in a number of jobs. An example would be analyzing quantitative data, which would be functional for many different occupations.
F. Values
   1. Describe an ethical choice from client's past.
   2. How are the client's values similar or dissimilar to family members.
   3. Values card sort is a semistructured method for introducing values.

          a. Identify best, neutral, and worst values.

    G. Occupational card sort

       1. Place cards in Like, Dislike, or Indifferent piles.

          a. Counselor supports detailed descriptions of why occupations are placed in a pile.

          b. Look for consistent themes.

       2. Look for occupational stereotypes or misperceptions.

    H. Student card sort

       1. Goal is to identify barriers to success as a student.

    I. Defining success

       1. How important is making money?

       2. How important are other roles?

       3. Are definitions internal or external?

          a. How good is the client at filtering external messages/pressures?

II. Narrowing and Prioritizing

    A. Decision making

       1. Do not follow a rigid order.

       2. Include emotions and personal reactions.

       3. The steps are only suggestions. Feel free to modify it for your practice and clientele.

    B. Career portfolio

       1. A collection of qualifications, goals, work samples, etc.

          a. Much more detailed than a resume.

       2. Making portfolios may be useful in group formats.

    C. **Support/Psychoeducational Groups**

       1. Groups offer support through job searches and when awaiting call-backs.

       2. Expert leaders or other members can offer advice, introduce new skills, or provide experiences to help others.

EXERCISES

1. Create a values card sort by brainstorming or by using a checklist. In dyads, play a counselor using the values card sorts with a client. Practice reflecting and summarizing the client's statements.

2. Which of the many other techniques presented excite you as something you might use with clients. Why? Practice using several techniques in dyads, switching between counselor and client roles.

3. How could you use some of the techniques described with a group? Design a psychoeducational group that meets for several sessions. Think sequentially, and consider which techniques you would use first, second, and third to create a growing experience for the group members.

REFERENCES

Bloch, D. P., & Richmond, L. J. (Eds.). (1997). *Connections between spirit and work in career development: New approaches and practical perspectives.* Palo Alto, CA: Davies-Black.

Bolles, N. B. (1995). *What color is your parachute?* Berkeley, CA: Ten Speed Press.

Brooks, D., & Brown, L. (1996). *Career choice and development.* San Francisco: Jossey-Bass.

Dail, H. L. (1983). *The lotus and the pool.* Boston: Shambhala.

Drummond, R. J., & Ryan, C. W. (1995). *Career counseling: A developmental approach.* Englewood Cliffs, NJ: Prentice-Hall.

Figler, H. (1979). *The complete job search handbook.* NY: Holt, Rinehart & Winston.

Gysbers, N. C., Heppner, M. J., Johnston, J. A., & Associates (1998). *Career counseling: Process, issues, and techniques.* Boston: Allyn & Bacon.

Gysbers, N. C., & Moore, E. J. (1987). *Career counseling: Skills and techniques for practitioners.* Englewood Cliffs, NJ: Prentice-Hall.

Isaacson, L. E., & Brown, D. (2000). *Career information, career counseling, and career development.* Boston: Allyn & Bacon.

Martin, R. J. (1987). People are castles: A therapeutic metaphor. In *Innovations in clinical practice: A source book,* 6 (pp. 38–45). Indianapolis, IN: Wiley.

Minuchin, S., & Fishman, H. C. (1981). *Family therapy techniques.* Cambridge, MA: Harvard Univ. Press.

Okiishi, R. (1987). The genogram as a tool in career counseling. *Journal of Counseling and Development, 60,* 139–143.

Rayburn, C. A. (1997). Vocation as calling: Affirmative response or "wrong number." In D. P. Bloch & L. J. Richmond (Eds.), *Connection between spirit and work in career development* (pp. 163–184). Palo Alto, CA: Davies-Black.

Richmond, L. J. (1997) Spirituality and career assessment: Metaphors and measurement. In D. P. Bloch & L. J. Richmond (Eds.), *Connection between spirit and work in career development* (pp. 209–236). Palo Alto, CA: Davies-Black.

Savakis, M. L. (1997). The spirit in career counseling: Fostering self-completion through work. In D. P. Bloch & L. J. Richmond (Eds.), *Connection between spirit and work in career development* (pp. 3–26). Palo Alto, CA: Davies-Black.

Schulman, B. H., & Mosak, H. H. (1967). Various purposes of symptoms. *Journal of Individual Psychology, 23,* 79–87.

Skovholt, T. M., Morgan, J. I., & Negron-Cunningham, H. (1989). Mental imagery in career counseling and life planning: A review of research and intervention methods. *Journal of Counseling and Development, 67*(5), 287–293.

CHAPTER 10

Assessment and Career Counseling

Rather, I believe that science must be understood as a social phenomenon, a gutsy, human enterprise, not the work of robots programmed to collect pure information.... Science, since people must do it, is a socially embedded activity. It progresses by hunch, vision, and intuition (pp. 21–22).

Stephen Jay Gould, 1981

In Chapter 8, The Career Counseling Process, an emphasis was placed on establishing a relationship and encouraging the client to share as much of her self-concept as possible (Cavanagh & Levitov, 2002; Wolberg, 1954). In addition to creating a flow of interaction as in any other form of counseling, the career counselor silently attends to a clinical critique of the client's personality, interaction style, and specific situation. In this chapter, we describe the factors considered by the counselor while the counseling process proceeds. Recommended background information is also considered, as well as the use of formal testing instruments.

It is important to stress, however, that assessment is not intended to interrupt the counseling process in which the emphasis is on the client's self-expression and growth. Borgen (1995), a noted researcher on career assessment, says:

Assessment, ideally conducted in a counseling context, becomes a dynamic process. It stimulates dialogue between client and counselor, through which are merged the expert perspectives each brings. Together they construct a narrative, but often one that is in process, tentative, and incomplete. (p. 438)

Although the description of assessment procedures sounds definitive and direct, counselors need to set a tone in which clients realize that formal assessment is provisional in nature and in which the client is a full participant. The goal is to collect information and construct pictures of career identity that may change or become differently constructed as the process continues over time. Above all, clients need to feel their own self-assessments are primary, respected, and open to change (Martin, 2000).

ASSESSING CLIENT INFORMATION

Career counseling begins with a thorough assessment of the client's current level of functioning. Choosing to ignore a full assessment hamstrings a counselor and may lead to a superficial counseling experience for the client. The purpose of seeking some specific client information is to detect interpersonal or intrapersonal factors that may inhibit the client from being successful. It also provides excellent data for picking the best assessment instrument(s) at a later point (Liptak, 2001).

Context for Presenting Concerns

The first part of the initial counseling session focuses on why the client has sought counseling. Are clients self-referred or coming in at the insistence of family or friends? Is she preparing to begin a search after completing some form of training or education, or is she changing jobs due to downsizing or a conflict with her current employer? During this part of the session, the counselor is attempting to hear the client at multiple levels. The counselor is paying attention to verbal and nonverbal behaviors that may suggest a mental illness (Hood & Johnson, 1991). It would be common in career counseling for clients to be experiencing depression or anxiety, and there is a need to determine if the client needs to address the noncareer mental health issues before focusing on career issues.

Beyond mental illness, the counselor makes objective observations of the client and assesses how the client presents himself. The ability of the counselor to create global impressions, to be able to think creatively, to connect loosely associated ideas, and to be socially sensitive to subtle nuances of behavior can be powerful when helping clients choose and prepare for pursuing a career (Fredman & Sherman, 1987). Specifically, some global impressions helpful for further counseling are: client motivation; client self-esteem and self-efficacy; client awareness of world of work; and career experience.

The first part of the first session focuses mostly on the reason(s) for seeking career counseling. This approach honors the client's initial concern and helps the counselor build rapport. The second part of the session may shift to noncareer issues that the counselor has determined are important. Counselors working with a particular population may have learned with experience that specific factors often affect career choice making (e.g., a female client lives in a community that has traditional roles for women). Some questions may not seem obviously career-related and may be confusing for the client. It is important to prepare the client for this shift and to normalize the questions that are about to be asked. This can be done through statements such as, "I'm about to ask you some questions that may have a bearing on our counseling. I have found it very useful to get a full picture of a person's current life before I can be most helpful. Do you have any questions for me before I start?" Such preparatory statements allow for a smooth transition and show respect for the client by offering them opportunities to interact within the counseling process.

One area of inquiry that may not seem directly related to career is other roles salient in the client's life. Family roles and leisure life may interact negatively with career activities by adding stress and exhaustion due to over-commitment of time and energy (Newman, 2000). On the other hand, noncareer roles may be so important to the client that a career choice must be very pragmatic. A client may be so focused on playing golf, for instance, that work is simply a means to an end, providing time off and enough money for pursuing the sport. Or, a political activist may be interested in the job as an avenue to gain information or to stimulate societal change. Finally, career counselors may be biased in assuming that career is a primary role defining a major portion of identity for the client. This may not be true at all, and inquiring about other roles will provide the career counselor with a full picture of the client's life.

Decision-Making Style and Social Support

Determining decision-making style (Liptak, 2001) and available family and peer support are important assessments that should take place at the front end of career counseling. Clients bring a wide array of cognitive and personality styles to the counseling process. Some clients need to have a decision made years before it is actually needed whereas others let life make decisions for them. Family and peers can influence the client by exhorting values, offering social status, or punishing the client. An assessment of both areas allows the counselor to prepare for barriers to career choices and for individualistic approaches that will need to be taken into account.

Decision Making

Assessing clients' decision-making styles can easily be accomplished by asking clients to describe difficult decisions or choices they have made within the last year, or some other time frame if this doesn't elicit an answer. Exploring the steps a client took to reach the decision illuminates how the client thinks, what he values in decision making, and what skills he does and does not possess. The time it took to make the decision is also a factor and may suggest what he expects from counseling. If a client has not ever made an important decision, remedial skills may be needed. Sometimes the phrase "making an important choice" elicits a reaction better than the term "decision making." Also, exploring easy versus difficult choices can provide a description of how a client makes distinctions in his life.

The next area to explore is what did and did not work. Helping clients clarify the part of the important decision that went well allows them to draw from that experience and apply it to the current situation (de Shazer, 1988; Walter & Peller, 1992). Conversely, identifying parts of the decision that did not work creates an atmosphere where the counselor's challenges seem helpful to the client.

Family and Peer Support

Family and peers impact the decisions humans make. In most cultural contexts, some careers are valued whereas others are devalued. For example, seeking education may be seen as a betrayal of the family as it removes the educated member from the family support system (Rotunno & McGoldrick, 1982). On the other hand, some families require an advanced degree before a member is considered an equal. Finally, some families expect a child to follow in a parent's footsteps (e.g., family business). If the child chooses a different career, the family responds as if it has been rejected. These types of family expectations can make the decision-making process difficult for clients. During the different steps of the career process, it is important to understand how familial pressure will support or hinder clients. A full genogram (see Chapter 9, Career Counseling Techniques) is not always necessary; however, a basic understanding of the family is important.

Peers can impact decisions in a slightly different manner. In mainstream American culture, different careers have different status levels. It is not uncommon for high school students to aspire to occupations that sound like they have a lot of prestige (e.g., medical doctor, scientist, rock star, model, etc.). Choosing the occupation is based upon achieving a desired response from others. This pattern may continue into college where students often choose their majors based on the expectation of a certain level of income after graduation. Students who change majors or leave school sometimes face the negative evaluations of others. It can be useful, therefore, to assess how clients expect their career choices to impact on their status with peers. To help a client explain a career choice to questioning friends, you may have the client do some research and gather information about related job opportunities and future prospects.

Leisure Activities

By asking about leisure time activities, a counselor can offer interest areas that a client has not considered as potential career fields. Also, inquiring about noncareer areas signals to the client that a balance between different areas of life is important (Brems, 2001). What are the client's hobbies? Hobbies allow people to express their values, interests, and abilities. Hobbies are also an excellent way to reenergize. Look for themes in the hobbies, such as competition, being outdoors, being alone or with a group, working as a team, goal-oriented or just a way to spend time, how much they cost, etc. All this information can be helpful when looking for themes related to occupations.

Interview Summary

It is important to note that although the initial session requires asking questions and gathering information, skilled counselors do not engage in the staccato of a question–answer rhythm ("Shotgunning" according to Brems, 2001, p. 141). Straight questioning with the counselor's agenda dominating the counseling process reinforces the client's misperception that the expert will find the solution. Instead, the skilled counselor uses general questions as much as possible, and clients are encouraged to explain their responses with full descriptions of their experience. Interspersing inquiries with reflections of content, meaning, and feelings is another technique used by skilled counselors to help maintain the conversational tone of an interview.

Even the word *interview*, a term typically used with assessment, implies a structure of pre-prepared questions that are asked in the same sequence with every client. Counselors can gain the information they need by varying the timing of questions according to the client's content.

Assessment does not necessarily occur in the first session. There need not be a press to complete a specified regime within a particular time frame. Flexibility on the counselor's part and following the lead of the client is the most appropriate practice. Unless specific information is essential for the next steps of counseling, many questions can be included at any time.

TO TEST OR NOT TO TEST, THAT IS THE QUESTION

Criticisms of the test-and-tell style of interviewing have led some professional career counselors to the belief that the use of any instrument interferes with quality interactions with clients. Figler (Figler & Bolles, 1999) points out that all tests work from a limited pool of occupational titles and therefore could curtail client exploration. He also refutes the misperception that interest inventories have predictive validity and that higher scores mean greater interest in a specific occupation. Figler believes that tests are crutches for counselors and that they create a dependency on external authority for clients. Instead, he recommends framing different questions that encourage the client to say what careers are of interest to them.

All the criticisms of using instruments in career counseling stress the many negative consequences that occur when formal assessment dominates the interaction process. Surveys and inventories are only considered helpful if they can be used within the context of client exploration. In learning the skills of career counseling, it may be better for the novice career counselor to gain experience in the process before using instruments. The client needs to be the true focus of career counseling, not test results. Skilled counselors are able to integrate test results into the context of the interaction with the client. Also, skilled counselors typically use formal assessments in small increments to stimulate or validate the client's self-examination. However, using instruments can be of great assistance in summarizing the information about a client.

The developmental level of the client is another factor that experienced counselors take into account when choosing whether or not to use testing instruments. For most adults with career experience, inventories only record what the client can easily report in the interview. However, for clients with less maturity and experience, surveys are a means of reality testing and learning about the world of work. In any case, when instruments are used, the counseling process must relay the message that the client determines what occupational choices are relevant, and the client's internal evaluation of potential choices is much more significant than any survey results. The instruments, in and of themselves, are of little value if the client does not have the opportunity to use the results for self-exploration and to integrate the results with self-knowledge. It cannot be emphasized enough that the use of instruments is not the dominant focus of competent career counseling.

Qualitative Assessment Methods

The chapter on career counseling techniques (Chapter 9) includes a number of qualitative activities for gathering client information and for assessing various aspects of the client's personality, interests, or values. Such activities include occupational card sorts and genograms. These techniques do provide the means to interact with the client while the counselor forms impressions and the client gains insight at the same time.

The terminology used by the counselor has implications for what is communicated to clients. Use of the word *test*, for career instruments, brings to mind achievement tests, which have right and wrong answers and definitive results. Interest survey, value checklists, and personality inventories are descriptive of the client's current self-portrait in the context of an external comparison to other workers. The use of terms such as *instruments, surveys,* or *inventories* indicates the intention of examining self-descriptors for career identity exploration and integration.

Tests Are Tools

When instruments are used appropriately, they serve as a door that leads the client to explore personal and career-related domains. Measurement instruments can provide a common language for the counselor and client to proceed through a process in which the client gains insight. This is the magic of psychological assessment. It opens a door for dialogue. Specifically, the client is able to respond to questions with personal information that is then rearranged to fit within the structure of a survey. The client can confirm or deny the results, explain it in more detail, compare it with previous information, or even rank order its accuracy. Implicit in such a description of instruments is the message that the client is an expert on herself, and the survey is only one of many methods of organizing the client's responses to particular stimuli.

CHOOSING APPROPRIATE INSTRUMENTS

Some counselors use the same instruments for all career clients regardless of presenting concerns or needs. This is another example of an approach to career services that does not reach the professional standard of examining the unique career identity of each client. Assigning a particular survey or several instruments must meet the needs of the client and be appropriate to the client's developmental level (Hoffman, 2002). The counselor chooses instruments, which have **norming groups** similar to the client with respect to age, ethnicity, and race (see the specific technical manual as well as the American Counseling Association Code of Ethics in Box 10.1). Instruments chosen for the client must have norms representative of the client's background. In this section, we will demonstrate a method for choosing an instrument that is purposeful and differential for each individual client, but first we must discuss validity and reliability.

Validity

"**Validity** refers to the truth of the observations" (Elmes, Kantowietz, & Roediger, 2003, p. 55). Valid tests measure what they claim to measure, so validity is important when counselors select a specific instrument from the wide variety available (e.g., interests, values, aptitudes). Validity scores are typically reported in the technical manual that accompanies the instrument, and counselors are advised to evaluate whether or not the selected instrument is valid, that is, measures characteristics relevant to the client's goals.

Reliability

"**Reliability** refers to the consistency of behavioral measures" (Elmes et al., 2003, p. 60). When working with people, we expect variability in performance. Therefore, little changes are normal if an instrument is administered twice over two time periods. However, large variations in scores suggest that the information provided by the instrument is minimally useful at best. Again, the instrument's reliability will be reported in the technical manual; counselors should expect good reliability scores. Do note that high reliability does not equal validity. The behavior of a small child who calls every animal a doggy is reliable, but not valid. On the other hand, validity requires reliability. See Box 10.1 for the ACA ethical code regarding use of assessment instruments.

Career Interest Inventories

The Career Diamond can be used to determine which interest inventory is appropriate for clients who are placed at different points in the developmental process. For clients who are placed at the beginning of the Career Diamond, where the client has not yet explored either career information or opened up to self-exploration, the *Self-Directed Search (SDS)* is the most suitable instrument (Holland, 1996).

The Career Diamond in Figure 10.1 shows a client who is just becoming aware of the career choice process. The X on the top line indicates the client is just starting to become self-aware, identifying a few personal characteristics

Figure 10.1   The X's placed near the A on the Career Diamond indicate the client is just beginning to explore both the Self and the World of Work. An instrument such as the SDS is a good tool to teach such naïve clients about the World of Work and about broad personal preferences related to occupational characteristics.

Box 10.1   American Counseling Association ACA Code of Ethics (eff. 1995, n.d.)

Section E: Evaluation, Assessment, and Interpretation

E.1. General

a. Appraisal Techniques. The primary purpose of educational and psychological assessment is to provide measures that are objective and interpretable in either comparative or absolute terms. Counselors recognize the need to interpret the statements in this section as applying to the whole range of appraisal techniques, including test and nontest data.

b. Client Welfare. Counselors promote the welfare and best interests of the client in the development, publication, and utilization of educational and psychological assessment techniques. They do not misuse assessment results and interpretations and take reasonable steps to prevent others from misusing the information these techniques provide. They respect the client's right to know the results, the interpretations made, and the bases for their conclusions and recommendations.

E.2. Competence to Use and Interpret Tests

a. Limits of Competence. Counselors recognize the limits of their competence and perform only those testing and assessment services for which they have been trained. They are familiar with reliability, validity, related standardization, error of measurement, and proper application of any technique utilized. Counselors using computer-based test interpretations are trained in the construct being measured and the specific instrument being used prior to using this type of computer application. Counselors take reasonable measures to ensure the proper use of

---

related to a career identity. The X on the bottom line suggests the client is also just beginning to identify possibilities in the world of work.

At this point in the process, the client needs to learn about personal likes and dislikes and about career information. The *SDS* matches the client's reported likes and dislikes with Holland's six occupational categories. As the client takes the Holland Code letters and explores categories in the *Occupational Finder* (Holland, 1996) or the *Educational Opportunity Finder* (Rosen, Holmberg, & Holland, 1997), the client learns about occupations and how jobs are distributed among broad categories. The client learns that identifying specific self-attributes can lead to a match with occupations that have similar characteristics. Such a matching process is the most basic method of self-assessment; the trait-factor approach originally proposed by Parsons (1909). Although this simple approach is basic, it is appropriate for clients who are just beginning the career exploration process and may include young clients

psychological assessment techniques by people under their supervision.

b. Appropriate Use. Counselors are responsible for the appropriate application, scoring, interpretation, and use of assessment instruments, whether they score and interpret such tests themselves or use computerized or other services.

c. Decisions Based on Results. Counselors responsible for decisions involving individuals or policies that are based on assessment results have a thorough understanding of educational and psychological measurement, including validation criteria, test research, and guidelines for test development and use.

d. Accurate Information. Counselors provide accurate information and avoid false claims or misconceptions when making statements about assessment instruments or techniques. Special efforts are made to avoid unwarranted connotations of such terms as IQ and grade equivalent scores. (See C.5.c.)

E.6. Test Selection

a. Appropriateness of Instruments. Counselors carefully consider the validity, reliability, psychometric limitations, and appropriateness of instruments when selecting tests for use in a given situation or with a particular client.

b. Culturally Diverse Populations. Counselors are cautious when selecting tests for culturally diverse populations to avoid inappropriateness of testing that may be outside of socialized behavioral or cognitive patterns.

---

or older clients who need experiences considering personal attributes and occupational characteristics.

Career materials for secondary students, even in middle school or junior high, often use such a matching method, based on the Holland system or other similar systems. Computer programs, such as *Choices* or *DISCOVER*, are matching systems, though the categories are somewhat different from Holland's. What is important to emphasize to students is that the matching of interests, values, and abilities to occupations are *only* creating possibilities. The goal is not to find a specific occupation that will predetermine career choice but to use the matching method to suggest characteristics of occupations (Campbell, Hyne, & Nilsen, 1992; Holland, Fritzsche, & Powell, 1997; Holland, Powell, & Fritzsche, 1997). Future career endeavors may very well have such characteristics but may not be the specific job titles found through the initial matching.

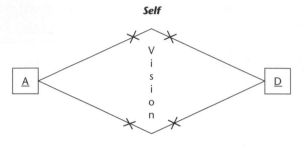

Figure 10.2   The X's are placed in the widest part of the Career Diamond, indicating the client has done some exploring of Self and the World of Work. A Vision may be forming, and a few Self priorities may have been set. The few personal priorities may have been integrated into realistic characteristics of an occupation or some aspect of the World of Work. An instrument such as the *CISS* or the *Strong* would help the client gain greater clarity for a final stage of exploring as the decision-making process begins.

Clients who are placed further along the bottom of the Career Diamond have some sense of their interests and some knowledge of occupations.

The four X's on the Career Diamond in Figure 10.2 show the space where a client has developed considerable self-awareness and has a good amount of knowledge about the world of work. The client needs to integrate a vision of self with the external demands in the world of work to come to a decision.

The space on the diamond is about the middle of the exploring phase or in the first part of the decision-making phase. Clients may need to continue exploring or they may have begun to make some choices and may need to confirm those options. For such clients, the ***Strong Interest Inventory (SII)***® (1994) would be appropriate. The *SII* offers empirical evidence of the client's shared interests with workers in different occupations. Clients are given validation that some occupations may have characteristics of interest to them and that the people in those occupations have interests in common with them.

For clients placed in the same area of the diamond but who demonstrate a lack of confidence in their skill or ability to perform tasks associated with occupations, the ***Campbell*™ *Interest and Skills Survey (CISS)***® (Campbell, 1994) is suitable. The *CISS* also compares clients' interests with the interests of workers in different occupations. However, it adds the client's self-estimate of abilities needed to perform the tasks of the occupations. By discussing any disparity between interests and confidence of abilities, clients can come to terms with the impact of their self-estimates as they make career choices.

The ***Career Assessment Inventory (CAI)*** (Johansson, 2002) is useful for clients who are placed in the same area of the Career Diamond and who

"CISS" is a registered trademark and "Campbell" is a trademark of David P. Campbell, Ph.D.

may be interested in careers associated with two-year community college or vocational school majors. Some careers requiring four-year college degrees are also included in the *CAI* tool, so the client can consider the options of several types of postsecondary training.

Ability Tests: Achievement and Aptitude Assessment

According to Seligman (1994), ability tests measure both the "degree of mastery of a body of knowledge" and a means to project "a person's likelihood of succeeding in an academic or occupational endeavor" (p 111). However, assessment of abilities has been shown to reflect bias in representing the true capacities of any given person. Gender and racial impartiality have been shown, and the tests do not include the impact of motivation, persistence, and attentiveness for academic and career achievement (Seligman, 1994). Clients could be unaware of the various abilities they possess and which abilities are related to specific occupations, so identifying aptitudes could help expand career self-concepts. However, the impact of tests for self-efficacy could also be limiting when individuals are compared to others who share different backgrounds. Career counselors can help clients assess their abilities by examining a number of sources related to abilities, including motivated skills, school grades, and previous work performance.

The following are some of the aptitude tests measuring general abilities and occupationally related skills. Contact information is provided at the end of this section for each instrument: *General Aptitude Test Battery (GATB)*; *OASIS-3*; and *Differential Aptitude Tests®, (DAT®)*. ACT's *Work Keys* ties skills (Reading for information; Listening/Writing; Applied Mathematics; Applied Technology; Teamwork; Locating Information; Observation) to abilities required for specific jobs related to a job's analysis. The *COPSystem (Career Occupational Placement System)* includes an ability battery, an interest inventory, and a work values survey, which are all linked to 14 occupational clusters. For individuals interested in the military, the *Armed Services Vocational Aptitude Battery (ASVAB)* identifies occupational aptitudes as well as interests. Clients should be referred to a military recruiter, or recruiters may be willing to come to a high school and conduct a group administration. The Scholastic Aptitude Test (SAT) and the American College Test (ACT) predict achievement for college academics. The ACT also contains an interest survey related to the World-of-Work Map and the DISCOVER career computer program (see Chapter 11).

Personality Surveys

The assessment of personality may aid the client in developing a vocabulary for describing the self (Hirsh & Kummerow, 1989). Through formal assessment, the client may become more aware of personality characteristics that are not in his awareness. The Career Diamond demonstrates the need for a personality instrument. If the counselor determines that the client has done little self-exploration, a personality inventory may further the career process.

The *Myers-Briggs Type Indicator (MBTI)*® instrument can be used with most clients placed all along the top of the diamond model. The *MBTI* has a major advantage of stressing the positive nature of all the described personality types. Weaknesses are seen as the result of overusing strengths and using the strengths in situations where they are not applicable. Leadership descriptions and the information specific to career give the client and the counselor an avenue for exploring personal attributes (Myers, McCaulley, Quenk, & Hammer, 1995).

Personality exploration in career counseling can be difficult. Clients may not expect to share personal self-descriptions. Or, a client may not understand what sort of a self-description is needed. The counselor may try to use reflection of feelings to encourage self-exploration but find that the technique falls flat, with the client offering only limited responses. Asking clients about their work experience, their likes and dislikes, or their values may also lead to brief, clipped answers. Using an instrument such as the *MBTI* tool offers the client and the counselor a format for examining the client's self-concept. The description of Myers Briggs letters gives the client and counselor a common language and a set of concepts for discussing how the client sees herself. The personality styles described in the materials related to career show how different people perform work-related tasks and how they interact with other workers. Such descriptions create a vehicle for imagining how the client, with her unique style, might behave in a work environment. As the counselor and the client project the client's attributes into a working role, the client can begin to own a picture of herself as a worker.

Counselors who find the *MBTI* instrument inappropriate for some clients may consider using the *16 Personality Factors (16PF)* tool (Cattell, Cattell, & Cattell) or the *California Psychological Inventory (CPI)*™ instrument (Gough, 1996). Both tests present personality descriptors and, in the most recent additions, provide career profiles. Clients who demonstrate some psychological sophistication may benefit from the *16PF* tool, whereas highly sophisticated clients may be better served by the *CPI* instrument.

Assessing Values

Value measurements are the least well-developed area of career assessment. Values are subjectively defined and applied by individuals in idiosyncratic ways. Instruments can be somewhat sophisticated, such as *The Values Scale* (http://www.life-values.com/), or fairly simple, such as a values checklist. The purpose of using a values measure is to encourage the client to weigh the choices that determine what is important for a self-defined, meaningful life. Values will often be expressed during counseling discussions and can be noted and clarified in the moment. Summaries of a collection of values heard over time can validate a client's sense of meaning and help determine the priorities a client has for making choices.

Values card sorts are not difficult to make by taking values mentioned before in session along with other values and writing each down on a small piece of paper. Either the client or the counselor or both together can generate a list of values. The client can then be instructed to put the values in priority order and explain why each is important and why one may be more important than another. The counselor might even write a summary of the explanations to give to the client for future reference.

Career Diamond and New Assessment Instruments

If the reader comes across a career, personality, or values instrument that has not been mentioned in this book, the Career Diamond can be used to rate it. Look at the difficulty of completing the instrument as well as the information provided. Place an X on the top or bottom half of the diamond that is indicative of the level of development for what the instrument measures. When a client is in a similar area of the expanding or deciding phase, then that instrument is more likely to be helpful. If the instrument is placed behind or too far ahead of the client's place on the diamond, the information will either be too simple or too advanced. In these situations, there is no purpose in using the tool, and other techniques would be more appropriate.

INTERPRETING ASSESSMENT RESULTS

> Personally, I use formally identified assessment with clients only rarely and reluctantly, primarily because it so heavily places the therapist in the expert role, implying that the therapist diagnoses and fixes people, once he or she has gathered enough information. It often means to clients that the therapist has secret methods for getting things out of the client and making judgments based on this information.
>
> *Martin, 2000, p. 209*

Clients respond well to career assessment material if they are actively involved in interpreting the results, are able to have the final word on the significance of the results, and can apply the information to the personal and professional expansions of the Career Diamond (Brown & Brooks, 1991). Therefore, taking several sessions to interpret one survey creates a process in which the client's self-exploration takes precedence over the instrument's results. In the next sections, we will explore methods for interpreting career and personality protocols. We will show how instruments can be chosen to

Box 10.2   Assessment Companies and Instruments

The following list contains some of the well-known assessment companies. Most websites contain license requirements, target audience, and the type of information provided by the assessment tool. Browsing these and other websites allows counselors to look for the instruments that will best serve particular clientele.

ACT http://www.act.org
1. *ACT Assessment*
2. *DISCOVER®*

CPP, Inc. (Formerly Consulting Psychologists Press) http://www.cpp.com/
1. *Strong Interest Inventory® (SSI®)*: Interest Inventory
2. *Myers-Briggs Type Indicator® (MBTI®)*: Personality Assessment
3. *The California Psychological Inventory™ (CPI™)*: Personality Assessment
4. *Career Beliefs Inventory (CBI)*: Beliefs Inventory

EdITS http://www.edits.net
1. *Career Occupational Preference System (COPSystem)*: Interest Inventory (Different versions of the COPS are prepared for different age groups.)
2. *Career Orientation Placement and Evaluation Survey (COPES)*: Values Inventory
3. *Career Ability Placement Survey (CAPS)*: Aptitude Test
4. *Making a Terrific Career Happen (MATCH)*: Interest, Abilities, and Values Exploration Instrument

JIST Works, Inc. http://www.jist.com/
1. *Career Exploration Inventory (CEI)*: Interest Inventory
2. *Job Search Attitude Inventory (JSAI)*: Assesses Motivation
3. *Leisure/Work Search Inventory (LSI)*: Connects leisure activities employment opportunities
4. *Barriers to Employment Success Inventory (BESI)*: Assesses challenges to obtaining work
5. *Occupational Outlook Handbook, 2004–2005 Edition*: Book

Nelson Assessment http://assess.nelson.com/
1. *General Aptitude Test Battery (GATB)*: Aptitude Test (Originally produced by United States Employment Service)

PAR, Psychological Assessment Resources, Inc. http://www.parinc.com/index.cfm
1. *Self-Directed Search®*: Interest Inventory
2. *O*NET Dictionary of Occupational Titles, 3rd Ed.*: Printed Version
3. *Career Thoughts Inventory™ (CTI™)*: Negative Career Thinking
4. *Career Decision Scale (CDS)*: Decision Making
5. *Screening Assessment for Gifted Elementary and Middle School Students, 2nd Ed. (SAGES-2)*: Achievement Inventory
6. *Wide Range Achievement Test 3 (WRAT3)*: Achievement Inventory
7. *Work Readiness Profile (WRP)*: For Clients with Disabilities

*Spanish Instruments Available

(continued)

(Box 10.2 continued)

Pearson Assessments (Formerly National Computer Systems, Inc.)
http://www.pearsonassessments.com

1. *Career Assessment Inventory™ Enhanced Version*: Interest Inventory
2. *CISS® (Campbell™ Interest and Skill Survey)*: Interest Inventory
3. *IDEAS™ (IDEAS: Interest Determination, Exploration and Assessment System®)*: Interest Inventory
4. *16PF® Fifth Edition*: Personality Assessment
5. *BASI™ (Basic Achievement Skills Inventory)*: Achievement Inventory
6. *WBST™ (Wonderlic® Basic Skills Test)*: Achievement Inventory

Pro-Ed, Inc. http://www.proedinc.com

1. *OASIS-3 Interest Complete Kit, Third Edition*: Interest and Aptitude Instruments

2. *Insights: A Self and Career Awareness Program for the Elementary Grades*: Career Development Activities
3. *Preparing Teens for the World of Work: A School-to-Career Transition Guide for Counselors, Teachers and Career Specialists*: Activity Book

The Psychological Corporation
http://www.harcourt.com/

1. *Career Interest Inventory (CII)*: Interest Inventory
2. *Differential Aptitude Tests®, Fifth Edition (DAT®)*: Aptitude Test
3. *Stanford Achievement Test Series, Tenth Edition – Just the Basics – Complete Battery*: Achievement Test

meet a need a client's need, and interpretations can be timed to facilitate client growth. The following is the authors' method of interpreting results in a meaningful manner that enhances a counseling relationship.

Interpreting Instruments

The following step-by-step plan for interpreting personality and interest surveys has been developed over years by monitoring how clients react to the information that is provided to them. It enables counselors to modify their suggestions to suit individual styles. Adaptations can be made in order to individualize the process to meet the client's developmental needs.

Step 1: Review the results before the client comes in.

This may seem like an obvious statement, but it is not. Many counselors find themselves very knowledgeable about an instrument they use regularly, and the need to prepare an interpretation seems unnecessary. Although the knowledge is there, it is best to avoid the cookie cutter style of interpretation in which interpretations follow the same format for every client. Instead, consider the following areas:

A. Look for general themes.

Interest inventory:

Is the client marking only yes to doing, thinking, creating, etc., types of occupations? Do most of the professions have high status? Is there one area where interests are similar to occupations in other areas that are not indicated by the instrument? Is there a general interest in many areas but no one field of shared interests? Are interests shown, but belief in skills low or vise versa?

Personality Survey:

Is the client indicating either introversion or extroversion? Did the client scores show a clear preference on some factors and a low propensity on others? Or are most factors somewhere in the middle range? Does the client verbally report characteristics to be one way, but the survey indicates something different?

B. Note anything that matches previous discussions.

Being able to personalize the assessment results increases the interpretation's validity. It also highlights the ways in which the information can be put to use. For example, if a person tends to be introverted, it may make sense that the client dislikes a job requiring intensive contact with the public. It may be that contact with people is difficult, but other aspects of the job could be more appealing. Thus, a transfer within the company may be the best choice whereas the client had originally considered trying an entirely different field. Many clients are not temperamentally inclined to make such connections. Counseling can provide a new perspective and create new opportunities for consideration.

Step 2: Ask the client what it was like to take the test.

Responding to items provided by an instrument can start a thinking process. Did the client think of anything new after taking the inventory? Was there any part of the survey that was particularly interesting or boring? Clients may have also spent time talking with friends or family about the testing experience. This may generate new information that was not collected during earlier counseling sessions. Counselors may even want to plant these questions in the client's mind before taking and assessing protocols.

Step 3: Choose whether or not you will use the instrument in session with the client.

Crites (1981) recommends interpreting assessment results without bringing the protocol into the session with the client. The presence of the impressive looking charts can get in the way of the counseling dialogue. If the counselor and client find themselves focused on the printed page, there is a risk that both parties will direct their attention to the results item by item in a sequential order. Although counselors-in-training may use such a focus to learn the structure of a test, this approach is not useful for clients' self-interpretation. Instead of keeping their eyes on the survey, clients need to reflect on the meaning of the report and apply the results to what they know about themselves. Rather than using the printed results counselors could:

A. Write an outline of discussion points.

Prepare a brief report that highlights the general themes that were identified in step 1. If more than one instrument was used, integrate all the material. Such a report would use language the client can understand. The counselor may let the client keep the report.

B. Use only one or two sections of the instrument per session.

Do not go through all of the instrument's results in sequential order. Appropriate planning would determine the order for examining the results according to the client's style and according to what has been previously discussed. Copies of a part of the results could be made to share with the client for each session. Remember, the client will be responding to the results at hand and expand the personal meaning of the information. Focusing on only some of the results in a single session will encourage self-exploration.

C. Share the results over multiple sessions.

The best situation for interpreting instruments is over time. The client needs to have time to digest the material and apply it to the situation at hand. Therefore, it can take two to five sessions to review one instrument. Extending the time for sharing results prevents the instrument from dominating the interaction and keeps the client coming back to the next session to receive more results. The message sent to the client is, "This piece of paper is not the primary focus, you are." By sending this message, counseling avoids the assumption the results will give "the answer" and implies that career decision making is a process that develops over time.

Step 4: Interpret the instrument from the general to the specific.

Begin with general categories, and see how the client responds to each. Many clients would prefer starting with specific occupations to find out what careers are identified as the best. Once these clients see that such and such occupations are the ones the instrument tells them to pursue, they no longer listen or respond to any generalizing of themes characteristic of many occupations. Hence, most manuals recommend starting with general categories. Constantly ask how this information reflects the client's self-concept. How accurate is it? With what part does the client agree or disagree? As the client opens up and starts to apply the information to past situations, such as thoughts and dreams, move to subcategories of the general classification. Move to specific occupations only after general categories have been thoroughly discussed. Basically, the movement is from a place of endless possibilities to a place of specific options. Such movement usually requires considering results over several sessions.

Although most manuals recommend progressing from the general to the specific, there are some clients who prefer the opposite procedure of considering the specific occupations first and then moving to the general categories. Clients who are categorized as sensing on the Myers Briggs Type Inventory, as well as those with Holland Codes including R, C, or many I's, tend to think in concrete terms before they are ready to expand their considerations to generalizing themes. Some people trained in the scientific method think in specifics first. Also, a client who is seeking validation for an already thoroughly considered career path might prefer to gain the specific information first. For such clients, the counselor must weigh all the factors and determine if reversing the recommended movement would work well.

Sometimes, immature career clients will discontinue career counseling and not return to scheduled sessions once they have seen the occupations ranked as highest in priority by the instrument. The counselor must make the clinical judgment: "Will this client benefit from using a specific to general approach or vice versa? Is the client able to take specifics first and still complete the thematic process? If the client's style prefers specifics first, will he maintain an open mind long enough to realize how occupational characteristics can be transferred to other occupations not included in the inventory?"

For mature career clients, it may be appropriate to ask what approach would work best for them, making it clear that generalizing the results provides the greatest benefit. Asking clients their preferred approach and explaining what would follow is called "bringing the process into the open." The client is made aware of the path taken in the counseling interaction and of the choices being made for a new direction. It is a very respectful technique for counselors who make use of it.

Once the overall approach is determined, the counselor can facilitate a learning experience in which the client discovers how to apply assessment results for self-exploration and for integrating external information with career self-concept. Following are techniques to promote the process:

A. Have the client provide examples.
    Whenever new information is added, ask the client to describe experiences that are related to the characteristics under discussion. These can

CASE STUDY 10.1   But I'm Only a Kid

A high school junior came to the counselor's office as per her father's request. Her father was a medical doctor but hated his job. He had recently taken a personality test and found himself to be an introvert. He told his daughter that if he had only known this at her age, he would have chosen a much different career. The father wanted her to take a personality test so they could decide what she was going to do after she graduated from college. The client had no idea what a personality test was and wasn't even sure if she wanted to go to college. Other information that was important: Her mother had a Ph.D. and her older brother was a first-year law student. There were two physicians in the grandparent generation.

How Would You Conceptualize This Case?

1. Would you have administered a test(s) to this client? Why or why not? If yes, which ones?

2. Would this case have been different if none of her family had gone to college?

3. The father wanted the counselor to give his daughter the test results so he could look at them. What would you have done?

What Actually Happened?

The client did not take a personality or an interest test, and the client was coached to explain to her father that career counseling does not always entail formal testing. The client was supported in not needing to know, "What I will do after college." In addition, information-gathering and decision-making strategies were taught. Client reported relief in gaining permission to focus on exploring versus choosing a career.

---

be examples of life events from school, work, home, and the like. Another way to encourage such processing is to have the client imagine how this piece would look at work. For example, one client had a high extroversion score on two independent tests. He reported that he would need a position that supported socializing on the job and a team approach. He said he would rather work 50 hours a week and able to talk with others than to work 40 hours a week but be stuck at his desk. This is an excellent example of how a client can predict the environment that will bring the most satisfaction.

B. Follow up between sessions.

   Ideally the client will be thinking about the information gained between sessions. She may be talking with family, friends, or a partner about what has been learned and what it means. At the beginning of each session, ask what the client has been thinking or doing since the last session. This sends a message that the counselor is interested in the client's gradual process. Finally, it allows the counselor to modify the test interpretation if new information provided by the client indicates such a change would be helpful. Consider an example in which part of the test interpretation plan was to look at the disparity between high interests (e.g., lawyer) and low self-reported abilities (e.g., academic skills). The client identifies a new area where she is very confident of skills (e.g., investigator). The counselor may choose to shift gears and look at opportunities within that area, spending less time determining if the client's self-report was accurate or not or if new skill development might be needed.

C. Integrate values, interests, and abilities.

Fitting all of the pieces together is an important part of the career process. How does being extroverted, liking the outdoors, excelling in science, not liking school, and wanting a high income come together in a coherent picture of the future? By comparison, how does being introverted, wanting to serve the community, not having enough money for school/training, and having to support a family impact career decisions? Clients need help in prioritizing those factors that require attention first, yet should not ignore an area that is less important but may still impact job satisfaction.

ASSESSMENT EXAMPLE: INTERPRETING RESULTS OF INTEREST INVENTORIES

Components of Interest Inventories

The following section is an example of how to go through an assessment instrument and compare it to others on the market. This same procedure can be used to evaluate aptitude tests, personality instruments, and so on.

Many interest inventories are organized with several occupational categories, starting with the broadest class to the more specific. (The following section draws heavily from the technical manuals for each instrument. Please refer to Campbell et al., 1992; Harmon, Hansen, Borgen, & Hammer, 1994; Johansson, 1986). For the *SII* tool and the *CAI* inventory, the category for the broadest occupational division is called General Themes, which are grouped by Holland codes (*RIASEC*). The *CISS* inventory uses the term Orientation Scales for the broadest category.

Subscales are in the next category called Basic Interest Scales for the *CAI* tool and the *SII* instrument and the Orientations & Basic Scales for the *CISS* inventory. Occupational Scales are listings of specific occupations and are usually presented last.

For the broader categories (see Table 10.1), the respondent is compared to the general population of all people who have ever taken the test. Higher scores show more interest than the statistical average for all people taking

Table 10.1   Campbell™ Interest and Skill Survey Individual Profile Report

00026476   Date Scored: 06/09/2005

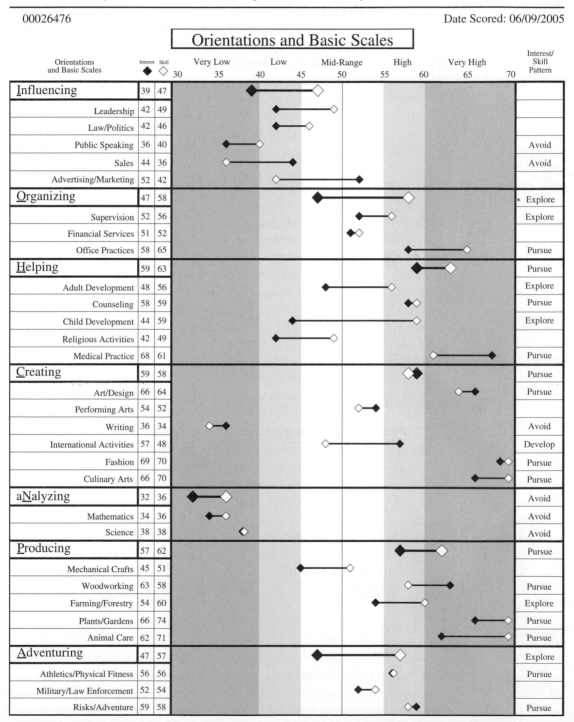

Orientations and Basic Scales	Interest ◆	Skill ◇	Interest/Skill Pattern
Influencing	39	47	
Leadership	42	49	
Law/Politics	42	46	
Public Speaking	36	40	Avoid
Sales	44	36	Avoid
Advertising/Marketing	52	42	
Organizing	47	58	‹ Explore
Supervision	52	56	Explore
Financial Services	51	52	
Office Practices	58	65	Pursue
Helping	59	63	Pursue
Adult Development	48	56	Explore
Counseling	58	59	Pursue
Child Development	44	59	Explore
Religious Activities	42	49	Explore
Medical Practice	68	61	Pursue
Creating	59	58	Pursue
Art/Design	66	64	Pursue
Performing Arts	54	52	
Writing	36	34	Avoid
International Activities	57	48	Develop
Fashion	69	70	Pursue
Culinary Arts	66	70	Pursue
aNalyzing	32	36	Avoid
Mathematics	34	36	Avoid
Science	38	38	Avoid
Producing	57	62	Pursue
Mechanical Crafts	45	51	
Woodworking	63	58	Pursue
Farming/Forestry	54	60	Explore
Plants/Gardens	66	74	Pursue
Animal Care	62	71	Pursue
Adventuring	47	57	Explore
Athletics/Physical Fitness	56	56	Pursue
Military/Law Enforcement	52	54	
Risks/Adventure	59	58	Pursue

Copyright © 1989, 1992 David P. Campbell, Ph.D. Published and distributed exclusively by NCS Pearson, Inc., P.O. Box 1416, Minneapolis, MN 55440. Reproduced with permission of NCS Pearson, Inc.

the instrument in the norming group. So, for the broader categories, an interpretation that the client has higher than average interest is accurate.

However, using the words *more* interest or *higher* interest for interpreting the specific occupational scores is not accurate. In the occupational category, the respondent's likes and dislikes are compared to people who have been in a specific occupation for at least three years and who say they like their work. Accurate interpretation for specific occupational comparisons is that the scores represent the degree to which the test-taker shares similar likes and dislikes with people in the field. It is important that counselors use appropriate interpretations so clients do not develop misconceptions.

Gender Differences

Different instruments deal with gender differences in different ways. The *SII* tool and *CAI* instrument keep men and women in separate norming groups and give scores comparing women to women and men to men (Harmon et al., 1985; Johansson, 1986). The dark dot or star used to indicate where the respondent's score falls on the distribution of scores is given for the comparison with appropriate sex (see Table 10.2). However, the distribution of scores for the opposite sex is also given by the *SII* tool, and a range of scores for the opposite sex is given by the *CAI* instrument. The dot or star placed on the bar for the respondent's sex is above a similar bar indicating the distribution of scores for the opposite sex. A line for the respondent's dot or star could be drawn up or down to the distribution for the opposite sex to make a comparison with the opposite sex.

Likewise, considering where the respondent's score would be within the range of scores for the opposite sex on the *CAI* instrument gives an indication of how the client's interests would compare with the opposite sex group. Sometimes, shared interest to workers in an occupation is shown when the comparison is made with the opposite sex but not when the comparison is made with the same sex. It may be relevant to discuss such interests. Note that Holland Code classifications may differ for men and women for the same occupation. When Holland letters are different by gender, the score's dot or star will be shown in the category of classification for the respondent's sex.

Procedural Checks

Interest inventories give information about the respondent's answers to the items. This information tells if the test-taker answered all the questions or if the answers were consistent for similar items. Failing to respond to a considerable number of items or inconsistent answers would render the results

Table 10.2 Strong Interest Inventory®

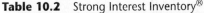

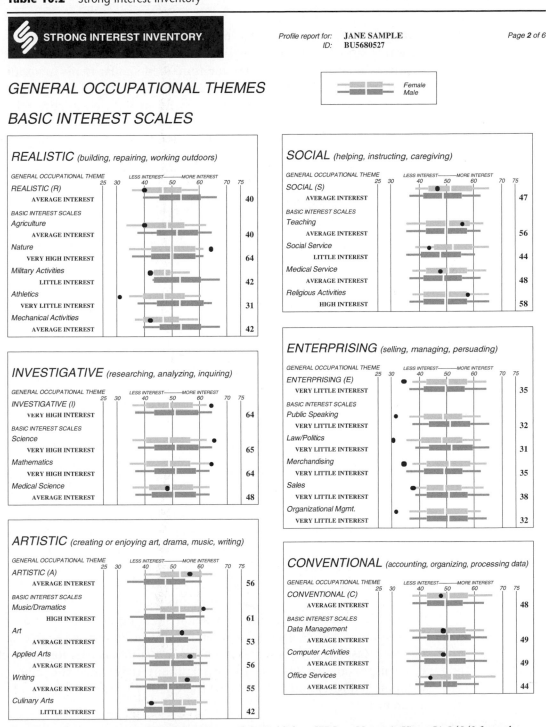

Modified and reproduced by special permission of the Publisher, CPP, Inc., Mountain View, CA 94043 from the Strong Interest Inventory® Instrument. © 1933, 1938, 1945, 1946, 1966, 1968, 1974, 1981, 1985, 1994, by CPP, Inc. Further reproduction is prohibited without the Publisher's written consent. Strong Interest Inventory is a registered trademark of CPP, Inc.

invalid. Usually, there is a chart indicating the percentage of answers in the various sections of the test. These percentages could indicate a negative or positive mindset, or if the respondent marked similar items in an inconsistent matter. If the percentages are weighted in the extreme, a pattern of interests may not be shown, and the profile would be interpreted as flat. Another possibility could be that a particular section shows a pattern of all likes or dislikes, such as the section for school subjects. If the counselor noted that the client disliked all or most school subjects, discussing the client's experience with formal education might be in order.

Special Scales

Special scales often offer general interpretations for the respondent's pattern of interests. Topics include occupational introversion/extroversion indicating if the client may prefer an occupation with high or low contact with people. Another topic may be commitment to education, suggesting whether the client appreciates schooling for its own sake or if training is seen as a means to an end. Still another may be an indication of the degree of occupational risk-taking behavior that may be of interest to a client. These scales are very broad and need to be suggested tentatively to clients, watching for their reactions and ultimately trusting the clients' self-opinions. See Box 10.3 for an outline summarizing the sections of interest inventories.

SUMMARY

A career counseling approach to assessment is client focused. The client is active in the interpretation of the results and is almost always considered correct if his view differs from the assessment results. By taking several sessions per instrument, our experience has been that clients look forward to coming back, learn more from the interpretations, and are able to apply this information to choosing and pursuing a career. By comparison, clients who experience test-and-tell may seem satisfied immediately following interpretations of results but are often not able to integrate the information. Finally, please note that there is not a super test that is best for every client. It is important to choose the instrument that suits the client's developmental level and accounts for the client's self-knowledge and career awareness.

Box 10.3   Components of Interest Inventories

I. Broadest Occupational Categories such as
   A. General themes for *SII* & *CAI*
   B. Orientations Scales for *CISS*
   C. For the broader career categories, the respondent is compared with all people taking the test. Higher scores in the broad categories mean the respondent shows more interest in the career area than the general population.

II. Subscales of Broader Categories such as
   A. Basic interest for *CAI;* Basic interest & skill scales for *CISS*
   B. Basic interest scales for *SII*
   C. See C above.

III. Occupational Scales
   A. Comparisons of test respondents who have worked in specific occupations and who state they like their jobs.
   B. For the occupational categories, the more the respondent agrees with the people in the occupation, the higher the score. Therefore, a high score for counselor would mean the respondent shares similar interests to counselors (not more interest, similar interests).
   C. Stars and the bell curve of most interest inventories have a depiction of the distribution of scores for all people taking the instrument. Usually, there is a dark dot, star, or diamond to indicate where the respondent's score falls within the distribution of scores.
   D. Gender Issues

   1. Various instruments deal with gender in different ways.
   2. *SII* and *CAI* keep men and women in separate norming groups and the dark dot is given for the gender of the respondent. However, the bell curve distribution for the opposite gender is also given and can be interpreted if the difference of a score for the appropriate gender is more than one than the score for the opposite gender.
   3. *CISS* uses a coed norm group, which has both men and women in the pool.

IV. Procedural Checks, Summary of Item Responses
   A. Interest inventories give information about the respondent's answers to the instrument questions. This information indicates:
      1. If the respondent completed all the questions and if the results are valid
      2. If the answers are or are not consistent
      3. The percentage of answers in different categories
   B. Interpretations of the patterns of answers can include:
      1. A positive or negative mindset if answers are mostly positive or mostly negative.
      2. All likes or dislikes results in a flat profile where it is difficult to determine a pattern of priorities. Interpretation of pro-

(continued)

(Box 10.3 continued)

file should focus on this issue alone.

V. Special Scales

A. Special scales are general interpretations of the respondent's approach to occupations. These interpretations are based on psychological studies of the inventory data of a respondent's demographic data. Topics include:

1. Introversion/extroversion
2. Approach to education
3. Risk-taking
4. Others

B. These scales are very broad and need to be suggested tentatively to the client for reaction, trusting the client's self-opinions.

STUDY OUTLINE: KEY TERMS AND CONCEPTS

I. Client Information
   A. Find out "why" the client has come in
   B. Assess:
      1. How the client presents one's self and interacts with you
      2. Client motivation, self-esteem, self-efficacy, awareness of the world of work, and past work experiences
      3. Other important life roles. Career may not be a primary role, just a means to an end.
      4. Family and peer support
      5. How the client has made tough decisions in the past
      6. Physical functioning: sleep, diet, exercise, alcohol/drug use, hobbies, etc.
   C. Be able to shift to noncareer issues

II. To Test or Not to Test
   A. Assessment is useful because it
      1. provides a common language for the client and counselor.
      2. can be used to validate a client's self-evaluation.
      3. can expand career or personal information for a young or inexperienced client.
   B. Counselors could allow an instrument's interpretation to dominate counseling interaction or use instruments to help clients explore.
   C. Qualitatively structured assessments can be useful: card sort, career genogram
   D. Use terms such as *instrument, survey,* or *inventory* to better communicate what the assessment is.
      1. Avoid the word *test.*

E. Information must be client interpreted and processed.

1. The client has the final say on what information is useful and/or correct

III. Choosing Appropriate Instruments

A. **Norm**: A standard, model, or pattern for a group's scores as measured by an assessment tool. Norms may reflect a local, regional, or national group's scores. Interpretations of test results are based on the performance of, or normed to, a particular group. In other words, the testing participant's scores are compared to the norms, or average scores, of a defined group. Norm-referenced assessment compares clients, or groups, to others who have taken the test previously.

B. **Norming group**: The manual of assessment instruments describes the composition of the group used to establish norming scores. Attempts are made to test a broad segment of the appropriate population so scores can be compared to similar testing participants. When a test is given to an individual whose age, national origin, etc. differs dramatically from the characteristics of the norming group described, interpretations of scores must be cautious.

C. **Validity**: The degree to which an instrument tests what it says it measures. Validity can be determined by comparing a test to other tests that are known to measure a similar characteristic. Or, the construction of the instrument can be designed to apply to defined criterion.

D. **Reliability**: The degree of consistency an instrument yields, showing consistent scores over time and when the test is administered multiple times.

E. An instrument(s) should only be chosen if it meets a client's need.

1. Do not give the same battery of tests to every client.

   a. *SDS*: Client has not explored career information or expanded knowledge of self.

   b. *SII* or *CISS*: Client is in the middle of the diamond model.

   c. *CAI*: Client is pursuing a 2-year or technical degree, not a 4-year degree.

   d. *MBTI*: Useful with clients at varying places in the diamond.

   e. *16PF*: Client would be more open to a more sophisticated instrument and a career profile.

   f. ***CPI***: Client has a high psychological sophistication. Use
       with individuals pursuing upper management or similar
       types of work
   g. **Values card sort**: Use to present different values that can
       impact career.
IV. Interpreting Assessment Results
   A. Review results before the client comes in.
      1. Note general themes.
      2. Note inconsistencies between client reports and assessment
          results.
   B. Get client's response to having taken the test.
      1. May want to ask client to think about these questions while
          taking the instrument.
   C. Choose whether you will use the actual results or a counselor-gen-
       erated summary.
      1. If using actual results, what part of it will you present in ses-
          sion 1, session 2, session 3, and so on?
      2. Counselor-generated summary may be best if integrating re-
          sults from multiple instruments.
   D. Typically present results from general to specific
      1. Reverse may better match a client's cognitive style
   E. Have clients provide examples to confirm or deny results.
   F. Have client imagine how a trait (e.g., extroversion) would look in
       a job.
   G. Is a client discussing this process with family and friends?
      1. If yes, what is being said?
      2. If no, why?
   H. Integrate client's values and interests with assessment results.

EXERCISES

   1. Students bring in one of the career instruments they have taken dur-
           ing the course. They hand the instrument to their partner, and the
           partner practices interacting with the client to interpret the test.
           Partners can use 5–10 minutes to notice themes, determine surprises,
           and choose which part of the instrument to present. It is important
           that students practice saying phrases that accurately reflect what the
           instruments' results truly mean. For example, "This dark dot indicates
           you share similar interests with people in this occupation." Students
           switch roles so each student gains practice interpreting results.

2. Students can access the card sort lists in the techniques chapter (Chapter 9). Have each student get note cards, and put each term and definition on a card. The students should bring their cards to class the day of this exercise. Students can develop three cards with values or occupations not given in the chapter and share them with the class.

REFERENCES

American Counseling Association. (n.d.). *American Counseling Association code of ethics (eff. 1995)*. Retrieved May 7, 2004, from http://www.counseling.org/site/PageServer?pagename=resources_ethics#ce

Borgen, F. H. (1995). Leading edges of vocational psychology: Diversity and vitality. In W. B. Walsh & S. H. Osipow (Eds.), *Handbook of vocational psychology* (2nd ed., pp. 427–441). Hillsdale, NJ: Erlbaum.

Brems, C. (2001). *Basic skills in psychotherapy and counseling*. Belmont, CA: Brooks/Cole.

Brown, D., & Brooks, L. (1991). *Career counseling techniques.* Boston: Allyn & Bacon.

Campbell, D. (1992). *Campbell Interest and Skill Survey.* Minnetonka, MN: National Computer Systems.

Campbell, D. P., Hyne, S. A., & Nilsen, D. L. (1992). *Manual: Campbell interest and skill survey*. Minneapolis, MN: National Computer Systems.

Cattell, R. B., Cattell, A. K., & Cattell, H. E. P. *16PF®* (5th ed.). Minneapolis, MN: Pearson Assessments.

Cavanagh, M. E., & Levitov, J. E. (2002). *The counseling experience: A theoretical and practical approach* (2nd ed.). Prospective Heights, IL: Waveland Press.

Crites, J. O. (1981). *Career counseling: Models, methods, and materials.* NY: McGraw-Hill.

de Shazer, S. (1988). *Clues: Investigating solutions in brief therapy*. New York: Norton.

Elmes, D. G., Kantowietz, B. H., & Roediger H. L., III (2003). *Research methods in psychology* (7th ed.). Belmont, CA: Thomson/Wadsworth.

Figler, H., & Bolles, R. N. (1999). *The career counselor's handbook.* Berkeley, CA: Ten Speed Press.

Fredman, N., & Sherman, R. (1987). *Handbooks of measurement for marriage and family therapy.* New York: Brunner/Mazel.

Gough, H. G. (1996). *CPI™ 434 Profile.* Palo Alto, CA: Consulting Psychologists Press.

Gould, S. J. (1981). *The mismeasure of man*. New York: Norton.

Harmon, L. W., Hansen, J. C., Borgen, F. H., & Hammer, A. L. (1994). *Strong applications and technical guide*. Palo Alto, CA: Consulting Psychologists Press.

Hirsh, S., & Kummerow, J. (1989). *Life types*. New York: Warner Books.

Hoffman, E. (2002). *Psychological testing at work*. New York: McGraw-Hill.

Holland, J. L. (1996). *The occupations finder* (4th ed.). Odessa, FL: Psychological Assessment Resources.

Holland, J. L. (2004). *Self-Directed Search™*. Odessa, FL: Psychological Assessment Resources.

Holland, J. L., Fritzsche, B. A., & Powell, A. B. (1997). *Self-Directed Search: Technical manual*. Odessa, FL: Psychological Assessment Resources.

Holland, J. L., Powell, A. B., & Fritzsche, B. A. (1997). *Self-Directed Search: Professional user's guide.* Odessa, FL: Psychological Assessment Resources.

Holmberg, K., Rosen, D., & Holland, J. L. (1997). *The leisure activities finder.* Odessa, FL: Psychological Assessment Resources.

Hood, A. B., & Johnson, R. W. (1991). *Assessment in counseling: A guide to the use of psychological assessment procedures.* Alexandria, VA: American Counseling Association.

Johansson, C. B. (1986). *Career assessment inventory: The enhanced version*. Minneapolis, MN: National Computer Systems.

Liptak, J. J. (2001). *Treatment planning in career counseling*. Belmont, CA: Brooks/Cole.

Myers, I. B., & Briggs, K. (1998). *The Myers-Briggs Type Indicator®*. Palo Alto, CA: Consulting Psychologists Press.

Myers, I. B., McCaulley, M. H., Quenk, N. L., & Hammer, A. L. (1998). *A guide to the development and use of the Myers-Briggs Type Indicator®* (3rd ed.). Palo Alto, CA: Consulting Psychologists Press.

Martin, D. G. (2000). *Counseling and therapy skills* (2nd ed.). Prospect Heights, IL: Waveland Press.

Newman, B. M. (2000). The challenges of parenting infants and young children. In P. C. McKenry & S. J. Price (Eds.), *Families and change: Coping with stressful events and transitions* (pp. 45–70). Thousand Oaks, CA: Sage.

Parsons, F. (1909). *Choosing a vocation.* Boston: Houghton Mifflin.

Rosen, D., Holmberg, K., & Holland, J. L. (1997). *The educational opportunities finder.* Odessa, FL: Psychological Assessment Resources.

Rotunno, M., & McGoldrick, M. (1982). Italian families. In M. McGoldrick, J. K. Pearce, & J. Giordano (Eds.), *Ethnicity and family therapy* (pp. 340–363). New York: Guilford Press.

Seligman, L. (1994). *Developmental career counseling and assessment* (2nd ed.). Thousand Oaks, CA: Sage.

Strong, E. K. (1994). *The Strong Interest Inventory.* Palo Alto, CA: Consulting Psychologists Press.

Walter, J. L., & Peller, J. E. (1992). *Becoming solution-focused in brief therapy.* New York: Brunner/Mazel.

Wolberg, L. R. (1954). *The technique of psychotherapy.* New York: Grune & Stratton.

CHAPTER 11

Managing Career Information and Technology

Tell me, and I'll forget. Show me, and I'll remember. Involve me, and I'll learn.

Marla Jones

Over time, descriptions of career information in counseling texts and journals have listed many materials produced by the government and by publishing companies. Technological advances have expanded resources still further. Some career clients themselves have greater access to multiple sources of information and have gained more motivation for becoming informed. Thus, career counselors are now challenged more than ever to become knowledgeable in a wide variety of resources: printed, computer-based career programs, and Internet sites.

EVALUATING INFORMATION

The needs of the client determine the information required and the type of material used. This chapter's review of the standard options points to some of the considerations that need to be taken into account, but professionals must also carefully weigh what is most effective for their particular clientele. Evaluating resources and managing limited budgets to obtain the best material for client purposes can be a time-consuming and daunting task.

Career counselors often wear the hat of a specialized librarian responsible for providing information and organizing a resource center. Clients may call upon the career counselor to explain where to find material and how to deal with computer glitches. Others constituents (i.e., teachers, parents, and other professionals) may ask questions, sometimes assuming the counselor has read and remembers all the information in the library or can find information embedded in thick books or on the computer quickly. It is important to remember that patrons of career resources can learn by finding information themselves. The maintenance of material and overseeing computer systems

---

Box 11.1   National Career Development Association (NCDA) Guidelines: Evaluating Career Information

NCDA provides guidelines for evaluating career and occupational information using the following criteria (http://www.ncda.org).

1. Information is accurate and free of bias and stereotyping on the bases of gender, socioeconomic status (SES), ethnicity, race, age, religion, or disability.
2. Information is clear, concise, readable, and interesting without grammatical errors.
3. Information uses language that is non-sexist and free of jargon, and a vocabulary appropriate for library patrons.

4. Graphics, pictures, and statistics are accurate, displaying an inclusive representation of demographic groups in regards to gender, race, ethnicity, SES, age, religion, or disability.
5. Descriptions of occupations include: duties, nature of the work, work settings and conditions, training required for entry, special requirements, methods of entry, earnings, benefits, typical advancement paths, employment outlook, related occupations, and sources for additional information.
6. It is also recommended that information entail suggestions for exploring the field and gaining experience.

---

is an organizational task; however, becoming a walking encyclopedia is not a requirement or even desirable.

Written materials and Internet sources require counselor evaluation of reading level, how material is organized, and ease of access. The *Career Development Quarterly* has a section recommending titles of books for career information and book reviews. Publishers will send catalogs with descriptions of books, books series, and computer programs. Free and inexpensive materials are described by subscription services online and off.

Counselors are responsible for updating material regularly and displaying the date of publication clearly; and it is recommended that material be no more than five years old. Lee (1996) notes that young people today have grown up with computers and their approach to searching for information is different than the traditional ways of organizing libraries and resource centers. Stimulating material with a technological flavor is appreciated, concrete information is preferred, and personal contact with service providers is demanded. Though most young people are striving for traditional goals of family and career, they want to keep their options open, are looking for the good-looking jobs, and fear boring, routine, McJobs. Career counselors might sense the press young people feel to find the latest information and to always be ahead of competition by learning on the leading edge (Lee, 1996).

ORGANIZING OCCUPATIONAL INFORMATION

Berman (1997) describes the career library organization for the University of Illinois, Chicago Circle. He says that using indexes such as the *Dictionary of Occupational Titles (DOT)* (U.S. Department of Labor, 1991) or the Dewey Decimal Classification are unnecessarily complex for use by students. Instead, Berman created a classification system of 101 categories, mostly occupational titles, and several classifications for directories, special populations, and career issues.

Other career services use several common organizational systems. Holland's (1997) work environments—Realistic, Investigative, Artistic, Social, Enterprising, and Conventional—provide categories to classify occupations. The RIASEC groupings also allow clients to use the same categories found on the *Self-Directed Search* or the *Strong Interest Inventory.* The *Occupations Finder* (Gottfredson & Holland, 1996) lists the Holland Codes for thousands of occupations, standardizing the classification of information titles. The World-of-Work Map (ACT, 2000), used for the DISCOVER computer system, provides another set of 26 categories for occupations that have Holland Code equivalents. Prediger (1981) also adds the *DOT* categories of Data, People, and Things to the World-of-Work Map.

The Guide to Occupational Exploration (GOE), published by the U.S. Employment Service (USES), uses 12 clusters of occupational groupings. The USES interest inventory measures likes and dislikes related to the *GOE* occupational clusters (http://www.doleta.gov/uses/).

O*NET, originally released in 1997 and still under development, takes data from the *DOT* and offers descriptions of over 1,100 occupations categorized by 300 characteristics, including functional skills that are used in a variety of jobs. The aim is for workers to be able to determine skills and to relate them to occupations in the database and for employers to list job openings using the same system. To serve adult career clients seeking employment, crossreferencing library materials with the O*NET system is useful.

The U.S. Department of Education has identified 16 career clusters, listing occupational levels from entry level through professional level within broad industry areas. Each cluster describes the academic and technical skills, as well as the knowledge needed, for occupational performance. Descriptions of occupational categories are at http://www.ed.gov/offices/OVAE/clusters.

The choice of an organizational system for categorizing occupational material is dependent on what would be useful for the clients seeking information. Other aspects of the career service might also be considered, such as systems that correlate to the interest inventories typically used.

PROCESSING INFORMATION

Career counselors might also remember Gelatt's (1991) description of information (see Chapter 8). All information, in print and in cyberspace, has been arranged by other human beings; and its arrangement is therefore subjectively influenced. An important but sometimes neglected service is to assist clients in processing information, to make the material relevant according to the clients' individual purposes and priorities. Broad-based information can be used to explore possibilities, whereas more specific facts are needed to narrow options according to the Career Diamond's process. Questions offered in Chapter 3 can assist practitioners in evaluating the needs of clients. Counselors need to consider the readiness of clients to deal with the information and evaluate what method of receiving information would be most useful to individual clients. Counselors must also know resources well enough to orient students as to how materials are organized and to recommend specific sources for particular information. Counselors assess clients' abilities to deal with information and their readiness to make choices. Library research tasks related to clients' individual purposes help clients apply information according to each individual's criteria.

In counseling sessions or informally in the library, counselors help clients to process information so they can make sense of the descriptions and determine how the data relates to their exploration and/or decision making. Clients need to gain an understanding that guides their selection of alternative choices by setting priorities that place some alternatives as most appealing and discarding others as not relevant to their interests.

To enhance their own development, clients must take responsibility for completing counselor research assignments, working consistently to locate information, reading descriptions, and analyzing the material. Dealing with occupational information takes time, energy, and motivation and may be indicative of career maturity. Most often clients need counseling sessions to process information and to determine the application of the external factors to personal characteristics. Coming to terms with the realities of occupational requirements and determining if the client has the requisite abilities and temperament is an important aspect of career counseling.

Gysbers et al. (1998) recommends encouraging clients to pace themselves while seeking information. If too much information is obtained too quickly, the client may be overwhelmed or may not value the content. Information is valued not only for its objective content but also its motivational impact. Here the counselor serves an educational function, teaching patrons to conduct information searches and to apply information to individual concerns. Simply providing reams of facts and occupational descriptions does not serve patrons well. In the library, career clients may need to discuss what the information they are finding means to them. User-friendly material is, of course, better integrated by clients. Facilitating the use of information can be done in individual counseling, workshops, or on the spot in brief encounters in the resource center. For maximum service to clients, career libraries often employ paraprofessionals, including students, who are trained and supervised by the career professional in charge.

CAREER RESOURCE CENTER: A MODEL

The following is a description of the center designed by the first author.

Career Resource Room

For over 10 years, the author managed several career development programs at three different universities. The Student Counseling Service (SCS) at a large midwestern university can serve as an example of organizing resources and accessible services. Allocating considerable resources visibly demonstrates the department's high regard for careers as an important area of service for students. For example, the Career Exploration Center at SCS includes a large room containing two walls of bookshelves filled with small books describing occupations, pamphlets and articles, thick directories, and even a small TV/VCR unit with videos. Another wall is lined with several computers containing DISCOVER, the center's webpage, Internet links, and practice tests for graduate school admissions. A printer is accessed by all the computers. In the center of the room are a couple of comfortable chairs and a table with chairs for quiet reading and perusing.

The shelves for written materials are organized and labeled by Holland Code letters. Each letter R, I, A, S, E, C is color coded for easy return of the books to the appropriate shelf and of articles to color-coded containers. A chart on the wall shows the colors and associated letters with descriptions of the Holland categories. The chart also translates job families from DISCOVER to the same color categories. Within the Holland category on each shelf, books are randomly placed. The random placement within categories is to encourage clients' exploration. If students are looking for a particular occupation within the category, with no order provided, they are forced to come across similar occupational titles and may choose to examine other options. There is a numbering system for inventory purposes, and a computer program that lists books and other material by major and by occupation. But the overall plan is to encourage the student to stumble across information they may not have considered before. The majority of the library patrons are freshman and sophomores who have not yet chosen a major or who are changing majors, so career exploration is considered their primary need. Hence the library organizational system supports the patron's needs as defined.

Career Assistants

To maintain the library and provide assistance to students, undergraduate work-study students are trained as paraprofessional career assistants (CAs). CAs lend an air of friendly accessibility to the resource center, and they are trained to take care of materials and equipment and to helpfully inquire about the students' exploration. Periodically, CAs interrupt the student's reading or online activities to ask how the information is meeting the student's career vision. They know at what point in the DISCOVER program it is useful to *rap* with the student, asking about the job families associated with the student's interests, abilities, or values. They can discuss what it means if interests and values indicate different occupations, and they show students what to print to bring to a career counselor. Resource center patrons gave high satisfaction ratings to the CAs who were seen as helpful and knowledgeable. CAs also host an open house each semester timed to coincide with course registration. They create advertising for the career library and specific programs, and design passive programming with displays and bulletin boards describing occupations associated with a rotating list of majors.

Training for the CAs is ongoing and designed to gradually increase skills in assisting patrons and to build camaraderie for the team of paraprofessionals. Experience as a CA is seen as a resume builder and as the opportunity to help peers. An important goal of the career center is to hire students majoring in different fields. CAs can refer students to other campus services and can help students find course information in the local college catalog as well as assist in the use of directories to find other colleges with different majors. The first author created a similar peer program using high school juniors and seniors to assist students in guidance offices in a high school and a middle school.

Supervision of young people serving as paraprofessionals is time consuming. Regardless of how well trained young people are, they seek regular input, need positive reinforcement, and their judgment is inconsistent. A graduate assistant or the career coordinator needs to be readily available to CAs. Although much service benefit is obtained through their efforts at relatively low cost, it is important to note that considerable professional time is needed for supervision.

Educational Information

The career center resource room also displays information in the form of well-designed handouts on topics commonly needed by undergraduates. Topics include a description of Holland Codes with related majors, student activities, and occupations; how to evaluate occupational information and descriptions of majors; and questions for informational interviews. A section of shelves is devoted to graduate school directories and handouts describing how to apply to graduate programs and write application essays. CAs offer handouts to students and can explain the contents. Materials are also used for outreach programs given to classes and student groups throughout campus.

Walk-In Career Counseling

Across the hall from the career resource room is an office housing graduate students from two university counseling programs for the master's and doctoral degrees. Walk-in career counselors are trained to see students for brief contacts on a first-come, first-served basis. The goal is to assess the student's needs, to describe the career development process, and to determine the next appropriate step for the student's career movement. Students will often seek information and then discuss their reactions to the descriptions of occupational activities with the walk-in counselors (e.g., discuss the results of the DISCOVER program). Another service on campus schedules informational interviews for students with alumni contacts. If there is a need and students are motivated for regular ongoing career counseling, walk-in counselors complete an intake form and make appointments with the senior staff. In essence, walk-in counselors provide career education to enhance the students' developmental process. When students would benefit from an introspective identity exploration through career counseling sessions or when other psychological issues are readily apparent, the students are referred for ongoing appointments. The walk-in service captures students' interest for a teachable moment on the spot, when students come to the library. Students respond well to the attention given to their immediate needs, and many return for second and third brief contacts.

Florida State University combines the roles of library paraprofessionals and walk-in career counselors using graduate students majoring in career counseling and higher education (Lenz, 2000). The training for these career advisors is extensive, including a series of paper "scavenger hunts" in which trainees, either individually or in teams, search difference computer-assisted career guidance systems and websites. Performance appraisals for CAs and training modules are based on the recommended competencies of the NCDA.

Special Populations

Some career information centers make an effort to include material written to appeal to specific groups. There are some materials describing issues related to the career experiences of racial and ethnic minorities, gender/sexual orientation, clients with disabilities, and information for those chronically unemployed. The model career resource center provides videos of minorities, women, and people with disabilities in various professional fields providing visual role models as encouragement for students.

Computer-Assisted Career Guidance Systems

Computer-assisted career guidance systems (CACGS) are a quick and efficient service method, and students appreciate the modern technological presentation of the trait-factor approach. Typically, programs such as DISCOVER, SIGI+, and CHOICES offer interest inventories, values checklists, and self-report assessments of abilities. The computer programs match the self-chosen attributes with factors characteristic for a number occupations. Occupational information is presented, decision-making steps are described, and sometimes coping strategies for transitional changes are given. CHOICES also includes templates for letters requesting college applications and financial aid.

CACGS are chosen for clients' developmental needs as are any structured interventions. CHOICES is appropriate for high school students and would be of limited value for post-secondary clientele. DISCOVER is most appropriate for ages 18 to 21, particularly college freshman and sophomores, though different versions of the program are designed for high school and more experienced adults. DISCOVER is designed to produce a list of any occupation related to personal characteristics. A summary grid shows which characteristics (interests, values, or abilities) are related to each occupational title. The effect is to produce a long list of possible occupations for consideration without any attempt to narrow the options. Thus, DISCOVER promotes exploration as in the first half of the Career Diamond. Research offering a comprehensive review of findings demonstrating the effectiveness of DISCOVER in promoting career development is published by American College Testing (Taber & Luzzzo, 1999).

SIGI+, however, is values driven, and it provides an interactive effect demonstrating how setting priorities can lengthen or shorten the list of occupations that meet the users' criteria. For example, if the user demands both high income and short working hours, the program prompt might say, there are only two occupations meeting these specifications. The program then prompts the user to answer, "Do you want to adjust your criteria?" Removing short hours may then increase the number of occupations. The users can visibly see the effect of demanding too stringent or too few criteria when the program informs them of the number of possibilities added or eliminated. SIGI+ works well for clients who have passed the initial exploration stage and who are approaching a decision as in the middle to second half of the Career Diamond.

CACGS provide immediate feedback to students, teach sequential steps to determining career choices, and offer suggestions for the next action to take. However, counselors need to be careful in assuming that all clients have the skills and cognitive functioning to use the systems well or that the programs are adaptable to individual needs. Computer systems are easily mind-numbing. Clients who are not alert to recording their true reactions and simply click in answers can create inaccurate feedback. This is why CAs interact with students while the students are working on DISCOVER, to encourage thoughtful reactions.

Listings of the sections for the programs discussed are in Table 11.1.

Iaccarino (2000) performed a literature review and an online survey of career services professionals. Other CACGS systems used for secondary students and adults include: CHOICES (Bridges, 2000), Career Information Delivery Systems* (http://www.noic.gov); Career Finder Plus (http://www.eurekanet.org/cfinder.html); CareerLeader (http://www.careerdiscovery.com); The Career Key (http://www.ncsu.edu/careerkey/index.html); CareerScope (http://www.vri.org); Career Visions Plus* (http://www.cdways.com/products/cvisions.html); CareerWAYS (http://www.cew.wisc.edu/cew/groups/carways.htm); Compute a Match System/Pesco 2001 (http://www.pesco.org); Embark.com (http://www.embark.com). Stars indicate the systems have versions available for middle school students.

Table 11.1 CACGS Program Sections

DISCOVER* (http://www.act.org)	SIGI+ (http://www.ets.org/sigi/)	CHOICES*
1. Beginning the career journey	1. Introduction	1. Relate interests to occupations
2. Learning about the world of work	2. Self-assessment	2. College letter writer to ask for information from selected colleges
3. Learning about yourself	3. Search	
4. Finding occupations	4. Information	3. Financial aid letter writer asking for information
5. Learning about occupations	5. Skills	
6. Making educational choices	6. Preparing	
7. Planning next steps	7. Coping	
8. Planning your career	8. Deciding	
9. Making transitions	9. Next steps	

Each system has its own strengths. Some have videos showing people on the job; some specialize in careers in business; some are tied to the *Occupational Outlook Handbook (OOH)*; some allow students to develop portfolios; some identify transferable skills; some measure interests, abilities, and values; and some include educational information as well as occupational information. Only counseling professionals familiar with the needs of their particular clientele and aware of budget constraints and community support can choose the system most effective for their services. The NCDA provides guidelines for selection and evaluation (http://ncda.org/acsi_pubs1.html). The website for Florida State University Center for the Study of Technology in Counseling and Career Development (http://www.career.fsu.edu/techcenter) supplies research studies for many programs and bibliographic information.

The respondents to Iaccarino's survey (2000) listed cost as the primary factor in choosing CACGS. Sampson et al. (1994) provide a cost analysis of a number of CACGS that also evaluates systems according to long list of complex issues: career assessment; matching capabilities for skills, ability, and education/training; number of searches accommodated; the quality and arrangement of occupational information; provision of educational information including financial aid information; sections for adult transitions; descriptions of career decision making and feedback to users regarding their choices; job search information or lists of resources; ability of the system to save information for multiple uses; user-friendly features; data collection for compiling reports regarding the system's use; support materials; training manuals; availability of demonstration copies; and explanation of all costs.

Costs for CACGS were found by Sampson et al. (1998) to be from $250 to $1,850 for a year's lease. However, in recent years, costs have been going down as state information systems produced more inexpensive systems (CIDS, described in next section) and as commercial providers developed online systems (described in online section).

Supplementing the use of CACGS with counselor contact enhances the use of the computer systems. Career workshops can provide an introductory session to prepare students; then students individually can use the program; then follow-up sessions discuss what students learned. Richard Pyle (2000) describes a three-session group with two computer-based homework assignments. Group members discuss what the computer program can offer, how the generated information is applied in the career process, and what next steps to take to continue career exploration. Individual career conferences can also be held with students or with students and their parents. Promoting exploration through the efficiency of a computer matching system that also provides occupational information can facilitate career development or movement along the Career Diamond process. However, discussions with a counselor are needed to clarify career information and to facilitate psychological development. At the 2000 NCDA convention, Dr. JoAnn Harris-Bowlsbey, winner of the 1999 Eminent Career Research Award, said, "Though use of computer-delivered material without human support is better than no assistance at all, the most effective way to help people with career planning is through a planned combination of technology and human support" (Harris-Bowlsbey, 2000). Indeed, researchers Garis and Niles (1990) note that CACG systems may not be used appropriately as stand-alone interventions.

Gati (1996) recommends that counselors help clients utilize computer-assisted career programs. The author notes that if the student elicits a very long list of occupational possibilities, the amount of information could be overwhelming and discourage students in further exploration. On the other hand, if a student uses the computer sorting occupational search and determines only a few possibilities, career exploration is too limited. In discussing computer-generated lists, the counselor can determine how the client is increasing or decreasing the number of alternatives considered. The counselor can also determine if the values the client lists are compatible with interests and abilities. Discussing these issues with clients can facilitate understanding that the client's choices determine the possible alternatives.

Ballantine and Sampson (1995) describe the use of CACGS within organizations by human resource departments to assist individual employees in clarifying their career goals. Companies use aggregate reports to understand employees' values and interests and then tie the employee information to company goals in team building and job designs. As companies attempt to maintain the motivation and commitment of employees in fluid job placements, considering both the individual and organizational perspectives through computer-generated data might serve both the company and the employee.

DISCOVER-e

Some websites are interactive in that users can take assessment surveys and match personal characteristics online as with CACGS and CIDS. As was mentioned previously, the model resource center has both the CD-ROM version of DISCOVER, in which students use the program on site, and the DISCOVER-e capability, in which students are given a user's code to access the program at home. The advantage of students using the program on site is the availability of CAs and walk-in career counselors who can further facilitate the patron's exploration. Also, the CD-ROM version has more sophisticated graphics that students find appealing and motivating. Using a computer system online adds convenience for users who can complete a program on home computers at any time. A disadvantage of handing out user numbers is that professional input could be lost if students do not return to the center. Still, the walk-in counselor can go online and find a summary of the sections the client used, and how much time was spent per section. Follow-up e-mails to clients can encourage continued contact between clients and counselors.

Career Information Delivery Systems

From the late 1970s through 1991, a congressional initiative entitled the National Occupational Information Coordinating Committee (NOICC) distributed career programs similar to CACGS. State Occupational Information Coordinating Committees (SOICCS) offered schools and community agencies free software that permitted the users to go online and use the system. Career Information Delivery Systems (CIDS) include four components: assessment, occupational search, occupational information, and educational information. The self-assessment category includes a values survey, an interest inventory, a skill identifying instrument, and a test that summarizes work experiences. Users establish criteria for the occupational search that can be changed if the matching occupations are not to the users liking, similar to SIGI+.

Although NOICC was disbanded in 1991, SOICCS are still operating. Inexpensive state computer programs have extended user sites to those who could not afford the systems developed in the private sector. Not only were leasing fees prohibitive for some career centers, but there was also the problem that maintaining and replacing the hardware or the computers themselves was an unaffordable budget item. Administrators sometimes question the cost effectiveness of designating computers for the single use of CACGS. Once CIDS programs increased the competition, the impact was to reduce costs for CACGS and to encourage development of online systems. For the model career center, DISCOVER costs were reduced in 2001 to such a degree that the original CD-ROM versions have been maintained and DISCOVER-e was added as a service.

GOVERNMENT AGENCIES' INFORMATION

Dictionary of Occupational Titles and *Guide for Occupational Exploration*

Traditionally, career libraries have housed a number of directories that included occupational information published by governmental agencies. These dense and thorough guides are filled with labor market data, but are difficult for students and laypeople to use. However, career counselors included the volumes in order to have a full listing of occupational descriptions that could be translated for library patrons. In the 1970s, when the first author was in training, much of the time in a career counseling course was spent learning how to use the classification system for *The Dictionary of Occupational Titles (DOT, 1991)*. Thankfully, current students are spared such training because the laborious system is not readily usable for clients.

In 1979, the government streamlined the *DOT (1991)* layered categorizing system and classified occupations by interest areas in the *Guide of Occupational Exploration (GOE, Farr, 2001)*. Though the *GOE* simplified the procedures for finding occupational descriptions, the occupational descriptions are still dense, and young people often need translations to understand the material. The value of such volumes is the extensiveness of the listings, 2,500 for the *GOE* and many more for the *DOT (1991)*. Job descriptions include work activities, skills and abilities required, related interests, training requirements, and other additional information. In the late 1980s during the beginning waves of downsizing and layoffs, the *DOT* (U.S. Dept. of Labor, 1991) was found inadequate for helping workers find jobs using their transferable skills. The *GOE* is still published, but some descriptions have not kept up with changes in occupations occurring over the last decade. By 1994, the Department of Labor modernized and began a new effort to classify occupations, titled the Occupational Information Network or O*NET.

O*NET

Figure 11.1 shows the domains of O*NET (http://www.onetcenter.org), an online system for classifying worker characteristics and relating these to occupational factors. The worker characteristics are in four boxes starting at the top, going around the left side of the O*NET circle and coming around to the bottom square. The occupational factors are in two boxes on the right. The database for O*NET classifies 1,172 occupations and provides information for all. As with the *DOT (1991)*, the new system allows employers to classify the characteristics of jobs and workers to identify skills and abilities. Job factors and workers' abilities can be matched in a cross-referencing system. Interested people can also find an interest profiler measuring Holland personality types and a values inventory entitled the *Work Importance Locator*. Like CACGS, the O*NET system will match interests and values with related occupational titles.

In 2004, the O*NET database was updated using alternate occupational titles to improve keyword search performance. The data collection program is updated twice a year. An *Ability Profiler* (2003) matches work skills to occupations. A Spanish version of the O*Net database translates occupational

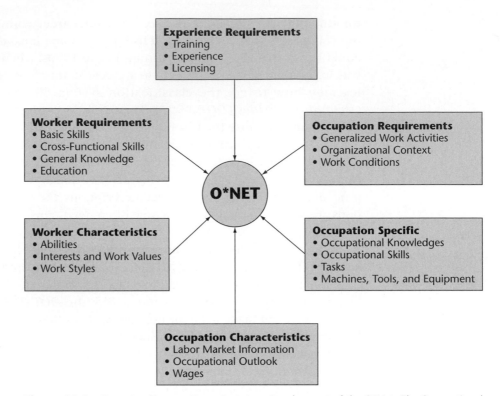

Figure 11.1   Domains (Source: From *Prototype Development of the O*Net: The Occupational Information Network,* by J. Nottingham and J. Gulec, updated, Raleigh: North Carolina Occupational Analysis Field Center.)

information using the same format. Another feature allows for a "crosswalk" (*Crosswalk Service Center, NCSC*) from one job classification to another. Educational and experience requirements are listed as well as apprenticeship information.

O*NET is linked to Career One Stop (http://www.careeronestop.org), which contains a job bank (America's Job Bank [AJB], http://www.ajb.org), a section describing job trends for states and cities throughout the nation, a listing of courses and training providers, and a list of public service offices assisting the unemployed. Employers can list occupations, and job seekers can list their skills, both according to the same system. AJB reported that 313,994 registered employers used the service in 2003, with 1,081,776 jobs, and 5,151,736 job seekers registered. Career counselors can network with other professionals through associations, find resources for education and certification training, and keep up with trends in the job market and Labor Department initiatives. Counselors can also use printable materials to orient clients to the Career One Stop services. Although AJB and O*NET are an excellent source of career information, the classification system is difficult for many young people who often find the simpler *Occupational Outlook Handbook* (*OOH*) more useful for exploration purposes.

Occupational Outlook Handbook

The Department of Labor provides another standard publication for career information centers, titled the *Occupational Outlook Handbook (OOH)*. It is available in print form, CD-ROM, and online (http://www.bls.gov/oco/). The information of interest is the government's projection of the outlook for individual occupations. Printed in book form, a subscription for quarterly updates is also available. The online and CD-ROM versions also contain short interest and values surveys. Recently, the first author mentioned the importance of values to a client at the end of a counseling session. The client left and went online to the *OOH*. Later in the day, an e-mail from the client indicated excitement about the combination of reputable government information and his personal priorities. Most clients are not as enthusiastic about information published by the government, but many find the resource reputable and the *OOH* system comparatively easy to use.

Department of Defense, Service Branches

The publication *America's Top Military Careers: The Official Guide to Occupations in the Armed Forces* (U.S. Department of Defense, 2000) describes positions and training available in the military. Young people considering military service would do well to research information to inform their conversations with recruiters. Gaining a job assignment and/or the training related to personal interests is enhanced if the potential recruit is informed. Each branch of the armed forces also has a specific website:

U.S. Army: http://www.armedforcescareers.com
U.S. Navy: http://www.navyjobs.com
U.S. Air Force: http://www.af.mil
U.S. Marine Corps: http://www.usmc.mil
U.S. Coast Guard: http://www.uscg.mil/jobs

OTHER INFORMATION SOURCES

Other Directories

Reference books for career libraries also typically include directories that list academic institutions, such as postsecondary technical schools, junior colleges, and four-year colleges and universities. The career resource centers in colleges include directories for graduate schools and sometimes volumes providing practice tests for admissions. Similar to the *DOT, GOE,* and *OOH,* the *Dictionary of Holland Occupational Codes* (Gottfredson & Holland, 1996) is a nongovernmental publication that is useful for finding occupations organized using RIASEC.

Websites

Many young people with access to computers enjoy using websites to gain information. However, the information displayed on websites can range from valuable to poor. One skill taught in career workshops that is needed by many clients is how to sift through the junk and find what is useful. Clients can learn how to use search engines efficiently by using key words that lower the number of hits and also increase the quality and relevance of the sites found. Hambley and Magnusson (2001) say that career counselors may need training in Internet usage in order to know how to retrieve high-quality career information. Baldwin (1998) suggests clients are more likely to use the Internet if they have a career counselor who is using it on a regular basis and is enthusiastic about information found.

Although the government agency sites are generally accurate, they are not always written in a form that captures the interest of young browsers. Many university websites provide educational information, and university career services have websites, often embedded within larger sites for the placement services or counseling centers. The model career service website (iastate.edu; students; student counseling; services; counseling; career/ or ksu.edu/acic/career/option.html#career) contains many of the handouts available in the resource center and is linked to other university sites.

Professional associations and organizations and private corporations and companies also have websites describing occupations. The National Career Development Association site (http://ncda.org) has links labeled the career development process, self-assessment, employment trends, educational information, apprenticeships, job search, and online counseling in addition to others. Other good sites are http://www. collegeboard.org/ and http://www.collegenet.com/.

It is helpful to create handouts describing career web surfing and a loose-leaf binder directory naming sites that patrons have found useful. Such a listing of sites must be updated regularly because sites come and go and the information varies in quality over time. Student paraprofessionals with a knack for web surfing enjoy the assignment of reviewing sites.

Job Search Sites

A large portion of career information on the Web consists of jobs openings (cyberuiting; e-recruiting) and available candidates (Kirk & Murrin, 1999). Students not yet participating in job search activities can get lost among the numerous listings from companies recruiting entry-level employees. Outplacement firms such as those who are members of the Association of Outplacement Consulting Firms International (AOCFI), include job search trends and a message board. The online career center (http//www. online-sports.com pages. careercenter.html) lists positions available and job seekers (Kirk & Murrin, 1999). Newsgroups offer career information and a vehicle for interacting with careerists who can offer advice, contacts, and a network resource. Online contacts can help job seekers prepare for interviews and some actual interviewing. Companies like Nike or Macy's ask multiple choice questions and eliminate half of the respondents because they do not fit in the organization's culture. Some job placement Internet sites such as Net.CareerWeb (http://www.cweb.com) offer job hunting advice, articles, and career changing techniques. The National School Network Exchange (http/nsn.bbn.com/) offers telementoring in which students and professionals can develop mentoring contacts. Mentors can be found through professional associations as well. Cybercoaching is also available for fees. If students who are exploring possibilities rather than job hunting are taught to circumvent the job listings, much up-to-date career information is available. Tables 11.2 and 11.3 show active job search sites and advice-giving cyberspace columns available as of June 2004.

Virtual Job Fairs

Miller and McDaniels (2001) describe online job fairs where job openings and resumes are exchanged for a specified time through the auspices of university career centers. Students and employers utilize e-mail services, chat rooms, and online job applications. In the future, even virtual interviews could be arranged with the combined use of computers and video equipment. Employers could offer tours of their companies and present public relations messages advertising the organizations' mission.

Table 11.2   Job Search/Career Planning Websites

Website	Address
Career Development Manual	http://www.cdm.uwaterloo.ca
Career Planning Process	http://www.bgsu.edu
Creative Job Search	http://mapping-your-future.org
Professionals Job Search Guide	http://www.mnwfc.org/cjs
Planning Manual	http://www.works.state.mo.us/tips/index.htm
The Riley Guide	http://www.rileyguide.com
Jobs listings/advice	http://www.monster.com

Table 11.3   Career Advice/Information Sites

Site	Address
The Wall Street Journal	http://career.wsj.com
San Francisco Examiner	http://.examiner.com/careersearch
Ask An Expert	www.askanexpert.com
The Dixon Report	http://www.pamdixon.com
Jobs Online	http://jobweb.org
Job Hunter's Bible	http://www.jobhuntersbible.com/index.html
Joyce Lain Kennedy	http://www.sunfeatures.com/
National Business Empl.	http://www.usjobnet.com

Career Information for International Opportunities

In the era of globalization, career information may need to take on an international flavor. Columbia and Rice universities offer model programs that supply information regarding study abroad prospects, occupational descriptions, and outreach presentations designed to broaden students' crosscultural understanding. Citing studies documenting American international illiteracy (National Governor's Association, 1989; Vobeja, 1986), Sanborn (1992) suggests future careerists may need to expect to travel globally and to interact with crosscultural customers regularly. Career counselors may be pressed to provide information that allows careerists to play international work roles.

CAREER COUNSELING ONLINE

Career counseling online is a practice that is coming of age. Although many career-related websites are currently limited to information, the next step of providing counseling online is becoming a reality. Many career coaching sites are available. Professional associations express concerns about the counselor–client relationship in online counseling as well as ethical issues, such as maintaining confidentiality.

Cohen and Kerr (1998) found that computer-mediated counseling was effective in reducing client anxiety, and client attitudes toward online counseling were positive. Comparing ratings of counselors' expertness, attractiveness, and trustworthiness were no different than ratings for face-to-face counseling. Matheson and Zanna (1998) note that eliminating in person interaction allowed clients to focus on their internal process rather than the presentation of their public image. The anonymous quality of online interactions also encourages clients to share personal feelings more quickly, as when clients call hotlines for crisis intervention (Rutter, 1987; Wark, 1982). Wellman (1996) and Sander (1996) comment that cyberspace exchanges increase the client's feelings of safety and ability to share embarrassing information. Cohen and Kerr (1998) suggest that computer counseling could avoid stereotyped reactions to clients' appearances and could decrease counselor assumptions. Also, the convenience of sending messages at anytime allows both the counselor and the client time to consider what their messages may mean.

However advantageous, confidentiality on the Internet is sometimes less than secure, though expensive Web-based message security systems are available (Manhal-Baugus, 2001). Clients may not know the competency of the counselor as easily unless there is a system for verifying credentials. Metanoia (http://www.metanoia.com) provides a list of professional websites along with a consumer guide about the counselors' credentials, though none of the counseling specialties listed include career. The counselor does not necessarily know from session to session if messages are from the same client or from someone else using the client's e-mail account. Misunderstandings over the Net may not be acknowledged and clarified. Licensing and certification requirements monitored by states are ineffective when counseling occurs across state lines. And, most important, there is little research to determine if online counseling is effective and what competencies are required.

The American Counseling Association and the National Board for Certified Counselors have both issued ethical guidelines for Web counselors that are applicable for personal and career counseling. Both suggest informed consent pages to describe the risks to confidentiality and the limits of the online counseling relationship. Verifying the identity of clients, including the identity of parent/guardians providing consent for minors, is ethically required. Counselors are ethically bound to provide links to websites for certification agencies and licensing boards and to determine crisis intervention resources for the client's geographical locality. Ethical codes are included in the Appendix B.

Arizona State University has several Internet career education programs. The online exchanges are intended to change irrational career beliefs and occupational stereotyping in order to encourage client cognitive restructuring. One program educates parents on how to help children enhance their career development. Another is designed to alter self-defeating attributions that block the motivation of at-risk youth (Clark, Horan, Tompkins-Bjorkman, Kovalski, & Hackett [2000]).

Boer (2001) distinguishes between placement job search websites and career coaching and career counseling websites. Placement and coaching services respond to clients' questions with expert information whereas online counselors create a private relationship with individual clients via e-mail. Online career counselors pay attention to the tone of the written messages, the client's use of language, and the implied affect. Coaches may respond in public forums or chat room settings. Boer also notes that counselors can apply counseling skills such as responding to affect online only if the written message is valued and treated as though the client were sitting in the counseling room face to face.

Sussman (1998) makes a case for counseling online by describing the accessibility of the service for underserved populations, those living in isolated geographical areas, those with transportation difficulties, and those who are reluctant to seek services and feel safer talking to someone from their homes. Lee (1998) portrays the current generation as fully comfortable with online communication, and Watts (1998) suggests that Internet services may be a part of the change occurring in the world of work, requiring career counselors to fully implement lifelong career counseling. The press to provide services through the increasingly used medium has resulted in NCDA creating Web counseling guidelines. NBCC (http://www.nbcc.org/ethics/webethics.htm) and NCDA (http://www.ncda.org/) also have their own websites offering a public display of professional guidelines and lists of certified counselors by geographical location.

Online counseling requires knowledge of resources available on the Internet to cite for client use. Just as counselors refer clients to library resources, online counselors are familiar with Internet resources and develop the skill to determine which sites are the most appropriate for each client. Helping clients work though the myriad information available is a must. When counseling via e-mail messages, the counselor must be able to pick up clients' cues in the tone of their writing and to respond concisely. Online career counseling also requires keeping up with the latest technology in both hardware and software. Boer's (2001) research and experience leads her to recommend that Internet counselors have experience with face-to-face career counseling and that a new credential for certifying online counselors be developed.

Boer (2001) distinguishes between online counseling and other career services offered on the Internet. Public usenet or online groups, Web forums, listservs, message boards, and chat rooms are exchanges between Internet users, not professional exchanges. Monster.com has developed toolkits on specific topics of interest to special populations such as older workers, those in military transition, career changers, and those interested in nonprofit organizations. Toolkits offer specialized information and links to message boards. Emis and Dillingham (2002) also report the effectiveness of an online record-keeping system for Texas high school students developing a career portfolio through supervised agricultural experience programs. Although these sites are useful to users, and career counselors may recommend them, they offer information, not counseling.

The use of assessment instruments with online clients follows a pattern similar to using instruments in face-to-face contact. First, counselors spend time listening to clients describe their situations, their goals, and their expectations for test results. Specific instruments are chosen for particular clients, and only assessments that have been tested as reliable via computer delivery are used. Clients are provided an access code for a secured site for test administration and scoring, protecting the confidentiality of the user's results. Clients and counselors discuss the results in follow-up sessions, assuring that interpretations are understood by the client and integrated with the client's overall purposes. Online counseling could promote a test-and-tell interchange rather than a fully professional integration of assessment results. Skilled counselors would need to develop Internet methods to encourage processing so clients don't leave their computers saying, "The test told me to be a _____."

Clearly, the Internet offers both promising opportunities and some risks for career counselors. As this field develops, it will become clearer what competencies and methods counselors need to provide competent and convenient service for clients.

SUMMARY

Implementing services to provide information to clients as per the bottom half of the Career Diamond is a daunting professional task. The practitioner must develop the skills of a specialized librarian organizing information, computer delivery systems, videos, and so on. The career practitioner also considers the educational needs of center users. Technology has added the need for additional competencies given the popularity of CD-ROM systems and online websites that provide information and interactive activities. In our changing world, new developments are rapidly adding technological interventions for career counseling, including counseling on the Internet. Career practitioners certainly must be lifelong learners if they are to keep up with exciting changes.

STUDY OUTLINE: KEY TERMS AND CONCEPTS

    I. Managing Career Information and Technology
       A. Evaluating occupational information
           1. NOICC guidelines

B. Organizing information
   1. Materials chosen according to the needs of population served
      a. Usefulness and motivating appeal to users
      b. Systems: Holland; *DOT; GOE;* O*NET
C. Processing information
   1. All materials are subjectively influenced.
   2. Integrating client priorities with occupational characteristics
D. Librarian and educator role
   1. Clients need to use slow pace in reviewing information.
   2. Too much information can be overwhelming.
   3. Career educator assists in application of information to client's career identity.
E. Model career resource center
   1. Materials
      a. Materials organized by Holland Code
      b. Within RIASEC category, materials randomly placed to encourage exploration
      c. Educational handouts of interest to center patrons
F. Career assistants
   1. Provide for maintenance of resources
   2. Serve as receptionists
   3. Initiate dialogues with clients regarding career information
   4. Create publicity materials
   5. Host open houses
   6. Gain ongoing training and camaraderie with CA group
   7. Good experience for resume
G. Walk-in career counselors
   1. Brief contacts—first-come, first-served
   2. Determine student needs, assign next career activity, explain information, review DISCOVER results, refer to ongoing career counseling
II. Computer-Assisted Career Guidance Systems (CACGS)
   A. DISCOVER, SIGI+, CHOICES
      1. Programs designed for different developmental levels
      2. Include personal assessment: Interests, abilities or skills, values
      3. Match personal characteristics with related occupational factors (trait-factor)
      4. Maximum benefit gain by users if they can provide accurate input and spend time considering choices
      5. Follow-up provided by career practitioners
   B. Computer Information Delivery Service (CIDS)

1. Inexpensive CACGS programs online.
2. Provided by NOICCs and SOICCSs
C. Government agencies' information
1. *DOT* and *GOE:* Extensive classification systems for worker traits and occupational factors
2. O*NET: Online classification system replacing *DOT*
a. Contains self-assessment surveys
b. Includes sections for job bank, job trends, training information, and list of services for unemployed
D. *OOH:* Gives brief occupational descriptions with future outlook
1. Available in print, online, and CD-ROM versions containing self-assessment surveys.
2. Defense Department Occupational material describes positions in military.
3. Other directories: School indexes; Dictionary of Holland Codes
4. Materials dealing with relevant issues for minority groups and women
E. Websites
1. Occupational information offered by companies, corporations, universities, and professional associations.
2. Information varies in quality.
3. Users need to learn how to do effective searches and how to judge quality of information.
4. DISCOVER-e
a. Online application of CACGS
b. Provides convenience for clients who are motivated to follow up services
III. Career Counseling Online
A. Reduces client anxiety
B. Rated highly by users
C. May encourage emotional sharing given anonymous interaction
D. Allows time between reactions
E. Ethical concerns: Confidentiality; counselor-client relationship; requires informed consent, verifying identities, links to certifying bodies.

EXERCISES

1. Students are to search the Web for three websites. The first should be of excellent quality and one that could be greatly beneficial. The second website should be of medium quality, and the final site should be just plain horrible. The student is to write up a one- to two-page description of why each site received the rating it did. Second, can the student teach those evaluation skills to a client?

REFERENCES

Baldwin, N. (1998). The world wide web as a career resource. In *Technology & career and employment counseling: A compendium of thought* (pp. 7-10). Toronto, Ontario: The Counseling Foundation of Canada.

Ballintine, M., & Sampson, J., Jr. (1995). The use of computer-assisted career guidance systems with adults at work. *Career Planning and Adult Development Journal,* Spring, 14–20.

Berman, L. A. (1997). The Chicago Circle career library. *Personnel and Guidance Journal,* October, 101–105.

Boer, P. M. (2001). *Career counseling over the internet: An emerging model for trusting and responding to online clients.* Mahwah, NJ: Erlbaum.

Clark, G., Horan, J. J., Tompkins-Bjorkman, A., Kovalski, T., & Hackett, G. (2000). Interactive career counseling on the internet. *Journal of Career Assessment, 8*(1), 85–93.

Cohen, G. E., & Kerr, B. A. (1998). Computer-mediated counseling: An empirical study of a new mental health treatment. *Computers in Human Services, 15*(4), 13–26.

Emis, L., & Dillingham, J. (2002, December). MyAgRecord: An online career portfolio management tool for high school students conducting supervised agricultural experience programs. Paper presented at the Annual Conference of the Association for Career and Technical Education, Las Vegas, NV.

Farr, M. J. (Ed.) (2001). *Guide for occupational exploration system.* Indianapolis, IN: JIST Works.

Garis, J. W., & Niles, S. G. (1990). The separate and combined effects of SIGI or DISCOVER and a career planning course on undecided university students. *Career Development Quarterly, 38,* 261–275.

Gati, I. (1996). Computer-assisted career counseling: Challenges and prospects. In M. L. Savickas & W. B. Walsh (Eds.). *Handbook of career counseling theory and practice* (pp. 169–190). Palo Alto, CA: Davies-Black.

Gelatt, H. B. (1991). *Creative decision making: Using positive uncertainty.* Lanham, MD: National Book Network.

Gottfredson, G. D., & Holland, J. L. (1996). *Dictionary of Holland occupational codes.* Odessa, FL: Psychological Assessment Resources.

Gysbers, N. C., Heppner, M. J., & Johnston, J. A. (1998). *Career counseling: Process, issues and techniques.* Boston: Allyn & Bacon.

Hambley, L. A., & Magnusson, K. (2001). The receptivity of career practitioners toward career development resources on the internet. *Canadian Journal of Counseling, 35*(4), 288-297.

Harris-Bowlsbey, J. H. (2000). Words to the wise. Paper presented at National Career Development Association conference, Pittsburg, PA.

Holland, J.L. (1997). *Making vocational choices.* Odessa, FL: Psychological Assessment Resources.

Iaccarino, G. (2000). Computer-assisted career guidance systems. In D. A. Luzzo (Ed.), *Career counseling of college students* (pp. 173-200). Washington, DC: American Psychological Association.

Kirk, J. J., & Murrin, J. (1999). *On-line Career Services: A brief update.* U.S. Department of Education, Educational Resources Information Center (ERIC #ED432673).

Lee, C. A. (1998). Characteristic of Generation X and implications for reference services and the job search. In D. A. Lorenzen (Ed.), *Career planning and job searching in the information age* (pp. 51-71). New York: Haworth Press.

Lenz, J. G. (2000). *Paraprofessionals in career services: The Florida State University mode.* U.S. Department of Education, Educational Resources Information Center (ERIC #ED453457).

Manhal-Baugus, M. (2001). E-therapy: Practical, ethical, and legal issues. *CyberPsychology and Behavior, 4*(5), 551-563.

Matheson, K., & Zanna, M. P. (1998). Persuasion as a function of self-awareness in computer-mediated communication. *Social Behavior, 4,* 99-111.

Miller, K. L., & McDaniels, R. M. (2001). Cyberspace, the new frontier. *Journal of Career Development, 27*(3), 199-206.

National Governor's Association. (1989). *America in transition: The international frontier.* Washington, DC: Author.

Prediger, D. J. (1981). Getting ideas out of DOT and into vocational guidance. *Vocational Guidance Quarterly, 29,* 293-305.

Pyle, K. R. (2000). Career counseling in an information age: The promise of "high touch" in a "high tech" age. *Career Planning and Adult Development Journal,* Fall, 7-27.

Rutter, D. R. (1987). *Communicating by telephone.* Oxford: Pergamon Press.

Sampson, J. P., Jr., Reardon, R. C., Reed, C., Rudd, E., Lumsden, J., Epstein et al. (1998). A differential feature-cost analysis of seventeen computer-assisted career guidance systems. Number 10 (8th ed.). Tallahassee: Florida State Univ., Center for the Study of Technology in Counseling and Career Development.

Sanborn, R. D. (1992). *Internationalizing career planning: A new perspective for college career centers.* U.S. Office of Education, Educational Resources Information Center (ERIC/CAPs #ED348624).

Sander, R. M. (1996). Couples group therapy conducted via computer-mediated communication: A preliminary case study. *Computers in Human Behavior, 12*(2), 301–312.

Sussman, R. J. (1998). Counseling online. *CTOnline, Special Report.* http://www.counseling.or/ctonline/sr598/sussman.htm.

Taber, B. J., & Luzzo, D. A. (1999). *A comprehensive review of research evaluating the effectiveness of DISCOVER in promoting career development.* Iowa City, IA: ACT Research Report Series.

U.S. Department of Defense (2000). *America's top military careers: The official guide to occupations in the armed forces.* Washington, DC: U.S. Government Printing Office.

U.S. Department of Defense, Office of the Assistant Secretary for Manpower, Installations, and Logistics (1984). *Military occupational and training data.* Washington, DC: U.S. Government Printing Office.

U.S. Department of Labor, Bureau of Labor Statistics. *Occupational outlook handbook (2002).* Washington, DC: U.S. Government Printing Office.

U.S. Department of Labor, Employment and Training Administration. (1991). *Dictionary of occupational titles,* Vol. I (4th ed.). Lincolnway, IL: VGM Career Horizons, NTC Publishing Group.

Vobeja, B. (1986, November 22). U.S. students called internally illiterate. *Washington Post,* 18–20.

Wark, V. (1982). A look at the work of telephone counseling center. *Personnel and   Guidance Journal, 61*(2), 110–112.

Watts, A. G. (1998). *A new concept of career for a new millennium: Implications for theory, policy and practice.* Keynote paper presented at the National Career Development Association Seventh Global Conference, re-shaping career development in the 21st century, Chicago, IL.

Wellman, B. (1997). An electronic group is virtually a social network. In S. Kiesler (Ed.), *The culture of the internet* (pp. 179-205*).* Mahwah, NJ: Erlbaum.

PART IV

Career Development and Education

CHAPTER 12

Career Development in Elementary School

When we observe the slow development of a child, we may be certain no evolution of human life is possible without the presence of a protecting community. The various obligations of life carry in themselves the necessity for a division of labor which not only does not separate human beings, but strengthens their bonds.

Alfred Adler, 1927

Professionals working with school-aged children will benefit from an understanding of the career literature as well as the general developmental literature. In this chapter, we focus on important developmental concepts that should supplement the theories in Chapters 4 and 5, add to the career literature, aid in the understanding of children, and aid in the preparation of effective school-based career exercises and programs. Super (1957) labels all but the oldest elementary school age children (ages 4–10) as developmentally in the fantasy stage, and Super (1983) describes the goals of early career education as developing children's basic academic skills and their readiness for functional autonomy, self-esteem, internal locus of control, and a future perspective. To that end, this chapter focuses on skill building (language development, analytical thought, problem solving); development of values and morals; learning interpersonal skills (listening, communicating, sharing, meeting others' needs, identifying people who can meet one's own needs); and learning intrapersonal skills (introspection, identifying own needs, motivations, goals, desires, passions). A second goal of the early years is exposure to the adult world of work. Grutter (2000) describes these years as a time of discovery and awareness. The young child begins to discover interests and to become aware of abilities, which is fostered through varied play, school activities, role-playing, and unconditional support.

Notice there is a lack of a constriction of the Career Diamond for elementary school (K–5) children (Figure 12.1). The job of children is to learn basic concepts about family, community, and societal values that will benefit them

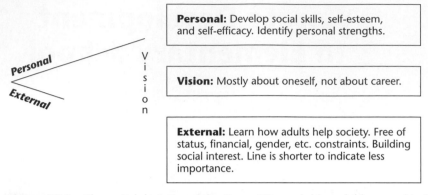

Personal: Develop social skills, self-esteem, and self-efficacy. Identify personal strengths.

Vision: Mostly about oneself, not about career.

External: Learn how adults help society. Free of status, financial, gender, etc. constraints. Building social interest. Line is shorter to indicate less importance.

Figure 12.1   The partial depiction of the Career Diamond shows children need to focus on Self development. The external world is less important. A Vision for the future may be building, but decision making is not in the picture.

as they grow up and enter the adult world. Specific to career, children can learn to appreciate how different professions benefit the world. Visions of the future can be fantastic for children, and even though they are highly unrealistic, the important themes developed during this phase can be tempered later. A fantastic future motivates a child to want to grow up and approach adulthood positively.

THE NATIONAL CAREER DEVELOPMENT GUIDELINES (NOICC, 1992) AND A CAREER DEVELOPMENT PROGRAM FOR KINDERGARTEN TO FIFTH GRADE

The National Career Development Guidelines

We recognize the important contribution made by career development researchers, and *The National Career Developmental Guidelines* (National Occupational Information Coordinating Committee [NOICC], 1992) is a significant work. Well-established guidelines are important because they can be used to develop and/or evaluate ongoing career development programs. First, they offer a common language for researchers, educators, and legislators. Second, they offer clearly defined goals for outcomes research. Finally, the goals are age specific and based upon the developmental literature.

NOICC launched its guidelines in 1987 by field testing them in several states, making revisions, and providing grants to aid states in implementing them (Lankard, 1991; Miller, 1992). These guidelines were created by collaborating with "the professional career counseling community, local program administrators, counselor educators and state guidance supervisors.

Coordination with similar efforts by professional organizations, career development researchers, and state departments of education was stressed" (Miller, 1992, ¶ 3). Although funding for NOICC ended in 1997 (NOICC Crosswalk and Data Center Annual Report, 2000), the guidelines can easily be found with an Internet search. One is likely to find the guidelines on State Occupational Information Coordinating Committees (SOICC) websites or even on the occasional school district website.

Within each age group (elementary, middle school, high school, and adult), three major areas are to be of focus: (a) self-knowledge, (b) educational and occupational exploration, and (c) career planning (NOICC, 1992). We are restricting our listings to the major categories; however, each major area has multiple goals (e.g., under Self-Knowledge: Knowledge of the Importance of Self-Concept, NOICC describes six specific goals). Each section is comprised of age-specific set goals, and readers are encouraged to obtain a full version (please see the NOICC, 1992, reference at the end of the chapter).

NOICC and Grade School

The guidelines presented in Table 12.1 are specific to grade-school programs, and the guidelines for later age groups will be presented in their corresponding chapters. The major focus of the grade-school years is to become aware of the self (including self-concept), understand changes in male/female career roles, develop helpful attitudes, and begin to understand the broad requirements of the world of work (Lankard, 1991). Ideally, parental and community involvement will be a significant part of the career programs. School-based programs are encouraged to prepare students in all three areas, and exercises presented throughout this chapter shall refer back to this section.

Career Development Program

Gysbers and Henderson (2000) developed a K–12 Life Career Development program, and we have summarized the major points and presented them in Box 12.1. The original work does contain tasks that are broken down per year in school. We chose to summarize and group the tasks together because "the range of topics needs to reflect students' developmental needs, the community's priorities, and significant state or national initiatives" (VanZandt & Buchan, 1997, p. 7). We recognize the need for a sound program that is thorough in its delivery of Life Career Development, but we also recognize the need for school programs to be flexible and creative given the realities of the region, city, or a specific school.

Table 12.1   NOICC Career Education Guidelines

Self-Knowledge	Educational and Occupational Exploration	Career Planning
Knowledge of the importance of self-concept.	Awareness of the benefits of educational achievement.	Understanding how to make decisions.
Skills to interact with others.	Awareness of the relationship between work and learning.	Awareness of the interrelationship of life roles.
Awareness of the importance of growth and change.	Skills to understand and use career information.	Awareness of different occupations and changing male/female roles.
	Awareness of the importance of personal responsibility and good work habits.	Awareness of the career planning process. (NOICC, 1992)
	Awareness of how work relates to the needs and functions of - society.	

Please note that actual career planning is only one-third of the program and that self-knowledge and interpersonal skills and life roles, setting, and events make up the other two-thirds. The genius of Gysbers and Henderson is the focus on the entire person, hence, Life Career Development. Finally, note how simplistic the initial tasks are, but how they grow in complexity as the child ages. Finally, if one looks at their program in the other developmental chapters (this section will be repeated in the next two chapters), one will notice that themes are repeated albeit in a more complex manner. The following list contains the tasks that should be included in a career program from kindergarten through fifth grade. The section ends with an example of a grade school career exercise.

There are critiques of using established career programs and failing to adapt them to one's local or regional context. Patton and McMahon (1999) state that many career programs are one-size-fits-all. Specifically, career programs often identify topics related to the world of work without fully adapting for developmental level and individual differences. Presentation of career education material is often linear (every child encounters the material at the same time and at the same speed) and the children are not able to work at their own pace. Patton and McMahon say that many career programs are not preparing children for the future, a changing economy in which individual development is key to determining career behavior. Thus, career counselors are advised to be flexible and creative when developing a new program or modifying and adapting an existing program.

Box 12.1   Life Career Development: Student Competencies by Domains and Goals

Self-Knowledge and Interpersonal Skills

1. Begin with students becoming aware of themselves and others. Move to identifying unique attributes of self and others (K–3). Later, move to recognition of different skills and abilities across individuals, and move to identifying skills and abilities one values (4–5).
2. Age appropriate information and strategies for enhancing physical and mental health.
3. Begin with students identifying how one is self-sufficient and has personal responsibilities. Next, identify differences between home and school expectations (K–3). Demonstrate knowledge of personal responsibilities. Recognize need of increasing self-control (4–5).
4. Learn about relationships with others. Learn how to make and keep friends. Begin to understand how one impacts others' feelings (K–3). Assess the effectiveness of cooperation. Begin to assess relationships within the family (4–5).
5. Teach students about listening and speaking roles and how to be good in both (K–2). Be able to understand how one listens and talks with well known people and not so well known people. Understand how communication impacts other people's actions. End with a focus on how other people communicate thoughts and feelings (3–5).

Life Roles, Settings, and Events

1. Young children will learn how to describe what they are learning at school. Later, school knowledge will be applied to home situations, and spe-

cific study skills are identified for different school subjects (K–3). Next, students can describe how they approach different subjects (study skills). Acquired study skills can be applied to work skills (4–5).
2. Begin with an introduction to the economic system, move to the need/usefulness of rules, and end with an understanding of consumerism (1–3). Introduce the interdependence of economies and the reality of paying taxes (4–5).
3. Become aware of roles in life and how they change over time (K–3). Learn about the impact important events can have upon people. Shift from specific roles to understanding the concept of a life-style (4–5).
4. Become aware of stereotypes by projecting people into a variety of adult roles. Look at differences between peers. Become aware of how different people do different activities. Learn about choosing specific work activities and that choices can be changed (K–3). Define and describe the concept of a stereotype and how stereotypes can impact a student. Look at the stereotypes of various jobs.
5. Be introduced to the concept of "the future" and think about the near future (up to three years for younger children, but 4th and 5th graders may even want to think about 20 years from now).

Life Career Planning

1. Begin with family work roles and move toward adult work roles. Include rewards one earns through work (K–3). Look at different roles within a worker,

(continued)

(Box 12.1 continued)

and understand that workers are inter-dependent (4–5).

2. Become aware of activities that are and are not enjoyable. Describe behaviors in others that they do not like. Describe valued accomplishments (K–3). Learn about attitudes and beliefs and how they effect decisions. Be able to define what values are and give examples of personal values.

3. Identify when autonomous decision making is acceptable. Learn to accept when decisions are made for the student. Think about the thinking (metacognition) that occurs prior to making a decision (K–3). Think about how one changes a decision and when that is and is not possible. Be introduced to formal decision-making strategies (4–5).

4. What to do if there are two good choices. Identify personal decisions that are difficult. Become aware that each student has his own decision-making process. Become aware of possible rewards or consequences of decisions prior to implementation (K–3). Learn how to generate alternatives, and later learn how to compare and contrast said alternatives (4–5).

5. Be introduced to the concepts "capabilities" and "interests." Recognize that the environment can impact the development of both (K–3). Understand that there are different ways to evaluate progress toward the completion of a task. Realize that values impact how one approaches goals (4–5).

Adapted from Gysbers and Henderson, *Developing and Managing Your School Guidance Program* (2000, pp. 327–334).

LEARNING ABOUT ONE'S SELF: GENDER, MORALS, SOCIAL SKILLS, AND SELF-ESTEEM/EFFICACY

Gender

A major goal of K–5 career development is to minimize gender stereotyping, which may lead to a career being eliminated because it is considered to be men's work or women's work (Gottfredson, 1996: Gottfredson & Lapan, 1997; Gysbers & Henderson, 2000). This is especially important because from 1981–2000, women went from earning 54.7 percent to 60.1 percent of associate degrees. From 1986–2000, women went from earning 50.8 percent to 56.3 percent of bachelor's degrees; and from 1981–2000, women went from earning 50.3 percent to 57.8 percent of master's degrees (National Center for Education Statistics, n.d.). As women continue to expand their formal education, more and more work environments will open to them, and if fewer males are pursuing education, their career options may shrink. Career education needs to keep as many jobs opportunities as possible open for both boys and girls.

Box 12.2   Making Careers Concrete

Goals: Learn job-related vocabulary. NOICC (1992): Interpersonal skills, awareness of the interrelationship of life roles. Gysbers & Henderson (2000): Interpersonal skills, becoming aware of stereotypes, becoming aware of duties that are and are not enjoyable, learn about listening and speaking.

Bachay (1997) created the in-school field trip for acclimating recently immigrated students to the school. The program has excellent potential for all students and is developmentally appropriate for 1st through 3rd grades because it is concrete, experiential, and inexpensive as the field trip occurs in the very school the students are attending.

1. Meet with the children, and explain to them that many of the skills they are learning in school will be later used in their jobs. This is an interactive discussion in which the group brainstorms about needed skills (e.g., math, writing, listening skills, teamwork skills).
2. Identify the adults in the school who are to be interviewed. The children are given directions to identify three job

duties and the associated skills employed in the job observed. These skills should be directly tied to what they learned in school and may be stimulated by the previous brainstorming session.

3. Students form interview teams and take a tour of the school. They have access to a variety of people ranging from custodial staff to administrators. Bachay had the students take a photograph to go along with the reports the interview teams were to prepare.
4. The students come together after the reports have been completed. They share their knowledge with the class.

Hints: (1) Each interview team develops a set of questions. These questions should be different so that each group can share new information. (2) A list of vocabulary words for each position is provided for the children to learn. (3) If possible, school employees (minorities and women) who work in nonstereotypical positions are interviewed. (4) A variation would include parents from various careers coming to school and being available for interviews.

Gottfredson's theory (1981, 1996, 1997) postulates that between the ages of 6 and 8, children become aware of sex roles and sex-appropriate behaviors. If an occupation is identified as belonging to the opposite sex, it is actively rejected. In addition, there is an inchoate understanding of social class and that certain occupations have more or less prestige. There is further support for the idea that young children stereotype occupations. Matlin (2001) reports that children become rigid about occupational sex-typing between K–4th grades. Research by Hageman and Gladding (1983) suggests that gender stereotyping of careers solidifies a little later with 6th graders being more rigid than 3rd graders. Hageman and Gladding found that 6th grade boys and children of low SES were the most rigid. Forty percent of the 6th grade girls listed nontraditional jobs as most appealing; however, 26 percent of the girls changed to feminine-oriented occupations when asked what job they would eventually have. On a positive note, the female students were dreaming about nontraditional occupations; and educators, counselors, and parents do have an opportunity to influence the process of eliminating potential occupations during the grade school years.

One way of impacting gender stereotyping is to actively find nonsexist career materials (Kyle & Hennis, 2000). This may include pictures or stories of women and people of color in traditionally White male roles, as well as pictures of men in traditionally female roles. Another option is to have adults in nontraditional work roles visit the class and talk about their careers. Actually providing potential role models offers identification figures for the children to see and question. Organizing a field trip to a place of employment in which both men and women are working is another idea. Finally, a guided play (see later in the chapter) could deliberately place boys and girls in nontraditional roles, expanding perspectives of work options.

Morals

> No one has yet fully realized the wealth of sympathy, kindness, and generosity hidden in the soul of a child. The effort of every true educator should be to unlock that treasure.
>
> *Emma Goldman*

Gysbers and Henderson (2000) posit that personal values impact how an individual sets and approaches goals. To that end, moral development is important because the morals and values that children internalize later impact career decision making. Kohlberg (1976, 1986) offers a theory of moral development that includes three levels (preconventional, conventional, and postconventional reasoning) with two stages per level (total of six). The specifics of each level and stage can be found in almost every child development and human development text on the market, so readers are referred to such sources.

What is important for this text is the conceptualization Kohlberg offered for moral development. He viewed moral development beginning with external values provided by others (e.g., parents and teachers) and a fear of punishment as guiding moral behavior. Next, the individual transitions between internalizing adult-provided values and seeking approval/rewards from others as guiding moral thought. Finally, the individual has a fully internalized value system, and that person is able to personalize it based upon his personal conscience. Adults can help children identify values, ex-

Box 12.3   Expanding Gender via the Mini-Society

Goal: NOICC (1992): Understand how to make decisions, awareness of different occupations, aware of the benefits of education. Gysbers & Henderson (2000): Introduction to economic situation, counteract gender stereotypes of various careers, introduce concept of the future.

Kourilsky and Campbell (1984) created the following intervention for grade-school children (3rd–6th). Students participated in three 45-minute sessions each week for 10 weeks. Both boys and girls increased their acceptance of females working in entrepreneurial careers. Here's how it works:

1. Teachers were trained for four weeks (total of 24 hours) in the pedagogy and economic concepts necessary to make the mini-society work.
2. The mini-society starts by the teacher presenting a scarcity problem (e.g., not enough buses in the city). The children are to develop a variety of alternative solutions, discussing the pros and cons of each. Then, as a group, the children make a decision to implement one of the strategies.
3. Next, the children are to develop a society that is "better" than the current one. The children choose the paid jobs. The mini-society has its own currency, so they have to develop their own exchange system.
4. Having currency leads to the need for products and services. Now the children begin setting up a system whereby products (e.g., pencils) and services (e.g., music lessons) can be purchased. Teachers can make money by consulting with the students on different entre-

preneurial projects. Later, the students may become "experts" and can become consultants to other students. Finally, the teacher may introduce the idea of stock. That is, some students will sell the stock of their company so that they can raise income to expand the business further.

5. As the society develops, the teacher and students must make decisions based upon the current economic, political, or social realities of the classroom (e.g., costs for cleaning up pollution; creating laws that would help or hinder certain business practices; dealing with a company's use of a river that would change leisure activities of the area).

There are so many modifications one can make based upon the region or student population. For example, if a person wants to be a doctor, she may have to pay back a student loan. By week 2–3, the child may be frustrated with the small amount of her paycheck she gets to keep. By week 10, the student loan would be paid off, and the doctor would be very well off. Companies may make donations to politicians to get a law passed or blocked. A natural disaster may require clean-up and repair costs. A strike could shut down production. The options are endless and can be both fun and educational. Finally, niche markets may be identified. The point to underscore is that few of the work activities are gender identified. The activities are performed by people with good ideas and implementation skills with no requirement for a person from either sex.

plain important values the child may misunderstand, and correct unacceptable values while promoting the child's internalization of such values.

School-based career programs need to include societal morals and values as an important part of the program (character education and values exploration). Exposing children to ethical dilemmas and aiding them in solving the situation builds awareness of complex life situations, decision making, and perspective taking. For example, a company has been severely fined for polluting a local river. The fishing population has been damaged, and local residents no longer spend summer days at the river. On the other hand, the company is in trouble financially, and changes in its production method may result in relocation or bankruptcy. (A variation would have the company rolling in money, but willing to relocate if the city gets too punitive. Will this change how the students approach the situation?) How can the students solve the pollution problem yet also keep the company local so that people don't lose their jobs? Teachers can help the students devise plans that help both the community and the company (clearly, 5th graders will solve this situation differently than 1st graders). The value that may be taught is that a businessperson needs to make a profit, but should not hurt the environment or community in the process.

Social Skills

Childhood is an opportunity to develop a foundation in social problem-solving skills (Gysbers & Henderson, 2000; NOICC, 1992). Social problem solving may be defined as the resolution of conflicts between two or more individuals in ways that are acceptable and satisfactory to all involved. Children who get along with peers, are liked, and are helpful are defined as well adjusted (WAC). On the other hand, children who are highly aggressive or anxious and withdrawn, and are disliked by peers are considered to be maladjusted (MAC) (Crick & Dodge, 1994; Vitaro & Pelletier, 1991). Dubow, Tisak, Causey, Hryshko, and Reid (1991) found that children or adolescents who improved their social problem-solving skills demonstrated gains in academic, emotional, and social functioning.

Crick and Dodge (1994) list the skills a child must have to successfully resolve conflicts. First, the child must encode (pay attention to) social cues. Second, the encoded cues must be interpreted. WAC accurately interpret social cues whereas MAC selectively interpret social cues, typically as hostile. The third step is to formulate social goals. WAC tend to form pro-social goals that strengthen relationships, like sharing or being helpful. MAC often create goals that damage relationships. For example, the goal may be to "get even" or to "avoid" a person. The fourth and fifth steps include generating possible problem-solving strategies and evaluating the probable effectiveness of those strategies. WAC create multiple strategies and are often able to choose an effective one. MAC expect situations to end poorly, and this interferes with their ability to generate and choose adaptive or effective strategies. Finally, the child must enact the response they have chosen.

Improving social problem-solving skills can become a routine part of the child's experience, and learning such skills is very important for the global economy (Gysbers & Henderson, 2000; NOICC, 1992). A foundation in social problem-solving skills in childhood can lead to successful career behavior as an adult. Teaching children how to solve social problems provides them a framework for later learning. Using stories or play-acting of typically occurring problems will help the child to know when to apply the new strategies. When a conflict occurs, an adult can gather the children together and help them interpret the situation. When appropriate, the adult helps the children to expand their way of understanding the situation. The next step is to help the children come up with acceptable solutions. Again, adult interventions can help the child to expand possible solutions. Finally, teaching children how to predict the outcome of their chosen solution can help them decide whether they've made a good choice. Multiple studies have found that variations of this type of teaching will improve the children's social skills (Feis & Simons, 1985; Gettinger, Doll, & Salmon, 1994; Ridley & Vaughn, 1982).

Although more difficult to access, family environment is a very important part of social skills training (Gysbers & Henderson, 2000). Boyum and Parke (1995) reports that: (a) mothers and fathers who express high levels of positive affect have children with better social skills, demonstrate higher levels of pro-social behaviors, and receive higher teacher ratings, (b) mothers high in negative expressions of affect have children who demonstrate more aggression, (c) parents who modulate their negative affect and provide precise negative feedback have children with lower levels of aggression and high levels of pro-social behavior, and (d) parent–child interactions are connected to peer ratings of the child. Thus, family dynamics set the stage for positive or negative social skills and peer interactions. Boyum and Parke suggest that children in need of training on how to recognize and respond to emotional messages need to be treated at the family level as opposed to the individual level (for a model on how to create a school-family collaboration, see Bemak, 2002). Given the difficulty in accessing families who may be high in negative affective expressions, when implementing social skills, training career counselors may need to make time allowances for children who live in families that send regular negative messages.

Self-Esteem, Self-Concept, and Self-Efficacy

Both NOICC (1992) and Gysbers and Henderson (2000) found that self-knowledge is important for career development. To that end, self-esteem, self-concept, and self-efficacy are three interdependent ingredients of success initially formed during the early years of childhood. An important goal of the grade school years is to set a solid foundation in all three areas. Later, that foundation will aid in career decision making. First, let's define each term.

Self-esteem refers to the relatively permanent emotions one connects to the self. Though somewhat stable, self-esteem varies with daily interpretations of successes and failures (Osborne, 1993). What a person feels about herself, the typical positive or negative emotions connected to the self, make up self-esteem. According to Osborne and Stites (Osborne, 1996), individuals low in self-esteem demonstrated an external locus of control. When life goes well, the person assumes positive external factors lead to the temporary success. By comparison, people with high self-esteem view success as caused by internal factors; success is expected over time; and success can be generalized to occur again. Thus, there is an internal locus of control (Osborne, 1996). A person's self-esteem entails how she interprets the world, what behaviors she is likely to attempt or not, and her decision making.

Self-concept is the way one thinks about himself. For example, when a person views the self as being a rebel, he may listen to underground music, dress against social norms, and read antiestablishment literature. By comparison, a person who sees himself as a leader may run for school government, organize a club, and try to excel academically. Individuals will try to act in ways that lead to consistent feedback with one's self-concept, even if it is negative (Swann, 1983).

It is important to note that self-esteem and self-concept do not have to agree, although they often do. We ask the reader to remember a time when one thought one way about a situation but felt totally opposite. For example, a client worked in an environment that did not suit his personality. His self-concept was one of a competent person providing quality services to customers; however, emotionally, the client felt doubt and insecurity. Even with a positive self-concept, he experienced negative emotions and lowered self-esteem because coworkers gave critical feedback. Renewed high self-esteem came with a change of working environment in which the person received positive feedback for the very same behaviors that led to coworker conflict in the previous job.

Self-efficacy refers to the assessment of one's abilities that led to success, overcoming barriers, and reaching goals (Bandura, 1989). An important distinction between self-efficacy and self-esteem/concept is action. What can

Box 12.4   Developing Self Skills

Goals: NOICC (1992): Knowledge of self-concept, awareness of the importance of growth and change, skills to interact with others. Gysbers & Henderson (2002): Become aware of the self, recognize individual skills and abilities.

Santrock (2002) outlined a strategy for raising self-esteem, self-concept, and self-efficacy in young children. The following is a description of the four steps.

1. Identify self-esteem level and which domains are viewed as lacking by the child (school, appearance, athletics). The domains that are lacking should be considered important to self-esteem and self-concept. First, identify the domains of life that are going well. A child may be overfocusing on specific negative situations and missing the global positive theme. In addition, skills from the domains that are going well may be useful when applied to the domains that are lacking. Also, the child may need to evaluate whether the lacking domain is really important to the self or not (Osborne, 1996). Unimportant domains can be ignored. Second, realistic assessment may identify domains that can and cannot be improved. Teaching children such self-evaluation skills can be helpful to them throughout life. Effort can improve performance in some domains and impact self-efficacy. Third, reevaluate ignored domains at a later point when self-esteem, self-concept, and self-efficacy have been improved. As a child experiences success, the child can reevaluate self-esteem and self-concept.

2. Adults need to provide emotional support to help the child to find social approval in groups that are caring and loving. Groups that artificially raise self-esteem by putting down others are to be avoided because such behavior does not improve self-efficacy. Please note, positive feedback from others is not enough to raise self-esteem (Harter, 1990; Osborne, 1996). The child has to interpret the outcome as successful and relate that success to the self.

3. Teaching skills that will increase self-efficacy leads to achievement. Throughout this process, the child learns how to evaluate improvement, success, or setbacks. Overly negative interpretations change to accurate assessments.

4. Finally, a child must learn how to cope with failure to gain success or reach one's goals because setbacks are a normal part of life. Self-esteem and self-concept also include persistence, ethics, courage, or teamwork, and not just a focus on goal achievement. Children need to learn to avoid denial, self-deception, or avoidance. Finally, some situations cannot be changed, and children can develop skills for tolerating or enduring some negative situations.

a person do? If a person encounters an obstacle in life and says, "I've over-come problems like this in the past. I'll just modify and integrate previously successful solutions and gain success," one has high self-efficacy. On the other hand, if a person says, "I've never encountered this before, but I'm sure I can figure it out and gain success," one has high self-esteem and a positive self-concept. Therefore, self-esteem is feelings; self-concept is thoughts; and self-efficacy is action.

LEARNING ABOUT THE EXTERNAL WORLD: PLAY

Preparation for later career development includes learning how careers benefit society (NOICC, 1992). Schools can build important skills by using play and providing adult guidance when needed. Why do children often play at being a police- or fireperson, teacher, soldier, or doctor? Because these are the professions they have seen regularly on TV or in their community. Many children have no idea what their parents do because many parents work outside of the home and only complain about undesirable aspects of their work (Brown, 2003). Parents, teachers, and counselors can expand a child's understanding of the work force by exposing children, through play, to the multitude of professions available. The goal is not to lead a child to choose a particular profession, but to highlight how each profession benefits society.

Play is an important vehicle for children to develop the skills necessary to becoming an adult. While playing, children interact with peers, explore adult roles in a safe manner, develop imaginative and sociodramatic skills, and release tension (Santrock, 1994). Furthermore, Russ, Robins, and Christiano (1999) found the ability to pretend in young children predictive of divergent thinking and the use of affect in play over a four-year period. Children who engaged in more pretend play are able to creatively approach problems with a variety of ideas. Russ et al. also found that children who are able to use affect in play used greater sophistication for problem solving four years later and demonstrated greater emotional variance. Both skills are definitely needed in the current global economy.

Benefits of Affect in Play

Encouraging affect in play is beneficial because it teaches children how to label and express affect and how to use affective cues to negotiate the environment. Russ (1993) provides the following principles when including affect:

1. Be accepting of the child's expression of feelings.
2. Give verbal permission for expression of feelings.

3. Create a permissive environment (but set limits when needed).
4. Develop a comfortable relationship with the child.
5. Label feelings that are expressed.
6. Listen to the child and empathize.
7. Enjoy the child's play and fantasy.
8. Have a variety of toys available—a variety that promotes unstructured play.
9. Follow the child's lead in determining the movement of play.
10. Depending on the child, stay uninvolved in the play itself. Only provide the guidance a child needs to get going, get unstuck, and feel comfortable (pp. 89–90).

In group situations, a teacher or counselor can help children organize the roles each child will play. If the children are not playing out the scenario like the real world, that is okay. It is the creativity and social interaction that are important, not "getting it right." The goal is to help children develop divergent thinking skills, affective sophistication, and creativity that will aid them as they mature. In addition, if the play can center around work situations, the children are learning about ways in which adults contribute to society.

Kyle and Hennis (2000) suggest setting up a learning center in which children can follow their interests, gather information, think, and problem solve. In a dramatic play area, children can act out dramas. Props can stimulate acting in career roles, and children can develop the role with some depth. In a science area, children can explore different work environments via models, pictures, and so on. The children can learn how to compare and contrast the environments. A play area with dolls, vehicles, and buildings can allow children to create an adult world. Here, children may control multiple dolls and develop role-switching skills. An art area encourages children to paint, draw, cut pictures out of magazines, and such, and each child explains his artwork. Finally, a library area provides a place in which children can look up information about different work environments.

Types of Play

Pretense/Symbolic Play, which peaks around 4 to 5 years of age and then gradually declines, consists of props, plots, and roles (Garvey, 1977). Roles may include reality roles such as a mom, dad, or doctor, or fantasy roles such as the superhero, dragon, or medieval knight. Props include using sticks for guns or drinking from an imaginary cup. Plots, although often simple, build the story creatively. Adults can support role exploration and aid in the creativity of play by:

1. Helping the child to expand the variety of activities enacted by role or particular profession. For example, doctors help people by finding the best medication; computer technicians make the computer work so children can play games and learn things.
2. Explaining a professional helps or benefits society. Police officers help people who are in trouble and protect innocent people; managers help employees do the best job they can.
3. Describing work ethics such as being honest, helpful, competing fairly, protecting the environment, remembering family time.
4. Explaining the variety of jobs available such as biologist, marketing director, executive managers, physicist.
5. Identifying negative traits by saying things such as, "Bosses who treat their employees poorly aren't nice people, people shouldn't steal from the workplace."

Constructive Play, the combination of repetitive activity that leads to skill development and symbolic representation of ideas, results in the construction of a product or solves a problem (Santrock, 1994). This type of play begins in preschool and continues through the elementary years. Adults can guide children by introducing projects that teach a desired value or trait and also provides ample opportunity for practicing skills. Group activities that require sharing, joint decision making, team participation, and problem solving are examples. Children may be instructed to write a story about an airplane pilot, develop a play about being a good president, or build a model rocket together. When the group struggles or has conflict, the adult can intercede and teach the students how to reconcile difficulties (Kostelnik, Whiren, & Stein, 1988).

Finally, we come to games, which peak between 10–12 years of age, but begin around age 6 and may last well into adulthood (Bergen, 1988; Eiferman, 1971; Rubin, Fein, & Vandenberg, 1983). Games require children to memorize a set of rules, teach the rules to others, resolve arguments about the rules, and apply those rules to a social setting, all with at least a minimum level of cooperation. Some games like Statue are more participation focused. (Swing a person in a circle and let them go. When the person stops moving, the person becomes a statue and explains what role is depicted.) Other games are competitive like checkers or chess. Adult participation in games is an excellent opportunity for children to observe and participate in social communication skills, taking turns, developing patience, and solving conflicts. This is not a time for adults to be "right" and children to be "wrong," but it is a time for adults to help children to learn about social exchanges.

Please note that the above section focuses on skills adults will need. A foundation in the skills that will lead to a healthy participation in the world

---

Box 12.5   Using Dress-Up Days to Expand Career Exposure

Goal: NOICC (1992): Awareness of different occupations. Gysbers and Henderson (2000): Introduce future, become aware of stereotypes.

Catlett (1992) noticed that when children came to school dressed up as a careerist, she saw attorneys, doctors, pilots, teachers, and nurses. She did not see miners, grocery store checkers, beauticians, and many others. Catlett questioned whether some careers are invisible to children. One idea would be to have a dress-up day in which the teacher forbids

students to pick the standard careers. Students are instructed to go home and research "invisible" careers and come back prepared to share with the class what was discovered.

Children can dress up as the career. Use art time to build replicas of different career items (e.g., make a microscope, stethoscope, chainsaw). One could even have a runway in which students display costumes and props while walking down the aisle as the teacher reads a description of the roles students model.

---

of work is excellent career education for young children, and play is a fun way to introduce and practice those skills in ways that are meaningful to children.

MAKING CAREER DEVELOPMENT WORK IN THE SCHOOL

Support from Teachers and Administrators

An important step in developing a successful career program is gaining the support of teachers and administrators (Brown, 2003). Successful programs require a commitment by the school. Niles and Harris-Bowlsbey (2002) made the following four recommendations. First, assessing the political environment is vital. If the school does not perceive a connection between career development and academic achievement, support is unlikely. Furthermore, it is important to communicate what benchmarks will demonstrate a program's success. Second, what are the needs of the specific population one is serving? Define outcome behaviors so teachers and administrators can visualize how the career program will be helpful. Third, if teachers are overworked and understaffed, they may feel career education activities are yet one more thing added to their workload. Such a barrier may be overcome with the school counseling staff presenting units in classes while teachers are given a planning period. Fourth, procure resources that are not vulnerable to other school needs so administrators could remove funding from the career program.

Support from Parents and Community

Like teachers and administrators, parents must be educated as to the bene-fit of a career program for young children. Rising school costs combined with decreased funding can lead to some parents questioning why a school is wasting money in this area. Brown (2003) wrote that one of the events that led to the failure of the 1970s career movement was the misperception of middle class parents who confused career education with vocational train-ing. The parents did not understand how career programs lead to academic achievement and professional training.

Brown (2003) made suggestions for parents to implement at home. First, parents need to understand the negative impact of gender-stereotyping work (see also Herr and Cramer, 1996). Parents may need to assess whether they are treating their sons and daughters differently. Counselors can offer con-crete suggestions to parents for supporting their children's curiosity in mul-tiple work domains. Second, parents need to be aware of how they talk about work at home. Many parents only share the boredom, coworker conflict, and other pressures. The child hears over and over how horrible work is. Although it is important for children to hear about adult struggles and ob-serve how adults cope and solve issues, children also need to hear a balanced perspective noting the positive aspects of work. Third, parents need to ac-curately assess their child's abilities. Brown says, "Parental pressures that push a child of limited ability toward academically competitive areas are just as harmful and wasteful as those that encourage academically able children to leave school and go to work as soon as possible" (p. 331). A career pro-gram that provides an excellent assessment of a child and accurately explains this to the parents can be a benefit to all concerned. Parents can provide ap-propriate stimulation for the child, encouraging the discovery of interests and awareness of abilities in a pressure-free environment.

There are multiple things parents can do at home to improve children's career development. Specifically, Herr and Cramer (1996) suggest parents can help children by: (a) helping and supporting the identification of self-characteristics, (b) learning about the world of work, (c) learning about work values, (d) teaching the economics of running a home and affording recre-ation and the need for work to earn money, (e) exposing children to a wide variety of information including books, films, and friends of the family, (f) giving children opportunities to work at home or in the community, and (g) having children practice decision-making skills. Combining elements of Brown (2003) and Herr and Cramer (1996) are nice topics for psychoe-ducational programs for parents, and they would also demonstrate the value of career services in the schools.

The community offers another avenue for support for career program-ming. Local businesses may offer financial support. In addition, community

Box 12.6   Getting to Know Important Adults in Your Life

Goal: NOICC (1992): Awareness of how work relates to the needs and functions of society, awareness of the interrelationship of life. Gysbers & Henderson (2000): Teach students about listening and speaking roles, school knowledge is applied to home, aware of life roles, begin with family work roles.

VanZandt and Buchan (1997) suggest, first, defining the meaning of the family and then brainstorming about enjoyable family activities (e.g., nuclear family, step-families, important nonrelated adults, extended family). Brainstorming should include different family members' perspectives or evaluations of the activity (teaching perspective shifting). Second, draw a picture (may need to divide it up into sections if the child has more than one home) of a favorite family activity. Third, students present their families to the class. Once four or five students have presented, "com-pare and contrast family sizes, make-up, and activities" (p. 73).

Niles and Harris-Bowlsbey (2002) suggest that students be assigned to learn about the various jobs of their nuclear and/or extended family (may include important nonrelated adults). They are to ask about education/training requirements as well as how the job benefits society. Students then present the information to the class (if information on nuclear families can lead to some students feeling badly about their family situation, then change this to include only extended family or close family friends). The younger the child, the closer career explorations need to be tied to the family's experience. As the child ages, exploration of careers can become more distant from actual family experience. Niles and Harris-Bowlsbey refer to this as the "proximity-distance scheme," which is useful for helping students to organize ca-reer information (p. 258).

members may provide excellent classroom visitors or sites for field trips. It is widely known that parents make for good guests in classrooms. Visitors can describe what they do and make a personal connection to the class or school. Community members offer additional role models for various jobs, which build a connection between the school and the community. Finally, community members who know administrators and teachers can serve as advocates to explain the importance of employees gaining skills needed in the workplace such as problem solving, creative thinking, and social cooperation.

SUMMARY

During the grade-school years, career development needs to focus on the foundation of skills and attitudes needed regardless of eventual career aspirations. Sometimes it is difficult to explain to laypeople how social skills, problem-solving skills, and building self-esteem/concept/efficacy are career development. A very, very important developmental attitude for young people is to avoid the sextyping of different occupations. "Men's work" or "women's work" are not distinctions appropriate for the workplace. Play is an excellent way to teach the myriad skills grade-school children need to develop in order to pursue future career options. Play can be fun for children and adults, and it is a meaningful way for children to organize and integrate information for later use. Finally, parents and community leaders are excellent sources for exposing children to the world of work and as a backdrop for developing meaningful career exercises.

STUDY OUTLINE: KEY TERMS AND CONCEPTS

I. Career Development in Childhood (K–5)
   A. Skill building
      1. Language
      2. Analytical thought
      3. Problem solving
   B. Developing morals and values
   C. Developing inter- and intrapersonal skills
      1. Listening and communicating
      2. Sharing
      3. Introspection
   D. Children are not in a position to make career decisions or even understand the realistic concept.
   E. Encourage discovery of interests and becoming aware of abilities.
   F. Diamond has no closure at this time.

II. Gender
   A. Women are becoming more educated than men.
   B. Gottfredson's Theory: Sex-typing of occupations occurs between ages 6–8. (Children eliminate options if connected to opposite sex.)
   C. Present career options in a nonsexist manner.

III. Morals
   A. Begin externally and are slowly internalized as the child enters adolescence.
   B. Identify, teach, and correct pro-social values.

IV. Social Skills
   A. WAC/MAC children and their approaches to social problem solving

    B. Crick and Dodge (1994) social skills list
       1. Encoding
       2. Interpretation
       3. Formulate
       4. Generating possibilities
       5. Evaluating the effectiveness of # 4
    C. Use classroom event to teach entire class social skills.

V. Self-Esteem, Self-Concept, and Self-Efficacy
    A. **Self-esteem**—feelings about the self
    B. **Self-concept**—thoughts about the self
    C. **Self-efficacy**—belief about actions that will lead to success
    D. To increase all three:
       1. Identify levels of all three.
       2. Provide support.
       3. Teach actual skills.
       4. Teach coping skills.

VI. Play
    A. Use play to introduce career-related materials and teach skills.
    B. Create safe place for emotion, expression, identification.
    C. Consider setting up learning centers, e.g., drama, science, play, and library.
    D. Pretense/symbolic play—use of props, plots, and roles
    E. Constructive play—repetitive activity designed to develop and master skills
    F. Games—master and apply rules to interactions

VII. Making Career Programs Work
    A. Teachers and administrators must support the program.
    B. Parents should advocate for career programs while teaching skills at home.
    C. Community
       1. Provide speakers and field-trip sites
       2. Communicate importance of career skills
       3. Provide financial and other support

EXERCISES

In small groups, design a fun program for K–5 students. Groups may want to design a program for a specific year or a program that is added to each year and grows over time. Remember to keep the developmental level of the children in mind. What is the goal of the intervention (exposure, countering stereotypes, skill building)? Is this to take place in a wealthy suburban school or a less affluent inner city school? What kind of financial and staff support can one expect from the school or community? Will/can families be involved?

Below are examples other authors have used.

1. Yontiac Motor Company (Catlett, 1992): First, Catlett and a third-grade teacher combined a section in economics on labor and capital with a look at child labor around the 1900s. Then the students joined the Yontiac Motor Company in which they were to produce 8-inch-long paper cars. Students had to fill out applications, sign employment contracts, and follow work rules. The students received wages that could be spent at the Yontiac store (e.g., candy, pencils, etc.). There were four different "assembly lines" that competed with each other. They had to deal with quantity versus quality issues as production changed through competition. The big surprise came when Yontiac vehicles were not selling, and three of the lines had to be shut down. (Students who no longer worked could read, something that was reported as being enjoyable.) Catlett reported that the children had a very negative reaction to the mass layoff. Each production line had to problem solve (skills they had learned earlier) as to which line would make the last orders. Finally, the class shared in a class discussion what it was like to work as a team and then lose one's job.

    Goal: Experience the multifaceted nature of work. Make skills learned in school practical to the work environment.

2. School as work (Inniss, 1982; Kyle & Hennis, 2000): Students earn money via attendance, grades, behavior, and performing certain activities. Based upon the developmental level of the child, students can be paid piecemeal, weekly, bi-weekly, or monthly. Have a store that allows the students to purchase items on set days (e.g., every Friday). Some items should cost enough that students must save or put the item on layaway. If children are absent, they are docked pay. Older students may also need to pay bills/fines.

    Goal: Connect certain behaviors with earning money. Connect earning money to buying items.

REFERENCES

Bachay, J. (1997). Welcome to our school community: A career development intervention for the newcomer. *Professional School Counseling,* *1*(2), 13–14.

Bandura, A. (1986). *Social foundations of thought and action*. Englewood Cliffs, NJ: Prentice-Hall.

Bandura, A. (1989). Human agency in social cognitive theory. *American Psychologist, 44*, 1175–1184.

Bemak, F. (2002). The SAFI model as a critical link between marginalized families and schools: A literature review and strategies for school counselors. *Journal of Counseling and Development, 80*(3), 322–331.

Bergen, D. (1988). Stages of play development. In D. Bergen (Ed.), *Play as a medium for learning and development: A handbook of theory and practice* (pp. 49–66). Portsmouth, NH: Heinemann.

Boyum, L. A., & Parke, R. D. (1995). The role of family emotional expressiveness in the development of children's social competence. *Journal of Marriage and Family, 57*(3), 593–608.

Brown, D. (2003). *Career information, career counseling, and career development* (8th ed.). Boston: Allyn & Bacon.

Catlett, J. L. (1992). The dignity of work: School children look at employment. *Elementary School Guidance & Counseling, 27*(2), 150–154.

Crick, N. R., & Dodge, K. A. (1994). A review and reformulation of social information-processing mechanisms in children's social adjustment. *Psychological Bulletin, 115*, 74–101.

Dubow, E. F., Tisak, J., Causey, D., Hryshko, A., & Reid, G. (1991). A two-year longitudinal study of stressful life events, social support, and social problem-solving skills: Contributions to children's behavioral and academic adjustment. *Child Development, 62*, 583–599.

Eiferman, R. R. (1971). Social play in childhood. In R. E. Herron & B. Sutton-Smith (Eds.), *Child's play* (pp. 270–298). New York: Wiley.

Feis, C. L., & Simons, C. (1985). Training preschool children in interpersonal cognitive problem-solving skills: A replication. *Prevention in Human Services, 3*, 59–70.

Garvey, C. (1977). *Play*. Cambridge, MA: Harvard Univ. Press.

Gettinger, M., Doll, B., & Salmon, D. (1994). Effects of social problem solving, goal setting, and parent training on children's peer relations. *Journal of Applied Developmental Psychology, 15*, 141–163.

Gottfredson, L. S. (1981). Circumscription and compromise: A developmental theory of occupational aspirations. *Journal of Counseling Psychology, 28*, 545–579.

Gottfredson, L. S. (1996). Gottfredson's theory of circumscription and compromise. In D. Brown & L. Brooks (Eds.), *Career choice and development* (3rd ed., pp. 179–232). San Francisco: Jossey-Bass.

Gottfredson, L. S., & Lapan, R. T. (1997). Assessing gender-based circumscription of occupational aspirations. *Journal of Career Assessment, 5*(4), 419–441.

Grutter, J. (2000). Developmental career counseling: Different stages, different choices. In J. M. Kummerow (Ed.), *New directions in career planning and the workplace: Practical strategies for career management professionals* (2nd ed., pp. 273–306). Palo Alto, CA: Davies-Black.

Gysbers, N. C., & Henderson, P. (2000). *Developing & managing your school guidance program* (3rd ed.). Alexandria, VA: American Counseling Association.

Hageman, M. B., & Gladding, S. T. (1983). The art of career exploration: Occupational sex-role stereo-typing among elementary school children. *Elementary School Guidance & Counseling, 17*, 280–287.

Harter, S. (1990). Self and identity development. In S. S. Feldman & G. R. Elliott (Eds.), *At the threshold: The developing adolescent* (pp. 352–387). Cambridge, MA: Harvard Univ. Press.

Herr, E. L., & Cramer, S. H. (1996). *Career guidance and counseling through the lifespan* (5th ed.). New York: HarperCollins.

Inniss, J. (1982). Operation employment: A taste of the world of work. In C. L. Thompson (Ed.), Idea exchange column. *Elementary School Guidance & Counseling, 16*(3), 235–240.

Kohlberg, L. (1976). Moral stages and moralization: The cognitive-developmental approach. In T. Lickona (Ed.), *Moral development and behavior*. New York: Holt, Rinehart & Winston.

Kohlberg, L. (1986). A current statement on some theoretical issues. In S. Modgil & C. Modgil (Eds.), *Lawrence Kohlberg*. Philadelphia: Falmer.

Kostelnik, M. J., Whiren, A. P., & Stein, L. C. (1988). Living with He-Man: Managing superhero fantasy play. *Young Children, 41*, 3–9.

Kourilsky, M., & Campbell, M. (1984). Sex differences in a simulated classroom economy: Children's beliefs about entrepreneurship. *Sex Roles, 10*, 53–66.

Kyle, M. T., & Hennis, M. (2000). Experiential model for career guidance in early childhood education. In N. Peterson & R. C. Gonzalez (Eds.), *Career counseling models for diverse populations: Hands-on applications by practitioners* (pp. 1–7). Belmont, CA: Wadsworth/Thomson Learning.

Lankard, B. A. (1991). *Strategies for implementing the national career development guidelines*. Columbus, OH: ERIC Clearinghouse on Adult Career and Vocational Education. (ERIC Document Reproduction Service No. ED338898).

Matlin, M. W. (2001). *The psychology of women* (4th ed.). Thomson/Wadsworth.

Miller, J. V. (1992). The national career development guidelines. Ann Arbor: MI: ERIC Clearinghouse on Counseling and Personnel Services. (ERIC Document Reproduction Service No. ED347493).

National Center for Education Statistics. (n.d.). Degrees conferred by sex and race. Retrieved August 15, 2002, from http://nces.ed.gov/fastfacts/display.asp?id=72.

National Occupational Information Coordinating Committee (NOICC). (1992). *The national career development guidelines project.* Washington, DC: U. S. Government Printing Office.

Niles, S. G., & Harris-Bowlsbey, J. (2002). *Career development interventions in the 21st century.* Upper Saddle River, NJ: Merrill Prentice Hall.

NOICC Crosswalk and Data Center (2000). *Annual report: July 1, 1998–June 30, 1999.* NCDC, Iowa. Retrieved May 16, 2004, from http://www.state.ia.us/ncdc/ncdc99.html.

Osborne, R. E. (1993). Self-esteem. In *Magill's survey of the social sciences: Psychology.* Pasadena, CA: Salem Press.

Osborne, R. E. (1996). *Self: An eclectic approach.* Boston: Allyn & Bacon.

Patton, W., & McMahon, M. (1999). *Career development and systems theory: A new relationship.* Pacific Grove, CA: Brooks/Cole.

Ridley, C. A., & Vaughn, R. (1982). Interpersonal problem solving: An intervention program for preschool children. *Journal of Applied Developmental Psychology, 3,* 177–190.

Rubin, K. H., Fein, G. G., & Vandenberg, B. (1983). Play. In E. M. Hetherington (Ed.), *Handbook of child psychology: Vol. 4, Socialization, personality, and social development* (4th ed., pp. 693–744). New York: Wiley.

Russ, S. W. (1993). Affect and creativity: *The role of affect and play in the creative process.* Hillsdale, NJ: Erlbaum.

Russ, S. W., Robins, A. L., & Christiano, B. A. (1999). Pretend play: Longitudinal prediction of creativity and affect in fantasy in children. *Creativity Research Journal, 12*(2), 129–139.

Santrock, J. W. (1994). *Child Development* (6th ed.). Madison, WI: Brown & Benchmark.

Santrock, J. W. (2002). *Life-Span Development* (8th ed.). Boston: McGraw Hill.

Super, D. E. (1957). *Vocational development: A framework for research.* New York: Teachers College Press.

Super, D. E. (1983). Assessment in career guidance: Toward truly developmental counseling. *Personnel and Guidance Journal, 61* (9), 555–562.

Swann, W. B., Jr. (1983). Self-verification: Bringing social reality into harmony with the self. In J. Suls & A. G. Greenwals (Eds.), *Social psychological perspectives on the self* (Vol. 2, pp. 33–66). Hillsdale, NJ: Erlbaum.

VanZandt, Z., & Buchan, B. A. (1997). *Lessons for life: Elementary grades* (Vol. 1). West Nyack, NY: The Center for Applied Research in Education.

Vitaro, F., & Pelletier, D. (1991). Assessment of children's social problem-solving skills in hypothetical and actual conflict situations. *Journal of Abnormal Child Psychology, 19,* 505–518.

CHAPTER 13

Career Development in Middle School

Life asks us to make measurable progress in reasonable time. That's why they make those fourth grade chairs so small—so you won't fit in them at age twenty-five!

Jim Rohn

In the last chapter, children were described building skills (language development, analytical thought, problem solving), developing values and morals, and learning interpersonal and intrapersonal skills. Once a child enters adolescence (middle and high school), development involves a sequence of growth whereby those foundational issues are chosen or rejected; owned or disowned; integrated or unresolved; and then applied to life. The adolescent is becoming aware of differences between personal and social views on race, ethnicity, gender, sexual orientation, SES, religious beliefs, values, emotional styles, interpersonal styles, and family roles. The adolescent, with this awareness, purposely chooses to develop the abilities that lead to success and joining the adult world. The flow of development is to build on previous development and integrate all factors into a complex personal identity.

THE NATIONAL CAREER DEVELOPMENT GUIDELINES (NOICC, 1992) AND A CAREER DEVELOPMENT PROGRAM FOR MIDDLE SCHOOL/JUNIOR HIGH (GRADES 6–8)

NOICC and Middle School

This section contains the goals appropriate for middle school-aged students. For an introduction to NOICC, please see Chapter 12. Within each age group (elementary, middle school, high school, and adult), three major areas are to be of focus: (a) self-knowledge, (b) educational and occupational exploration, and (c) career planning (NOICC, 1992). We are restricting our listings to the major categories; however, each major area has multiple goals. Each

Table 13.1   NOICC Career Education Guidelines

Self-Knowledge	Educational and Occupational Exploration	Career Planning
Knowledge of the influence of a positive self-concept	Knowledge of the benefits of educational achievement to career opportunities	Skills to make decisions
Skills to interact with others	Understanding the relationship between work and learning	Knowledge of the interrelationship of life roles
Knowledge of the importance of growth and change	Skills to locate, understand, and use career information	Knowledge of different occupations and changing male/female roles
	Knowledge of skills necessary to seek and obtain jobs	Understanding the process of career planning (NOICC, 1992)
	Understanding how work relates to the needs and functions of the economy and society	

section is comprised of age-specific set goals and readers are encouraged to obtain a full version. (Please see the NOICC, 1992, reference at the end of this chapter.)

It is important to notice that there is a shift away from focusing on the here-and-now and an insertion of the future into the middle school years. Specifically, career choices are concretely connected to adult life-styles, and students become aware that career decisions result in different types of lives lived. Ideally, businesses and industry will play a larger role in educating this age group. Although the development of self-concept is still important, one now sees a greater emphasis placed upon career information, including the requirements for entering various fields (see Table 13.1). Students need to start looking at the specific competencies they possess or are able to develop (Lankard, 1991).

Career Development Program

This section contains the second installment of Gysbers and Henderson's (2000) tasks for a Life Career Development program. Compared to the earlier tasks, an increasingly realistic look at the adult word is apparent. In addition, a move toward projecting one into the future is introduced. Students are still developing here-and-now skills to deal with everyday concerns, but an obvious connection to the adult world is emerging. As stated in the last chapter, the original work contains tasks that are broken down by each school year.

Box 13.1   Life Career Development: Student Competencies by Domains and Goals

Self-Knowledge and Interpersonal Skills

1. Begin with how one expands or changes abilities. Move toward comparison of abilities with others (accept the differences). End with accurate description of own skills and make predictions for the future.
2. Age-appropriate information and strategies for enhancing physical and mental health.
3. Assess how enacting personal responsibilities impacts others. Look at people in the immediate environment and how each has his own set of responsibilities. End with understanding of how taking care of responsibilities aids in quality of life.
4. Evaluate the skills involved when making and maintaining friendships. Look at peer interactions as opposed to child and adult interactions. End with a focus on effective family relationships, their impact on the family, and what keeps them going.
5. Learn about nonverbal communication. Focus on how communication impacts problem solving. End with an understanding of how listening and speaking can improve a relationship.

Life Roles, Settings, and Events

1. Begin to make connection between the learning environment and leisure activities. Make connection between knowledge and adult work experiences. Identify nonschool opportunities for learning.
2. Look at how governments use tax money. Describe the rights and responsibilities of being a citizen in a community and later a country.

3. Introduce the concept of having control over one's self and life-style choices. Be able to identify likely feelings in various situations. Begin to predict how one would feel in possible situations.
4. Assess the potential impact of stereotypes for each student. Look at how stereotypes of specific jobs are maintained. Assess how various groups of people get stereotyped.
5. Project self into the future. Look at possible changes in the world of work and how they may need to change for the future.

Life Career Planning

1. Teach students how to break down a task into steps. Learn to appreciate the completion of a difficult task. Connect satisfaction with completing a task and personal interests.
2. Assess how attitudes and values affect actions. Be able to describe similarities and differences in values across self and others. Make connection between values and life-style.
3. Understand how decisions made by others (e.g., school) can impact them. Connect past decisions to present behaviors. Look at how past family decisions may be impacting current personal decisions.
4. Learn how to predict the consequences for every alternative choice; then choose the best alternative. Be able to give personal examples of rewards or consequences from past decision making. Learn how to gather additional information prior to choosing an alternative.

(continued)

(Box 13.1 continued)

5. Identify five goals, based upon interests and capabilities, for the next five
   years. Learn multiple ways to assess

progress toward these goals. Look at
goals "I want" to complete versus goals
"I expect" to complete.

Adapted from Gysbers and Henderson, *Developing and Managing Your School Guidance
Program* (2000, pp. 327–334).

We chose to summarize and group the tasks together in order to suggest that
the goals are flexible pending the needs of the region, city, or a specific
school.

THE FIRST DIAMOND: MIDDLE SCHOOL

Grades 6 through 8 can be stormy years as children enter adolescence.
Cognitive developments, including abstract thought and idealism, puberty
with its sexual awakenings, social changes, and real choices that can have an
impact years later, all combine to form opportunities for high drama (Brown,
2003; Santrock, 2002). It is a process that can take 10 to 15 years, and with
appropriate adult support, later adolescence may be calmer (Santrock, 2002).
This is an exciting time as the early adolescent gains more choices than ever
before but is actually in transition because full adult responsibility is still
years away (Brown, 2003). Because the middle school student is aware of the
importance of work but is barely independent, adults can have an important
impact on the early formation of a career identity.

As seen in Figure 13.1, the Career Diamond is coming to its first end
point. The dotted lines suggest that although identity is forming, it is not
complete and is still permeable and open to adjustment. Most students in
this age group do not have the experience to truly know themselves, and
adults provide important experiences and feedback to aid in this process.
On the other hand, the external world is requiring the first career decision. Dating at least back to 1963, the career literature discusses the choice
students make prior to entering into high school, namely to pursue college
preparatory or vocational preparatory courses (Katz, 1963). Katz stated that
it is much easier to shift from the college preparatory track to the vocational
route than vice versa (see also Arbona, 2000; Donlevy, 2001).

At this point, the diamond vision takes on a sense of reality as fantastic
career options are left behind and actual career options are considered. Super
(1957) describes students as finishing the growth stage and entering the tentative substage of the exploration. The student can envision an identity of

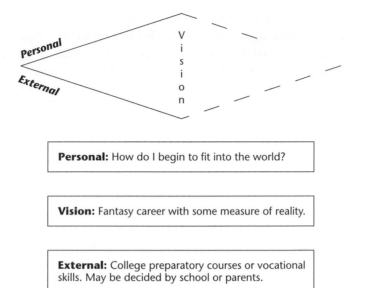

Personal: How do I begin to fit into the world?

Vision: Fantasy career with some measure of reality.

External: College preparatory courses or vocational skills. May be decided by school or parents.

Figure 13.1   The fantasy of childhood diminishes at the onset of realistically understanding the adult, external world. The 6th to 8th grader is poised to begin integrating self and external demands, but not fully able to do so at this time.

the self as a college student, mechanic, or office manager though the vision's use of realistic information may be lacking. With a vision comes the choice of classes that will lead to exploring the adult world a little more. Clearly, middle school students do not have the course choices that high school and college students have, but there may be some choices offered. Should the student take a shop class or computer class? Is the student in advanced English, math, or science or just taking the minimum requirements? These choices are very important and set the stage for decision making that will eventually lead to a career. Teaching students in the 6th grade how to think about the 7th and 8th grades creates a future focus, but the view emphasizes the near future and is within the early adolescent's capability to understand. Making choices is extended when students enter high school, and foundational skills learned when making earlier choices can be refined.

EARLY ADOLESCENCE AND THE INTERNAL SIDE OF THE DIAMOND

Cognitions

For all sad words of tongue and pen, the saddest are these, 'It might have been.'

— *John Greenleaf Whittier*

According to Piaget's theory, early adolescents are shifting from logical thinking that organizes and stabilizes the world (a type of thinking that operates on actual, before-the-eye events) toward an abstract ability to see what could be. The more sophisticated type of cognition is referred to as formal operations. Piaget describes the adolescent as capable of understanding the potential, the possible, and imagining all that could be. Such projection allows adolescents to see themselves in adult roles and as a part of society beyond family and friends (Flavell, 1963). However, most adolescents are "initially faltering and clumsy in the use of abstract thought" (Berk, 2002, p. 569). Berk suggests typical early adolescent behavior includes argumentativeness or indecisiveness. Such annoying behaviors are clearly related to inexperience with a new way of thinking and seeing the world. In regard to career development, indecisiveness is natural for this stage and represents an exploratory beginning rather than a permanent character flaw.

Piaget noticed that individuals demonstrate a burst of egocentrism when they enter a new domain of cognitive ability (Flavell, 1963). The good news is that this egocentrism subsides as the person masters the new way of thinking. For the early adolescent, egocentrism materializes in the form of the imaginary audience and personal fable (Elkind, 1967, 1978).

The *imaginary audience* refers to a heightened self-consciousness that can border on the extreme. Young people feel as though everyone is looking at them and noticing everything they do. Vartanian and Powlishta (1996) found that early adolescents are especially likely to react to the imaginary audience when in a new and novel situation (e.g., switching schools, meeting a new peer group). A protective function may develop as the adolescent restricts public behavior with the hopes of limiting embarrassment. On the other hand, adolescents may act or say things that bring them attention because they enjoy being on stage (Vartanian & Powlishta, 1996). In the career area, adolescents may only consider high prestige positions that gain maximum approval from others. On the other hand, adolescents are very sensitive to being different and may avoid considering any job that would bring ridicule from peers. (On a side note, Vartanian and Powlishta consider anticipating how others will react to be an adaptive social cognition that will aid the adolescent later in life.) If the adolescent believes she is unable to obtain a high prestige position, teachers and parents may hear "I don't know" as an answer to "What do you want to be when you grow up?" "I don't know" can be code for "I don't want to tell you."

The *personal fable* refers to the early adolescent's sense of being special, unique, and invincible. Moreover, their experience of the world is beyond the understanding of most people around them. Specific to career, idealism is reflected in the adolescent's view of a perfect future, a future that lacks the shortcomings most adults understand (e.g., injustice, discrimination) (Berk, 2002). Flavell (1963) writes that the adolescent is possessed by a naïve idealism whereby the young person is able to "reform and reshape reality … with a cavalier disregard for the practical obstacles which may face its proposals" (p. 224).

In terms of the Career Diamond, the early adolescent's vision is still fantasy based but is slowly shifting toward realistic considerations. The fantasy has lost the fantastic flair of a child who wants to grow up and be a knight. Instead, fantasies are based in actual adult roles, but with little understanding of realistic requirements or the negative aspect of occupations.

The opening quote of this section suggests a sad person looking back on one's life and seeing missed opportunities. This is an important quote to remember when working with early adolescents. As adults, many only see what could go wrong, but the young see endless possibilities. Teachers, parents, and career counselors need not interfere with an early adolescent's buoyant optimism. Career services at this stage might include the injection of realism when it's useful but a heavily negative approach does not bring about an understanding of the world of work. Mature understanding develops over time.

Gender and Socioeconomic Status (SES)

One of the ways people narrow career exploration is by identifying male and female work roles and eliminating choices. An important goal for career services is to reduce this artificial trap. With the emerging adolescent, pressure to conform to sex-typed behaviors and attitudes dramatically increases, and girls feel this pressure more strongly than boys (Basow & Rubin, 1999; Crouter, Manke, & McHale, 1995; Galambos, Almeida, & Petersen, 1990; Huston & Alvarez, 1990).

A second limiting factor can be socioeconomic status (SES). Lower expectations for achievement are barriers built by even teachers and school counselors. Dusek and Joseph (1983) found that teachers have more favorable expectations for Caucasian and middle-class children than for low-SES and/or minority children. This may occur because poor and minority students are more likely to be placed in lower ability groups in elementary school (Haller, 1985). Sadly, low SES and minority students, once tracked, may have limited options in the future. A vicious cycle of low expectations, low performance, lower expectations, worse performance may occur without peer or parental support. Adult intervention could provide a supportive emotional connection for children and models for alternative futures. Repeated contacts by supportive adults can make a huge difference in a young person's expectations for himself.

Box 13.2   Mapping Vocational Challenges for Middle School Students

Goals: Begin to recognize the circumspection process. NOICC (1992): Knowledge of different occupations and changing male/female roles. Knowledge of skills necessary to seek and obtain jobs. Understanding the process of career planning. Gysbers & Henderson (2000): Look at people in immediate environment and how each has her own set of responsibilities. Assess how various groups of people get stereotyped. Project self into the future. Identify five goals, based upon interests and capabilities, for the next five years.

Gottfredson and Lapan (1997) provide the following exercise to aid middle school children considering vocational interests, values, gender stereotyping, efficacy expectations, and parental support. This task should take about four 45- to 60-minute sessions. A workbook (see bottom of box) contains this exercise although career practitioners could develop their own materials accommodating specific student needs. The workbook contains a color-coded three dimensional map. The following is a simplified version of the exercise.

Session 1: Introduce the students to the importance of exploring vocational interests. Roughly 45 careers that span Holland's RIASEC model are presented to the students. Each career is described in a 3×4-inch box and includes "expected work activities, necessary skills and training, helpful high school classes, employment outlook, and expected median or mean national salary" (p. 436). Students read each box, and a class discussion focuses attention on different aspects of various careers. The session ends with the student writing a description of their parents' careers and their fantasy career.

Session 2: An interest inventory is completed (there is one in the MVC workbook or another could be used, such as the *Self-Directed Search*). All of the 45 occupations plus the parents' and fantasy careers are listed. The student marks the 15 occupations she likes the best and the 15 least liked. Students use the information regarding their interests as well as occupational information to explain their choices. Next, a 3×5-inch grid of 15 boxes is presented. The boxes are labeled High Interest, Medium Interest, and Low Interest on one side. Students put their choices of occupations into each of the 15 boxes.

Session 3: Regardless of whether or not the student likes a specific career, he is to mark his ability to successfully complete the educational and task requirements of the job.

Session 4: The workbook provides information from the U.S. Department of Labor on the various careers. How many women and minorities work in each occupation is a part of the information provided. Session 4 also includes a values exercise. Next, students look at their perspective on "sextype, efficacy expectations, work values, and parental support" (p. 438). Finally, students discuss how they think their parents and/or peers would respond to their selections.

The MVC activities are copyrighted material. Additional information on these activities as well as permission to use them can be obtained from Dr. Richard Lapan, 16 Hill Hall, University of Missouri-Columbia, MO 65211.

When teaching decision-making skills, it is important to stress that sex- or SES-stereotypes unnecessarily narrow viable options. Furthermore, students need continual exposure to nonsexist occupational materials displaying nontraditional workers (Kyle & Hennis, 2000). In support of the power of role models, Hoffman (2000) finds that girls who have employed mothers tend to have higher career goals, regardless of the family's SES.

With professional employment, it is important to note that it is a person's brain that makes the difference, not her sex or parents' employment. Vocational employment typically requires working with technology. There are many jobs that historically required heavy manual labor and became identified with male roles. Now such work may not require brawn as much as skills to operate machinery.

A maximum number of electives can create a school atmosphere in which females can take traditionally male classes and vice versa. Low-SES students could be encouraged to pursue advanced coursework by friendly teachers who relay, through words and actions, their belief that all students can achieve with appropriate support.

Ethnicity

> Even a remorseful majority, then, must be watchful lest it persist unconsciously in habitual patterns.
>
> —*Erik Erikson (1968, p. 305).*

Cross's revised (1971, 1978, 1991, 1995) racial identity model provides descriptions of a minority person's differing experience in developing an identity as compared to Caucasian Americans. Important to career development is the shift that can occur with the onset of adolescence, specifically, moving from the encounter stage to the immersion-emersion stage.

The onset of advanced cognitions allows the adolescent to think about the self and one's group from multiple perspectives. For example, minority adolescents may have to confront prejudice and discrimination, which are barriers to reaching their goals (Phinney & Rosenthal, 1992). Furthermore, Phinney (1989) reports that adolescents from multiple racial backgrounds have additional pressures. Phinney finds that African-American men worry about job discrimination and negative societal views of African-American men; and Latino adolescents struggle with bicultural difficulties. Cross (1991, 1995) would refer to such concerns as indicative of the encounter stage. Children are most likely in the pre-encounter stage whereby they do not even think of racial issues, and they easily identify with the majority culture. However, adolescence brings awareness, and awareness brings cognitive and emotional discomfort around issues of race and mistreatment (encounter stage). If the discomfort is intense enough, the person moves to the next stage of immersion-emersion and can develop an anti-White identity whereby everything White is rejected.

Career services need to honestly address the needs of minority students. People of color are discriminated against and this can impact post-high school education/training and later career decisions. On the one hand, career counselors need not create barriers and dispel hope (overfocus on discrimination). On the other hand, career counselors are not credible if reality is candy-coated or they dismiss the impact discrimination (perceived or experienced) has on minority youth. Frank discussions can assist adolescents to add this reality of racial inequality to career decision making.

Cross (1991, 1995) also describes the internalization stage (last stage) as a point at which positive identification with race includes acceptance and a bicultural identity. Ideally, a person in this stage can build bridges between minority cultural identification and ways to live with the majority culture. It would be unrealistic to expect middle or high school students to develop fully tolerant identities through career counseling, but career services can aid students in their struggles.

Identity

The teenage years are ones of struggling with identity (Erikson, 1968). The next chapter on middle and late adolescence will cover identity in a much more thorough manner; however, it is important to understand terms associated with identity development and to consider factors that may limit career development.

Marcia (1966, 1976, 1980, 1994), in analyzing Erikson's work, identified four ways in which adolescents approach and develop identity: identity diffusion, identity foreclosure, identity moratorium, and identity achievement. Marcia saw crisis and commitment as important parts of identity development. A crisis is defined as a time when the adolescent is struggling between meaningful alternatives. Commitment occurs when the adolescent chooses a meaningful alternative with the personal investment of defining the self. These two concepts directly relate to the four identity conditions.

First, there is identity diffusion. It would not be uncommon for adolescents in middle school to be in this domain simply through a lack of opportunity to experience a crisis. Identity diffusion occurs when a crisis has not occurred; the adolescent has not made any commitments, and may even show little interest in developing commitments. Second, identity foreclosure occurs when a young person has made a firm commitment, but has done so by accepting the injunction of another person, such as a parent, spiritual guide, or a gang leader. Third, identity moratorium exists when the adolescent is experiencing a crisis, but has not firmly made a commitment. To enhance development, the young person needs to avoid making a rash commitment simply to end the crisis and can grow by learning to endure the discomfort of not knowing. Finally, identity achievement occurs after a teenager has experienced a crisis, evaluated meaningful alternatives, and has made a commitment

A small point worth noting is the possibility for a person to be diffused in one area of life but to gain healthy achievement in another area. When working with students, diffusion in one personality domain, for example, spiritual belief, does not necessarily reflect diffusion in another area of personality, for example, career concerns.

The concept of foreclosure is important for the middle school years in that it suggests that early adolescents need exposure to a wide variety of career experiences. This can occur through reading, guest speakers, career field trips, career days at school, class projects, and the like. Because the adult world is still a few years off, quantity of exposure that slowly moves toward quality might be a good guideline. Default choices (saying whatever sounds good to peers or adults) could occur simply because the student lacks awareness of the range of career opportunities (Grutter, 2000).

Grutter (2000) also describes foreclosure that may not materialize until many years later. An early adolescent may appear to have gained career identity achievement by demonstrating knowledge about a field and appearing to make good academic and vocational decisions. However, if the career choice was gained without full self-exploration or the decision was externally driven, say from a parent, the young person may have eliminated true consideration of personal enjoyment in work. Specifically, career services should assess whether the student has engaged in getting to know the self (then achievement has occurred) or is ignoring the self (then foreclosure has occurred and it's being carefully disguised).

According to Grutter (2000), there can be another downside to rigid career identity achievement. If a student is dedicated to one profession and the occupation is eliminated in a changing economy, the student may know of no alternatives if early exploration was truncated. The global economy requires flexibility and the ability to change, sometimes rapidly. Therefore, exploring reasonable alternative occupations is vital. Career education must include the ever-present reality of change, not to squash the vision, but to create flexibility for the possibility of change.

Interests, Abilities, and Values

During childhood, a goal of career practitioners, teachers, and parents is to present enough opportunities for children to discover, or more accurately stumble upon, self-satisfying abilities and areas of interest. Ideally, childhood would be pressure free. A shift during the middle school years moves toward purposeful exploration. External messages may relay expectations for the early adolescent to be future focused with some goals for adulthood in mind. The early adolescent is also motivated to self-enhance (engage in behaviors that lead to positive feelings about the self), and positive achievement feelings can be gained by pursuing and mastering content related to adult roles (Brown, 1998). Therefore, both internal and external motivators exist for the early adolescent. What makes moving toward mastery even more likely is that the early adolescent typically doesn't have to start from scratch. Many of the areas of interest and abilities are extensions from childhood (Grutter, 2000). Early adolescents who are not discovering interests and abilities may feel behind their peers in their development (Brown, 1998).

Struggles between interests and abilities may include a lack of alignment, an unrealistic awareness of the connection between education/training and an occupation, or discovering likes that differ from parents (Grutter, 2000). Grutter suggests that many early adolescents have goals that are not consistent with their abilities. For example, the young person who wants to work for NASA but is taking lower-level science and math classes may need help recognizing realistic limitations, but also needs encouragement at the same time. On the other hand, a young person with high ability may plan for an occupation because it is easy or expected, without thoroughly considering personal preferences. Finally, supporting students who have reasonable interests in areas their parents do not favor can also be challenging but important. Working with middle school students, career counselors walk a fine line between encouraging career projections while at the same time slowly and strategically introducing realistic considerations without overwhelming or discouraging the young person.

In regard to values, middle school-aged children are preparing for an identity crisis that ends with an emerging adult identity (Erikson, 1968). An adolescent's internalization of values may vary from his parents, and these emerging values will guide the decisions and behaviors. No longer do children simply follow adults; adolescents base behavior on personal beliefs. Grutter (2000) states, "As an identity is shaped that is separate from the parents, values begin to emerge as major determinants of behavior" (p. 283). Exposing students to a wide variety of pro-social and pro-self values is paramount for adolescents to achieve pro-social identities.

The goal of exposing this age group to a variety of values involves the need for the early adolescent to learn examples of desirable values and to learn a vocabulary for self expression. Ethically bound dilemmas or exercises allow students the experience of making choices and applying different values, while getting to avoid the actual consequences.

Box 13.3   Exposing Youth to Careers

Goals: NOICC (1992): Skills to interact with others. Knowledge of skills necessary to seek and obtain jobs. Understanding how work relates to the needs and functions of the economy and society. Understanding the process of career planning. Skills to make decisions. Gysbers & Henderson (2000): Assess how enacting personal responsibilities impacts others. Learn about nonverbal communication. Focus on how communication impacts problem solving. Make connection between knowledge and adult work experiences. Identify nonschool opportunities for learning. Project self into the future. Teach students how to break down a task into steps.

Foaud (1995) developed the following six-week program to expose students to math and science occupations; however, it could easily be extended to each of the Holland domains, with each six-week program covering one of the domains. Please note how the children are given choices and are socialized into the adult world of work.

First, a logo contest was held to prepare students for the upcoming program. The winning student's logo was made into buttons and posters. Next, there was a field trip to a local university. Students were given a tour of the school, and a professor of physics did a presentation called "Science can be Fun." If covering each Holland domain, a faculty from other specific majors could describe related career opportunities.

Week 1: Classroom introduction to specific fields within a domain. Classroom discussion about the field is held. Students are taught career-specific vocabulary. Audiovisual presentations, reading about specific careers, and creating a bulletin board all serve to inform the students about related occupations. Students then help to brainstorm about local businesses that could provide live observation opportunities.

Week 2: Some field trips contain one tour for all students, and other field trips entail multiple mini-tours at which students choose the destination. Field-trip specific exercises are assigned as homework. Thank-you notes are written and sent to the businesses. Parents are invited to participate on the field trips as chaperones.

Weeks 3 and 4: Students develop of list of speakers they would like to invite to the school. Students then choose to attend two of the eight presentations lasting 30–40 minutes. Students prepare questions ahead of time and are taught how to ask them. In addition, appropriate behavior is discussed. Finally, thank-you notes are written and sent.

Week 5: Students who are interested in specific occupations are given an opportunity to shadow a professional for one half day. Appropriate shadowing behavior is taught. Students are given worksheets that provide additional information about the career and a follow-up form for evaluating the experience.

Week 6: Students and teachers get together to evaluate the program, the speakers, the field trip, and the shadowing exercise. The hope is to identify those experiences that are worth repeating and those that are best avoided.

Box 13.4   Values Clarification Exercise I

Goals: NOICC (1992): Knowledge of the importance of growth and change. Knowledge of the influence of a positive self-concept. Skills to interact with others. Knowledge of the interrelationship of life roles. Gysbers & Henderson (2000): Assess how enacting personal responsibilities impacts others. Look at people in immediate environment and how each has his own set of responsibilities. Make connection between knowledge and adult work experiences. Introduce the concept of having control over one's self and lifestyle choices. Be able to identify likely feelings in various situations. Begin to predict how one would feel in possible situations. Assess how attitudes and values affect actions. Make connection between values and life-style.

In addition to the values exercises in the technique/assessment chapters, here is an interesting group or individual project (Johnson, 1990). Students have 20 minutes to pick the six people who will be allowed to escape some horrible catastrophe. Only six can go, and here is the list:

A male bookkeeper who is in his early thirties

The bookkeeper's wife who is six months pregnant

An African-American, second-year medical student who is also a political activist

A famous historian-author in his early forties

An actress who can sing and dance

A female biochemist

A Rabbi in his mid-fifties

A male Olympic athlete who is skilled in all sports

A female college student

A police officer with a gun

This exercise is multileveled. First, why does an individual pick some people over others? Why is education valued but not dancing or singing, or vice versa? Is age a factor for preferential treatment? Is there a priority set for some occupations? Second, how do the students agree and disagree with each other? Do some students get steamrolled or are they steamrollers? The interpersonal interaction is valuable information about the self.

EARLY ADOLESCENCE AND THE EXTERNAL SIDE OF THE DIAMOND

Role of Parents and Teachers

It is common knowledge that many researchers have found SES differences in educational and vocational achievement. Ginzberg (1972) writes, "Children born into low income families have relatively little prospect of developing and accomplishing an occupational goal that requires graduating from college or professional school. The exceptional person can make it, but the vast majority will be unable to surmount the multiple hurdles along the way"

Box 13.5   Values Clarification Exercise II

Goals: NOICC (1992): Knowledge of the importance of growth and change. Knowledge of the influence of a positive self-concept. Skills to interact with others. Knowledge of the interrelationship of life roles. Gysbers & Henderson (2000): Assess how enacting personal responsibilities impacts others. Look at people in immediate environment and how each has her own set of responsibilities. Make connection between knowledge and adult work experiences. Introduce the concept of having control over one's self and life-style choices. Be able to identify likely feelings in various situations. Begin to predict how one would feel in possible situations. Assess how attitudes and values affect actions. Make connection between values and life-style.

Lewis (2000) offers another values exercise that has been modified to fit within the middle school population. What is important is not the actual person(s) the student selects, but why that person(s) was chosen. The skill in this exercise is to be able to listen for the meta message.

Students are given a list of people and told they face a very serious situation. The students are told that the situation is personal but the circumstances are not described. As they think about very important issues in their lives, who would they seek council from and why? Is this person male or female? How old is this

person? What would the outcome be? Knowing the interests of particular students may offer clues to generate additional questions to draw out the students' values.

A university professor who is an expert in this area
A teacher with whom the student feels very comfortable
An adult family member
A family member in his/her teenage years
A peer who has gone through this before
A friend whom the student really trusts and likes
A religious leader such as priest, minister, or rabbi
A physician
Other

If the students say it depends upon the issue, they are missing the point. Who do they see in their daily lives as being important advisors when dealing with big issues? Career practitioners need to resist the urge to give an example of a personal issue. In addition, some students may want to get help from multiple people. This is just fine. Have the student mark a percentage by each person they choose (ideally it will add up to 100). Notice that the list ranges from impersonal experts to very personal confidants. Note that the age range is from a peer to a potential elder. Gather this information as they talk about their choices.

Box 13.6   Understanding Finances

Goals: NOICC (1992): Understanding how work relates to the needs and functions of the economy and society. Knowledge of the benefits of educational achievement to career opportunities. Gysbers & Henderson (2000): Understand how decisions made by others (e.g., school) can impact them. Connect past decisions to present behaviors. Learn how to predict an ending per alternative choice; then choose the best alternative.

Divide students into groups of five or six. As a group, students identify occupations of varying financial levels. Following random assignments of one occupation to each student, the students begin to earn the amount of money that is realistically appropriate. A draw bag contains labels for negative events that can occur, such as sick child, cannot work, laid off, home or car repair. Similarly, some positive events are in-

cluded, such as promotion, bonus, get an extra part-time job.

Use the newspaper to identify the cost of buying a home or renting and groceries. Estimate utilities (may even have students interview their parents about the cost of their utilities). Students must manage a home, deal with child care, buy groceries, keep vehicles working, and plan for leisure/vacations. Regardless of the income level, bills must be paid on time. Obviously, some students with higher paying occupations could sell their belongings and buy cheaper cars or homes when emergencies occur. It will become clear that minimum wage occupations do not provide a living wage. You may also want to allow them to use credit cards to furnish their home or go on vacations. Then have them deal with the extra payments. Some research may be needed to make the financial numbers realistic for the local area.

(p. 173). Sadly, this sentiment is supported 30 years later by Blustein et al.'s (2002) work with high-SES and low-SES adolescents, who, by the way, were similar in intelligence and motivation levels.

On the other hand, Keith et al. (1998) studied over 15,000 students and found that parental involvement in the 8th grade strongly predicted academic achievement in the 10th grade. This relationship was more important than SES or previous school performance and was significant for African Americans, Caucasians, Native Americans, and Asian Americans. Furthermore, Bell, Allen, Hauser, and O'Connor (1996) report that parental pressure to achieve academically and vocationally surpassed family SES in impact.

Basically, parents need to be involved in their children's schooling. Career programs for this age group could include strategies for: (a) building relationships between teachers and parents, (b) having teachers create homework assignments that include parents, (c) teaching parents how to help their children at home, and (d) getting parents involved and invested in the goals of the school (Eccles & Harold, 1993).

Rather than determining specific occupational choices and risking premature foreclosure, Grutter (2000) suggests aiding adolescents in focusing their career interests. Over time (by early adulthood), those interests will stabilize and the individual will achieve full identity development. However, Grutter also notes that some adolescents will enter the work force right out of high school and may need assistance in identifying and developing marketable skills. The process of identifying skills may make it clear to the adolescents that postsecondary training will be needed whether further schooling is considered desirable or not.

Time with Peers Versus Parents: Experiencing the External World

Adolescents spend less and less time with their parents and more and more time with peers, and this has direct implications for career development. The average American teenager spends all day in school plus an additional 18 extracurricular hours a week with peers (Fuligni & Stevenson, 1995). Seniors in high school spend less than 15 percent of waking hours with family (in India, it is about 40 percent) (Larson & Verma, 1999). Anywhere from two to six million school-aged children are alone at home until the adult work day is over (Berman, Winkleby, Chesterman, & Boyce, 1993; Richardson, Radziszewska, Dent, & Flay, 1993), and between the 5th and 6th grade, children begin to self-disclose more to friends than parents (Buhrmester, 1996). Such a limited amount of time with nonschool-related adults does not offer much time for exposure to various occupations. School may be the major source for adolescents to gain an awareness of the world of work.

Early adolescents are, however, gaining experience with the external world (Grutter, 2000). Students spend the night at friends' homes and observe how other families discuss the world of work; they go to the mall or movies, budget money for items and food. Basically, the early adolescent is starting to make choices and experience consequences in ways that are closer to adult experiences. Introducing decision-making skills is appropriate.

Exposing teenagers to various occupational opportunities requires a well-designed career education program that is developmentally appropriate, informative, and interesting. Career counselors can expand the focus of early adolescents by asking questions such as, "Thinking of your parents and older siblings, extended family, friends' parents and older siblings, are there any jobs that capture your interest or ones you dislike?" Early adolescents can learn a great deal by observing adults and asking about jobs. A variety of class projects can be created based upon this age group's daily exposure to adults. Because some unrealistic beliefs about adulthood still occur, respecting opinions expressed while suggesting further considerations can stimulate career exploration.

SUMMARY

The middle school years are about transition. Transitioning from childhood fantasies to adult realities. Transitioning from prepubescence toward sexual maturity. Transitioning from concrete operations to formal operations. Transitioning from the nuclear family to the world of peers. These transitions rarely are emotionally and socially smooth, but they serve the purpose of beginning individual identity development. Career counselors can aid in the transitory period by laying the foundation for adult decision making and preparing the early adolescent for the first big decision: college or vocational training tracks in high school. Students envision the future through dreams, but those dreams need to become increasingly realistic.

STUDY OUTLINE: KEY TERMS AND CONCEPTS

I. The first diamond
   A. The first true future focus
      1. Preparing one's self for college preparatory or vocational preparatory classes
      2. Thinking about skills for first job
      3. Fantasy of self as an adult is somewhat reality based
II. Cognitions
   A. Abstract thinking
      1. Thinking about the potential, the possible, and imagining all that could be
      2. Idealistic and critical
      3. Inexperienced, which leads to interesting conclusions
      4. Imaginary audience: every one thinks about me as much as I think about myself
      5. Personal fable: I am unique and special, and the world will turn out differently for me
III. Gender and SES
   A. Gender
      1. Increased pressure to engage in sex-typed behaviors (worse for females)

2. May artificially pick sex-specific careers to avoid criticism from peers

3. School needs to avoid sex-typing careers or classes.

B. SES

1. Adults may have lower expectations for low-SES families

2. Low-SES students may be placed in lower-level courses

IV. Ethnicity: Cross's Model

A. Racial Identity

1. Middle school students are able to "encounter" and understand racial barriers

2. Awareness may lead to an anti-White and anti-selling out identity

3. Professionals want to set the stage for the internalization stage and avoid the anti-White identity

V. Identity

A. Marcia

1. Identity foreclosure occurs when a teenager makes a decision that is handed down by another, but is not personally committed.

2. Identity achievement occurs when a teenager chooses and personally invests in commitment after experiencing a crisis.

3. Identity moratorium is the place after a crisis but before a commitment.

4. Identity diffusion is a lack of commitment that may be due to a lack of a crisis (normal) or a lack of interest (problematic).

5. Students may be diffused in one area, have achievement in another, and be in moratorium in yet a third area (expect this).

B. Grutter

1. Foreclosure in career leads to a default decision.

2. Low achievers default due to a lack of awareness about career options.

3. High achievers can default due to parental or societal pressure or pursuing what is easy.

4. Default choices limit skill development, which is important for dealing with the global economy and guaranteed changes in the future.

VI. Interests, Abilities, and Values

A. Interests and abilities

1. Begin to align the two domains

      2. May see interests as unrealistic due to limited abilities

      3. May not understand which abilities to develop or to what extent

    B. Values

      1. Teach vocabulary for values

      2. Provide examples of pro-social values

      3. Have exercises in which students apply values in decision making

 VII. Role of Parents and Teachers

    A. Parents

      1. Be involved with child's schooling

      2. Pressure child to academically do well (healthy pressure only)

    B. Teachers

      1. Build bridge to parents

      2. Have homework that involves parents

      3. Teach parents how to help child at home

VIII. Time with Peers versus Parents: Experiencing the External World

    A. Parents

      1. Rapidly decreasing time and sharing of personal information since 5th grade

      2. Make family time to be with child(ren)

    B. Peers

      1. Allows teenager to see how others survive and prosper

      2. Begins shift toward peer-based world

      3. Career practitioners can use this experience to expand career awareness

EXERCISES

Research and Role Play:

Goals: Introduce the idea that current decisions are connected to the future. Connect education and training to desired future. Introduce the need to plan now for the next step of high school. Introduce the adult financial world.

Students are to gather want ads (newspaper or online), utility bills, home listings, housing rental ads, monthly car payments, insurance quotes, monthly food expenses, and any other important monthly bills. Have the students generate monthly overhead estimates for various income levels. (This is a good small group project. Have each group pick a different income range.) Then use the want ads to generate monthly income ranges. Once each range is created, students can share their information with the other groups.

Students pair off and role-play. (One plays the counselor, the other the middle school student.) First, have the student playing the middle school client identify the life-style they would like to have as a grownup. The goal is to communicate that this is a realistic life-style and not a fantasy one (e.g., rock star). Use the financial information to generate the typical overhead of the life-style. Second, use the want ads to identify the type of job needed to support said life-style. Third, look at the training/education requirements of this job. Fourth, use the middle school curriculum to explore and set a foundation for high school. Finally, suggest that this process will need to be repeated in high school so a foundation can be set for the next level of training.

REFERENCES

Arbona, C. (2000). The development of academic achievement in school-aged children: Precursors to career development. In S. D. Brown & R. W. Lent (Eds.), *Handbook of Counseling Psychology* (3rd ed., pp. 270–309). New York: Wiley.

Basow, S. A., & Rubin, L. R. (1999). Gender influences on adolescent development. In N. G. Johnson & M. C. Roberts (Eds.), *Beyond appearance: A new look at adolescent girls* (pp. 25–52). Washington, DC: American Psychological Association.

Bell, K. L., Allen, J. P., Hauser, S. T., & O'Connor, T. G. (1996). Family factors and young adult transitions: Educational attainment and occupational prestige. In J. A. Graber, J. Brooks-Gunn, & A. C. Petersen (Eds.), *Transitions through adolescence: Interpersonal domains and context* (pp. 345–366). Mahwah, NJ: Erlbaum.

Berk, L. E. (2002). *Infants, children, and adolescents* (4th ed.). Boston: Allyn & Bacon

Berman, B., Winkleby, M., Chesterman, E., & Boyce, T. (1992). After-school child care and self-esteem in school-aged children. *Pediatrics, 89,* 654–659.

Blustein, D. L., Chaves, A. P., Diemer, M. A., Gallagher, L. A., Marshall, K. G., Sirin, S., & Bhati, K. S. (2002). Voices of the forgotten half: The role of social class in the school-to-work transition. *Journal of Counseling Psychology, 49*(3), 311–323.

Brown, D. (2003). *Career information, career counseling, and career development* (8th ed.). Boston: Allyn & Bacon.

Brown, J. D. (1998). *The self.* Boston: McGraw Hill.

Buhrmester, D. (1996). Need fulfillment, interpersonal competence, and the developmental contexts of early adolescent friendship. In W. M. Bukowski, A. F. Newcomb, & W. W. Hartup (Eds.), *The company they keep: Friendship during childhood and adolescence* (pp. 158–185). New York: Cambridge Univ. Press.

Cross, W. E., Jr. (1971). The Negro-to-Black conversion experience. *Black World, 20*(9), 13–27.

Cross, W. E., Jr. (1978). The Thomas and Cross models of psychological nigrescence: A review. *Journal of Black Psychology, 5*, 13–31.

Cross, W. E., Jr. (1991). *Shades of Black: Diversity in African-American identity*. Philadelphia: Temple Univ. Press.

Cross, W. E., Jr. (1995). The psychology of nigrescence: Revising the Cross model. In J. G. Ponterotto, J. M. Casas, L. A. Suziuki, & C. M. Alexander (Eds.), *Handbook of multicultural counseling* (pp. 93–122). Thousand Oaks, CA: Sage.

Crouter, A., Manke, B., & McHale, S. (1995). The family context of gender intensification in early adolescence. *Child Development, 66*, 317–329.

Donlevy, J. (2001). Workforce development: Building effective programs for children in institutional settings—a look at the elite schools model. *International Journal of Instructional Media, 28*(3), 215–222.

Dusek, J., & Joseph, G. (1983). The bases of teacher expectancies: A meta-analysis. *Journal of Educational Psychology, 75*, 327–346.

Eccles, J. S., & Harold, R. D. (1993). Parent-school involvement during the early adolescent years. *Teachers College Record, 94*, 568–587.

Elkind, D. (1967). Egocentrism in adolescence. *Child Development, 38*(4), 1025–1034.

Elkind, D. (1978). Understanding the young adolescent. *Adolescence, 13*(49), 127–134.

Erikson, E. H. (1968). *Identity: Youth and Crisis*. New York: Norton.

Flavell, J. H. (1963). *The developmental psychology of Jean Piaget*. Princeton, NJ: Van Nostrand.

Fouad, N. A. (1995). Career linking: An intervention to promote math and science career awareness. *Journal of Counseling and Development, 73*(5), 527–534.

Fuligni, A. J., & Stevenson, H. W. (1995). Time use and mathematics achievement among American, Chinese, and Japanese high school students. *Child Development, 66*, 830–842.

Galambos, N. L., Almeida, D. M., & Petersen, A. C. (1990). Masculinity, femininity, and sex role attitudes in early adolescence: Exploring gender intensification. *Child Development, 61*, 1905–1914.

Ginzberg, E. (1972). Toward a theory of occupational choice: A restatement. *Vocational Guidance Quarterly, 20*(3), 169–176.

Gottfredson, L. S., & Lapan, R. T. (1997). Assessing gender-based circumscription of occupational aspirations. *Journal of Career Assessment, 5*(4), 419–441.

Grutter, J. (2000). Developmental career counseling: Different stages, different choices. In J. M. Kummerow (Ed.), *New directions in career planning and the workplace: Practical strategies for career management professionals* (2nd ed., pp. 273–306). Palo Alto, CA: Davies-Black.

Gysbers, N. C., & Henderson, P. (2000). *Developing & managing your school guidance program* (3rd ed.). Alexandria, VA: American Counseling Association.

Haller, E. J. (1985). Pupil race and elementary school ability grouping: Are teachers biased against Black children? *American Educational Research Journal, 22*(4), 465–483.

Hoffman, L. W. (2000). Maternal employment: Effects of social context. In R. D. Taylor & M. C. Wang (Eds.), *Resilience across contexts: Family, work, culture, and community* (pp. 147–176). Mahwah, NJ: Erlbaum.

Huston, A. C., & Alvarez, M. M. (1990). The socialization context of gender role development in early adolescence. In R. Montemayor, G. R. Adams & T. P. Gullotta (Eds.), *From childhood to adolescence: A transitional period?* (pp. 156–179). Newbury Park, CA: Sage.

Johnson, D. W. (1990). *Teaching out: Interpersonal effectiveness and self-actualization.* Upper Saddle River, NJ: Prentice-Hall.

Katz, M. (1963). *Decisions and values: A rationale for secondary school guidance.* New York: College Entrance Examination Board.

Keith, T. Z., Keith, P. B., Quirk, K. J., Sperduto, J., Santillo, S., & Killings, S. (1998). Longitudinal effects of parent involvement on high school grades: Similarities and differences across gender and ethnic groups. *Journal of School Psychology, 36,* 335–363.

Kyle, M. T., & Hennis, M. (2000). Experiential model for career guidance in early childhood education. In N. Peterson & R. C. Gonzalez (Eds.), *Career counseling models for diverse populations: Hands-on applications by practitioners* (pp. 1–7). Belmont, CA: Wadsworth/Thomson Learning.

Lankard, B. A. (1991). *Strategies for implementing the national career development guidelines.* Columbus, OH: ERIC Clearinghouse on Adult Career and Vocational Education. (ERIC Document Reproduction Service No. ED338898).

Larson, R., & Verma, S. (1999). How children and adolescents spend time across the world: Work, play, and developmental opportunities. *Psychological Bulletin, 125,* 701–736.

Lewis, H. (2000). *A question of values: Six ways we make the personal choices that shape our lives.* Crozet, VA: Axios Press.

Marcia, J. E. (1966). Development and validation of ego identity status. *Journal of Personality and Social Psychology, 3*, 551–558.

Marcia, J. E. (1976). Identity six year after: A follow-up study. *Journal of Youth and Adolescence, 5*, 145–150.

Marcia, J. E. (1980). Identity in adolescence. In J. Adelson (Ed.), *Handbook of adolescent psychology* (pp. 159–187). New York: Wiley.

Marcia, J. E. (1994). The empirical study of ego identity. In H. A. Bosma, T. L. G. Graafsma, H. D. Grotevant, & D. J. De Levita (Eds.), *Identity and development* (pp. 67-80). Newbury Park, CA: Sage.

National Occupational Information Coordinating Committee (NOICC). (1992). *The national career development guidelines project*. Washington, DC: U. S. Government Printing Office.

Peterson, N., & Gonzalez, R. C. (2000). *The role of work in people's lives: Applied career counseling and vocational psychology*. Stamford, CT: Brooks/Cole.

Phinney, J. S. (1989). Stages of ethnic identity development in minority group adolescents. *Journal of Early Adolescence, 9*, 34–49.

Phinney, J. S., & Rosenthal, D. A. (1992). Ethnic identity in adolescence: Process, context, and outcome. In G. R. Adams, T. P. Gullotta, & R. Montemayor (Eds.), *Adolescent identity formation* (pp. 145–172). Newbury Park, CA: Sage.

Richardson, J., Radziszewska, B., Dent, C., & Flay, B. (1993). Relationship between after-school care of adolescents and substance use, risk taking, depressed mood, and academic achievement. *Pediatrics, 92*, 32–38.

Santrock, J. W. (2002). *Life-span development* (8th ed.). Boston: McGraw Hill.

Super, D. E. (1957). *Vocational development: A framework for research*. New York: Teachers College Press.

Vartanian, L. R., & Powlishta, K. K. (1996). A longitudinal examination of the social-cognitive foundations of adolescent egocentrism. *Journal of Early Adolescence, 16*(2), 157–178.

CHAPTER 14

Career Development in High School and Late Adolescence/Young Adulthood

Some students go to college. All students go to work.

Kris Gossom

Late adolescence and young adulthood are overlapping stages of life that may independently or consecutively apply to a young person. Middle adolescence consists of the high school years, those of 14–18. The teenager is on the verge of entering the adult world of work, and current decision making has an important impact on future career directions. Late adolescence may last until age 24, include continued training (e.g., post-secondary education or an apprenticeship), and delay the responsibilities of adulthood. For many, however, adulthood begins at 18 and includes employment in a profession (e.g., entry level management in retail or the food industry), setting up a household, and beginning a family.

Career counselors are charged with assessing clients in the 18–25 age group as to whether they fit more into the late adolescence or early adulthood group. Furthermore, because the ages 18–25 represent a transition out of high school and into the world of work, most clients will have needs across both domains. This chapter is divided into two sections, but the heaviest focus is on middle adolescence as Chapter 15 will take a full look at adulthood.

MIDDLE ADOLESCENCE: AGES 14–18

Adolescence is an exciting phase. Getting a driver's license and a car becomes a reality. Forming adult, intimate relationships that could lead to marriage and a family occur with some frequency. Finally, being free from the rules and strict guidance of one's parents feels exciting. It is a time of idealized logic and buoyant optimism (Santrock, 1999). It is also a time of decision making that can alter one's life path.

For children prior to high school, reflecting the reality of the adult world was too distant, and a fully realistic vision of the future was not the developmental goal. Both elementary and middle schools offer career services to establish conceptual and attitudinal foundations for later career choices. Although a transition to a more informed career focus can occur in middle school, early adolescence still contains elements of fantasy. High school is a different world. First, the adolescent has had some time to practice formal operations cognitive skills as per Piaget's (1970) descriptors. Second, many adolescents are experiencing their first jobs, checking accounts, and monthly bills (e.g., car payment, cell phone bill, etc.). Third, the adult world is becoming ever more present, and even if adolescents are not ready for the adult world, time is signaling that the world is ready for them.

However, high school is certainly not the last opportunity for making important career decisions. The threat in a message saying "This is it. Figure it out or suffer for the rest of your life" is not appropriate or useful. Encouragement for creating an adaptable vision works best. Career counselors capitalize on the high school years by enhancing psychological development so young people can make the maximum contribution to society. Adolescents can deal with the anxiety of entering the adult world and learn how to integrate personal and external factors implicit in career identity. Society benefits by helping student maximize their potential through a process of identifying satisfying career pursuits that will bring economic independence.

THE NATIONAL CAREER DEVELOPMENT GUIDELINES (NOICC, 1992) AND A CAREER DEVELOPMENT PROGRAM FOR HIGH SCHOOL (GRADES 9–12)

NOICC and High School

This section contains the goals appropriate to high school-aged students. For an introduction to NOICC, please see Chapter 12. Within each age group (elementary, middle school, high school, and adult), three major areas are to be of focus: (a) self-knowledge, (b) educational and occupational exploration, and (c) career planning (NOICC, 1992). We are restricting our listings to the major categories; however, each major area has multiple goals. Each section is comprised of age-specific set goals, and readers are encouraged to obtain a full version. (Please see the NOICC, 1992 reference at the end of this chapter.)

During the high school years, the development of competency grows in importance with actual occupational or educational exploration occurring. In addition, students should be able to find, evaluate, and understand various sources of career information. Ideally, students are learning how to prepare themselves for finding, acquiring, maintaining, or changing jobs/

Table 14.1   NOICC Career Education Guidelines

Self-Knowledge	Educational and Occupational Exploration	Career Planning
Understanding the influence of a positive self-concept	Understanding the relationship between educational achievement and career planning	Understanding the interrelationship of life roles
Skills to interact positively with others	Understanding the need for positive attitudes toward work and learning	Understanding the continuous changes in male/female roles
Understanding the impact of growth and development	Skills to locate, evaluate, and interpret career information	Skills in career planning (NOICC, 1992)
	Skills to prepare to seek, obtain, maintain, and change jobs	
	Understanding how societal needs and functions influence the nature and structure of work	
	Skills to make decisions	

education/training situations. This last point includes a realistic understanding of how work, the economy, and individual life-styles are interconnected. Finally, students are able to engage in career planning and decision making as seen in Table 14.1 (Lankard, 1991).

Career Development Program

This section contains the third and final installment of Gysbers and Henderson's (2000) Life Career Development program for use in the school system. Career counselors should immediately notice the sophistication that is apparent with the various tasks. The grade school years contained concepts such as introduce, but this part of the program assumes that students are able to understand advanced economic concepts, complex social skills, and project the self into the adult world. In line with the two previous sections, we have summarized and grouped the tasks together as opposed to breaking them down by school year. Our hope is that career counselors will build or adjust the program to meet regional, city, or specific school needs and realities.

Career Diamonds

The Career Diamond (Figure 14.1) focuses on the primary decision for adolescents, which is applying for postsecondary training or finding work right after graduation. This diamond opens immediately into another diamond once

Box 14.1   Life Career Development: Student Competencies by Domains and Goals

Self-Knowledge and Interpersonal Skills

1. Work on valuing unique characteristics and abilities. Assess how abilities develop. Learn to appreciate differences in self and others. End with encouraging uniqueness.
2. Acquire age-appropriate information and strategies for enhancing physical and mental health.
3. Begin with identifying when the student does and does not take responsibility for himself. Look at how he manages the environment. Assess how avoidance of responsibility interferes with success and how taking responsibility increases the likelihood of success.
4. Assess need for relationships with both peers and adults. Look at how his actions can impact how another person responds and treats the student. Look at family and social relationships and assess what is and is not working. End with an understanding of how we are interdependent upon each other.
5. Evaluate group communication skills. Learn how to use communication to help others and encourage problem solving. End with an assessment of current communication skills and strategies for continual improvement.

Life Roles, Settings, and Events

1. Be able to identify unique study skills and how one approaches personal learning. Evaluate said skills and learning, and look for opportunities of improvement. Look at how such skills will aid/hinder her in the world of work. End with an evaluation of what she currently learns and how approaches to learning may change in her future.
2. Take a detailed look at taxation and government. Look at being a consumer, a consumer's legal rights, and a consumer's responsibilities. End with how citizenship and consumerism is an integral part of our economic system.
3. Assess how life roles, events, and specific settings impact life-styles, and consequently, how life-styles can differ based upon changes in the above list. Assess how current life-style was developed and how adjustments in life roles, events, and specific settings could result in a preferred life-style.
4. Look at how each student currently is affected by stereotypes. Assess the stereotypes of others around them and how those stereotypes limit their choices. Look at how personal stereotypes have changed over time. End with a focus on stereotypes and their impact on career identity.
5. Understand how current decisions can impact the future. Predict concerns that will arise with age. Prepare for being flexible in life roles and choices. End with a focus on how concerns are connected to situations and life roles, and how a change in one will change a person's concerns.

Life Career Planning

1. Look at how workers need to cooperate when dealing with a large or difficult task. Understand the need for workers to have laws or contracts that

(continued)

(Box 14.1 continued)

protect them. Identify the rights and responsibilities of workers. Predict changes in the rights and responsibilities of workers in the future.

2. Explain and rank order values. Give personal examples of using attitudes and values to make a decision. Assess how personal values impact their decisions, behaviors, and life-style. Be able to explain why it is important to understand one's attitudes and values.

3. Look at past legal decisions that impact the students. Assess how others make decisions. Predict how decisions the students have already made will impact them in the future. Be able to use a formal decision-making process effectively.

4. Be able to describe why the creation of multiple alternatives prior to making a decision is important. Be able to assess the varying levels of risk per alternative. Describe the consequences paid by another person who made an important decision. Have the ability to self-assess, make decisions, weigh consequences, and seek additional information.

5. Be able to describe personal values, interests, and capabilities. Understand why it is important to set realistic goals and work toward achieving them. Assess changes in values, interests, and capabilities. Look at how one has dealt with past goals and make predictions for the future.

Adapted from Gysbers and Henderson, *Developing and Managing Your School Guidance Program* (2000, pp. 327–334).

high school has ended. Whether pursuing training/education or working, the late adolescent will confirm likes/dislikes and abilities, and increase knowledge of the world of work. What was once fantasy will be day-to-day reality. The second diamond focuses on adjusting to the first decision. If the young person stays in the first full-time job, then how to advance in the field becomes an issue. If a change is indicated, determining training needs or other opportunities becomes relevant.

The adolescent's developmental task is to come to a clear understanding of personal identity. Although adjustments can be made, the sense of self is typically stable, and the foundation is set. The world of work is becoming more and more realistic but is still permeable. Part-time jobs and a more accurate understanding of parents' or other adults' experiences allows the adolescent to gain some career understanding, ruling out some occupations while still considering others. However, until the young person participates in occupational activities, a dotted line indicates an inexperienced understanding of the external world.

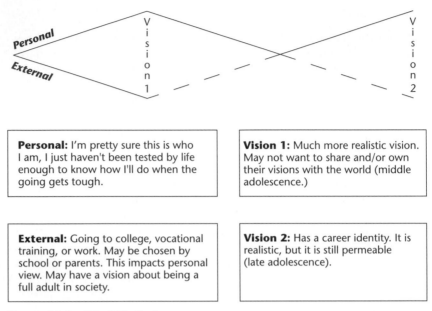

Personal: I'm pretty sure this is who I am, I just haven't been tested by life enough to know how I'll do when the going gets tough.

Vision 1: Much more realistic vision. May not want to share and/or own their visions with the world (middle adolescence.)

External: Going to college, vocational training, or work. May be chosen by school or parents. This impacts personal view. May have a vision about being a full adult in society.

Vision 2: Has a career identity. It is realistic, but it is still permeable (late adolescence).

Figure 14.1   9th–12th Graders

The first vision, which occurs in high school, can be quite realistic. Super (1985) finds that developmental patterns present in 9th grade boys correlated significantly with adult career behavior. Middle adolescents have an idea about what they would never want to do and are slowly narrowing down the options for what would be desirable. This vision may still have some unrealistic elements because the adolescent does not fully understand the amount of training/education or years of experience required. Yet, the adolescent, based upon a good sense of the self, can project into the future and imagine what life will be like when the goal has been met. This vision is a major motivator for career planning, encouraging the young person to tolerate disliked training, paying dues at the workplace, and exercising patience. It is vital that career counselors assist high school students in forming a well-delineated vision full of detail and experiential imagery.

The second vision refers to post-high school experiences that have reduced or eliminated unrealistic beliefs about the world of work. Based upon actual experience, the late adolescent (ages 18–25, Arnett, 2000, refers to this as "emerging adulthood") understands what it is going to take to achieve his career goals. Realistic planning can begin and a sense of pacing himself can be expected. In addition, the late adolescent may become more familiar with career options and have a greater understanding of occupational characteristics than the middle adolescent. Therefore, the late adolescent may

Box 14.2   The Career Diamond: Formal Assessment

Goals: NOICC (1992): Skills to interact positively with others. Skills to make decisions. Skills to locate, evaluate, and interpret career information. Gysbers & Henderson (2000): Work on valuing unique characteristics and abilities. Learn to appreciate differences in self and others. Prepare for being flexible in life roles and choices. Assess how personal values impact their decisions, behaviors, and life-style.

Students can take a personality instrument such as the *Myers-Briggs Type Indicator,* which is quick to administer and self-scoring. After the students have taken the *MBTI,* but before they receive the results, a career practitioner can provide a mini-workshop. The workshop includes descriptions of each trait (E-I, S-N, T-F, and J-P). Strengths and weaknesses are explained as well as how primary, auxiliary, and tertiary scores impact the expression of any given type. Finally, the different types are described. Students can guess what their type is and which domain is their primary, auxiliary, and tertiary. Then when students score the instruments, they can see how close their original guesses were. This is great fun, and the students are often surprised by how accurate the *MBTI* is.

Students can also write a paper describing their results. First, they describe their understanding of the *MBTI* and their particular type. Second, they provide evidence (thoughts, feelings, and behaviors) that either supports or contradicts the test results. Finally, they can project what their "type" would be like in the workplace and what kinds of careers would be attractive and unattractive.

Their second task is to take a career interest inventory like the *Self-Directed Search.* A career practitioner explains the theory behind an interest inventory and the different areas represented in the instrument. Students can again predict how they scored. Using their "type" results, students analyze personality factors that might affect performance in each work domain (this forces applying the self to the external world). Finally, the instruments inventory results are reviewed and students consider their predictions in comparison.

An important area for discussion could be the impact of high income and/or prestige in making occupational choices. How to deal with occupational demands that are not in line with personal strengths can also be discussed. Finally, it is vital that students gain the perspective that instruments are tools for exploration, instruments do not provide answers, and only they determine their career goals.

change occupational choices, and the diamond immediately opens back up. These types of changes can suggest to the late adolescent that all career decisions are temporary, setting a useful attitude for later adulthood. For middle and late adolescents, several Career Diamond processes may occur in a relatively short period of time.

MIDDLE ADOLESCENCE AND THE SELF SIDE OF THE DIAMOND

Cognitions

Adolescent thinking has several properties characteristic of the developmental stage. First, adult thinking patterns are not fully developed because adolescents haven't gained extensive experience. Second, just because adolescents can make informed, logical, and mature decisions in one area of life does not mean they can make similar decisions in other areas of life. Third, idealism and a personal sense of uniqueness may lead to some lofty goals but limited planning (Elkind, 1967, 1978). Career counselors can enhance growth as thinking patterns mature and encourage career development. Middle adolescents start to identify some possible occupational choices and design a plan to determine whether they want to continue pursuing original goals or to make a change. Changing goals need not be problematic, especially given the career counselors desire to instill decision-making skills and the need for adaptability in the global economy.

The maturing of cognitive abilities adds sophistication to researching information and determining personal priorities. However, adolescents will vary in their ability to make informed decisions, depending upon the life domain and their previous experience. One strategy is to identify successful choices that have been made in some areas of life. The seasoned career practitioner helps the adolescents to see where they have been successful and assists them to generalize those skills to new domains of life. Recognizing how they made choices in other areas builds confidence and speeds up the learning curve for career decision making.

The middle adolescent is finally in a place where decision-making skills can be taught and properly used. Decision-making theory for career education programs could be designed using the Career Diamond along with the outline of questions found in the techniques chapter (Chapter 9). Decision-making curriculums can also include concepts such as planned happenstance, positive uncertainty, and informed opportunism as described in Chapter 6 on the global economy. Finally, teaching about decision making can include exploring unique ways individuals make choices, taking into account intuitive methods as well as rational ones (intuitive clues may offer insights that can be rationally examined later).

Although the steps to career decision making are often presented in a logical and rational manner, personal preferences and emotional leanings impinge in every phase of the process. If the focus is too logical, the decision-making process is fatally flawed. The exercise in Box 14.3 is an example of how skills based on the reality of high school also teach skills for future career decision making.

Box 14.3   You Have Say in Your Immediate Future

Goals: NOICC (1992): Understanding the relationship between educational achievement and career planning. Skills to make decisions. Skills in career planning. Gysbers & Henderson (2000): Look at how one manages the environment. Learn how to use communication to help others and encourage problem solving. Understand how current decisions can impact the future. Be able to use a formal decision-making process effectively.

Schlossberg (2001) designed the following program to aid 9th graders in understanding how choices in high school connect to the world of work, goal setting, and career exploration. The program consists of six 45-minute group sessions that span approximately two months. Notice how the skills taught can easily be generalized to the world of work.

Session 1: The purpose of the program is explained, and students are organized into teams. Good listening skills are taught and modeled. Students then identify behaviors that would lead to a successful school experience as well as aid in making friends. The first team task is to identify learned behaviors and make suggestions for making friends. Second, potential student problems are presented, and the teams must generate a list of emotions and behaviors that could emerge. Next, the teams brainstorm about potential solutions and present them to the class. Finally, each student is asked to pick one positive behavior and try it within a week's time.

Session 2: The goal is to expose students to the ideas that: (a) the current and future world of work will change, (b) planning is important, and (c) it is possible to have potential career goals based upon desired characteristics. Students receive a handout that looks at the shifting job market and makes predictions about future job needs. A second handout introduces students to the concepts of Data, People, Things, or Ideas as presented in the *Dictionary of Occupational Titles*. The third handout provides a grid for planning (one step leads to the next step), and it indicates the importance of planning. The weekly assignment has students interviewing an adult about his career planning and career missteps.

Session 3: This session exposes the students to high school requirements, how to plan a four-year curriculum around interests while also meeting high school graduation requirements, and underscores the need to be responsible for one's future. Four handouts are given: (a) list of high school courses, (b) requirements for graduation, (c) sample four-year plans, and (d) a sentence completion task. Counselors present information regarding the graduation requirements, and the teams compete to see who remembered the most points from the presentation. The second team project has students completing the following sentences and sharing the information with team members (e.g., I'm most happy when…; I've been successful at…). The entire class discusses the

(continued)

(Box 14.3 continued)

need to be responsible for planning and making decisions. There is a second counselor presentation on various school curricular areas, requirements, and electives. Students then mark what electives are most interesting. The weekly assignment is to prioritize electives, evaluate personal academic strengths and weaknesses, and share their four-year plan with their parents.

Session 4: This session introduces the availability of counseling services, connects decisions made about the first year of high school to the following years, and creates a tentative plan spanning the four years of high school. The three worksheets are: (a) a tentative educational plan spanning all four years, (b) an autobiographical timeline containing important life events, and (c) a sheet for assessing interests and strengths. Teams discuss, with help from wandering counselors, future aspirations and how current educational plans set the foundation for success. Counseling services are explained. A variety of future options ranging from enlisting in the military to vocational/technical training to two- and four-year colleges are introduced. Finally, students are told about the local and national standardized tests they will be taking while in high school.

Session 5: Students choose the classes for the 10th grade. Students meet with a teacher in each subject who must sign a form ensuring the class is appropriate. Teams discuss reasons for and ramifications of changing four-year plans. The weekly assignment is to identify an area where the student desires improvement and an area in high school that will be fun and productive.

Session 6: Students evaluate the program. Items include things they liked and disliked about the program, what they are looking forward to in high school, and what they are concerned about in high school. Teams discuss these various topics, and counselors answer questions. Finally, students are encouraged to take charge of their high school career by accepting personal responsibility, but also by seeking help when needed.

Gender

Gender stereotyping is another area creating limits for career development in middle adolescence. Marsh (1989) found that adolescents differ in the way they judge their academic qualities. Consistent with cultural stereotypes, boys and girls evaluate themselves higher in gender-stereotyped domains. Schools may further support gender-stereotypes by reinforcing boys and girls who choose gender-specific classes, and school counselors may even advise students to consider traditional occupations rather than nontraditional options (Eccles & Hoffman, 1984; Haring & Beyard-Tyler, 1984; Stipek, 1992). In the classroom, Henderson and Dweck (1990) found that math teachers were likely to say young women lack ability when they don't understand concepts, whereas math teachers are likely to tell young men that poor performance is due to a lack of effort. Consequently, young women doubt their abilities and do not pursue careers in the area of math or science. In the last two years of high school, young women also reduce their participation in gifted programs, listing pressure from peers and parents and the attitudes of teachers and counselors as reasons for this decision (Read, 1991).

Model programs suggest methods to motivate students regardless of gender. Mason and Kahle (1988) designed and implemented a program for 9th graders. First, science teachers who volunteered for the program were sensitized to overt and covert behaviors that send different messages to boys and girls. This was done via workshops where information and teaching materials were distributed. In addition, hands-on activities taught the teachers how to create more exciting learning environments for all students. Over the course of the experiment, the teachers received visits, mailings, and telephone calls to help them achieve the goals of the program. The results showed that students who were in the experimental classrooms had more positive perceptions of science, engaged in more extracurricular science activities, and increased their interest in science-related careers as compared to the control group. Both boys and girls became better motivated. Such programs require strong support by school districts as well as ongoing teacher training.

It is clear that a high school can positively influence the expansion of career options. If students are not taking classes in the sciences and math fields, whether the student is male or female, some occupations may be forever closed to them. Career counselors can assist high school students in determining class schedules and school activities that are career specific but gender neutral. For example, to pursue many technical, science, or medical occupations, sequential math and science courses are needed. Another example might come from a liberal arts focus where foreign languages and/or advanced writing courses would be helpful. Also, extracurricular activities can aid in developing career skills and provide additional learning opportunities (e.g., school newspaper, science club, etc.).

A variety of role models within the schools can influence student attitudes. If students only see female English teachers and male math teachers, the school is sending a message supporting gender stereotypes, regardless of the rhetoric stating that girls can do math and boys can enjoy English.

Extracurricular activities also provide an important piece for later career choice. Grant (2000) followed seven gifted females from high school through college. He found that despite changes in their academic majors, tasks and skills they acquired from K–12 extracurricular activities remained consistent with their career aspirations. Although this sample is small, it does point to the importance of school experiences outside the classroom. Extracurricular activities provide opportunities to develop organization, delegation, listening and following, and public speaking skills, to name just a few. Career counselors can help young people explore these experiences, building students' confidence and making associations to occupational choices.

Socioeconomic Status (SES)

In regards to socioeconomic status (SES), Blustein et al. (2002) interviewed late adolescents from different socioeconomic backgrounds and found influential factors affecting the career development of high school students. Two student groups were identified: high socioeconomic status (HSES), and low socioeconomic status (LSES). First, Blustein et al. found that both groups of late adolescents had "similar internal educational resources and barriers (e.g., motivation, and cognitive abilities)," and were working in similar low-status, unskilled, low-paying jobs (p. 320). However, the HSES individuals saw their current jobs as the means to prepare themselves for future opportunities. The LSES group viewed their current jobs as representing the trap that would restrict them for the rest of their careers. To determine the source of the attitudinal differences, Blustein et al. investigated the students' backgrounds.

HSES individuals were more likely to have intact families with postsecondary educational and professional career experiences (who could offer advice about college and professional careers), acceptable housing and health care (not a distraction), and financial resources to provide support for further education. By comparison, the LSES individuals, despite having families who wanted to be helpful, were more likely to have little or no exposure to the professional world of work (parents have no experience and the adolescent has to make decisions alone), were struggling with issues of poverty (e.g., bad housing, lack of health care creating practical distractions), were more likely to be divorced or having relational disruptions (more distractions), and were emotionally fragmented and overwhelmed by life circumstances (still more distractions) (Blustein et al., 2002). Obviously, HSES parents are in a position to offer emotional, experiential, and financial support, whereas LSES parents may have limited resources and may even need the support of their child in dealing with their own lives.

Career counselors may need to be more available to the personal side of students who fall in the LSES group and be sensitive to disruptions that could distract students from focusing on career planning. On the other hand, career counselors should not assume that HSES students are disruption free because divorce and/or financial problems might be a factor for any adolescent's career development.

Ethnicity

The United States is a diverse nation, and its schools clearly demonstrate the variety of peoples within its borders. The National Center for Education Statistics (NCES) reports that in 2001 public schools had the following racial/ethnic groups represented in significant numbers: (a) White, non-Hispanic 28.8 million , (b) Black, non-Hispanic 8.1 million (c) Hispanic 7.7 million, (d) Asian/Pacific Islander 1.9 million, and (e) American Indian/Alaska Native .5 million (n.d.b). These statistics indicate that schools must be able to meet the psychological and educational needs of a variety of people. High school and college graduation rates can demonstrate how race and ethnicity affect educational achievement and hence career mobility.

In 1997, the U. S. Census Bureau reported that 82 percent of all adults over 25 had completed high school, and 24 percent had a bachelor's degree. However, a closer look shows a difference in high school completers and college graduates by race. For example, 94 percent of White and 87 percent of Black 25–29-year-olds have a high school diploma; however, only 63 percent of Hispanic people have a high school diploma. Bachelor's degrees follow a similar trend with 36 percent of White, 21 percent of Black, and 15 percent of Hispanic people completing a bachelor's degree (NCES, n.d.a). This trend places minority individuals at a continuing disadvantage when competing in the workplace. Because Whites pursue more education, they are better able to enter into higher paying, professional employment. Career counselors can adapt services to help all people maximize their potential, overcome barriers to occupational achievement, and make contributions to the diverse needs of the global economy.

A second factor complicating the picture is diversity within groups. For example, different Hispanic populations have different high school graduation rates—73 percent of Cubans but only 51 percent of Mexican-Americans graduate from high school (Therrien & Ramirez, 2000). Career counselors need to become well acquainted with the different racial groups in their region to identify the unique needs of diverse school populations and to design specific programs to meet specific needs.

Career counselors need to be able to: (a) assess the needs of their student population, (b) identify the unique and specific barriers for each group, (c) design multiple programs, (d) educate the administration and community on how to best meet those different needs, that is, selling the programs, and (e) implement those multiple programs. Again, quality programs require financial support and adequate staff; however, programs may have to be adjusted based on financial and staffing restraints, while trying to maintain a core of quality services. In school districts where funding is tentative, providing evidence of success through program evaluations and describing high achieving graduates could provide the data to lobby for support for career education efforts.

Identity

> Did you ever see an unhappy horse? Did you ever see a bird that had the blues? One reason why birds and horses are not unhappy is because they are not trying to impress other birds and horses.
>
> —*Dale Carnegie*

There is a misnomer in the way western culture looks at the process of becoming an adult. "Independence" is the cry, and self-sufficiency is the goal. Can a young person learn to live all by herself? The irony of adolescence is that in order to become independent of one's family, one must become interdependent within society (Gysbers & Henderson, 2000; Scandura, 2002). Few people in modern economies grow all of their own food, raise and slaughter their own animals, build and maintain a home, spin yarn and make all of their own clothes, and provide all of their own medical care. Obviously, no one is truly independent. We all rely on each other to play our part in society, and the combination of our joint efforts results in the wealth of items and services we take for granted. The goal of independence is balanced by recognizing interdependence.

Erikson's (1968) classic work, *Identity, Youth and Crisis,* describes the process of moving from childhood through adolescence to adulthood. Erikson's approach portrays young adults maturing to a point where they make contributions to society; but the psychological focus emphasizes individual growth rather than interpersonal social development. A more realistic view recognizes that individual identity development is affected by the political or societal context that provides roles for young people who are entering adult society (Hoover, Marcia, & Parris, 1997). Both the individual and societal processes influencing adult identity will be considered in the following sections.

Erikson (1968) observed and predicted that technological advances have and will continue to lengthen the time between childhood and adulthood. Recently, Arnett (2000) expanded the adolescent developmental period to age 25. As adolescence is extended, it becomes a way of life that includes special rules for behavior, a specific generational style of language, types of dress, and specific interests. Adolescent life-styles reject the current adult way of life.

Unless teenagers are choosing damaging norms or behaviors, exploring new social behaviors can be beneficial as new styles adapt to societal changes. The skills and norms practiced and refined by youth might define acceptable social habits as the new generation comes into power. Career counselors can capitalize on teenagers' creativity by helping them consider how some of their novel behaviors could influence the future. In addition, teaching adolescents to distinguish between comical norms that serve no social purpose and interesting norms that may point to future social progress is an important skill. Just think of Bill Gates or Michael Dell, who changed the way the computer industry operates. At one point, both of them were adolescents who envisioned technological improvements and later defined an industry that impacted the whole of society.

One of the struggles for adolescents creating a new way of life comes in defining the self. Erikson (1968) wrote that teenagers constantly define, overdefine, and redefine themselves, and this process may include a ruthless comparison to others. The goal is to thoroughly test new ideas and old values. Therefore, adults can expect adolescents to highly value an occupation one day and be totally turned off by it the next day. Such is the nature of career exploration as the adolescent begins to develop skills in analyzing why a specific occupation would be valued or not. The evaluative process fits nicely with the deciding phase of the Career Diamond, as the adolescent attempts to integrate a sense of self with the anticipated external adult world.

A main goal of Erikson's fourth stage (Industry versus Inferiority) is delayed gratification. The older child learns to enjoy the process of working hard toward a goal. When the goal is achieved, then an even greater joy may be experienced. Career counselors can encourage this important foundational block. Especially relevant is the integration of the past and future that Erikson (1968) found to be so important during adolescence. He wrote that teenagers must integrate who they were as children and who they will become as adults. The process is further complicated by the teenager's susceptibility to the perceptions and expectations of others. Erikson indicated that the adolescent might struggle with feelings of being a baby and at the same time feel elderly. On the one hand, scared of change. On the other hand, excited and eager for change. When an adolescent becomes trapped within this dichotomy, Erikson described the young person as living life as if encased in molasses.

Erikson (1968) portrayed some teenagers as showing a snobbish hostility toward society and projecting an attitude of being above or beyond society. Such an adolescent stance is not a productive way to create belonging nor does such an outlook include an attempt to gain a sense of mastery. Erikson also noted that some teenagers demonstrating alienated attitudes might come from wealthy families. Because the adolescent has been associated with the parents' accomplishments, an identity based on one's own achievement might be difficult to come by. Furthermore, the adolescent might have received many unearned rewards. Career counselors need to be sensitive to teenagers who have highly successful parents and who may feel like they live under a long shadow. A negative identity might solve the psychological dilemma of those who have been privileged. On the other end of the economic scale, poor teenagers may think their efforts will never be rewarded and the only way they can escape poverty is also through a negative antisocial identity (e.g., drug dealer). Career counselors can help teenagers at risk of developing a negative identify by facilitating visions of pro-social careers where unique talents are rewarded and a legacy of mistaken attitudes is overcome.

Finally, many teenagers just want to be unique. Erikson (1968) found that some adolescents appeared to avoid or sabotage opportunities for success. He wrote that these adolescents absolutely resist success because it robs them of their chance to be different. The 1980s heavy metal group Skid Row captures this sentiment in the song *Youth Gone Wild*. One stanza is:

> Boss screamin' in my ear about who I'm supposed to be.
> Getcha 3-piece Wall Street smile and son you'll look just like me.
> I said, "Hey man, there's something you ought to know.
> I tell ya, Park Avenue leads to skid row."

This song describes a young person who has a successful job where professional attire and manners are needed, yet he is willing to throw it all away because he sees the poor and downtrodden living on the edge of Wall Street wealth. The pro-social concern for others fuels a desire to reject the social system. Counselors can offer clients release for such existential angst and support the unique expression of a human struggle to come to terms with society's inequities.

Hoover, Marcia, and Parris (1997) view the formation of identity not as an individual process, but as an interaction between a powerful culture and a malleable individual. For example, when asked who one is, most people answer with their vocation or avocation. Because society has attached status to these domains, people can imply all sorts of things about the self. Hoover, Marcia, and Parris posit that political systems institutionalize the procedures and polices that allow for identities (e.g., vocations) to serve the common good. As individuals choose an established role that fits their individual preferences, they obtain the status that goes along with the role. This brings up the irony of teenage rebellion. As the adolescent rejects established adult roles and is a "nonconformist," that adolescent typically is conforming to a teen subculture (e.g., punk rock, gangsta rap). Hoover, Marcia, and Parris cleverly point out that a person cannot be unique all by one's self. In order to be unique, one has to have norms with which to disagree and other people to recognize the uniqueness.

Even more importantly, Hoover, Marcia, and Parris (1997) describe identity as a bonding between the self and society. Considering "Who am I?" includes the person's communal culture. Identity only exists in comparison to and in connection with others. For example, a person who works on a widget assembly line is more than just a warm body. That person allows for the rest of society to have and use widgets. Work, even unskilled labor, is more than just a product. It is the way adults take care of each other. A way for adults to let other people know they are important and valued.

Hoover, Marcia, and Parris (1997) state, "Individual choices are cued, shaped, and constrained by powerful influences emanating from social forces great and small" (p. 45). Why is this so? Because humans are naturally social in nature. We need to belong. Therefore, society has the power to support or disrupt attachments at the individual, family, or social level. For example, some corporations regularly move employees from place to place, which disrupts family and social attachments. By comparison, some companies define their organizations as family, make contributions to the community, and organize social events entertaining employees.

Finally, parents play an important part of the formation of identity. Hoover, Marcia, and Parris (1997) suggest that parents may be admired by their adolescent children who yearn for parental acceptance but experience only the void of parents' absence given long working hours. This lack of contact, which appears to currently be supported by society, further enables teenagers to develop a way of life that is different from adulthood. Adolescents cannot emulate adults if they never see them. Also, adolescents have little opportunity to observe their primary role models performing career tasks, which further hampers the transition from adolescence to adulthood. Career counselors can be very helpful by providing role models and by thoroughly discussing what students observe. Bringing in community speakers, setting up job shadowing or internships, and helping teenagers to research careers promotes identity development. Actively engaging learners increases the likelihood of students retaining and inculcating new concepts and skills. One idea would present teenagers with problems commonly faced in a work environment that captured their interests. Students brainstorm solutions, and then a professional from the field could evaluate their suggestions (e-mail communications could facilitate the exchange). Such exercises can build bridges between the here-and-now and the future.

INTERACTION OF THE INTERNAL AND EXTERNAL

Interests, Abilities, and Values

Middle adolescence sees a narrowing of interests, a prioritizing of future training, the ownership of values, and the struggle between values and interests (Grutter, 2000). Much is happening in a short period of time.

Grutter (2000) writes that young people attempt first to align interests and abilities. That is, students identify what they enjoy and then assess whether their abilities are sufficient for success. If an alignment occurs, the adolescent has a career area to pursue. If the abilities are not sufficient, then a different career area needs to be identified. Through this process of exploration and assessment comes a natural narrowing of interests (Grutter, 2000).

Adolescents also evaluate the values handed down by society and parents and accept, modify, or reject them. Kohlberg (1976, 1986) describes the process of personalizing values as postconventional moral reasoning. The person takes ownership of values and further solidifies the personal awareness that is so important to career development.

The narrowing of interests and ownership of values can lead to conflicts between the internal priorities and external requirements (Grutter, 2000). For example, the student may be interested in material wealth but values service-oriented occupations. On the one hand, highly lucrative careers may require competition and a focus on the financial results versus the human impact of various decisions (e.g., such as laying off people). On the other hand, the student may value cooperation and helping others and dislike competition. An important part of adolescence is resolving interest and value conflicts in a way that allows the adolescent to move forward in career development. Some sacrificing will occur, and the integration between the internal and external narrows the diamond toward closure, for the time being.

Grutter (2000) recommends that adolescents continue to consider alignment issues over time. Career counselors can monitor students who become stuck and are unable to align interests and abilities or resolve value and interest conflicts. In these struggles and with new experiences in the external world (part-time work, volunteering, or internships), career maturity develops.

The following examples describe how and why some middle and late adolescents step out of career development (Grutter, 2000). First, the student may miss the connection between education and a specific career. The student stops working in school or elsewhere and blocks ability enhancement. Second, some students may struggle with the reality that what they would enjoy doing will not pay the bills. For example, very few can get paid to test video games or be a professional athlete. Third, the adolescent may want the perfect job. Most teens do not have the training or experience to work in their perfect job. They will have to learn to work in related activities that bring them closer and closer to what they envision for their ideal future. Finally, adolescents may overestimate their worth, appear superior to coworkers, and demonstrate a lack of the teamwork skills, thus thwarting advancement. Career counselors can help students anticipate these struggles and prepare them for success.

The Career Diamond of middle and late adolescence is more than just a decision point for taking time off, technical training, or going to college. It can be a turning point for personal commitment. Grutter (2000) describes youth as a place where a sense of purpose can be developed. She wrote, "It's the difference between 'having a mission in life'—and seeing how work relates to that mission—and just having a job" (pp. 285–286). Fully examining interests, abilities, and values is very important. Career counselors who relay a critical sense of the importance of self examination will encourage clients who are willing and capable of engaging in the process.

Finally, self-examination also prepares students to excel in interviews. The language the adolescent develops around interests, abilities, and values lends itself to specific descriptions about who one is and what one is good at. "The more specific they can be about who they are, what they want, and what they're good at, the more likely it is that employers will be interested. The 'whatever job you have available' approach falls on deaf ears in most employing organizations" (Grutter, 2000, p. 288).

MIDDLE ADOLESCENCE AND THE EXTERNAL SIDE OF THE DIAMOND

Role of Parents

Many adolescents have seen their parents' failures. They have heard descriptions of missed opportunities and have seen their parents suffer due to downsizing, being fired, or the company moving out of state or out of the country. Some adolescents have vicariously experienced their parents' job transfers, mistreatment from employers, and difficult dynamics among coworkers. Many adolescents live in nice homes and drive nice cars but never see their parents because parents are working long hours. To intensify a bleak picture, adolescents may have older siblings, cousins, neighbors, or friends who have gone to college, graduated, moved back home, and found jobs well below their abilities and educational preparation.

Box 14.4   But I Can Be Anything I Want—What Now?

Goals: NOICC (1992): Understanding the impact of growth and development. Understanding the relationship between educational achievement and career planning. Skills to make decisions. Skills in career planning. Gysbers & Henderson (2000): Assess how avoidance of responsibility interferes with success and how taking responsibility increases the likelihood of success. Learn how to use communication to help others and encourage problem solving. Be able to describe personal values, interests, and capabilities. Explain and rank order values. Assess how personal values impact their decisions, behaviors, and life-style. Understand why it is important to set realistic goals and work toward achieving them.

Multipotentiality is the realistic ability to achieve in any number of career fields. Unfortunately, "You can be anything you want" can lead some gifted adolescents to

being nothing at all. Kerr and Ghrist-Priebe (1988) developed a one-day career counseling intervention to introduce gifted students to career decision making and the availability of counseling services. Of note, 52 percent of the students requested additional counseling services. Two months later, 55 percent remembered a specific goal they had set, 31 percent had changed their educational plans, and another 38 percent reported the workshop helped to confirm their plans.

Step 1: Students meet at college or university. Place students in gender balanced groups. After introductions are made and the day's schedule is presented, students complete the *Self-Directed Search (SDS), Edwards Personal Preference Schedule (EPPS),* rank 30 values (from a checklist), and answer a questionnaire about academic and extracurricular activities.

Step 2: Students choose a place on campus to visit and are guided by a college-

Furthermore, teenagers spend less and less time with their families (Larson & Verma, 1999), which may suggest that family influences lessen as the adolescent gains independence. However, assuming families have little impact would be inaccurate. Penick and Jepsen (1992) found that family functioning is a stronger predictor of career development than gender, SES, and educational achievement. Specifically, parental pressure to achieve academically and vocationally surpassed family SES in its impact (Bell, Allen, Hauser, & O'Connor, 1996). Family expectations also surpassed the influence of relational disruptions (e.g., distant parents, divorce, etc.) (Blustein et al., 2002). Furthermore, Schultheiss et al. (2002) wrote that traditional career theory may not be fully accurate in assuming that career decisions are made at the individual level. Their research suggests that family members serve as central resources and are very important in the decision making of college students.

Discussing what adolescents have seen and how they have made sense out of their observations may be important. Discouraging experiences may be

student host. Next, students pick one course within their interest area and attend a class.

Step 3: Lunch with counselors. Two to three students eat with a counselor and discuss the morning activities, their current academic preparation, and future plans.

Step 4: Individual and group counseling sessions (after lunch). The individual sessions were 50 minutes and included: (a) a discussion of values, needs, and interests via interpreting the *SDS, EPPS,* and ranking of values; (b) identifying and clarifying student concerns (counselors used open-ended questions and communicated curiosity in the student's interests); (c) underscoring the need to set goals (goal-setting handout depicted a map indicating the need for weekly, monthly, and yearly steps to achieve goals); and (d) motivating the students

to continue the process of career decision making that had begun.

The group session consisted of one counselor and four to seven students. Students describe specifics regarding the life-style they would like to live. Next, barriers to life-style goals as well as avenues for obtaining the goals were identified. The group discussion is facilitated by the counselors who also encourage the students to set high aspirations and provide information when needed. One of the techniques used has the students imagining their perfect workday 10 years in the future.

Step 5: Conclude the day with a restatement of the purpose of the workshop and the hope that students will continue to actively participate in the process of developing their career identities. Provide the students the opportunity to anonymously schedule additional counseling sessions.

a part of reality, but obstacles also present opportunities. Teenagers may need reminding that the future is yet to be written and flexibility is a must. Parents are major sources of emotional support. Even if financial and experiential resources are missing, a good parent–child relationship can free the adolescent to pursue her dreams (Kenny et al., 2003). If, however, the family is experiencing major disruptions, regardless of financial and experiential support, the adolescent may be consumed with strong emotion (e.g., worry, anger, hurt) and be unable even to consider career issues. Therefore, career services in high school need to include a realistic assessment of the family (Hall, 2003). Both the family's strengths (sources of support) and weaknesses (barriers to career development) can be honestly examined in a supportive atmosphere.

One career intervention with families is a one-time psychoeducational presentation that includes the importance of the family on career development. Alternatively, this could be written up in a small packet and sent home (available in both English and Spanish). The goal would be to teach families how they can help and hinder their student's career development. Recommendations could include ways for providing support to students as well as recognizing the impact of common family disruptions. Referrals (including sliding-fee-scale agencies) could be included for major concerns. Finally, the career practitioner may want to include information about the services available at the school. Career education packets send a message to the parents that career services are important and helpful and could serve as an invitation for active parental involvement in their students' career development.

A second career intervention comes from Solberg, Close, and Metz (2002). They suggest that schools can design Web pages (English and Spanish) that direct parents to information about colleges, how to help their child study, and when and how to contact school staff about their child's performance. Such attempts to include families in their students' school lives underscore the importance of family influences for career development and serves as a bridge to the community that pays for career services.

LATE ADOLESCENCE: AGES 18–25

It makes little sense to lump the late teens, twenties, and thirties together and call the entire period *young adulthood*. The period from ages 18–25 could hardly be more distinct from the thirties.
—*Arnett, 2000, p. 477*

A flawed assumption is that 18–19-year-olds are in a position to make career decisions for the rest of their life. First, many late teens are experiencing reduced parental control and/or independent living for the first time. Second, cultural milestones such as turning 21 are still a couple of years away. Many 18–19-year-olds are still living in the here-and-now and not realistically and seriously thinking about the future. Remember, age 25 is six to seven years away, the same distance between the senior year of high school and the 6th grade. The importance and relevance of education or training will become clearer as the late adolescent works and/or attends postsecondary educational institutions.

Emerging Adulthood

Arnett (2000) posits that adolescence does not end at 18–19 with adulthood immediately following. Instead, he describes the next seven years as emerging adulthood, a transition between the two phases. This age group may or may not attend college. If emerging adults do attend college, Arnett suggests that most students follow a nonlinear pattern (e.g., they take longer than

Box 14.5   Simulating a Mini-World

Goals: NOICC (1992): Understanding the impact of growth and development. Understanding the relationship between educational achievement and career planning. Understanding how societal needs and functions influence the nature and structure of work. Understanding the interrelationship of life roles. Gysbers & Henderson (2000): Learn to appreciate differences in self and others. Encouraging uniqueness. Look at how one manages the environment. Look at how said skills will aid/hinder them in the world of work. Understand how current decisions can impact the future. Predict concerns that will arise with age. Prepare for being flexible in life roles and choices. End with a focus on how concerns are connected to situations and life roles, and how a change in one will change a person's concerns.

Similar to the popular video game *The Sims,* students follow a person through high school, postsecondary training/education, and entrance into the career market. This exercise takes at least a semester and can last an entire year.

Students write a paper about their fantasy person. This person should be realistic, have aspirations, interests, and hobbies (they can even assign the fantasy person an *MBTI* type). Meanwhile, the teacher creates random events cards. Some cards are positive, "You scored high on the SAT and received a full ride to the college of your choice"; some cards are neutral, "You work at a part-time job and save $3,000 over the summer"; and some cards are negative, "A family emergency delays your

plans for six months." There needs to be enough number cards that students are exposed to a variety of situations. In addition, it may be helpful to have different sets of cards for each stage: high school, education/training, and entering a career. Cards also include noncareer life events such as, "Your car breaks down and it will cost $1,000 to fix it" or "You get married and have a baby."

A specific time limit is set (e.g., every two class periods represents one month for the fantasy person). Students draw one card and respond to it in writing (fun cards can be "Draw three cards and deal with everything"; "Draw three cards and pick the best one given your plans"; or "Draw three cards and pick the worst one given your plans"). When the next time period begins, a new card is drawn. An accelerated calendar can allow students to "live" through a couple of years in a short period.

The true impact of this game comes from responding to the cards. Students write what they would do and predict the best- and worst-case scenarios. The teacher decides how successful responses are. It is highly desirable for students to ask other students' fantasy person to help them so a cooperative community response to the problem can occur. It is important for the cards to have realistic events. It is even more vital for the teacher to be as realistic as possible when deciding what happens to a student's fantasy person after they respond to each card. Every student needs to experience setbacks and positive surprises.

four years). Specifically, there will be periods of attendance, periods of nonattendance, and some combination of seeking an education while working.

In middle adolescence, work is typically in the service industry, is not cognitively challenging, requires minimal skills, and serves the purpose of gaining spending money. By comparison, Arnett suggests that the emerging adult will view current work as building a foundation for later work. It is during this period that work and identity come together. Questions emerge, such as:"What kind of work am I good at? What kind of work would I find satisfying for the long term? What are my chances of getting a job in the field that seems to suit me the best?" (Arnett, 2000, p. 474).

Whether or not a young person is pursuing an education, this can be a time for trying out novel work experiences. Short-term job programs such as summer employment, internships, AmeriCorps, or the Peace Corps allow young people to travel to new locations, work for a period of time, and come back with new experiences (Arnett, 2000). These experiences can be important to identity development and in determining a direction for the future. Thus, 18–25-year-olds can finally explore, with freedom, a variety of potential career options. Though decision-making skills are used to analyze current experiences and future options, decisions need not take on the aura of finality.

Realities of Late Adolescence

The emerging adult, due to limited experience, must deal with environmental factors that can influence career decision making. Feldman (2002) suggested three primary influences affecting young adults.

First, political or social trends may create a myth around a certain career. In the 1950s, being an engineer was revered. The 1990s saw the computer industry as the new desirable field. Hot careers may artificially entice young people away from careers in which they have genuine interest or ability.

Second, booming economies can make more monies available for education. However, more money often coincides with more choices, and young people may be hesitant to make a choice and lose the opportunity to do something better. Sluggish economies restrict available support for training/education, but the need to have a secure, stable career increases the desirability of making a choice and sticking to it. So, students may sacrifice a better overall match for safety. In addition, booming economies may pay good salaries to individuals who do not have advanced training/education. Hence, young people could choose to enter the job market as opposed to pursuing training/education.

Third, current trends suggest late adolescents change jobs and/or majors with some frequency, delaying final career decision making. Furthermore, the goal of obtaining the perfect job paralyzes or severely restricts career decision making. Young people may want a high paying career that also provides a lot of vacation time and is located in an ideal geographical location. Compromising is difficult, and the young person may miss opportunities to have a good-enough job that could serve as a steppingstone to the perfect job.

Feldman (2002) concludes by suggesting that career services for young adults may place too much emphasis on keeping options open and delay sophisticated considerations for sequential decision making. It is time for choices to be made, even while remaining open to new opportunities. Second, interests are useful for beginning the process of career exploration in middle adolescence. However, adolescents in the 18-plus age group must move toward a realistic assessment of their skills and talents. It's not enough to have a dream. Late adolescents need to be able to articulate how they are going to achieve their dream and what realistic alternatives might replace less likely pursuits.

Dependent while Independent

On the one hand, the late adolescent has more freedom than ever before. On the other hand, the adult world requires skills that many late adolescents barely possess. Scandura (2002) points out that graduation ceremonies celebrate a level of learning and independence, but earning a degree for the self is often followed by employment that may make challenging demands and require interdependence (e.g., team work). Furthermore, young people have to deal with conflicts between their visions of the adult world and the realities of the adult world. Dealing with undesirable supervisors who wield power for career progress (e.g., promotions, assignment of duties) can lead to negative feelings about a career choice. Romantic relationships and the birth of children hamper independence and force the consideration of others when making decisions about the future. Scandura paints a portrait of young people launching from home only to find their lives more restricted, not by parents or laws, but by a lack of experience and power and by the demands of the job. Helping young people cope with these experiences is the challenge for career counseling.

Scandura (2002) suggests that career practitioners consider dependency issues when working with late adolescents. Specifically, what is the young person's response toward authority, independence, and worker autonomy? Will the young person conform or rebel? Is he able to be self-motivated or more passive, hoping supervisors will provide direction? Anticipating clients' responses to different work systems may aid in planning interventions in career counseling. For example, Scandura says that nonconforming individuals may have a higher job turnover rate and supervisors may find them more

CASE STUDY 14.1 The Premack Principle

One of the authors had the privilege of knowing a young man from middle school through his late twenties. This is the story of how he became a very successful webmaster.

Middle school was a drag for Steven. He would just do the bare minimum to keep the teachers and adults off his back. It was a real shame because everyone knew he was quite bright. In high school, he told the school counselor he was not interested in taking college preparatory courses. The counselor engaged him in conversation, asking what he was interested in. He said he was totally immersed with his home computer. In the early 1990s, the Internet was coming into its own, and Steven loved to build Web pages. In fact, he would forego many activities to work on his computer. Steven also worked part time on a job programming computers and developing his Web editing skills. As local small businesses decided to start websites, Steven earned more money setting up their pages. He told the counselor he didn't want to waste time studying books because computers were much more fascinating.

How Would You Conceptualize This Case?

1. What counseling stance would be effective with Steven, given his devotion to computer activities and his lack of interest in school subjects?
2. Would it be appropriate and effective to include Steven's parents in counseling? What about Steven's teachers? Would it be a good idea for the counselor to arrange a meeting to consult with Steven's teachers?
3. Could Steven benefit from doing research about computer-related careers?

What Actually Happened?

The counselor challenged Steven to find ways to use his computer skills for each of his classes. Steven consulted with his teachers about websites to help students learn course material. Before long, Steven had become the school's expert on Web design and was also learning a great deal in each course because he put course content on websites. One day Steven complained to the counselor that he was interested in so many subjects that he had no idea how he would be able to choose a major for college. Seeing how successful and hardworking Steven had become, the counselor had to ask, "Steven what happened? You were such a slacker, and now you could qualify as a workaholic." Steven smiled sheepishly and said, "I was just waiting to create a computer-based education. Why would I try hard when school was not technologically relevant?"

This story illustrates important concepts. Namely, high school students need to find something that totally captures their interests. Even if they never pursue adolescent interests as an adult, the skills identified and developed while young may be generalized to another career. The Premack Principle states that pairing a frequent activity with an infrequent behavior increases the infrequent activity. By tying course content to the client's obsession, the counselor induced Steven to learn course content. Another point is that we never know what occupations have yet to be developed; Steven's computer interests grew with the industry. Steven's story may become more common as new technologies are developed.

difficult to deal with when compared to interdependent or passive individuals. Considering the interaction between family and work might also be appropriate. What happens if partners marry and only one of the couple can work in a desired field? If children are born, how will that change career plans? Basically, Scandura (2002) says that career practitioners should expect dependency issues to reemerge as late adolescents leave the comfort of their childhood home and enter the adult world.

SUMMARY

Early childhood is oriented toward building foundational skills for life. The middle school years encompass major transitions from a childhood to early adolescence, including changes in cognitive abilities, expanding freedom, and beginning to set a personal direction. Middle and late adolescence is a time of preparation: preparing for an adult world that is in the near future; preparing for independence from one's family, but interdependence on society; preparing for the ups and downs of being young in the world of work. It can be a very exciting time because the adolescent can put into place her plans for success. Capturing the young person's passion for life and fully articulating the vision launches students into the adult world. Adolescence offers time to consider many opportunities and to experience the unfolding self. The vision and sense of self can coalesce into occupational choices promising success, satisfaction, and ability to make a contribution.

Super and Sverko (1996) refer to Super's "mini-cycle" that reoccurs as economic forces and/or changes in personal needs result in transitions. Each change in adulthood requires the person to reexplore and reestablish the self to new conditions, just as the adolescent explored and initially established a career identity during the first three diamonds. The Career Diamond captures the process of the mini-cycle, with the adult initially exploring or opening up a new diamond. The mini-cycle ends when the adult sets priorities and makes new choices. Hence, the diamond contracts, and the adult is reestablished in a new or adjusted career identity. Adult career services recapitulate middle and late adolescent career development with the added experience and additional responsibilities of adulthood.

STUDY OUTLINE: KEY TERMS AND CONCEPTS

I. Middle Adolescence
   A. The adult world is in the near future.
   B. Decisions made now may impact the rest of one's life.

      C. Often experiencing a first job and own money

      D. Not the last opportunity for making career decisions

  II. The Second Diamond

      A. A decision has to be made.

         1. High school will end and a new diamond will open up.

      B. Must integrate the internal and external

         1. The external world is still permeable.

      C. Must deal with not having the ideal job for a while

         1. Goal is to work as close to ideal job as possible.

      D. Vision for late adolescence will be more reality based.

      E. Vision for early adulthood will still have some fantasy to it.

 III. Cognitions

      A. Still coming to grips with abstract/logical thinking

         1. Good news is that the student typically has a few years' experience by this point

      B. Advanced cognitive skills in one area of life does not equal advanced skills in all areas.

         1. Career practitioners can help the student to generalize already existing skills.

      C. May have high goals but limited planning

         1. Time to teach true decision-making skills

 IV. Gender and SES

      A. Schools and teachers may inadvertently support gender-stereotyping in course selection and feedback on academic performance.

         1. Schools need teachers who violate gender-stereotypes (e.g., female math teacher).

         2. Teachers need to be sensitive to the impact they have on students and the classroom climate they create.

      B. High SES adolescents benefit from having family members who can provide financial, experiential, and emotional support.

      C. Low SES adolescents are at a disadvantage because their families typically experience more relational disruptions, lack professional experience, limiting availability of advice, and cannot provide financial support.

  V. Ethnicity

      A. We are a diverse country with approximately 39 percent of our K–12 students non-White.

      B. Whites earn the most four-year degrees, followed by Blacks and then Hispanics.

      C. There is a variety of academic achievement within groups.

    1. "One-size-fits-all" programs designed for minority groups will not work.

 VI. Identity

  A. Prepare adolescent for interdependence not only independence

  B. Erikson

    1. Teenagers will evaluate and attempt to integrate the old traditions with new values/norms.

     a. Teach adolescent how to evaluate useful versus frivolous norms.

    2. Adolescent needs to continue building delayed gratification skills.

    3. Some teenagers find a place in society by being an outcast.

     a. May become hostile or snobbish toward society

     b. Wealthy teenagers may not develop an identity separate from the family name. They need help in establishing their own accomplishments.

  C. Hoover, Marcia, and Parris

    1. Society cues, shapes, and constrains individual choices, thus greatly impacting identity development.

    2. One cannot be unique by one's self.

    3. Identity is a bond between the individual and society.

    4. Parents are important to identity development; however, many parents are unavailable and their children are unable to emulate them.

 VII. Interests, Abilities, and Values

  A. Interests and abilities need to be in alignment if a career choice is to be successful.

  B. Continue to refine skills and abilities

  C. Adolescents may miss connection between training/education and a desired career, want the perfect job, or overestimate their worth.

 VIII. Role of Parents

  A. Teenagers may have seen a lot of the negative aspects of the world of work.

    1. Career practitioners need to know what adolescents have seen.

  B. Parental pressure to succeed surpasses family SES in its impact of achievement.

  C. Career practitioners need to build bridges to parents and include them in the career development when possible.

 IX. Late Adolescence

A. Arnett
  1. Ages 18–25
  2. Often living in the here-and-now
  3. May have a nonlinear education path
     a. combination of starting, taking time off, and working
  4. May have a nonlinear start to their career
     a. underemployed, low income
  5. Opportunity to travel, work in a variety of fields, and explore
B. Feldman
  1. Be aware of political/social trends that make jobs "hot" but may be a mismatch
  2. May want the perfect job, which restricts career development
  3. Staying too open may restrict career decision making.
     a. Need to be making some temporary decisions (narrowing of the diamond)
C. Scandura
  1. Dependent while experiencing independence
     a. Independent of parents
     b. Dependent upon employer/teacher for training
     c. Dependent upon coworkers/other students for help (teamwork)
  2. Learning to deal with incompetent or unhelpful superiors at workplace
  3. Adapting to the realities of the work environment, forming adult relationships (partnering), and having children

EXERCISES

Role-play with one student as the counselor and one student playing one of three roles. It may help to have a third student observe and takes notes about the process. The goal is to come up with a plan for high school that also connects to the world of work after graduation; however, the plan is developed within the context of the student's personality, motivation, aptitude, and social situation. It may help to obtain course offerings and graduation requirements from two or more high schools in the area.

The conclusion of this exercise occurs when a tentative four-year plan has been created. It is critically important that the students do not focus overly on the four-year plan, that a major emphasis is the creation of a relationship with the student. If we are to expect a student to bring her personal awareness into career planning, we must bring personal issues into the counseling session. A rote, concrete use of linear decision making to get to an outcome will not allow for the personal issues to become integrated with career issues. Hopefully, this relationship would span the four years of high school as the student's career identity matures.

Role 1: Student is college bound. Choose whether she is pursuing the sciences, liberal arts, or a professional degree.

Role 2: Student is technical training bound. This student would become a skilled technician.

Role 3: Student is at risk of dropping out of school.

---

*Please feel free to expand each role based upon regional realities.

REFERENCES

Arnett, J. J. (2000). Emerging adulthood: A theory of development from the late teens through the twenties. *American Psychologist, 55*(5), 469–480.

Bell, K. L., Allen, J. P., Hauser, S. T., & O'Connor, T. G. (1996). Family factors and young adult transitions: Educational attainment and occupational prestige. In J. A. Graber, J. Brooks-Gunn, & A. C. Petersen (Eds.), *Transitions through adolescence: Interpersonal domains and context* (pp. 345–366). Mahwah, NJ: Erlbaum.

Blustein, D. L., Chaves, A. P., Diemer, M. A., Gallagher, L. A., Marshall, K. G., Sirin, S., & Bhati, K. S. (2002). Voices of the forgotten half: The role of social class in the school-to-work transition. *Journal of Counseling Psychology, 49*(3), 311–323.

Eccles, J., & Hoffman, L. (1984). Sex roles, socialization, and occupational behavior. In H. Stevenson & A. Siegel (Eds.), *Child development research and social policy* (pp. 367–420). Chicago: Univ. of Chicago Press.

Elkind, D. (1967). Egocentrism in adolescence. *Child Development, 38*(4), 1025–1034.

Elkind, D. (1978). Understanding the young adolescent. *Adolescence, 13*(49), 127–134.

Erikson, E. H. (1968). *Identity, youth and crisis*. New York: Norton.

Feldman, D. C. (2002). When you come to a fork in the road, take it: Career indecision and vocational choices of teenagers and young adults. In D. C. Feldman (Ed.), *Work careers: A developmental perspective* (pp. 93–125). San Francisco: Jossey-Bass.

Grant, D. F. (2000). The journey through college of seven gifted females: Influences on their career related decisions. *Roeper Review, 22*(4), 10–12.

Grutter, J. (2000). Developmental career counseling: Different stages, different choices. In J. M. Kummerow (Ed.), *New directions in career planning and the workplace: Practical strategies for career management professionals* (2nd ed., pp. 273–306). Palo Alto, CA: Davies-Black.

Gysbers, N. C., & Henderson, P. (2000). *Developing & managing your school guidance program* (3rd ed.). Alexandria, VA: American Counseling Association.

Hall, A. S. (2003). Expanding academic and career self-efficacy: A family systems framework. *Journal of Counseling and Development, 81*(1), 33–39.

Haring, M., & Beyard-Tyler, K. (1984). Counseling with women: The challenge of nontraditional careers. *School Counselor, 31*, 301–309.

Henderson, V., & Dweck, C. (1990). Motivation and achievement. In S. Feldman & G. Elliot (Eds.), *At the threshold: The developing adolescent* (pp. 308–329). Cambridge, MA: Harvard Univ. Press.

Hoover, K., Marcia, J., & Parris, K. (1997). *The power of identity: Politics in a new key*. Chatham, NJ: Chatham House.

Kenny, M. E., Blustein, D. L., Chaves, A., Grossman, J. M., & Gallagher, L. A. (2003). The role of perceived barriers and relational support in the educational and vocational lives of urban high school students. *Journal of Counseling Psychology, 50*(2), 142–155.

Kerr, B. A., & Ghrist-Priebe, S. L. (1988). Intervention for multipotentiality: Effects of a career counseling laboratory for gifted high school students. *Journal of Counseling and Development, 66*, 366–369.

Kohlberg, L. (1976). Moral stages and moralization: The cognitive-developmental approach. In T. Lickona (Ed.), *Moral development and behavior* (pp. 31–53). New York: Holt, Rinehart & Winston.

Kohlberg, L. (1986). A current statement on some theoretical issues. In S. Modgil & C. Modgil (Eds.), *Lawrence Kohlberg* (pp. 485–546). Philadelphia: Falmer.

Lankard, B. A. (1991). *Strategies for implementing the national career development guidelines*. Columbus, OH: ERIC Clearinghouse on Adult Career and Vocational Education. (ERIC Document Reproduction Service No. ED338898).

Larson, R., & Verma, S. (1999). How children and adolescents spend time across the world: Work, play, and developmental opportunities. *Psychological Bulletin, 125*, 701–736.

Marsh, H. W. (1990). Age and sex effects in multiple dimensions of self-concept: Preadolescent to adulthood. *Journal of Educational Psychology, 81*, 417–430.

Mason, C. L., & Kahle, J. B. (1988). Student attitudes toward science and science-related careers: A program designed to promote a stimulating gender-free learning environment. *Journal of Research in Science Teaching, 26*(1), 25–39.

National Center for Education Statistics. (n.d.a). Percentage of 25- to 29-year olds who attained selected levels of education, by race/ethnicity: March 1971 and 2000. Retrieved October 21, 2002 from http://nces.ed.gov/quicktables/Detail.asp?Key=523.

National Center for Education Statistics. (n.d.b). Public school membership, by race/ethnicity and state: School year 2000–01. Retrieved October 21, 2002 from http://nces.ed.gov/quicktables/Detail.asp?Key=768.

National Occupational Information Coordinating Committee (NOICC). (1992). *The national career development guidelines project. Washington, DC: U.S. Government Printing Office.*

Penick, N., & Jepsen, D. (1992). Family functioning and adolescent career development. *Career Development Quarterly, 40*, 208–222.

Piaget, J. (1970). *The science of education and the psychology of the child.* New York: Orion Press.

Read, C. R. (1991). Achievement and career choices: Comparisons of males and females. *Roeper Review, 13*, 188–193.

Scandura, T. A. (2002). The establishment years: A dependence perspective. In D. C. Feldman (Ed.), *Work careers: A developmental perspective* (pp. 159–185). San Francisco: Jossey-Bass.

Schlossberg, S. M. (2001). The effects of a counselor-led guidance intervention on students' behaviors and attitudes. *Professional School Counseling, 4*(3), 156–160.

Schultheiss, D. E., Palma, T. V., Predragovich, K. S., & Glasscock, J. M. (2002). Relational influences on career paths: Siblings in context. *Journal of Counseling Psychology, 49*(3), 302–310.

Solberg, V. S., Close, W., & Metz, A. J. (2002). Promoting success pathways for middle and high school students: Introducing the adaptive success identity plan for school counselors. In C. L. Juntunen & D. R. Atkinson (Eds.), *Counseling across the lifespan: Prevention and treatment* (pp. 135–157). Thousand Oaks, CA: Sage.

Stipek, D. (1992). The child at school. In M. H. Bornstein & M. E. Lamb (Eds.), *Developmental psychology: An advanced textbook* (3rd ed., pp. 579–628). Hillsdale, NJ: Erlbaum.

Super, D.E. (1985). Coming of age in Middletown. *American Psychologist, 40*(4), 405–414.

Super, D. E., & Savickas, M. L., & Super, C. M. (1996). A life-span, life-space approach to career development. In D. Brown & L. Brooks (Eds.), *Career choice and development* (3rd ed., pp. 121–175). San Francisco: Jossey-Bass.

Therrien, M., & Ramirez, R. R. (2000). The Hispanic population in the United States: March 2000. *Current population reports, P20-535.* Washington, DC: U.S. Census Bureau.

U.S. Census Bureau (1997). Press release. *United States Department of Commerce News.* Retrieved October 21, 2002 from http://www.census.gov/Press-Release/cb97-122.html.

PART V

Career Issues Across the Life-Span

CHAPTER 15

Career Counseling for Adults

When work is a pleasure, life is a joy! When work is a duty, life is slavery!

Maxim Gorky, The Lower Depths, *1903*

In the three previous chapters, we integrated the developmental and career literature to consider the career education/counseling needs of specific age groups. Adult development is much more variable than previous periods of growth and cannot be defined by short, well-delineated stages. However it is possible to identify important concepts that apply to adult clients seeking career services.

Given the pressures of the global economy, adults may periodically need career services. As workplaces adapt to compete, workers must adapt, too. Simple hierarchies may still define relationships among many workers, yet downsizing patterns and collegial teams have changed some interactive patterns. New technologies require learning new skills and thinking in different ways. Diverse backgrounds for workers demands that all people learn to understand differing cultural norms, values, and communication/interaction patterns. So, the changing economy requires change even if workers remain in one work environment—though most workers will change workplaces regularly.

Adults with work experience who face career changes will undergo the same expanding and contracting process described throughout the book. However, identity development has taken form, and adult awareness of personal and external factors adds richness and depth to individual counseling or career workshops. Although life transitions for adults may be individually unique, presenting concerns often follow common themes examined in this chapter. Settings for the delivery of services vary widely and can be found in many sectors of the community. New approaches to services, such as career coaching and consulting with organizations, are also examined.

THEORY OF WORK ADJUSTMENT AND PERSON-ENVIRONMENT-CORRESPONDENCE

Dating from the 1959 Work Adjustment Project, the theory of Work Adjustment (TWA) (Dawis & Lofquist, 1984) has been evolving to its current form (Dawis, 1996). Person-Environment-Correspondence (PEC) (Lofquist & Dawis, 1991) was fully articulated in 1991 and more recent writings incorporate both TWA and PEC (Dawis, 1994, 1996). TWA and PEC offer explanations describing how adult workers adapt to work environments, incorporating the internal and external factors at play in the workplace.

TWA and PEC Theory

As seen in Figure 15.1, TWA defines a number of terms to describe the fit between the individual and the work environment. Individuals can be described by their personality structures and personality styles. Personality structure consists of abilities and values. Abilities are aptitudes suggesting the level of mastery an individual can achieve. Please note that abilities do not suggest honed skills. Skills are learned, practiced, and can be meas-

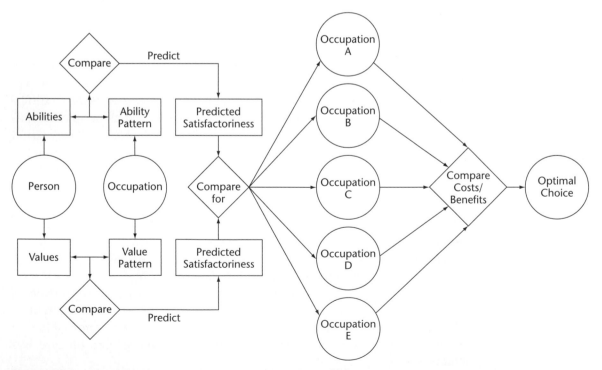

Figure 15.1   Use of the Theory of Work Adjustment in Career Choice

ured. Ability level is the person's aptitude for mastering certain skills. Values determine the importance of specific reinforcers (e.g., salary, title, social contact, geography) that motivate workers (Dawis & Lofquist, 1984; Dawis, 1996).

Personality style is made up of celerity, pace, rhythm, and endurance (Dawis & Lofquiest, 1984; Dawis, 1996; Lofquist & Dawis, 1991), and all four constructs exist on a continuum. Celerity refers to the speed at which an individual is comfortable working. Running is a good metaphor for pace. Some workers are sprinters whereas others are long-distance runners (although some individuals try to sprint through a marathon). Thus, pace is defined as the level of effort an individual typically exerts. Rhythm and pace go together. Rhythm involves the timing of output such as "steady, cyclical, or erratic" (Dawis, 1996, p. 85). Finally, endurance describes the length of time required to successfully complete task requirements.

Similar to the individual, the work environments consist of an environmental structure and environmental style. Each work environment is made up of various individuals, each with a personality structure. The collective personality structure adds all the personalities together to create typical ability and value patterns. The collection of personality structures makes up the environment structure (Dawis, 1996). Career clients often describe difficult work dynamics in which the client's personality does not fit the environmental structure, representing a mismatch at the personal level.

Environment style consists of celerity, pace, rhythm, and endurance expectations needed to get the job done (Dawis, 1996). Two examples are an emergency room and a gemsmith. An emergency room requires cyclical, intense work periods as well as down times. Medical personnel need high celerity (be fast) with a high level of effort (pace). Also, some surgeries could last up to 16 hours, requiring high endurance. By contrast, a gemsmith is ill advised to be fast when cutting gems, and the celerity requirements are low. In addition, several outstanding gems may be worth more money than many poorly cut stones (low pace). The work environment has a steady rhythm and probably requires varying amounts of endurance, depending upon the stone size and complexity of the cuts.

These two agents, the individual and the work environment, influence each other with the goal of achieving satisfaction for the individual worker and satisfactoriness for the work environment (Dawis & Lofquist, 1984; Dawis, 1996). When their biological and psychological needs (work needs) are met by the work environment, individuals gain satisfaction. Clearly, salary is connected to basic needs, shelter, transportation, and food; however, prestige, challenge, belonging, etc. are examples of important psychological needs. The collection of these needs is referred to as work reinforcers. Individuals develop their work skills and interact with the work environment in order to receive the reinforcers provided. By comparison, the work environment has task requirements and skill requirements to be successfully productive. Individuals who successfully employ the proper work skills to meet the task requirements enable the work environment to achieve satisfactoriness. Correspondence occurs when both the individual and the work environment have needs/expectations met, and both agents actively attempt to create and maintain correspondence (Dawis & Lofquist, 1984; Dawis, 1996).

Individual cognitive functions play an important role in worker satisfaction (Lofquist & Dawis, 1991). The individual must perceive available information, evaluate the information according to personal values and the expectations of the work environment, and deal with the emotions that accompany the cognitive evaluation (Dawis, 1996; see Lofquist & Dawis, 1991). Failure to accurately perceive information, failed critiques, or negative emotions will interrupt satisfaction. The individual also perceives herself. Perception of the self impacts self-esteem, self-concept, and self-efficacy, key ingredients for meeting the needs of the work environment (Dawis, 1996). It is important for the career counselor to assess the client's perceptual accuracy in regard to the work environment and self. Sometimes workers' fears presented in counseling represent misunderstandings of company directives or policy information or of personal abilities and performance. A useful intervention is to recommend the client check out information with trusted colleagues or supervisors.

Adjustment

Workers and work environments are said to be in correspondence if the needs of both the workers and the system are satisfied. Workers demonstrate job satisfaction if the environment meets their survival and psychological needs. Work environments reward workers and judge worker performance as satisfactory if the job requirements are met and the system is supported.

At some point in the interaction, workers and work environments fail to meet one or both of the other's needs/expectations. Adjustment style can be assessed across individuals and work environments to reveal varying levels of flexibility, activeness, reactiveness, and perseverance. Low levels of discorrespondence can be tolerated, but higher levels would not be acceptable and would require an adjustment. Tenure, the time a worker remains or is retained on the job, is important for both agents. First, tenure equals continued employment for the individual. Second, tenure reduces the costs of hiring and training new workers. Correspondence is positively correlated to tenure whereas discorrespondence is positively correlated with tardiness, absenteeism, and turnover (Lofquist & Dawis, 1991). Flexibility is measured by the amount of discorrespondence that can be tolerated by the worker or work environment (Dawis, 1996).

Change in the worker or work environment is referred to as adjustment. There are two ways in which either side adjusts to the other: active mode and reactive mode. When workers are in the active mode, they are trying to get the environment to change. By comparison, workers who make changes in themselves to better match the work environment are said to be in the reactive mode. The same process can be found in the work environment—it can be active or reactive. Therefore, the goal of returning to correspondence could include the worker changing, the work environment changing, or both changing (Dawis, 1996; Lofquist & Dawis, 1991).

Also of note is who initiates change as opposed to who actually changes. Even though workers may strike (active mode), the work environment may hold steady by hiring scabs, so the workers either take less salary or benefits or are fired. In this case, the workers end up changing even though they attempted to change the environment. On the other hand, the work environment may press for higher levels of production. Workers may leave in response to the pressure, and the work environment has to backpedal, reducing demands, to keep its employees (Dawis, 1996).

Finally, we come to perseverance. Both workers and work environments have an amount of time each is willing to work on adjusting (Dawis, 1996). Failure to achieve correspondence can last only so long before one or both parties physically (quitting, firing) or psychologically (at work in body only, marginalized employees) separate from each other. Clearly, higher levels of perseverance suggest longer tenure whereas lower levels suggest turnover.

The current economy may influence the reciprocity between workers and worker environment. When employers have access to cheaper workers overseas, U.S. workers have less bargaining power and are required to meet work environment demands regardless of the impact on worker needs. When the long-term tenure of employees is no longer cost effective, there is little pressure for the work environment to meet worker demands for improved satisfaction rewards.

Adjustment style and personality/environment style are important to consider when designing career services. First, if the client is struggling with the work environment, then career counselors can estimate how much the environment might tolerate before expelling the client. Second, career counselors can use TWA/PEC theory to predict how much change the client can endure. For example, Dawis (1996) says that celerity and flexibility are inversely related. Workers or work environments that are quick to initiate the

Figure 15.2   Critique of TWA and PEC

active mode are less likely to tolerate discorrespondence. On the other hand, endurance and perseverance are clearly connected. Finally, Dawis suggests that knowledge about pace and rhythm could aid career specialists in predicting how the active mode or reactive mode will play out.

The shape in Figure 15.2 applies the Career Diamond process to the TWA/PEC approach. This theory describes how the world of work functions and is not a theory describing how to provide career services. The exploration phase is truncated, a vision is lacking, and the matching of worker skills and efforts to environmental demand is the primary focus. For example, Dawis (1996) says,

> TWA-based assessment requires information about abilities and values for the person and ability requirements and reinforcers for work environments. This information can be obtained in a number of ways, the most dependable being through the use of psychometric instruments. (p. 103)

Such a test-and-tell/trait-factor approach defines human beings in a limited way. Although the theory accounts for both the internal and external factors, the whole process is narrow. The application of this theory results in focusing on a match that meets minimum requirements as opposed to promoting human growth and expression. A longitudinal focus for the individual or the changing work environment is lacking. However, clients who find satisfaction in nonwork roles may not seek fulfillment in work and may be satisfied with jobs that simply match their current abilities. In addition, if family or geographical considerations limit a client's search for work, this basic matching approach may work well given the client's priorities. However, for counselors who add to the basic matching procedure, time for understanding all of the client's self-expression will help clients understand their choices in the context of the whole of their lives.

Instruments measuring satisfaction, satisfactory performance, need preferences, aptitudes, and preferences for patterns of reinforcers are available. Career counselors would most likely use the work adjustment model to help workers who need help in understanding their satisfaction needs and the requirements of their work environment.

TWA/PEC theory suggests that over time the worker may change and begin to integrate the environmental factors into his identity. The first author's father illustrates a pattern where the worker inculcates the external influences of the work environment. He was a sergeant in the military for 30 years, well adapted to the work environment. Though he claimed to dislike his working conditions and constantly referred to his retirement, over time he took on the characteristics of the work environment. He gave his children military ranks, inspected their rooms weekly, maintained rigid discipline within the family, and spit shined his civilian shoes. When he did retire, his life resembled the routines and interactions patterns he disliked at work. Career counselors can help adult clients determine if work styles are reflective of their natural personalities outside work.

LIFE TRANSITIONS

In the 1980s when downsizing and the effects of economic globalization began, many authors described major life transitions. Although these transitions may seem commonsensical, they are not automatic for the client who experiences deep emotions when making a career change.

Bridges (1980) describes a three-step response to natural transitions such as retirement or children leaving home that can be generalized to job change. The first stage is dealing with the loss, the middle phase is recognizing the implications of change, and the final stage is accepting the change and adapting to new roles. Often clients can use past experiences in which changes were required to remember helpful coping mechanisms.

Brammer (1991) describes adult changes as broadly dealing with the fear of the unknown and "journeying through" the process with the courage to face fears and take risks. Brammer portrays the first reaction to change (Adaptation) as coping. The second reaction (Renewal) occurs when the person sets new goals after clarifying values. The third step (Transformation) involves a shift in thinking and feeling as though a new life is born, and the final stage (Transcendence) entails the discovery of inspirations for new life meanings.

Schlossberg and coauthors created the most complete transition model. She identifies the many areas requiring adjustment as subjects for counselors to explore with clients (Schlossburg, 1984; Schlossburg & Robinson, 1996; Schlossburg, Waters, & Goodman, 1995). According to Schlossburg, clients need to approach transitions by analyzing how a change will affect the many aspects of their lives including: roles, routines, and relationships. Important aspects of the self may be challenged including assumptions, attitudes, values, and beliefs. Each client needs to assess her unique situation, support systems, and resources. Finally, strategies for self-care and coping mechanisms can be determined. When such a thorough analysis is made, the client can approach a new vision with a perspective that a different life could be possible and meaningful. Adding to counseling the impact of relationships and social systems expands the client's perspective. To life's meaning, Schlossburg includes relationships and reminds clients their worth is based on more than their occupations. Box 15.1 gives a technique to identify important relationships and support systems.

It may be that older workers, who have lived life-styles where consistent change was not assumed and where career identities were forged in only a few organizations within one profession, have approached transitions with greater difficulties than will younger workers who are being socialized into a more fluid economy. However, to presume clients can make regular career changes without dealing with the implications for career identity and the whole of one's life-style might also miss some important human considerations.

EMOTIONAL AND COGNITIVE CONSTRUCTS EXPERIENCED DURING TRANSITIONS

Adults experiencing career transitions may have many emotions and attitudes to process in career counseling. The life-style and career visions from youth may feel lost, and fears that nothing can fill the void may dominate. Feelings of betrayal, anger, and hurt may pervade descriptions of expectations denied, worker relationships, and unappreciated contributions. Empathetic support is appropriate though career counselors balance understanding with an eye toward creating a new vision for the future. Within the context of the client's story, most often there are opportunities to note client strengths and to tie abilities to new opportunities.

Many emotions are related to societal messages and expectations. The work ethic in the U.S. society implies unemployment is the equivalent to not deserving respect. In addition, not all work is equally valued because some occupations have higher status than others. One of the fears of job-changers is that the next position will not be viewed as deserving equivalent status. Career practitioners provide the opportunity for clients to openly explore societal messages and to determine the implications and costs of adhering to such judgmental constructs. Supportive listening can release emotions and allow clients to gain kinder attitudes toward themselves. Releasing the negative energy allows clients to move past difficult experiences and opens up new possibilities. As new visions begin to vaguely appear, clients may pull for reassurance, and though the counselor cannot guarantee the future, offering hope that the client can manage change and create something new is invaluable.

Box 15.1   Career Ecomap

The ecomap is designed to pictorially represent with whom and how a person is connected to his environment. It is particularly useful for adult clients changing careers. Counselor and client may, for example, want to identify where positive and negative relationships exist, what services are available to the client, and who or what is competing for time and energy. Ideally, as the client looks at her situation globally, a strategy to bring the network together to solve problems becomes clearer. Some questions that will aid in forming an ecomap are:

> Who works in your immediate area? What is your relationship with each of them?
>
> Who are the important managers/administrators? Are they to be considered as a group (one place on the ecomap) or as individuals?
>
> What services are available to you (e.g., human resource department, union, legal aid, food bank, church)?
>
> Is it safe to talk with coworkers about your situation, or should you keep your concerns within your family and nonworker friends? (Boundary setting.)
>
> Who would be most likely to help you? Least likely? Cannot due to their own situation?
>
> Whom do you wish were still available (e.g., old boss, retired coworker, last minister at church)?

> With whom do you wish to disconnect, limiting contact as much as possible?

As information is gathered, it is plotted on the ecomap. Similar to a genogram, people and offices/agencies each have their own shape, and other symbols indicate the relationship between the client and said person/agency (see Figure 15.3). Note that questions around the flow of energy toward or away from the client indicate if the client gains support from the area or offers support or if the support is mutual.

Case Example of Use of Ecomap

Bob was considering a career change. He could stay with his current job as a middle manager, seek a similar job with another company, or change fields. His circumstances at work have been stressful and unsatisfying. There were also strains in his marriage, with his in-laws, and with his parents. In creating the ecomap, Bob visually depicted the number of conflicts and the numerous areas where his energy flowed outward, with only a few areas where he felt supported. Bob took the diagram home and used it to open a dialogue with his wife in which both talked about "the arrows" in both their lives. Ultimately they decided Sally would find a full time teaching job in a smaller community where the family would live and Bob would start a consulting firm located closer to home.

Source: Sherman & Freeman, 1986.

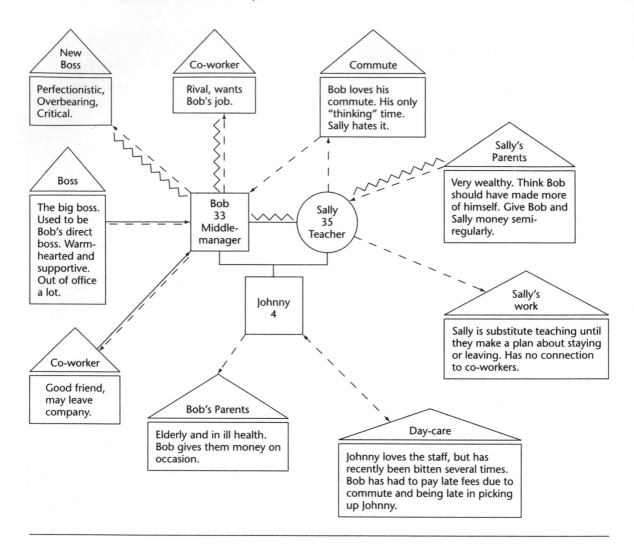

Figure 15.3 Career Ecomap

PROCHASKA'S MODEL FOR CHANGE: "I WANT TO CHANGE CAREERS, BUT..."

Although clients may present by saying they are ready to make a career change, it may seem that they spend more time talking about the work they have been doing and about their experience in the latest work environment.

Understanding the process of change allows counselors to facilitate the client's movement.

Prochaska, Norcross, and Diclemente (1994) provide a model of change that offers additional insight for career counseling. The stages of change established by this research include a pre-contemplation period followed by contemplation. Pre-contemplation is described as a stage in which clients lack a readiness to make a decision, and this is similar to the beginning point of the Career Diamond. Contemplation is a process of raising consciousness where clients expand their awareness of information and its application to personal experience. This stage is comparable to the two components of the Career Diamond's expanding self and information. Contemplation begins with a general acceptance of new information and a broad relationship of the information to the self as in the exploring stage of the diamond. Preparation comes about through a change of self-image that sets the stage for taking action as in the vision pictured in the center of the Career Diamond. The openness to new information grows with the setting of new personal priorities. Integration of new information to one's self-image is similar to the deciding side of the diamond. Prochaska describes the psychological movement of growing self-awareness and the gradual internalization of new information as the necessary predecessor of a decision to change. Only when the process of expanding awareness and integration takes place can a new decision become possible. Prochaska's model of change validates the applicability of the Career Diamond to the transitions of mature adults.

An adult client may indicate that a career change is needed, either because of external forces or personal dissatisfaction. However, the client may not be ready to participate in the process represented by the diamond because the client is not yet ready to make a change, even if a job has been lost. Clients in this situation may be in the pre-contemplation stage. Prochaska's model reminds us that the process of changing career identity is difficult and takes time. In addition, its description of how clients approach change includes suggestions as to how counselors can facilitate the career change process for adults.

Pre-Contemplators

For pre-contemplators, career counselors must patiently encourage an awareness of the value of change and the cost/benefit ratio of remaining with the status quo. Pre-contemplators are not willing to accept that change is needed. They mainly want the possibility of change to go away. If others are suggesting career changes may be necessary, the pre-contemplator just wants others to stop saying such things. Although counselors for pre-contemplators are supportive and reflect the painful feelings demonstrated by facing change, the counselors do not soften the view of negative consequences associated with failing to change.

Clients may be in denial and literally unaware of the need to face demanding realities. Clients facing needed career changes benefit most by counselors directly and frequently recommending the need for reality checks and by insisting that clients can take responsibility for their choices. For pre-contemplators, counselors may want to follow this approach: (a) do not enable denial but patiently provide support; (b) do not push or demand change but recognize the realities indicating the necessity for a career change. Depending upon the client, the counselor may be drawn via concern (as in a) or frustration (as in b) to act for the client. Only the client can establish the personal priorities needed to determine what changes would meet her needs for career satisfaction. Facing hard choices demanded by external realities is difficult. Counselors support the client and facilitate a gradual acceptance of external demands before change is actually considered. One option is a counseling group that can offer a venue for acceptance. Group members can experience the support gained by realizing, "I'm not the only one," as well as by job searching or budgeting ideas or suggestions for explaining unemployment to family and friends.

Contemplators

Contemplators begin to admit that change may be necessary and are willing to look at the cost/benefit ratio that a career change may mean. A shift in attitude from running away from reality to facing information pointing to needed change occurs, but the resolve to actually change is not strong. Facing the loss of "the way it was," may be painful; and the client may experience much grief before letting go of the past and rejoining the present. All that the client had invested to gain the "just lost" career is emphasized, and the difficulties of change dominate the client's thinking.

Some clients may be able to admit fears and concerns that they cannot change whereas others will deny any fear. Some may direct feelings outward as anger toward others or toward the circumstances that seem unfair. Psychological defenses break down so there is a readiness to talk but not to act. Some clients may be preparing to act whereas other clients may be demonstrating a decision-making style of waiting endlessly until there are no choices left. Some clients may show a fear of failure whereas others are fearful of the loss of earned success. Some clients may obsessively examine every detail of their feelings, and others may hold onto drama of the circumstances, eliciting sympathy from others. Some clients may wear out anyone willing to listen to the point that no one feels any compassion. Some worry excessively about the consequences of change and wait for the perfect, magic moment when change will no longer be threatening. Others may spend time with wishful thinking, creating an image of how circumstances may change to rescue them. Still others may make changes impulsively and then resent the natural consequences for which they are unprepared. Others may focus only on negative consequences. Some may misuse information to fit personal needs. Contemplators are trying to face change but cannot let go of their established career identities. They seem unwilling to reevaluate their identities or to see unused facets of their personalities that could present new opportunities.

Becoming a Client: Preparation and Action

Eventually contemplators become tired of ruminating. Counselors can capitalize on the recognition that such clients are opening to change and focus attention on the changing perspectives (preparation stage). With the hint that change may be acceptable, counselors should support the momentum of considering what changes might be the easiest as first steps. Clients can be encouraged to think before they act. The process of developing a new career identity, the search for relevant information, and the integration of a new career self-image with current realities can gradually begin.

The final stage of integrating realistic considerations with personal priorities includes considering the realistic consequences of a decision to change. At this point, the client can weigh pros and cons for self and significant others without getting bogged down in the process. New self-evaluations and thoughts on how to deal with the reactions from others helps the client recognize that change is possible and beneficial, even if there is a cost to be paid. Input from others can be welcomed as a helpful support for change, rather than a means to force unwanted change.

Once the decision is made, Prochaska describes the action stage of change as one also requiring a considerable commitment of time and energy. Counselors can help clients plan for change, adjust to changes made, and maintain the new behaviors. The model for change consistently reminds us that at each step a patient counselor creates space to support the client. From the Career Diamond's perspective, the model has opened to new decisions and closed at a new point. After the changes have been acted on and adjustments to a new self-image have been maintained, the process will begin again.

The last two stages, maintenance and termination, focus on maintaining changes and avoiding relapse to previously unhealthy functioning; the main focus is on psychological career issues. The maintenance stage may apply to some career clients who continue to revert to fears of regretting the new decision or who are overwhelmed by the demands of a new career choice.

Counselors can patiently remind clients of the previous process in which the new choice seemed to open better possibilities and to support the client in recognizing the insights previously made. Once the new decision is accepted, the counselor can genuinely compliment the client who has shown the courage to change and to gain the skills to make yet another change when the time comes. When the client is settled into a new life choice, the change is solidified and the old patterns are terminated as are counseling sessions. Counselors are reminded to schedule follow-up sessions with clients to check in and offer assistance with the client's adjustment to new career choices.

The Prochaska description of change says that adult changers have to release an established career identity in the midst of creating a new career self-image. The older client may have feelings of loss and possibly anger that color the exploring process. An added task of career counseling is dealing with such issues.

UNDECIDED VERSUS INDECISIVE

When adults present for career services, they may misrepresent or misunderstand their needs and goals. In the struggle to make a choice, career theory has labeled some adult clients as **undecided** and others as **indecisive**. Undecided clients are described as ready and capable of coming to a decision; however, they lack skills in decision making. Career services can teach clients the decision-making steps, identify or clarify personal preferences, and support clients as they develop and apply new skills for the world of work. Indecisive clients are unable to make decisions, even if decision-making skills exist (Grutter, 2000), and they may have broader psychological problems.

The distinction between undecided and indecisive is an attempt to delineate those clients who respond well to standard career counseling and those who do not. The rationale is that indecisive clients are not capable of deciding, and the indecision is a symptom of mental illness or a personality disorder not readily amenable to change (Crites, 1981). Brown and Brooks (1991) add to the description of indecision a lack of cognitive clarity. Without cognitive clarity, a client cannot assess her own strengths and weaknesses and apply this self-knowledge to environmental demands. This inability to determine a career identity may stem not from mental illness per se but from cognitive distortions such as those described by Krumboltz (1993). Examples of such cognitions are when the person: (a) does not believe change is possible, (b) does not put forth the necessary effort to change, (c) eliminates viable alternatives, or (d) perceives that goals are not achievable. Heppner and Hendricks (1995) continue the concept of dividing clients as undecided versus indecisive, determining client variables that influence career counseling. However, when working with adults, it may be that some clients labeled as indecisive, those who spend an exorbitant amount of time avoiding a decision, may be pre-contemplators who are not ready to decide.

CAREER COACHING

Coaching is a new approach to career services. Coaching is a combination of mentoring, encouraging, facilitating new and creative options, consulting, and planning. The approach uses some counseling skills, such as active listening and empathy, while identifying client strengths and promoting the full realization of whatever vision the client has for life. There is little attention paid to the past because the focus is geared to what is needed to move ahead. Certainly, obstacles and fears are acknowledged, but the thrust of coaching is to trust the individual's inner resources and capacity to create the conditions needed to get what is desired. A major rationale for the coaching process is the rapid change occurring today in all fields. Coaches support people in renewing their motivation and setting goals to deal with almost any endeavor, from career changes to health enhancement to retirement planning.

The field began with consultants helping corporations change to the new management systems required for the global economy. Total quality management and team training were examples of early attempts to create collaborative working cultures with less hierarchy and greater adaptability. Outplacement services by career professionals helped executives find new areas of employment during downsizing periods. In today's economy, coaches define their role as "helping adults manage change effectively" (Hudson, 1999, p. 7). Some career changes require workers to master new technological skills, and some coaches offer such training and ongoing consulting. Many coaches have experience in the business community and can offer mentoring advice. Given rapid staff changes, mentoring within organizations is rare and short lived. In "whole life coaching" (Williams, 2002), clients gain assistance in determining their values and purpose beyond economic success.

Some coaches consult with companies seeking systems changes as well as work with individuals within the system. They may help executives determine their personal goals and ascertain how those goals fit with the organizational priorities. Hargrove (1999) describes "empowering people to create a future they truly desire based on unearthing what they passionately care about," (p. 20). He ties the leader's passion to values and a guiding vision that will inspire small teams of employees to work for the cause rather than following prescriptions defined by others. The executive coach will identify behavioral and interaction patterns that block the CEO from reaching company goals. If the interaction between the CEO and the executive team is inconsistent, the coach helps change patterns that have become obstacles.

A major function of the coach is to act as a catalyst for encouraging renewed interest and energy in career pursuits. Coping with change is disheartening at times. Previous expectations are shattered, and new conceptions are needed. It takes encouragement to look ahead with hope rather than spend too much time remembering what has been. A coach may briefly acknowledge the strain of letting go of the past, but the focus of coaching is to motivate the person to face the future. Like the crest of the Career Diamond, a vision of the future becomes the motivator for making personal changes and dealing with external requirements. Also like the diamond, there is an emphasis on building self-esteem and identifying strengths.

Much of what the coaching literature describes is fully in keeping with career counseling from the perspective of the Career Diamond. What the coaching model captures is the overriding dominance of the self as responsible for career development and career paths as expressions of career identity. The emphasis on a positive focus with constructive feedback and support for creating a renewed vision stemming from the person's values is also fully within the context of career counseling. That a person's past is deemphasized in coaching may be the major distinction between some counseling and coaching; but career counseling most often looks to family of origin patterns as defining personal style and motivators, not as a primary focus. Career counselors typically do not act in the consulting role of offering business mentoring or strategizing. And although counselors certainly provide hopeful support when clients express doubts, the coaching literature has a greater flavor of motivational language, such as abundancy thinking and effortlessness (Grodzki, 2002).

Lynn Grodzki (2002) quotes Harriet Simon Salinger, who locates career counseling and coaching on a continuum with psychoanalytic therapy at one end and sports coaching on the other. The middle is where counseling becomes less oriented to pathology, interpretations, transference, and years of analysis and more oriented to client fulfillment, contentment, confidence, and participating in satisfying relationships. In this middle ground, coaching and counseling may overlap in approach.

There are, however, some important differences. Counseling tends to take place on a regular basis and in professional private settings. Coaches meet clients in homes and restaurants and consult on the phone or Internet, offering flexibility that meets clients' needs. Coaches also socialize with clients and assume dual relationships that are considered unethical for counselors. Finally, if coaches perceive personal problems that prevent clients from benefiting from coaching, they refer clients to therapy. One coach described the career-focused clientele as the "worried well" who want a supportive consultant, not a therapeutic counselor. Also, the pace of coaching is more demanding in a results-oriented active mode. If the client needs extended time and space to examine personal issues, counseling is needed. Counselors who do both therapy and coaching tend not to interchange the services with the same client because the interactions tend to be different.

It may be that the clientele is the major distinguishing factor between coaching and career counseling. Clients who are impatient with the slower counseling pace may favor coaching, given the demands of a fast-paced work environment where self-examination would be considered a deterrent to a success-oriented image. Such clients may respond to direct behavioral feedback, but not to a drawn-out self-discovery process. They may expect answers and solutions to come quickly just as they are expected to perform at work. Yet skilled counselors are able to adapt their interacting styles to the mode of the client, and certainly career counselors have experience with clients who want the answer. For example, one type of interaction was noted in several articles describing coaching. Grodzki (2002) offers an intervention with a client where the coach says:

> All of us have to deal with negative self-talk from time to time. Your negative self-talk is clearly getting in your way when you sit in meetings. As your coach, I'd like to support you to think more positively about yourself and have a confident demeanor. What is the best way to start? (p. 16)

And, Robert Niederman (2002) describes another coaching interaction:

> I want to tell you something. I want to tell you how I felt just now walking down the hall with you. Would you be open to that? . . . It reminded me of being a little kid; it was as if my big father is charging ahead because he is so much more important and his time is so much more valuable than mine. It made me feel that you believe that you are very important but that I'm not. (p. 28)

Both interactions are very respectful, asking the customers if they are open to feedback. The feedback is behavioral with no attempt to unearth connections to previous experience. The behavior is tied to interactions that could be relevant at work, and the first quote shows a direct connection to the goals for change.

These interventions could have easily been included in scripts describing career counseling. Although the career coach writers say they don't interchange counseling with coaching, they do follow the client's lead and use a range of counseling interventions. Coaches do not, however, use techniques more in keeping with a psychoanalytic tradition by encouraging transference and such. Career counselors may need to seek training in coaching to gain additional expertise directly related to the business world. They may need to learn the language and other nuances. And if coaching were combined with counseling, the ethical standards of counseling may need to be maintained. Career counselors may also consider the type of clientele they are comfortable with before adopting a coaching approach.

There are professional associations and training for coaches, including the International Coach Federation (ICF) and Coach University in Brandon, Florida. Criteria for ethical practice and professional standards are in place. However, an Internet search found such an array of long-distance coaching services, it is difficult to determine the quality of services offered. Coaches are available through websites, by telephone, and in most major cities. Costs range from $10 per e-mail to $200 to $350 per hour to $1,000 retainers for three sessions a month to $250,000 for one year's organizational consultation and executive coaching.

QUESTERS AND CAREER-PRENEURS

Several authors have written about mid-life career changers who have made major changes in career and life-styles by choice. Career counselors may take note of the qualities of these models. Kanchier (1987) identifies the characteristics of people who have taken the risk of making sizeable changes as purposeful, autonomous, intimate, and androgynous, as well as achievement and growth oriented. She makes the recommendation that all adults remain aware of their satisfaction in their current life-styles and reevaluate regularly. Moore (2000) describes successful women who have followed the pattern of renewing their preferences and options multiple times. She coins descriptors such as *co-preneurs,* (husband-wife entrepreneurs); *market creator* (discovering and filling a new niche); *parallel pather* (moonlighting with a career purpose); *spiral careerist* (capitalizing on opportunities and problems); *punctuated careerist* (actively going for opportunities with forceful energy); *pandemonium careerist* (making major moves across occupations and fields) (Moore, 2000, p. 8–26).

All careerists can adopt an entrepreneurial mode as described by Figler and Bowles (1999). Workers become "me-incorporated," an individual career center that looks to the market for opportunities to sell themselves. Actually, such a description implies a cultural materialistic standard where innovation, profit, and self-centered values are primary. Some workers who are temperamentally not suited to an enterprising approach as per the Holland Code and those whose values lean more toward stability, security, and other-centered behavior may not adapt easily to such attitudinal and behavioral patterns.

Career counselors can facilitate a personal assessment to help adults analyze work environments where their services are needed. However, the "me-incorporated" language may or may not be appropriate for all clients.

CAREER CONSULTING FOR ORGANIZATIONS

The August 2001 issue of *The Monitor on Psychology*, a publication of the American Psychological Association, included an article showing how psychologists perform a number of roles in the workplace (Carpenter, 2001). One consultant described consulting work assisting company employees deal with adjustments to crosscultural issues in doing business internationally. Career practitioners also design programs to assist employees dealing with businesses, factories, and other workplaces that are permanently closing. Outplacement services assist executives to find new jobs so employees leave companies without resentment. Although job security is not guaranteed, sometimes job changes within a company offer employees new challenges and the opportunity to develop new skills for future employment. Career counselors could be particularly well suited to assisting employees to take advantage of the opportunities available in-house and to assist employers in retaining an active, productive work force. Other career counselors help employees deal with work stress and relationships between workers and other factors affecting the psychological health of employees and their productivity. Use of instruments related to career counseling sometimes provides needs assessments, outcome measures, and feedback for clients. For example, the *MBTI* or variations such as the *Personal Profile System* (1994) are often used for team building and for examining leadership styles.

Counseling psychology and education is the home of theories and practices for career services, and the changing economy is in need of quality services based on sound professional standards. Those from other fields, such as business managers, populist writers, and entrepreneurs, often offer services that counselors could provide with greater breadth and depth. Frequent changes for individual companies and agencies in a more fluid economy result in less in-house services for employees' career assistance. The void of permanent employee assistant programs offers more opportunities for career practitioners to offer consultation services on a short-term basis. The author has some experience consulting with a major automobile manufacturer and can describe such services as a model for consultation for other career issues.

Consultation for Plant Closings

As factories change locations in the global economy, many workers and some supervisors and executives do not move to the new plant's site. Workers with years of seniority may be eligible for severance benefits that could finance new career opportunities. Others may be open to further education while still others look for new jobs immediately. Counselors are in a unique position to offer career services because they are trained in the specialty whereas most other professional helpers are not. Counselors can offer educational programs preparing workers for change and teach job search skills. Support groups and individual counseling can help workers deal with emotional issues, processing information, and decision making. To meet the needs of displaced personnel, community agencies or corporations hire counseling professionals to organize services. The following discussion describes one such consulting project developed by the first author.

Early inquiries from plant managers requesting career services opened a dialogue defining what the company needed and what the author and her colleague would agree to provide. The company executives were concerned that permanently laying off thousands of employees would create much negative publicity and were anxious to create a public relations message that employees would receive assistance in finding new jobs. They were also concerned that laid off employees could demonstrate mental health problems and extreme reactions, such as suicide, which would create a negative public image for the company. Although having a professional counselor would not guarantee preventing mental health difficulties or finding replacement jobs, several packages of services were offered, along with a rationale for why such services could prove useful. A needs assessment could project those employees in need of ongoing individual counseling and those who could gain assistance in support groups and workshops. Consultation for managers and labor leaders was another service offered.

The company decided to buy a package of support groups, job search workshops, individual counseling, and consultation for management and labor union representatives. A brief needs assessment utilizing the instrument, *My Vocational Situation* (Holland, Daiger, & Power, 1980), determined those employees with greater needs who were offered individual counseling and those who might be able to deal with the layoff with a series of workshops. Employees could also self-refer for individual counseling or support groups. Peer counselors, workers from the assembly line, were chosen and trained to help facilitate workshops. Referrals to community services were also arranged. The author also attended regularly scheduled meeting for leaders responsible for making the closing run smoothly, and plant leaders could seek individual consultations for specific situations. The contract ran for six months for one plant and for 18 months for another factory (Mosley-Howard & Andersen, 1993).

With a basic structure in place, the author built support by touring the plant and visiting with employees, foremen, line leaders, and managers. She consulted with the human resource department that held the responsibility for transferring a few workers to other plants across the nation, learning about those limited opportunities and setting up agreements for cross-referrals. To build trust with workers and union leaders, she ate lunch in the plant cafeteria and was eventually invited to eat in the "workers' only" music room, where assembly workers played instruments and sang to entertain each other during breaks. To maintain a level of respect, the plant physicians recommended the use of the term Doctor to reflect the author's credentials. To create a welcoming mode, the more approachable first name basis seemed friendlier. A compromise developed as the workers called the author Dr. Pat.

The literature regarding plant closings describes a grieving cycle similar to the emotions experienced with other major losses. Initial reactions by some workers denied the plant would actually close. It seemed impossible that thousands of people would be quickly displaced, and that huge building complexes—landmarks in the community for generations—would be torn down. Anger and blame personalized the company and the union as uncaring as well as all-powerful. Sadness sometimes approached a sense of helplessness as the reality took hold. Workers needed to describe the work they had contributed and to tell the stories of plant politics between union and management and within the ranks between workers and line-leaders or foremen. Clients experiencing the range of emotions before acceptance were not ready for career counseling because they needed time for psychological work. Within the grieving paradigm, however, much is learned about clients, their strengths, coping mechanisms, vulnerabilities, and, most importantly, their values. Such background issues prepared counselor and client for the expanding and integrating of career counseling.

Leaders in a plant-closing atmosphere add a personal sense of responsibility to others to their own individual issues. Few opportunities for emotional release existed for those who were expected to model controlled behavior and acceptance of reality during the massive changes taking place. Some executives experienced self-blame for letting others down and obsessed about

CASE STUDY 15.1   The Union Forever

A factory for a major corporation announced it was closing and a few thousand employees would be laid off. A wife and husband came for counseling because of their concern for their future. The couple was in their late forties, and he (skilled laborer) had worked for the plant since graduating from high school. Employees with his level of seniority had been offered a significant financial package if they would waive their rights to future jobs with the company. The union contract stipulated "a call back" to work was only possible if the company opened another plant within the United States. Call-backs occurred in order of seniority and usually required a move to another state. There was the distinct possibility that no one would be called back because there were plans to relocate some factories outside of the country. The husband had hated his job for years but was frightened by the loss of security. He had felt protected by working for a huge multinational corporation and was angry that "blood money" was offered to disconnect him from a company that had been his working home. The wife did not want to move from the city where she had spent her whole life.

A franchise company was selling trucks delivering a snack and sandwich service with exclusive routes. Owner-operators purchased trucks that were outfitted with a soda machine, refrigerator, small stove, and an open window with displays for snacks. The driver owned rights to a route where he sold food at prearranged sites for breakfast, lunch, and dinner. The wife strongly supported accepting the financial offer and using the money to buy a truck and route. The topic angered the husband.

How Would You Conceptualize This Case?

1. What were the husband's interests and needs?
2. What were the wife's interests and needs?
3. How could the counselor attend to the interests of the couple so both the husband and wife would mutually benefit?

what they could have done to prevent the layoffs. Executives also had to deal with their emotions very carefully for fear that their reactions would be interpreted as disloyalty to the company.

Clients in groups and workshops learned about the career transition process and how to deal with the loss of their expectation of permanent job security. A major theme became self-responsibility for career movement as workers gained personal insight and a belief in their ability to manage the difficult change (Andersen & Mosley-Howard 1989). Counselors earned trust and respect by utilizing the same skills used for creating career education and counseling programs in other settings. Although the work gave much satisfaction and a sense of making an important contribution, it was also very emotionally consuming and physically exhausting.

What Actually Happened?

The husband needed to deal with feelings of betrayal by the company. To give up his role as an employee of a well-known corporation made him feel as though he was lost and all alone. To own a business was a risk. What would happen if he failed? The wife needed to maintain a sense of home and community. The counselor arranged to see the wife and husband separately for several sessions. The husband described his years working in the factory. Over the years, many conflicts were experienced between the union and management, but he felt safe as long as he and his buddies stood together. He hated the dull routine, working on the assembly line, doing the same tasks over and over. Yet he enjoyed his breaks and lunchtimes when he socialized with other workers. Finally, he recognized his most hurtful losses were his friendships. His greatest satisfaction, and an important strength, was conversing with others. He recognized if he were operating a lunch truck, a major part of his time could be talking with customers and no time would be spent doing the routine tasks on the factory line that he hated. Still, he was afraid he would not be able to handle the business aspects, such as keeping accurate accounts of expenses and ordering the right amount of supplies.

The wife expressed her fears in individual counseling as well. She knew both she and her husband valued the family ties and neighborhood relationships they had established over the years. To relocate would entail losing a lifetime of connections. She did not work outside the home. She felt her work with the parish church, running a soup kitchen, was a meaningful contribution to the community.

When the couple came to counseling together, the husband eventually agreed to take the financial offer and buy the truck route. The wife agreed to join her husband in the business training offered by the franchisers and to help with bookkeeping tasks and ordering procedures. The wife sent a Christmas card to the counselor for years saying how much the couple enjoyed their business and working together.

Consulting for other career situations and needs would entail services and counseling interventions similar to those discussed here. Learning about the psychological patterns and career needs of specific situations experienced by adults in the working world adds some content, but the basic skills are the same skills utilized by career practitioners across many career programs in many settings. Over time, career literature has described the specific needs of particular populations who require assistance dealing with career issues intertwined with personal circumstances, such as displaced homemakers or mid-career changers. If more people with particular needs become known, more descriptions of workshop content and other process needs might be developed. And, if the economy continues the current trend toward frequent job/field changes for all workers, public agencies may be called upon to meet the career needs for many clients regularly. Professional career practitioners can rise to the occasion by valuing their skills and adapting to needs. Eventually, the profession may create greater sophistication in determining how the needs of differing populations vary.

SUMMARY

Adult and younger workers follow a similar Career Diamond process of exploring self and expanding occupational information before prioritizing personal values and choices through a narrowing movement integrating internal and external factors. The process for adults is somewhat more complex than for those with less experience because identities have been formed and have been influenced by previous adaptations to work environments. Additional theories and professional practices have been developed to answer adult needs.

Career coaching represents an approach that is similar to traditional career counseling, with the exception that coaches sometimes offer services in a variety of settings and also offer advice regarding business strategies. Fast-paced, action-oriented coaching also includes a motivational press, and coaches socialize with clients, contrary to counseling ethics forbidding dual relationships. Otherwise, coaching's emphasis on listening skills, client strengths, and encouragement of client change and self-responsibility is within the realm of career counseling. Coaching methods are preferred by successful clients who want to look ahead, rather than engage in therapy that may review past experiences in a slower-paced self-discovery process. Questers and career-preneurs represent models for the "worried well" that seek coaching services. Whether making strategic movements within corporations or starting new businesses, success models are always looking ahead and adapting to new opportunities.

Transitions to new careers are more difficult for many adults. Prochaska et al. (1994) describe a process where adults spend time talking about potential change and maybe complain prior to actually considering changes or preparing for eventual action. Even after action has been taken, it takes time to solidly maintain new changes. Societal messages regarding joblessness and potential loss of status are issues some clients need to work through. Several models for major life transitions have been proposed, the most thorough being that explicated by Schlossburg (1984). Using an ecomap creates a picture of the multiple areas adults consider when facing major transitions.

Career practitioners are needed in many community settings, as the economy requires numerous job changes. Consulting for organizations can offer

career services during downsizing and business closings. Career practitioners can also assist employees to change positions within companies and help
them deal with job stress as well as employee relationships and other factors contributing to satisfying, productive work lives.

STUDY OUTLINE: KEY TERMS AND CONCEPTS

   I. Adult Career Issues
      A. Adult development
         1. Is no longer tied to physical maturation
         2. The stages are much longer and may contain adults in vari-
            ous life situations.
            a. All children/adolescents are to attend school.
            b. Adults may be in school, employed, single, married,
               widowed, with or without children, caring for elderly
               parents, etc.
  II. Undecided vs. Indecisive
      A. Previous literature distinguished between clients not yet
         decided (**undecided**) and those unable to make decisions
         (**indecisive**).
      B. Prochaska's model may explain why some resistant clients seem
         indecisive; they may not yet be ready to enter a decision-making
         process.
 III. Difficult Transitions
      A. Prochaska's Model
         1. Precontemplation: Coming in due to external pressure (A in
            Career Diamond)
         2. Contemplation: Recognizing there is a problem (beginning
            the exploring phase)
         3. Preparation: Making small changes and preparing for action
            (ending the exploring phase and beginning the deciding
            phase)
         4. Action: Making changes (D in deciding phase).
  IV. Person-Environment Correspondence
      A. Workers
         1. Workers want rewards from the work environment.
         2. Workers want a positive relationship with the work
            environment.
      B. Work environment
         1. Has requirements to be successful and wants workers to be
            able to meet those requirements

    C. Correspondence
- 1. The degree to which the needs of the worker and needs of the work environment are being met.

V. Career Coaching
    A. Counseling, listening skills used
- 1. Emphasis on client strengths
- 2. No attention to past
- 3. Motivational

    B. Helping adults make multiple career changes
- 1. Attention to values, visions, self-esteem

    C. Whole life coaching for balance between personal and career

    D. Advice for business strategies
- 1. Similar to but distinctive from career counseling
- 2. Clientele: "Worried well"
- 3. Fast paced
- 4. Behavioral, action oriented
- 5. Different ethics: Dual relationships
- 6. Professional association, training, and certification

VI. Questers and Career-Preneurs
    A. Description and terms for careerists as "me-incorporated"

VII. Emotional and Cognitive Constructs
    A. Loss of career expectations
    B. Life-style changes
    C. Societal messages regarding job loss and job status

VIII. Major Life Transitions
    A. Bridges: Natural life changes
    B. Brammer: Journey to a new place in life
    C. Schlossburg: Pervasive nature of change in many areas of life
- 1. Roles
- 2. Routines
- 3. Support systems
- 4. Relationships
- 5. Personal identity

IX. Consultation for Organizations
    A. Career practitioners consult with organizations regarding many topical areas.
- 1. Crosscultural adjustment
- 2. Business, plant closings, outplacement
- 3. Changing positions within organization
- 4. How to deal with stress and other wellness issues
- 5. Relationships between workers

    B. Consultation for plant closing

1. Negotiating package of services
2. Needs assessment
3. Career education programs
   a. Support groups
   b. Job search workshops
   c. Individual career counseling
   d. Consulting with management and union leaders
   e. Grieving cycle
   f. Leaders issues

EXERCISES

1. Determine a particular group of adult career changers who could use the services of career practitioners. What psychological issues might be relevant to that specific group? Design a psychoeducational group that would offer career information and a series of experiential exercises to change attitudes and allow for coming to terms with the group's unique experiences.

2. Write an imaginary case study for one of the group members who is also receiving individual career counseling and who has family issues that are a part of his context.

REFERENCES

Andersen, P., & Mosley Howard, S. (1989). *Emotional effects and social process of a plant closing.* Presentation: American Counseling Association, Cincinnati, OH.

Brammer, L. (1991). *How to cope with life transitions: The challenge of personal changes.* New York: Hemisphere.

Bridges, W. (1980). *Transitions: Making sense of life's changes.* Reading, MA: Addison-Wesley.

Brown, L. & Brooks, D (1996). *Career choice and development.* San Francisco: Jossey-Bass.

Carlson Learning Company. (1994). *Personal profile system.* Minneapolis, MN.

Carpenter, S. (2001). Monitor on psychology. *American Psychological Association, 32*(7), 48–60.

Crites, J. O. (1981). *Career counseling: Models, methods, and materials.* New York: McGraw-Hill.

Dawis, R. V. (1994). The theory of work adjustment as convergent theory. In M. L. Savikas and R. W. Lent (Eds.), *Convergence in career development theories: Implications for science and practice* (pp. 33-43). Palo Alto, CA: CPP Books.

Dawis, R. V. (1996). The theory of work adjustment and person-environment-correspondence counseling. In D. Brown & L. Brooks (Eds.), *Career choice and development* (3rd ed., pp. 75–120). San Francisco: Jossey-Bass.

Dawis, R. V., & Lofquist, L. H. (1984). *A psychological theory of work adjustment*. Minneapolis: Univ. of Minnesota Press.

Figler, H., & Bolles, R. N. (1999). *The career counselor's handbook*. Berkeley, CA: Ten Speed Press.

Grodzki, L. (2002). *The new private practice*. New York: Norton.

Grutter, J. (2000). Developmental career counseling: Different stages, different choices. In J. M. Kummerow (Ed.), *New directions in career planning and the workplace: Practical strategies for career management professionals* (2nd ed., pp. 273–306). Palo Alto, CA: Davies-Black.

Hargrove, R. (1999). *Masterful coaching*. San Francisco, CA: Jossey-Bass/Pfeiffer.

Heppner, M. J. & Hendricks, F. (1995). A process and outcome study examining career indecision and indecisiveness. *Journal of Counseling & Development, 73*(4), 426–437.

Holland, J. L., Daiger, D. C., & Power, P. G. (1980). *My vocational situation*. Palo Alto, CA: Consulting Psychologists Press.

Hudson, F. M. (1999). *The handbook of coaching*. San Francisco, CA: Jossey-Bass.

Kanchier, C. J. (1987). *Questers: Dare to change your job and your life*. Saratoga, CA: R & E.

Krumboltz, J. D. (1993). Integrating career and personal counseling. *Career Development Quarterly, 42*(2), 143–148.

Lofquist, L. H., & Dawis, R. V. (1991). *Essentials of person-environment-correspondence counseling*. Minneapolis: Univ. of Minnesota Press.

Moore, D. P. (2000). *CareerPreneurs: Lessons from leading women entrepreneurs on building a career without boundaries*. Palo Alto, CA: Davies-Black.

Mosley-Howard, S., & Andersen, P. (1993). Using my vocational situation with workers facing a plant closing. *Journal of Career Development, 19*(4), 289–300.

Myers, I. B., & McCaulley, M. H. (1998). *Manual: A guide to the development and use of the Meyers-Briggs Type Indicator*. Palo Alto, CA: Consulting Psychologist Press.

Niederman, R. (2002). Coaching CEOs and executive teams. In L. Grodzki (Ed.), *The new private practice* (pp. 25–37). New York: Norton.

Prochaska, J. O., Norcross, J. C., & Diclemente, C. C. (1994). *Changing for good*. New York: Avon.

Schlossberg, N. K. (1984). *Counseling adults in transitions: Linking practice with theory.* New York: Springer.

Schlossberg, N. K., & Robinson, S. P. (1996). *Going to plan B: How you can cope, regroup, and start your life on a new path.* New York: Simon & Schuster.

Schlossberg, N. K., Waters, E. D., & Goodman, J. (1995). *Counseling adults in transition.* New York: Springer.

Sherman, R., & Freeman N. (1986). *Handbook of structured techniques in marriage and family therapy.* New York: Brunner/Mazel.

Williams, R. (2002). Dysfunction or discovery: A former therapist becomes an executive coach. In L. Grodzki (Ed.), *The new private practice* (pp. 50–66). New York: Norton.

CHAPTER 16

Spirituality and Career Counseling

*You work that you might keep peace with earth and the soul of the earth
. . . and when you work with love, you bind yourself to one another and
to God. . . . Work is love made visible.*

Kahlil Gibran

The self-awareness needed to consider vocational pursuits makes the area of personal values and meaning an obvious extension of career counseling. Some clients easily move into raising issues of life's meaning. When values and issues of broad significance remain implicit but are not openly expressed, it is the counselor's role to bring these topics into the open and to give the client the opportunity to consider those concerns. Although counselors are neither spiritual leaders nor experts in religion, existential concerns—the search for the value of a life lived—provide the venue for integrating profound personal intentions into the counseling experience.

Bergin (1991) reports the results of a values survey of mental health professionals. Most counselors agreed with the necessity of finding fulfillment and satisfaction in work. A high percentage of counselors also agreed that having a purpose for living is an important part of a healthy life-style. Some counseling clients may explore values and personal meaning that are not connected to an overall philosophy, religion, or sense of spirituality. Other clients may express a search for meaning labeled as a spiritual search that may or may not have a philosophical cohesion but that does impart a feeling of deep meaning. Still other clients may participate in an organized religion with a set of beliefs that are applied to daily life. Counselors can facilitate the client's search for meaning within the context of the client's chosen structure of meaning without sharing an adherence to the client's specific system of thought.

Counseling literature includes discussions of broad-based values as well as spiritual concerns that are related to other life issues for clients (see the works of Anderson & Worthen 1997; Ballenger & Watt, 1996; Elhany,

McLaughlin, & Brown, 1996; Moules, 2000; Prest & Keller, 1993; Rey, 1997; Walsh, 1998; Weaver, Koenig, & Larson, 1997). Spiritual values provide direction and a moral, ethical compass for making life's decisions. Career counselors can encourage clients to consider the meaning of career choices within the clients' own set of values and spiritual framework.

CALLING TO VOCATION

In earlier times, the meaning of work was tied to phrases such as a calling to a vocation or the mission of one's life (Bolles, 1995). The term **calling** means that a higher power is determining the specific kind of work the individual should do. It suggests that meaningful work is expressive of more than the individual's private desires. Although today the depiction of career as a divine calling is uncommon in the secular world outside of the ministry, aspiring to a meaningful purpose in one's work is still a common human need. Indeed, many of the concepts directly tied to religious traditions or biblical interpretations bear a resemblance to secular career ideas. Current career counseling may not explicitly use the term spiritual calling, but underlying the profession are humanistic values that are similar in many ways to religious beliefs.

CORE HUMANISTIC VALUES

Flow (1993) describes the core values of meaningful work shared by many clients. These values include service to others and contributing to the community while developing one's self. Although a religious person may add the practice of seeking God's guidance through prayer or reading the scripture, both secular humanitarians and religious adherents share the value of serving others. The goal of achieving meaning beyond economic and personal gains is also common.

Huntley (1997) describes a sociological analysis of American culture where a calling serves as the means for individuals to relate to others and the wider society through their work. Studs Terkel quotes a worker saying, "I think most of us are looking for a calling, not a job" (1972, p. xxiv).

Cochran (1990) describes careerists he called meaning searchers, people who created lives "radiant with meaning," whatever their chosen vocation. The meaning they found in work was not defined by job titles that are too concrete to convey life's purpose. Instead, their purpose in life was to contribute to society and to create a significant legacy.

SELF-EXPRESSION AS MEANING

Self-fulfillment is the work value that is truly expressive of the person's identity. In modern times, the search for self-expression in work has taken on an almost spiritual meaning. Expressions such as "follow your bliss" convey the concept that individuals can use their own inner satisfactions to determine the career path that expresses their identity (Campbell & Moyer, 1988). The book *Do What You Want, the Money Will Follow* (Sinetar, 1987) expresses the hope that activities that bring personal satisfaction can generate income as well. *Soul Work* (Bloch & Richmond, 1998) asserts that if workers are passionate about their work, success will come. All these authors describe a search for meaning beyond matching interests and abilities to a job title. They suggest that the individual's true inner voice expresses a meaningful wisdom. Further meaning is gained when the person's work also becomes a contribution to others and society.

Natale and Neher (1997) discuss the differences between the typical cultural norms of the corporate workplace and individual meaning. Standard corporate expectations require adherence to the hierarchical structure. An individual's sense of values is subsumed under a bottom line mentality and accountability to the organization. Individuals, on the other hand, gain meaning through inner integrity. Personal values are based on personal authority, experience, feelings, and discernment of abilities. Personal values can be maintained at work only if individuals can interpret their private meaning as connected to the external system.

Note the parallel with the Career Diamond. Individual considerations are placed on the top with the externals on the bottom leading to a process of integrating the two. Another career-related pictorial depicts the significance of an individual's values. Richmond (1997) draws a funnel (Figure 16.1) where interests, knowledge, skills, and values enter the wide top part of the shape, and all the personal characteristics run into the narrow bottom exit.

The funnel is similar to the second half of the Career Diamond (Figure 16.2) showing a narrowing, prioritizing, and integrating process that comes to an end point as a decision is made at the end of the diamond. Counselors who expand the standard checklists of career-related values to a full discussion of life's meaning are extending the process to a level full of significance and profound relevance.

The funnel image illustrates the process of taking a large number of values and determining those that are most important, whereas the second half of the Career Diamond illustrates the integration of personal characteristics with external demands in a process where, when the two sides come together, a decision is made.

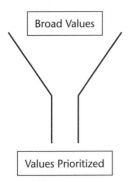

Figure 16.1   Richmond (1997) uses a funnel to depict the broad values that are considered when decisions are made (the wide top of the funnel) and the sorting that refines considerations (narrow bottom of the funnel) so the decision can meet the most important priorities.

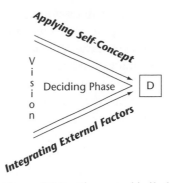

Figure 16.2   The second half of the Career Diamond shows the Vision created by earlier exploring. To bring the Vision into reality, personal priorities are set and integrated with realistic external factors, a narrowing refinement that leads to a Decision.

PROCESS INTERVENTIONS

Counselors can facilitate quests for meaning by reflecting expressions that seem significant to the client and by asking basic questions such as, "What gives your life purpose?" Clients usually have underlying motivations for the choices they have made such as, "I want to help people"; "I want to bring decent writing into the world"; "I want to build something of lasting value"; "I want to be part of a team of members working together for a common purpose"; or "I want to have a voice in improving my profession."

Basic motivations for doing a job may not, however, touch the deeper meanings a client has for life. The answers clients give to questions of meaning and purpose offer clues as to how much time and effort the client wants to spend considering these issues. For example, clients who indicate little interest in deeper meaning might say, "I want to make enough money to put my kids through college" or "I want to retire by age 62 so I can play golf every day."

Reflection of Meaning

In career counseling, reflections of meaning are slightly different than reflections of content or feelings. The expression of values may be implied, in which case it is up to the counselor to bring out the underlying meaning, or strong emotions regarding values that may be revealed in the client's tone of voice. The counselor then has a choice of reflections, emphasizing the emotion or the implicit belief or value, or both. The counselor chooses to mirror the client's values when accentuating his emotions would not be helpful and when pointing to meaning would be more encouraging. Although identifying and releasing feeling is healing and allows the client to become aware of internal experience, sometimes an overemphasis on feeling prevents the client from moving forward in considering options. For example, reflecting depressive or inferiority feelings will not induce movement toward the goal of considering career choices. However, if the negative feelings are associated with the value of say, making a contribution to society, then reflecting the value encourages clients to see themselves in a positive light. Values and beliefs are ideas tied to strong feelings. Movement in counseling can occur when the counselor makes skillful choices of when to reflect emotion, when to state an implied value, and when to do both.

A number of themes can be seen in the values commonly expressed in career counseling. Clients often express their desire to build careers that mean more than the means to earn money. Career choices may also be grounded in the need to make a positive contribution that is self-expressive. Finding solutions to world problems may be a motivating value for some clients whereas others see the family as their major value in contributing to society.

ANTI-MATERIALISM

Some authors have contrasted the values of making money with meaningful "soul-work" (McClenahen, 1991; Moore, 1992; Policoff, 1985). The prevailing ethic in our society sometimes seems to emphasize working as a means to earn more to buy more. Spiraling consumption (Fox, 1995) requires a lifestyle of workaholism that leads people to self-centered, isolated, stressful lives. Amy Saltzman (1991) coined the term *downshifting* for reducing the emphasis on career striving and doing more satisfying and meaningful activities outside of work. Career counselors can facilitate clients' examination of how much materialism reflects their values and whether consuming less would provide more life satisfaction. Balancing career efforts with other meaningful activities can be an important aspect of clarifying values for clients.

CREATIVITY

Fox (1995) describes a concept of work as the creation and evolution of a spiritual way of being, in which an inner spirit feeds external career efforts. In his *Spirituality and Work Questionnaire*, the questions offer counseling interventions that can be interspersed throughout the process of exploring meaning. Some of his questions are, "Do I experience joy in work, and do others experience it as a result of my work?" "Do I experience awe and wonder through it? And would it be a blessing for generations to come?" Fox's conceptions are captured in the title of his book, *The Reinvention of Work.* The self-development he describes includes the way people approach work as well as what they do.

Such work may not be what one does to earn a living. The effective career counselor is able to enhance lives by paying attention to avocations as well as jobs. Robert Frost expresses the dream of many in his words, "My object in life is to unite/ My avocation and my vocation/ As my two eyes make one in sight" (1949). Many clients decide to work in jobs that pay the bills while expressing their creativity in after-work activities. Counselors can help clients view their lives as a whole picture in which the most meaningful activities take place outside of work.

SAVING THE PLANET

Some articles on spirituality describe the meaningfulness of ecology and preserving the planet (Moules, 2000). The elevation of ecology to the level of spirituality occurs when the interconnection of all life is held as a value. American Indian values describe the sacredness of nature and the inspiration gained by humans in honoring their connection to the land and to animals. Participating in volunteer activities related to ecology gives meaning and a deep sense of contribution to some clients. Macy (1990) describes the term *eco-self* as a metaphor used in counseling to describe a person's interconnection to others and to the earth and the universe. Some writers tie an ecological sensibility to negating consumerism and materialism. Creating a life-style respectful of the earth and internally communing with nature can have far-reaching implications for career and life-style choices.

FAMILY VALUES

Economic pressures force families to adapt to the demands of working life. It is difficult for all but the most well-paid workers to provide a comfortable living for their families without two incomes. Some working parents are making choices to budget their income so that one of them can stay home with young children for at least a period of time. The family bond created by couples carefully cooperating to make the quality of their home life a major priority is an important expression of values. The stay-at-home parent may feel a sense of purpose in staying home with the children but may also feel isolated in a world where many parents work.

Although changing gender roles have created a variety of arrangements for parents sharing child care, there continue to be pressures no matter what choices are made. Some mothers who stay home with children feel their intelligence questioned and may not gain understanding from others regarding economic pressures. Fathers who stay home face skeptical reactions (Pleck, 1999). Many writers describing family/career issues have dealt with the practicalities of balancing these demands. However, the values expressed by the choice of life-style are not often discussed in the dual-career literature. When the meanings of creating a satisfying relationship and of keeping the family as the central priority are explored with clients, practical considerations often fall into place. Career counselors can validate couples' choices of family values, offering understanding for the difficulties and pressures whether the choice includes both parents working or not.

In more than 50 percent of intact American families, both parents are working; however, there is a difference between dual-earners and dual-careerists (Goldenberg & Goldenberg, 2002). The Goldenbergs define dual-earners as couples who must work to make ends meet. By comparison, dual-careerists tend to be more affluent, see their careers as an important part of their identity, and value nonfiscal parts of employment, such as achievement or responsibility. When couples choose the dual-career route, they may also be expressing important values. The couple may be committed to egalitarian roles for both partners and determined to share home responsibilities and parenting. Again, practical considerations and pressures often dominate, but the struggles can be worth the effort if the values are explicitly kept in the forefront.

Knudson-Martin (2001), a marital counselor, writes of the intersection between religion and gender. She describes couples struggling to maintain unsatisfying and unequal relationships because they believe their religion dictates a subservient role for women and a dominant, responsible role for men. Without imposing the ideal of equality, the counselor can facilitate an exploration of the couple's faith-based relationship values. Most couples come to an agreement where respect and caring become more important than who is in charge. By opening the counseling to the examination of religious ideals, couples may be relieved of their sense of being stuck and be more receptive to the faith values that can help resolve issues. Such a process of examining values and spiritual issues holistically follows a counseling pattern that could be applicable to other intersections of career and family.

McKenry and Price (2000) cite numerous studies regarding the psychological and social impact of economic stress on families. These authors recommended that counselors inquire about the effect of change (e.g., job changes) on the family. They point to positive coping mechanisms such as social support, cognitive restructuring, and self-help strategies as a way to buffer the stress. The meaning of change has implications for a person's values and spirituality, and when we address meaning in counseling, we bring the whole person into the process as opposed to artificially focusing on one small facet of life.

NATURE AND COMMUNITY

Some people seek solace in nature and find that natural settings induce a calm inner space for dealing with life's issues. Counselors can ask clients if there is a special place where the client goes to ponder important concerns. Clients may report that a walk in the woods or a drive along the seashore helps them gain perspective, yet they do not visit the natural setting regularly. Encouraging clients to consistently practice any habit for self-renewal helps them get in touch with their inner strengths. Clients can be taught to use a common relaxation tool in which they imagine themselves in their special place. This exercise can be extended for use as a means to contemplate meaning.

Whether or not a client is a member of an organized religious community, finding or creating a network of people who share similar beliefs can enhance meaning making. There are many creative ways to make and keep contacts with others today. The Internet is a primary example of a way in which clients can find others who are exploring common values. Even distant communities can share support and meaningful connections.

Counselors can help clients solidify personal meanings by assigning the task of writing a personal mission statement. An individual's sense of meaning can be described in a declaration of purpose. Avowing meaningful goals provides motivation for continuing to do the daily activity of work. Mission statements require regular rewriting, or the inspiration no longer invigorates a person. Some clients appreciate the value of inscribing on a plaque a succinct proclamation of meaning consisting of a few motivating words.

SPIRITUALITY

Spirituality is defined by Bloch and Richmond (1998) as "the ability to find communion with that which is the deepest within ourselves and the greatest outside ourselves" (p. 18). Despair is sometimes expressed by a client whose job lacks personal meaning or when the loss of a job or business opens up doubts about the meaning of an individual's life. Cochran (1990) notes that career counselors sometimes miss the client's search for meaning by approaching counseling with an overly positivistic attitude. Meaning may come by discovering negative circumstances that need changing or by facing the lack of meaning in one's life. Clients may recognize that the meaning of their lives has not been a major consideration as they have busied themselves with the practical activities of earning a living. An invitation to integrate profound questions of meaning with career considerations gives the client an opportunity to examine the issues. If there are cues that existential issues are concerning the client, the next question can be, "What role does spirituality play in your life?"

EXISTENTIAL ISSUES AND CLINICAL JUDGMENT

Existential counseling presumes that life is meaningless and that each person must create any meaning life will have (Frankl, 1959/1984). This school of thought also describes the void and anxiety felt by anyone who has avoided the struggle of defining a purpose for life. The counseling task during a client's existential crisis is to create an atmosphere of safety in which the doubts can be expressed while also maintaining hope. Decisions for the future based on fear do not offer the self-expression of meaning that the client is seeking. The client needs inspiration and energy to fill the void created by a lack of direction. The key is that only the client is an effective source of resolution. The counselor facilitates the self-examination but cannot "minister" in ways that provide specific spiritual instruction. The meaning to be found is unique to the individual, and however painful the struggle, reassurances and the counselor's own beliefs are not helpful. Instead, the counselor can create space for the client's search and on occasion offer vehicles to encourage an existential journey.

It is important to note that sometimes discouragement is so pervasive that the client is not able to deal with profound issues. The client may need to focus on problem solving to resolve a difficult situation. After resolution is found, there may be another opportunity to reflect on life's meaning. Career counselors determine the client's needs and manage the process of counseling to help the client meet those needs in the sequence that is appropriate for her.

SYNCHRONICITY

Many people, whether adhering to a religious tradition or not, still believe in the notion that things happen for a reason. For clients, a belief that unknown influences are affecting their lives is often expressed when career changes occur. That change creates new meaning that takes on an aura of unknown forces at work. **Synchronicity** is a label used by Carl Jung (1933) to describe the interconnectedness of seemingly random events. Life's events may be neither random nor meaningless. Instead anything that happens may be "synchronized" to other seemingly unrelated events. Meaning might be found by paying attention to the underlying implications of everyday events. Jung suggests an event that seems unrelated to what a person expects may actually be a call for the person to seek an unrecognized purpose.

Some religions use a similar concept of a relationship between suffering and inspiration. What appears to be a negative experience teaches something to an individual, even if the purpose behind the experience is unknown. Within such beliefs is the implication that it is better to accept negative experiences and try to learn from them. Assuming that all events have an unknown purpose behind them, resisting denies the validity of the purpose. It is best simply to let life take its course. Maybe at a later time, the meaning of the experience will be revealed. Clients may state such beliefs, and the meanings can be reflected back to see what develops as the words open the client's awareness.

The client may find hope and comfort in the belief that a change may have a good purpose, or the client may reveal ambivalence. It might be appropriate to let the client stay with the feeling of conflict about whether the change had a good purpose, a bad purpose, or perhaps no purpose at all. After an interlude, the counselor may cue the client to "Describe both your feelings of hope and despair." Getting in touch with beliefs tinged with only half acceptance allows the client to fully live the experience in the moment. Growth often occurs when such mixed feelings are accepted and acknowledged, releasing new energy to focus on a new quest.

FLOW: MEANING BEYOND THE SELF

The term **flow** is used to describe a state in which work becomes so absorbing that the worker feels a oneness with the tasks. Flow is described in studies by Csikszentmihalyi (1990), which were discussed in an earlier chapter. The assumption is that the worker has such a harmonious connection with the career tasks that the effort is not taxing, but satisfying. In fact, when working under flow conditions, a person can feel energized by the tasks. Harmony with work allows individuals to enact (e.g., putting one's identity into action) their own identity in a unique way, offering a sense that the career was meant to be.

To place flow within a spiritual context, Csikszentmihalyi (1990) compared the concept with *yu* as described by Taoist scholar Chuang Tzu. The author suggests that both *yu* and flow allude to experiencing work activity as connected to positive feelings of deep meaning. Csikszentmihalyi used the term *harmoniously ordered consciousness* to tie flow to the eastern sense of oneness with universal forces. The worker is participating in the flow of life, and the effort is both a personal expression and a participation in all of life. Work becomes a pleasurable experience connected to a universal flow of energy. The flow of the person's feelings and internal consciousness joins the universal flow of life's movement. Both the person's mind and sense of being are synchronized in harmony with the energy that connects all living things, and work takes on the meaning of contributing to life itself. Work is a meditative experience, renewing self and giving of self, offering a spiritual sense of meaning. Tillich (1963) uses a metaphor of God as a stream with all human beings in the stream. This metaphor validates the faith that swimming against the stream may be counterproductive and being carried by the stream offers purposeful movement (Prest & Keller, 1993).

Our culture recognizes the phenomenon in athletics, and we refer to it as "being in the zone." So we are not asking clients to become eastern philosophers, but taking something we all recognize in one life domain and looking for opportunities to experience it in our vocation or avocation.

HARMONY

Bloch (1997) points out that gaining the experiential meaning of flow requires that the western mindset suspend a subject–object duality; instead, the worker and the work become a part of a flowing experience. Another source of harmony includes feeling the connection with the work one is meant to do, or the experience of a calling. Still another source of feeling connected is a natural sense of love within authentic relationships with others at work. Bloch talks about a Buddhist scholar Krishnamurti, who wrote *On Right Livelihood* (1974). Finding the right livelihood in the Buddhist tradition includes the expression of universally positive values that contribute to the common good and express peaceful caring to others. David Tiedeman (1997) speaks to the need for career counseling theory to include the concept of **complementarity,** in which dualistic thinking is abandoned and a holistic view is gained. With complementarity as a world view, being in context with others and experiencing the flow of work creates meaning beyond the self.

Counseling as Flow: In Touch with Client's Healing Spirit

Barlow and Bergin (2001) allude to a growing interest in spiritual issues in psychotherapy. The authors described **meta-empathy** as "perceptions and feelings that appear to be influenced by an alternate reality beyond that which is sense-perceivable" (p. 77). Without any direct information, counselors have intuitive insights regarding client needs, and such empathy, according to the authors, could be considered an influence from an other-worldly power. For example, a client was being treated for dysthymia when Bergin recognized that the depressive mood was not the real issue. Instead, the client's identity, goals, and purpose in life were the underlying cause. Such a case has a direct connection to career counseling where personal meaning and purpose are the crux of the occupational search.

Paul Fleischman (1993) is a talented psychiatrist who has won awards for his insights into the human psyche. He also writes of a spirit at work in counseling.

> There is a healing spirit. By "spirit" I mean a mood, an intangible yet definable ambiance that underlies and facilitates that restoration of well-being. In some circumstances, the healing spirit alone can reverse psychopathology, but more often it participates in complicated processes that include technical, psychological, and medical interventions which are buoyed up by it. (p. 17)

Counselors need not leave their sense of spirituality out of counseling as was once advised. Without imposing specific beliefs, counselors would do well to be in touch with the healing force that Fleischman and other authors describe.

Spirituality was defined earlier as a deep internal feeling inspired by our adherence to values beyond ourselves (Bloch & Richmond, 1998). Barlow and Bergin (2001) defined spirituality as "those invisible phenomena associated with thoughts and feelings of enlightenment, vision, transcendence, harmony and truth" (p. 81). Such a broad definition includes many spiritual practices that might be helpful to therapists and clients alike. Rizzuto (1993) also points to spirituality as healthy, saying, "... a socially sound faith ... allows for sublimation of personal developmental joys and pains ... (and) may be an essential component of individual and societal health" (p. 33).

MEDITATION

Eastern philosophical practices encourage tuning in to the connection between the individual's subconscious and an external consciousness through meditation. Bloch (1997) depicts meditation as a process of synthesis in which meaning is created beyond the basics of matching interests and abilities to jobs. When human beings meditate, they can synthesize specifics as well as patterns of personal and external information into a holistic sense of purpose. The discovery of meaning is unique to each individual and occurs within the private experience of meditating about the relationships between aspects of self and external inputs. In order to synthesize the factors, both internal and external, executive functioning of the left brain must be suspended to allow the creativity of the right brain to combine both in unique and private ways. Meditation is a means to clear the mind of linear associations and to promote synthesizing in this way. Eastern thought also sees meditation practice as the means to infuse individual syntheses with the universal forces that inform all of life with meaningful connections.

Intentionality

Regular practice of meditation creates a clear mind connected to the flow of energy that enables the mind's vision to influence external events. For Bloch (1997), such an experience is a spiritual practice. In meditation, the still mind can envision the person striving for goals, performing well, and succeeding in career-related activities. Such visualizations and affirmations can center the person and influence the person to do what is needed. Another view is that meditation actually influences external variables to make the changes visualized. For western cultures, a parapsychological sense of people managing external energy has only marginal acceptance as a reality in everyday life.

However, the major validating method of science has provided some basis for considering such interconnections of energy. The Buddhist concept of connecting the still mind to universal forces was seen as a part of the quantum physics reality that Tiedeman (1997) describes. Chaos theory also describes different realities that may interconnect in nonlinear ways. Scientific thought seems to be coming to explanations of the interconnectedness of all life.

Energy forces are also described by the Indian system of charkas, which associate different parts of the body with colors that symbolize human endeavors. Jung (Von Franz & Hillman, 1971) suggests that in other cultures, supreme realities might be labeled as universal matter or the energy connecting all life. The experience of interconnections between universal energy sources during meditation may be similar to the experience of prayer as practiced in different traditions. If meditation connects the individual to eternal sources, the mind's visualizations, or intentions, could influence outcomes in a way that is beyond human understanding and is truly drawing on outside forces.

Specific methods for meditative and visualization practices are described in the next section. Whether a counselor chooses to believe in the various explanations for the successful outcomes of meditative practices or not, using the techniques might tap into a unique private meaning for some clients.

Meditative Practice

There are many ways to assist people in finding the inner voice that provides support and direction. Some religions teach prayer, chanting, or meditation. Mediation is designed to clear the mind and to create a still space. As scattered thoughts enter the mind, they are released, and the mind refocuses on stillness. It takes effort and regular practice to fully clear the mind to a blank space. However, the practice of letting go of extraneous thoughts is useful and encourages stress relief as well as renewed perspective. Some eastern religions believe that the still mind is in touch with the flow of life interconnecting all things of the universe. Such a connection to life's flow creates a sense of deeper purpose uncluttered with meaningless personal thoughts.

Another method for gaining a peaceful retreat is the practice of mindfulness. In walking meditation, the mediator attends to every sound and movement happening in the moment. By becoming sensitive to immediate experiencing, this practice also creates a new focus for the mind and relief from typical meaningless internal chatter. Mindfulness can become a habit or a method used in everyday experiences. Focusing attention on the sounds and movement of anything can release a person from internal thoughts and encourage a sense of being in the here and now. The movie *Karate Kid* showed the master teacher setting up tasks for the young boy and demonstrating the practice of mindfulness in painting a fence. The young man learned to be aware of the movement of painting up and down the wood while focusing his attention only on the task. From this perspective, a meditative practice can lead to mindfulness for all the activities of life.

The most common meditation method is to be aware of the body's breath. If the mediator focuses only on the breath coming in and going out of her nose and lungs, the still place can be experienced. One simple method adds another tool to retain the focus on the breath. As the mediator breathes in, she counts one and as she breathes out, she counts two. One in, two out, three in, four out. Counting continues until the number 10 is reached and then the counting returns to one. The counting and attention to the breath creates a focus of attention. When extraneous thoughts enter the mind, the counting is interrupted. With each interruption, the count returns to one. The mediator may find she is regularly returning to one, or discover that she has counted to a number over 10. Overcounting usually means mindfulness has been lost and a foggy-like mind state has interfered. Eventually (with regular practice), the discipline of linking breath and counting becomes natural, and only a few stray thoughts interrupt. At such a time the counting can be eliminated, and the mediator can focus only on the breath.

Bloch and Richmond (1998) provided another meditation practice from the aboriginal people of Australia called *dadirri* and presented by Krishnamurti (1974).

> Sit very quietly and be still
> not only physically,
> not only in your body,
> but also in your mind.
> Be very still
> and then, in that stillness,
> attend.
> Attend to the sounds outside this building,
> the Cock crowing,
> the birds singing,
> somebody coughing,
> Somebody leaving.
> Listen first to the things
> outside you,
> Then listen to what is going on
> in your mind.
> And you will then see,
> if you listen very, very attentively,
> in that silence, that
> the outside sound
> and the inside sound
> are the same. (p. 162)

Again, this meditation practice seeks to bring the person to a silent space where personal worries are calmed and renewal offers fresh perspective.

One more meditation method uses a mantra, a word repeated over and over to still the mind. *Um* has been popularized as a sound mantra, but other traditions have other sounds or phrases. Some people enthusiastically try new spiritual practices, and some combine cultural traditions. The first author's mother meditated by repeating, "Jesus loves me," and gained a calm, meaningful peace.

Certainly, some clients may have their own practices, and introducing new methods may not be needed. Asking "Do you have a spiritual practice that calms you and helps you gain a new outlook?" determines the client's habits for seeking renewal. If clients have minimal contemplation habits, helping them create or expand such practices might encourage deeper more meaningful space for considering important concerns.

MEANING THROUGH RELIGION

In a survey of counselors conducted by Bergin in 1991, only 40 to 50 percent of the respondents agreed that spirituality is of psychological importance, and the same percentage said that they have an active religious affiliation (Bergin, 1991). However, Bergin and Jensen (1990) pointed out in another study that 72 percent of the public agreed with the statement, "My religious faith is the most important influence in my life." Despite the seeming disparity between counselors' and the general public's opinions, asking about spirituality may be useful for any career client who is mature enough to weigh significant questions. When a client names a particular religion, counselors can facilitate a process where the client can clarify the application of religious values to career considerations.

Applying faith values in career counseling sessions may not be comfortable for some clients who have strong religious convictions. The domination of materialism and achievement in our society may suggest to religious clients that career counseling is not a venue for exploring deeper meanings. "What role does spirituality play in your life?" may be a welcome invitation for some religious clients. However, such a basic question may not give full permission to discuss religious issues to other clients. The focus on self that is so much a part of most career counseling may subtly deny finding meaning in a theistic system. God may be an important figure guiding decisions for some clients, and prayer may be a vehicle for finding direction. Counselors who demonstrate an openness and respect for religious beliefs and practices can facilitate a search for meaning within a religious tradition without entering into theological areas or interpreting scriptures.

Clients with affiliations to traditional religions may seek direction from God through prayer or scriptures. Facilitating religious clients' searches within the framework they define is more efficacious than trying to circumvent the belief system that is their internal strength and a major resource. If the client asks for a specific religious interpretation, the counselor can ask, "What do you think, and how would this question be answered within your faith?" If the client is caught in doubt about the appropriate interpretation indicated by his religion, then a referral to a spiritual leader may be appropriate. The role of counseling can be defined as a process that helps clients deal with the personal meanings and values that can be faith based. Clients identify the frameworks for their values and determine their ultimate priorities. Counselors facilitate the process and follow the lead of clients who determine their own direction.

It is important for counselors to recognize the variety of theological interpretations even within the same denominations of the same religion.

Christian theologians offer differing ideas when discussing the role of work in the lives of the faithful. All interpreters regard work as a necessary duty to meet the requirements of the natural order. However, most Christian writers also place career as a secondary goal and spirituality as primary (Huntley, 1997).

Some theologians denounce work that becomes too dominating in one's life and therefore detracts from spirituality. Workaholism can be considered a form of idolatry because it forces workers to deny natural life rhythms and encourages a separation from interdependence with nature's cycles. Work could become a means to deny true meaning in life and one's relationship with the transcendent.

Another biblical interpretation affirms work as a vehicle to express Christian values. Work is a divine gift corrupted only by the human distortions of self-centered strivings for status, power, and material gain. The most controversial Christian interpretation describes God and workers as involved together in the continual ongoing process of creativity (Huntley, 1997). The co-creation interpretation depicts unselfish work as expressing the spiritual nature within human beings. Work provides the opportunity for people to serve others and to reconcile with nature. Critiques of the co-creation approach caution against placing man too high on a near-God level because God alone truly creates (Huntley, 1997). The most prevalent and recurring Christian theme is that of work as a calling. A calling can be shown through the natural gifts given to an individual. Using natural talent while honoring appropriate values is heeding the calling. So, paying attention to internal messages that show the way to career pursuits is actually responding to direction from the creator. The person of faith prepares to hear what the calling is. The calling combines self-expression with God's will because a faithful person is internally in tune with any spiritual missive. However, Rayburn (1997) notes examples of biblical figures who objected to a calling because they felt they did not have the appropriate skills to fulfill the designated roles. But according to Christian theology, whether a person feels ready or not, failure to answer a call ends in negative consequences.

Given the multiple ways to interpret work within a religious context, counselors need to allow the client to come to private interpretations. A person's struggle with moral issues and the role of career strengthens an individual and provides direction on the chosen path of powerful meaning.

Some religious clients may interpret career indecision or difficulties as a punishment from a higher power. Such guilt-ridden clients may need to explore the role of forgiveness in their faith and to examine what they need to do to get past negative experiences. Rituals are often powerful means for creating transitions, for letting go of the past, and preparing for the future. Helping the client create a meaningful ritual can be most productive. A counselor could ask, "What spiritual practices have been a part of your life?" The failure of a business, for instance, was seen by one client as the consequence of being too greedy in pushing ahead for material gain. He created a ritual where he regularly made a ledger of debts, assets, and income and then prayed for guidance before making financial decisions. For some clients, it may be preferable to refer to a religious leader who could assist in creating a ritual.

Counselors can also make referrals to different denominations and different faiths. The social support offered by religious affiliations may be needed by clients in addition to the faith support. It can be useful to a counselor to know the names of ministers in the area and programs sponsored by different religious organizations that may be important resources for clients. Communicating to referral agents the purpose of sending career clients to them and how counseling intersects with questions of purpose could build valuable bridges for clients using multiple services.

People active in a religious community tend to have the following characteristics: an ability to cope with crisis and life's difficulties; fewer incidents of depression; fewer incidents of suicide, delinquency, and divorce; and a greater ability to cope with physical illness (Bier, 1999). Certainly career counselors can validate the strength that religious participation offers clients.

Spiritual genograms (Frame, 2000) or spiritual ecomaps (Hodge, 2000) are techniques used to explore the historical impact of spirituality and religious practices for a client's family. The genograms described in Chapter 9 picture a person's family history. A spiritual genogram labels the religious convictions of family members across generations, helping a client view the family influences on his spirituality. The ecomaps described in Chapter 15 pictorially represent a person's connections to the community or environment. The client participates in positive and negative relationships as well as social services and activities, and the ecomap diagrams the connections. A spiritual ecomap shows the relationships and activities that enhance or detract from the client's spiritual experience.

SUMMARY

Chapter 6 on the global economy deals with the effects of rapid changes in the workplace and reviews several writings that suggest the individual's personal purpose in life is the main rudder available to careerists continually changing jobs or even career fields. Coping with the demands of external change leaves the person as the center of stability, and the major source of meaning in a life regularly disrupted. When life changes, clients try to pull their experiences together into a pattern that makes sense of it all. Reflecting on one's life and determining what choices are consistent with personal values can be a guide for choosing the next options. Career counselors need to be prepared to facilitate a client's search for purpose by facilitating the contemplation process. By reflecting the meanings the client suggests, the values and themes of the client's internal world become explicit.

The transitions created by disruptions in employment can represent a crisis of meaning when previous assumptions regarding life and its meaning are destroyed. Unless the client has a working value system that includes regular change, there is little available to make sense of life's events. Work structures day-to-day activities and takes up so much time that while working, many people feel little need to consider meaning beyond meeting daily obligations.

When employment is absent, not only is time unoccupied but also thoughtful activity is often more open to personal musings. Young people facing the end of schooling and workers without jobs often consider what their lives will mean over time. In a society that defines a person's identity with an occupational title, unemployment represents a challenge to selfhood. Work provides an anchor mooring a person's place in society and a sense of identity. Without the purpose offered by work, a person's significance is easily questioned.

Transitions require changes that are often more than finding another similar job. To change, people may need to let go of a major role. Giving up a part of a self-image feels like being uprooted. Considering the meaning of experiences brings forth significant areas that may have been dormant a long time. Change can be required because there have been changes in significant relationships as in divorces or when children grow up and become independent adults. Uncertainty clouds any picture of what change will bring to one's life. A pause is needed to evaluate what has been and to sketch a new vision of the future. Counseling allows clients to review their lives and the meanings already created and to determine new meanings or purpose. Clients can begin a journey toward renewed motivation for another phase. In changing work and social roles, clients create a new expression for the contribution they can make externally and for the new meanings they will build internally.

STUDY OUTLINE: KEY TERMS AND CONCEPTS

I. Expanding Career Counseling beyond Finding a Good Job
   A. Meaning making and finding fulfillment
      1. Unless properly trained, career counselors do not have to be experts on religion and are not expected to provide "Christian Counseling."

2. Existential questions, which contain spirituality, are the purview of career counselors.

B. Provides direction for decision making

C. Clients may have a calling to a specific field. This typically includes religious work but may include secular work.

1. **Calling**: Serves as the means for individuals to relate to others and the wider society through their work

D. Coworkers with similar beliefs may share values, and this can lead to a good fit.

E. Individual values may be placed behind (or even violated by) corporate needs. This robs workers of their internal integrity and the meaning they have set for their lives.

II. Interacting with Clients

A. Assess how one could make the world (community) better. What would give a client purpose?

1. Basic motivations do not count (e.g., make lots of money).

B. Just like reflecting feelings (giving words to obvious but unstated emotions), clients may benefit from reflecting the values they communicate.

1. Overemphasis on reflecting emotions may overshadow reflecting values.

C. Downshifting: Avoiding the downward spiral of make more, buy more, become self-centered and isolated, and live a stressful life

1. Replace downward spiral with balance of making enough money, but also contributing to the world.

D. Paid work may not allow for values to be expressed. In this case, career counselors assess the client's avocation.

1. Eco-self: Preserving parts of the planet

2. Focusing on family time and raising the next generation (dual-earners vs. dual-careerists)

E. Look for some clients, based upon religious beliefs, to place particular pressures on certain people (e.g., men must be the financial pillar of the family) while limiting others (e.g., women must take care of children first and work in meaningless jobs subservient to men).

F. Assist clients in identifying self-renewal behaviors (e.g., alone time, being in nature, nonwork reading, exercise/meditation) and in practicing them.

III. Spirituality

A. **Spirituality**: An inspired sense of meaning defining personal values that range from self-expression to purposes beyond the self. Spirituality can include religious faith, contributions to the common good, harmony with nature, or whatever imbues a person with a sense of purpose, ultimate truth, and/or transcendence.

B. Assess the importance of spirituality and religiosity in one's clients.

C. Individuals who lack a purpose often experience a void in life and may also make decisions out of fear instead of a guiding purpose.

D. Career counselor's spiritual belief cannot provide answers. Must aid the client in finding a direction.

E. Crisis may interfere with spiritual questions. Solve crisis first, then return to meaning making.

F. **Synchronicity**: The interconnectedness of seemingly random events.

IV. Flow (Csikszentmihalyi)

A. **Flow**: A feeling state in which the person is so focused on the activity that concentration is only on the task at hand and the person is unaware of all other external distractions.

1. Westerners may understand "in the zone."

B. May need to abandon dualistic thinking. Move toward holistic thinking and opportunities for complementarity.

C. **Complementarity**: A universal context in which all people are interconnected, and each person's work contributes to the common good.

D. **Meta-empathy**: Career counselor uses "intuition" when coming to insights with the client. May not be factually based.

1. May need to teach clients how to use and trust "intuition."

E. Use of meditation may be appropriate.

1. Western clients may not accept this practice.

2. Western science supports benefits of meditation.

V. Spirituality and U.S. Culture

A. Despite 72 percent of Americans believing that religious faith is one of the most important influences in their lives, only 40 to 50 percent view religion as having psychological importance.

B. Ask clients about religious beliefs and practices. Then apply to career decision making.

C. Because a variety of interpretations are possible for the same religious texts, career counselor openness is vital.

1. Clients need to provide own interpretations.

2. May refer client back to religious text or spiritual leader for answers/direction.

D. Forgiveness of self or other can be important.

      1. Engaging in established religious practices may aid the client in healing.

   E. Use spiritual genograms or spiritual ecomaps to aid clients in better understanding their religious past and current connections.

EXERCISES

In small groups of no more than five people, discuss how spiritual values have intersected with career issues in your life and for members of your family. Small groups then share summary themes with the whole class.

1. In small groups, share the "touchy" values issues that would be difficult to explore with clients. For example, would helping a client deal with an unwanted pregnancy be a strain? What if the client was trying to decide if she wanted to have an abortion? Or, what would it be like if a client said, "Do you believe in Jesus? I can only talk to a born-again Christian who will understand me"?

2. Each small group determines a list of "touchy" subjects and shares with the class why the subject would be difficult and recommendations for handling the situation with a client.

REFERENCES

Anderson, D., & Worthen, D. (1997). Exploring a fourth dimension: Spirituality as a resource for the couple therapist. *Journal of Marital and Family Therapy, 23*, 3–12.

Ballenger, E., & Watt, R. T. (1996, February). *Spirituality and religion in social work education: Valuable or values conflict.* Paper presented at the conference for the Council on Social Work Education, Washington, DC.

Barlow, S. H., & Bergin, A. E. (2001). The phenomenon of spirit in a secular psychotherapy. In B. D. Slife, R. N. Williams, & S. H. Barlow (Eds.), *Critical issues in psychotherapy* (pp. 77–91). Thousand Oaks, CA: Sage.

Bergin, A. E. (1991). Values and religious in psychotherapy and mental health. *American Psychologist, 46*(4), 394–403.

Bergin, A. E., & Jensen, J. P. (1990). Religiosity of psychotherapists: A national survey. *Psychotherapy, 27*, 2–7.

Bier, W. C. (1999, August). Spiritual influences in healing and psychotherapy. Award Address: Annual convention of the American Psychological Association.. *Psychology of Religion Newsletter,* American Psychological Association Division 36, 25:1.

Bloch, D. P. (1997). Spirituality, intentionality, and career success: The quest for meaning. In D. P. Bloch & L. J. Richmond (Eds.), *Connections between spirit and work in career development* (pp. 185–208). Palo Alto, CA: Davies-Black.

Bloch, D. P., & Richmond, L. J. (1998). *Soul work: Finding the work you love, loving the work you have.* Palo Alto, CA: Davies-Black.

Bolles, R. N. (1995). *The 1995 what color is your parachute.* Berkeley, CA: Ten Speed Press.

Campbell, J., & Moyer, B. (1988). *The power of myth.* NY: Doubleday.

Cochran, L. (1990). *The sense of vocation: A study of career and life development.* Albany: State Univ. of New York Press.

Csikszentmihalyi, M. (1990). *Flow: The psychology of optimal experience.* NY: Harper Collins.

Elhany, A., McLaughlin, S., & Brown, P. (1996, February). *The role of religion and spirituality   in social work education and practice.* Paper presented at the conference of the Council on Social Work Education, Washington, DC.

Fleischman, P. R. (1993). *Spiritual aspects of psychiatric practice.* Cleveland, SC: Boone Chance Press.

Flow, D. (1993). A business owner's mission: Working as a Christian in a car sales firm. In R. J. Banks (Ed.), *Faith goes to work: Reflections from the marketplace* (pp. 17–23). NY: Alban Institute.

Fox, M. (1995). *The reinvention of work.* San Francisco, CA: Harper San Francisco.

Frame, M. W. (2000). The spiritual genogram in family therapy. *Journal of Marital and Family Therapy, 26*(2), 211–216.

Frankl, V. E. (1959/1984). *Man's search for meaning* (Rev. & Updated). New York: Washington Square Press.

Frost, R. (1949) *Complete poems of Robert Frost.* Austin, TX: Holt, Rinehart, & Winston.

Gibran, K. (1951). *The prophet.* NY: Knopf.

Goldenberg, H., & Goldenberg, I. (2002). *Counseling today's families* (4th ed.). Pacific Grove, CA: Brooks/Cole.

Hansen, S. (1997). *Integrative life planning.* San Francisco: Jossey-Bass.

Hodge, D. R. (2000). Spiritual ecomaps: A new diagrammatic tool for assessing marital and family spirituality. *Journal of Marital and Family Therapy, 20*(2), 181–194.

Huntley, H. L. (1997). How does "God-talk" speak to the workplace: An essay on the theology of work. In D. P. Bloch & L. J. Richmond (Eds.), *Connections between spirit and work in career development* (pp. 115–136). Palo Alto, CA: Davies-Black.

Jung, C. G. (1933). *Modern man in search of a soul.* Orlando, FL: Harcourt Brace.

Knudson-Martin, C. (2001). Spirituality and gender in clinical practice. *Family Therapy News, 32,* 4–5.

Krishnamurti, J. (1974). *On right livelihood.* San Francisco: Harper San Francisco.

Macy, J. (1990). The greening of the self. *Common Boundary, 8*(4), 22–25.

McClenahen, J. S. (March 4, 1991). It's no fun working here anymore. *Industry Week,* 20–22.

McKenry, P. C., & Price, S. J. (2000). *Families and change.* Thousand Oaks, CA: Sage.

Moore, T. (1992). *Care of the soul: A guide for cultivating depth and sacredness in everyday life.* NY: Harper Collins.

Moules, N. J. (2000). Postmodernism and the sacred: Reclaiming connection in our greater-than-human worlds. *Journal of Marital and Family Therapy, 26*(2), 229–240.

Natale, S. M., & Neher, J.C. (1997). Inspiriting the workplace: Developing a values-based management system. In D. P. Bloch & L. J. Richmond (Eds.), *Connections between spirit and work in career development* (pp. 237–256). Palo Alto, CA: Davies-Black.

Pleck, J. H. (1999). Are "family-supportive" employer policies relevant to men? In A. Vail (Ed.), *Taking sides: Clashing views on controversial issues in family and personal relationships* (4th ed., pp. 136–144). Guilford, CT: Dushkin/McGraw-Hill.

Policoff, S. P. (1985). Working it out. *New Age Journal, 73,* 34–39.

Prest, L. A., & Keller, J. F. (1993). Spirituality and family therapy: Spiritual beliefs, myths and metaphors. *Journal of Marital and Family Therapy, 19,* 137–148.

Rayburn, C. A. (1997). Vocation as calling: Affirmative response or "wrong number." In D. P. Bloch & L. J. Richmond (Eds.), *Connections between spirit and work in career development* (pp. 163–184). Palo Alto, CA: Davies-Black.

Rey, L. D. (1997). Religion as invisible culture: Knowing a lot and knowing with conviction. *Journal of Family Social Work, 2*(2), 159–177.

Richmond, L. J. (1997). Spirituality and career assessment: Metaphors and measurement. In D. P. Bloch & L. J. Richmond (Eds.). *Connections between spirit and work in career development* (pp. 209–236). Palo Alto, CA: Davies-Black.

Rizzuto, A. (1993). Exploring sacred landscapes. In M. L. Randour (Ed.), *Exploring sacred landscapes: Religious and spiritual experiences in psychotherapy* (pp. 27-46). New York: Columbia Univ. Press.

Saltzman, A. (August, 1991). Downshifting: The search for ways to change your life and reinvent success. *Inc.,* 70–71.

Sinetar, M. (1987). *Do what you want, the money will follow: Discovering your right livelihood.* Mahwah, NJ: Paulist Press.

Terkel, S. (1972). *Working.* New York: Pantheon Books.

Tiedeman, D. V. (1997). Ready, set, grow: An allegoric induction into quantum careering. In D. P. Bloch & L. J. Richmond (Eds.), *Connections between spirit and work in career development* (pp. 61–86). Palo Alto, CA: Davies-Black.

Tillich, P. (1963). *The eternal now.* New York: Scribner's.

Von Franz, M. L., & Hillman, J. (1971). *Lectures on Jung's typology.* Dallas, TX: Spring.

Walsh, F. (1998). Beliefs, spirituality, and transcendence. In M. McGoldrick (Ed.), *Revisioning family therapy: Race, culture, and transcendence in clinical practice* (pp. 62–77). New York: Guilford Press.

Weaver, A. J., Koenig, H. G., & Larson, D. F. (1997). Marriage and family therapists and the clergy: A need for clinical collaboration, training, and research. *Journal of Marital and Family Therapy, 23,* 13–25.

APPENDIX A

Career Counseling Competencies

Revised Version, 1997

- Introduction to Career Counseling Competency Statements
- Minimum Competencies
- Professional Preparation
- Ethical Responsibilities
- Career Counseling Competencies and Performance Indicators
  - Career Development Theory
  - Individual and Group Counseling Skills
  - Individual/Group Assessment
  - Information/Resources
  - Program Promotion, Management, and Implementation
  - Coaching, Consultation, and Performance Improvement
  - Diverse Populations
  - Supervision
  - Ethical/Legal Issues
  - Research/Evaluation
  - Technology

INTRODUCTION TO CAREER COUNSELING

Competency Statements

These competency statements are for those professionals interested and trained in the field of career counseling. For the purpose of these statements, career counseling is defined as the process of assisting individuals in the development of a life-career with focus on the definition of the worker role and how that role interacts with other life roles.

NCDA's Career Counseling Competencies are intended to represent minimum competencies for those professionals at or above the Master's degree level of education. These competencies are reviewed on an ongoing basis by the NCDA Professional Standards Committee, the NCDA Board, and other relevant associations.

Professional competency statements provide guidance for the minimum competencies necessary to perform effectively a particular occupation or job within a particular field. Professional career counselors (Master's degree or higher) or persons in career development positions must demonstrate the knowledge and skills for a specialty in career counseling that the generalist counselor might not possess. Skills and knowledge are represented by designated competency areas, which have been developed by professional career counselors and counselor educators. The Career Counseling Competency Statements can serve as a guide for career counseling training programs or as a checklist for persons wanting to acquire or to enhance their skills in career counseling.

MINIMUM COMPETENCIES

In order to work as a professional engaged in Career Counseling, the individual must demonstrate minimum competencies in 11 designated areas. These 11 areas are: Career Development Theory, Individual and Group Counseling Skills, Individual/Group Assessment, Information/Resources, Program Management and Implementation, Consultation, Diverse Populations, Supervision, Ethical/Legal Issues, Research/Evaluation, and Technology. These areas are briefly defined as follows:

- Career Development Theory: Theory base and knowledge considered essential for professionals engaging in career counseling and development.

- Individual and Group Counseling Skills: Individual and group counseling competencies considered essential for effective career counseling.

- Individual/Group Assessment: Individual/group assessment skills considered essential for professionals engaging in career counseling.

- Information/Resources: Information/resource base and knowledge essential for professionals engaging in career counseling.

- **Program Promotion, Management and Implementation**: Skills necessary to develop, plan, implement, and manage comprehensive career development programs in a variety of settings.

- **Coaching, Consultation, and Performance Improvement**: Knowledge and skills considered essential in enabling individuals and organizations to impact effectively upon the career counseling and development process.

- Diverse Populations: Knowledge and skills considered essential in providing career counseling and development processes to diverse populations.

- **Supervision**: Knowledge and skills considered essential in critically evaluating counselor performance, maintaining and improving professional skills, and seeking assistance for others when needed in career counseling.

- **Ethical/Legal Issues**: Information base and knowledge essential for the ethical and legal practice of career counseling.

- **Research/Evaluation**: Knowledge and skills considered essential in understanding and conducting research and evaluation in career counseling and development.

- Technology: Knowledge and skills considered essential in using technology to assist individuals with career planning.

PLEASE NOTE: *Highlighted competencies are those that must be met in order to obtain the Master Career Counselor Special Membership Category.*

PROFESSIONAL PREPARATION

The competency statements were developed to serve as guidelines for persons interested in career development occupations. They are intended for persons training at the Master's level or higher with a specialty in career counseling. However, this intention does not prevent other types of career development professionals from using the competencies as guidelines for their own training. The competency statements provide counselor educators, supervisors, and other interested groups with guidelines for the minimum training required for counselors interested in the career counseling specialty. The statements might also serve as guidelines for professional counselors who seek in-service training to qualify as career counselors.

ETHICAL RESPONSIBILITIES

Career development professionals must only perform activities for which they "possess or have access to the necessary skills and resources for giving the kind of help that is needed" (see NCDA and ACA Ethical Standards). If a professional does not have the appropriate training or resources for the type of career concern presented, an appropriate referral must be made. No person should attempt to use skills (within these competency statements) for which he/she has not been trained. For additional ethical guidelines, refer to the NCDA Ethical Standards for Career Counselors.

CAREER COUNSELING COMPETENCIES AND PERFORMANCE INDICATORS

Career Development Theory

Theory base and knowledge considered essential for professionals engaging in career counseling and development. Demonstration of knowledge of:

1. Counseling theories and associated techniques.

2. Theories and models of career development.

3. Individual differences related to gender, sexual orientation, race, ethnicity, and physical and mental capacities.

4. Theoretical models for career development and associated counseling and information-delivery techniques and resources.

5. Human growth and development throughout the life span.

6. Role relationships which facilitate life-work planning.

7. Information, techniques, and models related to career planning and placement

Individual and Group Counseling Skills

Individual and group counseling competencies considered essential to effective career counseling. Demonstration of ability to:

1. Establish and maintain productive personal relationships with individuals.

2. Establish and maintain a productive group climate.

3. Collaborate with clients in identifying personal goals.

4. Identify and select techniques appropriate to client or group goals and client needs, psychological states, and developmental tasks.

5. Identify and understand clients' personal characteristics related to career.

6. Identify and understand social contextual conditions affecting clients' careers.

7. Identify and understand familial, subcultural and cultural structures and functions as they are related to clients' careers.

8. Identify and understand clients' career decision-making processes.

9. Identify and understand clients' attitudes toward work and workers.

10. Identify and understand clients' biases toward work and workers based on gender, race, and cultural stereotypes.

11. Challenge and encourage clients to take action to prepare for and initiate role transitions by:
    • locating sources of relevant information and experience,
    • obtaining and interpreting information and experiences, and acquiring skills needed to make role transitions.

12. Assist the client to acquire a set of employability and job search skills.

13. Support and challenge clients to examine life-work roles, including the balance of work, leisure, family, and community in their careers.

Individual/Group Assessment

Individual/group assessment skills considered essential for professionals engaging in career counseling. Demonstration of ability to:

1. Assess personal characteristics such as aptitude, achievement, interests, values, and personality traits.

2. Assess leisure interests, learning style, life roles, self-concept, career maturity, vocational identity, career indecision, work environment preference (e.g., work satisfaction), and other related life-style/ development issues.

3. Assess conditions of the work environment (such as tasks, expectations, norms, and qualities of the physical and social settings).

4. Evaluate and select valid and reliable instruments appropriate to the client's gender, sexual orientation, race, ethnicity, and physical and mental capacities.

5. Use computer-delivered assessment measures effectively and appropriately.

6. Select assessment techniques appropriate for group administration and those appropriate for individual administration.

7. Administer, score, and report findings from career assessment instruments appropriately.

8. Interpret data from assessment instruments and present the results to clients and to others.

9. Assist the client and others designated by the client to interpret data from assessment instruments.

10. Write an accurate report of assessment results.

Information/Resources

Information/resource base and knowledge essential for professionals engaging in career counseling. Demonstration of knowledge of:

1. Education, training, and employment trends; labor market information and resources that provide information about job tasks, functions, salaries, requirements, and future outlooks related to broad occupational fields and individual occupations.

2. Resources and skills that clients utilize in life-work planning and management.

3. Community/professional resources available to assist clients in career planning, including job search.

4. Changing roles of women and men and the implications that this has for education, family, and leisure.

5. Methods of good use of computer-based career information delivery systems (CIDS) and computer-assisted career guidance systems (CACGS) to assist with career planning.

Program Promotion, Management, and Implementation

Knowledge and skills necessary to develop, plan, implement, and manage comprehensive career development programs in a variety of settings. Demonstration of knowledge of:

1. Designs that can be used in the organization of career development programs.

2. Needs assessment and evaluation techniques and practices.

3. Organizational theories, including diagnosis, behavior, planning, organizational communication, and management useful in implementing and administering career development programs.

4. Methods of forecasting, budgeting, planning, costing, policy analysis, resource allocation, and quality control.

5. Leadership theories and approaches for evaluation and feedback, organizational change, decision-making, and conflict resolution.

6. Professional standards and criteria for career development programs.

7. Societal trends and state and federal legislation that influence the development and implementation of career development programs.

Demonstration of ability to:

8. Implement individual and group programs in career development for specified populations.

9. Train others about the appropriate use of computer-based systems for career information and planning.

10. Plan, organize, and manage a comprehensive career resource center.

11. Implement career development programs in collaboration with others.

12. Identify and evaluate staff competencies.

13. Mount a marketing and public relations campaign in behalf of career development activities and services.

Coaching, Consultation, and Performance Improvement

Knowledge and skills considered essential in relating to individuals and organizations that impact the career counseling and development process. Demonstration of ability to:

1. Use consultation theories, strategies, and models.

2. Establish and maintain a productive consultative relationship with people who can influence a client's career.

3. Help the general public and legislators to understand the importance of career counseling, career development, and life-work planning.

4. Impact public policy as it relates to career development and workforce planning.

5. Analyze future organizational needs and current level of employee skills and develop performance improvement training.

6. Mentor and coach employees.

Diverse Populations

Knowledge and skills considered essential in relating to diverse populations that impact career counseling and development processes. Demonstration of ability to:

1. Identify development models and multicultural counseling competencies.

2. Identify developmental needs unique to various diverse populations, including those of different gender, sexual orientation, ethnic group, race, and physical or mental capacity.

3. Define career development programs to accommodate needs unique to various diverse populations.

4. Find appropriate methods or resources to communicate with limited-English-proficient individuals.

5. Identify alternative approaches to meet career planning needs for individuals of various diverse populations.

6. Identify community resources and establish linkages to assist clients with specific needs.

7. Assist other staff members, professionals, and community members in understanding the unique needs/characteristics of diverse populations with regard to career exploration, employment expectations, and economic/social issues.

8. Advocate for the career development and employment of diverse populations.

9. Design and deliver career development programs and materials to hard-to-reach populations.

Supervision

Knowledge and skills considered essential in critically evaluating counselor or career development facilitator performance, maintaining and improving professional skills. Demonstration of:

1. Ability to recognize own limitations as a career counselor and to seek supervision or refer clients when appropriate.

2. Ability to utilize supervision on a regular basis to maintain and improve counselor skills.

3. Ability to consult with supervisors and colleagues regarding client and counseling issues and issues related to one's own professional development as a career counselor.

4. Knowledge of supervision models and theories.

5. Ability to provide effective supervision to career counselors and career development facilitators at different levels of experience.

6. Ability to provide effective supervision to career development facilitators at different levels of experience by:

- knowledge of their roles, competencies, and ethical standards
- determining their competence in each of the areas included in their certification
- further training them in competencies, including interpretation of assessment instruments
- monitoring and mentoring their activities in support of the professional career counselor; and scheduling regular consultations for the purpose of reviewing their activities

Ethical/Legal Issues

Information base and knowledge essential for the ethical and legal practice of career counseling. Demonstration of knowledge of:

1. Adherence to ethical codes and standards relevant to the profession of career counseling (e.g., NBCC, NCDA, and ACA).

2. Current ethical and legal issues which affect the practice of career counseling with all populations.

3. Current ethical/legal issues with regard to the use of computer-assisted career guidance systems.

4. Ethical standards relating to consultation issues.

5. State and federal statutes relating to client confidentiality.

Research/Evaluation

Knowledge and skills considered essential in understanding and conducting research and evaluation in career counseling and development. Demonstration of ability to:

1. Write a research proposal.

2. Use types of research and research designs appropriate to career counseling and development research.

3. Convey research findings related to the effectiveness of career counseling programs.

4. Design, conduct, and use the results of evaluation programs.

5. Design evaluation programs which take into account the need of various diverse populations, including persons of both genders, differing sexual orientations, different ethnic and racial backgrounds, and differing physical and mental capacities.

6. Apply appropriate statistical procedures to career development research.

Technology

Knowledge and skills considered essential in using technology to assist individuals with career planning. Demonstration of knowledge of:

1. Various computer-based guidance and information systems as well as services available on the Internet.

2. Standards by which such systems and services are evaluated (e.g., NCDA and ACSCI).

3. Ways in which to use computer-based systems and Internet services to assist individuals with career planning that are consistent with ethical standards.

4. Characteristics of clients which make them profit more or less from use of technology-driven systems.

5. Methods to evaluate and select a system to meet local needs.

NCDA opposes discrimination against any individual on the basis of race, ethnicity, gender, sexual orientation, age, mental/physical disability, or creed.

Revised by the NCDA Board of Directors, April 1994.

The Ethics of Technology-Based Counseling

National Board for Certified Counselors, Inc.
and
Center for Credentialing and Education, Inc.
3 Terrace Way, Suite D
Greensboro, NC 27403

This document contains a statement of principles for guiding the evolving practice of Internet counseling. In order to provide a context for these principles, the following definition of Internet counseling, which is one element of technology-assisted distance counseling, is provided. The Internet counseling standards follow the definitions presented below.

A TAXONOMY FOR DEFINING FACE-TO-FACE AND TECHNOLOGY-ASSISTED DISTANCE COUNSELING

The delivery of technology-assisted distance counseling continues to grow and evolve. Technology assistance in the form of computer-assisted assessment, computer-assisted information systems, and telephone counseling has been available and widely used for some time. The rapid development and use of the Internet to deliver information and foster communication has resulted in the creation of new forms of counseling. Developments have occurred so rapidly that it is difficult to communicate a common understanding of these new forms of counseling practice.

The purpose of this document is to create standard definitions of technology-assisted distance counseling that can be easily updated in response to evolutions in technology and practice. A definition of traditional face-to-face counseling is also presented to show similarities and differences with respect to various applications of technology in counseling. A taxonomy of forms of counseling is also presented to further clarify how technology relates to counseling practice.

NATURE OF COUNSELING

Counseling is the application of mental health, psychological, or human development principles, through cognitive, affective, behavioral, or systemic intervention strategies, that address wellness, personal growth, or career development, as well as pathology.

Depending on the needs of the client and the availability of services, counseling may range from a few brief interactions in a short period of time to numerous interactions over an extended period of time. Brief interventions, such as classroom discussions, workshop presentations, or assistance in using assessment, information, or instructional resources, may be sufficient to meet individual needs. Or, these brief interventions may lead to longer-term counseling interventions for individuals with more substantial needs. Counseling may be delivered by a single counselor, two counselors working collaboratively, or a single counselor with brief assistance from another counselor who has specialized expertise that is needed by the client.

FORMS OF COUNSELING

Counseling can be delivered in a variety of forms that share the definition presented above. Forms of counseling differ with respect to participants, delivery location, communication medium, and interaction process. Counseling *participants* can be **individuals, couples,** or **groups**. The *location* for counseling delivery can be face-to-face or at a distance with the assistance of technology. The *communication medium* for counseling can be what is **read** from text, what is **heard** from audio, or what is **seen** and **heard** in person or from video. The *interaction process* for counseling can be **synchronous** or **asynchronous**. Synchronous interaction occurs with little or no gap in time between the responses of the counselor and the client. Asynchronous interaction occurs with a gap in time between the responses of the counselor and the client.

The selection of a specific form of counseling is based on the needs and preferences of the client within the range of services available. Distance counseling supplements face-to-face counseling by providing increased access to counseling on the basis of **necessity** or **convenience**. Barriers, such as being a long distance from counseling services, geographic separation of a couple, or limited physical mobility as a result of having a disability, can make it **necessary** to provide counseling at a distance. Options, such as scheduling counseling sessions outside of traditional service delivery hours or delivering counseling services at a place of residence or employment, can make it more **convenient** to provide counseling at a distance.

Table 1   A Taxonomy of Face-To-Face and Technology-Assisted Distance Counseling

Counseling

- Face-To-Face Counseling
  - Individual Counseling
  - Couple Counseling
  - Group Counseling
- Technology-Assisted Distance Counseling
  - Telecounseling
    - Telephone-Based Individual Counseling
    - Telephone-Based Couple Counseling
    - Telephone-Based Group Counseling
  - Internet Counseling
    - E-Mail-Based Individual Counseling
    - Chat-Based Individual Counseling
    - Chat-Based Couple Counseling
    - Chat-Based Group Counseling
    - Video-Based Individual Counseling
    - Video-Based Couple Counseling
    - Video-Based Group Counseling

A Taxonomy of Forms of Counseling Practice. Table 1 presents a taxonomy of currently available forms of counseling practice. This schema is intended to show the relationships among counseling forms.

DEFINITIONS

Counseling is the application of mental health, psychological, or human development principles, through cognitive, affective, behavioral, or systemic intervention strategies, that address wellness, personal growth, or career development, as well as pathology.

Face-to-face counseling for individuals, couples, and groups involves synchronous interaction between and among counselors and clients using what is seen and heard in person to communicate.

Technology-assisted distance counseling for individuals, couples, and groups involves the use of the telephone or the computer to enable counselors and clients to communicate at a distance when circumstances make this approach necessary or convenient.

Telecounseling involves synchronous distance interaction among counselors and clients using one-to-one or conferencing features of the telephone to communicate.

Telephone-based individual counseling involves synchronous distance interaction between a counselor and a client using what is heard via audio to communicate.

Telephone-based couple counseling involves synchronous distance interaction among a counselor or counselors and a couple using what is heard via audio to communicate.

Telephone-based group counseling involves synchronous distance interaction among counselors and clients using what is heard via audio to communicate.

Internet counseling involves asynchronous and synchronous distance interaction among counselors and clients using e-mail, chat, and videoconferencing features of the Internet to communicate.

E-mail-based individual Internet counseling involves asynchronous distance interaction between counselor and client using what is read via text to communicate.

Chat-based individual Internet counseling involves synchronous distance interaction between counselor and client using what is read via text to communicate.

Chat-based couple Internet counseling involves synchronous distance interaction among a counselor or counselors and a couple using what is read via text to communicate.

Chat-based group Internet counseling involves synchronous distance interaction among counselors and clients using what is read via text to communicate.

Video-based individual Internet counseling involves synchronous distance interaction between counselor and client using what is seen and heard via video to communicate.

Video-based couple Internet counseling involves synchronous distance interaction among a counselor or counselors and a couple using what is seen and heard via video to communicate.

Video-based group Internet counseling involves synchronous distance interaction among counselors and clients using what is seen and heard via video to communicate.

STANDARDS FOR THE ETHICAL PRACTICE OF INTERNET COUNSELING

These standards govern the practice of Internet counseling and are intended for use by counselors, clients, the public, counselor educators, and organizations that examine and deliver Internet counseling. These standards are intended to address *practices* that are unique to Internet counseling and

Internet counselors and do not duplicate principles found in traditional codes of ethics.

These Internet counseling standards of practice are based upon the principles of ethical practice embodied in the NBCC Code of Ethics. Therefore, these standards should be used in conjunction with the most recent version of the NBCC ethical code. Related content in the NBCC Code are indicated in parentheses after each standard.

Recognizing that significant new technology emerges continuously, these standards should be reviewed frequently. It is also recognized that Internet counseling ethics cases should be reviewed in light of delivery systems existing at the moment rather than at the time the standards were adopted.

In addition to following the NBCC® Code of Ethics pertaining to the practice of professional counseling, Internet counselors shall observe the following standards of practice:

Internet Counseling Relationship

1. In situations where it is difficult to verify the identity of the Internet client, steps are taken to address impostor concerns, such as by using code words or numbers.

2. Internet counselors determine if a client is a minor and therefore in need of parental/guardian consent. When parent/guardian consent is required to provide Internet counseling to minors, the identity of the consenting person is verified.

3. As part of the counseling orientation process, the Internet counselor explains to clients the procedures for contacting the Internet counselor when he or she is off-line and, in the case of asynchronous counseling, how often e-mail messages will be checked by the Internet counselor.

4. As part of the counseling orientation process, the Internet counselor explains to clients the possibility of technology failure and discusses alternative modes of communication, if that failure occurs.

5. As part of the counseling orientation process, the Internet counselor explains to clients how to cope with potential misunderstandings when visual cues do not exist.

6. As a part of the counseling orientation process, the Internet counselor collaborates with the Internet client to identify an appropriately trained professional who can provide local assistance, including crisis intervention, if needed. The Internet counselor and

Internet client should also collaborate to determine the local crisis hotline telephone number and the local emergency telephone number.

7. The Internet counselor has an obligation, when appropriate, to make clients aware of free public access points to the Internet within the community for accessing Internet counseling or Web-based assessment, information, and instructional resources.

8. Within the limits of readily available technology, Internet counselors have an obligation to make their Web site a barrier-free environment to clients with disabilities.

9. Internet counselors are aware that some clients may communicate in different languages, live in different time zones, and have unique cultural perspectives. Internet counselors are also aware that local conditions and events may impact the client.

Confidentiality in Internet Counseling

10. The Internet counselor informs Internet clients of encryption methods being used to help insure the security of client/counselor/supervisor communications.

   Encryption methods should be used whenever possible. If encryption is not made available to clients, clients must be informed of the potential hazards of unsecured communication on the Internet. Hazards may include unauthorized monitoring of transmissions and/or records of Internet counseling sessions.

11. The Internet counselor informs Internet clients if, how, and how long session data are being preserved.

   Session data may include Internet counselor/Internet client e-mail, test results, audio/video session recordings, session notes, and counselor/supervisor communications. The likelihood of electronic sessions being preserved is greater because of the ease and decreased costs involved in recording. Thus, its potential use in supervision, research, and legal proceedings increases.

12. Internet counselors follow appropriate procedures regarding the release of information for sharing Internet client information with other electronic sources.

   Because of the relative ease with which e-mail messages can be forwarded to formal and casual referral sources, Internet counselors must work to insure the confidentiality of the Internet counseling relationship.

Legal Considerations, Licensure, and Certification

13. Internet counselors review pertinent legal and ethical codes for guidance on the practice of Internet counseling and supervision.

Local, state, provincial, and national statutes as well as codes of professional membership organizations, professional certifying bodies, and state or provincial licensing boards need to be reviewed. Also, as varying state rules and opinions exist on questions pertaining to whether Internet counseling takes place in the Internet counselor's location or the Internet client's location, it is important to review codes in the counselor's home jurisdiction as well as the client's. Internet counselors also consider carefully local customs regarding age of consent and child abuse reporting, and liability insurance policies need to be reviewed to determine if the practice of Internet counseling is a covered activity.

14. The Internet counselor's Web site provides links to websites of all appropriate certification bodies and licensure boards to facilitate consumer protection.

Adopted November 3, 2001

Name Index

Subject Index

435